HANDBOOK OF ANTI-ENVIRONMENTALISM

Handbook of Anti-Environmentalism

Edited by

David Tindall

Professor, Department of Sociology, University of British Columbia, Canada

Mark C.J. Stoddart

Professor, Department of Sociology, Memorial University of Newfoundland, Canada

Riley E. Dunlap

Dresser Professor and Regents Professor of Sociology Emeritus, Oklahoma State University, USA

Edward Elgar PUBLISHING

Cheltenham, UK • Northampton, MA, USA

© David Tindall, Mark C.J. Stoddart and Riley E. Dunlap 2022

All rights reserved. No part of this publication may be reproduced, stored in a retrieval system or transmitted in any form or by any means, electronic, mechanical or photocopying, recording, or otherwise without the prior permission of the publisher.

Published by
Edward Elgar Publishing Limited
The Lypiatts
15 Lansdown Road
Cheltenham
Glos GL50 2JA
UK

Edward Elgar Publishing, Inc.
William Pratt House
9 Dewey Court
Northampton
Massachusetts 01060
USA

A catalogue record for this book
is available from the British Library

Library of Congress Control Number: 2022931169

This book is available electronically in the **Elgar**online
Sociology, Social Policy and Education subject collection
http://dx.doi.org/10.4337/9781839100222

Printed on elemental chlorine free (ECF)
recycled paper containing 30% Post-Consumer Waste

ISBN 978 1 83910 021 5 (cased)
ISBN 978 1 83910 022 2 (eBook)

Printed and bound in the USA

Contents

List of contributors	viii
Foreword: foreign-funded radicals	x
James Hoggan	

PART I   INTRODUCTION AND OVERVIEW

1   The contours of anti-environmentalism: an introduction to the *Handbook of Anti-Environmentalism*   2
Mark C.J. Stoddart, David Tindall and Riley E. Dunlap

PART II   THEORETICAL PERSPECTIVES

2   Understanding countermovements   23
Suzanne Staggenborg and David S. Meyer

3   Against environmentalism for the common good: a theoretical model   43
Nicholas Scott

PART III   ANTI-ENVIRONMENTALISM DISCOURSE AND FRAMING

4   'Total preservation is just as bad as total logging': forests and environmental attitudes and behaviours in an anti-environmentalist countermovement   63
David Tindall, Mark C.J. Stoddart and Valerie Berseth

5   Climate change scepticism in front-page Czech newspaper coverage: a one man show   84
Petr Ocelík

PART IV   VALUES, ATTITUDES AND PUBLIC OPINION

6   Understanding opposition to the environmental movement: the importance of dominant American values   108
Riley E. Dunlap

7   The effect of public opinion on environmental policy in the face of the environmental countermovement   133
Kerry Ard, Tiffany Williams and Paige Kelly

8   Anti-environment, or pro-livelihood? Dissecting environmental conflict and its key drivers in Northern New South Wales   153
Vanessa Bible

PART V SOCIAL NETWORKS AND ANTI-ENVIRONMENTALISM

9   Climate change counter movement organisations: an international deviant network?   173
    Ruth E. McKie

10 Fossil networks and dirty power: the politics of decarbonisation in Australia   192
    Adam Lucas

11 Regime of obstruction: fossil capitalism and the many facets of climate denial in Canada   216
    William K. Carroll, Shannon Daub and Shane Gunster

12 The Koch Brothers and the climate change denial social movement   234
    Patrick Doreian and Andrej Mrvar

PART VI EXTRACTIVE DEVELOPMENT AND ANTI-ENVIRONMENTALISM

13 Neoliberal governance of environmentalism in the post-9/11 security era: the case of pipeline debates in Canada   248
    S. Harris Ali

14 Fashioning anti-environmentalism in Turkey: the campaign against the Bergama movement   268
    Hayriye Özen

PART VII AGRICULTURE AND ANTI-ENVIRONMENTALISM

15 Food sovereignty and anti-regulation from the left   284
    James S. Krueger

16 Agrarian reform movement in the Betung Kerihun National Park: mobilisation of hunter–gatherer communities against nature protection in Kalimantan   304
    Martin C. Lukas

17 Wind energy development and anti-environmentalism in Alberta, Canada   329
    Aleksandra Afanasyeva, Debra J. Davidson and John R. Parkins

PART VIII ETHNICITY AND RACE

18 The end of population-environmentalism: dissonance over human rights and societal goals   345
    Pamela McMullin-Messier

19 The environmental state and the racial state in tension: does racism impede environmentalism?   365
    Ian R. Carrillo

Adam Lucas is Senior Lecturer in the School of Humanities and Social Inquiry at the University of Wollongong, Australia.

Martin C. Lukas is Senior Researcher at artec Sustainability Research Center at the University of Bremen, Germany.

Ruth E. McKie is Senior Lecturer in Quantitative Criminology at De Montfort University, UK.

Pamela McMullin-Messier is Professor in the Department of Sociology at Central Washington University, USA.

David S. Meyer is Professor in Sociology at University of California, Irvine, USA.

Andrej Mrvar is Professor of Social Science Informatics at the University of Ljubljana, Slovenia.

Petr Ocelík is Assistant Professor in the Department of International Relations and European Studies and International Institute of Political Science at Masaryk University, Czech Republic.

Hayriye Özen is Professor in the Department of Sociology at Izmir University of Economics, Turkey.

John R. Parkins is Professor and Department Chair in the Department of Resource Economics and Environmental Sociology at the University of Alberta, Canada.

Nicholas Scott is Associate Professor in the Department of Sociology and Anthropology at Simon Fraser University, Canada.

Suzanne Staggenborg is Professor in the Department of Sociology at the University of Pittsburgh, USA.

Mark C.J. Stoddart is Professor in the Department of Sociology at Memorial University of Newfoundland, Canada.

David Tindall is Professor in the Department of Sociology at the University of British Columbia, Canada.

Todd E. Vachon is Assistant Professor in the School of Management and Labor Relations at Rutgers University, USA.

Haydn Washington is Adjunct Lecturer at the PANGEA Research Centre, School of Biological, Earth and Environmental Sciences at University of New South Wales, Australia.

Tiffany Williams is a doctoral student at Michigan State University, USA.

Foreword: foreign-funded radicals
James Hoggan

My journey from corporate PR consultant to co-founder of a new media website investigating climate change disinformation was eye-opening. We launched DeSmogBlog (n.d.) in January 2006 to 'clear up the PR pollution that clouds climate science'. We wrote about Darth Vader PR campaigns in the US, Canada, Australia and the UK, largely funded by the coal and oil industries. Finding myself in the midst of a nasty international dispute about the climate crisis, I realized the strategies used to mislead people with anti-science propaganda and anti-environmentalism are much more developed and robust than those used to educate people about science and the environment.

My interest in environmental disinformation started in 2003 when I was invited to join the board of the David Suzuki Foundation, Canada's best-known science-based environmental organization. Consultants at my public relations firm thought accepting would be a mistake. They questioned the wisdom of associating with environmental activists. We worked for the establishment. Environmentalists make the establishment nervous.

Suzuki Foundation board members had concerns of their own. Wasn't public relations spin part of the problem? Wasn't it responsible for much of the public confusion? It's hard to argue with that. Public relations does have its dark side. Without bad actors manipulating public opinion, our path toward solutions would be quicker. We'd see more light, less heat.

Even though I owned the most successful PR shop in Vancouver, I didn't see myself as part of that dark side. We represented the establishment on difficult public issues: governments, hospitals, universities, big business (especially real estate development), banks, biotech, forestry, mining, oil and gas, and even the cruise ship business.

When I accepted the appointment, I didn't know a lot about the environmental challenges the world was facing. But when I join a board, I read my board package. I attend board meetings. I listen to briefings and read reports.

When Al Gore came to a board dinner, I paid attention. And given the chance to talk to famous scientists like Callum Roberts about marine conservation or Camilo Mora about climate disruption, I jumped.

Two pieces of writing around that time upended my worldview: a *New Yorker* series called 'The Climate of Man' by Elizabeth Kolbert,[1] which became a best-selling book *Field Notes From a Catastrophe* (2006), and *Boiling Point* by Ross Gelbspan (2004). These books opened my eyes to how serious the climate crisis is.

Over time, I realized that environmentalists are not crazy or even radicals. They're telling the truth: humans are rapidly destroying the oceans, driving record levels of species to extinction and dangerously overheating the climate. Environmental collapse is not just a future risk. It is well underway.

The late Interface Carpets CEO Ray Anderson, also a Suzuki Foundation board member, would often say at meetings, 'The house is on fire.' But you would not have known what he was talking about from the state of public discourse.

I became preoccupied with a question. Why, despite all the alarming scientific evidence, are we doing so little to address the big environmental challenges? Why, when we know so much, are we doing so little? I realized that if we want to do something about the climate crisis, we need to do something about the state of public discourse. The ability to have an honest public conversation is a tremendous public resource, but what is happening now is a deliberate attempt to stop us from doing the heavy thinking.

I became interested in the role that propaganda and pseudoscience play in change resistance, and the ways in which manufactured doubt and controversy can be used to stall the growth of public concern and block public policy solutions. I co-founded DeSmogBlog to raise awareness and help people become savvy about the global problem of climate change disinformation. It gained millions of readers and was named one of the best blogs of 2011 by *Time* magazine (Walsh, 2011). In 2009, I wrote *Climate Cover-Up* with Richard Littlemore (2009) to take a deeper look at anti-science propaganda and the widespread echo chamber of media and think tanks that magnify it. The book won awards and made its way onto the bookshelves of climate scientists around the world, yet I was shocked people were not more outraged by all the evidence of deception.

As a PR specialist, I have spent 30 years dealing with tough issues, straddling the worlds of government and industry, business and the environment, and I see this dysfunctional dialogue and corruption in the public square as a pressing problem. If we do not find a way to work this out, to disagree more constructively, we may never arrive at timely solutions to critical collective problems. When faced with an onslaught of over-the-top advocacy, people lose interest, hope or simply the thread of what's being said. This leads to escalating polarization and eventually gridlock and weak public policy.

Although DeSmog has investigated and written about anti-climate science campaigns in the US, Australia and elsewhere, the following example from Canada illustrates the misleading rhetoric we should all be concerned about.

Early in January 2012, I was watching the Canadian Broadcasting Corporation's evening news program *The National*, when Kathryn Marshall, a spokesperson for a group called 'Ethical Oil' was interviewed.

Her message was as simple as it was strange: Ethical oil is like fair trade coffee or conflict-free diamonds. It burns the same as conflict oil in your gas tank and it costs the same, but it is morally superior.

She said the then-proposed Northern Gateway pipeline project, which would take diluted Alberta bitumen from the oil sands to the coast of British Columbia, would be good for Canada and would allow export 'of our ethically produced oil to different countries that can then reduce their dependency on conflict oil from nations like Nigeria, Saudi Arabia and Iran that have atrocious human rights records and really don't care about the environment at all' (CBC News, 2012).

She said Canadians should 'make sure that foreign interests and their foreign-funded front groups and lobby groups' didn't interfere with the pipeline approval and did not 'hijack a Canadian process' (CBC News, 2012).

Her talking points were a mix of conservative agitator Ezra Levant (2010)'s 'ethical oil' narrative and the 'research' of a former aquaculture industry PR person, Vivian Krause. In examining funding for environmental groups, Krause (n.d.) concocted a conspiracy theory that US interests were funding Canadian environmental efforts in a plot to landlock Canadian oil to benefit the US industry. As full of holes as the theory is, it was latched onto by numerous pro-oil, anti-climate action people in government, media and industry.

Marshall dominated media with this story about foreign funded radicals for weeks. The public narrative about pipelines and climate change shifted to one about Canadian sovereignty.

It was bad enough when it was just industry and its front groups making these specious arguments. But it got worse when the then-Conservative government under Prime Minister Stephen Harper piled on. Conservative senator Nicole Eaton charged these 'foreign funded radicals' with political manipulation (Senate of Canada, 2012). 'There is influence peddling,' she said. 'There are millions of dollars crossing the borders masquerading as charitable donations.'

Natural Resources Minister Joe Oliver claimed environmentalists and other radical groups were trying to block trade and undermine Canada's economy, 'threatening to hijack our regulatory system to achieve their radical ideological agenda' (*The Globe and Mail*, 2012). Environment Minister Peter Kent hinted money-laundering was involved. Senator Don Plett asked where environmentalists would 'draw the line' on where they receive money from: 'Would they take money from al-Qaeda, the Hamas or the Taliban?' (Riley, 2012).

In 2019, When Jason Kenney was elected premier of Alberta, home of Canada's oil sands and leading source of greenhouse gas emissions, he reanimated the foreign-funded radicals' campaign. Kenney was a cabinet minister in the Harper Government when the campaign was cooked up in 2012. Soon after he became premier, Kenney announced a public inquiry into foreign funding of 'anti-Alberta' energy groups. As part of his 'fight back strategy', he opened a 'war room to counter misinformation'. He also unveiled a commission to investigate the 'shadowy funding' of environmental groups (Dawson, 2019). I know, it all seems a bit Russian.

Just as Canada's 'ethical oil' is a public relations fiction, so too is the US's 'clean coal'. Neither actually exists. The 'clean coal' brand was created by an advertising agency, R&R Partners, and promoted by the Hawthorn Group, a public relations shop working for the American Coalition for Clean Coal Electricity (ACCCE), an industry front group fighting climate change regulations (Hoggan and Littlemore, 2009, pp. 201–202). The 'ethical oil' concept came from a 2010 book of the same name by Ezra Levant, a conservative political activist and writer. Alykhan Velshi, a senior adviser to Prime Minister Harper, then built it into a strategic campaign, funded by the oil and gas industry.

Countless campaigns like these are polluting public conversations around the world. They are often designed by people like Washington political consultant Richard Berman.

On 30 October 2014, *The New York Times* published an article about a speech Berman gave at a Colorado Springs event sponsored by the Western Energy Alliance, a group whose members specialize in extracting natural gas through hydraulic fracturing. Berman said oil and gas industry officials need to exploit emotions like fear, greed and anger and turn them against environmental groups. His speech was secretly recorded and leaked to the *Times* by an industry executive who was offended by Berman's tough talk. 'Think of it as an endless war,' Berman told executives. 'You can either win ugly or lose pretty' (Lipton, 2014).

Berman was trying to raise $3 million for an advertising and public relations campaign called Big Green Radicals. 'There is nothing the public likes more than tearing down celebrities and playing up the hypocrisy angle,' his colleague said, showing billboard advertisements planned for Pennsylvania that featured Robert Redford and the words, 'Demands green living. Flies on private jets' (Lipton, 2014).

Berman is no stranger to conspiracy theories. He claims environmental groups are funded by Russian oil interests. He set up his own EPA, the Environmental Policy Alliance, to create confusion around the Environmental Protection Agency. Its stated purpose is to uncover the funding and hidden agenda of environmental and conservation groups.

Washington insiders call Bergman 'Dr Evil' because his aggressive campaigns are designed to demonize not just environmental and conservation groups but non-controversial ones like the Humane Society, Mothers Against Drunk Driving, green building groups, and sports and fishing organizations concerned about pollution.

The more I delved into the war on fact-based reality, the angrier I got. The disinformation was so blatant and shameless. And much of it involved ad hominem attacks. But the main source of my anger was the effectiveness of the tactics. Toxic conversations like these stall our ability to think collectively, act in our own interests and solve the many dangerous environmental problems stalking everyone on Earth.

The attacks on science and the environment are global.

There's the 'climategate' hoax (Nature, 2010). Late in 2009, just before the Copenhagen Climate talks, an unknown hacker stole more than 1000 emails from climate scientists at the Climate Research Unit of the University of East Anglia. The hacked emails were then used to dupe much of the free world's media into writing misleading front-page stories suggesting climate scientists were falsifying data, and raising the possibility that global warming was a hoax. What really happened was that, within 48 hours of the theft, front groups in the US, including the Cato Institute, Americans for Prosperity, the Heritage Foundation and the Competitive Enterprise Institute – all heavily funded by oil and gas – launched an international PR blitz aimed at discrediting climate scientists and disrupting the Copenhagen Climate talks. Although numerous independent inquiries exonerated the climate scientists, 'climategate' was the biggest global warming story of 2009 even though it was a made-up scandal.

Then there's Rupert Murdoch. He's used the influence of his massive global media empire – which includes newspapers like *The Times* of London and broadcasters like Fox News – to cast doubt on climate science (Cave, 2020). In a campaign to divert public attention from the link between Australia's bushfires and the 'bogeyman of climate change' his flagship newspaper *The Australian* campaigned to shift blame for the fires away from conservative political inaction onto 'greenies' falsely claiming environmentalists and arsonists were the cause of the fires, and that it was an arson emergency not a climate emergency.

There is truth in the proverb that sunlight is the best disinfectant. Transparency can bring honesty back into public conversations. That's why I continue to write about environmental propaganda. People aren't as outraged as they should be. When asked in interviews why I started DeSmogBlog, I would answer that when you turn on the lights, the critters scuttle back into the corners. But I learned that was seldom true. Usually, the critters get bigger, meaner and more aggressive.

In my most recent book, *I'm Right and You're an Idiot: The Toxic State of Public Discourse and How to Clean It Up*,[2] I took a deeper look at the propaganda problem. I interviewed philosophers, moral psychologists, media gurus, cognitive scientists, social psychologists, public intellectuals and spiritual leaders about toxic public discourse.

I spoke to best-selling authors like Wade Davis, David Suzuki, Ronald Wright, Thich Nhat Hahn, Joan Halifax, Karen Armstrong, Marshall Ganz, Peter Senge and Otto Scharmer. I even interviewed the Dalai Lama.

Why, I wanted to know, are we shouting at each other rather than listening to what the science is trying to tell us? And why all the name-calling and ad hominem attacks? How have we come to a time when facts don't seem to matter?

One of the first people I interviewed was Yale social scientist and law professor Dan Kahan, an expert in risk communication.

He said something that stuck with me: 'Just like we can pollute the natural environment, we can pollute public conversations.' Not with greenhouse gas emissions, but with disinformation, unyielding one-sidedness and a warlike approach to public debate.

HOW PROPAGANDA WORKS

Canadian social scientist Alex Himelfarb, who served in various public service roles under three Canadian prime ministers, told me these campaigns are not about persuasion. 'The strategy is to minimize public spaces where dialogue might occur, and where it does occur, confuse it, obscure it,' he said. 'The idea is to kill the debate, not foster it.'

It's almost too easy. 'They don't have to convince the public of anything to limit public will,' Himelfarb said. 'They just have to make it seem as if all the proponents for change are pursuing their own special interests and sow doubt that anybody is telling the whole truth.'

Jason Stanley, who teaches a course in the philosophy of language and propaganda at Yale, told me that when bitumen from Fort McMurray is called 'ethical oil' and coal from West Virginia is called 'clean coal', real discussion about the pros and cons gets lost. This language, according to Stanley, is not so much about making substantive claims as it is about silencing.

He called the foreign-funded radicals' campaign a linguistic strategy for stealing others' voices. 'The idea is to silence people by painting them as grossly insincere, undermining public trust in them, so nothing they say can be taken at face value.'

Polluting the public square with this style of rhetoric suggests there are no facts or objectivity and everyone is trying to manipulate you for their own interests. Disinformation is bad enough. But, if you can convince the public that everyone is biased, public conversations become impossible. Unfortunately, an even darker force is at work in this propaganda.

After spending time with Jonathan Haidt and Dan Kahan, I realized the true engine of propaganda is division and polarization. Whose side you are on becomes more important than what you have to say.

Social psychologist Jonathan Haidt, who teaches at New York University's Stern School of Business and studies the social psychology of teams, argues that human beings are tribal. We naturally gather into teams. If you can get people to engage in the psychology of teams, open-minded thinking shuts down.

'Our righteous minds have been designed by evolution to unite us into teams, divide us against other teams, and blind us to the truth,' he said. 'We are divided in these highly polarizing ways not because some of us are good and others are evil but because our minds were designed for groupish righteousness.'

Yale Law School's Kahan takes it further, arguing we want to be misled. He studies cultural cognition, the tendency of individuals to form beliefs about disputed matters that reflect the values of their cultural identities.

According to Kahan, we resist information that threatens our identity. When we are under the spell of cultural cognition, we develop elaborate rationalizations to justify our beliefs even if they are false and evidence points in another direction. We engage in selective thinking. We look for what confirms our beliefs, and ignore information that contradicts those beliefs. When scientific evidence is cloaked with team meaning, our minds close.

When we massage 'my-side bias' into issues, we convince people that, as Kahan says, 'This isn't something people like us believe. If you believe this you can't be one of us; you must be one of them.' Loss of faith in facts, reason and public discourse is the outcome. You are wrong before you start because you are on the wrong side. Disinformation is not the toxic heart of propaganda, tribalism is.

It's not just bad actors who pollute and polarize public conversations. Carol Tavris, author of the best-selling *Mistakes Were Made But Not By Me*, told me the moment we make a decision we begin to see all the reasons we are right about it. We overlook information that suggests we could be wrong. This self-justification protects us from the uncomfortable feelings of cognitive dissonance that come from recognizing we've made a mistake. The more time, effort, money and public face we attach to our decisions, the harder it is to admit we are wrong. We find ways to defend our mistakes rather than facing the alternative, which is to admit doing something stupid, unethical or incompetent even though we are good, smart and decent.

Self-justification is a powerful process. Tavris believes the feeling of having two conflicting views of ourselves can be as uncomfortable as hunger or thirst. The mind is highly motivated to reduce this discomfort. Because of this, we have trouble accepting evidence that we made a mistake or did something harmful or are holding an outdated belief.

'The greatest danger we face on the planet is not only from bad people doing corrupt, evil and bad things, but also from good people who justify the bad, evil and corrupt things they do in order to preserve their belief that they are good kind and ethical people,' Tavris said.

The miserable state of public discourse can lead us to believe the problem is evil on the side of our opponents.

Rodger Conner, who teaches non-litigation strategies for social and political change at Vanderbilt Law School in Nashville, points out that most of us are not evil, that good people can do bad things for good reasons. If we don't understand this, we can fall into something he calls the advocacy trap.

It starts when people disagree with us. We do not like being contradicted or criticized in public. When people disagree with us, we question their views and try to correct them with facts and evidence. But if they persist, we question their motives and intentions. Eventually they aren't just wrong, they're wrongdoers. We perceive them as aggressors. They turn from opponents into enemies. Eventually, defeating our opponent becomes more important than our original purpose.

It is difficult to engage or collaborate with someone you consider untrustworthy or despicable. In the advocacy trap, public disagreements become perpetual shoving matches, endless battles between good and evil. It is not enough to be right and share facts. We must also extract ourselves from advocacy trap polarization.

How do we re-open the commons? According to Conner, it starts with us. Being right is not enough. We escape the polarizing spell of the advocacy trap – and propaganda – when we choose a stance of respect, empathy and compassion. People can be completely wrong but still be decent people.

Campaigns like 'foreign-funded radicals' are deliberate attempts to fracture society and pollute public discourse. They create division. That is their purpose. This cannot be ignored. We need to defuse this polarization. The ability to have honest conversations is a tremendous public resource. We need to restore public confidence in the commons. We cannot do that if we are held captive in the polarizing spell of the advocacy trap.

Best-selling author and TED Prize winner Karen Armstrong sowed the seeds of a theme that emerged in many of the interviews. She suggested we follow the golden rule: 'Look into your own heart, discover what gives you pain, and refuse under any circumstances whatsoever to inflict that pain on anyone else. Never treat others as you would not like to be treated yourself.'

Sometimes, according to San Francisco attorney and psychotherapist Bryant Welch, the best strategy is to simply not engage because that undercuts the 'projective devices that adversaries use to justify their aggression'. If the victim remains silent rather than responding aggressively, it is harder to sustain the aggression and the perpetrator is left to stew in their own ugliness. We all like to view ourselves as justified in what we say and do. Perpetrators who are denied the self-justification that comes with an angry response are slowed in their aggression.

David Suzuki and I had tea with the renowned Vietnamese monk Thich Nhat Hanh at The University of British Columbia in August 2011. We were speaking about species extinction when Thich Nhat Hanh said we should bring a spiritual dimension to the work of protecting the environment. 'You're not saying we shouldn't be activists, are you?' I asked. He looked at me in a quiet, piercing way and said slowly, 'Speak the truth, but not to punish.'

I have been thinking about this advice ever since. It was one of the most profound moments of this entire three-year journey of research and writing, the seminal moment, because it gathered together the deepest voices and most profound threads of this long book into one elegant sentence.

As I was finishing the book, someone sent me a Public Broadcasting Service special in which Bill Moyers and Harvard's Marshall Ganz discussed how to achieve political change (Bill Moyers, 2013). Ganz said we should never be afraid of the controversy that arises from speaking the truth. There is nothing wrong with a good fight over injustice. He said he has no time for people who criticize polarization and say, 'Let's just get along better.' He argued that polarization can have positive outcomes.

I was puzzled by this, so I called him. He told me that taking a conciliatory stance in the face of wrongdoing is a strategic and moral mistake that severely compromises what he calls the 'adversarial mechanisms' that citizens rely on to bring out the truth. We live in a democracy in which leaders are expected to raise the level of debate in pursuit of the truth. In his view, contention lies at the heart of democracy. Ganz recommended I read Rabbi Hillel (AJWS Staff, n.d.) and sent me a few articles. The Rabbi, who lived at the time of Jesus, taught that conflict falls into two categories: arguments for the sake of heaven and arguments for the sake of victory. The goal of argument and public debate should not be to crush someone who disagrees with you, but to bring forward the truth. Argument is necessary and people should be encouraged to hold different opinions, to challenge issues, to question motivations and points of view, and to take part in passionate discussion. Paralysis is what is bad.

Ganz added that many of his students slip into conflict avoidance too often and easily. They have a mistaken idea that if everyone talks things out, everyone will eventually agree and we can all move forward with consensus. But, Ganz argues, the illusion of agreement is for authoritarian regimes. Democracies are made healthier when citizens are free to loudly and actively challenge injustices. He was quick to note that while he believes contention lies at the heart of democracy, it must ultimately be constructive. In an argument for the sake of heaven, Hillel explains that each side listens willingly and seriously to the other's views and analyzes those points using reason, logic and respect. Debate used for power rather than truth leads to gridlock.

Of the many interviews I conducted for *I'm Right and You're an Idiot*, my conversation with the Dalai Lama stands out. The Dalai Lama believes our destructive emotions are the real troublemakers and that we must learn to deal with them. As the interview ended, the Dalai Lama pointed at my forehead and told me many people think the Western mind is more sophisticated. 'But in Tibet we operate from the heart and this is very strong. So combine these two, Tibetan heart and Western mind, and then we will have real success. Real success.' We need more warm-heartedness, more compassion. Valuable advice for a public square polluted with unyielding one-sidedness.

Feelings play a powerful role in public discourse. Ganz called it a dialogue of the heart. We participate in emotional dialogue through stories, so we need to be careful about the narratives we create. We want to defuse, not exacerbate polarization. It's through pluralistic, empathetic narrative that more people will come to care about the right things. Environmental advocates, educators and scientists need to excel at emotional dialogue. We need to replace narratives that divide us with those that bring us together. That is how we avoid being drawn into the polarization strategy of propaganda.

Empathy and evidence need to replace disinformation and division. This is a challenge. The science of how to mislead people about science is advanced and muscular. The well-funded propaganda machines fighting environmental regulation know far more about stoking division than environmental scientists know about persuading us to support science-based public policies to protect the environment.

The 70-plus interviews I did for *I'm Right and You're an Idiot* convinced me we need to be careful not to be duped into fuelling the polarization that gives propaganda its sting. We need to speak up for what is right while we self-police and ask ourselves if we are intensifying or defusing polarization.

As George Orwell wrote, 'It appears to me, that one defeats the fanatic precisely by not being a fanatic oneself, but on the contrary by using one's intelligence.'[3]

The polarizing strategies preferred by these anti-science, anti-environment groups require that we explore the art of pluralistic advocacy so culturally diverse people who are motivated by different narratives, characters and dramas can see themselves in the stories we share and can share their own stories. The goal is to find a narrative that people relate to and embed a message that will lead to open-minded consideration.[4] This pluralistic approach to public narrative is an attempt to defuse polarization.

Environmental risk communication will fail unless it is inclusive, a dialogue of the heart where all sides have something worthwhile to contribute and each respects the other's views.

I am not an academic, but I have learned a lot from the academics in my book – Bruno Latour, Peter Senge, Karen Armstrong, Steve Rosell, Carol Tavris, Paul Slovic, Alex Himelfarb and many more. Some have become mentors and friends. Their work has improved my work as a public affairs consultant, and their words, through my books and lectures, have helped the communication work of others.

I was pleased to write the preface for this valuable work because we desperately need to find new, reliable ways to deal with the polarizing power of propaganda. Scientists, educators and environmental activists need guidance from social scientists.

In the world of environmental communication, we are learning as we go. For years, we thought facts and outrage changed minds in ways they do not. We need to explore reliable new ways to speak, listen and connect in the face of environmental disinformation and polarization.

For that we need ongoing research that helps educate us as it explores and advances the principles of effective science communication and highlights the harms of anti-environmentalism.

NOTES

1. Elizabeth Kolbert's (2005a, 2005b, 2005c) three-part essay in the *New Yorker*.
2. Personal communication via interviews with the subsequently mentioned authors, experts and faith leaders were undertaken between 15 August 2011 and 14 October 2015. Details of each interview can be found in Hoggan and Litwin (2019).
3. From Letter to Richard Rees (3 March 1949) in Orwell and Angus (1968, pp. 478–9).
4. Personal communication via interview with Dan Kahan, from Hoggan and Litwin (2019).

REFERENCES

AJWS Staff (n.d.) Arguing for the sake of heaven. Mishnah, Pirkei Avot 5:17. *Sefaria* (online). Available from: https://www.sefaria.org/sheets/114018?lang=bi (accessed 2 November 2015).
Bill Moyers (2013) Marshall Ganz on making social movements matter (video online). Available from: billmoyers.com/segment/marshall-ganz-on-making-social-movements-matter/ (accessed 2 November 2015).
Cave, D. (2020) How Rupert Murdock is influencing Australia's bushfire debates. *The New York Times*. Available from: https://www.nytimes.com/2020/01/08/world/australia/fires-murdoch-disinformation.html.
CBC News (2012) Pipeline debate heats up (video online). *CBC News: The National*. Available from: https://www.cbc.ca/player/play/2186004232 (accessed 29 December 2015).
Dawson, T. (2019) Alberta announces inquiry into 'shadowy' foreign funding of environmental groups. *National Post*. Available from: https://nationalpost.com/news/politics/alberta-announces-public-inquiry-into-shadowy-foreign-funding-of-environmental-groups.
DeSmog (n.d.) About us. *DeSmog*. Available from: www.desmogblog.com/about.
Gelbspan, R. (2004) *Boiling Point*. New York: Basic Books.
Hoggan, J. and Littlemore, R. (2009) *Climate Cover Up: The Crusade to Deny Global Warming*. Vancouver: Greystone Books.
Hoggan, J. and Litwin, G. (2019) *I'm Right and You're an Idiot: The Toxic State of Public Discourse and How to Clean it Up*. 2nd edn. Gabriola Island: New Society Publishers.
Kolbert, E. (2005a) The Climate of Man–I. *The New Yorker*. Available from: https://www.newyorker.com/magazine/2005/04/25/the-climate-of-man-i.
Kolbert, E. (2005b) The Climate of Man–II. *The New Yorker*. Available from: https://www.newyorker.com/magazine/2005/05/02/the-climate-of-man-ii.
Kolbert, E. (2005c) The Climate of Man–III. *The New Yorker*. Available from: https://www.newyorker.com/magazine/2005/05/09/the-climate-of-man-iii.
Kolbert, E. (2006) *Field Notes From a Catastrophe*. New York: Bloomsbury Press.
Krause, V. (n.d.) The tar sands against overseas exports of Canadian oil: Activism or economic sabotage? *Fair Questions Blog*. Available from: https://fairquestions.typepad.com/rethink_campaigns/activism-or-sabotage.html.
Levant, E. (2010) *Ethical Oil: The Case For Canada's Oil Sands*. Toronto: McClelland & Stewart.
Lipton, E. (2014) Hard-nosed advice from veteran lobbyist: 'Win ugly or lose pretty'. *The New York Times*. Available from: https://www.nytimes.com/2014/10/31/us/politics/pr-executives-western-energy-alliance-speech-taped.html?_r=1.
Nature (2010) Closing the Climategate. *Nature*. 468(345). DOI: 10.1038/468345a.

Orwell, S. and Angus, I. (eds) (1968) *The Collected Essays, Journalism and Letters of George Orwell, Vol. IV: In Front of Your Nose, 1945–1950*. London: Martin Seeker & Warburg, pp. 478–9.

Riley, S. (2012) Gloves are off in war on greens. *Ottawa Citizen*. 16, May, p. A11.

Senate of Canada (2012) Debates of the Senate, 41st Parl, 1st Sess, 148(54). *Senate of Canada* (online). www.parl.gc.ca/Content/Sen/Chamber/411/Debates/054db_2012-02-28-e.htm#70 (accessed 27 October 2015).

The Globe and Mail (2012) An open letter from Natural Resources Minister Joe Oliver. *The Globe and Mail*. Available from: https://www.theglobeandmail.com/news/politics/an-open-letter-from-natural-resources-minister-joe-oliver/article4085663/.

Walsh, B. (2011) Best Blogs of 2011: DeSmogBlog. *Time Magazine* (online). Available from: http://content.time.com/time/specials/packages/article/0,28804,2075431_2075447_2075499,00.html.

PART I

INTRODUCTION AND OVERVIEW

1. The contours of anti-environmentalism: an introduction to the *Handbook of Anti-Environmentalism*

Mark C.J. Stoddart, David Tindall and Riley E. Dunlap

The term 'anti-environmentalism' brings many things to mind. As Meyer and Staggenborg note in their classic *American Journal of Sociology* article, 'any social movement of potential political significance will generate opposition' (Meyer and Staggenborg, 1996, p. 1630). When opposition to a movement also takes on social movement organizational forms, tactics, or discursive strategies, we are looking at a countermovement. Along these lines, anti-environmentalism includes grassroots mobilization by workers in extractive industries like forestry or oil who fear for the livelihood impacts of environmental policy and who act in defense of their community and family economic wellbeing (Dunk, 1994; Lewin, 2019; Tindall et al., 2021). It also includes anti-environmental think tanks that produce material promoting skepticism about the seriousness of problems like climate change to promote anti-environmentalism and block policies to ameliorate these problems (Boynton, 2015; Brulle, 2014; Dunlap and Jacques, 2013; McLevey, 2014). Going beyond a focus on countermovements, anti-environmentalism can also be enacted through concerted government programs of rolling back environmental policies or regulations, as seen under Donald Trump's Republican administration in the United States, or Stephen Harper's Conservative government in Canada (MacNeil, 2014; Turner and Isenberg, 2018). In these cases, as Fisher and Jorgenson (2019) note, we see that policy shifts towards stronger 'environmental states' are neither uni-directional nor inevitable. The progressive environmental policy regimes that emerged across many Western countries since the 1970s can clearly be undone, as is readily apparent in the United States, Canada and Australia. This *Handbook* considers all these types of anti-environmentalism, which we define as 'classic anti-environmentalism'.

However, this *Handbook* adopts a broader scope in its exploration of anti-environmentalism. The purpose of this introductory chapter is to set out the spectrum of anti-environmentalisms. This includes classic forms of anti-environmentalism that are frequently corporate driven and often organized by public relations firms as 'astroturf' organizations; that is, corporate-supported movements designed to resemble grassroots movements (Beder, 1998; Brulle and Aronczyk, 2019). However, it also includes what we term 'critical' or 'reflexive' anti-environmentalisms. The latter forms of anti-environmentalism often stem from critical conversations within and across social movements that tend to be progressive and share the goals of social justice and sustainability to varying degrees. They grow from tensions produced by critical reflections and debates about the unintended or negative impacts of environmentalism within and among these social movements that otherwise share common goals, interests and political orientations. This spectrum of anti-environmentalisms is the conceptual foundation that orients this volume. The remainder of the chapter proceeds as follows: first, we provide a brief overview of the history of environmentalism, as this sets the background context for the emergence and development of anti-environmentalism. Second, we provide an overview of classic anti-environmentalism. Third, we introduce the notion of critical or reflexive anti-environmentalism and examine its variations. Finally, we provide a brief overview of the structure of the *Handbook*.

A BRIEF HISTORY OF ENVIRONMENTALISM

Environmental movements can be defined by multiple waves. The first wave is often characterized by the emergence of naturalist and advocacy groups like the Audubon Society and the Sierra Club in the late nineteenth century. First wave environmentalism (often called preservationism) reflected several intersecting influences and anxieties, including the Romantic movement in visual art, which asserted the intrinsic value of rural landscapes, mountains, forests and oceans that had previously been seen largely as threatening, hostile or undeveloped places. Key public intellectuals of first wave environmentalism, such as Henry David Thoreau and John Muir, translated this Romantic interpretation of nature to audiences through their writings. The rapid spread of industrial development in North America provoked an interest in protecting and preserving relatively undisturbed landscapes, especially wilderness areas (Nash, 1967). Many participants in first wave environmentalism were inspired by participation in outdoor recreation activities like hiking, mountaineering, skiing and birdwatching. As such, there was a high level of cross-over between outdoor recreation clubs and advocacy for protected areas (Reichwein, 2014; Schrepfer, 2005).

At the same time, there was another branch of early environmentalism (often called conservationism) led by figures such as Gifford Pinchot that pushed for the wise management of natural resources such as forests to ensure that they would not be depleted and remain available for human use, sometimes leading to conflict with preservationists like Muir (Hays, 1951). Nonetheless, they complemented one another as both opposed the unregulated exploitation and depletion of natural resources. A major legacy of first wave environmentalism was the establishment of a national park system in the United States, an innovation that gradually spread across much of the world. However, first-wave environmentalism gradually faded in visibility, especially in the early days of the Great Depression, while leaving its mark via parks, wilderness areas and the National Park Service, and organizations like the Sierra Club, Audubon Society, National Parks & Conservation Association, and Izaak Walton League (Mertig et al., 2002).

A second, somewhat less notable, wave emerged with the election of US President Franklin Delano Roosevelt, whose efforts to deal with the devastating impacts of the 1929–1933 depression and its aftermath included launching federal programs such as the Civilian Conservation Corps (CCC), Soil Conservation Service and Tennessee Valley Authority (Petulla, 1977). The CCC, in particular, employed over three million young, single, jobless men during its existence from 1933 to 1942 to work on a wide range of conservation activities. Among its most notable accomplishments were planting over three billion trees to combat soil erosion and regenerate forest land; building roads, trails, and fire lookouts in federal and state parks; constructing bridges and dams for erosion control; and fighting forest fires. More generally, its efforts contributed to a broader conception of conservation that contributed to the evolution of environmentalism (Maher, 2009).

Following World War II, the US (and then many other nations) gradually experienced growing affluence leading to more leisure time and sparking more interest in outdoor recreation such as visiting state and national parks. Many environmentalists grew concerned about the overuse of public lands as well as their continued exploitation by extractive industries and launched campaigns to expand and protect wilderness and primitive areas and precious sites such as the Grand Canyon. Their campaigns evolved into a full-fledged Wilderness Movement in the 1950s that constituted a third wave of environmentalism (McCloskey, 1972). Its efforts led to passage of the US Wilderness Act in 1964; however, subsequent battles raged over adding many primitive and roadless areas, wildlife refuges, and new parks (e.g., the Redwood National Park) to the National Wilderness Preservation System created by the act, and these kept the Wilderness Movement active and mobilized (Harvey, 1991; McCloskey, 1972). Campaigns such as the one to establish the Redwood National Park gave the movement and organizations leading these campaigns, such as the Sierra Club and Wilderness Society, a great deal of publicity that helped expand their memberships (Mertig et al., 2002). Some of these traditional organizations began to broaden their focus to environmental degradation writ large as widespread pollution became more obvious (McCloskey, 1972), positioning them to play a significant role in the modern environmental movement that was emerging in the 1960s and constitutes the fourth (and most significant) wave of environmentalism.

In the United States, environmentalism evolved into its contemporary and most notable form as part of the 1960s protest cycle (Boynton, 2015; Dunlap and Mertig, 1992; Mertig et al., 2002; Staggenborg and Ramos, 2016). This protest cycle was spurred by the US civil rights movement and led to the emergence of several spin-off movements including the women's movement, gay and lesbian rights movements, and Indigenous rights movements, as well as the environmental movement (which also benefited greatly from the contributions of more traditional conservation and wilderness organizations). The growing visibility of ecology as a scientific discipline, as well as the popularity of movement intellectuals and key books like Rachel Carson's *Silent Spring*, also played a role in solidifying the new environmental movement (Jamison et al., 1991; Mertig et al., 2002; Walker, 2020). Whereas first wave environmentalism focused primarily on wilderness and establishing protected areas, this fourth and largest wave focused on a broader range of issues including the proliferation of pesticide use, air and water pollution, and nuclear power and weapons testing.

The first Earth Day, held in 1970 with a focus on teach-ins and public education, was a critical event in the timeline of modern environmentalism (Rome, 2013). During this period, not only did several traditional conservation organizations like Sierra Club and National Audubon Society rapidly expand their memberships, but new environmental groups like the Natural Resources Defense Council (NRDC) and Friends of the Earth were founded and then quickly grew (Mertig et al., 2002). Of particular significance was the emergence of Greenpeace. Formed in Vancouver, Canada, in 1971 as the Don't Make a Wave Committee, Greenpeace originated as a protest group against nuclear weapons testing. But in contrast to older groups like the Sierra Club and newer ones like NRDC, Greenpeace was notable for playing to the logic of mass media. With journalists among its founding members, Greenpeace protesters engaged in peaceful but illegal civil disobedience that offered drama and spectacle for environmental news coverage (Corrigall-Brown, 2016; Dauvergne and Neville, 2011; Weyler, 2015).

More radical groups like Greenpeace favored civil disobedience and extra-institutional forms of protest, and other early groups like Environmental Action encouraged various (if rather mild) forms of 'ecotage' (Love and Obst, 1972). However, as the 1970s progressed there was also increasing institutionalization of the environmental movement, especially in the US where the large national organizations—both traditional ones and recently formed ones—became the dominant force in the movement (Mertig et al., 2002). They concentrated in Washington, DC to pursue policy reform via a range of conventional strategies, including both administrative and congressional lobbying, overseeing policy implementation, litigation, and electoral support for pro-environmental politicians (as exemplified by the League of Conservation Voters). In the process they became highly formalized organizations, relying on professional staffs to pursue their goals as well as manage the organizations and expand their memberships. A key strategy for the latter was direct mail campaigns that built large memberships consisting of individuals who had little if any involvement with the organizations other than paying annual dues and sometimes contributing to specific campaigns—a very weak type of environmental activism to say the least (Fisher, 2006; Mertig et al., 2002).

At the international level, environmentalism was given a major boost by a 1972 United Nations meeting in Stockholm, which led to the creation of the United Nations Environment Programme or UNEP (Caldwell, 1992). Fifteen years later, the UN's World Commission on Environment and Development (established in 1983 and chaired by former Norwegian Prime Minister Gro Harlem Brundtland) released its report, *Our Common Future*, in 1987. Also known as the Brundtland Report, this volume drew enormous attention around the world and helped mainstream the concept of sustainable development (Macnaghten and Urry, 1998). This version of sustainability promised that economic development and environmental wellbeing could proceed in tandem, provided the needs of future generations were not sacrificed to meet the needs of present generations. This version of sustainability, with its emphasis on balancing the three pillars of economically, environmentally, and socially sustainable development has since come to dominate governmental and corporate environmental discourse (Baker, 2006). However, it has also been criticized as being too abstract, pliable and adaptable to multiple—and often contradictory—political and economic interests (Adkin, 1998; Washington, 2015).

The 1980s and 1990s represented another shift in the evolution of the environmental movement. While well-institutionalized groups continued to dominate the environmental movement with a focus on political engagement in global capital cities, there was also a surge of grassroots (Freudenberg and Steinsapir, 1992) and radical environmentalism through networks like Earth First! (Davis, 1991) that furthered the use of out-of-system protest tactics originally popularized by Greenpeace (Weyler, 2015). Environmental justice movements also emerged through Black community activism in the US, which pointed to racialized disparities in which communities were put at risk of exposure to toxic waste and pollution (Bullard, 1990). Environmental justice movements were particularly important for opening lines of debate within the environmental movement about the costs of institutionalization and social distance from affected communities, as well as the limits of race-blind eco-politics focused on protected areas or endangered species that were far-removed from the experience of many of the communities subjected to environmental harms (Pellow and Brulle, 2005).

The contemporary moment represents yet another version of the modern environmental movement. With the diffusion of social media platforms, we have seen more horizontal and networked forms of environmental movement mobilization and contention, such as Extinction Rebellion (XR), fossil fuel divestment movements, and youth climate strikes, which operate independently from more established and institutionalized environmental organizations (Apfel, 2015; Stuart et al., 2020). At the same time, established and institutionalized groups like the World Wide Fund for Nature or WWF (originally named World Wildlife Fund) continue to have prominent roles in generating movement-produced research, engaging in the political sphere, or serving as news sources in mainstream television, radio or newspaper coverage of environmental issues (Corrigall-Brown, 2016; Konishi, 2018). Plus, despite the potential for more horizontal forms of communication through social media, institutionalized groups like Greenpeace and WWF also serve as key conduits for environmental protest information to their large groups of followers on social media outlets like Twitter, Facebook or YouTube (Gerhardt et al., 2018; Katz-Kimchi and Manosevitch, 2015). As such, in addition to its worldwide diffusion, contemporary environmentalism is characterized by a diversity of components that include both larger institutionalized groups, which remain relevant as political actors, and more diffuse networks of grassroots protest. It is also characterized by a diversity of tactics, from radical forms of disruptive protest to moderate tactics of lobbying and public education. Finally, contemporary environmentalism is also characterized by a diversity of discursive approaches that range from mainstream sustainable development, to environmental justice, through to radical critiques of the unsustainability of capitalist economies (Caniglia et al., 2015; Dryzek, 1997).

'CLASSIC' ANTI-ENVIRONMENTALISM

Much previous research on anti-environmentalism focuses on social movements that mobilize in specific opposition to the environmental movement. These forms of 'classic' anti-environmentalism connect conservative or neoliberal political ideologies that emphasize the free market over government regulation with corporate—particularly fossil fuel sector—interests in maintaining profitability in the face of mounting environmental concern (Boynton, 2015; Brulle and Aronczyk, 2019; Walker, 2020).

As Dunlap (Chapter 6) notes in this volume, US anti-environmentalism emerged in the 1970s as a response to the challenges posed by environmentalism to core American values of 'personal freedom, individual rights ... success, material comfort and progress'. While anti-environmentalist sentiment was expressed by businesses that were targets of the environmental movement, it cohered into a countermovement through the Sagebrush Rebellion and its successor the Wise Use Movement (Brulle and Aronczyk, 2019). The latter—a key example of classic anti-environmentalism—was exemplified early on by forestry workers in the western US, with significant corporate support from the forestry industry, mobilizing in the 1990s against the environmental groups that sought protections for remnant old growth forests and endangered species that relied on those old growth forests for habitat. Their anti-environmentalism linked a form of rural, breadwinner masculinity against an image of environmentalism as an outside force that cared more for trees and spotted owls than for workers and rural communities (Burke, 1995). Particularly in the US, the Wise Use Movement gradually expanded into a widespread effort to open federal land for development and to oppose a wide range of environmental regulations (Brick and Cawley, 1996; Switzer, 1997). The discourse of the Wise Use movement has since been mainstreamed in US political discourse through integration into the Tea Party, as well as through Koch-funded groups like Americans for Prosperity (Brulle and Aronczyk, 2019).

Wise Use also proved influential beyond US borders and inspired the mobilization of SHARE our Resources in British Columbia, Canada. SHARE similarly mobilized forestry communities against environmentalists, adopting a 'jobs versus environment' frame that positioned environmentalists, old growth forests, and wildlife against the economic wellbeing of rural British Columbia (Doyle et al., 1997; Tindall et al., 2021). Tindall et al. (2021) refer to SHARE as a 'quasi-astroturf group' because it was created and guided by corporate actors but gained life through the mobilization of local forestry workers and communities. In contrast to other Wise Use campaigns, however, it was less successful at projecting an image of grassroots protest through the media to broader bystander publics. Its affiliations with forestry companies and public relations firms were more apparent to news-workers, which resulted in questions about its legitimacy as a grassroots countermovement (Doyle et al., 1997).

The most prevalent contemporary example of organized anti-environmentalism is the climate change denial or sceptic movement (Brulle, 2014; Dunlap and McCright, 2015). The main thrust of the climate sceptic movement is to undermine efforts to ameliorate climate change by challenging the scientific consensus that climate change is real, human-caused and serious and requires a concerted global policy response and economic transformation (Cook et al., 2016) by promoting uncertainty about climate science. Strategies for doing this include producing research and holding conventions—often with assistance from a handful of contrarian scientists—outside the structures of peer-reviewed climate science, but which gives an aura of scientific credibility to participants' claims (Boykoff, 2013; Brulle and Aronczyk, 2019; Dunlap and McCright, 2015, Freudenburg and Muselli, 2013; McCright and Dunlap, 2010; Oreskes and Conway, 2011; Young and Coutinho, 2013). The counterclaims of the climate sceptic movement include denial that climate change is occurring at all by challenging the evidential basis of trend data; acknowledging that climate change is occurring but denying that it is human-caused and instead asserting that it is naturally occurring; or acknowledging that climate change is occurring but arguing that it is not serious enough to justify the proposed political or economic interventions to address it. Carroll et al. (2018) describe a newer 'soft' form of climate denial that is strategically used by the fossil fuel sector in Canada. As the political and scientific imperatives for climate action become stronger, bolstered by public opinion, fossil fuel companies publicly acknowledge the reality of climate change, while working in the political sphere to manage climate action in ways that protect their profitability.

Like its Wise Use predecessor, the climate sceptic movement draws on corporate resources for support, but also draws on anxieties about environmental protection among segments of the public that rely on fossil fuel intensive economies. Large oil companies like Exxon have been heavily implicated as supporters of the climate change denial machine, which is widely seen as a front for protecting the interests of the fossil fuel sector (Cook et al., 2019; Farrell, 2016a; Rowlands, 2000; Walker, 2020). As Brulle et al. (2020) find, for example, media and political attention to climate change correlates with promotional advertising by fossil fuel companies. Other research has identified the important role of conservative think tanks and countermovement entrepreneurs like the Koch brothers in driving climate scepticism (Brulle, 2014; Boussalis and Coan, 2016; Dunlap and Jacques, 2013; Farrell, 2016b; McLevey, 2014, Walker, 2020), a topic explored in this volume by Doreian and Mrvar (Chapter 12).

Eyerman and Jamison's (1991) 'cognitive approach' to social movements emphasizes the role of key intellectuals and books in the emergence, diffusion and institutionalization of the modern environmental movement through the 1960s and 1970s. This approach highlights that movement intellectuals are essential to shaping the 'knowledge interests' that underpin social movement claims-making and strategic action (Jamison et al., 1991). Just as environmentalism has evolved through the influence of key intellectuals and authors, so too does anti-environmentalism work as an intellectual movement as well as a social movement. For example, Danish political scientist Bjørn Lomborg enjoys media visibility as a self-proclaimed 'sceptical environmentalist' who argues that environmental movements exaggerate the severity of environmental problems and that environmental harms are not significant enough to require the costly fixes proposed by environmental advocates (Besley and Shanahan, 2004). In Canada, former Greenpeace activist Patrick Moore developed a second career as public defender of extractive resource sectors against environmentalist demands for new protected areas, or more rigorous regulation and oversight of resource extraction sectors. Well-known Canadian journalist Rex Murphy has similarly been a vocal defender of the Alberta oil sands and voice for climate sceptic claims (Murphy, 2015). Vivian Krause is a journalist and blogger who has found a platform for the frame that environmentalist opposition to the Alberta oil sands is part of a concerted foreign funded campaign to undermine Canada's oil-based economy, which has found resonance with many Conservative politicians.

Arlie Hochschild's (2016) recent book *Strangers in their Own Land* takes an ethnographic approach to examining the culture and beliefs of Tea Party Republicans in Louisiana, which typically include climate scepticism and anti-environmentalism. One of her main concerns is the 'Great Paradox' that characterizes environmental politics in Louisiana and across the US. That is that red states (that vote Republican) consistently suffer more from industrial pollution, yet also show greater opposition to environmental regulation. For Hochschild, treating the Great Paradox as an example of a public that is duped by corporate interests and actors like the Koch Brothers gives us an incomplete picture. Rather, much of the anti-environmentalism that pervades the American right draws from a shared 'deep story' that profoundly distrusts government intervention, trusts in the free market as emblematic of the American Dream, and asserts a defense of Christian faith, family, whiteness, and traditional masculinity against the political and cultural shifts provoked by the social movements of the 1960s protest cycle. The movement–countermovement dynamic thus also relies on the persistence of 'empathy walls' that serve as 'an obstacle to deep understanding of another person, one that can make us feel indifferent or even hostile to those who hold different beliefs' (Hochschild, 2016, p. 5). Some commentators on Hochschild's work also raise the question of whether researchers should take such 'deep stories' at face value or cast a critical eye on narratives that contain many false assumptions and incorrect facts and may be a form of impression management by participants (Jasper, 2018; McVeigh, 2017; Polletta and Callahan, 2017; Ray, 2017; Shapira, 2017). Still, as Hochschild's work illustrates, it is important to distinguish corporate-led or 'astroturf' forms of anti-environmentalism that protect elite economic interests from the grassroots forms of anti-environmentalism that express anxieties with the livelihood impacts of environmental regulation on families and communities. These forms of anti-environmentalism may work together and complement each other, but it is analytically important to note that they are driven by different political, social and cultural forces.

For example, the tumultuous relationship between environmentalism and resource extractive labor is well studied (Mayer, 2009; Norton, 2003). John Bellamy Foster (1993) takes the conflicts over old growth forestry in the US Pacific Northwest as a starting point. He places much of the blame for the jobs-versus-environment framing of environmental issues at the doorstep of environmental groups that adopt wilderness frames that distance them from forestry workers. One result is that industry-funded anti-environmentalism becomes the de facto 'voice of the workers' in a loggers-versus-owls dichotomy (Foster, 1993, p. 13). Similarly, Dunk (1994) draws on interviews with forestry workers in north-western Ontario, Canada, to examine how jobs-versus-environment frames are interpreted. He argues that forestry workers are generally aware of their paradoxical role in relation to nature, as being simultaneously embedded in nature through their labor while also contributing to its destruction via deforestation. Forestry workers often do not view forestry conflicts through the jobs-versus-environment frame. They are aware of the problems of technological rationalization, shrinking markets, and practices of over-cutting. However, they adopt an oppositional stance towards environmentalists, who are symbolically linked with the urban, the outsider, and with expert knowledge. By contrast, forestry workers define their self-identities through the local, the rural, and common-sense knowledge. In their chapter in this volume (Chapter 4), Tindall, Stoddart and Berseth examine similar issues amongst pro-forestry activists in British Columbia.

Similar social and cultural dynamics are at play in American coal communities. Looking at environmental justice movements in the coal dependent Appalachian region, Bell and Braun (2010) examine the gendered dimension of coal mining identity and environmental resistance. Coal is central to regional identity and dominant forms of masculinity that valorize coal sector employment and reinforce a 'culture of silence' around the environmental health impacts of coal mining. By contrast, women are over-represented in environmental justice movements. In part, this is because they can step outside the regional coal mining identity by adopting a motherhood identity, which allows political space to engage in debate about issues like downstream water pollution, air pollution, and the occupational health impacts that harm residents of coal-dependent communities. Lewin (2019) similarly emphasizes the cultural importance of a shared sense of 'coal heritage' among Appalachian coal workers to understand their anti-environmentalism. There is a shared valorization of coal labor in the region because it is challenging, relatively well-paid, and makes a significant contribution to the American energy system in a 'national division of labor' (Lewin, 2019, p. 52). Conversely, there is a shared sense that the region is looked down upon by many Americans and that their communities will lose out on any transition away from fossil fuels. The communication strategies of coal companies are well aligned with regional values and identity. This reinforces the cultural power of the coal heritage narrative and feeds distrust of environmentalist discourse about just transitions for fossil fuel dependent communities.

Classic forms of anti-environmentalism are generally corporate-driven and organized through conservative think tanks and PR-designed astroturf organizations and campaigns. They connect corporate interests and conservative public intellectuals with segments of the public that share conservative worldviews or who share anxieties about the impacts of environmental policies on extractive sector communities and workers. While organized anti-environmentalism is present across much of the world, it has been most successful at gaining public and political traction in the United States, which serves as the geopolitical center for the movement. Outside the US, anti-environmentalism has become more visible in other Anglo-American countries, such as Canada, Australia and the United Kingdom, where it has often found affiliation with conservative party politics. While several of the chapters in this volume provide a close analysis of this classic form of organized anti-environmentalism, we also broaden the scope to examine what we might call critical or reflexive forms of anti-environmentalism.

CRITICAL/REFLEXIVE ANTI-ENVIRONMENTALISM

In addition to 'classic anti-environmentalism', this volume explores other forms of anti-environmentalism that we define as critical or 'reflexive' (Davidson, 2012; 2019) forms of anti-environmentalism. These multiple forms of anti-environmentalism highlight perceived problems within the environmental movement and are often raised by those generally sharing political orientations similar to those of environmentalists. In some ways, we might think of critical/reflexive anti-environmentalism as a form of 'insider opposition' and productive critique that draws attention to alternative ways of conceptualizing sustainability or doing eco-politics (Agyeman et al., 2003), rather than the outside opposition of classic anti-environmentalism that seeks to obstruct or undermine environmental movement objectives. At the same time, these critical interventions have become subject to debate and critique by environmental scholars, as examined by Kopnina et al. (Chapter 22) in this volume.

A great deal of reflexive anti-environmentalism focuses on the unintended consequences of environmental movements. While the creation of parks and protected areas systems is the major legacy of first wave environmentalism, environmental historians highlight how protected areas entrenched racialized and gendered power dynamics of who was seen to belong in these protected spaces and who was excluded from the 'commodified wilderness experiences' they provided (Reichwein, 2014, p. 11). As Schrepfer (2005) notes, first wave environmentalism was born from mountaineering experiences and rooted in recreational interactions with nature. These experiences were often framed as part of a 'masculine sublime' where barren, uninhabited mountainous nature was a stage for constructing a particular form of adventurous, risk-seeing masculinity. The creation of parks and protected areas privileged the recreational and touristic use of these spaces by predominantly 'Anglo, white, urban, middle-class mountaineers' (Reichwein, 2014, p. 105). By contrast, historical and ongoing Indigenous land use and inhabitation were largely obscured, other than occasional enactments of white 'playful fantasies' of 'playing Indian' in the wilderness (p. 105).

Critical studies of parks and protected areas have continued to draw attention to the ways in which they have faced resistance by local communities as a form of land enclosure (MacEachern, 2001). Laudati's (2010) study of Bwindi Impenetrable National Park in Uganda, for example, shows that the discourse about the national park as a form of economic development through nature protection and ecotourism failed to translate into benefits for adjacent host communities, but instead created new social inequalities. The creation of the park involved pushing people out of this protected landscape and enclosing forest resources that local communities had depended upon. By contrast, most of the benefits of gorilla ecotourism flowed out of the region to international companies, with only 6 percent of tourism revenues reaching local communities. Nixon similarly examines South African game lodges and protected areas as spaces that stage romanticized 'encounters with the "timeless" Africa of charismatic megafauna' (Nixon, 2011, p. 176). For Nixon, this is an example of the 'slow violence' of environmental racism that inscribes colonial stereotypes that treat 'blacks as barbarous poachers whose relationship to wildlife was one of illegality and threat while depending, conversely, on mythologizing whites as stewards of nature whose conservationist principles evidenced a wider civilizational superiority' (p. 190).

While perhaps harder to read as anti-environmentalism, there have also been tensions and points of conflict within the environmental movement that have led to debates over what constitutes authentic environmentalism. One of the deepest tensions within the movement is between deep ecological or eco-centric environmentalisms versus humanist or social justice-oriented environmentalisms (Chodorkoff, 2014; Hay, 2002; Humphrey, 2000; Luke, 1997; Washington et al., 2017). From the former perspective, environmentalism does not align to the traditional left–right political spectrum and should be concerned primarily with ecosystem and species health, with a politics guided by environmental science. For some eco-centric advocates, ecological health must take priority over social development, which leads to support for population control or restrictions on immigration. From the latter perspective, environmentalism aligns with other left-leaning or progressive political issues. This perspective holds that ecological sustainability cannot be achieved without also challenging social power inequalities. In North America, the issue of immigration has been one flashpoint of debate between these different visions of environmentalism, which is explored in this volume by McMullin-Messier (Chapter 18).

Anti-environmentalism may also consist of tensions across different social movements. There have been alliances between environmentalism and Indigenous rights movements during conflicts over forestry practices, oil extraction, and new oil and gas pipelines. However, the tensions that emerge in these relationships are also well documented. As Callison notes, Indigenous groups often face a 'conundrum' because they often must 'demonstrate a special relationship with the land' to have a voice in the political or media spheres (Callison, 2014, p. 71). However, environmental organization reliance on wilderness frames often sits uneasily with Indigenous relationships with place, in part because they risk erasing Indigenous people from lands they have occupied for thousands of years (Bacon, 2019; Braun, 2002).

For example, Coats (2014) distinguishes the 'conservationist approach' of environmental opponents of Alberta oil sands development from the 'Indigenous rights' approach taken by Indigenous oil sands opponents. The conservationist approach is rooted in frames centered on risks to habitat and fresh water, as well as linking the oil sands to global climate change. The conservationist approach targets provincial and federal governments and promotes technological and market solutions to climate change and fossil fuel dependency. By contrast, Indigenous Rights approaches begin from an analysis of settler–colonial dynamics, wherein the downstream environmental risks and health impacts are disproportionately borne by Indigenous communities and need to be understood as 'only the latest in a string of injustices' that should be addressed as part of efforts to 'assert Indigenous treaty rights, improve living standards, exercise their right to self-determination, and heal Mother Earth' (Coats, 2014, p. 271; also see Lameman, 2014; Thomas-Muller, 2014). Tensions between these approaches are exacerbated because environmental groups working from the conservation approach are often better resourced and more influential in public and policy arenas. Furthermore, tensions emerge between the support in principle for Indigenous rights that is shared by many environmental activists and organizations, and the economic development interests of many within Indigenous communities (Vasey, 2014).

Although more scholarly attention has been paid to Indigenous and environmental opposition to oil and gas development, there have also been emerging tensions over renewable energy transitions. For example, in Sámi territories across the Nordic countries, onshore wind energy infrastructure has disrupted Sámi reindeer herding practices. Aili Keskitalo, President of the Sámi Parliament in Norway, argues that when the un-reflexive development of renewable energy places additional burdens on Indigenous communities who must 'give up our traditional lands and practices to save the world', this is a new form of colonialism 'dressed in green finery' (Keskitalo, 2018).

Another key example of environmentalist–Indigenous conflict is the fallout from environmental campaigns against sealing from the 1970s onwards. As documented in the film *Angry Inuk*, anti-sealing campaigns have alienated Inuit communities from environmental groups and made alliance building difficult because they have undermined Inuit livelihoods and community wellbeing (Arnaquq-Baril, 2016). One response was the adoption of a #sealfie social media campaign by Inuit to reframe anti-sealing campaigns as a form of discrimination and cultural bias (Graugaard, 2018; Rodgers and Scobie, 2015). While Greenpeace abandoned their earlier participation in anti-sealing campaigns, they continue to deal with a legacy of distrust within Inuit and other Indigenous communities because of their association with opposition to sealing. In the Nunavut community of Clyde River, for example, Greenpeace worked with the Clyde River Solidarity Network to support local opponents of seismic activity for offshore gas exploration that would pose risks to local wildlife and hence disrupt Inuit hunting practices. To begin working with the Clyde River community, Greenpeace first issued an apology for the economic and social harms caused by their anti-sealing campaigning. However, some Inuit leaders remain sceptical of the Greenpeace apology, viewing it as a strategic political move in their Save the Arctic campaign, rather than a sincere attempt at decolonizing their environmental politics and 'following the lead' of Inuit communities (Rodgers and Ingram, 2019).

Environmental justice movements and scholarship are another important source of critical reflection on the problems of mainstream environmentalism. The environmental justice perspective attends to the ways in which environmental risks and harms are disproportionately and inequitably distributed within and across societies (Agyeman et al., 2003; Čapek, 1993; Guha and Alier, 1997). Key early environmental justice scholarship emerged in the US context and documented that African American and Latinx communities were more likely to be located near hazardous facilities and exposed to toxic pollution, a phenomenon defined as environmental racism (Bullard, 1990). Though some critics suggested that class may be more important than race in accounting for unequal exposure to environmental harms, further research strengthened the case for environmental racism (Mohai et al., 2009). From an environmental justice perspective, the absence of attention to issues of environmental racism and social justice among the large, institutionalized environmental organizations is not simply a blind spot, but represents a wholesale failure to adequately conceptualize sustainability as an eco-political project. By contrast, environmental justice scholars advance the notion of 'just sustainabilities', which re-orients environmental policy change to integrate concerns with social justice and inequality (Agyeman et al., 2003).

Other critical interventions into environmentalism have come from within academia. To take an example that has been the subject of contention but continues to be well read in environmental social sciences and humanities, environmental historian William Cronon's (1995) essay on the 'trouble with wilderness' focuses on environmentalism's preoccupation with saving or protecting 'wilderness' places. He argues that the cultural construction of wilderness, rooted in European romanticism and American frontier mythologies, is problematic because it perpetuates nature–culture binaries that are at the core of much of our unsustainable social–ecological relationships. Similarly, Timothy Luke (1997) argues that an eco-politics that privileges the protection of an idealized, uninhabited wilderness has the effect of setting aside special environments and wildlife as nature museums for recreational and touristic visitors. For Luke, this lets the normal, unsustainable operation of consumer capitalism proceed unimpeded outside these protected zones. However, for eco-centric critics, these critiques are counter-productive because they undermine the ecological importance of large untouched natural areas and the biodiversity and ecological values that they protect.

We also find critics of environmentalism within environmental sociology, where one of the long-standing theoretical debates has been between proponents of Ecological Modernization Theory (EMT) and Treadmill of Production (TOP) Theory. Put briefly, EMT asserts that capitalism has a history of adapting to moments of crisis and the further ecological modernization of capitalism to ensure its sustainability is more viable than pursuing alternatives to capitalism (Fisher and Jorgenson, 2019; Mol et al., 2013). From this perspective, sustainability solutions involve more efficient use of resources, resource substitution, and technological innovation. Ecological modernization is driven by constellations of governments, corporate actors, and environmental movements working in collaboration and conflict. Individual-level environmentalism is also important, both through political consumerism, such as shopping according to environmental values, and ecological citizenship, such as voting for pro-environmental political parties (Spaargaren and Mol, 2008). While EMT generally adopts a positive view of environmentalism as a force for pro-environmental social change, the TOP perspective is suspicious of organized environmentalism.

In contrast to EMT, TOP theory adopts an eco-Marxist perspective that sees capitalism as fundamentally unsustainable because of its core logic of endless growth and the imperative to ensure and increase value for corporate shareholders (Gould et al., 2008; Schnaiberg and Gould, 2000). This Treadmill imperative of endless economic growth is powered by three mutually reinforcing social forces: the interests of corporations in profitability; the interests of workers-citizens in pay checks and consumerist lifestyles; and the interests of governments in maintaining the consent and wellbeing of both corporations and citizens. According to the TOP, social movement actors have the *potential* to disrupt the Treadmill by aligning with workers-citizens and challenging corporations and governments. A social movement politics of social–ecological synthesis embraces ecological sustainability goals while also working to reduce social inequality. However, the TOP perspective argues that most mainstream environmentalism engages in a politics of managed scarcity, where governments and corporations are provoked to adopt just enough sustainability to keep the Treadmill running, with little attention to social inequality or injustice. This eco-politics of managed scarcity means that affluent social groups will retain privileged access to environmental goods—clean air and water, healthy food, beautiful recreational environments—and will be able to insulate themselves from the worst effects of environmental decline. Disadvantaged groups, by contrast, will see the amplification of exposure to environmental risks or harms, such as toxic waste, air and water pollution, or climate disasters. From a TOP perspective, most environmentalism feeds a politics of managed scarcity and is oriented around maintaining the institutional legitimacy of environmental organizations. As such, a great deal of environmentalism is either irrelevant or actively harmful (Gould et al., 1993).

OVERVIEW OF THE *HANDBOOK*

The rest of this *Handbook* explores the spectrum of anti-environmentalisms as follows. Part II introduces theoretical frameworks for understanding anti-environmentalism. Suzanne Staggenborg and David S. Meyer (Chapter 2) revisit and update their foundational analysis of social movement/countermovement dynamics, with a focus on classic forms of anti-environmentalism. They argue that a relational approach to movement/countermovement dynamics in the contexts of political opportunities and available resources is essential to better understand how pro-environmental social and political change occurs or is obstructed. Nicholas Scott (Chapter 3) draws on the pragmatic sociology and justification theory of Boltanski and Thévenot to construct a typology of anti-environmentalisms that accounts for the multiple forms of critical/reflexive anti-environmentalism. For Scott, these critical/reflexive countermovements are valuable because they can provoke new forms of environmentalism that are more attuned to questions of justice.

Part III examines the cultural dynamics of anti-environmentalism with a focus on discourse and framing. David Tindall et al. (Chapter 4) examine the forestry-based Share Our Resources (SHARE) countermovement that was active in British Columbia, Canada, at the height of protests over the protection of old growth forests. Drawing on survey data from this peak period of environmental movement and countermovement mobilization, Tindall et al. examine the divergence and surprising convergence of frames used by members of these opposed groups. Petr Ocelík (Chapter 5) examines the discursive strategies used to promote climate scepticism in the media sphere in the Czech Republic. While climate scepticism is most often associated with the US and other anglophone countries, Ocelík's analysis illuminates how climate sceptic actors have also been successful at gaining media visibility and shaping the climate debate in post-socialist societies.

Part IV turns to issues of anti-environmental values, attitudes and public opinion. First, Riley E. Dunlap (Chapter 6) revisits early work on the environmental movement and its promotion of alternative social values and attitudes. This chapter includes a new preface wherein Dunlap reflects on how the antagonistic relationship between environmentalism and anti-environmentalism continues to shape public opinion, value conflicts and public policy. Kerry Ard et al. (Chapter 7) assess the relative importance of political party affiliation, corporate lobbying, and public opinion on US policy-makers' pro-environmental and anti-environmental voting patterns, thereby illuminating how public opinion translates (or fails to translate) into the political sphere. While public opinion does effectively influence Democrat policymakers, it has less impact for Republican policymakers, whose voting patterns are more influenced by corporate lobbying. Vanessa Bible (Chapter 8) examines environmental attitudes among resource extraction workers in Australia and argues that it is overly simplistic to define them simply as anti-environmental in their orientations. Anti-environmental attitudes are largely linked to livelihood concerns for extractive industry workers, but these livelihood concerns can be leveraged by corporate and political forces for anti-environmentalism.

Part V shifts focus to social network analyses of anti-environmentalism. Ruth E. McKie (Chapter 9) examines the international diffusion of climate sceptic movements beyond their traditional US base. While there are shared communicative strategies around supporting fossil fuel sectors, using economic development arguments to impede climate action, and emphasizing market-based environmental solutions, McKie also shows that although the climate sceptic movement forms an international network, the communicative strategies of this countermovement are geographically varied. Adam Lucas (Chapter 10) examines Australia's slow and intermittent trajectory towards climate change action. A network of economic and political elite actors that is well connected within the political sphere has been effective at obstructing Australian climate policy and protecting fossil fuel sector interests against public support for decarbonization and climate action. William K. Carroll et al. (Chapter 11) similarly examine how fossil fuel sector interests have worked through social network connections to articulate the Canadian oil sector—as exemplified by the Alberta oil sands—into a form of 'symbolic nationalism' that impedes climate policy responses that challenge ongoing fossil fuel extraction. Patrick Doreian and Andrej Mrvar (Chapter 12) use network analysis to identify the central role and disproportionate influence of the Koch Brothers in US anti-environmental movements. Their analysis shows how the Koch influence has diffused into a public and political force for climate scepticism and anti-environmentalism through the US mainstream media and Republican Party.

The subsequent parts of the *Handbook* examine anti-environmentalism in particular substantive contexts, with Part VI focusing on extractive development and Part VII focusing on agriculture and land use. S. Harris Ali (Chapter 13) examines the discursive strategies used by the Canadian government under Conservative Prime Minister Stephen Harper to protect the interests of the oil sector from the environmental movement, which was portrayed as an enemy of Canadian economic development. Hayriye Özen (Chapter 14) examines anti-environmental movements that arose in defense of gold mining in Turkey. Özen notes that the movement relied on discursive strategies of deflecting attention from environmental concerns by not directly addressing these concerns, but instead shifting discussion to a nationalistic discourse that portrayed anti-mining activists as a foreign-led attempt to undermine economic development.

The chapters in Part VII mark a distinct shift in the volume from analyses of classic anti-environmentalism to analyses that address critical/reflexive forms of anti-environmentalism. James S. Krueger (Chapter 15) turns to the food sovereignty movement to disturb the environmentalism/anti-environmentalism binary, as this movement has characteristics associated with environmentalism (opposition to industrial agricultural practices), as well as with classic anti-environmentalism (opposition to government intervention and regulation). Martin C. Lukas (Chapter 16) examines conflict between nature protection agencies and Indigenous hunter–gatherer communities around Betung Kerihun National Park in Indonesia and identifies how critical events can provoke local anti-environmental mobilization against parks and protected areas as nature conservation projects. Aleksandra Afanasyeva et al. (Chapter 17) examine opposition to wind power development in rural Alberta, Canada and note that it is inaccurate to characterize this opposition solely as anti-environmentalism. Wind power opponents often share pro-environmental views and call for more socially acceptable forms of renewable energy development.

Part VIII draws attention to the ways in which ethnicity and race complicate our understandings of environmentalism and anti-environmentalism. Pamela McMullin-Messier (Chapter 18) examines how questions of over-population and immigration policy became divisive for the US environmental movement and led to an anti-environmentalism that targeted the 'greening of hate' and used environmental discourse to legitimate an anti-immigration political agenda. Ian R. Carrillo (Chapter 19) centers race and racism in our understanding of the social and political dynamics of anti-environmentalism. He argues that race-blind approaches fail to grasp how anti-environmentalism and environmental injustice are bound up with the racial state formations that perpetuate racial inequality.

Part IX examines environmentalism/anti-environmentalism dynamics in the diverse contexts of labor unions, academic institutions and religious settings. Todd E. Vachon (Chapter 20) takes a closer look at the classic 'jobs versus the environment' assumptions about anti-environmentalism of US labor movements. Rather than seeing labor-based anti-environmentalism as a reflection of workers' personal attitudes and interests, Vachon highlights the political economic structures that have made good quality unionized jobs increasingly scarce. In this context, labor movement anti-environmentalism is an understandable response to preserving union jobs, but this also creates situations where union members become the public faces and voices for corporate anti-environmental interests. Victor W.Y. Lam (Chapter 21) looks at the religious sphere, where Christianity has often been implicated as a cultural source of human exceptionalism and anti-environmental values. Lam examines the protest movement against the proposed Trans Mountain pipeline expansion in British Columbia, Canada, which has drawn together activists from Indigenous, religious and environmentalist affiliations. Such protest movements serve as spaces to cultivate 'reflexive religious anti-environmentalism' that challenges anti-environmental currents within religious spheres. Helen Kopnina et al. (Chapter 22) turn their gaze on academia. They argue that critical strains of research and writing in the environmental sciences, humanities, and social sciences serve as an 'indirect' form of anti-environmentalism because academic critiques of environmentalism can undermine the much-needed political efforts of environmental movements and bolster the claims of classic anti-environmentalists.

The final chapter (Chapter 23) highlights some of the main themes of research on anti-environmentalism, and describes some of the different theoretical approaches to this (and related) topics. In this chapter we argue for greater efforts to incorporate syntheses of key analytical concepts from environmental social sciences and social movement studies as a theoretical foundation for ongoing research on the social and political dimensions of anti-environmentalism.

CONCLUSION

In their classic piece on countermovements, Meyer and Staggenborg (1996) set out two overarching research challenges: to understand 'the conditions under which countermovements emerge in response to movements' and to analyze 'the dynamics of movement–countermovement relations once a countermovement has arisen' (p. 1631). Expanding on this framework, the chapters in this *Handbook of Anti-Environmentalism* demonstrate that anti-environmentalism is not a monolithic social force but represents a spectrum of interests and objectives. It is often corporate led, ideologically conservative, and obstructionist to pro-environmental social and political change. However, it may also be critical but oriented towards provoking environmental movements to embrace self-reflexivity and more holistic or inclusive ways of working towards sustainability. The conceptual distinction between classic anti-environmentalism and critical/reflexive anti-environmentalism is thus an important contribution of the dialogue generated across the *Handbook*.

REFERENCES

Adkin, L.E. (1998) *The Politics of Sustainable Development: Citizens, Unions and the Corporations*. Montreal, QC: Black Rose Books.
Agyeman, J., Bullard, R.D. and Evans, B. (2003) *Just Sustainabilities: Development in an Unequal World*. Cambridge, MA: MIT Press.

Apfel, D.C. (2015) Exploring divestment as a strategy for change: An evaluation of the history, success, and challenges of fossil fuel divestment. *Social Research: An International Quarterly*. **82**(4), pp. 913–37.

Arnaquq-Baril, A. (2016) *Angry Inuk*. Toronto, ON: National Film Board of Canada.

Bacon, J.M. (2019) Settler colonialism as eco-social structure and the production of colonial ecological violence. *Environmental Sociology*. **5**(1), pp. 59–69.

Baker, S. (2006) *Sustainable Development*. New York: Routledge.

Beder, S. (1998) *Global Spin: The Corporate Assault on Environmentalism*. White River Junction, VT: Chelsea Green.

Bell, S.E. and Braun, Y.A. (2010) Coal, identity, and the gendering of environmental justice activism in central Appalachia. *Gender & Society*. **24**(6), pp. 794–813.

Besley, J.C. and Shanahan, J. (2004) Skepticism about media effects concerning the environment: Examining Lomborg's hypotheses. *Society & Natural Resources*. **17**(10), pp. 861–80.

Boussalis, C. and Coan, T.G. (2016) Text-mining the signals of climate change doubt. *Global Environmental Change*. **28**, pp. 89–100.

Boykoff, M.T. (2013) Public enemy no. 1? Understanding media representations of outlier views on climate change. *American Behavioral Scientist*. **57**(6), pp. 796–817.

Boynton, A. (2015) Formulating an anti-environmental opposition: Neoconservative intellectuals during the environmental decade. *The Sixties: A Journal of History, Politics and Culture*. **8**(1), pp. 1–26.

Braun, B. (2002) *The Intemperate Rainforest: Nature, Culture, and Power on Canada's West Coast*. Minneapolis, MN: University of Minnesota Press.

Brick, P.D. and R.M. Cawley (eds) (1996) *A Wolf in the Garden: The Land Rights Movement and the New Environmental Debate*. Lanham, MD: Rowman & Littlefield.

Brulle, R.J. (2014) Institutionalizing delay: Foundation funding and the creation of US climate change counter-movement organizations. *Climatic Change*. **122**(4), pp. 681–94.

Brulle, R.J. and Aronczyk, M. (2019) Organized opposition to climate change action in the United States. In: Kalfagianni, A., Fuchs, D. and Hayden, A. (eds) *Routledge Handbook of Global Sustainability Governance*. New York, NY: Routledge, pp. 218–29.

Brulle, R.J., Aronczyk, M. and Carmichael, J. (2020) Corporate promotion and climate change: An analysis of key variables affecting advertising spending by major oil corporations, 1986–2015. *Climatic Change*. **159**(1), pp. 87–101.

Bullard, R.D. (1990) *Dumping in Dixie: Race, Class, and Environmental Quality*. Boulder, CO: Westview.

Burke, W.K. (1995) The wise use movement. In: Berlet, C. (ed.) *Eyes Right!: Challenging the Right Wing Backlash*. Boston, MA: South End Press, pp. 135–54.

Caldwell, L.K. (1992) Globalizing environmentalism: Threshold of a new phase in international relations. In: Dunlap, R.E. and Mertig, A.G. (eds) *American Environmentalism*. New York, NY: Taylor & Francis, pp. 63–76.

Callison, C. (2014) *How Climate Change Comes to Matter: The Communal Life of Facts*. Durham, NC: Duke University Press.

Caniglia, B.S., Brulle, R.J. and Szasz, A. (2015) Civil society, social movements, and climate change. In: Dunlap, R.E. and Brulle, R.J. (eds) *Climate Change and Society: Sociological Perspectives*. New York, NY: Oxford University Press, pp. 235–68.

Čapek, S.M. (1993) The 'environmental justice' frame: A conceptual discussion and an application. *Social Problems*. **40**(1), pp. 5–24.

Carroll, W., Graham, N., Lang, M.K., Yunker, Z. and McCartney, K.D. (2018) The corporate elite and the architecture of climate change denial: A network analysis of carbon capital's reach into civil society. *Canadian Review of Sociology*. **55**(3), pp. 425–50.

Chodorkoff, D. (2014) *The Anthropology of Utopia: On Social Ecology and Community Development*. Porsgrunn: New Compass Press.

Coats, E. (2014) A proposal for a coherent, powerful, indigenous-led movement. In: Black, T., D'Arcy, S., Weiss, T. and Russell, J.K. (eds) *A Line in the Tar Sands: Struggles for Environmental Justice*, Toronto, ON: Between the Lines, pp. 267–78.

Cook, J., Supran, G., Lewandowsky, S., Oreskes, N. and Maibach, E. (2019) America misled: How the fossil fuel industry deliberately misled Americans about climate change. Fairfax, VA: George

Mason University Center for Climate Change Communication. Available from: https://www.climatechangecommunication.org/america-misled/.
Cook, J., Oreskes, N., Doran, P.T., Anderegg, W.R., Verheggen, B., Maibach, E.W., Carlton, J.S., Lewandowsky, S., Skuce, A.G., Green, S.A. and Nuccitelli, D. (2016) Consensus on consensus: A synthesis of consensus estimates on human-caused global warming. *Environmental Research Letters.* **11**(4), p. 048002.
Corrigall-Brown, C. (2016) What gets covered? An examination of media coverage of the environmental movement in Canada. *Canadian Review of Sociology/Revue Canadienne de Sociologie.* **53**(1), pp. 72–93.
Cronon, W. (1995) The trouble with wilderness, or, getting back to the wrong nature. In: Cronon, W. (ed.) *Uncommon Ground: Toward Reinventing Nature.* New York, NY: W.W. Norton & Company, pp. 69–90.
Dauvergne, P. and Neville, K.J. (2011) Mindbombs of right and wrong: Cycles of contention in the activist campaign to stop Canada's seal hunt. *Environmental Politics.* **20**(2), pp. 192–209.
Davidson, D. (2012) Analysing responses to climate change through the lens of reflexivity. *The British Journal of Sociology.* **63**(4), pp. 616–40.
Davidson, D.J. (2019) Emotion, reflexivity and social change in the era of extreme fossil fuels. *The British Journal of Sociology.* **70**(2), pp. 442–62.
Davis, J. (1991) *The Earth First! Reader: Ten Years of Radical Environmentalism.* Salt Lake City, UT: Peregrine Smith.
Doyle, A., Elliott, B. and Tindall, D. (1997) Framing the forests: Corporations, the BC Forest Alliance, and the media. In: Carroll, W.K. (ed.) *Organizing Dissent: Contemporary Social Movements in Theory and Practice.* Toronto, ON: Garamond Press, pp. 240–68.
Dryzek, J.S. (1997) *The Politics of the Earth: Environmental Discourses.* New York, NY: Oxford University Press.
Dunk, T. (1994) Talking about trees: Environment and society in forest workers' culture. *Canadian Review of Sociology/Revue Canadienne de Sociologie.* **31**(1), pp. 14–34.
Dunlap, R.E. and Jacques, P.J. (2013) Climate change denial books and conservative think tanks: Exploring the connection. *American Behavioral Scientist.* **57**(6), pp. 699–731.
Dunlap, R.E. and McCright, A.M. (2015) Challenging climate change: The denial countermovement. In: Dunlap, R.E. and Brulle, R.J. (eds) *Climate Change and Society: Sociological Perspectives.* New York, NY: Oxford University Press, pp. 300–332.
Dunlap, R.E. and Mertig, A.G. (eds) (1992) *American Environmentalism: The US Environmental Movement, 1970–1990.* New York, NY: Taylor & Francis.
Eyerman, R. and Jamison, A. (1991) *Social Movements: A Cognitive Approach.* State College, PA: Penn State Press.
Farrell, J. (2016a) Corporate funding and ideological polarization about climate change. *PNAS.* **113**(1), 92–7.
Farrell, J. (2016b) Network structure and influence of the climate change counter-movment. *Nature Climate Change.* **6**(4), pp. 370–74.
Fisher, D. (2006) *Activism, Inc.: How the Outsourcing of Grassroots Campaigns is Strangling Progressive Politics in America.* Stanford, CA: Stanford University Press.
Fisher, D.R. and Jorgenson, A.K. (2019) Ending the stalemate: Toward a theory of anthro-shift. *Sociological Theory.* **37**(4), pp. 342–62.
Foster, J.B. (1993) The limits of environmentalism without class: Lessons from the ancient forest struggle of the Pacific Northwest. *Capitalism Nature Socialism.* **4**(1), pp. 11–41.
Freudenberg, N. and Steinsapir, C. (1992) Not in our backyards: The grassroots environmental movement. In: Dunlap, R.E. and Mertig, A.G. (eds) *American Environmentalism.* New York, NY: Taylor & Francis, pp. 27–37.
Freudenburg, W.R. and Muselli, V. (2013) Reexamining climate change debates: Scientific disagreement or scientific certainty argumentation methods (SCAMs)? *American Behavioral Scientist.* **57**(6), pp. 777–95.
Gerhardt, H., Kristoffersen, B. and Stuvøy, K. (2018) Saving the Arctic: Green peace or oil riot? In: Gad, U.P. and Strandsbjerg, J. (eds) *The Politics of Sustainability in the Arctic.* New York, NY: Routledge, pp. 149–62.

Gould, K.A., Pellow, D.N. and Schnaiberg, A. (2008) *The Treadmill of Production: Injustice and Unsustainability in the Global Economy*. Boulder, CO: Paradigm.

Gould, K.A., Weinberg, A.S. and Schnaiberg, A. (1993) Legitimating impotence: Pyrrhic victories of the modern environmental movement. *Qualitative Sociology*. **16**(3), pp. 207–46.

Graugaard, N.D. (2018) 'Without seals, there are no Greenlanders': Colonial and postcolonial narratives of sustainability and Inuit seal hunting. In: Gad, U.P. and Strandsbjerg, J. (eds) *The Politics of Sustainability in the Arctic*. London; Routledge, pp. 74–93.

Guha, R. and Alier, J.M. (1997) *Varieties of Environmentalism: Essays North and South*. New York, NY: Routledge.

Harvey, M.W.T. (1991) Echo Park, Glen Canyon and the postwar wilderness movement. *Pacific Historical Review*. **60**(1), pp. 43–77.

Hay, P.R. (2002) *Main Currents in Western Environmental Thought*. Bloomington, IN: Indiana University Press.

Hays, S.P. (1951) *Conservation and the Gospel of Efficiency: The Progressive Conservation Movement 1890–1920*. Cambridge, MA: Harvard University Press.

Hochschild, A.R. (2016) *Strangers in Their Own Land: Anger and Mourning on the American Right*. New York, NY: The New Press.

Humphrey, M. (2000) 'Nature' in deep ecology and social ecology: Contesting the core. *Journal of Political Ideologies*. **5**(2), pp. 247–68.

Jamison, A., Eyerman, R., Cramer, J. and Laessoe, J. (1991) *The Making of the New Environmental Consciousness: A Comparative Study of Environmental Movements in Sweden, Denmark and the Netherlands*. Edinburgh: Edinburgh University Press.

Jasper, J.M. (2018) Strangers in their own land. *Sociological Forum*. **33**(2), pp. 556–9.

Katz-Kimchi, M. and Manosevitch, I. (2015) Mobilizing Facebook users against Facebook's energy policy: The case of Greenpeace unfriend coal campaign. *Environmental Communication*. **9**(2), pp. 248–67.

Keskitalo, A. (2018) Indigenous guardianship and self-governance: Ecosystems and thriving communities, presented at Arctic Circle, 20 October, Reykjavik, Iceland.

Konishi, M. (2018) The impact of global NGOs on Japanese press coverage of climate negotiations: An analysis of the new 'background media strategy'. *Environmental Communication*. **12**(4), pp. 558–73.

Lameman, C. (2014) Kihci Pikiskwewin – speaking the truth. In Black, T., D'Arcy, S., Weiss, T. and Russell, J.K. (eds) *A Line in the Tar Sands: Struggles for Environmental Justice*. Toronto, ON: Between the Lines, pp. 118–26.

Laudati, A. (2010) Ecotourism: The modern predator? Implications of gorilla tourism on local livelihoods in Bwindi Impenetrable National Park, Uganda. *Environment and Planning D: Society and Space*. **28**(4), pp. 726–43.

Lewin, P.G. (2019) 'Coal is not just a job, it's a way of life': The cultural politics of coal production in central Appalachia. *Social Problems*. **66**(1), pp. 51–68.

Love, S. and Obst, D. (eds) (1972) *Ecotage*. New York, NY: Pocket Books.

Luke, T.W. (1997) *Ecocritique: Contesting the Politics of Nature, Economy, and Culture*. Minneapolis, MN: University of Minnesota Press.

MacEachern, A. (2001) *Natural Selections: National Parks in Atlantic Canada, 1935–1970*. Montreal, QC and Kingston, ON: McGill-Queen's Press.

Macnaghten, P. and Urry, J. (1998) *Contested Natures*. Thousand Oaks, CA: Sage.

MacNeil, R. (2014) Canadian environmental policy under Conservative majority rule. *Environmental Politics*. **23**(1), pp. 174–8.

Maher, N.M. (2009) *Nature's New Deal: The Civilian Conservation Corps and the Roots of the American Environmental Movement*. New York, NY: Oxford University Press.

Mayer, B. (2009) Cross-Movement coalition formation: Bridging the labor–environment divide. *Sociological Inquiry*. **79**(2), pp. 219–39.

McCloskey, M. (1972) Wilderness movement at the crossroads, 1945–1970. *Pacific Historical Review*. **41**(3), pp. 346–61.

McCright, A.M. and Dunlap, R.E. (2010) Anti-reflexivity. *Theory, Culture & Society*. **27**(2–3), pp. 100–133.

McLevey, J. (2014) Think tanks, funding, and the politics of policy knowledge in Canada. *Canadian Review of Sociology/Revue Canadienne de Sociologie.* **51**(1), pp. 54–75.

McVeigh, R. (2017) Deep story or self-serving narrative? Understanding the paradox of conservative politics. *Contemporary Sociology.* **46**(5), pp. 510–12.

Mertig, A.G., Dunlap, R.E. and Morrison, D.E. (2002) The environmental movement in the United States. In: Dunlap, R.E. and Michelson, W. (eds) *Handbook of Environmental Sociology.* Westport, CT: Greenwood Press.

Meyer, D.S. and Staggenborg, S. (1996) Movements, countermovements, and the structure of political opportunity. *American Journal of Sociology.* **101**(6), pp. 1628–60.

Mohai, P., Pellow, D. and Roberts, J.T. (2009) Environmental justice. *Annual Review of Environment and Resources.* **34**, pp. 405–30.

Mol, A.P.J., Spaargaren, G. and Sonnenfeld, D.A. (2013) Ecological modernization theory: Taking stock, moving forward. In: Lockie, S., Sonnefeld, D.A. and Fisher, D. (eds) *Routledge International Handbook of Social and Environmental Change.* New York, NY: Routledge, pp. 31–46.

Murphy, R. (2015) The emerging hypercarbon reality, technological and post-carbon utopias, and social innovation to low-carbon societies. *Current Sociology.* **63**(3), pp. 317–38.

Nash, R.F. (1967) *Wilderness and the American Mind.* New Haven, CT: Yale University Press.

Nixon, R. (2011) *Slow Violence and the Environmentalism of the Poor.* Cambridge, MA: Harvard University Press.

Norton, P. (2003) A critique of generative class theories of environmentalism and of the labour–environmentalist relationship. *Environmental Politics.* **12**(4), 96–119.

Oreskes, N. and Conway, E.M. (2011) *Merchants of Doubt: How a Handful of Scientists Obscured the Truth on Issues from Tobacco Smoke to Global Warming.* New York, NY: Bloomsbury.

Pellow, D.N. and Brulle, R.J. (eds) (2005) *Power, Justice and the Environment.* Cambridge, MA: MIT Press.

Petulla, J.M. (1977) *American Environmental History.* San Francisco, CA: Boyd & Fraser.

Polletta, F. and Callahan, J. (2017) Deep stories, nostalgia narratives, and fake news: Storytelling in the Trump era. *American Journal of Cultural Sociology.* **5**, pp. 392–408.

Ray, R. (2017) A case of internal colonialism? Arlie Hochschild's *Strangers in Their Own Land. British Journal of Sociology.* **68**(1), pp. 129–33.

Reichwein, P. (2014) *Climber's Paradise: Making Canada's Mountain Parks, 1906–1974.* Edmonton, AB: University of Alberta Press.

Rodgers, K. and Ingram, D. (2019) Decolonizing environmentalism in the Arctic? Greenpeace, complicity and negotiating the contradictions of solidarity in the Inuit Nunangat. *Interface: A Journal for and about Social Movements.* **11**(2), pp. 11–34.

Rodgers, K. and Scobie, W. (2015) Sealfies, seals and celebs: Expressions of Inuit resilience in the Twitter era. *Interface: A Journal on Social Movements.* **7**(1), pp. 70–97.

Rome, A. (2013) *The Genius of Earth Day: How a 1970 Teach-in Unexpectedly Made the First Green Generation.* New York, NY: Hill and Wang.

Rowlands, I.H. (2000) Beauty and the beast? BP's and Exxon's positions on global climate change. *Environment and Planning C: Government and Policy.* **18**(3), pp. 339–554.

Schnaiberg, A. and Gould, K.A. (2000) *Environment and Society: The Enduring Conflict.* Caldwell, NJ: Blackburn Press.

Schrepfer, S.R. (2005) *Nature's Altars: Mountains, Gender, and American Environmentalism.* Lawrence, KS: University Press of Kansas.

Shapira, H. (2017) Who cares what they think? Going about the right the wrong way. *Contemporary Sociology.* **46**(5), pp. 512–17.

Spaargaren, G. and Mol, A.P. (2008) Greening global consumption: Redefining politics and authority. *Global Environmental Change.* **18**(3), pp. 350–59.

Staggenborg, S. and Ramos, H. (2016) *Social Movements.* Oxford: Oxford University Press.

Stuart, D., Gunderson, R. and Petersen, B. (2020) The climate crisis as a catalyst for emancipatory transformation: An examination of the possible. *International Sociology.* **35**(4), pp. 433–56.

Switzer, J.V. (1997) *Green Backlash: The History and Politics of Environmental Opposition in the U.S..* Boulder, CO: Lynne Rienner.

Thomas-Muller, C. (2014), The rise of the native rights-based strategic framework: Our last best hope to save our water, air, and earth. In: Black, T., D'Arcy, S., Weiss, T. and Russell, J.K. (eds) *A Line in the Tar Sands: Struggles for Environmental Justice*. Toronto, ON: Between the Lines, pp. 240–52.

Tindall, D., Howe, A. and Mauboulès, C. (2021) Tangled roots: Personal networks and the participation of individuals in an anti-environmentalism countermovement. *Sociological Perspectives*. **64**(1), pp. 5–36.

Turner, J.M. and Isenberg, A.C. (2018) *The Republican Reversal: Conservatives and the Environment from Nixon to Trump*. Cambridge, MA: MIT Press.

Vasey, D. (2014) The environmental NGO industry and frontline communities. In: Black, T., D'Arcy, S., Weiss, T. and Russell, J.K. (eds) *A Line in the Tar Sands: Struggles for Environmental Justice*. Toronto, ON: Between the Lines, pp. 64–75.

Walker, J. (2020) *More Heat than Life: The Tangled Roots of Ecology, Energy, and Economics*. Singapore: Palgrave Macmillan.

Washington, H. (2015) *Demystifying Sustainability: Towards Real Solutions*. New York, NY: Routledge.

Washington, H., Taylor, B., Kopnina, H., Cryer., P. and Piccolo, J.J. (2017) Why ecocentrism is the key pathway to sustainability. *The Ecological Citizen*. **1**(1), pp. 35–41.

Weyler, R. (2015) *Greenpeace: How a Group of Ecologists, Journalists, and Visionaries Changed the World*. Emmaus, PA: Rodale.

Young, N. and Coutinho, A. (2013) Government, anti-reflexivity, and the construction of public ignorance about climate change: Australia and Canada compared. *Global Environmental Politics*. **13**(2), pp. 89–108.

PART II

THEORETICAL PERSPECTIVES

2. Understanding countermovements
Suzanne Staggenborg and David S. Meyer

Activists have taken to the streets around the world to demand forceful action to confront climate change. In doing so, they face different constellations of opponents everywhere. In most—but not all—of the democratic world, the reality of climate change is accepted, and political debates turn on strategies for response. In the United States, however, climate change deniers have enjoyed firm perches within the federal government, including the White House during the Trump administration. Activists have targeted the federal government, and they have faced opposition from both the government and supporters of a fossil fuel economy. The Trump administration resisted even modest environmental measures and sought to roll back policies implemented by the preceding Obama administration. But governmental inaction is not new; it has long been buoyed by environmental countermovements promoting skepticism about the reality, roots and prospective remedies of the climate action movement (Brulle and Aronczyk, 2020). Our research on countermovements aims to help in understanding this phenomenon, and consideration of the environmental case helps us refine and expand a theory that we began developing more than two decades ago (Meyer and Staggenborg, 1996).

Many modern social movements attract countermovements, which oppose their social change goals. Movement–countermovement conflicts are a critical element of contemporary politics, and the rise of a countermovement affects the ability of a movement to mobilize supporters and make progress on its policy goals. Opposing movements can endure for many years and may have multiple impacts on one another. Countermovement mobilization often increases and maintains support for the initiating movement by creating threats that sustain organizations and activities. While threats help organizers mobilize their bases of support, however, they also create obstacles to political and policy gains. The net effect is government that is stymied in responding to critical issues, including climate change but also inequality, immigration, health care, and gun violence. The presence of an opposing movement is an essential element in the structure of political opportunities, creating both provocation and obstacles for those who want to promote social change.

Our goal in this chapter is to lay out the conditions under which countermovements emerge and succeed as a basis for understanding anti-environmentalism. We draw on the theoretical ideas in our earlier work, but we also consider how that framework might be altered nearly 25 years later, due to both our previous oversights and the ways in which the political landscape in advanced industrialized societies has changed. In our original analysis, we explored movement–countermovement interaction in a variety of social movements, but our prime exemplar was the abortion conflict. At that point, the abortion debate in the United States had sustained volatile movements on both sides for many years. More than two decades later, that movement–countermovement pair continues to animate a wide variety of political action with no resolution in sight. In this chapter we reflect on how anti-environmental movements compare to anti-abortion movements, as well as conflicts over other issues, as we continue to think about movement–countermovement interactions. The stakes for environmentalism are truly extraordinary insofar as the climate change countermovement has impeded progress in halting climate change and seriously endangered the planet.

WHY COUNTERMOVEMENTS EMERGE

In 1996, we identified three reasons why a countermovement might emerge in response to a movement, and we now add a fourth and fifth factor: First, insofar as the movement is successful, opponents are likely to want to emulate it. Second, when established interests are threatened, they are likely to strike back. Third, the availability of political allies encourages the formation of a countermovement. Fourth, social media and internet communications allow for the rapid spread of movement ideas and the easy countering of them by opponents, thereby supporting the emergence of a countermovement. Fifth, resources facilitate countermovement mobilization. In our initial conceptualization, we largely neglected the issue of resources, focusing instead on opportunities and political context. To some extent, this reflected our focus on the abortion debate, in which both sides have been able to sustain sufficient financial and human resources over an extended period of time. We implicitly assumed a rough symmetry of resources and strategies but looking at the climate debate and other cases, we need to reconceptualize this issue. While the anti-abortion movement has received support from conservative organizations and churches, the vast network of conservative organizations, corporations, foundations and think tanks supporting the anti-environmental movement has resulted in a huge asymmetry between environmental movements and countermovements (Brulle and Aronczyk, 2020; Dunlap and McCright, 2015).

Signs of Movement Influence

When social movements demonstrate extensive and vigorous support, attain broad visibility, and attract notable allies, they appear likely to make progress in attaining their goals, posing a threat to their opponents. In a democratic polity, large public demonstrations, for example, send the message to allies and to elected representatives that significant numbers of voters care about an issue, and are willing to undertake political action. Public opinion polls reveal the extent of citizen support for issues promoted by a movement, and activism can persuade pollsters to ask about movement issues. Effective activism can draw media attention to movement issues, helping to increase the visibility of those issues and put them on the public agenda. By raising the public profile of their concerns, movements can force government to respond to them and, sometimes, win support. Passage of legislation that advances movement goals would of course be a strong indicator of influence, but even the suggestion that policies will change in the direction of movement concerns is likely to spur opposition.

Protest movements can create opportunities for institutional action by exploiting, extending, or prying open a 'policy window' (Kingdon, 1984), which then encourages other actors to mobilize around the issues in different venues. Following political opportunity theory (Eisinger, 1973; Tilly, 1978; Meyer, 2004), we expect the relationship between movement influence and countermovement emergence to be curvilinear (Meyer and Staggenborg, 1996, pp. 1635–6). Ineffective movements are far less likely to provoke countermovements because they create no real threat, but movements that win definitive victories are also unlikely to spur countermovements. It is movements that credibly threaten to have some influence that are most likely to rouse countermovements because opponents see the possibility of influencing policy outcomes by organizing a movement in response. However, victories are rarely definitive after only one policy outcome, and a single victory often incites opposition.

State structures also affect the ability of a movement to score policy victories and foreclose countermovement mobilization. States with divided governmental authority, such as the federal structures of the United States, Canada and Germany, are most likely to experience prolonged movement–countermovement conflicts. In states with federal structures, opposing movements are likely to find a mix of governmental support and opposition at different levels. When one level such as the national one is unfavorable, movement or countermovement activists can switch their efforts to a more favorable arena such as the state or provincial legislature. In contrast, unitary governments like Britain and France are less likely to see prolonged movement–countermovement conflicts because they are better able to avoid internal conflict in making and implementing policies. In such cases, the state bears the burden of countering a movement.[1] It's not that competitors in the public debate won't develop and deploy movement structures and tactics, but rather that one side can win the unambiguous support of government, making subsequent mobilization less necessary or urgent.

The case of the American abortion conflict shows how movement–countermovement conflicts can endure for decades, even after the movement wins what seems like a decisive victory. In 1973, the abortion rights movement won a major victory when the Supreme Court legalized abortion throughout the country. But that victory fueled the political conflict, as the anti-abortion countermovement picked up steam and continued the battle at both state and national levels. Federal systems do vary in the opportunities they provide for actions by opposing movements (see Schwartz and Tatalovich, 2018). In comparing abortion politics in Canada and the United States, we found that differences in the political structures and cultures of the two federal polities produced differences in their abortion conflicts (Meyer and Staggenborg, 1998). Both countries have experienced long-standing battles over abortion, but political parties in Canada exert far more control over individual members than they do in the United States, making it more difficult for individual members to continually raise the abortion issue. As they depend on institutional party support, Canadian politicians have little interest in cultivating a set of divisive social movement organizations to fund and animate individual campaigns. Canadian courts have also been weaker historically, making it more difficult for the countermovement to use them to erode abortion rights. Partly a reflection of institutional political structures, the Canadian political culture is also less prone to mobilization on explicitly moral issues; Canadians are less religious, and religion plays a far more limited role in party politics than in the United States. As a result, it has been more difficult for the Canadian anti-abortion countermovement to sustain vigorous protest mobilization or cultivate institutional allies, much less effect change, than its American counterpart.

The environmental movement in the United States, like the abortion rights movement, won some major victories in the 1970s, including the creation of the Environmental Protection Agency in 1970 and landmark environmental legislation such as the Clean Water Act of 1972 and the Endangered Species Act of 1973. Environmental organizations became established in Washington, DC, and promoted a new awareness of environmental threats. This progress greatly alarmed industry and conservatives opposed to government regulation generally. The first Earth Day in 1970 was a vivid demonstration of the strength of environmental sentiment in the population and an incentive for conservatives to create an anti-environmental countermovement. In doing so, they were able to build on existing right-wing movements and their conservative allies in the United States. Right-wing movements opposed to civil rights, government regulation and immigration had long existed in the United States (Diamond, 1995; Lipset and Raab, 1978), and a New Right emerged in the 1970s opposed to policies such as the Equal Rights Amendment, legal abortion and gay rights. Opposition to environmentalism also took off, with support from conservative legislators, industry, and right-wing think tanks (Beder, 2002; Brulle and Aronczyk, 2020; Dunlap and McCright, 2010, 2011; Oreskes and Conway, 2010). Opponents were animated by ideology, networked alliances and corporate interests. This mobilization, in turn, spurred growth of the environmental movement (Spears, 2020).

Political battles played out in both local and national politics over a variety of environmental issues, most visibly, nuclear power (Joppke, 1993). The battles over environmental issues were waged in a range of venues, and industry forces deployed a repertoire of approaches that would be mirrored in a range of other movement–countermovement conflicts. Opponents of environmental regulation appeared at public hearings, engaged in electoral politics, and lobbied legislators, but rarely organized protest demonstrations. They questioned the science underpinning regulatory efforts, sometimes producing contrary scientific claims. Grafting claims about politics onto a raging culture war, they accused environmentalists of being elitist and out of touch with authentic Americans. Anti-environmentalists emphasized potentially negative effects on economic growth, employment and lifestyles, and opposed government action to restrict market and corporate decisions (Oreskes and Conway, 2010; Shulman, 2008). In effect, environmental countermovements made reactive claims and sought to halt government action, an advantageous position in American politics.

Movement Threats to Established Interests

Movements that begin to exert influence are likely to threaten some established interests, such as industries or government elites. A policy developed in response to movement constituents can seem threatening to other groups and provide opportunities for counter-mobilization. While most movements are 'conflict movements' that face opposition, some movements are 'consensus movements' that enjoy widespread support (McCarthy and Wolfson, 1992)—at least for a while. But movements that attempt to promote political, policy or cultural change, and the uncertainty associated with virtually any kind of change, can inflame public opposition. The nature of opposition to a movement varies, and not all opposition takes the form of a countermovement similar in shape to the initiating movement. Moreover, both movements and countermovements vary in size and scope. Some countermovements, such as the pro-nuclear power movement, are initiated by elites and rely on elite resources (Useem and Zald, 1982), while others originate with grassroots supporters and enjoy widespread support or consist of a mixture of elite and grassroots support. It is generally too simple to describe a movement as having a grassroots or elite base, because most ongoing campaigns require both forms of support. Countermovements that oppose environmental regulation can be particularly powerful because they include a wide variety of organizations that 'act in different political and cultural arenas and employ different time horizons to achieve a range of objectives' (Brulle and Aronczyk, 2020, p. 219). Tindall et al. (2020) describe one local campaign as 'quasi-astroturf', an ostensibly grassroots campaign initiated and motivated by outside monied interests, but nonetheless containing sincere and active local participants.

Movements create different kinds of threats, which results in the emergence of different types of countermovements. Some movements threaten economic interests, such as the fossil fuel industries, and some economic threats are much broader than others. Other movements pose threats that are primarily symbolic or moral in nature rather than challenging the allocation of some scarce resource (e.g., public lands or government spending). Movement issues may symbolize a broad set of values and behaviors, thereby threatening a range of people who are drawn into a countermovement for different reasons. And some movements threaten both material interests and cultural concerns. Opponents of cultural and political change have a clear interest in framing the threats they face as broad, rather than limited to specific interests. The ways in which movement demands are framed affect how threatening they are to existing interests and values. For example, the movement against drunk driving, in contrast to the earlier Prohibition movement, faced little opposition so long as it focused on the drunk driver as the problem rather than on the alcohol industry (Gusfield, 1981; McCarthy, 1994). McCarthy and Wolfson (1992) argued, however, that the movement was gradually changing from one of consensus to one of conflict as it began to focus on broader reforms beyond the individual culpability of drunk drivers, such as raising the legal drinking age and restricting alcohol advertisements. Frames that threatened the alcohol and automobile industries were more likely to provoke elite-generated countermovements (McCarthy, 1994). The alcohol industry, like the tobacco industry, was willing to cooperate with efforts that emphasized individual choices and responsibilities, partly to forestall larger efforts at regulation. As the American political system includes multiple political institutions with the potential to influence policy that respond to different constituencies and timetables, proactive change is extremely difficult to achieve. In this regard, the political playing field for movements is virtually always tilted in favor of the forces that work to prevent change (Meyer, 2015).

The conflict over guns in the United States is one that involves multiple interests and has symbolic meaning, which helps to explain why the gun control movement has had such a difficult time creating change. A strong countermovement to the gun control movement attracts people who support gun ownership for different reasons, such as hunters and homeowners who feel they need guns to protect themselves. Opponents of gun regulation took over the National Rifle Association, which previously encompassed a range of opinions on government policy and was more of a service organization than a political force (Winkler, 2011). Although the NRA continues to serve hobbyists and sport shooters, the now dominant approach of the organization—and the firearms industry that supports it—frames guns as a means of self-defense. Although there were ideological interests behind this move, the turn also represented a pragmatic business strategy. Hunting and sport shooting have steadily declined in American life, such that maintaining a robust market for firearms necessitated expanding the audience. The NRA, far and away the dominant organization within the movement against gun regulation, attracts many white, rural, working and middle-class men who are concerned about a loss of status and prestige associated with the rise of feminism, gay rights, and other issues; in defending guns, they are also defending 'frontier masculinity' (Melzer, 2009).

Guns have symbolic meaning, which helps to explain their appeal to groups such as white men who feel themselves to be declining in economic standing (Mencken and Froese, 2019). Over a period of decades, the NRA expanded its rhetorical agenda to mirror that of the hard right of the Republican Party, particularly on social issues. In effect, a political battle about national and state policies on firearms grew into a cultural conflict that invoked strong identities. This transformation may be typical for long-lived movement–countermovement battles.

A dispute about policy accretes connections to other causes and constituencies; in the current political alignment, this entails partisan polarization (Laschever and Meyer, 2021). As a result, resolution of any policy dispute that becomes heavily embedded in partisanship becomes much harder to manage with compromise. The countermovement battle becomes a contest not only over differences in the increments of policy, but also values, politics and identity.

Abortion provides a particularly clear example of a policy dispute that over time became a moral conflict insofar as the issue symbolizes changes in gender relations and sexual behavior. While some constituents of the anti-abortion countermovement, such as liberal Catholics, may oppose abortion strictly on religious grounds, others also oppose changes in sex, gender and 'family values' that they associate with abortion (Cuneo, 1989; Luker, 1984; Klatch, 1987; Markson, 1982). In *Abortion and the Politics of Motherhood*, Kristin Luker (1984) argued that the abortion conflict was a battle over the meaning of motherhood. In her analysis, the abortion rights movement attracted women committed to careers and women's rights, who saw motherhood as only one part of their lives, while the anti-abortion countermovement appealed to women who had committed themselves to the more traditional female roles of wife and mother, and who felt threatened by changing gender relations. This type of concern might change over time and an issue like abortion could lose its symbolic importance. In a symposium on Luker's classic book, Jon Shields (2012) argues that anti-abortion movement supporters have been influenced by feminism and have become less traditional in their gender ideology, moving closer to abortion rights movement constituents. He contends that the conflict over abortion is about the rights of women versus the rights of fetuses rather than being a conflict over gender. Lori Freedman and Tracy Weitz (2012) point out that there is no longer any debate about women being in the labor force and that a majority of women who have abortions are already mothers. These comments suggest that the meaning of abortion has changed over time. However, other observers argue that abortion continues to symbolize broader concerns, which change along with shifts in public opinion, such as 'women's growing freedom and power, including their sexual freedom and power' (Pollitt, 2014, p. 31).

While women's labor force participation is no longer controversial, a stance against abortion rights remains connected to other socially conservative positions, including positions that limit civil rights protections for LGBTQ people. The point is that the linkages of issues are dynamic and respond to larger shifts in public opinion and political alignments. Increasingly in American politics, extremely partisan politics lead to a sorting and shifting of opinion such that those with a liberal position on a favored issue will, through both pragmatic political dealing and social ties, develop liberal positions on others, and conservative positions on even ostensibly unrelated issues, such as abortion rights and tax policy, will also cluster. In abortion politics, while both rights and restrictions claimed support within both parties in the 1970s, serious aspirants for office essentially had to adopt the preferred position of their party. Ostensible outliers who held unusual combinations of policy positions were increasingly defined by association with the most salient issue position. Thus, as Kelsy Kretschmer (2009) notes, Feminists for Life was dismissed as a group of inauthentic feminists, and Catholics for a Free Choice was similarly disparaged as wayward by the organized Catholic Church.

Although environmental issues might be expected to feature greater levels of consensus and a less moralistic and partisan politics, we see the same trajectory toward increased polarization. Initially, the United States experienced more consensual politics when the Environmental Protection Agency was established in 1970 by Republican President Nixon and the landmark environmental legislation of the 1970s, including the Clean Water Act of

1972 and the Endangered Species Act of 1973, was enacted. But any hope that environmental issues could escape partisan politics and larger identity meanings has since eroded. Partly, this is a function of the threats represented by regulatory policies about issues such as pollution and nuclear power. Compliance with regulations increased industry costs, and movement victories on these issues alarmed both industry and conservative activists. In the 1970s, a growing New Right linking business interests with grassroots social conservatives began to exercise electoral power. Opposition to government regulation of industry on environmental issues united two critical constituencies with ostensibly different interests: manufacturers and fossil fuel businesses that wanted to avoid higher costs, and ideological conservatives opposed to all sorts of regulation on principle.

That movement won a major victory in 1980 with the election of Republican President Ronald Reagan, who opposed government intervention in the economy. Reagan pursued an aggressively anti-environmental agenda that included reduced regulations on car mileage and pollution (Dunlap and McCright, 2010). As a symbol of resolve, he disconnected solar panels that his predecessor, Jimmy Carter, had installed on the roof of the White House (Jacobs, 2016). Reagan appointed agency heads who would pursue his policy agenda and promote political understanding that would support ongoing resistance to environmental regulations. Notably, Reagan's first Secretary of the Interior, James Watt, worked to open federal lands for development. Watt also explicitly linked the interests of businesses seeking to reduce government regulation with the evangelical goals of religious conservatives. Outside of government, opposition to environmental initiatives was supported by well-funded right-wing activists who launched a 'wise use' countermovement organized in the late 1980s to promote development over environmental protection (Palast, 2016). This movement exploited sentiments among residents in areas such as the Pacific Northwest, where loggers and others economically dependent on the timber industry saw a threat in the protection of endangered species, most notably the spotted owl. The countermovement provoked cultural conflict between loggers seeking to protect their jobs and way of life and 'outsiders' such as environmentalists, hippies and gay people (Stein, 2001, p. 122).

It is important to note that the peculiar electoral rules in American politics, which welcome very long and expensive campaigns for office, barely coordinated by weak political parties, allow monied interests more influence than in other political contexts. The strong mobilization of an ongoing campaign against environmental regulation also kept environmental activists engaged. As a result, the existence of opposing movements exacerbated growing tendencies in American politics toward social and political polarization, where any regulation was framed as extreme. Thus, the 1980s saw an anti-environmental regulation movement grow and make significant inroads in politics, exercising increasing influence within the Republican Party. The ideological bases of this movement were surprisingly diverse, including religious fundamentalists who claimed to follow a divine mandate to use the earth, business conservatives wary of government regulation, and industries likely to be affected by regulation. Conflicts around environmental action mapped onto cultural conflicts that energized activists. Business support meant that campaigns against environmental regulation benefited from a significant infusion of resources. Although there were some similarities between advocates on both sides of the issue, the tactics differed, reflecting both different resources and the presence of allies in government. Large demonstrations were mostly the province of environmental activists. Both sides engaged in public education campaigns, though anti-environmentalists often questioned scientific findings. Both sides also engaged in party politics and elections.

The success of one side in mobilizing provoked and encouraged its opponents. As Dunlap and McCright (2011, p. 146) describe, initial efforts by the Reagan Administration to diminish environmental protections created backlash, and environmental opponents learned 'to question the *need* for environmental regulations by challenging evidence of environmental degradation, rather than the *goal* of environmental protection.' This became critical in the battle over climate change as the countermovement framed the issue in terms of the 'uncertainty' about the human origins of climate change (Oreskes and Conway, 2010). Organizers against action on climate change invested in debunking the scientific consensus, even funding scientists and permanent organizations, like the Heartland Institute, that expressed skepticism about the scientific consensus on climate (Mayer, 2016). Dunlap and McCright (2011) examine the 'climate change denial machine' that was created by the fossil fuels industry, corporations, conservative foundations, right-wing think tanks, front groups, the conservative media, and 'astroturf' organizations and campaigns. In comparison to the abortion rights movement, which does not threaten powerful corporate interests, the environmental movement presents significant threats to multiple interests, both material and symbolic. Consequently, the anti-environmental countermovement is much more complex, making it extremely powerful (Brulle and Aronczyk, 2020). Although anti-environmental countermovements have some grassroots support, they receive extensive resources from elites. Framing has been accomplished by expert attacks on those scientists who share a strong consensus on the causes of climate change. While there are some divisions among elites over climate change, particularly within corporate America, elite support for anti-environmentalism has remained strong (Dunlap and McCright, 2011, p. 148).

Support from Allies

Available support from institutional actors, elites of various sorts, and other allies is another predictor of countermovement emergence, which is related to threats to existing interests. Under some circumstances, government authorities, businesses and other powerful interests may have an incentive to assist in the organization of a movement or countermovement. These elites, who enjoy disproportionate access to meaningful resources such as information, money or attention, are located in a range of different spheres, including government, business and culture. We assume that the default position of any actor will be neutral neglect except when provoked by a threat to material or value interests. Government bureaucrats will be concerned first with performance of their jobs; business executives will want to make money; cultural elites will want to engage in the arts, media or other pursuits. The first question, of course, is whether they can be activated; such interests may remain uninvolved when a movement poses a challenge, or they may oppose the movement without supporting the mobilization of a countermovement. State and local officials responded differently to anti-civil rights countermovements in the American South during the 1950s and 1960s and these responses affected the success of the movement and intensity of the countermovements in different locales (Andrews, 2004; Luders, 2010). When a movement poses a significant threat to elite interests, it may demonstrate to elites that the movement form is worth emulating, leading elites to support countermovement organization. For example, Voss (1993) shows that employers supported the formation of employers' associations to counter the success of the US labor movement. The nuclear power and tobacco industries determined that countermovements were needed to oppose the anti-nuclear and anti-smoking movements (Useem and Zald, 1982; Troyer, 1989). Both movements and countermovements typically need support from allies who can provide resources. Differences in their ability to mobilize resources from elite and grassroots sources will alter the longevity and outcomes of the conflict.

Movements may succeed when they are strategic about calculating how to avoid elite interference. Organizers can sometimes create threats or target actors who will have less incentive to oppose movement goals. In the case of the American civil rights movement, Luders (2010) argues that the outcomes of protests targeted at businesses depended on the types of costs anticipated by economic actors. He distinguishes between 'concession costs' that result from movement victories, such as the loss of a cheap source of labor, and 'disruption costs' that stem directly from the protests, such as the loss of business during a sit-in campaign (2010, p. 3). Luders found that the most successful campaigns were waged when business interests lacked significant concession costs, but disruption costs were high.

Allies are also potentially available from within state and local governments. Although government officials are bound by the law and the constraints of their jobs, individuals enter those jobs with political commitments and outside connections. A number of researchers have demonstrated the importance of 'insider' support for social movements (e.g., Skrentny, 2002; Pettinicchio, 2019). Banaszak's (2009) study of feminist activists working inside and outside government shows that bureaucrats can work on behalf of movement interests from within the state, and they can bring information resources to social movement actors working outside. The ability (or inability) to mobilize bureaucratic resources and information has been critical to the development of movement conflict on climate change.

The anti-environmental movement, including its climate change denial contingent, has been nurtured over decades by elite allies who have provided extensive resources. In comparing the opposing movements around environment in the United States to others on issues such as abortion, we are struck by the large resource disparities in environmental conflicts. While the modern environmental movement enjoys extensive grassroots support and an established collection of national organizations, as well as the support of scientists and liberal politicians, the anti-environmental movement has benefited from the backing of right-wing organizations that expanded greatly with the mobilization of the New Right in the 1970s. These groups are supported by big business political action committees such as the National Conservative Political Action Committee, and conservative think tanks such as the Heritage Foundation (Diamond, 1995; Himmelstein, 1990). Right-wing donors, including the Koch brothers and other wealthy benefactors, poured huge amounts of money into think tanks and countermovement organizations opposed to environmental regulations and efforts to cut greenhouse gas emissions. Billionaire fossil fuel barons who became part of the Koch donor network provided the 'dark money' that promoted climate change denial on an unimaginable scale (Mayer, 2016). Climate change denial also benefited from prior efforts to cast doubt on scientific findings on issues such as cigarette smoking; many of the same 'merchants of doubt' used similar tactics on a range of issues that threatened elite interests (Oreskes and Conway, 2010).

At the same time, climate change activists have benefited tremendously from the information and legitimacy offered by government actors supporting and promoting a scientific consensus on the causes and consequences of climate change. Most notably, James Hansen, who directed the NASA Goddard Institute for Space Studies (GISS) for more than thirty years, provided a consistent resource for the movement, initially delivering testimony to Congress and later engaging in civil disobedience to draw attention to the issue of climate change. Housed at Columbia University, GISS was founded and funded by NASA, and Hansen's activism became increasingly valuable and controversial. Scientific research on both climate change and risk communication also came from other government agencies, including the National Oceanic and Atmospheric Administration, and the Environmental Protection Agency. University-based scientists funded by government grants also became both players in the conflict and the subject of controversy. Through political appointments, different presidential administrations have tried to amplify or silence scientific findings; but even in administrations hostile to recognizing climate change, institutional science has provided a powerful resource for environmental activists, countered only partly by climate skeptics funded by countermovement groups. Similarly, while many celebrities have engaged in activism on behalf of climate action, including the full range of movement activity up to routinized civil disobedience campaigns, conservative celebrities have been far less visible in promoting their views on the larger anti-climate action movement.

Overall, the availability of allies for the opposing movements has been asymmetrical: climate change activists have enjoyed support from scientists, both on and off government payrolls, and from a variety of cultural elites. Business interests, particularly in the fossil fuel industries, have organized vigorously against them, using the extensive resources at their disposal (Carroll, 2017; Carroll et al., 2018). But business interests have been far from unified. Some large companies such as Amazon and Apple have vigorously promoted their own environmental initiatives, partly as a matter of business sense, and partly in response to outside and inside pressures (Baig, 2019; Winston, 2019). Resource disparities clearly need to be examined in studies of opposing movements, which are likely to adopt political strategies that exploit the resources they do have.

Social Media and New Communication Technologies

The rise of internet communications and rapid spread of social media, as well as technologies such as smartphones, has made it easier to mobilize both movements and countermovements, altering the value of certain resources, and diminishing the importance of the gatekeepers of conventional media. In the twentieth-century political world that we considered in our 1996 article, mainstream media played a critical role in bringing attention to the messages and actions important to movements. Those media were both actors that covered events and activists, but also arenas of contest and debate. Importantly, access to those arenas was managed by gatekeepers, who deemed some issues and actors important and only certain positions legitimate. Success in those arenas allowed access and influence in other political arenas (Ferree et al., 2002).

Although mainstream media remain important to social movements, they no longer enjoy a monopoly on the reporting and evaluation of news. Social media allow entrepreneurial actors of all sorts, including movement organizers, the chance to reach supporters and bystanders with essentially unfiltered messages (Rohlinger, 2019). This monumental change has made new kinds of movements possible. In the 2011 Arab Spring, for example, social media were essential to the rapid mobilization of movements opposed to repressive regimes in many Middle Eastern countries, though face-to-face organizing was also important (Castells, 2012; Tufekci, 2017). Activists could not have achieved comparable visibility with conventional media, which are far easier to monitor and censor. Countermovements can also emerge rapidly using social media tools and we might expect their character to change in response to social media. Opposing movements can respond quickly to the issues and language that are most successful at mobilizing online support.

The diminished importance of gatekeepers is also critical. Fringe groups, which had more difficulty locating supporters in the absence of the internet, can reach substantial niche audiences through websites and social media. Caren et al. (2012), for example, describe how an online movement community of white nationalists was created among geographically dispersed individuals. Through the internet, isolated individuals who subscribe to beliefs outside the mainstream can find one another and remain anonymous if they choose, thereby lowering the cost of participation in an extremist movement or countermovement. False information spreads easily, bolstering movements such as the anti-vaccine movement. In the case of climate change denial, the internet has spread misinformation widely. Moreover, the proliferation of myths and misstatements online may increase cynicism rather than scrutiny insofar as consumers of information are unable to distinguish among various sources and fail to recognize the fact-checking done by mainstream media.

Cynicism about sources and facts is particularly critical in the ongoing debate about climate change. The move to take strong measures to combat climate change is predicated on the recognition of a particularly grave environmental threat. To forestall action, particularly restrictive regulations or new taxes and fees, countermovement forces have attacked the scientific understanding of the climate peril. Despite the strong scientific consensus that the earth is rapidly warming due to human intervention (Cook et al., 2016), the countermovement has questioned the veracity of this observation as well as its implications. Opponents of climate action have funded prominent scientists—and others—to question critically the work of climate scientists (e.g., Banerjee, 2012). Deploying ostensibly well-credentialed and well-qualified skeptics to question the reality of climate change, opponents of action have been able to undermine a sense of urgency and provide their allies with a rationale for inaction. They have also questioned the motives of climate scientists, who, they contend, promote a sense of crisis for crass financial motives (e.g., Qiu, 2018). For example, prolific conservative anti-tax and anti-regulation crusader Stephen Moore (2018) said, 'In America and around the globe governments have created a multi-billion dollar Climate Change Industrial Complex … A lot of people are getting really, really rich off of the climate change industry.' Asserting that university-based climate scientists have a financial interest in promoting alarm, opponents attempt to undermine their scientific credibility.

Following a playbook deployed previously in fighting regulations on a range of issues, including acid rain, auto safety, guns, and tobacco, countermovement spokespeople have touched on what Hirschman (1991) has described as the three pillars of the rhetoric of reaction: perversity, jeopardy and futility. The claim is that efforts at regulation or pricing or even research will be costly, and ineffective, that they will threaten economic growth and/or social justice, and that, by virtue of the immensity of the problem of carbon discharge, they are unlikely to have any impact anyway. The repertoire of arguments and counter-frames need not win acceptance through a legal trial or peer review; to be effective they must simply strengthen the will and resources of opponents of government action. To the extent that new social media undermine trust in authoritative determinations of fact, the countermovement cause is aided.

MOVEMENT–COUNTERMOVEMENT INTERACTIONS

When a conflict persists for many years, we can think of movement and countermovement as *opposing movements* with their own structures and agendas, which 'influence each other both directly and by altering the environment in which each side operates' (Meyer and Staggenborg, 1996, pp. 1632–3). Opposing movements create both opportunities and obstacles for one another through their interactions. One way in which opposing movements influence one another is through their impacts on mobilization; the nature of the opposition influences the amount and type of support that a movement or countermovement receives. A second way in which opposing movements influence one another is through their impact on strategies and tactics (Meyer and Staggenborg, 2008).

Ongoing Mobilization of Opposing Movements

The outcomes of movement and countermovement activities affect the growth and decline of each side. Both opportunities and threats can mobilize collective action depending on what type of openings they create for strategies and tactics. A positive policy outcome for a movement can encourage further mobilization and collective action, as in the case of US Supreme Court decisions and other government actions that spurred mobilization of the civil rights movement (McAdam, 1982). But some positive reforms discourage movement action while unfavorable government actions lead to protests (Meyer, 1993a, 1993b). When a countermovement is present, a victory for the movement is likely to motivate support for its opposition, and growth of the countermovement is then likely to keep movement supporters mobilized. When one side suffers a defeat, more supporters of that side are likely to mobilize in response unless the defeat is so complete as to cut off further action, which would be rare in a divided system of government such as American federalism.

In the case of the American abortion conflict, we can see how victories and defeats affected the opposing movement and kept both sides alive (Staggenborg, 1991, 1995). As abortion rights groups began to mobilize in the 1960s, anti-abortion groups also formed, but it was not until 1973, when the movement won legalized abortion nationwide with the Supreme Court's *Roe v. Wade* decision, that the countermovement really expanded. Blocked by the courts, countermovement activists turned to Congress where they lobbied, unsuccessfully, for a Human Life Amendment before succeeding in getting Congress to pass the Hyde Amendment banning federal funding of abortion in 1976. The countermovement also worked at the state and local levels in support of funding cutoffs and restrictions on abortion. While the abortion rights movement might have declined after its major victory in 1973, insofar as supporters thought the battle was over, countermovement activities prevented this from happening. Instead, the movement remained mobilized and began building its capacity to lobby Congress and block restrictions in the courts. The threats to abortion rights in Congress, and the election of anti-abortion President Ronald Reagan in 1980, greatly spurred mobilization of the abortion rights movement in the 1970s and early 1980s. The threat subsided somewhat, however, with the defeat of anti-abortion legislation in Congress together with a Supreme Court decision in 1983 that struck down many restrictive abortion laws, essentially reaffirming *Roe v. Wade*. Between 1983 and 1989, it was more difficult for the abortion rights movement to mobilize support because it seemed to many supporters that the battle had been won. In 1989, however, the movement was revitalized by a partial defeat, the Supreme Court decision in *Webster v. Reproductive Health Services*, which permitted significant restrictions on abortion and seemed to invite further limitations. This ruling encouraged anti-abortionists to work for state anti-abortion laws that might generate a court case to overturn *Roe*. The threat also renewed the abortion rights movement as supporters once again became alarmed. This pattern continued with the 1992 Supreme Court decision in *Planned Parenthood of Southeastern Pennsylvania v. Casey*, which allowed some key restrictions on abortion but did not overturn *Roe*. Each opposing movement claimed defeat, rousing its supporters with the new threats.

This history shows—as do more recent events—that a victory by one side is rarely decisive; partial victories or defeats often work to perpetuate the conflict by keeping both sides mobilized. The net result in the American abortion debate has been relatively ready access to reproductive rights in some states and for women who could pay for services and travel, but much more uneven access for women with fewer economic resources. With relatively modest shifts over the past forty years, this result has been far more stable than activists on either side of the debate would have imagined. Moreover, in a federal system, there are alternative venues in which to pursue the fight when there is a defeat in one arena such as the federal legislature.

The story of stasis and stalemate is recurrent in countermovement battles, reflecting not consensus, but vigorous struggle by opposing movements. As we have seen, mobilization of the US environmental movement spurred extensive opposition to environmentalism from the right wing, beginning in the 1970s and increasing in the Reagan years. In response, environmentalists also mobilized their troops. Anti-environmental threats from the Reagan administration spurred the growth of national environmental organizations, such as the Sierra Club and the Wilderness Society, which experienced dramatic increases in their memberships (Mitchell et al., 1992). The Clinton administration came into office in 1993 with strong commitments to environmental action, including explicit attention to the problem of climate change. But little progress was made, and after the Republicans gained control of the House of Representatives in 1994, the administration had to reduce the political fronts on which it faced opposition (Royden, 2002). Similarly, during the Trump administration, outrage at appointments to the EPA and other agencies, withdrawal from the Paris Accord, and support for the fossil fuel industries in the face of climate change spurred growth of the environmental movement.

Well before Trump's election, climate activists contested countermovement denial of global warming and protested the lack of government action. In September 2014, climate activists organized the first large-scale climate change march in New York City during talks by the United Nations on climate change, as coordinated protests took place in 162 countries around the world (Fisher, 2018, p.113). In 2017, climate activists joined the Trump Resistance movement for both a March for Science and another People's Climate March in April 2017. As the outrages of the Trump administration against the environment accumulated, the movement continued to fight back (Meyer and Tarrow, 2018; Fisher, 2019; Skocpol and Tervo, 2020). But the Trump administration also faced opposition from state governments and from industry as it sought to revoke many of Obama's policies (e.g., Eisenstein, 2019). It is hard to promote dramatic policy change—even from within government. Social movements mobilize with dramatic rhetoric and press for large reforms, but the policy battles generally play out in increments.

Strategies and Tactics of Opposing Movements

Strategies and tactics include movement demands, frames, targets, chosen arenas of conflict, and the actual forms of collective action employed. Opposing movements influence one another with their strategies and tactics, but some opposing movements are more tightly 'coupled' than others, resulting in a stronger strategic influence on their opponents (Zald and Useem, 1987). In a tightly coupled conflict, when one side chooses to operate in an arena, the other side follows suit when there is the possibility of a real contest. In general, movements and countermovements try to choose venues that are favorable to them, but if one side looks to be making gains in an arena, the opposing movement will be compelled to compete in that arena, regardless of its favorability. An opposing movement that suffers a defeat in one institutional venue is likely to shift targets and arenas to continue the fight.

Particularly in democratic countries with federal structures, opposing movements can press their claims in multiple venues. When one venue or level of government becomes unreceptive to movement goals, often because of countermovement inroads, the movement can shift its focus to alternative arenas. In the American abortion conflict, the opposing sides shifted arenas of action, tactics and demands in response to interactions with one another and shifts in political opportunities and public policy outcomes (Meyer and Staggenborg, 2008). Even as environmental organizations facing hostile national governments can shift their attention to state and local targets, as many did during the Trump administration, they really cannot afford to retreat from any political battle. When elite allies block success in one venue, such as Congress, they may aid movement mobilization in other arenas by creating motivating threats. Climate activists, for example, worked with favorable governments such as California during the hostile Trump years. But the anti-environmental movement is extremely powerful and well resourced, with a diverse set of organizations and strategies for countering environmental actions (Brulle and Aronczyk, 2020). Anti-environmentalists have aligned with right-wing movements such as the Tea Party movement—very much an extension of the 'wise use' movement—to build grassroots support as well as a national base (Van Dyke and Meyer, 2014). An extensive network of right-wing think tanks, such as the Heartland Institute, promotes libertarian and conservative ideologies that appeal to Tea Party activists opposed to government intervention (Dunlap and McCright, 2010, 2011). Countermovement organizations employ an array of tactics including litigation and electoral politics, working through the Republican Party. The environmental movement, with allies such as the Trump resistance group Indivisible, is scrambling to compete with a powerful opponent using a variety of tactics in multiple arenas.

Our 1996 article postulated a sort of mirror image of tactics and downplayed resources. Looking at the battle of climate change, we see that that vision was, at best, incomplete. Proponents of urgent action on climate change enjoy the strong support of institutional science and international allies, and they are relatively well resourced, particularly by the standards of public interest movements. But the industry and ideological opponents of action on climate change have stable support, including extensive financial support. Although both sides engage in virtually every arena of American life, variations in the initiation of efforts reflect differential resources. For example, the movement for action on climate change has mobilized the support of young people on college and high school campuses, but the student activists have faced far more resistance from Boards of Trustees than from other students (e.g., Knox, 2019). Indeed, Stanford's decision to divest its holdings in coal, a partial victory for climate change activists, was possible only because of the presence of a billionaire activist alumnus on the Board of Trustees, Tom Steyer (Carroll, 2014). In general, the climate change movement has had more success cultivating support among students than among trustees. Countervailing strategies reflecting different resources and bases of support are critical to movement growth.

CONCLUSION

Opposing movements are an important element of the political opportunity structure, and interactions among movements, countermovements and the state are critical to our understanding of how social change occurs. Few movements avoid arousing countermovements when they show signs of success and threaten existing interests and values, thereby motivating opposition alliances and making resources available to them. The internet and social media spread information (and disinformation) about movement tactics and successes and make it rather easy to organize a countermovement. When we wrote about countermovements in the 1990s, there was relatively little theorizing and empirical research on this phenomenon. Since that time, we are gratified to see many more empirical studies of opposing movements in a wide variety of conflicts (e.g., Alimi and Hirsch-Hoefler, 2012; Blok, 2008; Crowley, 2009; Dixon, 2008; Lind and Stepan-Norris, 2011; Peleg, 2000). In reconsidering movement–countermovement dynamics nearly twenty-five years after our 1996 paper was published, we are pleased that other scholars have used our work to further develop our understanding of the role of countermovements in the mobilization, strategies and outcomes of social movements. We also recognize some blind spots in our earlier work and we hope to encourage new research on some neglected issues. Here we note two areas of needed research.

First, research is needed to provide comparisons of like movements across different contexts or structures of political opportunity. Our initial approach suggested that the kind of pattern we identify here, of countermovements in a federal system, is one in which each side in a countermovement pair is not only able to aggregate resources, but also to cultivate institutional niches in government, producing a longer-lasting dispute. But from our current vantage point the nature of disputes in the United States is striking in its distinctiveness. Most importantly for environmentalism, the nature of the arguments about climate change and the relative power of the fossil fuel industry in the United States are unparalleled elsewhere. To be sure, opponents of action on climate change have been able to maintain themselves and effectively make claims on policy in other federal states, such as Canada. As fossil fuel interests are also prominent in Canadian politics, we need to look beyond federalism as a simple explanation. America's combination of weak political parties and long, expensive and lightly regulated electoral campaigns not only gives industry exceptional influence but enables self-described skeptics to hold institutional power. This finding points to the need for more comparative research on the nature of political opportunities for claimants in countermovement conflicts. Given America's disproportionate political sway and negative environmental impact, understanding the global spread of anti-environmentalism is critical.

A second question concerns how countermovement pairs differ from one another. One critical difference lies in the nature and scope of movement and countermovement objectives. Climate change activists have ambitious designs that will remake not only the energy grids of countries around the world but also global values and lifestyles. In contrast, opponents of climate action mostly want to resist change. In virtually all democracies, those who defend the status quo have structural political advantages; in the United States, where power is divided among several distinct government bodies, those advantages are extreme (Meyer, 2015). The environmental climate action movement wants to slow and reverse a rapidly increasing global condition, requiring urgent, ongoing efforts and international cooperation; its opponents want only to slow the movement for climate action.

The type and volume of resource disparities is another key factor in explaining differences in countermovement conflicts. Some countermovements, such as the climate change denial movement, have access to extensive resources that help to explain their success. Moreover, some opponents are much less visible than others; the behind-the-scenes work of the 'merchants of doubt' who fueled the anti-environmental movement with 'dark money' is a case in point (Mayer, 2016; Oreskes and Conway, 2010). Both sides in the battle over climate change have extensive networks of allies, but the infrastructures vary significantly. The resisters to climate action include a complex set of organizations and activists that are, to a large extent, funded and directed by those with strong financial interests in the fossil fuel industry. There are also cultural elements to the conflicts, such as the opposition of right-wing activists to government regulation of industries and individuals. Environmental activists have strong moral concerns about saving the planet, and they enjoy substantial support from institutional science and from young people as well as international support. These differences are reflected in movement goals and strategic approaches, even as each side adapts to its opponents. The dynamics of conflicts between opposing movements over environmental issues are similar in many ways to those of other pairs, but the resource disparities and complexity of threatened interests set them apart.

Ongoing disputes framed largely in terms of moral values, such as the conflicts over abortion or LGBTQ rights, are likely to play out differently depending upon resources. There are no obvious business interests implicated in the reproductive rights question and the moral issues seem unresolvable, so that neither side has been able to vanquish the other decisively. In contrast, we have seen more rapid acceptance of gay rights and same-sex marriage, as gay men and lesbians—a potentially important market for businesses—make visible social gains. In the American dispute over gun rights, the gun industry is a core supporter of the gun rights movement, but its scope and power does not approach that of the fossil fuel industry. Nonetheless, that movement has succeeded in holding campaigns at bay for even limited gun regulation by coupling focused organizing with a cultural appeal. In short, countermovements differ from one another in important ways, and we need to examine how institutional opportunities and the character of resources, asymmetrical or not, affect the development of opposing movements over time.

The outcomes of the ongoing struggle between environmentalists and their opponents are very much undecided and of critical importance. Those outcomes will be determined by the effectiveness of each side in responding to circumstances largely outside of its control. The Covid-19 global pandemic, raging as we write, is likely to be one of those circumstances. Anti-environmentalists may be able to use the economic damage done by the global health crisis to fight environmental regulations and curtail funding for mass transportation and recycling. Alternatively, we can imagine environmental activists using the pandemic to resurrect public support for rigorous science and the economic crisis to build support for public spending on infrastructure. Given acceptance of a massive investment enterprise, activists could be successful in shaping projects to promote sustainability and climate sense. In this light, the current crisis may provide the needed shock to allow activists to make a Green New Deal.

NOTE

1. The extended debate over the United Kingdom's withdrawal from the European Union provides an interesting test, and likely a validation of this point. A binding referendum for Brexit didn't resolve the political debate, but once the Conservative Party won a national election running on the issue, there was no doubt that the government would be able to deliver on its promise. At the same time, we've seen concentrated areas of opposition work to develop alternative governmental venues for action. In Northern Ireland and particularly in Scotland, Remain activists have worked to increase the autonomy and influence of local governments as sites where they can continue to resist Brexit. The United Kingdom is becoming less united.

REFERENCES

Alimi, Eitan Y. and Hirsch-Hoefler, S. (2012) Structure of political opportunities and threats, and movement–countermovement interaction in segmented composite regimes. *Comparative Politics*. **44**(3), pp. 331–49.

Andrews, K.T. (2004) *Freedom is a Constant Struggle*. Chicago, IL: University of Chicago Press.

Baig, E.C. (2019) Apple on the environment: Doing right for the planet is good for business. *USA Today*. Available from: https://www.usatoday.com/story/tech/talkingtech/2019/04/11/apple-on-the-environment-doing-right-by-the-climate-is-good-for-business/3427400002/.

Banaszak, L.A. (2009) *The Women's Movement inside and outside the State*. New York, NY: Cambridge University Press.

Banerjee, N. (2012) Prominent climate change denier now admits he was wrong. *The Christian Science Monitor*. Available from: https://www.csmonitor.com/Science/2012/0730/Prominent-climate-change-denier-now-admits-he-was-wrong.

Beder, S. (2002) *Global Spin: The Corporate Assault on Environmentalism*. Revised edn. Totnes: Green Books.

Blok, A. (2008) Contesting global norms: Politics of identity in Japanese pro-whaling countermobilization. *Global Environmental Politics*. **8**(2), pp. 39–66.

Brulle, R. and Aronczyk, M. (2020) Environmental countermovements: Organised opposition to climate change action in the United States. In: Kalfagianni, A., Fuchs, D. and Hayden, A. (eds) *Routledge Handbook of Global Sustainability Governance*. London, UK and New York, NY, USA: Routledge, pp. 218–30.

Caren, N., Jowers, K. and Gaby, S. (2012) A social movement online community: Stormfront and the White Nationalist Movement. *Research in Social Movements, Conflicts and Change*. **33**, pp. 163–93.

Carroll, R. (2014) Stanford University ending investments in coal companies. *Reuters*. Available from: https://www.reuters.com/article/us-carbonstanford-divestment/stanford-university-ending-investments-in-coal-companies-idUSBREA460L620140507.

Carroll, W.K. (2017) Canada's carbon-capital elite: A tangled web of corporate power. *Canadian Journal of Sociology*. **42**(3), pp. 225–60.

Carroll, W., Graham, N., Lang, M.K., Yunker, Z. and McCartney, K.D. (2018) The corporate elite and the architecture of climate change denial: A network analysis of carbon capital's reach into civil society. *Canadian Review of Sociology*. **55**(3), pp. 425–50.

Castells, M. (2012) *Networks of Outrage and Hope: Social Movements in the Internet Age*. Malden, MA: Polity Press.

Cook, J., Oreskes, N., Doran, P.T., Anderegg, W.R.L., Verheggen, B., Maibach, E.W., Carlton, J.S. et al. (2016) Consensus on consensus: A synthesis of consensus estimates on human-caused global warming. *Environmental Research Letters*. **11**(4).

Crowley, J.E. (2009) Fathers' rights groups, domestic violence and political countermobilization. *Social Forces*. **88**(2), pp. 723–56.

Cuneo, M.W. (1989) *Catholics against the State: Anti-Abortion Protest in Toronto*. Toronto: University of Toronto Press.

Diamond, S. (1995) *Roads to Dominion: Right-Wing Movements and Political Power in the United States.* New York, NY: Guilford Press.

Dixon, M. (2008) Movements, countermovements and policy adoption: The case of right-to-work activism. *Social Forces.* **87**(1), pp. 473–500.

Dunlap, R.E. and McCright, A.M. (2010) Climate change denial: Sources, actors and strategies. In Lever-Tracy, C. (ed.) *Routledge Handbook of Climate Change and Society.* Abingdon: Routledge, pp. 270–90.

Dunlap, R.E. and McCright, A.M. (2011) Organized climate change denial. In: Dryzek, J.S., Norgaard, R.B. and Schlosberg, D. (eds) *The Oxford Handbook of Climate Change and Society.* New York, NY: Oxford University Press, pp. 144–60.

Dunlap, R.E. and McCright, A.M. (2015) Challenging climate change: The denial countermovement. In: Dunlap, R. and Brulle, R. (eds) *Climate Change and Society: Sociological Perspectives.* New York, NY: Oxford University Press, pp. 300–333.

Eisenstein, P.A. (2019) Automakers push back on Trump plan to relax mileage rules. Expected White House plan would trigger legal actions and 'untenable' uncertainty, 17 OEs warn. *The Detroit Bureau.* Available from: https://www.thedetroitbureau.com/2019/06/automakers-push-back-on-trump-plan-to-relax-mileage-rules/.

Eisinger, P.K. (1973) The conditions of protest behavior in American cities. *American Political Science Review.* **67**(1), pp. 11–28.

Ferree, M.M., Gamson, W.A., Gerhards, J. and Rucht, D. (2002) *Shaping Abortion Discourse: Democracy and the Public Sphere in Germany and the United States.* Cambridge: Cambridge University Press.

Fisher, D. (2018) Climate of resistance: How the climate movement connected to the resistance. In: Meyer, D.S. and Tarrow, S. (eds) *The Resistance.* New York, NY: Oxford University Press, pp. 109–24.

Fisher, D. (2019) *American Resistance.* New York, NY: Columbia University Press.

Freedman, L. and Weitz, T.A. (2012) The politics of motherhood meets the politics of poverty. *Contemporary Sociology.* **41**(1), pp. 36–42.

Gusfield, J. (1981) *The Culture of Public Problems: Drinking-Driving and the Symbolic Order.* Chicago, IL: University of Chicago Press.

Himmelstein, J.L. (1990) *To the Right: The Transformation of American Conservatism.* Berkeley, CA: University of California Press.

Hirschman, A.O. (1991) *The Rhetoric of Reaction.* Cambridge, MA: Belknap Press.

Jacobs, M. (2016) America's never-ending oil consumption. *The Atlantic.* Available from: https://www.theatlantic.com/politics/archive/2016/05/american-oil-consumption/482532/.

Joppke, C. (1993) *Mobilizing against Nuclear Energy: A Comparison of Germany and the United States.* Berkeley, CA: University of California Press.

Kingdon, J. (1984) *Agendas, Alternatives, and Public Policies.* Boston, MA: Little, Brown.

Klatch, R.E. (1987) *Women of the New Right.* Philadelphia, PA: Temple University Press.

Knox, L. (2019) Saving the planet hasn't persuaded colleges to divest from fossil fuels. Will saving money do the trick? *The Chronicle of Higher Education.* Available from: https://www.chronicle.com/article/Saving-the-Planet-Hasn-t/247057.

Kretschmer, K. (2009) Contested loyalties: Dissident identity organizations, institutions, and social movements. *Sociological Perspectives.* **52**(4), pp. 433–54.

Laschever, J.E. and Meyer, D.S. (2021) Growth and decline of opposing movements: Gun control and gun rights, 1945–2015. *Mobilization.* **26**(1), pp. 1–20.

Lind, B. and Stepan-Norris, J. (2011) The relationality of movements: Movement and countermovement resources, infrastructure, and leadership in the Los Angeles tenants' rights mobilization, 1976–1979. *American Journal of Sociology.* **116**(5), pp. 1564–609.

Lipset, S.M. and Raab, E. (1978) *The Politics of Unreason, Second Edition: Right-Wing Extremism in America, 1790–1977.* Chicago, IL: University of Chicago Press.

Luders, J.E. (2010) *The Civil Rights Movement and the Logic of Social Change.* New York, NY: Cambridge University Press.

Luker, K. (1984) *Abortion and the Politics of Motherhood.* Berkeley, CA: University of California Press.

Markson, S.L. (1982) Normative boundaries and abortion policy: The politics of morality. In: Lewis, M. (ed.) *Research in Social Problems and Public Policy*. Greenwich, CT: JAI Press, pp. 21–33.

Mayer, J. (2016) *Dark Money: The Hidden History of the Billionaires behind the Rise of the Radical Right*. New York, NY: Doubleday.

McAdam, D. (1982) *Political Process and the Development of Black Insurgency*. Chicago, IL: University of Chicago Press.

McCarthy, J. (1994) Activists, authorities, and media framing of drunk driving. In: Larana, E., Johnston, H. and Gusfield, J.R. (eds) *New Social Movements: From Ideology to Identity*. Philadelphia, PA: Temple University Press.

McCarthy, J. and Wolfson, M. (1992) Consensus movements, conflict movements, and the cooptation of civic and state infrastructures. In: Morris, A.D. and Mueller, C.M. (eds) *Frontiers in Social Movements Theory*. New Haven, CT: Yale University Press, pp. 273–98.

Melzer, S. (2009) *Gun Crusaders: The NRA's Culture War*. New York, NY: New York University Press.

Mencken, F.C. and Froese, P. (2019) Gun culture in action. *Social Problems*. **66**(1), pp. 3–27.

Meyer, D.S. (1993a) Institutionalizing dissent: The United States structure of political opportunity and the end of the nuclear freeze movement. *Sociological Forum*. **8**(2), pp. 157–79.

Meyer, D.S. (1993b) Peace protest and policy: Explaining the rise and decline of peace protest in postwar America. *Policy Studies Journal*. **30**(1), pp. 253–70.

Meyer, D.S. (2004) Protest and political opportunities. *Annual Review of Sociology*. **30**, pp. 125–45.

Meyer, D.S. (2015) *The Politics of Protest: Social Movements in America*. New York, NY: Oxford University Press.

Meyer, D.S. and Staggenborg, S. (1996) Movements, countermovements, and the structure of political opportunity. *American Journal of Sociology*. **101**(6), pp. 1628–60.

Meyer, D.S. and Staggenborg, S. (1998) Countermovement dynamics in federal systems: A comparison of abortion politics in Canada and the United States. *Research in Political Sociology*. **8**, pp. 209–40.

Meyer, D.S. and Staggenborg, S. (2008) Opposing movement strategies in U.S. abortion politics. *Research in Social Movements, Conflicts and Change*. **28**, pp. 207–38.

Meyer, D.S. and Tarrow, S. (eds) (2018) *The Resistance: Dawn of the Anti-Trump Movement*. New York, NY: Oxford University Press.

Mitchell, R.C., Mertig, A.G. and Dunlap, R.E. (1992) Twenty years of environmental mobilization: Trends among national environmental organizations. In: Dunlap, R.E. and Mertig, A.G. (eds) *American Environmentalism: The U.S. Environmental Movement, 1970–1990*. Washington, DC: Taylor & Francis, pp. 11–26.

Moore, S. (2018) Follow the (climate change) money. *Heritage Foundation Commentary*. Available from: https://www.heritage.org/environment/commentary/follow-the-climate-change-money.

Oreskes, N. and Conway, E.M. (2010) *Merchants of Doubt*. New York, NY: Bloomsbury Press.

Palast, G. (2016) *The Best Democracy Money Can Buy: A Tale of Billionaires & Ballot Bandits*. New York, NY: Seven Stories.

Peleg, S. (2000) Peace now or later?: Movement–countermovement dynamics and the Israeli political cleavage. *Studies in Conflict and Terrorism*. **23**(4), pp. 235–54.

Pettinicchio, D. (2019) *Politics of Empowerment: Disability Rights and the Cycle of American Policy Reform*. Stanford, CA: Stanford University Press.

Pollitt, K. (2014) *Pro: Reclaiming Abortion Rights*. New York, NY: Picador.

Qiu, L. (2018) The baseless claim that climate scientists are 'driven' by money. *The New York Times*. Available from: https://www.nytimes.com/2018/11/27/us/politics/climate-report-fact-check.html.

Rohlinger, D. (2019) *New Media and Society*. New York, NY: New York University Press.

Royden, A. (2002) U.S. climate change policy under President Clinton: A look back. *Golden Gate University Law Review*. **32**(4), pp. 415–78.

Schwartz, M.A. and Tatalovich, R. (2018) *The Rise and Fall of Moral Conflicts in the United States and Canada*. Toronto: University of Toronto Press.

Shields, J.A. (2012) The Politics of Motherhood revisited. *Contemporary Sociology*. **41**(1), pp. 43–8.

Shulman, S. (2008) *Undermining Science: Suppression and Distortion in the Bush Administration*. (Updated with a new preface edition). Berkeley, CA: University of California Press.

Skocpol, T. and Tervo, C. (eds) (2020) *Upending American Politics: Polarizing Parties, Ideological Elites, and Citizen Activists from the Tea Party to the Anti-Trump Resistance*. New York, NY: Oxford University Press.

Skrentny, J.D. (2002) *The Minority Rights Revolution*. Cambridge, MA: Belknap Press.

Spears, E.G. (2020) *Rethinking the American Environmental Movement post-1945*. New York, NY: Routledge.

Staggenborg, S. (1991) *The Pro-Choice Movement: Organization and Activism in the Abortion Conflict*. New York, NY: Oxford University Press.

Staggenborg, S. (1995) The survival of the pro-choice movement. *Journal of Policy History*. **7**(1), pp. 160–76.

Stein, A. (2001) *The Stranger Next Door: The Story of a Small Community's Battle over Sex, Faith, and Civil Rights*. Boston, MA: Beacon Press.

Tilly, C. (1978) *From Mobilization to Revolution*. Reading, MA: Addison-Wesley Publishing.

Tindall, D., Howe, A. and Mauboules, C. (2020) Tangled roots: Personal networks and the participation of individuals in an anti-environmentalism countermovement. *Sociological Perspectives*. Available from DOI: 10.1177/0731121420908886.

Troyer, R.J. (1989) The surprising resurgence of the smoking problem. In: Best, J. (ed.) *Images of Issues: Typifying Contemporary Social Problems*. New York, NY: Aldine de Gruyter, pp. 159–76.

Tufekci, Z. (2017) *Twitter and Tear Gas: The Power and Fragility of Networked Protest*. New Haven, CT: Yale University Press.

Useem, B. and Zald, M.N. (1982) From pressure group to social movement: Organizational dilemmas of the effort to promote nuclear power. *Social Problems*. **30**(2), pp. 144–56.

Van Dyke, N. and Meyer, D.S. (eds) (2014) *Understanding the Tea Party Movement*. Aldershot: Ashgate.

Voss, K. (1993) *The Making of American Exceptionalism: The Knights of Labor and Class Formation in the Nineteenth Century*. Ithaca, NY: Cornell University Press.

Winkler, A. (2011) *Gun Fight: The Battle over the Right to Bear Arms in America*. New York, NY: Norton.

Winston, A. (2019) Corporate action on climate change has to include lobbying. *Harvard Business Review*. Available from: https://hbr.org/2019/10/corporate-action-on-climate-change-has-to-include-lobbying.

Zald, M.N. and Useem, B. (1987) Movement and countermovement interaction: Mobilization, tactics, and state involvement. In: Zald, M.N. (ed.) *Social Movements in an Organizational Society*. New Brunswick, NJ: Transaction Books, pp. 247–72.

3. Against environmentalism for the common good: a theoretical model
Nicholas Scott

INTRODUCTION

Anthropogenic climate change, habitat destruction and the ongoing mass extinction of nonhuman species of life on earth pose uniquely 'wicked' problems (Lazarus, 2008) with contradictory, shifting demands that garner no single (or easy) solution. These intertwined ecological crises represent the gravest collective action dilemma humanity has ever faced. As such, they challenge humans 'to achieve unprecedented heights of global consensus and cooperation', and to seize 'a world-historical opportunity for the emergence of a common global society, with failure to do so likely to bring intensifying calamity for all parties' (Broadbent et al., 2016, p. 1). However, the formation of common worlds that coordinate widespread cooperation around shared visions of a common good presents a politically daunting task—not least for an ecological common good wherein humans not only have responsibilities to other humans but also nonhuman beings and their habitats.

Environmental movements, policies and campaigns continue to forge new common ground for making progressive, if incremental change, such as with Greta Thunberg, the Intergovernmental Panel on Climate Change, the Stern report and Al Gore's film, *An Inconvenient Truth*. But environmentalism in the early twenty-first century is unfolding against the postcolonial, neoliberal backdrop of exploding socio-economic inequalities, hyper-political partisanship and a rising tide of anti-elite populism around the world on the left and the right (Roth, 2018). This fractious political context has created a fortuitous political opportunity structure for fighting established environmental movements and policies. Undercutting political support and social license for environmentalism while mobilizing resistance against policies to reduce greenhouse gas emissions and lessen the destruction of more-than-human environments, some counter-movements against environmentalism pose a decisive threat to the emergence of a new, green world order. All this points at the need to better understand anti-environmentalism with all its moral complexities.

Counter-movements against environmentalism are nothing new. Like the White Citizens' Councils that arose in response to the Civil Rights Movement (Gale, 1972), anti-environmentalists retaliated against mass environmental movements of the 1960s and early 1970s that threatened traditional values and practices, most notably 'the beliefs that man's primary purpose is to produce and consume, that material resources are practically unlimited, and that a major function of the state is to make it easy for individuals and corporations to exploit the environment in order to increase wealth and power' (Albrecht, 1972). In fact, major frames of anti-environmentalism in the late 60s—environmental movements are secretly controlled by foreign radicals; forcing corporations to curb their pollution will precipitate massive job loss (Albrecht, 1972)—still resonate today. What is new, however, is the scale and irrefutable evidence of human-caused climate change and widespread knowledge of pending ecological collapse. The stakes of anti-/environmental conflict have never been higher.

To advance theoretical understandings of contemporary currents of anti-environmentalism and related counter-movements, this chapter explores the ways in which different counter-movements situated across the political spectrum advance moral appeals to the common good. I draw on pragmatic sociology (Boltanski and Thévenot, 2006[1991]; Blokker, 2011) as a fresh approach to contentious politics based on competing moral philosophies of the common good. These philosophies identify higher common principles for mobilizing actions that appeal to a shared humanity and the mutual flourishing of all persons, as individuals and as a collective. Movements *for* the environment are not the only ones that attempt to articulate their demands as good for everyone. Counter-movements *against* environmentalism, I suggest, also gain social and political force and legitimacy where they successfully mount moral critiques on the basis of supporting a common humanity. While competing common goods can be viewed as powerful moral frames, they also mobilize nonhuman actors and qualified objects (e.g. built environments and hydrocarbons), and are thus better construed as 'moral assemblages' that draw together heterogeneous agencies (Scott, 2020).

In what follows, I briefly review pragmatic sociology (Boltanski and Thévenot, 2006[1991]) before fleshing out the central ideals, actors and infrastructures of five moral assemblages of anti-environmentalism. Echoing similar efforts to distinguish prominent types of environmentalism (Brulle, 2009; Dryzek, 2013), my typology seeks to evoke a diversity of anti-environmentalisms ranging from reactionary responses that tend to mobilize conservative political standpoints to more critical forms of anti-environmentalism that typically align with liberal or progressive standpoints. I take up the five assemblages in turn, situating each in relation to the traditional political spectrum and foregrounding a variety of illustrative examples, including a 'paradigmatic case' (Flyvbjerg, 2006) that encapsulates each assemblage's theoretical features. My cases mostly focus on Canada. However, I also touch on cross-contextual examples of anti-environmentalism from other parts of the world to show broader applicability. To illustrate topical nuances in these cases I draw on a variety of sources, including reports from mass media (*Global News*, *CBC*, *Globe and Mail*, *Tyee*, *The New York Times*, *The Independent*, *The Guardian* and *The Washington Post*), relevant grey literature (e.g. *Canadian Dimension*, *Vancouver Magazine*, *Smithsonian Magazine*, *Everyday Feminism Magazine* and *Urban Land Magazine*) and academic research, including groundbreaking work on animal rights and environmental racism (Donaldson and Kymlicka, 2013; Taylor, 2014b). The chapter concludes by tracing inter-assemblage confluences between anti-environmentalisms, and highlighting the need to build bridges between progressive anti-environmental counter-movements.

ASSEMBLING ANTI-ENVIRONMENTALISM

Pragmatic sociology offers a theory of public justification and critique (for an overview see Blokker, 2011). In *On Justification*, Boltanski and Thévenot (2006[1991]) examine how people craft moral appeals to the common good (i.e. visions of a shared humanity in which every person can flourish), in order to broaden the legitimacy of their claims in public controversies. Linking political philosophy with sociology, they demonstrate that, in practice, people appeal to a plurality of contradictory common goods (e.g. equity, profit, technical efficiency), depending on the situation. Each common good features a distinctive moral framing or 'grammar' of worth (Blokker, 2011), on which actors rely to qualify certain subjects but also objects whose material support helps people deal with the profound uncertainty associated with competing common goods, particularly during conflicts when the attribution of moral worth is at stake. Boltanski and Thévenot (2006[1991]) elaborate common goods into 'common worlds', wherein qualified objects that populate one world (say, the tools and products of engineering in an industrial world) do not necessarily carry moral worth in another (e.g. a civic world equipped for social justice and liberal democracy). Applications of pragmatic sociology have illuminated, *inter alia*, the moral production of space, place, cities and mobilities (Thévenot, 2002; Blok and Meilvang, 2015; Holden, 2017; Holden and Scerri, 2015; Conley and Jensen, 2016). Extending it beyond its initial, anthropocentric focus, further applications have explored possibilities for an ecological common good (Lamont and Thévenot, 2000; Latour, 1998), showing how ecology is a 'moral assemblage' of more-than-human materials, social practices and modes of judgment (Scott, 2020; Blok, 2013). While considering different environmentalisms, pragmatic sociology has yet to take up the diversity of anti-environmentalisms.

Anti-environmental counter-movements, conceived broadly as both protest actions and more institutionalized policy work and media campaigns, draw upon a plurality of mainly anthropocentric moral assemblages. This chapter identifies and examines four anthropocentric assemblages of anti-environmentalism. The first, *inefficient environmentalism*, contests environmentalism where it places short-term thinking ahead of long-term planning, industrial productivity and fiscal responsibility. The second assemblage, *unprofitable environmentalism*, advances Adam Smith-inspired political attacks on regulations and policies that hinder market expansion and shareholder returns. The third moral assemblage, *inequitable environmentalism*, challenges environmental movements using Jean-Jacques Rousseau-inspired public judgments of social inequality, oligarchy and tyranny. The fourth, *settler environmentalism*, critiques colonial environmentalism, especially Eurocentric models that assimilate native and local ways of knowing into positivistic techno-science. These anthropocentric anti-environmentalisms do not necessarily occupy only one place on a traditional, left–right political spectrum. However, *inequitable* and *settler environmentalism*, at least in the Canadian and North American contexts on which I focus, animate strong left-liberal counter-movements while *inefficient* and *unprofitable environmentalism* resonate more strongly with counter-movements on the right. Finally, I explore a fifth moral assemblage, what I call *unecological environmentalism*. Unlike, all the other anti-environmentalisms, *unecological environmentalism* decentres humans as the primary moral agents in, and beneficiaries of, the fight against climate change, biodiversity loss and habitat destruction. Indicative of the culturally and geographically challenging nature of opening up a common global society to nonhuman persons, *unecological environmentalism* sits uneasily with respect to simplistic left–right political spectrums.

This chapter advances the thesis that counter-movements draw upon a plurality of contradictory moral assemblages of the common good to try and revise, defeat or revolutionize environmentalism. Each counter-movement appeals to a principle of the common good and denounces a social infrastructure it sees as undermining this good. In terms of their critiques, counter-movements against environmentalism show moral versatility. Some try to revise or correct public policy and public opinion by enhancing commitment to a pre-existing, if insufficiently supported, common good; others more radically seek to 'flip the moral script' by denouncing the common good upon which an environmental movement or policy is predicated and replacing it with another. Pragmatic sociology refers to these kinds of critique, respectively, as 'reformist' and 'radical' (Boltanski and Chiapello, 2005). Still other counter-movements, advancing what I call 'revolutionary critique', reject the entire notion of higher principles and common goods of humanity because they exclude nonhuman persons and their explicit right to flourish. The moral versatility of different kinds of anti-environmental counter-movements extends, moreover, to the dynamic relations between them, such as when *unprofitable* and *inefficient environmentalism* combine to bolster the capitalistic division between 'the economy' and 'the environment'. I highlight such relations in the chapter's conclusion and trace inter-assemblage confluences between progressive anti-environmentalisms, highlighting the need to build bridges between counter-movements against *unecological*, *inequitable* and *settler environmentalism*.

Inefficient Environmentalism

One particularly powerful moral assemblage of anti-environmentalism champions the ideals of techno-scientific efficiency, fiscal restraint and long-term planning for the future. *Inefficient environmentalism* animates counter-movements that appeal to objective, technical solutions that transcend place and local knowledge. Prototypical actors include many engineers, planners and economists, such as international celebrity anti-environmentalist Bjorn Lomborg, an economist who has infamously denounced public efforts to cut carbon as fiscally irresponsible compared to technological and engineering solutions for climate change. More generally, counter-movements against *inefficient environmentalism* embrace small 'c' conservatives and libertarians seeking to curb unnecessary taxation, lavish public spending and intervention within private industry by political elites. *Inefficient environmentalism* advances anti-environmental politics in a conservative direction, one weary of expanding government to fight either social oppression or ecological crises at the expense of industry and the larger economy. It diverges from progressive anti-environmentalisms (taken up below) by exalting 'the economy' and bracketing it off as something separate from 'the environment'. Once pitted against economic growth, innovation, long-term prosperity and jobs, the environment becomes easier to mobilize against by deploying radical (rather than reformist) denouncements that replace moral concern for the environment with that of the economy.

Inefficient environmentalism in twenty-first-century Canada, as elsewhere, is unfolding against the political and economic backdrop of cutting carbon pollution and reducing our dependence on fossil fuels to head off the worst effects of climate change. In 2015, Justin Trudeau was elected Prime Minster of Canada partly based on the promise of taking a fresh approach to environmental action (coming on the heels of Conservative governments that were openly hostile to environmentalists). This shift by Trudeau and his centrist Liberal Party purportedly transcends a false dichotomy erected by Conservatives between 'the economy' and 'the environment'. It requires 'ecofiscal' compromises that open the door to further exploitation of fossil fuels in the context of simultaneously strengthening environmental policies, notably a national carbon pricing plan. Such compromises have triggered counter-movements on both sides of the political spectrum. Tougher environmental regulations on extractive industries and pollution pricing imposed by Trudeau's government, as the ecofiscal cost of expanding Canada's fossil fuel industries, are seen by many pro-petroleum actors as a dangerous political interference into critical industries on which the long-term health of Canada's economy depends while the country gradually transitions to renewable energies.

For instance, in spring 2018 thousands of people protested in downtown Calgary in support of expanding oil pipelines (Heidenreich, 2018). A year later, Canada Action, a self-described 'grassroots movement encouraging Canadians to take action and work together in support of our vital natural resources sectors', assembled what it called 'the Largest Oil and Gas Rally in Canadian History' in the same city (Canada Action, 2019). This pro-petroleum counter-movement, headquartered in Calgary and running deep into western Canadian political culture, animates more than one form of anti-environmentalism, featuring, for example, a strong current of *unprofitable environmentalism* (taken up in the next section). But it clearly confronts *inefficient environmentalism* where, rather than the free market or quarterly returns, pro-pipeline counter-movements such as Canada Action position a 'responsible', even regulated petroleum industry within a long-term 'sustainability' frame as vital for future jobs, innovation and economic prosperity. For pro-petroleum counter-movements, Canada's very ability to function efficiently as a nation depends directly on oil and gas.

The social infrastructure problematized by counter-movements against *inefficient environmentalism* draws together political elites and public authorities who are widely seen as having little understanding of how their plans and policies impact everyday taxpayers and households, especially outside of cosmopolitan urban settings. When urban elites such as Prime Minister Trudeau and bike-friendly politicians like former Vancouver mayor (2008–2018) Gregor Robertson (Proctor, 2018) advanced ambitious visions to tax carbon emissions and curtail gasoline consumption and automobile dependence, they risked political backlashes from Canada's suburban, car-and-gas dependent majority. In many cases this backlash is fanned by other state actors, such as conservative political parties and formal lobbyists like the Canadian Association of Petroleum Producers, which holds considerable public sway in establishing the 'facts' about Canada's oil sands. In other cases, private counter-movement organizations play a more significant role, particularly those that 'take on the appearance of citizen-based grassroots movements' and use media savvy in the public sphere to make up for lack of governmental and legal support (Adams et al., 2015, p. 6). The success of counter-movements against *inefficient environmentalism* varies widely between national and urban contexts. It is more difficult to fight against environmentalism in the many places (e.g. Sweden, Germany) where scientific evidence of ecological crises like climate change (e.g. IPCC reports) are broadly believed by people; it is easier in places (e.g. United States, Australia) where the scientific frame is less accepted (Broadbent et al., 2016) and susceptible to rejection campaigns (Tranter and Booth, 2015).

A paradigmatic case of *inefficient environmentalism*, one that has prototypical value in establishing a metaphor 'for the domain that the case concerns' (Flyvbjerg, 2006, p. 230), lies in a 2015 referendum in Metro Vancouver (a federation of 21 municipalities, one Electoral Area and one Treaty First Nation, including the City of Vancouver) that asked voters to approve or reject a new 0.5 percent sales tax to help fund a major initiative to expand environmentally sustainable mobility projects (public transit, cycling and walking). Canada falls within a cluster of Anglo societies where the scientific frame for ecological crises such as climate change is unsettled and debated, which helps contextualize the referendum's results. The 'Yes' side (to fund sustainable mobilities) was widely expected to win, enjoying strong backing from the region's Transportation Authority and Mayors' Council (representatives from the 21 municipalities and Tsawwassen First Nation), which spent nearly $7 million on its campaign; it was leading with 57 percent in favour of the new tax and 43 percent against according to polls shortly before the vote. Instead, in a dramatic turn, the vote results were

62 percent against and 38 percent in favour (Johnson and Baluja, 2015). There was virtually no opposition—with the exception of the Canadian Taxpayers Federation (CTF). Portraying itself as a grassroots advocacy group against wasteful spending, CTF 'spokespeople regularly get more [news] coverage than elected officials', and has only about five members, encapsulating what Putnam (2000) called a fake grassroots, 'astroturf' organization (Lamont, 2016, n.p.). Nevertheless, on a shoestring budget of $40 000, the CTF humbled Vancouver's urban political elite, using media messaging that emphasized how much ordinary households would pay every year under the new tax and the financial impropriety of the regional Transportation Authority. 'No' votes, notably, were concentrated heavily in postwar, car-dominated suburbs (Johnson and Baluja, 2015).

Metro Vancouver's referendum highlights emerging political opportunities available to even bare bones, astroturf counter-movements against *inefficient environmentalism* to exploit urban–suburban divides tied to everyday mobilities, urban form and the built environment. With these divides increasingly dictating the results of Canadian elections and with sprawling, car-dependent suburbs growing faster than dense urban centres (Ibbitson, 2018; Walks, 2007), uneven technological and economic dependence on automobility and gasoline will continue to mediate and moderate scientific imperatives to address climate change, habitat degradation and biodiversity loss—particularly in national contexts already prone to debating the validity of environmental science itself. Making matters more challenging, populist *anti*-science counter-movements against *unprofitable environmentalism* are gaining ground on the far right, expanding and diversifying radical critiques of any environmental movements and policies that harm 'the economy'.

Unprofitable Environmentalism

A second moral assemblage of anti-environmentalism fights for the ideal of a truly profitable market, one unfettered by government regulation or 'red tape' so that it can create jobs and make more individuals (both people and corporations) wealthy. Whereas small 'c' conservative movements against *inefficient environmentalism* can still imagine an important, if limited role for government to address ecological crises—for example, where banks say such crises threaten economic growth (Roman, 2019)—many capital 'C' Conservatives in Canada have increasingly turned towards an ultra free market orthodoxy focused on getting government out of the economy's way. *Unprofitable* and *inefficient environmentalism* share some common frames and resources. Both galvanize right-wing actors, defend petroleum industries, endorse capitalism, attack taxes and radically denounce environmentalism. However, whereas *inefficient environmentalism* appeals to an industrial capitalism that treats nonhuman environments as natural resources in need of long-term, techno-scientific management by experts, *unprofitable environmentalism* appeals to an unconstrained, neoliberal capitalism (Walks, 2009) in which nonhuman environments are hyper-commoditized things to be bought, sold and moved as fast as possible to accelerate the short-term monetary exchanges that generate wealth. Furthermore, counter-movements against *unprofitable environmentalism* show stronger ties to broader, right-wing populist movements that have recently spread around the world.

More than other assemblages of anti-environmentalism, *unprofitable environmentalism* benefited when political winds in wealthy Anglo nations filled the sails of the far right. Brexit and Trump reflect the rise of right-wing populism, itself a response to exploding inequalities triggered by neoliberalist and austerity policies that pre-date, and were magnified by, the Great Recession. These same political conditions have animated populist, left-liberal counter-movements advancing pro-environmental objectives, such as Earth Day and the March for Science (Roth, 2018). But with pro-petroleum, pro-car activists gaining power (and debating whether science proves climate change is a problem), 'people power' that connects anti-environmentalism to this agenda, for the moment, finds a fortuitous political opportunity structure—even in Canada. I say 'even' because Canada, especially under the feminist, pro-immigrant rule of Prime Minster Trudeau, is generally viewed as a sharp contrast with Brexit and Trump. However, while Trudeau has been in power federally, populist right-wing premiers have seized power at the provincial level, notably in Ontario, Canada's most populous province and home of its automobile sector, and Alberta, home of the oil sands and site of the Largest Oil and Gas Rally in Canadian history.

The social infrastructure denounced by counter-movements against *unprofitable environmentalism* features liberal elites, environmental justice activists and 'politically correct' people and organizations who are portrayed as aiming to ban beef burgers, long flights and SUVs while killing jobs related to oil, gas and the car. Counter-movements against *unprofitable environmentalism* link social justice and 'globalism' to unacceptable attacks by mainstream environmental movements and policies on fossil fuels and automobility. For example, in February 2019, protestors (under police escort) drove a convoy of trucks, called United We Roll, from Alberta to Ottawa, Ontario (Canada's capital), to rev their engines and demonstrate in an effort to unite Canadians around building more oil and gas pipelines and to fight off new government regulations for assessing the environmental impact of petroleum infrastructure. However, United We Roll—so named to resonate with Jason Kenney's United Conservative Party (UCP), which was then vying for Alberta's provincial power in an election campaign—earned international media attention for becoming:

> a space for far-right groups to spew racism and xenophobia. Signs denouncing open borders, protesting Canada signing on to the global migration pact and accusing the prime minister of treason hung alongside signs supporting pipelines. Some convoy participants wore hats that said 'Make Canada Great Again', a nod to U.S. President Donald Trump's slogan that has become associated with denigrating Mexicans, asylum seekers and banning Muslims from entering the U.S. (Wright, 2019).

This pro-petroleum, anti-regulation convoy was not very large—about two hundred trucks. Yet, framed in the media as 'Canada's tea party' (Loreto, 2019), United We Roll briefly carried outsized influence on a par with that of the Canadian Taxpayers Federation. Controversially, it gained public support from Andrew Scheer, leader of the Conservative Party of Canada, Trudeau's official opposition. Scheer met United We Roll in Ottawa on Parliament Hill, proclaiming: 'We're standing with you' (Wright, 2019, n.p.). Originally calling itself the Yellow Vest Convoy, before changing the name because of its racist insinuations about Muslims and immigrants, United We Roll also found support from various right-wing figures who have been capitalizing on a rising wave of economic angst and populism—including Jason Kenney, who was elected a couple of months later as Alberta's premier.

A paradigmatic case of *unprofitable environmentalism* concerns Premier Jason Kenney, with his blanket hostility towards environmental actors and policies. A seasoned social conservative activist, Kenney returned to Alberta in 2016 from federal politics to merge the province's right and far-right parties into the UCP. Framing himself as Canada's 'fiercest carbon-tax killer' he won a majority government on a deeply polarizing campaign against the Trudeau government, British Columbia, environmentalists and anyone else standing in the way of more oil and gas extraction and new pipelines to tidewater. The first piece of legislation Kenny's government passed, fulfilling a central campaign promise, repealed the province's $30-per-tonne 'job-killing' carbon tax introduced by the previous Alberta government. This means the province will fall under Trudeau's federal carbon pricing plan, the constitutionality of which Kenney fought in federal court on the obviously dubious basis that climate change is a local issue that need and should not fall under wider, national jurisdiction (in March 2021, the Supreme Court of Canada ruled that the 'federal carbon price' is constitutional). Besides unravelling Trudeau's ecofiscal justification for expanding oil and gas extraction and investing in new pipelines, Kenney is actively battling against environmentalists (e.g. Greenpeace and the Pembina Institute) who spread what he calls 'myths and lies' about Alberta's oil sands, placing blame for Alberta's recent economic woes not with the collapse in the price of oil but rather with anyone who suggests the oil underneath Alberta should stay in the ground.

Kenney, echoing moves by authoritarian leaders such as Brazilian president Jair Bolsonaro and US president Donald Trump, presents a tangible threat to environmental movements and policy standing in the way of profitable resource extraction. Backed by a $30 million 'energy war room', Kenney threatened to 'fund lawsuits against offending environmentalists and to call a public inquiry into the role of money from U.S. foundations' (Weber, 2019) drawing on campaign style tactics. He effectively aims to merge long-standing international conspiracy frames of environmentalists as outsider extremists (Albrecht, 1972) with newer digital tactics to 'other' and 'out' oil sands critics by contesting majority science and revealing the real 'truth' about Alberta's resources and their contribution to climate change. His antipathy for carbon pricing, a market-driven solution to shift consumers away from carbon-intensive products and services, shows that Kenney's anti-environmentalism is driven not so much by an interest in long-term markets as it is by short-term threats to the profits, wealth and luxurious lifestyles that many folks and corporations in Alberta have, as elsewhere, reaped from fossil fuels. Kenney and Alberta's war against environmentalism, arguably motivated by money, marks one of Canada's most decisive attacks against the emergence of a green world order.

Inequitable Environmentalism

A third moral assemblage of anti-environmentalism draws on the ideal of social justice, highlighting how environmentalism helps create and reproduce complex social inequalities—racism, sexism, classism, ageism, ableism, *inter alia*—across a variety of axes and their intersections. *Inequitable Environmentalism* pivots anti-environmentalism in a left-liberal direction. Environmental justice (EJ) movements (Cole and Foster, 2001), notably, counter mainstream environmental movements by emphasizing human equity: 'instead of focusing on the preservation of nature in itself, EJ movements seek social justice for people who live, work, play, and learn in the most polluted environments in the world' (Bell and Braun, 2010, pp. 794–5). Starting from the empirical premise that people of colour and marginalized bodies and communities are disproportionately exposed to environmental hazards, often through zoning ordinances and business practices that privilege the carbon-intensive lifestyles of wealthy, white elites (Taylor, 2014a), EJ movements hit back at environmental campaigns that perpetuate this systemic oppression through ongoing discrimination.

Vegansim and animal rights (AR) movements, for example, have been condemned on the basis of environmental justice by 'vegans of colour' and others for reproducing white supremacy and oppression by mounting patronizing campaigns and protests for plant-based diets that overlook the high costs and sociospatial privileges of accessing, preparing and storing healthy food (Brueck, 2017; Joy, 2016). PETA (People for the Ethical Treatment of Animals), for example, has been called out for its overtly racist and sexist campaigns (Glasser, 2011), as when it sent rescuers into New Orleans after Hurricane Katrina to save animals—excluding the (predominantly African–American) humans. Dis/ability activists and scholars have also castigated the AR movement for obsessing with able-bodied fitness, ignoring equitable access to AR events, and for equating people with cognitive disabilities and nonhuman animals as 'marginal cases' who deserve a lesser moral status than neurotypical adult humans (Donaldson and Kymlicka, 2016, p. 86). As wealthy countries expand vegetarian and vegan diets, and the world as a whole moves in the opposite direction through rising meat and dairy consumption, political tension between AR and EJ movements is poised to grow.

EJ movements contend that underlying the oppressive content of some environmental campaigns are broader inequities regarding who gets to participate and gain positions of power within mainstream environmentalism. Up until the late nineteenth century, North American environmental organizations 'were bastions of upper middle class White male recreation, adventure-seeking, policymaking, and nature protection' (Taylor 2014b, p. 4); mass environmentalism in the civil rights era showed a middle-class bias (Albrecht, 1972). More recent research on racial, gender and class diversity among staff in American conservation and preservation organizations, government environmental agencies, and environmental grant-making foundations shows that while these movements and institutions have made progress over time on gender diversity, these gains have mostly gone to white women; racial diversity in general lags far behind gender diversity; cross-class collaborations remain rare; and men remain far more likely to occupy leadership positions (Taylor, 2014b). Such intersectional gaps in social diversity are compounded by mainstream environmental movements and institutions' democratic deficits.

The social infrastructure criticized by counter-movements against *inequitable environmentalism* entails authoritarian and elitist power structures that corrode the practices of liberal democracy which underlie support for the principles of social justice. In *Bowling Alone* (2000), Putnam takes environmental movement organizations (e.g. Greenpeace; Environmental Defence Fund) to task for their 'direct mail recruits' of so-called 'members' who evaporate as soon as they stop receiving mail, suggesting that mass environmental movements have grown detached from the rank and file and lack social capital. Presaging Putnam's analysis, in 1996, 16 founders of Greenpeace declared in a public letter that 'Greenpeace's leaders are paid too much, have lost their focus and must become more democratic' (Lean, 1996). More recently, Naomi Klein observed that elitist green groups have actually facilitated the spread of neoliberal environmental depredation where they have not been 'willing to give up their elite status,' harking 'back to the elite roots of the movement, and the fact that when a lot of these conservation groups began there was kind of a noblesse oblige approach to conservation. It was about elites getting together and hiking and deciding to save nature' (Mark 2013, n.p.).

Oligarchy represents a creeping threat to democratic environmentalism. Many of the non-governmental organizations that currently dominate national environmental movements in Canada and North America more broadly (e.g. the David Suzuki Foundation) have adopted relatively top-down, authoritarian structures that rely on professional staff, funding from capitalism-friendly foundations (e.g. Pew, Rockefeller Brothers Fund), and the higher levels of non-transparency that come with securing foundation money (Jay, 2013). In this light, movements whose members fund and democratically set agendas and choose leaders (e.g.

The Council of Canadians) could be viewed as counter-movements against *inequitable environmentalism*. Oligarchical environmental organizations and policies compound environmentalism's social diversity problem in a global context of growing social inequality, particularly where they endorse a conception of environmentalism that privileges corporate collaboration, luxury experiences of nature, and soaring returns on private investment.

For a 'paradigmatic case' of *inequitable environmentalism* consider green gentrification. The Barcelona Laboratory for Urban Environmental Justice and Sustainability (see http://www.bcnuej.org/green-gentrification/) defines green gentrification as 'processes started by the implementation of an environmental planning agenda related to green spaces that lead to the exclusion and displacement of politically disenfranchised residents'. Green gentrification carries prototypical value for *inequitable environmentalism* in part because it focuses attention on the city, where the United Nations (2018) predicts 70 percent of humanity will live by 2050, up from 55 percent today, and where political battles over ecological crises and social inequality have become increasingly intertwined (United Nations Human Settlements Programme, 2009). A global exemplar of green gentrification—and Canadian export—is Vancouverism, a profitable style of environmental planning named for the city that branded it. Vancouverism entails transforming urban space through lofty, glassy condo towers atop commercial podiums with expansive, protected views of nature and easy connections to new rail transit, bike lanes and central parks (Kiger, 2014). While Vancouverism merges environmentalism with urban planning by tackling ecological crises such as excessive dependence on fossil fuel-powered cars, it also constructs a luxurious, green urban core from which those without wealth are increasingly excluded—even communities that have long lived there.

A local group on the ground fighting against Vancouver's green gentrification called the Youth Collaborative for Chinatown (YCC) shows a typical counter-movement dynamic against *inequitable environmentalism*. Already facing extraordinary redevelopment pressures, Chinatown, along with the city's Downtown Eastside, one of Canada's poorest neighbourhoods, overlaps and interconnects with the last remaining undeveloped land in Vancouver's core, for which the City has a $1.73 billion plan to build condo towers, cafés, pubs, a floating restaurant and high-end retail that will further enrich some of the wealthiest developer–oligarchs in the world (Stewart, 2017). The emerald jewel of this plan is a new $200-million park designed by the creators of The High Line in New York City, another exemplar of elite-driven green gentrification (Bliss, 2017). Using grassroots, community-oriented tactics (e.g. organizing mahjong events, night markets and walking tours) while lobbying city officials, the YCC has helped mobilize the neighbourhood against the rapid, high end development that has been displacing an aging Chinese population. In so doing, the YCC advances both reformist and radical critiques, seeking to revise Vancouver's environmental planning agenda and replace its strong orientation towards a neoliberal market with one based on social justice for an historically marginalized population. The fight to make sustainable urban development more equitable will only grow, as Vancouver and other wealthy global metropolises compete with each other to become 'the world's greenest city' (City of Vancouver, 2017).

Settler Environmentalism

A fourth moral assemblage of anti-environmentalism animates counter-movements that appeal to the defence of local and traditional knowledge and ecological heritage against imperialism and colonialism. *Settler environmentalism* shares an overarching orientation against oppression with *inequitable environmentalism*; together, they elaborate a left-liberal dynamic wherein progressive counter-movements denounce conservative actors and campaigns. What sets *settler environmentalism* apart is its long view of history and emphasis on local, Indigenous authority, putting it starkly at odds with actors focused on *inefficient environmentalism*. The same techno-scientific, universal solutions with which engineers, economists and planners attempt to transcend place and context become obstacles and liabilities for those aiming to preserve and invigorate localized communities, Indigenous knowledge and unceded territories.

As 'digital repertoires of action' transform tactics through web-based social media (Roth, 2018), simply sharing content online can turn everyday moments into sparks for anti-environmentalist outrage. For example, in 2015 a video of a Kanaka Maoli man in Hawaii sitting next to, and performing a healing ceremony for a beached monk seal went viral after bystanders called the police because they thought the man was 'harassing' the seal, and the police then pepper-sprayed him and broke his bones while he was trying to leave. In the video, a woman cries, 'I was so scared he was going to hurt her [the seal]' (Joy, 2016, n.p.). Such apparent cultural chauvinism is by no means an isolated phenomenon, encapsulating larger tensions between AR and the struggles of Indigenous peoples. AR movements often overly focus on the 'cruel' and 'inhumane' practices of racialized and colonized populations in contrast to the supposedly 'civilized' treatment of animals by the majority (Donaldson and Kymlicka, 2016).

Beyond AR, a somewhat camouflaged formation of *settler environmentalism* revolves around 'invasion ecology'. An extensive scientific and popular movement trying to eradicate 'alien species' and 'introduced exotics' (Simberloff, 2013), invasion ecology encompasses respected ecologists, local conservation non-profits, intergovernmental interventions and even restaurants and annual cook-offs specializing in invasive plants and animals, such as seaweed soup and Asian carp burgers. Ostensibly, invasion ecology contests the domination of imperial species that threaten native ones, often by trying to eradicate the usurpers. While some non-native species clearly precipitate environmental nightmares (e.g. Burmese pythons in south Florida, brown tree snakes in Guam), a counter-movement has coalesced around the knowledge that others are relatively harmless (or even ecologically beneficial), and that by painting all introduced species as outsider, foreign usurpers based on their origin rather than their long-term environmental impact, invasion ecology works to reinforce inflammatory xenophobic rhetoric around non-native *humans* qua refugees and 'immigrant aliens' (Crawford, 2018). However, links between mainstream environmentalists and anti-immigration groups are hard to find, and the counter-movement against invasion ecology, appealing to a zoological and botanical kind of cosmopolitanism, may also contribute to *settler environmentalism* (see Mastnak et al., 2014). In an anthropocentric, reactionary twist, both sides of the clash over non-native nonhumans may play into the hands of human settlers who have failed to examine their own histories of colonialism at the expense of the colonized peoples they have undermined.

The social infrastructure pilloried by counter-movements against *settler environmentalism* rests on Euro-centric and positivistic science and technology and the bureaucracies that labour to rationalize and extend objective techno-science over native territories. Through modern bureaucracies managed by experts, successive federal and provincial governments in Canada have come to carefully map, measure and mobilize the nonhuman environment as a resource and economic commodity to be carved up, bought and sold at scale with industrial efficiency. This techno-scientific way of conceiving natural environments clashes, notably, with the ways in which many First Nations, Inuit and Métis communities imagine more-than-human environments. For example, as Anishinaabe scholar Deborah McGregor (2014) argues, many Indigenous peoples conceive of water and other elements of the world not as a thing to be ruthlessly exploited—a settler–colonial approach that has directly undermined the health of many First Nations communities by polluting and destroying water—but rather as a living being to which people owe ethical responsibilities. For McGregor, so long as traditional knowledge is itself considered in a respectful, ethical and collaborative way, it could play a part, not only in advancing Indigenous rights and self-determination, but also in shifting Western Euro-Canadian governance paradigms towards less exploitive relations with water wherein humans move towards fulfilling their moral responsibilities to nonhuman beings.

A paradigmatic case of *settler environmentalism* concerns the recent push at the centre of Canadian politics for economistic, fossil fuel-friendly environmental policies. As mentioned above, Prime Minster Trudeau was elected on the promise of prioritizing both 'the economy' and 'the environment' through ecofiscal compromises that balance tougher environmental policies against 'responsible' resource development. The Trudeau government exemplified this approach in 2018 when it purchased the Trans Mountain pipeline from Texas-based Kinder Morgan for CAD 4.5 billion, in order to revive a highly controversial project to expand the pipeline and bolster the profitability of oil sands development in Northern Alberta, with the quid pro quo that Alberta's government will start pricing the province's nation-leading, and growing, GHG emissions (Government of Canada, 2019). The National Energy Board (NEB) (now the 'Canadian Energy Regulator'), tellingly headquartered in Calgary rather than Ottawa, has played a pivotal role in publicly justifying the pipeline expansion on the basis of techno-scientific standards and objective, economic evidence. Initially, the NEB's case, according to a 2018 Federal Court of Appeal decision to temporarily halt pipeline construction, notably failed to consider the impact of rising tanker traffic on endangered southern resident killer whales or adequately consult with First Nations (Nikiforuk, 2018). Since then, however, court challenges to stall the Trans Mountain expansion, such as British Columbia's bid to control the flow of oil across its borders, have failed, igniting protests against Canada's pipeline by anti-colonial actors on the left.

Beyond the Trans Mountain pipeline's longstanding legal troubles, Trudeau's 'third-way' marriage of environmentalism to resource exploitation has inspired a formidable counter-movement of diverse actors, including Indigenous peoples, some members of British Columbia's New Democratic Party government, the City of Burnaby (within Metro Vancouver), and my own university, which happens to be located on top of Burnaby Mountain, underneath which the Trans Mountain pipeline runs. Mass protests against the pipeline project on Burnaby Mountain in fall of 2014 entailed considerable civil disobedience, leading to the arrests of students, professors and community members (Collis, 2015). Various protests have unfolded across the region since then, including large demonstrations organized by Extinction Rebellion and Climate Convergence Metro Vancouver after the NEB re-approved the Trans Mountain expansion in February 2019. This counter-movement against pipeline and oil sands expansion, like counter-movements against green gentrification, advances both reformist and radical critiques, seeking to reform Canada's environmental agenda by uncoupling Trudeau's eco-fiscal compromise and replacing the fiscal part with an emphasis on local political power, Indigenous rights and traditional knowledge. Together, counter-movements against *inequitable* and *settler environmentalism* protect political space for refining environmentalism rather than contesting its existence.

Unecological Environmentalism

A fifth moral assemblage of anti-environmentalism, a 'black swan' with unpredictable and possibly extreme consequences, advances the ideal of political agency and positive rights for nonhuman beings. *Unecological environmentalism*, not unlike *unprofitable environmentalism*, critiques mainstream environmentalism in general, not for the sake of an abstract 'economy' and short-term profits cynically removed from the nonhuman environments on which they ultimately depend, but rather for a strikingly different reason: anthropocentrism. Each of the previous assemblages of anti-environmentalism draws upon a common good—long-term planning and industrial efficiency; a profitable marketplace; social justice and equity; traditional knowledge and local heritage—that places humans and their flourishing at the apex of moral progress. However, why should nonhuman beings not also enjoy legal and political standing as morally legitimate persons? Why should nonhuman animals, plants, mushrooms and even individual communities of organisms not only morally require negative freedoms, or protections against being summarily murdered or tortured as someone else's instrument, but also positive obligations from humans that support their ability to flourish? In other words, why should nonhuman beings not be part of 'our' common good? While currently a long way from mainstream environmentalism in theory and practice, counter-movements against *unecological environmentalism* have nevertheless leapt ahead in recent decades through scholarship, legal actions and grassroots activism, all of which threaten not simply to revise or radically denounce environmentalism but to revolutionize it.

As scientific research continues to demolish longstanding myths about what makes humans unique, from tool use and intelligence to sociality and empathy (de Waal, 2016), a range of counter-movements across an array of political registers have sought to challenge human supremacism and shift nonhuman beings from instrumental 'things' to bona fide 'persons' with the same moral and legal standing that humans and corporations enjoy. In February 2018, for example, a group of philosophers and activists called the Nonhuman Rights Project submitted an amicus curiae brief to the New York Court of Appeals to grant legal personhood for two chimpanzees being isolated in cages by their owners, taking direct aim at a legal edifice that says only humans and their corporate collectives constitute persons (Sebo, 2018). Certain 'celebrity species' have received outsized attention, such as great apes (Cavalieri and Singer, 1993) and whales (Cavalieri, 2006), but the movement for nonhuman rights is slowly spreading to other animals, plants and even complex, multi-organism beings or ecosystems at risk of collapse, as when Toledo voters in 2019 passed the 'Lake Erie Bill of Rights', a charter amendment that defines the lake as a legally legitimate 'person' (McGraw, 2019). A growing international 'rights of nature' movement has extended individual rights to particular forests and watersheds in Ecuador, New Zealand, India and Colombia, with strong support by many Indigenous peoples who have long viewed forests and water as morally significant, living beings towards which humans ought to act responsibly and ethically (McGregor, 2014).

The social infrastructure assailed by counter-movements against *unecological environmentalism* rests on legal regimes, industrial agriculture, animal breeding, medical testing, resource extraction, automobility, aviation and sprawling built environments that have enshrined the status of nonhuman beings as the property of humans while pushing as many as one million plant and animal species to the risk of extinction (IPBES, 2019). Put simply, this is the infrastructure holding up modern ways in which humans live together, which helps explain why counter-movements against *unecological environmentalism* carry revolutionary potential.

Two central conceits perpetuated by modern ways of living together are: (1) in order to belong to a political community and have one's subjective good considered as part of its common good requires the higher cognitive capacities, reasoning skills and rationality that only humans enjoy; (2) the city is the space that happens when and where rational humans make a 'civilized' place for themselves away from the unruly beasts and unruly natures above which humans have managed to elevate and remove themselves.

A paradigmatic case of *unecological environmentalism* entails the 'zoopolis' (Donaldson and Kymlicka, 2013), a scholarly project and political philosophical foundation for a new, more inclusive animal rights (AR) movement. What makes the zoopolis paradigmatic is that Donaldson and Kymlicka (2013) start with the assumption that sentience and a subjective good alone are sufficient to qualify a being not only for basic negative rights (e.g. not to be killed or tortured), but also positive rights and responsibilities that are conducive to their flourishing. If an additional, higher cognitive capacity or political agency were also required, some Habermasian level of communicative rationality, then many humans (young children, people with cognitive disabilities or dementia) should lack such rights. That is neither the case nor the purpose of human rights (to protect the most vulnerable). In seeking to advance positive rights for animals, Donaldson and Kymlicka (2013) lay out what kinds of relations humans ought to share with nonhuman animal persons. They argue that domesticated animals require citizenship; liminal animals (living in human communities but not domesticated and untrusting of humans) require denizenship, or a set of responsibilities and rights that go beyond universal protections but not as far as citizenship; and wild animals require a flexible form of territorial sovereignty. What specific positive rights and responsibilities are appropriate reflects the nature of our relationship with a species, and depend on humans who know an individual animal well enough to help elicit their subjective, individualized good and facilitate their political agency.

A core strength of the zoopolis entails its extension of positive moral obligations to all animals (although, curiously, to the total exclusion of plants) improving on previous, ad hoc approaches that recognize only specific species. While it has not coalesced into a unified counter-movement, the zoopolis connects a wide array of already unfolding practical interventions, including: inclusive design for all animals, green cities and corridors for animal mobilities, new models of animal care work (e.g. socialization programs in correctional facilities), animal-friendly economies and even 'animal ombudsmen' on city councils (Donaldson and Kymlicka, 2016). Of course, the zoopolis has a long way to go before revolutionizing 'business as usual' when it comes to addressing everyday, institutionalized violence towards nonhuman beings. A core challenge facing a 'zoopolitical revolution' (Donaldson and Kymlicka, 2016) rests on effecting systemic social change with broader coalitions through liberal democratic politics. The critiques of the wider AR movement with respect to social injustice and settler colonialism brought up earlier in this chapter suggest that justice and personhood for nonhuman animals, besides bearing an uneasy relationship with traditional left–right politics, presents a multi-faceted moral struggle cutting across different assemblages of anti-environmentalism.

CONFLUENCES

So where does this all leave anti-environmentalism? As the wide range of cases explored in this chapter evoke, a strong sense of moral versatility characterizes a plurality of assemblages of anti-environmentalism, assemblages that appeal to contradictory visions of the common good.

This analysis can help future studies conceptualize morally diverse anti-environmentalisms, not only by identifying distinctive moral frames or 'grammars' of worth and competing styles of critique but also the larger, more-than-human assemblages of qualified objects, practices and modes of judgement that underpin anti-environmental counter-movements across the political spectrum. In so doing, future studies might better comprehend the moral–political compromises, critiques and contexts that characterize mobilizations against environmentalism that have yet to emerge and illuminate how progressive counter-movements might consolidate and magnify their impact in an increasingly unequal, hyper-partisan world beset by ecological emergency.

To conclude, I consolidate this sense of moral versatility among anti-environmentalisms by retracing a couple of salient confluences between different assemblages that speak broadly to how these assemblages fit together politically. While each moral assemblage features distinctive actors, contested social infrastructures and competing ideals of the common good, some notable patterns emerge. For one, *inequitable* and *settler environmentalism* animate both radical and reformist critiques—holding onto the idea of environmentalism by trying to refine it—while *inefficient* and *unprofitable environmentalism*, in contrast, emphasize radical denouncements that more simply seek to undercut it. Each assemblage conceives of, and formats, 'the environment' in a different way. Notably, *inefficient* and *unprofitable environmentalism* do so by bracketing 'the environment' off from 'the economy', making it easier to coherently denounce environmental movements and policies. These patterns convey left-liberal and right-wing distinctions among anti-environmentalisms, which in turn carry important implications for which assemblages gain access to political opportunities and levers of state power in an age of Brexit, Trump and Kenney.

A second salient confluence relates to the fact that most moral assemblages of anti-environmentalism are anthropocentric. This presents a significant challenge to reassembling common worlds in a global context of exploding inequalities, hyper-partisanship and rising populism in a manner that advances an ecological common good inclusive of nonhuman beings.

A notable exception to this entails *unecological environmentalism*. While less prominent than other counter-movements against environmentalism, such as 'Canada's fiercest carbon-tax killer' leading Alberta against Canada's emerging green order, efforts to establish positive rights and personhood for nonhuman beings have nevertheless begun to coalesce into a revolutionary challenge to human-centric environmentalism. I suggest that counter-movements fighting against *unecological environmentalism*, such as the zoopolis, have a higher chance of realizing this potential where they build bridges with counter-movements against *inequitable* and *settler environmentalism*. Such bridges include: ameliorating complex social inequities within environmental movements (e.g. the lack of women and people of colour in positions of leadership in environmental organizations); incorporating traditional and Indigenous knowledge into environmental policies and campaigns in a responsible and ethical way (e.g.

by reinforcing Indigenous rights); and eliminating the sexism, racism and cultural chauvinism lurking within popular animal rights movements (e.g. PETA).

Ultimately, oppressions and injustices against humans and nonhumans that corrode the common good are mutually reinforcing and interlocking (Glasser, 2011). Different axes of domination, therefore, need to be addressed simultaneously. Failure to ameliorate gross environmental injustices inflicted on nonhuman persons feeds into an overarching system of domination that reproduces complex inequities among humans. Ultimately, counter-movements for a more just and more ecological environmentalism depend on one another.

REFERENCES

Adams, A.E., Shiver, T.E. and Messer, C.M. (2015) Movement–countermovement dynamics in a land use controversy. *Human Ecology Review*. **21**(1), pp. 3–25.

Albrecht, S.L. (1972) Environmental social movements and counter-movements: An overview and an illustration. *Journal of Voluntary Action Research*. **1**, pp. 2–11.

Bell, S.E. and Braun, Y.A. (2010) Coal, identity, and the gendering of environmental justice activism in Central Appalachia. *Gender & Society*. **24**(6), pp. 794–813.

Bliss, L. (2017) The High Line's next balancing act. *Bloomberg CityLab*. Available from: https://www.bloomberg.com/news/articles/2017-02-07/the-high-line-and-equity-in-adaptive-reuse.

Blok, A. (2013) Pragmatic sociology as political ecology: On the many worths of nature(s). *European Journal of Social Theory*. **16**(4), pp. 492–510.

Blok, A. and Meilvang, M.L. (2015) Picturing urban green attachments: Civic activists moving between familiar and public engagements in the city. *Sociology*. **49**(1), pp. 19–37.

Blokker, P. (2011) Pragmatic sociology: Theoretical evolvement and empirical application. *European Journal of Social Theory*. **14**(3), pp. 251–61.

Boltanski, L. and Chiapello, E. (2005[1999]). *The New Spirit of New Capitalism*. London: Verso.

Boltanski, L. and Thévenot, L. (2006[1991]). *On Justification: Economies of Worth*. Princeton, NJ: Princeton University Press.

Broadbent, J., Sonnett, J., Botetzagias, I., Carson, M., Carvalho, A., Chien, Y.-J., Edling, C. et al. (2016) Conflicting climate change frames in a global field of media discourse. *Socius: Sociological Research for a Dynamic World*. **2**, pp. 1–17.

Brueck, J.F. (2017) *Veganism in an Oppressive World: A Vegans-of-Color Community Project*. Sanctuary Publishers.

Brulle, R.J. (2009) The U.S. environmental movement. In: Gould, K. and Lewis, Y.L. (eds) *Twenty Lessons in Environmental Sociology*. New York, NY: Oxford University Press, pp. 211–27.

Canada Action (2019) Largest oil and gas rally in Canadian history. *Canada Action*. Available from: https://www.canadaaction.ca/largest_oil_and_gas_rally.

Cavalieri, P. (2006) Whales as persons. In: Kaiser, M. and Lien, M. (eds) *Ethics and the Politics of Food*. Wageningen: Wageningen Academic Publishers, pp. 28–36.

Cavalieri, P. and Singer, P. (eds) (1993) *The Great Ape Project: Equality Beyond Humanity*. London: Fourth Estate.

City of Vancouver (2017) Greenest city: 2020 Action Plan. 2016–2017 implementation update. *City of Vancouver*. Available from: http://vancouver.ca/files/cov/greenest-city-action-plan-implementation-update-2017.pdf.

Cole, L.W. and Foster, S.R. (2001) *From the Ground Up: Environmental Racism and the Rise of the Environmental Justice Movement*. New York, NY: New York University Press.

Collis, S. (2015) After Burnaby Mountain: Does this change everything? *Contours: After Burnaby Mountain*. **6**, pp. 24–33.

Conley, J. and Jensen, O.B. (2016) 'Parks not parkways': Contesting automobility in a small Canadian city. *Canadian Journal of Sociology: Special Issue: Canadian Mobilities/Contentious Mobilities*. **41**(3), pp. 399–424.

Crawford, A. (2018) Why we should rethink how we talk about 'alien' species. *Smithsonian Magazine*. Available from: https://www.smithsonianmag.com/science-nature/why-scientists-are-starting-rethink-how-they-talk-about-alien-species-180967761/.

De Waal, F. (2016) *Are We Smart Enough to Know How Smart Animals Are?* New York, NY: W.W. Norton.

Donaldson, S. and Kymlicka, W. (2013) *Zoopolis: A Political Theory of Animal Rights*. Oxford: Oxford University Press.

Donaldson, S. and Kymlicka, W. (2016) Make it so: Envisioning a zoopolitical revolution. In P. Cavalieri (ed.) *Philosophy and the Politics of Animal Liberation*. London: Palgrave, pp. 71–116.

Dryzek, J.S. (2013) *The Politics of the Earth: Environmental Discourses*. Oxford: Oxford University Press.

Flyvbjerg, B. (2006) Five misunderstandings about case-study research. *Qualitative Inquiry*. 12(2), pp. 219–45.

Gale, R.P. (1972) From sit-in to hike-in: A comparison of the civil rights and environment movements. In: Burch, W., Cheek, N. and Taylor, L. (eds) *Social Behavior, Natural Resources and the Environment*. New York, NY: Harper and Row, pp. 280–305.

Glasser, C.L. (2011) Tied oppressions: How sexist imagery reinforces speciesist sentiment. *Brock Review*. 12(1), pp. 51–68.

Government of Canada (2019) Greenhouse gas emissions. *Government of Canada*. Available from: https://www.canada.ca/en/environment-climate-change/services/environmental-indicators/greenhouse-gas-emissions.html.

Heidenreich, P. (2018) Thousands of Calgary protesters loudly demand B.C. stop blocking Trans Mountain pipeline project. *Global News*. Available from: https://globalnews.ca/news/4136541/trans-mountain-pipeline-protest-calgary/.

Holden, M. (2017) *Pragmatic Justifications for the Sustainable City: Acting in the Common Place*. London: Routledge.

Holden, M. and Scerri, A. (2015) Justification, compromise and test: Developing a pragmatic sociology of critique to understand the outcomes of urban redevelopment. *Planning Theory*. 14(4), pp. 360–83.

Ibbitson, J. (2018) City growth dominated by car-driving suburbs, whose votes decide elections. *The Globe and Mail*. Available from: https://www.theglobeandmail.com/canada/article-city-growth-dominated-by-car-driving-suburbs-whose-votes-decide/.

IPBES (2019) *Summary for Policymakers of the Global Assessment Report on Biodiversity and Ecosystem Services of the Intergovernmental Science-Policy Platform on Biodiversity and Ecosystem Services*. Bonn, Germany: IPBES secretariat. Available from: https://www.ipbes.net/news/ipbes-global-assessment-summary-policymakers-pdf.

Jay, D. (2013) Where's the democracy in the environmental movement? *Canadian Dimension*. Available from: https://canadiandimension.com/articles/view/wheres-the-democracy-in-the-environmental-movement.

Johnson, L. and Baluja, T. (2015) Transit referendum: Voters say no to new Metro Vancouver tax, transit improvements. *CBC News*. Available from: https://www.cbc.ca/news/canada/british-columbia/transit-referendum-voters-say-no-to-new-metro-vancouver-tax-transit-improvements-1.3134857.

Joy, M. (2016) 4 ways mainstream animal rights movements are oppressive. *Everyday Feminism Magazine*. Available from: https://everydayfeminism.com/2016/03/animal-rights-oppressive/.

Kiger, P.J. (2014) How Vancouver invented itself. *Urban Land Magazine*. Available from: https://urbanland.uli.org/development-business/how-vancouver-invented-itself/.

Lamont, D. (2016) Canadian Taxpayers Federation has 5 members – why should we care what they think? *CBC News*. Available from: https://www.cbc.ca/news/canada/manitoba/canadian-taxpayer-federation-opinion-lamont-1.3802441.

Lamont, M. and Thévenot, L. (eds) (2000) *Rethinking Comparative Cultural Sociology: Repertoires of Evaluation in France and the United States*. Cambridge: Cambridge University Press.

Latour, B. (1998) To modernize or to ecologize? That's the question. In: Castree, N. and Willems-Braun, B. (eds) *Remaking Reality: Nature at the Millennium*. London: Routledge.

Lazarus, R.J. (2008) Super wicked problems and climate change: Restraining the present to liberate the future. *Cornell Law Review*. 94, 1153–234.

Lean, G. (1996) Greenpeace 'fatcat' leaders condemned by founders. *The Independent*. Available from: https://www.independent.co.uk/news/greenpeace-fatcat-leaders-condemned-by-founders-1350418.html.

Loreto, N. (2019) With United We Roll rally, Canada's right revs up its engines. *Washington Post*. Available from: https://www.washingtonpost.com/opinions/2019/02/21/with-united-we-roll-rally-canadas-right-revs-up-its-engines/?noredirect=on&utm_term=.db96c9ec2598.

Mark, J. (2013) Naomi Klein. *Earth Island Journal*. Available from: http://www.earthisland.org/journal/index.php/magazine/entry/naomi_klein/.

Mastnak, T., Elyachar, J. and Boellstorff, T. (2014) Botanical decolonization: Rethinking native plants. *Environment and Planning D: Society and Space*. **32**(2), pp. 363–80.

McGraw, D. (2019) Ohio city votes to give Lake Erie personhood status over algae blooms. *The Guardian*. Available from: https://www.theguardian.com/us-news/2019/feb/28/toledo-lake-erie-personhood-status-bill-of-rights-algae-bloom.

McGregor, D. (2014) Traditional knowledge and water governance: The ethic of responsibility. *AlterNative: An International Journal of Indigenous Peoples*. **10**(5), pp. 493–507.

Nikiforuk, A. (2018) National Energy Board pushed to correct errors in original 2016 Trans Mountain Report. *The Tyee*. Available from: https://thetyee.ca/News/2018/09/14/National-Energy-Board-Correct-Errors-In-Trans-Mountain-Report/.

Proctor, J. (2018) Bike lane barometer: Judging Vancouver Mayor Gregor Robertson's legacy: After 10 years in office, mayor's many accomplishments likely eclipsed by expansion of bike routes. *CBC News*. Available from: https://www.cbc.ca/news/canada/british-columbia/gregor-robertson-bike-lanes-mayor-vancouver-1.4481920.

Putnam, R. (2000) *Bowling Alone*. New York, NY: Simon and Schuster.

Roman, K. (2019) Climate change threatens 'both the economy and the financial system,' says Bank of Canada. *CBC News*. Available from: https://www.cbc.ca/news/politics/climate-change-bank-of-canada-financial-system-review-1.5137625.

Roth, S. (2018) Introduction: Contemporary counter-movements in the age of Brexit and Trump. *Sociological Research Online*. **23**(2), pp. 496–506.

Scott, N. (2020) *Assembling Moral Mobilities: Cycling, Cities, and the Common Good*. Lincoln: University of Nebraska Press.

Sebo, J. (2018) Should chimpanzees be considered 'persons'? *New York Times*. Available from: https://www.nytimes.com/2018/04/07/opinion/sunday/chimps-legal-personhood.html.

Simberloff, D. (2013) *Invasive Species: What Everyone Needs to Know*. Oxford: Oxford University Press.

Stewart, M. (2017) Is Vancouver ready for the High Line effect? *Vancouver Magazine*. Available from: https://www.vanmag.com/vancouver-high-line-effect.

Taylor, D.E. (2014a) *Toxic Communities: Environmental Racism, Industrial Pollution, and Residential Mobility*. New York, NY: NYU Press.

Taylor, D.E. (2014b) The state of diversity in environmental organizations. Available from: https://orgs.law.harvard.edu/els/files/2014/02 FullReport_Green2.0_ FINALReducedSize.pdf.

Thévenot, L. (2002) Which road to follow? The moral complexity of an 'equipped' humanity. In Law, J. and Mol, A. (eds) *Complexities: Social Studies of Knowledge Practices*. Durham, NC: Duke University Press, pp. 53–87.

Tranter, B. and Booth, K. (2015) Scepticism in a changing climate: A cross-national study. *Global Environmental Change*. **33**, pp. 154–64.

United Nations (2018) World urbanization prospects: The 2018 revision. The Population Division of the Department of Economic and Social Affairs. *United Nations*. Available from: https://esa.un.org/unpd/wup/.

United Nations Human Settlements Programme (2009) *Planning sustainable cities: Global report on human settlements 2009*. London: Earthscan.

Walks, A. (2007) The boundaries of suburban discontent? Urban definitions and neighbourhood political effects. *The Canadian Geographer*. **51**(2), pp. 160–85.

Walks, A. (2009) The urban in fragile, uncertain, neoliberal times: Towards new geographies of social justice? *The Canadian Geographer*. **53**(3), pp. 345–56.

Weber, B. (2019) Environmental groups shrug off Jason Kenney's 'war room' threat. *CBC News*. Available from: https://www.cbc.ca/news/canada/edmonton/environmental-groups-alberta-energy-jason-kenney-1.5142290.

Wright, A. (2019) United We Roll wasn't just about oil and gas. Scheer knew that and worked the crowd anyway. *CBC News*. Available from: https://www.cbc.ca/news/opinion/united-we-roll-1.5030419.

PART III

ANTI-ENVIRONMENTALISM DISCOURSE AND FRAMING

4. 'Total preservation is just as bad as total logging': forests and environmental attitudes and behaviours in an anti-environmentalist countermovement

David Tindall, Mark C.J. Stoddart and Valerie Berseth

INTRODUCTION

From the 1950s through to the 1970s, Port Alberni earned the distinction of having one of the highest per capita incomes of all towns in Canada. And its wealth was directly related to forestry. MacMillan Bloedel was its central employer, with a pulp mill, newsprint mills and sawmills. Logs came from all over Vancouver Island, from private forest lands [MacMillan Bloedel acquired early railway grant lands on the Island] and Crown lands. In the early 1980s, the town hit hard times. Newspaper headlines read 'Hundreds of forest jobs lost forever' and 'Hard times never worse.' There was a brief rally after that, but things did get worse in the 1990s. This time no one expects a reversion to the good times for forestry. (Marchak et al., 1999, p. 124)

If we don't have forestry in the forestry communities, what are the options? If we don't have a land base to have forestry, or the land base for any particular use other than parks and wilderness, how can we afford the parks and wilderness when we can't afford the social costs, housing, food, education, medical? (Port Alberni interview participant.)

This chapter uses a case of 'classic' anti-environmentalism to explore the polarization that exists between movements and countermovements, and their relation to the general public.[1] By classic anti-environmentalism, we are referring to social movements that mobilize in opposition to, or attempt to disrupt and undermine, an environmental movement (see Chapter 1 in this volume). Movements and countermovements are often assumed to be diametrically opposed in their values, attitudes, and behaviours. By looking at countermovements in relation to movements and the general public, we see a more complex picture of not only diverging but also, surprisingly, converging beliefs and attitudes around natural resource use and environmental protection. This chapter centres on a peak period of forestry conflicts in British Columbia (BC), Canada. This is also a period where similar conflicts over the protection of old growth forests and industrial forestry practices were unfolding across the west coast of North America, often drawing environmentalists into conflict with the Wise Use Movement (see Chapter 1 in this volume). While conflicts over forestry practices and protection have subsided somewhat in recent years, many of the dynamics that underlay movement–countermovement interactions regarding forestry are being repeated in conflicts over other natural resources, most notably oil and gas development, and coal mining.

Since the emergence of BC as a distinct political entity, forestry has been central to the provincial economy. As Hoberg writes, 'Forests are an essential part of the heritage and identity of British Columbians, and forest policy has long been central to BC politics' (Hoberg, 1996, p. 272). In the 1960s, environmentalism gained momentum as a potent political force in BC and provincial forests became a central object of political conflict (Wilson, 1998). In addition to increased participation in outdoor recreation, higher levels of education and economic security translated into demands for improved forestry practices and wilderness protection. The salience of wilderness for BC environmentalism peaked during the Clayoquot Sound protests of the early 1990s. Opposition to old-growth logging in this region of Vancouver Island resulted in the largest mass-arrests in BC history (Gibbons, 1994; Hatch, 1994; Tindall and Robinson, 2017). Drawing on Beck (1992), we may conceive of environmentalism as a particularly meaningful realm of 'sub-politics' in BC, wherein traditionally non-political social spheres are increasingly opened to democratization and political action. Environmental social movements have become an avenue for concerned citizens to engage in political action beyond the formal structures of party politics and electoral democracy.

Building on the literature on environmental countermovements, this chapter draws on quantitative and qualitative data to examine beliefs about forestry, environmental attitudes, definitions of 'sustainability' and preferences for post-materialist values (and related phenomena) among members of an anti-environmental movement in Port Alberni, BC. While our analysis begins with the beliefs and attitudes of countermovement members, we also compare anti-environmentalists with their environmentalist counterparts in both rural and urban areas. We further compare countermovement and environmental movement participants with members of the general public in Port Alberni (where the countermovement group was based) and Greater Victoria, the provincial capital and the largest urban centre on Vancouver Island. Our analysis focuses on two main topics of concern. First, we examine beliefs about job loss and the forest industry. Next, we examine participants' attitudes toward environmental protection, support for post-materialist values, participation in environmentally friendly behaviours and identification with environmentalism. The insights gained here about the complexity of countermovement participants are helpful for guiding further research on contemporary countermovements and environmental conflicts.

Countermovements and Anti-Environmentalism in Forestry-Related Conflicts

The environmental movement in BC has received significant academic attention for its prolific history of conflict with logging interests and record-setting pro-environmental demonstrations (Wilson, 1998; Hoberg, 1996; Magnusson and Shaw, 2002; Tindall et al., 2015; Tindall and Robinson, 2017). Comparatively less attention has been paid to environmental countermovements, though they were also significant players in BC's forestry politics (Doyle et al., 1997; Tindall et al., 2021). Where environmental countermovements have been explored in BC and elsewhere, they have been depicted as a corporate strategy used to prevent environmentalist alliances with forestry workers that might link environmental and social justice concerns (Austin, 2002; Doyle et al., 1997; Foster, 1993; Simon, 1998). However, research with forestry workers in Canada and the United States complicates this picture of forestry workers, including those actively involved in countermovements, as dupes to a corporate dominant ideology (Dunk, 1994; Reed, 2003; Satterfield, 2002). Moreover, as Scott (Chapter 3 in this volume) outlines, countermovements from the left and right of the political spectrum draw on a variety of anti-environmental moral positions to counteract environmental movements. There is a need to interrogate the views that underpin countermovement arguments and behaviours and their relation to environmentalist stances.[2]

Scholarship on environmental values, beliefs, attitudes and norms provides nuance to the study of environmental countermovements. Stern et al. (1999)'s value-belief-norm (VBN) theory suggests that people are more likely to support and engage in actions on behalf of environmental movements if they feel their values align with a movement's stated principles, if they perceive a tangible threat to something they value, and if they expect that their actions will contribute to protecting the environment. Stern et al. (1999)'s theory has been fruitfully used to explain support for the environmental movement and we can expect that similar dynamics underpin countermovements as well. There has been growing interest in understanding how countermovements relate to movements and what we know about social change. Although it may be expected that members of an environmental countermovement hold anti-environmental views, VBN research has shown that environmentalism is not unidimensional or neatly divided into different camps (de Groot and Steg, 2007; Huddart-Kennedy et al., 2009). In this chapter, we focus on beliefs and attitudes related to the forestry industry and environmentalism (and related phenomena) to better understand how Share members are differentiated from their environmental counterparts and the general public. Our analysis sheds light on whether environmental countermovements are defined by anti-environmental beliefs and attitudes, and whether this translates into anti-environmental behaviours.

Port Alberni and the Share Movement

Figure 4.1 provides a map of Vancouver Island, and identifies the location of Port Alberni, Victoria, and several of the other towns and geographical locations mentioned in this chapter.[3] Port Alberni is a forestry-based community on central Vancouver Island. Its population has remained largely the same today as it was during the peak of the anti-logging protests. In 1996 its population was 18,468. Port Alberni's residents are also older on average than the rest of the province, with 61 per cent of the population below 64, compared to 67 per cent for the province. Port Alberni is a community with a strong historical connection to forestry, which made it prosperous (Marchak et al., 1999). However, with a downturn in the forest industry and accompanying loss of forestry sector jobs, Port Alberni is a community that has struggled (Barnes et al., 1999).[4] In 1996 the average income for individuals in Port Alberni (CAD 24,387) was just slightly less than for the province overall (CAD 26,295). This gap has continued to widen since the time of our interviews, with Port Alberni's average income at CAD 36,259 in 2015 compared with the provincial average of CAD 45,616. Not only had Port Alberni been hit by problems and restructuring in the forest industry (low prices for wood products, a reduced timber supply, etc.), but it was near the centre of the maelstrom of controversy over the logging of old growth forests in Clayoquot Sound.[5]

The southern tip of Clayoquot Sound is about a 90-minute drive from Port Alberni. It is a visually spectacular area of fjords and mountains covered by ancient rainforest. A 1993 provincial government decision designated more than two-thirds of the area for logging. During the summer of 1993, the conflict over Clayoquot Sound became an issue of international importance. The area was visited by celebrities, tourists, forestry workers and citizens from across the province, the country, and from around the world. Over the course of the summer more than 850 citizens were arrested for engaging in civil disobedience – primarily for blockading logging roads. The scale of protest for this type of demonstration is unprecedented in Canadian history.[6]

Figure 4.1   Map of Vancouver Island, showing the location of Port Alberni and Clayoquot Sound

In response to this and related protests, the provincial government undertook several forestry and land-use initiatives in the 1990s including the establishment of a Commission on Resources and Environment, the creation of several new provincial parks on Vancouver Island, the establishment of rigorous new legislation regarding forest practices and the implementation of recommendations from the Clayoquot Sound Scientific panel (Tindall et al., 2015).

This series of events strongly affected the residents of Port Alberni.[7] In reaction to the creation of new parks and new forest policy that was perceived to favour environmentalists over forestry communities, a voluntary, pro-forestry organization was formed: Share Our Resources of Port Alberni. This is one of several Share Groups that formed in the province to mobilize for the interests of resource-based communities under the umbrella of Share BC. Formed in 1990, Share BC emerged as a 'coalition of community-based groups'.[8] During the early 1990s total membership in Share groups swelled to 20,000 members.[9]

According to an early Share document, Share groups aimed to 'support and promote the ideal of sustainable development based on the premise that healthy communities require a solid economic base which supports a good quality of life and that the integrity of the environment must be maintained in realizing this goal.' To this end, Share supported the concept of 'shared decision making' and believed that the costs of achieving sustainable development should be 'shared equitably'. Share emerged because its founders felt that conservation and development issues had been characterized by disputes involving government, industry and environmental organizations, while resource-dependent rural communities did not have the opportunity to

Table 4.1   Data sources

1.	Share Members Survey. Self-administered questionnaire in 1999–2000. Random sample (N = 129).
2.	Telephone interview survey with a random sample of the Port Alberni general public in 1998–1999 (N =100).
3.	Semi-structured qualitative interviews were conducted in person with a quota sample of Port Alberni residents in 1997, including members of Share. (N = 13, this is a subset of a larger interview study on Vancouver Island.)
4.	Phone interview survey with a random sample of the general public in Greater Victoria in 1999–2000 (N = 150).
5.	Interview survey with members of Victoria Wilderness preservation movement organizations in 1998, second wave of a panel survey originally based on a random sample (N = 61).
6.	A self-administered survey of members of the Friends of Clayoquot Sound, a rural-centred environmental group based in Tofino that focuses specifically on forestry issues on the west coast of Vancouver Island in 2005 (N = 211).

meaningfully engage in these disputes. In response, the Share concept emerged to ensure that rural, forestry-based community members had a voice in decision making that affected them.

During the blockades in 1993, many Port Alberni forest workers and other residents had face-to-face interactions with the protesters at Clayoquot Sound (Tindall et al., 2021). Further, many Port Alberni forestry workers were laid off because of reduced cutting in Clayoquot Sound. Not surprisingly, relations between environmentalists and other community members in Port Alberni and the surrounding communities of Ucluelet and Tofino became tense.

METHODOLOGY

The details for the data sources for this analysis are summarized in Table 4.1. We will also provide a brief description below. Over several decades, the lead author has conducted a research programme examining various aspects of environmentalism and anti-environmentalism in BC, including investigations of social networks, values, identities, gender, inter-group relations, micromobilization, activism, media coverage, and framing. Some works associated with the research programme include: Tindall and Begoray (1993), Doyle et al. (1997), Tindall (2002), Tindall et al. (2003), Tindall (2004), Cormier and Tindall (2005), Robinson et al. (2007), Robinson and Tindall (2008), Stoddart and Tindall (2011), Tindall et al. (2012), Malinick et al. (2013), Pechlaner and Tindall (2013), Tindall et al. (2015), Tindall and Robinson (2017), and Tindall et al. (2021). The data reported on in this chapter were collected as part of this research programme.

This chapter is based on several sources of data, as noted in Table 4.1. A self-administered questionnaire was distributed to a random sample of members of Share Our Resources in Port Alberni (N = 129) in 1998. We also conducted a telephone interview survey with a random sample of the Port Alberni general public (N = 100) in 1999. The analysis presented here is based primarily on responses to belief and attitude items from these first two sources. (More details are given in Tindall et al., 2021.) The third source is a set of semi-structured qualitative interviews that were conducted in person with a quota sample of Port Alberni residents (N = 13), including members of Share in 1997. This source is drawn upon primarily to provide qualitative context for the results.

The data used for comparison between Port Alberni residents, Vancouver Island environmentalists and the general public is drawn from three additional sources. Interviews were conducted with a random sample of the general public in Greater Victoria (N = 150) in 1999–2000. We also draw on data collected as part of a longitudinal study of environmental movement participation. In 1998, telephone interviews that included both closed-ended and open-ended questions were conducted with members of Victoria-based environmental organizations.[10] Finally, a self-administered survey was used to collect data from members of the Friends of Clayoquot Sound, a rural-centred environmental group based out of Tofino that focuses specifically on forestry issues on the west coast of Vancouver Island (N = 211).[11]

RESULTS

Beliefs about Job Loss in the BC Forest Industry

While it prospered in earlier decades, by the time of our study in the late-1990s, Port Alberni was a community that had been substantially affected by downturns in the forest resources economy (Marchak et al., 1999; Barnes et al.,1999). We asked interview respondents if they had any concerns about the state of forest communities. Their responses indicated a great deal of concern about the sustainability of these communities, with a particular focus on the consequences of lost forestry jobs.

> Total preservation is just as bad as total logging. And they [sic] was never a happy medium and when you take an economy that's so fragile like British Columbia. I mean, what have they got in here? Two, three million people, in this province, totally dependent on resource management and we destroy one industry, which is the mining, and we almost destroy the other, which is logging. And then you expect to generate enough revenue to run the province? (Fred, interview respondent.)

> [I have] real concern. We've lost a tremendous amount of jobs right here in Port Alberni and that applies all over Vancouver Island right from Port Hardy down to and not necessarily including Victoria but it has implications on Victoria of course. (John, interview respondent.)

In our surveys, we asked several questions about the causes of job loss in the forest industry. Research participants were asked to gauge the relative importance of overcutting, technological change and environmental protection as factors in forestry job loss. Critics have pointed to unsustainable timber harvest rates in BC (Marchak et al., 1999). Technological developments and increased mechanization led to reduced employment and overcapacity of mills (Marchak et al., 1999). Declining prices and trade agreements also negatively affected the industry. During our interviews with Port Alberni residents, some respondents acknowledged these trends. However, many countermovement interviewees suggested that the main cause of job loss in the forestry sector was environmental groups[12] and their successful lobby to have new parks and protected areas created, and new forestry policies and legislation established. Our survey participants echo the themes from our open-ended interviews (see Table 4.2). Here, blame for job loss is assigned to environmental protection measures that are defined as 'unnecessary' (52.3 per cent agree or strongly agree), the actions of environmental groups (41.1 per cent agree or strongly agree) and mechanization and market conditions (42.2 per cent agree or strongly agree).

Regarding environmental protection and the actions of environmental groups, one interview respondent commented:

> the goal posts keep changing. When I first started here, it was the Carmanah Valley and Western Canada Wilderness said we only want to save part of the Valley, well look what happened to us. It's

Table 4.2 Beliefs about the causes of job loss in the forest industry (% who completely agree or mostly agree)

	SHARE Anti-environmental countermovement	Rural General Public (Port Alberni)	Urban General Public (Victoria)	Urban Environmental Movement (Victoria)	Rural Environmental Movement (Tofino)
1. Most jobs in the forest industry have been lost because of a reduced timber supply due to overcutting.	5.5	21.0	39.6	31.7	48.7
2. Most jobs that have been lost in the forest industry are due to things like mechanization and market conditions (e.g., supply and price of wood fibre).	42.2	62.5	67.1	83.1	74.5
3. Most jobs that have been lost in the forest industry are due to *unnecessary* environmental protection (e.g., the creation of parks, the Forest Practices Code, etc.).	52.3	25.5	12.3	2.0	1.9
4. Most jobs that have been lost in the forest industry are due to *necessary* environmental protection (e.g., the creation of parks, the Forest Practices Code, etc.).	12.5	18.6	29.2	13.6	14.4
5. Most job losses in the forest industry are due to the actions of environmental groups.	41.1	35.0	8.2	1.6	1.0
	Sample N = 129*	Sample N = 100*	Sample N = 150*	Sample N = 61*	Sample N = 211*

Note: * N for individual items may be lower than Sample N due to item non-response.

not the Carmanah, it's not the Walbran, it's not the Clayoquot, it's not the Memphis, it's forever and ever and ever and I just see it as a make work program for preservationists. If they don't have an issue, they don't have a job. And if they don't have an issue they're not going to get donations so all they're doing, as far as I'm concerned, they're not coming up with any solutions, they're not protecting animals, they're not protecting fish. I don't see them out there doing any of those good things, all they're doing is making problems. If they were out there doing a lot of the good things – I mean we did need to wake up, we were doing things that maybe we could improve on which in some areas weren't done very well and maybe we got the wake-up call from these groups but now the pendulum is swinging too far over. I get quite emotional about it. (Mike, interview respondent.)

A variety of written responses on the Share Questionnaires also reinforced the blame attributed to environmentalists and the resentment of their perceived influence on the lives of Port Alberni residents:

Conservation has become a priority at the expense of families, communities and the economy. (Nancy, survey respondent.)

... because of environmental groups ... within 10 years (or sooner) there will be no more forest industry. (Ted, survey respondent.)

as with many of the people who work in the industry and live in the rural communities, our concern has always been that decisions are dictated wholly from Victoria and by the efforts of world organizations – i.e. Greenpeace, Sierra Club – without our involvement. (Susan, survey respondent.)

the forest industry thrived prior to the 'new religion.' By that I mean the worship of trees. Tree worship has practically brought the forest industry to its knees. Before the people that worship trees convinced government to change the 'old order'... forest workers were among the highest paid in the world ... (Joyce, survey respondent.)

When we compare the Share (countermovement) members with environmental group members and the general public, a few interesting points stand out (see Table 4.2). First, only a minority of Share survey respondents agree that mechanization and market conditions are a major cause of forestry job loss (42.2 per cent). This contrasts with the other groups surveyed, where a majority of each group agreed with the statement: 83.1 per cent of urban environmental group members, 74.5 per cent of rural environmental group members, 67.1 per cent of the Victoria general public and 62.5 per cent of the general public in Port Alberni. Nevertheless, while constituting a minority, a sizeable number of Share respondents agreed with this statement, and thus this seems like a relevant and fairly widespread framework for interpreting changes to the forest economy in BC. In making sense of the restructuring of the forest industry, mechanization and market conditions is the only interpretive framework that is (somewhat) shared by both the environmental movement and by members of the countermovement.[13]

Second, the attribution of blame for job loss as being due to environmentalists and unnecessary environmental legislation is not shared by environmental movement group members. Only 1.6 per cent of urban environmental organization members (see item 5 of Table 4.2) and 1 per cent of members from rural centred environmental organizations are willing to assign blame for job loss to the actions of environmental groups.[14] Similarly, only 2 per cent of urban environmentalists (see item 3 of Table 4.2) and 1.9 per cent of environmentalists from rural centred groups are willing to attribute job loss to unnecessary environmental protection (while a somewhat larger minority does accept that 'necessary' environmental protection has created job loss; see item 4). General public opinion breaks down along clear urban–rural lines. The rural public is closer to the Share standpoint on this issue, while the urban public more closely resembles the attitudes of urban and rural environmentalists.

Finally, a substantial minority (see item 1 of Table 4.2) of environmental movement group members view overcutting as major cause of job loss in the forestry sector (31.7 per cent of urban environmentalists and 48.7 per cent of environmentalists from the rural centred group). For environmental group research participants, overcutting is second in importance only to mechanization and market conditions as an explanation for job loss. However, only a very small proportion of Share members view this as a major factor (5.5 per cent). Here, the perspective of Share members is different from all of the other groups we studied, including the rural general public. Share members' attribution of blame for job loss (item 5 in Table 4.2) as due to environmentalists seems to be matched by an aversion to attributing blame directly to overcutting of forests by their industry (item 1 in Table 4.2).

Definitions of Sustainability in the Forest Industry

During our interviews it became obvious that there was a strong commitment among interviewees to forestry as a lifestyle.[15] Lifestyles involve several different dimensions. The forestry lifestyle involves working outdoors, the sense of accomplishment from hard physical work, the rural setting of forest communities and related ties to the surrounding land base. Other elements of a forestry lifestyle suggested during interviews include the high wages traditionally earned by forestry workers in BC (and in Port Alberni in particular) and a desire for there to be a single breadwinner so that one parent could be at home with children. Our survey respondents also show a high level of commitment to this notion of forestry as a lifestyle (Table 4.3). A large majority of Share members agree that 'working in forestry is a lifestyle as well as a job' (81.9 per cent). As with the intergenerational notion of sustainability, both urban and rural members of the general public also seem to accept the interpretation of Share members (74 per cent of the urban general public and 87 per cent of the rural general public). While there is a gap between these groups and environmentalists, it is noteworthy that a majority of environmental group research participants also accept this idea (53.2 per cent of urban environmentalists and 65.7 per cent of rural environmentalists). Even if environmentalists are less inclined to view sustainable forestry as the perpetuation of the status quo, they share the notion that forestry labour is part of a distinctive lifestyle, not only an occupation. This might be another area of convergence between the environmental movement and the countermovement.

Attitudes and Values

Several researchers have described a distinction between: (1) people who are primarily concerned about economic values, who see the natural environment in anthropocentric terms (e.g., primarily as resources for human use), and who have faith in the ability of humans to control the environment; and (2) people who are primarily concerned about non-economic values, who see environmental issues in non-economic and often non-instrumental terms (e.g., biocentric terms, believing that nature has intrinsic value), and who doubt the ability of humans to control the environment.[16] Table 4.4 provides comparisons across the groups in our study with regard to environmental attitudes.[17] The pattern of responses reported regarding environmental attitudes (see Table 4.4) suggests that members of Share Our Resources mostly

72   *Handbook of anti-environmentalism*

Table 4.3   *Definitions of sustainability in the forest industry (% who completely agree or mostly agree)*

	SHARE Anti-environmental countermovement	Rural General Public (Port Alberni)	Urban General Public (Victoria)	Urban Environmental Movement (Victoria)	Rural Environmental Movement (Tofino)
1. 'Sustainable forestry' means that forestry workers' children can continue to work in the forest industry doing similar jobs as their parents.	57.0	63.3	51.4	34.0	33.3
2. Working in forestry is a lifestyle as well as a job.	81.9	87.0	74.0	53.2	65.7
	Sample N = 129*	Sample N = 100*	Sample N = 150*	Sample N = 61*	Sample N = 211*

Note: * N for individual items may be lower than Sample N due to item non-response.

fall into the first category, while environmental movement group members tend to fall into the second category.[18] The general public appears to be somewhere in between the two categories. Three areas of divergence between Share members and environmental movement members are particularly noteworthy. First, about half of Share members agree that there has been too much emphasis on conserving natural resources (see item 3 of Table 4.4) and not enough on using them (50.4 per cent agree or strongly agree). This contrasts sharply with members of urban environmental groups, only 2 per cent of whom hold this view. Second, a large majority of environmental organization members agree that over-consumption of resources (see item 1 of Table 4.4) is a major cause of environmental problems (83.3 per cent of urban environmentalists and 77.7 per cent of rural environmentalists). By contrast, only about a third of Share members agree with this view (37.2 per cent). Third, the view that natural resources must be preserved for the future (item 9 of Table 4.4), even if people must do without, is held almost unanimously by urban environmentalists (96.1 per cent). However, this view is held by only 20.6 per cent of Share members.

Differences in views are often reflected in the diverse ways in which people socially construct and evaluate the world. For example, during the interviews we asked respondents several questions about what they thought were important characteristics of parks. Several of the Share Our Resources members talked about human recreation as the primary purpose of parks. These respondents claimed not to understand or support wilderness parks because these types of parks were too far away from main highways with limited accessibility, so human use was too low to justify their existence. This is a different view from that of wilderness-oriented outdoor recreationists, who place high value on wilderness parks precisely because of the unique experiences to be obtained in such places, or of environmentalists who stress the conservation value of parks.

We also asked interview respondents about values related to materialism and post-materialism. Inglehart (1995) posits that those who provide greater importance on

Table 4.4   Environmental attitudes (% who completely agree or mostly agree)

	SHARE Anti-environmental countermovement	Rural General Public (Port Alberni)	Urban General Public (Victoria)	Urban Environmental Movement (Victoria)	Rural Environmental Movement (Tofino)
1. Most environmental problems are a result of societal over-consumption of resources (e.g., over-use of paper products, over-packaging, reliance on single occupancy vehicles, etc.).	37.2	n/a	n/a	83.3	77.7
2. We should relax our efforts to control pollution in order to improve the economy.	8.5	12.1	4.0	2.0	n/a
3. There has been too much emphasis on conserving natural resources and not enough on using them.	50.4	n/a	n/a	2.0	n/a
4. Pollution control measures have created an unfair burden on industry.	16.4	17.0	11.4	6.0	n/a
5. Where natural resources are privately owned, society should have no control over them.	29.5	n/a	n/a	4.0	n/a
6. We should maintain our efforts to control pollution even if this slows down the economy and increases unemployment.	24.4	48.0	64.4	n/a	n/a
7. If an industry cannot control its pollution, the industry should be shut down.	53.5	67.7	71.1	88.0	n/a
8. Managers and owners of polluting industries should be punished with fines or imprisoned.	53.5	n/a	n/a	96.0	n/a
9. Natural resources must be preserved for the future, even if people must do without.	20.6	57.0	70.7	96.1	n/a
	Sample N = 129*	Sample N = 100*	Sample N = 150*	Sample N = 61*	Sample N = 211*

Note: * N for individual items may be lower than Sample N due to item non-response.

post-materialism also express higher levels of concern for the environment. While Inglehart's (1995, 1997) post-materialist values index has been critiqued for its relevance to national-level differences in environmental values (Kidd and Lee, 1997; Brechin, 1999; Dunlap and York, 2008), it has been used to examine value differences within nations (Booth, 2017; Tindall and Robinson, 2017; Tindall et al., 2021). We found differences in the priorities given to different post-materialism index items (low numbers indicate high priority, and high numbers correspond to lower priority; see Table 4.5).[19] As expected, members of environmental movements rated post-materialist values as having the highest priority, while Share members gave them

Table 4.5 Comparing post-materialist values between an anti-environmentalism countermovement, a rural resource-based community, an urban community in British Columbia, and an environmental organization (rural centred) (late 1990s)

	SHARE Anti-environmental countermovement	Rural General Public (Port Alberni)	Urban General Public (Victoria)	Rural Environmental Movement (Tofino)	Sig.
PMV Short Index: Mean	3.26	2.60	2.74	2.10	****
PMV Short Index: SD	(1.37)	(1.48)	(1.27)	(1.26)	

Notes: Significance for the F test for One Way ANOVAs. * p. ≤ .05, ** p. ≤ .01, *** p. ≤ .005, **** p. ≤ .001

the lowest priority, and the general public fell in between. It is notable, though, that survey responses across groups leaned toward prioritizing post-materialist values on the whole – common among publics in Western nations in the 1990s.

Interview data pointed to differences in how movement and countermovement members viewed forests – as spaces needing protection from human interference, or as the basis for economic security. Most Share members supported opening provincial and federal parks to logging, with the understanding that parks could provide economic security, sustainable ecological benefits, and recreation. For example:

> I think there's a balance that can be done. I find it difficult that up in the Queen Charlottes, where there's timberline rotting because it's a park. And I think that probably in the world today, when you shorten materials elsewhere, that you could probably use that to benefit the people. At the same time, you need to make sure that you're keeping certain areas which are sort of growing back to themselves. Doing their thing. I think that if care and all regulations are in place, there are certain things that can take place. (Alex, interviewee.)

> I think you can have the best of both worlds, you can have the resources making money for the economy, and on the other hand you can have the park areas for the tourists, for the animals, whatever, because I see it in our forest lands, I mean, I'm in areas that have been locked since the 1920s, I've been in areas that have had forest fires, prescribed fires, natural fires, all different things and I still see the same type of plants, I see the same animals come back to them. (Lisa, interviewee.)

While an analysis of environmental attitudes and values seems to highlight dramatic differences in worldviews between the environmental movement and the Share countermovement, our survey results also reveal a possible area of convergence. In terms of environmental attitudes (reported in Table 4.4) about half of Share members agree that if an industry cannot control its pollution, the industry should be shut down (see item 7 of Table 4.4; 53.5 per cent mostly agree or completely agree). The same proportion agree that managers and owners of polluting industries should be punished with fines or imprisoned (see item 8 of Table 4.4; 53.5 per cent mostly agree or completely agree). While these opinions are not as widely held among Share members as among environmentalists, the differences between the groups are much less substantial here than elsewhere. On questions of industrial pollution and corporate responsibility for environmental harm, there may be more similarity than difference between environmental movement and countermovement members.

Environmentally Friendly Behaviours

The beliefs, attitudes and values of members of Share Our Resources generally tend to diverge sharply from those of environmental movement members. While there are occasional issues on which there is noticeably less divergence, the overall picture that emerges is of social groups who adhere to differing worldviews. Given the oppositional relationship between the environmental movement and the Share countermovement, this difference does not come as a surprise. However, when we turn to look at environmentally friendly behaviours (Tindall et al., 2003), this picture becomes more complicated. Environmentally friendly behaviours (EFBs) refer to activities that people can do in everyday life to help protect the environment. These activities include things like car pooling, recycling, conserving energy, using environmentally friendly cleaning products, and buying organic food. By contrast with writing letters to government, or attending protest rallies, EFBs are much less explicitly linked to the activism of groups that are perceived as outsiders and anti-forestry. EFBs can be done by individuals without the mediation of environmental movement groups and so represent a more diffuse form of environmentalism that can be practised by individuals working inside the forestry sector (also see Skoglund and Böhm, 2020).

We asked Share members and environmental movement members about whether they've engaged in 17 distinct types of EFBs (see Table 4.6). Surprisingly, on this measure of pro-environmental behaviour, there are more similarities than differences between environmentalists and countermovement members. On an EFB index created by summing the number of the 17 behaviours in Table 4.6, Share members scored 11.56, which is not substantially less than the EFB index score for either rural environmentalists (13.27), or urban environmentalists (14.63). In particular, a large proportion of Share members recycle at home (92.2 per cent), pick up litter (92.2 per cent), conserve energy (91.4 per cent), use a reusable mug instead of paper or Styrofoam (85.2 per cent) and compost (80.5 per cent). Where we do see more divergence between Share members and environmentalists is on whether participants regularly walk, bicycle or take public transport instead of driving. While a majority of environmentalists do this (82.8 per cent of urban environmental group members and 66.3 per cent of rural environmental group members), only about a third of Share members do this (34.4 per cent). This discrepancy probably, in part, reflects the rural settings in which those with connections to forestry are often located, where public transit and cycling are often not viable modes of transportation.

Countermovement Members and Environmental Identification

In this section we look at identification with environmentalism on two different measures. First, Share members, environmental group members and members of the general public were asked how strongly they identify as an environmentalist. Second, all research participants were asked how strongly they identify as a member of the environmental movement. There are notable differences in responses between these two different aspects of environmentalist identity across all samples (see Table 4.7). It is not surprising that most environmental movement affiliated participants strongly identify themselves as environmentalists (90.2 per cent of urban environmentalists and 89.4 per cent of rural environmentalists). What is surprising is that nearly half of Share members identify themselves as environmentalists (44.5 per cent),

Table 4.6 Environmentally friendly behaviours (% who engage in EFBs)

	SHARE Anti-environmental countermovement	Urban Environmental Movement (Victoria)	Rural Environmental Movement (Tofino)
1. Recycling at home.	92.2	98.3	98.6
2. Recycling at work.	74.0	100.0	76.0
3. Regularly walking, bicycling or taking public transport instead of driving a single occupancy car.	34.4	82.8	66.3
4. Car pooling on a regular basis (e.g. to work, school, etc.).	22.0	33.3	19.7
5. Reusing and/or refusing unnecessary packaging and plastic bags.	79.7	95.1	93.8
6. Conserving energy (e.g. turning off unused lights).	91.4	98.4	97.1
7. Buying organic or local produce.	72.4	98.4	96.6
8. Growing your own vegetables and/or fruit.	64.8	86.9	74.5
9. Using environmentally friendly household cleaning products.	68.0	93.3	89.9
10. Regularly re-using and mending things instead of discarding them.	72.7	96.7	91.8
11. Planting trees.	68.0	85.2	67.8
12. Picking up litter.	92.2	93.4	92.8
13. Using a re-usable mug instead of paper or Styrofoam cups for beverages.	85.2	91.8	88.5
14. Helping to maintain parks or natural habitats.	46.9	70.0	54.8
15. Composting.	80.5	96.7	89.4
16. Conserve water in the home or yard.	75.8	85.2	91.3
17. Participating in the clean-up of streams, lakes and watersheds.	39.8	32.8	36.2
Mean score on EFB index	11.56	14.63	13.27
	Sample N = 129*	Sample N = 61*	Sample N = 211*

Note: * N for individual items may be lower than Sample N due to item non-response.

a greater proportion than members of the general public in either Victoria (36 per cent) or Port Alberni (25.5 per cent).

However, while a substantial proportion of Share members identify as environmentalists, very few identify as members of the environmental movement (6.3 per cent). This contrasts much more sharply with participants in environmental organizations (63.9 per cent of urban environmental group members and 78.2 per cent of rural environmental group members identify as members of the movement). This finding is not surprising, as membership in a Share implies opposition to the environmental movement it is mobilized against.

Regarding being 'environmentalists', in interviews several members of Share commented that they were the 'real environmentalists' because they lived and worked in nature, and had practical knowledge of forests and nature, unlike environmental movement activists who they depicted as being based in cities and as having abstract rather than practical knowledge (see also Dunk (1994) on this topic). Here it should be noted that Afanasyeva et al. (Chapter 17 in this volume) make similar observations in their chapter, about the views of conservative rural critics of wind power.

Table 4.7 Identification with environmentalism (% who very strongly agree or strongly agree)

	SHARE Anti-environmental countermovement	Rural General Public (Port Alberni)	Urban General Public (Victoria)	Urban Environmental Movement (Victoria)	Rural Environmental Movement (Tofino)
1. I identify myself as an environmentalist.	44.5	25.5	36.0	90.2	89.4
2. I identify myself as a member of the environmental movement.	6.3	5.0	15.4	63.9	78.2
	Sample N = 129*	Sample N = 100*	Sample N = 150*	Sample N = 61*	Sample N = 211*

Note: * N for individual items may be lower than Sample N due to item non-response.

DISCUSSION AND CONCLUSIONS

In this chapter, we have drawn on qualitative and quantitative data from interviews and surveys to explore the views of Share Our Resources members on forestry, sustainability, and other environmental issues.

Comparisons between countermovement members and members of environmental movement groups seem to complicate any simple picture of Share members as only 'anti-environmentalists' who stand in binary opposition to the environmental movement. As such, our findings fit in with other ethnographic and interview research on forestry and extractive industry workers (Dunk, 1994; Reed, 2003; Satterfield, 2002; Ellis, 2013; Lewin, 2019). Of course, there are more differences than similarities between members of these opposing groups in their views of forestry and environmental issues. There is a substantial gap between Share members and environmentalists in how they interpret job loss and the future of forestry communities. In the view of Share members, the main causes of job loss in the forest industry include environmental group actions, environmental legislation, and mechanization and market conditions. Unlike environmentalists, they do not view overcutting as a major contribution to job loss. Thus, countermovement members are inclined to attribute responsibility for job loss to environmentalists, or to abstract economic forces, rather than to mismanagement (such as overcutting) by the forest industry. Share members and environmentalists also adhere to different worldviews where environmental values are concerned. Share members tend to adopt a worldview that sees nature in more utilitarian and economic terms. Similarly, Share members identify more strongly with materialist values than do environmental movement members or the general public. By contrast, environmental movement group members tend to hold a more biocentric and postmaterialist view of nature.

However, there are also some surprising points of convergence between Share members and environmental movement group members. Questions about responsibility for industrial pollution demonstrate as much similarity as difference. Here, a substantial proportion of Share members support more stringent measures for controlling industrial polluters.

The notion of a simple binary opposition between these social movements is further complicated when we look at environmentally friendly behaviour. Share members engage in surprisingly high levels of EFBs. A high proportion of our respondents recycle, have bought organic and local food, and conserve energy. Based on measures of EFBs, Share members look more similar than different compared to environmental group members. Recent work by Skoglund and Böhm (2020) on the mundane, everyday environmentalism of energy company employees can help us interpret this rather surprising finding. As Skoglund and Böhm note, EFBs are appealing as a form of mundane micro-activism because it embodies a pro-solutions orientation and is distanced from the outsider and 'anti' associations of the organized environmental movement. Our results likewise suggest that EFBs are less tied into political conflicts over forestry resources, where Share members come into conflict with 'outsider' and 'anti' environmental groups in their role as countermovement participants. As a result, it may be a more appealing facet of environmentalism for Share members to adopt inside the forest industry context.

The final point of similarity is that while Share members do not identify as members of the environmental movement, a surprisingly large proportion do personally identify as environmentalists. The distinction between identification as an environmentalist and identification with the environmental movement is another particularly interesting finding. We might infer that the willingness of many Share members to identify as environmentalists relates in part to members' high levels of participation in EFBs. Participation in EFBs may be an expression of Share members' own sense of environmentalism, which is separate from the organized environmental movement and the values it embodies. But also, as several respondents noted in interviews, some participants in the Share countermovement see themselves as the 'real environmentalists' because of their geographical proximity to, and practical knowledge of nature.

As our analysis shows, we should not take as axiomatic that countermovement participants (at the individual or community level) are simply a front for corporate interests and ideology, or that there is a simple binary polarization between environmentalism and countermovements. Rather, this should be addressed through empirical research on how attitudinal or value divergence and convergence plays out in particular social contexts and episodes of environmental conflict. The case presented here tells a more nuanced story of important differences between Share members and members of rural and urban environmental movement groups in terms of beliefs, attitudes and values pertaining to the environment in general and forestry in particular. At the same time, there are surprising points of convergence between members of these politically opposed social movement groups, including shared understandings of the cultural significance of forestry, and overlapping interests regarding pollution and environmental protection. While Share members demonstrate a lot of anger and resentment toward environmentalists, the nature of forest community–environmental movement interactions is complex. Even central combatants in the conflict have expressed that there have been positive effects from such interactions on occasion. For example, one member of Share our Resources stated:

> I got involved [in Share Our Resources] because of the outlandish comments and actions of the preservation groups. I also got involved because of the seemingly indifference and lack of action from M&B [the major forestry company in the community at the time]. I became alarmed because if the preservationists weren't checked they could wreak havoc on forest dependent communities … Not all the preservationists' efforts were negative. They have taught many, including me, to tread more softly on the earth. (Sarah, survey respondent.)

Our findings are relevant for studies of countermovements within and beyond forestry conflicts. In particular, our findings point to the need to carefully consider the fault lines between movements and countermovement, and their basis in social, economic and ecological values. The Share Our Resources Port Alberni case also demonstrates the importance of conducting empirical research on both politicized actions (e.g. demonstrations, campaigns, blockades) and everyday actions (e.g. conserving energy, recycling, or picking up litter) to capture the nuances of such conflicts. By identifying areas of similarity in views and shared environmental practices, we can illuminate potential points of convergence between environmental movements and countermovement. These points of value convergence may offer important openings for joint conversations about the environmental, economic and social sustainability of rural or extractive resource dependent communities.

NOTES

1. We would also like to thank the following people, who served as research assistants on this project: Céline Mauboulès, Kamaljit Inman-Bates, Chantelle Marlor, Gabriela Pechlaner, Dan Kruk, Emily MacNair, Andrea Rivers and Noelani Dubeta. We would also like to thank Victor Lam for his helpful comments on an earlier draft of this chapter, as well as the many survey and interview participants who gave up their time to provide us with their views and experiences. This research was supported through several research grants from the Social Sciences and Humanities Research Council of Canada, and several internal grants from the UBC-HSS Fund.
2. Some countermovement groups have been described as 'fronts' for industry, or 'astroturf' organizations (Mix and Waldo, 2015; Walker, 2016). And indeed, some commentators have referred to the Share organizations in BC using these terms. In our view, while aspects of the Share case are somewhat ambiguous, this characterization is not entirely accurate. It is true that the formation of the Share organizations involved guidance and financial resources from the representatives of the corporate world (see Wilson, 1998; Doyle et al., 1997), however, our research provides evidence that there were real flesh and blood people from the affected communities active in these organizations, unlike some of the front organizations described by Oreskes and Conway (2011) in their research on some key groups linked to the tobacco and fossil fuel industries involved in opposing anti-smoking campaigns, and action on climate change. On this issue, it might be fruitful to think of a grassroots–astroturf continuum, with pure grassroots organizations at one end, and pure industry fronts at the other end. Share is somewhere in the middle of this continuum.
3. The map displayed in Figure 4.1 is in the public domain. Information about the map is available at: https://commons.wikimedia.org/wiki/File:Vancouver_clayoquot_sound_de.png.
4. See Barnes et al. (1999) for a discussion of two phases of industrial forestry (Fordist and Post-Fordist) and how these patterns of management and production have been related to jobs and the forestry economy in Port Alberni.
5. For more on the BC environmental movement see Tindall (1994) and Wilson (1998).
6. The preceding statement was true when this chapter was originally written. However, an ongoing protest (that had lasted over a year at the time of publication) near Fairy Creek on Vancouver Island (several hours from Clayoquot Sound by car) resulted in an even larger number of protesters being arrested, by part way through 2021. Some works documenting the Clayoquot Sound protest include: Breen-Needham et al. (1994), Berman et al. (1994), Krawcyk (1996), MacIssac and Champagne (1994), McLaren (1994), Lowther and Sinner (2008), Robinson and Tindall (2008), Moore (2015) and Tindall and Robinson (2017).
7. Text in this section is partly based on material reported in Mauboulès (2001).
8. The 'Share Movement' in BC parallels the 'Wise Use Movement' in the United States. For some work on the latter, see: Helvarg (1994), Echeverria and Eby (1995), Switzer (1997) and Moore (2015).
9. At the time of our survey, Share Our Resources of Port Alberni had a membership of over 1000, a substantial proportion of the total population of Port Alberni. Further, in terms of social network ties, data obtained from our general public survey – but not reported here – show that over one in three members of the general public has social ties to someone who is a member of Share. Thus in

'social capital terms' (Coleman, 1988) this organization has the potential to influence a substantial number of people.
10. Details for this study are given in Tindall (2004).
11. Details of this latter survey are given in Tindall and Robinson (2017).
12. We use the term 'environmental groups' to refer to mainstream environmental organizations like the Sierra Club, the Western Canada Wilderness Committee and Greenpeace. While there is some variation among these groups, they are commonly recognized as environmental groups. However, we should note that the terms 'environmental group' and 'environmentalist' are somewhat problematic. A number of respondents referred to these groups as 'preservationist groups' and contrasted them with groups like Share Our Resources which was described as being a real environmental group. Also in criticizing 'preservationists' many respondents from the forestry sector would refer to themselves as the 'real environmentalists'. Nevertheless, it was clear from our interviews that respondents knew what we meant when we used the term 'environmental groups'.
13. On this theme, see Dunk (1994) and Lewin (2019).
14. We use the term 'rural centred' (or similar wording) to describe the members of Friends of Clayoquot Sound, because the organization was based in a small town in a rural area, but it should be noted that members and supporters of the organization were spread out beyond the local area.
15. In a different context, Dunk (1994) has suggested that culture can serve as a barrier preventing forest workers and environmentalists from becoming allies. In his study of Thunder Bay forest workers the distinction between practical working class culture and abstract university-based middle class culture reinforced pre-existing cleavages between rural forest workers and urban-based environmentalists. The forest workers in Dunk's study, like those in this study, also had a strong commitment to forestry as a lifestyle. It should be noted, however, that unlike the informants in Dunk's ethnography, a substantial proportion of our survey respondents blamed environmentalists for job losses in the forestry sector. Lewin (2019) has made similar observations in the context of studying residents of a coal mining town in Appalachia.
16. These researchers include: Cotgrove (1982) and his distinction between the 'Dominant Paradigm' and the 'Alternative Environmental Paradigm', Catton and Dunlap (1978) and their distinction between the 'Dominant Western World View/Human Exceptionalism Paradigm' and the 'New Environmental Paradigm', and Inglehart (1990) and his distinction between 'Materialist' and 'Post-Materialist' values.
17. A number of the survey questions listed in Table 4.4 were adopted from Van Liere and Dunlap (1981).
18. While we use the term 'values' at the beginning of this paragraph, we would like to note that, while attitudes are a distinct concept, they tend to be associated with values (see Tindall, 2003), and thus it makes sense to talk about these things in association with one another. (In part, attitudes are somewhat more specific manifestations of attitudes.) The items in Table 4.4 are measures of attitudes.
19. We use low scores to indicate more importance, and high scores to indicate less importance because the original scale developed by Inglehart was based on ranking. It might be useful to keep in mind the metaphor of a race among a number of people, where the winner places 1st and other finishers have higher scores (2nd, 3rd, etc.).

REFERENCES

Austin, A. (2002) Advancing accumulation and managing its discontents: The U.S. antienvironmental countermovement. *Sociological Spectrum.* **22**(1), pp. 71–105.

Barnes, T.J., Hayter, R. and Hay, E. (1999) 'Too young to retire, too bloody old to work': Forest industry restructuring and community response in Port Alberni, British Columbia. *The Forestry Chronicle.* **75**(5), pp. 781–7.

Beck, U. (1992) *Risk Society: Towards a New Modernity*. London: Sage Publications.

Berman, T., Ingram, G.B., Gibbons, M., Hatch, R.B., Maingon, L. and Hatch, C. (eds) (1994) *Clayoquot and Dissent*. Vancouver: Ronsdale Press.

Booth, D.E. (2017) Postmaterialism and support for the environment in the United States. *Society & Natural Resources*. **30**(11), pp. 1404–20.

Brechin, S.R. (1999) Objective problems, subjective values, and global environmentalism: Evaluating the postmaterialist argument and challenging a new explanation. *Social Science Quarterly*. **80**(4), pp. 793–809.

Breen-Needham, H., Duncan, S.F., Ferens, D., Reeve, P. and Yates, S. (eds) (1994) *Witness to Wilderness: The Clayoquot Sound Anthology*. Vancouver: Arsenal Pulp Press.

Catton, W.R.J. and Dunlap, R.E. (1978) Paradigms, theories, and the primacy of the HEP–NEP Distinction. *The American Sociologist*. **13**(4), pp. 256–9.

Coleman, J.S. (1988) Social capital in the creation of human capital. *American Journal of Sociology*. **94**, pp. S95–S120.

Cormier, J.J. and Tindall, D.B. (2005) Wood frames: Framing the forests in British Columbia. *Sociological Focus*. **38**(1), pp. 1–24.

Cotgrove, S. (1982) *Catastrophe or Cornucopia: The Environment, Politics, and the Future*. Chichester: Wiley.

De Groot, J.I. and Steg, L. (2007) Value orientations and environmental beliefs in five countries: Validity of an instrument to measure egoistic, altruistic and biospheric value orientations. *Journal of Cross-Cultural Psychology*. **38**(3), pp. 318–32.

Doyle, A., Elliott, B. and Tindall, D. (1997) Framing the forests: Corporations, the B.C. forest alliance and the media. In: Carroll, W.K. (ed.) *Organizing Dissent: Contemporary Social Movements in Theory and Practice*. 2nd edn. Toronto: Garamond Press, pp. 240–68.

Dunk, T. (1994) Talking about trees: Environment and society in forest workers' culture. *Canadian Review of Sociology & Anthropology*. **31**(1), pp. 14–34.

Dunlap, R.E. and York, R. (2008) The globalization of environmental concern and the limits of the postmaterialist values explanation: Evidence from four multinational surveys. *Sociological Quarterly*. **49**(3), pp. 529–63.

Echeverria, J. and Eby, R.B. (1995) *Let the People Judge: Wise Use and the Private Property Rights Movement*. Covelo: Island Press.

Ellis, C. (2013) The symbiotic ideology: Stewardship, husbandry, and dominion in beef production. *Rural Sociology*. **78**(4), pp. 429–49.

Foster, J.B. (1993) The limits of environmentalism without class: Lessons from the ancient forest struggle of the Pacific Northwest. *Capitalism, Nature, Socialism*. **4**(1), pp. 11–41.

Gibbons, M. (1994) The Clayoquot papers. In: Berman, T., Ingram, G.B., Gibbons, M., Hatch, R.B., Maingon, L. and Hatch, C. (eds) *Clayoquot & Dissent*. Vancouver: Ronsdale Press, pp. 73–104.

Hatch, R.B. (1994) The Clayoquot show trials. In: Berman, T., Ingram, G.B., Gibbons, M., Hatch, R.B., Maingon, L. and Hatch, C. (eds) *Clayoquot & Dissent*. Vancouver: Ronsdale Press, pp. 105–54.

Helvarg, D. (1994) *The War on the Greens: The Wise-Use Movement, the New Right and Anti-Environmental Violence*. San Francisco, CA: Sierra Club Books.

Hoberg, G. (1996) The politics of sustainability: Forest policy in British Columbia. In: Carty, R.K. (ed.) *Politics, Policy and Government in British Columbia*. Vancouver: University of British Columbia Press, pp. 272–89.

Huddart-Kennedy, E., Beckley, T.M., McFarlane, B.L. and Nadeau, S. (2009) Rural–urban differences in environmental concern in Canada. *Rural Sociology*. **74**(3), pp. 309–29.

Inglehart, R. (1990) *Culture Shift in Advanced Industrial Society*. Princeton, NJ: Princeton University Press.

Inglehart, R. (1995) Public support for environmental protection: Objective problems and subjective values in 43 societies. *Political Science and Politics*. **28**(1), pp. 57–72.

Inglehart, R. (1997) *Modernization and Postmodernization: Cultural, Economic and Political Change in 43 Societies*. Princeton, NJ: Princeton University Press.

Kidd, Q. and Lee, A.R. (1997) Postmaterialist values and the environment: A critique and reappraisal. *Social Science Quarterly*. **78**(1), pp. 1–15.

Krawcyk, B.S. (1996) *Clayoquot: The Sound of My Heart*. Victoria: Orca Book Publishers.

Lewin, P.G. (2019) 'Coal is not just a job, it's a way of life': The cultural politics of coal production in central Appalachia. *Social Problems*. **66**(1), pp. 51–68.

Lowther, C. and Sinner, A. (eds) (2008) *Writing the West Coast: In Love with Place*. Vancouver: Ronsdale Press.

MacIssac, R. and Champagne, A. (1994) *Clayoquot Mass Trials: Defending the Rainforest*. Gabriola Island: New Society Publishers.

Magnusson, W. and Shaw, K. (eds) (2002) *A Political Space: Reading the Global through Clayoquot Sound*. Minneapolis, MN: University of Minnesota Press.

Malinick, T.E., Tindall, D.B. and Diani, M. (2013) Network centrality and social movement media coverage: A two-mode network analytic approach. *Social Networks*. **35**(2), pp. 149–58.

Marchak, M.P., Aycock, S.L. and Herbert, D.M. (1999) *Falldown: Forest Policy in British Columbia*. Vancouver: David Suzuki Foundation and Ecotrust Canada.

Mauboulès, C.M. (2001) *Forest Workers ... An Endangered Species: Countermovement Mobilization on the West Coast of Vancouver Island*. Unpublished MA Thesis. University of British Columbia.

McLaren, J. (1994) *Spirits Rising: The Story of the Clayoquot Peace Camp*. Gabriola: Pacific Edge Publishing.

Mix, T.L. and Waldo, K.G. (2015) Know(ing) your power: Risk society, astroturf campaigns, and the battle over the Red Rock coal-fired plant. *The Sociological Quarterly*. **56**(1), pp. 125–51.

Moore, N. (2015) *The Changing Nature of Eco/feminism: Telling Stories from Clayoquot Sound*. Vancouver: University of British Columbia Press.

Oreskes, N. and Conway, E.M. (2011) *Merchants of Doubt: How a Handful of Scientists Obscured the Truth on Issues from Tobacco Smoke to Global Warming*. New York: Bloomsbury Publishing.

Pechlaner, G. and Tindall, D.B. (2013) Changing contexts: Environmentalism, aboriginal community and forest company joint ventures, and the formation of Iisaak. In: Tindall, D.B., Trosper, R.L. and Perreault, P. (eds) *Aboriginal Peoples and Forest Lands in Canada*. Vancouver: University of British Columbia Press, pp. 260–78.

Reed, M.G. (2003) *Taking Stands: Gender and the Sustainability of Rural Communities*. Vancouver: University of British Columbia Press.

Robinson, J.L. and Tindall, D.B. (2008) Defending the forest: Chronicles of protest at Clayoquot Sound. In: Lowther, C. and Sinner, A. (eds) *Writing the West Coast: In Love with Place*. Vancouver: Ronsdale Press, pp. 232–47.

Robinson, J.L., Tindall, D.B., Seldat, E. and Pechlaner, G. (2007) Support for First Nations' land claims amongst Members of the Wilderness Preservation Movement: The potential for an environmental justice movement in British Columbia. *Local Environment*. **12**(6), pp. 579–98.

Satterfield, T. (2002) *Anatomy of a Conflict: Identity, Knowledge, and Emotion in Old-Growth Forests*. Vancouver: University of British Columbia Press.

Simon, A. (1998) Backlash! Corporate Front groups and the struggle for sustainable forestry in British Columbia. *Capitalism, Nature, Socialism*. **9**(4), pp. 3–36.

Skoglund, A. and Böhm, S. (2020) Prefigurative partaking: Employees' environmental activism in an energy utility. *Organization Studies*. **41**(9), pp. 1257–83.

Stern, P.C., Dietz, T., Abel, T., Guagnano, G.A. and Kalof, L. (1999) A value-belief-norm theory of support for social movements: The case of environmentalism. *Human Ecology Review*. **6**(2), pp. 81–97.

Stoddart, M. and Tindall, D.B. (2011) Eco-feminism, hegemonic masculinity and environmental movement participation in British Columbia, Canada, 1998–2007: 'Women always clean up the mess'. *Sociological Spectrum*. **31**(3), pp. 342–68.

Switzer, J.V. (1997) *Green Backlash: The History and Politics of Environmental Opposition in the U.S.*. Boulder, CO: Lynne Rienner.

Tindall, D.B. (1994) *Collective Action in the Rainforest: Personal Networks, Collective Identity, and Participation in the Vancouver Island Wilderness Preservation Movement*. Unpublished Doctoral Dissertation. University of Toronto.

Tindall, D.B. (2002) Social networks, identification, and participation in an environmental movement: Low–medium cost activism within the British Columbia Wilderness Preservation Movement. *Canadian Review of Sociology and Anthropology*. **39**(4), pp. 413–52.

Tindall, D.B. (2003) Social values and the contingent nature of public opinion and attitudes about forests. *The Forestry Chronicle*. **79**(3), pp. 692–705.

Tindall, D.B. (2004) Social movement participation over time: An ego-network approach to micro-mobilization. *Sociological Focus*. **37**(2), pp. 163–84.

Tindall, D.B. and Begoray, N. (1993) Old growth defenders: The battle for the Carmanah Valley. In: Lerner, S. (ed.) *Environmental Stewardship: Studies in Active Earthkeeping*. Waterloo: University of Waterloo Geography Series, pp. 269–322.

Tindall, D.B. and Robinson, J.L. (2017) Collective action to save the ancient temperate rainforest: Social networks and environmental activism in Clayoquot Sound. *Ecology and Society*. **22**(1), p. 40.

Tindall, D.B., Cormier, J. and Diani, M. (2012) Network social capital as an outcome of social movement mobilization. *Social Networks*. **34**(2), pp. 387–95.

Tindall, D.B., Davies, S. and Mauboulès, C. (2003) Activism and conservation behavior in an environmental movement: The contradictory effects of gender. *Society and Natural Resources*. **16**(10), pp. 909–32.

Tindall, D.B., Howe, A.C. and Mauboulès, C. (2021) Tangled roots: Personal networks and the participation of individuals in an anti-environmentalism countermovement. *Sociological Perspectives*. **64**(1), pp. 5–36.

Tindall, D.B., Robinson, J. and Stoddart, M.C.J. (2015) A view from sociology: Environmental movement mobilization over old growth temperate rainforests in British Columbia. In: Redpath, S., Gutierrez, R., Wood, K.A. and Young, J. (eds) *Conservation Conflicts: Navigating towards Solutions*. Cambridge: Cambridge University Press, pp. 152–64.

Van Liere, K.D. and Dunlap, R.E. (1981) Environmental concern: Does it make a difference how it's measured? *Environment and Behavior*. **13**(6), pp. 651–76.

Walker, E.T. (2016) Between grassroots and 'astroturf': Understanding mobilization from the top-down. In: Courpasson, D. and Vallas, S. (eds) *The SAGE Handbook of Resistance*. Thousand Oaks, CA: Sage Publications, pp. 269–79.

Wilson, J. (1998) *Talk and Log: Wilderness Politics in British Columbia, 1965–96*. Vancouver: University of British Columbia Press.

5. Climate change scepticism in front-page Czech newspaper coverage: a one man show

Petr Ocelík

Today's wicked environmental problems have given birth to manifold environmental movements and comparably diverse social forces that emerged to counter their achievements and agenda for the future (Dunlap and Brulle, 2015; White et al., 2012). Climate change is such a problem (Grundmann, 2016), requiring a major transformation of fundamental societal functions (Geels, 2002), but which is, nevertheless, resisted by path-dependencies of an established socio-technical regime (Geels, 2014) and varied societal actors who profit from the current arrangement. This notably includes the 'denial machine' (Begley, 2007), a broad and diverse campaign undermining the scientific basis of climate change, attacking related policies, and investing large resources also into media outreach (Dunlap and McCright, 2011). Mass media provide an important platform for information dissemination as well as competition among diverse stakeholders (Stoddart et al., 2016), thereby influencing 'a range of processes from climate science to informal notions of public understanding' (Boykoff, 2011, p. 3). Barkemeyer et al. (2017) further summarize that print media is assumed to have the strongest agenda-setting impact while quality newspapers serve also as 'inter-media agenda setters' shaping the agendas of television news and other medias (McCombs, 2004).

This chapter presents a single-case study of front-page climate change newspaper coverage in the Czech Republic, a post-communist European Union member state with an industry-based economy and coal-dominated power system (Vlček and Černoch, 2019). More specifically, two questions guided the analysis. First, how has the prevalence of climate change scepticism in the coverage evolved over time? Second, what counter-framing strategies have been employed therein by the sceptics? The chapter begins with a theoretical framework, which situates the sceptic counter-movement's strategies in a mass media context. Next, background information on the Czech case is provided. The next section describes the data and methods, which rely mostly on a discourse network analysis approach and descriptive statistics. The findings show a substantial presence of climate change scepticism during the second presidency of Václav Klaus followed by its steep decline and a shift towards the expertization and domestication of coverage. The chapter concludes with a discussion of the findings, including the persisting openness of cultural and institutional opportunities for climate change scepticism and the complementary balancing role of media consensus.

MASS MEDIA AND CLIMATE CHANGE SCEPTICS' STRATEGIES

Mass media have a crucial role as a main source of information on the climate change issue for the general public as well as for stakeholders and decision-makers (Barkemeyer et al., 2017; Pidgeon, 2012; Schäfer and Schlichting, 2014). As for the former, public agendas are importantly shaped by the salience of the issue in the media discourse (Kiousis, 2004;

McCombs, 2004) and resulting public opinion dynamics can then facilitate particular policy responses (Leifeld, 2017). As for the latter, media provide visible sites for policy debates where various actors struggle to define legitimate courses of action that prevent or promote specific policy change (Broadbent, 2016; Leifeld, 2013; Stoddart and Tindall, 2015). The ability to gain media representation is thus central to a discursive contest (Trumbo, 1996) where policy actors attempt to maintain or challenge the dominant interpretations of the issue by promoting competing alternatives, also called 'frames' (Koopmans and Statham, 1999). Framing involves emphasizing specific attributes of the issue while suppressing others in order to construct a relatively consistent interpretation scheme that condenses the 'world out there' (Benford and Snow, 2000; Entman, 1993). Importantly, framing is employed strategically by a plurality of actors relying on specific cultural and ideological resources who strive to outcompete alternative frames promoted by others (Ocelík et al., 2017; Oliver and Johnston, 2000; Van Gorp, 2007). Policy opponents are thus incentivized to employ frames countering unwanted developments. Counter-framing responds to a previous frame and its impacts on the audience's opinions by advocating a position opposing the preceding frame (Chong and Druckman, 2007).

Benford and Hunt (2003) distinguished four counter-framing strategies. First, the most straightforward strategy is *problem denial*, which rejects the existence of climate change and thereby disavows the need for adopting societal and policy changes. Second, *counter attributions* provide alternative explanations of the problem and identify who else or what else is to blame, thereby directing public attention to other issues. In this case, various natural processes such as increased volcanic activity or the Earth's orbital changes are mentioned as sources of climate change. Third, *counter prognoses* offer alternative predictions and/or solutions to the problem. Such scenarios typically marginalize the impacts of climate change and emphasize the role of technological innovation and human ability to adapt to changes. Fourth, *attacks on collective character* involve undermining the credibility of the 'pro-climate camp' by attributing to them hidden agendas and conspiracy motives and portraying its members as irrational, emotional, ideological, and so on (Benford and Hunt, 2003; see Vidomus, 2011).

Use of counter-framing strategies can be linked with different types of climate change scepticism as defined by their scope and degree of doubt (see Capstick and Pidgeon, 2014; Hobson and Niemeyer, 2012; O'Neill and Boykoff, 2010). Capstick and Pidgeon (2014) provide a useful distinction between epistemic and response scepticism. *Epistemic scepticism* refers to questioning climate change as a physical phenomenon and doubting its underlying scientific evidence (Capstick and Pidgeon, 2014). In the media, the manufacturing and dissemination of scientific uncertainty about climate science is a widespread practice through which the interests of the denialist machine are supported (see Dunlap, 2013). Pollack (2003) interestingly argues that the media discreditation campaign on climate science follows the pattern earlier found in the cases of acid rain, DDT pesticide, and stratospheric ozone layer depletion. Attacks on climate science have been further facilitated by the journalistic norm of 'balance', which potentially introduces an information bias by presenting competing views in a nominally balanced way without examining the validity of the arguments (Pooley, 2009 cited in Boykoff, 2011). The conflicting sides thus receive roughly equal attention in media coverage (Entman, 1989). Boykoff and Boykoff (2004, 2007) show that balanced reporting – amounting to an immensely inaccurate communication of the state of knowledge in climate science – had been strongly present until the 2000s (see Boykoff, 2011). Although the 'balance bias' has greatly diminished in the US quality press (Schmid-Petri et al., 2017), recent studies suggest that it is still widespread among TV weathercasters (Timm et al., 2020) and within the blogosphere (Van Eck et al., 2019).

Response scepticism refers to questioning the value of actions taken to tackle climate change ranging from the individual to the global level. Importantly, this includes scepticism towards political responses especially addressing climate change mitigation, which are deemed inefficient and/or counterproductive (Capstick and Pidgeon, 2014). Lomborg's well-known and influential publications (2001, 2007) epitomize this stance, which posits that since the net impacts of climate change will be far from catastrophic there is no need to prioritize mitigation efforts (Friel, 2010). In the media, this position can be further strengthened by a dominance of narratives stressing economic benefits generated by the fossil fuel industry and, more generally, socioeconomic concerns linked to the transition towards a decarbonized economy (Bacon and Nash, 2012; Lehotský et al., 2019). In their analysis of the UK quality press, Doulton and Brown (2009) identify a rationalist discourse emphasizing the primacy of economic growth as necessary for future adaption to climate change impacts. Dryzek (2013) describes a broader Promethean discourse asserting that human inventiveness and ability to manipulate the world enable us to resolve any environmental problems. Complementary to this, defenders of the status quo strategically disengage themselves from debating environmental issues, which decreases the issues' salience and reduces the number of actors involved (Baumgartner et al., 2009; Tosun and Schaub, 2017). Thus, as Lehotský et al. (2019) argue, the high salience of issues such as economic growth or performance of the fossil fuel industry and the low salience of environmental issues are likely to co-create discursive opportunities favourable to climate change scepticism.

CLIMATE CHANGE SCEPTICISM IN THE CZECH REPUBLIC

The cultural and historical roots of climate change scepticism have been traced to the Western Bloc countries, which in the mid-twentieth century largely shared 'a dominant social paradigm that valued individual rights, laissez-faire government, free enterprise and private property', implying a resolute disregard for environmental policies (Dunlap and McCright, 2011, p. 302). Such a paradigm opened the door to anti-regulatory economics and provided a firm ideological basis to actors promoting denial (Dunlap and McCright, 2015). Not surprisingly, climate change scepticism thus has been most present in advanced industrial countries with neoliberal political economies (Dunlap and Brulle, 2015).

This case study focuses on the Czech Republic, a post-communist country with mixed attributes of consensual and majoritarian democracy (Lijphart, 2012) characterized by a bicameral parliament, multiparty system, proportional representation, and prevailing practice of coalition governments (Černý and Ocelík, 2020). The rapid shutdown of heavy industry during the economic transformation allowed the country to comfortably achieve the European Union's (EU) 2020 (European Environmental Agency, 2019) as well as the EU2030 (European Environmental Agency, 2018) climate targets without major policy changes. Adoption of more ambitious mitigation policies has been prevented by the strong position of energy incumbents (Černý and Ocelík, 2020; Ocelík et al., 2019) and overall polarization of the climate policy subsystem (Wagner et al., 2020). As a result, the Czech Republic remains a coal-dependent economy (Vlček and Černoch, 2019), with the fifth highest CO_2 emissions per capita in the EU (European Environmental Agency, 2019). This is also reflected by the country's low mean ranking of 31 in the Climate Change Performance Index for the studied timeframe 2009–2018 (see Burck et al., 2019).

The Czech Republic underwent transition to democracy and a free market economy during the 1990s. Despite this very different historical trajectory, Hanley (1999) shows that Anglo-American New Right ideas became strongly anchored among the Czechoslovakian dissent and, later, gave rise to the post-revolutionary dominance of Thatcherite neoliberalism. Late in 1989, a grey zone technocrat working at the Forecasting Institute of the Czechoslovak Academy of Sciences, Václav Klaus, suddenly turned into one of the leaders of the Velvet Revolution and subsequently became Minister of Finance. Klaus swiftly profiled himself as a staunch promoter of rapid neoliberal reforms under the label of 'capitalism without adjectives' and became a charismatic leader of the conservative government in 1992 (Saxonberg, 1999). Klaus also engaged in a long-lasting ideological dispute on the nature of civil society with then President Václav Havel by defending a position where private wealth is a barrier to any state economic intervention and individual self-interest is a base for good citizenship (Myant, 2005; Pontuso, 2002). As Fagan (2004, p. 5) describes, during the 1990s, 'the environmental movement was politically marginalized and castigated as an anti-market relic of the socialist era that sought to usurp the liberal individualist agenda.' Though the socioeconomic impacts of neoliberal policies and a financing scandal within the *Civil Democratic Party* chaired by Klaus led to the fall of his second government in 1997, the anti-environmental discourse has remained to this day (Shriver and Adams, 2013).

Six years later, Václav Klaus became the second Czech president and served two full terms until 2013. His presidency was inseparably defined by his sustained opposition to any climate agenda, ranging from a deep denial of climate change to response scepticism over climate policies. The release of *An Inconvenient Truth* in 2006 was followed by the activation of the Czech climate sceptic community spearheaded by Klaus (see Vidomus, 2018), who rejected the movie's message as an arrogant instance of climate alarmism (Hluštík and Černý, 2009). Klaus has not only been active in the media but also collaborated closely with laissez-faire and conservative think-tanks – most prominently with the *Center for Economics and Politics* (founded by Klaus himself), which organized a seminar series on climate change. The book *Blue Planet in Green Shackles* (Klaus, 2007) summarized his views on the issue and gained significant public attention. The disappointment of the Copenhagen Conference of Parties and the Climategate controversy provided further encouragement to assaults on climate science. Such developments created political opportunity structures for the broader climate scepticism movement including contrarian scientists, publicists and bloggers (see Vidomus, 2018). Climate scepticism was also present at the governmental level, most notably in the government led by the *Civil Democratic Party* between the years 2010 and 2013. Significantly, this included the Minister of Environment Tomáš Chalupa, who was ideologically close to Václav Klaus and who promoted an environmental deregulation agenda (see Vidomus, 2018). Although the Czech climate sceptic movement has been considerably less active since the end of the Klaus presidency in 2013, the strong position of industry incumbents and widespread presence of anti-environmental rhetoric among political elites (see Binka, 2008; Osička and Černoch, 2017) provide resources for its renewal. Moreover, recent research has shown the continued presence of climate scepticism within the scientific community (see Wagner et al., 2020).

Considering the above, the comparatively lower public acceptance of climate change and perception of its seriousness are hardly surprising. A recent survey by the Czech Academy of

Sciences indicates that 86 per cent of the public agrees that climate change is occurring but 49 per cent agrees that climate change is caused to a *similar* extent by natural processes and human activity (Hanzlová, 2019). According to Zvěřinová et al. (2016), 17 per cent of the public agrees that there is a scientific dispute about the existence of climate change. A Eurostat survey (2017) documents that climate change was seen as the most serious global problem only by 6 per cent of the Czech public in 2017, the third lowest score in the EU28 (12 per cent average). The score ranged for the studied timeframe between a minimum of 6 per cent and a maximum of 34 per cent, recorded in 2009 (see Eurostat, 2009). Krajhanzl et al. (2018) further show that the public is most concerned with natural impacts of climate change, such as increased incidence of floods (68 per cent) and droughts or heat waves (67 per cent), and only secondarily with societal impacts, such as climate-driven migration.

Media coverage of climate change has followed a similar pattern to that observed in other European countries, reaching a maximum in the period from 2007 to 2010 (Boykoff et al., 2018; Lehotský, 2018). As elsewhere, this period of increased attention can be linked to internationally important events such as the publication of the fourth IPCC Assessment Report, the success of the film *An Inconvenient Truth*, the Copenhagen Conference, and the Climategate controversy. Nevertheless, Czech media coverage was especially influenced by the vocal presence of President Klaus, who adeptly used his privileged position and was the most represented person commenting on the issue (Lehotský, 2018; Vávra et al., 2013; Vidomus, 2018). In their analysis of newspaper coverage between the years 1997 and 2010, Vávra et al. (2013) show that climate change is covered more in terms of its environmental dimension rather than societal. In his study of media coverage in the period from 1997 to 2015, Lehotský (2018) documents a dominant coverage focus on climate change impacts both at the global and local level. In accordance with Olausson (2014), Lehotský (2018) further argues that media coverage shows a tendency towards 'domestication', emphasizing local threats such as floods in order to engage national audiences.

DATA AND METHODS

The data corpus contains all front-page articles during the period of interest on the issue of climate change in the four major national newspapers that satisfy the 'quality press' criterion (McCombs, 2004; see Barkemeyer et al., 2017). The newspapers' editorial ideology ranges from the liberal right perspective of *Lidové noviny* and *Hospodářské noviny* through *Mladá fronta Dnes*' centrist position to the traditional social democratic standpoint of *Právo* (see Volek and Urbániková, 2017). It is worth noting that chairman of governing party *ANO 2011* and current Prime Minister Andrej Babiš acquired the MAFRA publishing house that publishes *Lidové noviny* and *Mladá fronta Dnes* in 2013.

The *Anopress IT Czech media monitoring database* (Anopress, n.d.) was used for data collection through the following keyword search query (English/Czech keyword): {*global warming/globální oteplování*} OR {*climate change/klimatická změna*} OR {*climate change/změna klimatu*}. The timeframe for the search was set between 1 January 2009 and 31 December 2018 and divided into two periods. The first period (2009–2013) starts with the year of the Copenhagen Conference and ends with the last year of the Klaus presidency. The second (2014–2018) covers the post-Klaus presidency period.

The analysis was limited to front-page articles because placement is a key indicator of the visibility or prominence of an article (see McCombs, 2005). This approach assumes that if climate scepticism receives quality press coverage at the most prominent position (i.e. the front page) it is likely to be represented also in the less prominent positions and in other, less influential media. The search returned 6012 articles including 376 front-page articles from which, after examining their relevance, 303 were included in the analysis. The number of front-page articles across the years ranged between 18 in 2014 and 113 in 2009 (see Figure 5.1).

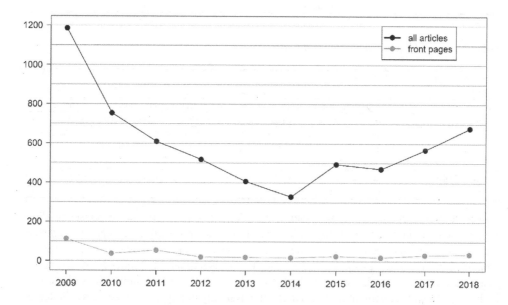

Figure 5.1   Annual frequency of articles covering climate change issue

All relevant articles were read and their contents manually coded by two independent coders if statements (1) referred to relevant policy positions or responses (e.g. 'energy transition is necessary to tackle climate change') or (2) expressed relevant normative evaluations (e.g. 'regulatory responses to climate change threaten individual freedoms') (Koopmans, 2002). Both direct and indirect (reported) statements have been coded. *Discourse Network Analyzer* (Leifeld, 2019) was used for coding. Each coding unit (statement) consisted of six variables: topic (concept in the default setting); strategy (if present); person; organization (if present); dis/agreement with the topic; and the statement's primary level of reference (non-specified, domestic or lower, higher than domestic, or combined).

The coding followed an abductive approach and the resulting corpus consisted of 800 coding units representing 34 topics, 4 pre-defined strategies, 241 persons, 168 organizations, 704 agreements, and 96 disagreements.

The descriptive analysis examined how the presence of sceptic statements and counter-framing strategies evolves over time. The prevalence of climate change scepticism for a given period was measured as the frequency of dis/agreements with topics that refer to (1) the

Table 5.1 Epistemic and response climate change scepticism

Denialism type	Defining topics
Epistemic scepticism	anthropogenic climate change (disagreement)
	scientific consensus (disagreement)
Response scepticism	adaptation measures (disagreement)
	mitigation measures (disagreement)
	adaptation over mitigation (agreement)
	socioeconomic threats (agreement)
	sociopolitical threats (agreement)

Table 5.2 Counter-framing strategies

Counter-framing strategy	Description
Problem denial	Denial of the existence of climate change as such or anthropogenic causes of climate change
Counter diagnoses	Alternative explanation of climate change – climate change as a result of natural processes
Counter prognoses	Alternative prognoses and/or solutions – it is not clear what the impacts of climate change will be; nature and societies will easily adapt; responses to climate change are inefficient and threatening to socioeconomic development
Attacks on collective character	Attacks on the credibility of the 'pro-climate camp' – typically, political and scientific controversy, hidden agenda, funding-dependency

causes of climate change or related scientific evidence and (2) particular responses to climate change or their implications (see Table 5.1). The first group of topics captures epistemic scepticism, while the second group refers to response scepticism. Likewise, the prevalence of counter-framing strategies for a given period was measured as the frequency of coding units that included the particular strategy. Importantly, not every coding unit that is classified as including a sceptic statement includes a counter-framing strategy, and vice versa. Statements of the latter category must contain the general characteristics as defined in Table 5.2.

Matrices for *actor congruence networks* consisting of actors (persons) tied via topics they share were extracted for both studied periods. The corresponding networks have weighted ties representing actors' cumulative similarity in the use of topics, that is, the closer the actors are within the front-page coverage, the higher the edge weight is between them. The resulting network is used to identify the structural position of climate sceptics.

COPENHAGEN CONFERENCE AND AFTERMATH: SCEPTICS ON A ROLL

The first analysed period starts in 2009, the year of the Copenhagen Conference, and ends in 2013, the last year of Václav Klaus's presidency. In accordance with the general trend in Europe (see Boykoff et al., 2018), the year 2009 shows the highest overall coverage in comparison to the rest of the studied timeframe although this trend is much less visible in the case of front-page coverage (see Figure 5.1). The front-page coverage includes comparatively more sceptic statements and is more polarized as the share of disagreements accounts for 16 per cent of the total number of statements (447). The statements refer mostly to international topics and events (see Table 5.3).

Table 5.3   Descriptive statistics

	2009–2013	2014–2018
Number of articles	189	114
Number of statements	447	353
Polarization	72	31
(% of disagreements in the period total)	(16.11%)	(8.78%)
Domestication (ratio of domestic to international statements)	0.43	1.63
Number of sceptic statements	36	11
(% of the period total)	(8.05%)	(3.12%)
Use of counter-framing strategies	94	6
(% of the period total)	(21.03%)	(1.70%)

Although climate change as a priority political agenda is the most prevalent topic (10.51 per cent of the period total), climate scepticism is very visible. *Epistemic scepticism* is represented by disagreeing statements on the topics of ACC (anthropogenic climate change) and scientific consensus on ACC (see Figure 5.2). Václav Klaus (2009) provides an exemplary instance of such a position by arguing that, '[although] global climate is, in fact, not changing, global warming alarmists successfully persuaded politicians (and also a number of reasonable people) that we face a catastrophe – based on this idea, they attempt to limit our freedom and to hinder prosperity.' A similar line of argumentation can be found in articles by prominent conservative commentators such as Martin Weiss and Daniel Kaiser. Kaiser (2009) contends that '[c]laiming allegiance to the theory of anthropogenic global warming is considered to be almost something as a participation fee, which needs to be paid by anyone who wants to engage in debates on environment.' The questioning of scientific consensus on ACC is less prevalent and relates almost exclusively to the Climategate controversy.

Response scepticism is present mainly through concerns about socioeconomic and sociopolitical threats that arise as undesirable by-products of misplaced climate polices (see Figure 5.2). The former argues that climate protection regulation endangers economic growth and competitiveness, typically linked with a general critique of the key accomplices – the European Union (EU) and renewable energy. Bjorn Lomborg's influential thesis that adaptation is markedly more effective than mitigation further provides supposed expert-base legitimation of such a position. The latter describes the climate agenda as a blind ideology or religion that paves the way towards a subjugated or even totalitarian society, with the EU, environmental movement and interventionist states as the main culprits. Accordingly, Klaus cautions that '[t]he global temperature is misused for a radical intervention of state and politics into a human society, which is what we are now witnessing' (Buchert, 2009). Such appeals are sometimes supported by reminiscences of the Communist regime.

Among the counter-framing strategies (Benford and Hunt, 2003), *attacks on collective character* is the most prevalent (13.87 per cent of the period's total) and is used mainly against environmental activists and policy actors supporting the climate agenda (see Figure 5.3). The depictions of the environmental movement range from characterizations based on attributed naivety and irrationality to an exposition of the movements' orchestrated assault on democratic and market-based institutions. Regarding the latter, Václav Klaus warns: 'It is apparent that ecologists do not want to change climate. They want to change us and our behavior' (Buchert, 2009). The European Union is seen as an ally of such efforts and a stronghold

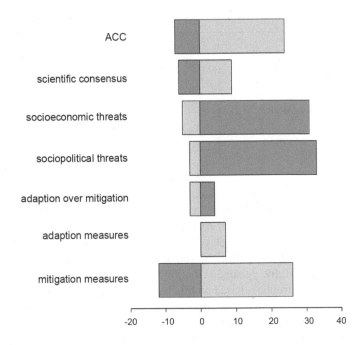

Notes: The x-axis displays the number of disagreements (negative counts) and agreements (positive counts) with the selected topic. Dark grey represents climate sceptic statements. Light grey represents other statements.

Figure 5.2   Distribution of dis/agreements on selected topics (2009–2013)

of bureaucratism. Commentator Martin Weiss (2009) also criticizes the role of conformist journalists, who supposedly profit from the fashionable climate change topic and 'in symbiosis with politicians produce toxic media waste: non-events which pretend to be events.'

The *problem denial* strategy (2.68 per cent) is employed in two ways. The first is a general rejection of the scientific consensus aided by labelling climate change as a 'theory' or 'hypothesis' (see Kaiser, 2012). The second is a rather bizarre reporting of weather conditions experienced by Václav Klaus mostly during his official visits abroad. 'It was unexpectedly cold in Florida, that is in the South, during March [...] It is really warm in the much more northern Washington now during the end of September [...] The hypothesis of global warming is thus, on average, not confirmed' (Klaus, 2010). The *counter attributions* (2.68 per cent) and *counter prognoses* (1.79 per cent) strategies are also markedly less prevalent than attacks on collective character. The former identifies natural processes as causes of climate change, while the latter questions mitigation-oriented responses. As Lomborg (2009) argues, 'drastic and incredibly expensive reduction of CO_2 emissions is completely unnecessary and will have practically zero impact on a global temperature until the half of century.' Likewise, Klaus (2009) claims that human society is sufficiently adaptable to cope with 'small climate changes'. According to this strategy, adequate responses thus should abandon restrictions introduced during 'the era of socio-ecological market economy' in order to encourage rational human activity (Klaus, 2009).

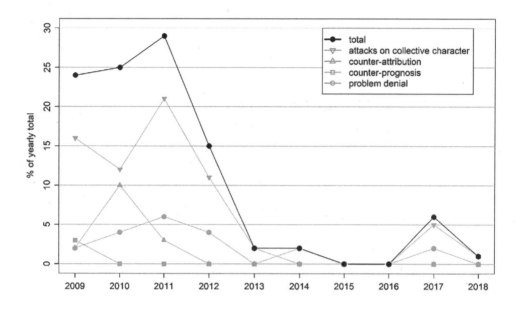

Figure 5.3   Annual prevalence of counter-framing strategies

When identifying the key actors and their groups, the actor congruence network (Figure 5.4) exhibits a segmentation into several clusters with a visible division between climate sceptics and exponents of ACC. The climate sceptic cluster includes Czech President Václav Klaus, conservative commentators Daniel Kaiser and Martin Weiss, economist Bjorn Lomborg, and geologist Václav Cílek (2010), who speculates about the possibility of a short-term global cooling. The cluster shares a general disagreement with ACC and with the priority of a climate change agenda. However, socioeconomic and sociopolitical threats resulting from climate action are markedly more prevalent and create the core of the sceptics' argumentation (see Figure 5.2). Lomborg thus not surprisingly occupies a bridging position between the two main clusters by recognizing climate change as a serious challenge while highlighting the inefficiency of mitigation shared by the other sceptics. Interestingly, the topic of sociopolitical threats is almost monopolized by Václav Klaus, who is also the person with the largest number of coded statements (11.86 per cent of the period total).

Greenpeace activist Jan Rovenský and US President Barack Obama are the most represented people in the ACC exponents cluster (see Figure 5.4), which promotes the importance of the climate agenda as such with a focus on the negative impacts of climate change. More specifically, environmental activists try to draw attention to the topic of coal mining and use, especially regarding the modernization of the largest Czech coal-fired power plant Prunéřov (Rovenský, 2009). Two experts have also been identified among the most represented persons

94 *Handbook of anti-environmentalism*

– climatologist Jan Pretel and Director of the *Czech Hydrometeorological Institute* Mark Rieder. Together with Václav Jirásek, a spokesperson for the state-owned company *Povodí Labe*, they mostly discuss the topics of drought and infrastructural adaptation, which became prominent in the second period.

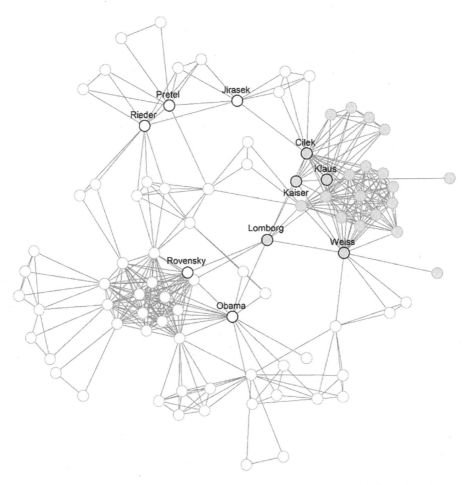

Notes: The edges represent shared agreements or disagreements with particular concept(s). The nodes refer to persons occurring in the coverage. The grey nodes indicate persons agreeing more than disagreeing with at least one of the climate scepticism related topics (see Table 5.1). The labels are displayed only for persons with the number of statements above the top decile. Isolates are not displayed.

Figure 5.4   *Normalized actor congruence network (w > 1), 2009–2013*

AFTER THE KLAUS PRESIDENCY: TOWARDS EXPERTIZATION

The second analysed period starts in 2014, the first full year after Václav Klaus's presidency, and ends in 2018. The year 2014 recorded the lowest overall coverage within the studied timeframe followed by its gradual increase (see Figure 5.1). The front-page coverage includes markedly fewer sceptic statements and is less polarized as the share of disagreements accounts for less than 9 per cent of the total number of statements (353). The results further show a visible shift towards domestic topics and events, which are about 1.6 times more represented than international ones (see Table 5.3).

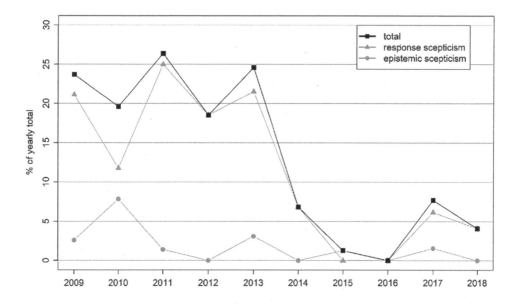

Figure 5.5   Annual prevalence of epistemic and response scepticism

The substantial decrease in climate scepticism applies mainly to *epistemic scepticism* (see Figure 5.5), which is represented by only three statements questioning ACC while the scientific consensus is no longer directly contested. Moreover, two of the three occurrences are of a reported character and refer to Václav Klaus and US President Donald Trump. Likewise, *response scepticism* is much less prevalent, with the notion of socioeconomic threats and opposition to mitigation efforts being the most frequent counter-arguments (see Figure 5.6). More specifically, response scepticism is expressed mainly through concerns about EU-driven over-regulation and resulting in excessive costs incurred particularly in the energy industry. The steep decline in the number of climate sceptic statements between the periods (see Table 5.3) corresponds with the rapidly fading role of Václav Klaus, who had 53 statements in the previous period (11.86 per cent of the period total) and only 2 statements in the second period (2.83 per cent). Likewise, counter-framing strategies are almost absent, with a combined prevalence of 1.7 per cent in the second period (see Figure 5.3). There are only 2 instances of *problem denial* and 4 instances of *attacks on collective character*, while *counter attributions* and *counter prognoses* are completely absent.

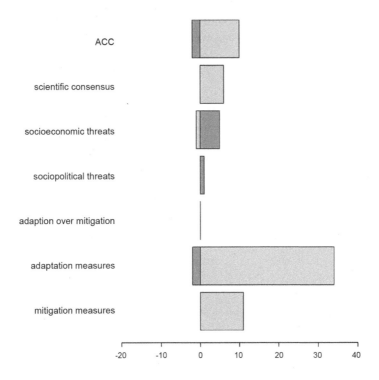

Notes: The x-axis displays the number of disagreements (negative counts) and agreements (positive counts) with the selected topic. Dark grey represents climate sceptic statements. Light grey represents other statements.

Figure 5.6 Distribution of dis/agreements on selected topics (2014–2018)

The actor congruence network (Figure 5.7) is no longer segmented according to the division between climate sceptics and exponents of ACC but resembles rather a core–periphery structure. The sceptics are located on the very periphery, represented by US President Donald Trump, who received attention due to the announced withdrawal from the Paris Climate Agreement, and a commentator from *Lidové noviny* Zbyněk Petráček (2018), who criticizes naive attempts to 'control' the climate and climate fearmongering. With one important exception of Richard Brabec, the rest of the most represented people are from academia. Their primary fields range from landscape planning (Michael Pondělíček), geology (Václav Cílek) and ecology (David Pithart) through hydrology (Mark Rieder) and meteorology (Jan Šrámek) to climatology (Aleš Farda, Radim Tolasz, Miroslav Trnka). This is a clear indication of an expertization of the front-page coverage, with a focus on climate change impacts analysis. The experts' cluster is formed especially around topics of biodiversity loss, drought and other extreme weather events. Václav Cílek also mentions negative sociopolitical impacts in terms of climate change-driven migration (Martinek, 2015). Lastly, Richard Brabec, the Minister of Environment, is the only Czech politician among the most represented people. Brabec claims that climate change is a priority policy issue with serious impacts on the Czech Republic and emphasizes the importance of adaptation efforts. Importantly, his statements do not address any mitigation measures.

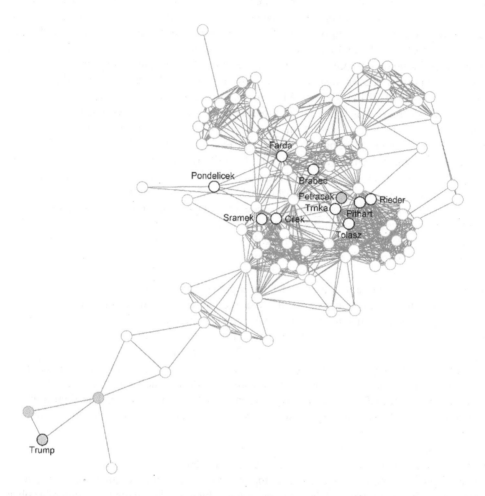

Notes: The edges represent shared agreements or disagreements with particular concept(s). The nodes refer to persons occurring in the coverage. The grey nodes indicate persons agreeing more than disagreeing with at least one of the climate scepticism related topics (see Table 5.1). The labels are displayed only for persons with the number of statements above the top decile. Isolates are not displayed.

Figure 5.7   *Normalized actor congruence network (w > 1), 2014–2018*

WHAT'S NEXT FOR CZECH CLIMATE SCEPTICISM IN NEWSPAPER COVERAGE: A DOOR LEFT AJAR

This chapter has mapped how the prevalence of climate change scepticism in Czech daily newspapers' front-page coverage evolved within the timeframe of 2009–2018, while focusing on the use of specific counter-framing strategies. It was shown that the majority of sceptic claims have been made by former President Václav Klaus, who utilized his privileged position and was not only the most prominent Czech sceptic but also the most represented actor on the issue. Such development helped to legitimize climate change scepticism as one of the two sides in a seemingly scientific dispute and, presumably, considerably delayed the formation of a *media consensus* (Blanco-Castilla et al., 2018) on climate change, which has emerged in the quality press only in more recent years. The substantial presence of both epistemic and response scepticism (Capstick and Pidgeon, 2014) was documented in the first studied period (2009–2013), corresponding to a large extent with Klaus's second presidency, while a rapid decrease was found in the subsequent period (2014–2018). The most prevalent counter-framing strategy was based on *attacks on collective character* of opponents, which oscillated from attributions of naivety through the exposition of a hidden agenda to the assignment of enemy status (Benford and Hunt, 2003). Similarly, Cann and Raymond (2018, p. 446) found that sceptics' counter-framing strategies shifted from scientific uncertainty arguments to 'more personal attacks on the integrity of climate scientists and their allies.'

Akin to the so-called Anglo-American model (AAM), Czech climate scepticism combines populist ideology with conservative values. Lockwood (2018) argues that, whereas populism juxtaposes the pure and deserving people against the corrupted elites collaborating with nefarious minorities, conservative values add emphasis on national sovereignty and market-based responses, which are in conflict with the 'progressivist agenda' of the cosmopolitan elites–minorities alliance. In line with this model, the exponents of anthropogenic climate change are portrayed as a united front consisting of the over-regulating EU, untrustworthy climate science community, and conformist mainstream media representing the corrupted elites, as well as the ideologically zealous environmental activists in the position of the nefarious minority. Such depictions are in line with Vidomus's findings (2013), which identified three *specific* traits of the Czech climate-sceptic counter-movement: the unique role of Václav Klaus, an assumed resistance to ideological reasoning acquired especially during the Communist regime, and a 'natural' congruence of climate- and Euro-scepticism (Vidomus, 2013). The final trait was further amplified by the Eurozone crisis and the related increase in the salience of economic topics (see Cross and Ma, 2015).

Klaus, together with a few other climate sceptics, succeeded in establishing a relatively polarized debate on the status of climate change and adeptly 'localized' the AAM within the European post-communist context. Replacing the 'red scare' with the 'green scare' (Jacques, 2006) was an important part of Klaus's storytelling, which facilitated the formation of a coherent and persuasive narrative resonating well with the audience (see Shanahan et al., 2011). Moreover, climate scepticism was also represented within the conservative *Civil Democratic Party*, which led the government for the majority of Klaus's second presidency (see Vidomus, 2018). The mainstreaming of climate scepticism is consistent with the AAM as documented in the USA (Dunlap and McCright, 2011) and Australia (Tranter, 2017) and contrasts with Western and Northern Europe where typically only smaller right-wing populist political parties pursue the sceptic agenda (Lockwood, 2018). Likewise, the presence of climate scepticism in news coverage is comparable with the higher levels found in the USA (Schmid-Petri et al., 2017), Australia (Tranter, 2017), and the United Kingdom (Painter and Gavin, 2016) rather than with Finland (Kukkonen and Ylä-Anttila, 2020), Germany (Grundmann and Scott, 2014) or Portugal (Horta et al., 2017) or even Canada (Stoddart et al., 2016), Ireland (Wagner and Payne, 2017) or New Zealand (Chetty et al., 2015). The AAM thus should be understood in the context of climate scepticism's ideological origins rather than as a (counter-)movement empirically occurring *only* in the Anglo-American world. The Czech case further supports Dunlap and Jacques' argument (2013, p. 708) that conditions of 'a recent history of staunch conservative governments, influential conservative think tanks, and a strong fossil fuels sector' enable diffusion of climate scepticism.

In contrast to the sceptics' dramatic storyline, ACC exponents mostly focused on a general promotion of the climate agenda and less so on addressing specific climate change impacts and related policy responses. As Lehotský's findings (2018) for the period 1997–2015 showed, although the topic of energy was highly prevalent in the climate change media discourse, it was represented mainly through general terms and not introducing particular topics of energy transition, renewables development, or energy efficiency – thus maintaining a discursive separation of the topics of climate change and coal as well as a low profile of energy industry incumbents (Černý and Ocelík, 2020; Lehotský et al., 2019). Stoddart et al. (2017), Vesa et al. (2020) and Ylä-Anttila et al. (2018) identified a similar trend where incumbent actors tend to use advocacy strategies but do not seek media visibility. This is also consistent with a higher prevalence in the news coverage of international events in comparison to domestic topics – a continuous trend documented by Vávra et al. (2013) in the 1997–2010 period.

The subsequent period of 2014–2018 following the end of the Klaus presidency exhibited a markedly different structure of front-page coverage. The prevalence of climate scepticism reached a near zero level, indicating the exceptional position that Klaus had enjoyed in the media and more broadly in public discourse (see Vidomus, 2018). Importantly, the decrease in climate sceptic visibility also corresponds with the overall decline of climate change issue salience in the media and public discourses after the Copenhagen Conference (Boykoff et al., 2018), when the Eurozone crisis and later migration crisis came to the centre of attention (see Cross and Ma, 2015; Greussing and Boomgaarden, 2017). Besides the marginalization of sceptic voices, two main trends were identified. The first is the overall *expertization* of the front-page coverage focusing on local climate change impacts, with drought becoming the most prevalent topic (cf. Kukkonen and Ylä-Anttila, 2020). This is in line with a more general tendency towards *domestication* (see Olausson, 2014) of climate change as shown by Lehotský (2018) and also found elsewhere (see Broadbent et al., 2016). The second trend is the dominance of adaptation over mitigation reasoning typically in the form of infrastructural adaptation measures (cf. Horta et al., 2017). In contrast to the previous period, climate change was to a large extent framed as a depoliticized problem, with localized impacts to be solved through technical expertise. This is similar to the eco-modernization framing of climate responses as identified in Ireland (Wagner and Payne, 2017).

These findings raise a question about the potential revival of the climate sceptic counter-movement. Although Václav Klaus left the president's office in 2013, 'elite cues', which as Brulle et al. (2012) showed importantly influence public opinion, are still present. The recent emergence of a radical environmental movement in the Czech Republic has further intensified the 'cultural war' by broadening the group of the involved actors – most importantly, serving Czech President Miloš Zeman, a long-time supporter of industry incumbents who recently claimed that he does not know whether climate change occurs due to natural cycles or human-made activity (Zeman, 2019). In the wake of the COVID-19 crisis, current Prime Minister Andrej Babiš said that the EU should forget about the Green Deal and focus on pandemic management instead (Euractiv, 2020). The leader of the opposition, the conservative *Civil Democratic Party*, still includes a number of high-ranking politicians with climate sceptic attitudes. Thus, both institutional and cultural opportunity structures (see Osička and Černoch, 2017) remain relatively open to counter-movement mobilization. Alongside political mobilization efforts (Brulle et al., 2012), this shows the importance of strengthening and maintaining the media consensus (Blanco-Castilla et al., 2018), which would counteract such tendencies. Nevertheless, media visibility of climate protection per se is not sufficient for countering the climate sceptic agenda (Stoddart et al., 2017; Van Rensburg and Head, 2017). As a potential remedy, Van Rensburg and Head (2017) suggest that communicative strategies should avoid narrow scientific views and instead focus more on the economic dimension of climate (non)responses.

Considering the above, there appear to be several promising directions for future research. First, the research would benefit from studies conducted outside the Anglo-American and old-EU states to overcome its rather limited empirical scope. Second, studies of transnational networks would shed light on the diffusion of the climate sceptic agenda from its traditional centres. Third, just as sceptic (counter-)framing evolves, research on the efficacy of climate protection-oriented communicative strategies seems to be especially relevant.

ACKNOWLEDGEMENTS

I am grateful to Anežka Konvalinová and Sebastián Mariňák for their dedicated assistance with the coding as well as to Michaela Hronová for her help with background materials. I would also like to thank the editors of this monograph for valuable feedback as well as to Marína Urbániková for a useful suggestion and to Colin Kimbrell, who provided language editing services. An earlier version of the research was presented at the Comparing Climate Change Policy Networks workshop held at the University of Bern, October 2019. The research was supported by the 'Perspectives of European Integration in a Changing International Environment II' (MUNI/A/1044/2019) fund and is a part of the COMPON project (http://compon.org).

REFERENCES

Anopress (n.d.) *Czech Media Database. Anopress.* Available from: https://monitoring.anopress.cz/Anopress.

Bacon, W. and Nash, C. (2012) Playing the media game: The relative (in)visibility of coal industry interests in media reporting of coal as a climate change issue in Australia. *Journalism Studies.* **13**(2), pp. 243–58. Available from DOI: 10.1080/1461670X.2011.646401.

Barkemeyer, R., Figge, F., Hoepner, A., Holt, D., Kraak, J.M. and Yu, P.-S. (2017) Media coverage of climate change: An international comparison. *Environment and Planning C: Politics and Space.* **35**(6), pp. 1029–54. Available from DOI: 10.1177/0263774X16680818.

Baumgartner, F.R., Berry, J.M., Hojnacki, M., Kimball, D.C. and Leech, B.L. (2009) *Lobbying and Policy Change: Who Wins, Who Loses, and Why.* Chicago, IL: The University of Chicago Press.

Begley, S. (2007) The truth about denial. *Newsweek.* Available from: https://web.archive.org/web/20071021024942/http://www.newsweek.com/id/32482.

Benford, R.D. and Hunt, S. (2003) Interactional dynamics in public problems marketplaces: Movements and the counterframing and reframing of public problems. In: Holstein, J.A. and Miller, G. (eds) *Challenges and Choices: Constructionist Perspectives on Social Problems.* New York, NY: Aldine de Gruyter, pp. 153–86.

Benford, R.D. and Snow, D.A. (2000) Framing processes and social movements: An overview and assessment. *Annual Review of Sociology*. **26**(1), pp. 611–39. Available from DOI: 10.1146/annurev.soc.26.1.611.

Binka, B. (2008) *Zelený extremismus: Ideje a mentalita českých environmentálních hnutí*. Masarykova univerzita.

Blanco-Castilla, E., Teruel, L.R. and Molina, V.M. (2018) Searching for climate change consensus in broadsheet newspapers. Editorial policy and public opinion. *Communication and Society*. Servicio de Publicaciones de la Universidad de Navarra. **31**(3), pp. 331–46. Available from DOI: 10.15581/003.31.3.331-346.

Boykoff, M.T. (2011) *Who Speaks for the Climate?: Making Sense of Media Reporting on Climate Change*. Cambridge: Cambridge University Press.

Boykoff, M.T. and Boykoff, J.M. (2004) Balance as bias: Global warming and the US prestige press. *Global Environmental Change*. **14**(2), pp. 125–36. Available from DOI: 10.1016/j.gloenvcha.2003.10.001.

Boykoff, M.T. and Boykoff, J.M. (2007) Climate change and journalistic norms: A case-study of US mass-media coverage. *Geoforum*. **38**(6), pp. 1190–204. Available from DOI: 10.1016/j.geoforum.2007.01.008.

Boykoff, M., Daly, M., Reyes, R.F., McAllister, L., McNatt, M., Nacu-Schmidt, A., Oonk, D. et al. (2018) World newspaper coverage of climate change or global warming 2004–2018 – April 2018. Center for Science and Technology Policy Research, Cooperative Institute for Research in Environmental Sciences, University of Colorado Boulder. Available from DOI: 10.25810/4C3B-B819.1.

Broadbent, J. (2016) Comparative climate change policy networks. In: Victor, J.N., Montgomery, A.H. and Lubell, M. (eds) *The Oxford Handbook of Political Networks*. Oxford: Oxford University Press. Available from DOI: 10.1093/oxfordhb/9780190228217.013.38.

Broadbent, J., Sonnett, J., Botetzagias, I., Carson, M., Carvalho, A., Chen, Y.-J., Edling, C. et al. (2016) Conflicting climate change frames in a global field of media discourse. *Socius: Sociological Research for a Dynamic World*. pp. 1–17. Available from DOI: 10.1177/2378023116670660.

Brulle, R.J., Carmichael, J. and Jenkins, J.C. (2012) Shifting public opinion on climate change: An empirical assessment of factors influencing concern over climate change in the U.S., 2002–2010. *Climatic Change*. Kluwer Academic Publishers. **114**(2), pp. 169–88. Available from DOI: 10.1007/s10584-012-0403-y.

Buchert, V. (2009) Klaus opět udeřil v nové knize: Klima je zneužíváno politiky. *Mladá fronta Dnes*. 21 August.

Burck, J., Hagen, U., Marten, F., Höhne, N. and Bals, N. (2019) *Climate Change Performance Index – Results 2019*. Available from: www.germanwatch.org/en/16073 (accessed 10 January 2019).

Cann, H.W. and Raymond, L. (2018) Does climate denialism still matter? The prevalence of alternative frames in opposition to climate policy. *Environmental Politics*. **27**(3), pp. 433–54. Available from DOI: 10.1080/09644016.2018.1439353.

Capstick, S.B. and Pidgeon, N.F. (2014) What is climate change scepticism? Examination of the concept using a mixed methods study of the UK public. *Global Environmental Change*. **24**(1), pp. 389–401. Available from DOI: 10.1016/j.gloenvcha.2013.08.012.

Černý, O. and Ocelík, P. (2020) Incumbents' strategies in media coverage: A case of the Czech coal policy. *Politics and Governance*. **8**(2), pp. 272–85. Available from DOI: 10.17645/pag.v8i2.2610.

Chetty, K., Devadas, V. and Fleming, J. (2015) The framing of climate change in New Zealand newspapers from June 2009 to June 2010. *Journal of the Royal Society of New Zealand*. **45**(1), pp. 1–20. Available from DOI: 10.1080/03036758.2014.996234.

Chong, D. and Druckman, J.N. (2007) Framing public opinion in competitive democracies. *American Political Science Review*. **101**(4), pp. 637–55. Available from DOI: 10.1017/S0003055407070554.

Cílek, V. (2010) Studené zimy teď' budou běžné, domnívá se Cílek. *Právo*. 12 February.

Cross, M.K.D. and Ma, X. (2015) EU crises and integrational panic: The role of the media. *Journal of European Public Policy*. **22**(8), pp. 1053–70. Available from DOI: 10.1080/13501763.2014.984748.

Doulton, H. and Brown, K. (2009) Ten years to prevent catastrophe?: Discourses of climate change and international development in the UK press. *Global Environmental Change*. **19**(2), pp. 191–202. Available from DOI: 10.1016/j.gloenvcha.2008.10.004.

Dryzek, J.S. (2013) *The Politics of the Earth: Environmental Discourses*. 3rd edn. Oxford: Oxford University Press.
Dunlap, R.E. (2013) Climate change skepticism and denial. *American Behavioral Scientist*. **57**(6), pp. 691–98. Available from DOI: 10.1177/0002764213477097.
Dunlap, R.E. and Brulle, R.J. (eds) (2015) *Climate Change and Society: Sociological Perspectives*. New York, NY: Oxford University Press. Available from DOI: 10.1093/acprof:oso/9780199356102.001.0001.
Dunlap, R.E. and Jacques, P.J. (2013) Climate change denial books and conservative think tanks: Exploring the connection. *American Behavioral Scientist*. **57**(6), pp. 699–731. Available from DOI: 10.1177/0002764213477096.
Dunlap, R.E. and McCright, A.M. (2011) Organized climate change denial. In: Dryzek, J.S., Norgaard, R.B. and Schlosberg, D. (eds) *The Oxford Handbook of Climate Change and Society*. New York, NY: Oxford University Press. Available from DOI: 10.1093/OXFORDHB/9780199566600.003.0010.
Dunlap, R.E. and McCright, A.M. (2015) Challenging climate change: The denial countermovement. In: Dunlap, R.E. and Brulle, R.J. (eds) *Climate Change and Society: Sociological Perspectives*. Oxford: Oxford University Press, pp. 300–332. Available from DOI: 10.1093/acprof:oso/9780199356102.003.0010.
Entman, R.M. (1989) How the media affect what people think: An information processing approach. *The Journal of Politics*. **51**(2), pp. 347–70. Available from DOI: 10.2307/2131346.
Entman, R.M. (1993) Framing: Toward clarification of a fractured paradigm. *Journal of Communication*. **43**(4), pp. 51–8. Available from DOI: 10.1111/j.1460-2466.1993.tb01304.x.
Euractiv (2020) Czech PM urges EU to ditch Green Deal amid virus. *EURACTIV*. Available from: https://www.euractiv.com/section/energy-environment/news/czech-pm-urges-eu-to-ditch-green-deal-amid-virus/ (accessed 2 April 2020).
European Environmental Agency (2018) Trends and projections in Europe 2018 Tracking progress towards Europe's climate and energy targets. EEA Report 16/2018. Available from: https://www.eea.europa.eu/publications/trends-and-projections-in-europe-2018-climate-and-energy.
European Environmental Agency (2019) Country profiles – greenhouse gases and energy 2019. *European Environment Agency*. Available from: https://www.eea.europa.eu/themes/climate/trends-and-projections-in-europe/climate-and-energy-country-profiles/copy_of_country-profiles-greenhouse-gases-and (accessed 24 March 2020).
Eurostat (2009) Climate change. Special Eurobarometer 322: Europeans' attitudes towards climate change. EU Open Data Portal. Available from: https://data.europa.eu/euodp/en/data/dataset/S703_72_1_EBS322.
Eurostat (2017) Climate change. Special Eurobarometer 459: Climate change. EU Open Data Portal. Available from: https://ec.europa.eu/clima/sites/clima/files/support/docs/report_2017_en.pdf.
Fagan, A. (2004) *Environment and Democracy in the Czech Republic: The Environmental Movement in the Transition Process*. 1st edn. Cheltenham, UK and Northampton, MA, USA: Edward Elgar Publishing.
Friel, H. (2010) *The Lomborg Deception: Setting the Record Straight about Global Warming*. New Haven, CT and London, UK: Yale University Press.
Geels, F.W. (2002) Technological transitions as evolutionary reconfiguration processes: A multi-level perspective and a case-study. *Research Policy*. **31**(8–9), pp. 1257–74. Available from DOI: 10.1016/S0048-7333(02)00062-8.
Geels, F.W. (2014) Regime resistance against low-carbon transitions: Introducing politics and power into the multi-level perspective. *Theory, Culture & Society*. **31**(5), pp. 21–40. Available from DOI: 10.1177/0263276414531627.
Greussing, E. and Boomgaarden, H.G. (2017) Shifting the refugee narrative? An automated frame analysis of Europe's 2015 refugee crisis. *Journal of Ethnic and Migration Studies*. **43**(11), pp. 1749–74. Available from DOI: 10.1080/1369183X.2017.1282813.
Grundmann, R. (2016) Climate change as a wicked social problem. *Nature Geoscience*. **9**(8), pp. 562–3. Available from DOI: 10.1038/ngeo2780.
Grundmann, R. and Scott, M. (2014) Disputed climate science in the media: Do countries matter? *Public Understanding of Science*. **23**(2), pp. 220–35. Available from DOI: 10.1177/0963662512467732.

Hanley, S. (1999) The new right in the new Europe? Unravelling the ideology of 'Czech Thatcherism'. *Journal of Political Ideologies*. **4**(2), pp. 163–89. Available from DOI: 10.1080/13569319908420794.

Hanzlová, R. (2019) Tisková zpráva: Postoje české veřejnosti ke změně klimatu na Zemi – říjen 2019. *Public Opinion Research Centre, Czech Academy of Sciences*. Available from: https://cvvm.soc.cas.cz/media/com_form2content/documents/c2/a5055/f9/oe191202.pdf (accessed 6 November 2020).

Hobson, K. and Niemeyer, S. (2012) 'What sceptics believe': The effects of information and deliberation on climate change scepticism. *Public Understanding of Science*. **22**(4), pp. 396–412. Available from DOI: 10.1177/0963662511430459.

Horta, A., Carvalho, A. and Schmidt, L. (2017) The hegemony of global politics: News coverage of climate change in a small country. *Society and Natural Resources*. **30**(10), pp. 1246–60. Available from DOI: 10.1080/08941920.2017.1295497.

Hluštík, D. and Černý, P. (2009) Al Gore se bál Klause, chlubí se Hrad. *Lidové noviny*. 5 March.

Jacques, P. (2006) The rearguard of modernity: Environmental skepticism as a struggle of citizenship. *Global Environmental Politics*. **6**(1), pp. 76–101. Available from DOI: 10.1162/glep.2006.6.1.76.

Kaiser, D. (2009) Sloupek Lidových novin. *Lidové noviny*. 21 July.

Kaiser, D. (2012) Sloupek Lidových novin. *Lidové noviny*. 22 January.

Kiousis, S. (2004) Explicating media salience: A factor analysis of *New York Times* issue coverage during the 2000 U.S. presidential election. *Journal of Communication*. **54**(1), pp. 71–87. Available from DOI: 10.1111/j.1460-2466.2004.tb02614.x.

Klaus, V. (2007) Modrá, nikoli zelená planeta. *Dokořán*. Available from: https://www.kosmas.cz/knihy/134393/modra-nikoli-zelena-planeta/ (accessed 26 March 2020).

Klaus, V. (2009) Úhel pohledu. *Lidové noviny*. 8 January.

Klaus, V. (2010) Zápisník z cest. *Právo*. 23 September.

Koopmans, R. (2002) *Codebook WP 2. Project: The Transformation of Political Mobilisation and Communication in European Public Spheres*. Work package: WP 2 (Content coding of claim-making) WP Coordinator: Ruud Koopmans Deliverable number: D 2.1. 5th Framework Programme at the European Commission. Available from: https://europub.wzb.eu/Data/Codebooks%20questionnaires/D2-1-claims-codebook.pdf (accessed 28 October 2019).

Koopmans, R. and Statham, P. (1999) Political claims analysis: Integrating protest event and political discourse approaches. *Mobilization: An International Journal*. **4**(1), pp. 203–21. Available from DOI: 10.17813/MAIQ.4.2.D7593370607L6756.

Krajhanzl, J., Chabada, T. and Svobodová, R. (2018) Vztah české veřejnosti k přírodě a životnímu prostředí. *Munispace – čítárna Masarykovy univerzity*. Masarykova univerzita.

Kukkonen, A. and Ylä-Anttila, T. (2020) The science–policy interface as a discourse network: Finland's Climate Change Policy 2002–2015. *Politics and Governance*. **8**(2), p. 200. Available from DOI: 10.17645/pag.v8i2.2603.

Lehotský, L. (2018) *Coal Mining and Climate Change in the Czech Republic: Two Cases of Media Narratives*. Masaryk University. Available from: https://is.muni.cz/th/hm81t/Lehotsky_dissertation_final.pdf (accessed 15 December 2018).

Lehotský, L., Černoch, F., Osička, J. and Ocelík, P. (2019) When climate change is missing: Media discourse on coal mining in the Czech Republic. *Energy Policy*. **129**, pp. 774–86. Available from DOI: 10.1016/j.enpol.2019.02.065.

Leifeld, P. (2013) Reconceptualizing major policy change in the advocacy coalition framework: A discourse network analysis of German pension politics. *Policy Studies Journal*. **41**(1), pp. 169–98. Available from DOI: 10.1111/psj.12007.

Leifeld, P. (2017) Discourse network analysis: Policy debates as dynamic networks. In: Victor, J.N., Montgomery, A.H. and Lubell, M.N. (eds) *The Oxford Handbook of Political Networks*. pp. 301–25. Available from DOI: 10.1093/oxfordhb/9780190228217.013.25.

Leifeld, P. (2019) Discourse network analyzer. Available from: http://github.com/leifeld/dna/.

Lijphart, A. (2012) *Patterns of Democracy: Government Forms and Performance in Thirty-six Countries*. New Haven, CT: Yale University Press.

Lockwood, M. (2018) Right-wing populism and the climate change agenda: Exploring the linkages. *Environmental Politics*. **27**(4), pp. 712–32. Available from DOI: 10.1080/09644016.2018.1458411.

Lomborg, B. (2001) *The Skeptical Environmentalist: Measuring the Real State of the Earth.* Cambridge: Cambridge University Press. Available from: http://www.cambridge.org/ch/knowledge/isbn/item1114451/The Skeptical Environmentalist/?site_locale=de_CH (accessed 2 April 2020).

Lomborg, B. (2007) *Cool it: The Skeptical Environmentalist's Guide to Global Warming.* New York, NY: Knopf.

Lomborg, B. (2009) Úhel pohledu. *Lidové noviny.* 21 January.

Martinek, J. (2015) Klimatolog Cílek: Je to teprve začátek. Do pohybu se mohou dát stamiliony. *Právo.* 7 November.

McCombs, M.E. (2004) *Setting the Agenda: Mass Media and Public Opinion.* 2nd edn. Polity.

McCombs, M.E. (2005) Look at agenda-setting: Past, present and future. *Journalism Studies.* **6**(4), pp. 543–57. Available from DOI: 10.1080/14616700500250438.

Myant, M. (2005) Klaus, Havel and the debate over civil society in the Czech Republic. *Journal of Communist Studies and Transition Politics.* **21**(2), pp. 248–67. Available from DOI: 10.1080/13523270500108758.

O'Neill, S.J. and Boykoff, M. (2010) Climate denier, skeptic, or contrarian? *Proceedings of the National Academy of Sciences of the United States of America.* National Academy of Sciences. **107**(39), pp. E151–E151. Available from DOI: 10.1073/pnas.1010507107.

Ocelík, P., Osička, J., Zapletalová, V., Černoch, F. and Dančák, B. (2017) Local opposition and acceptance of a deep geological repository of radioactive waste in the Czech Republic: A frame analysis. *Energy Policy.* **105**, pp. 458–66. Available from DOI: 10.1016/j.enpol.2017.03.025.

Ocelík, P. Svobodová, K., Hendrychová, M., Lehotský, L., Everingham, J.-A., Ali, Saleem, A., Badera, J. and Lechner, A. (2019) A contested transition toward a coal-free future: Advocacy coalitions and coal policy in the Czech Republic. *Energy Research & Social Science.* **58**, pp. 1–13. Available from DOI: 10.1016/J.ERSS.2019.101283.

Olausson, U. (2014) The diversified nature of 'domesticated' news discourse. *Journalism Studies.* **15**(6), pp. 711–25. Available from DOI: 10.1080/1461670X.2013.837253.

Oliver, P. and Johnston, H. (2000) What a good idea! Ideologies and frames in social movement research. *Mobilization: An International Quarterly.* **5**(1), pp. 37–54. Available from DOI: 10.17813/maiq.5.1.g54k222086346251.

Osička, J. and Černoch, F. (2017) Anatomy of a black sheep: The roots of the Czech Republic's pro-nuclear energy policy. *Energy Research & Social Science.* **27**, pp. 9–13. Available from DOI: 10.1016/J.ERSS.2017.02.006.

Painter, J. and Gavin, N.T. (2016) Climate skepticism in British newspapers, 2007–2011. *Environmental Communication.* **10**(4), pp. 432–52. Available from DOI: 10.1080/17524032.2014.995193.

Petráček, Z. (2018) Sloupek Lidových novin. *Lidové noviny.* 21 November.

Pidgeon, N. (2012) Climate change risk perception and communication: Addressing a critical moment? *Risk Analysis.* **32**(6), pp. 951–6. Available from DOI: 10.1111/j.1539-6924.2012.01856.x.

Pollack, H.N. (2003) *Uncertain Science ... Uncertain World.* Cambridge: Cambridge University Press.

Pontuso, J.F. (2002) Transformation politics: The debate between Václav Havel and Václav Klaus on the free market and civil society. *East European Thought.* **54**, pp. 153–77. Available from DOI: 10.1023/A:1015993401680.

Rovenský, J. (2009) Po Greenpeace zbyl na komíně transparent. *Mladá fronta Dnes.* 12 June.

Saxonberg, S. (1999) Václav Klaus: The rise and fall and re-emergence of a charismatic leader. *East European Politics and Societies.* **13**(2), pp. 391–416. Available from DOI: 10.1177/0888325499013002020.

Schäfer, M.S. and Schlichting, I. (2014) Media representations of climate change: A meta-analysis of the research field. *Environmental Communication.* **8**(2), pp. 142–60. Available from DOI: 10.1080/17524032.2014.914050.

Schmid-Petri, H., Adam, S., Schmucki, I. and Häussler, T. (2017) A changing climate of skepticism: The factors shaping climate change coverage in the US press. *Public Understanding of Science.* **26**(4), pp. 498–513. Available from DOI: 10.1177/0963662515612276.

Shanahan, E.A., Jones, M.D. and McBeth, M.K. (2011) Policy narratives and policy processes. *Policy Studies Journal.* **39**(3), pp. 535–61. Available from DOI: 10.1111/j.1541-0072.2011.00420.x.

Shriver, T.E. and Adams, A.E. (2013) Discursive obstruction and elite opposition discursive obstruction and elite opposition to environmental activism in the Czech Republic. *Social Forces*. **91**(3), pp. 873–93. Available from DOI: 10.1093/sf/sos183.

Stoddart, M.C.J. and Tindall, D.B. (2015) Canadian news media and the cultural dynamics of multilevel climate governance. *Environmental Politics*. **24**(3), pp. 401–22. Available from DOI: 10.1080/09644016.2015.1008249.

Stoddart, M.C.J., Haluza-DeLay, R. and Tindall, D.B. (2016) Canadian news media coverage of climate change: Historical trajectories, dominant frames, and international comparisons. *Society and Natural Resources*. **29**(2), pp. 218–32. Available from DOI: 10.1080/08941920.2015.1054569.

Stoddart, M.C.J., Tindall, D.B., Smith, J. and Haluza-DeLay, R. (2017) Media access and political efficacy in the eco-politics of climate change: Canadian national news and mediated policy networks. *Environmental Communication*. **11**(3), pp. 386–400. Available from DOI: 10.1080/17524032.2016.1275731.

Timm, K.M.F., Maibach, E.W., Boykoff, M., Myers, T.A. and Broekelman-Post, M.A. (2020) The prevalence and rationale for presenting an opposing viewpoint in climate change reporting: Findings from a U.S. national survey of TV weathercasters. *Weather, Climate, and Society*. **12**(1), pp. 103–15. Available from DOI: 10.1175/WCAS-D-19-0063.1.

Tosun, J. and Schaub, S. (2017) Mobilization in the European public sphere: The struggle over genetically modified organisms. *Review of Policy Research*. **34**(3), pp. 310–30. Available from DOI: 10.1111/ropr.12235.

Tranter, B. (2017) It's only natural: Conservatives and climate change in Australia. *Environmental Sociology*. Routledge. **3**(3), pp. 274–85. Available from DOI: 10.1080/23251042.2017.1310966.

Trumbo, C. (1996) Constructing climate change: Claims and frames in US news coverage of an environmental issue. *Public Understanding of Science*. **5**(3), pp. 269–83.

Van Eck, C.W., Mulder, B.C. and Dewulf, A. (2019) 'The truth is not in the middle': Journalistic norms of climate change bloggers. Available from DOI: 10.1016/j.gloenvcha.2019.101989.

Van Gorp, B. (2007) The constructionist approach to framing: Bringing culture back in. *Journal of Communication*. **57**(1), pp. 60–78. Available from DOI: 10.1111/j.0021-9916.2007.00329.x.

Van Rensburg, W. and Head, B.W. (2017) Climate change sceptical frames: The case of seven Australian sceptics. *Australian Journal of Politics & History*. **63**(1), pp. 112–28. Available from DOI: 10.1111/ajph.12318.

Vávra, J., Lapka, M., Dvořáková-Líšková, Z. and Cudlínová, E. (2013) Obraz změn klimatu v českých denících v letech 1997–2010. *AUC Philosophica Et Historica*. **2013**(2), pp. 9–33. Available from DOI: 10.14712/24647055.2014.1.

Vesa, J., Gronow, A. and Ylä-Anttila, T. (2020) The quiet opposition: How the pro-economy lobby influences climate policy. *Global Environmental Change*. Available from: https://researchportal.helsinki.fi/en/publications/the-quiet-opposition-how-the-pro-economy-lobby-influences-climate (accessed 13 July 2020).

Vidomus, P. (2011) Kontrahnutí v perspektivách sociologie sociálních hnutí. *Czech Sociological Review*. **48**(2), pp. 325–59.

Vidomus, P. (2013) Climate scepticism in the Czech Republic: An introduction. *Sociální Studia*. **10**(1), pp. 95–127.

Vidomus, P. (2018) *Oteplí se a bude líp: Česká klimaskepse v čase globálních rizik – Petr Vidomus | KOSMAS.cz - vaše internetové knihkupectví*. Kosmas. Available from: https://www.kosmas.cz/knihy/240774/otepli-se-a-bude-lip-ceska-klimaskepse-v-case-globalnich-rizik/ (accessed 15 December 2018).

Vlček, T. and Černoch, F. (2019) *The Energy Sector and Energy Policy of the Czech Republic*. 2nd edn. Masaryk University Press.

Volek, J. and Urbániková, M. (2017) Čeští novináři v komparativní perspektivě [Czech journalists in comparative perspective]. Available from: https://www.kosmas.cz/knihy/237421/cesti-novinari-v-komparativni-perspektive/ (accessed 26 January 2020).

Wagner, P.M. and Payne, D. (2017) Trends, frames and discourse networks: Analysing the coverage of climate change in Irish newspapers. *Irish Journal of Sociology*. **25**(1), pp. 5–28. Available from DOI: 10.7227/IJS.0011.

Wagner, P.M., Ylä-Anttila, T., Gronow, A., Ocelík, P., Schmidt, L. and Delicado, A. (2020) Information exchange networks at the climate science–policy interface: Evidence from the Czech Republic, Finland, Ireland, and Portugal. *Governance*. Available from DOI: 10.1111/gove.12484.

Weiss, M. (2009) Úhel pohledu. *Lidové noviny*, 19 February.

White, D.F., Rudy, A.P. and Wilbert, C. (2012) Anti-environmentalism: Prometheans, contrarians and beyond. In: Pretty, J., Ball, A., Benton, T., Guivant, J., Lee, D.R., Orr, D., Pfeffer, M. et al. (eds) *The SAGE Handbook of Environment and Society*. Los Angeles, CA: SAGE, pp. 124–41. Available from DOI: 10.4135/9781848607873.n8.

Ylä-Anttila, T., Vesa, J., Eranti, V., Kukkonen, A., Lehtimäki, T., Lonkila, M. and Luhtakallio, E. (2018) Up with ecology, down with economy? The consolidation of the idea of climate change mitigation in the global public sphere. *European Journal of Communication*. **33**(6), pp. 587–603. Available from DOI: 10.1177/0267323118790155.

Zeman, M. (2019) Vánoční poselství prezidenta republiky Miloše Zemana. Available from: https://www.hrad.cz/cs/video/vanocni-poselstvi-prezidenta-republiky-milose-zemana-15226.

Zvěřinová, I., Ščasný, M., Czajkowski, M. and Kyselá, E. (2016) Výzkum preferencí obyvatel pro klimatické politiky. Institute for Democracy and Economic Analysis. Available from: https://idea.cerge-ei.cz/files/IDEA_Studie_20_2016_Preference_klimatickych_politik.pdf (accessed 24 March 2020).

PART IV

VALUES, ATTITUDES AND PUBLIC OPINION

6. Understanding opposition to the environmental movement: the importance of dominant American values

Riley E. Dunlap

PREFACE TO CHAPTER 6

This chapter was written in 1976, when I was at Washington State University (WSU), and presented at the Annual Meeting of the Society for the Study of Social Problems (SSSP) that year. I want to explain why it is being included in this volume with only a small number of editorial improvements. The first is personal, while the second is the historical perspective on American environmentalism and anti-environmentalism it contributes to this volume.

In terms of the first reason, I submitted the paper to a top journal some time after the SSSP meeting and it was not accepted. About that time I began a collaboration with my WSU colleague the late William R. Catton, Jr on a series of papers aimed at defining, justifying and helping establish a field of 'environmental sociology', and put this paper aside for a while. I eventually resubmitted it to another journal and received a very encouraging revise-and-resubmit. Unfortunately, by then I was suffering from severe clinical depression, and even a simple revision was more than I could handle. Later on I felt the paper needed extensive updating and reluctantly filed it away, as I have done with a number of papers when struggling with bouts of depression during my career. But not publishing this particular paper always troubled me. The work I invested in understanding values and investigating 'American values' ended up being a crucial link in the progression of my early intellectual interests in partisan cleavages in support for environmentalism (Dunlap and Gale, 1974) to an examination of American values to an effort to formulate and operationalize the 'dominant social paradigm' and an emerging 'new environmental paradigm' within our society (Dunlap and Van Liere, 1978, 1984). The latter in turn fed into Catton's and my development of the paradigmatic nature of the emerging field of environmental sociology (Catton and Dunlap, 1978, 1980). I am happy to have an opportunity, however belatedly, to publish this paper.

The second and more important reason for including this chapter is that, despite being so dated, my co-editors and I feel it provides insights into the goals and strategies of the early US environmental movement and the growth of opposition in the form of a nascent anti-environmental counter-movement—a force that has grown far more powerful during recent decades as it has gained increasing support from various waves of rising conservatism.

I drew heavily on the second edition of Turner and Killian's influential text, *Collective Behavior* published in 1972, when social movements were seen as a special type of collective behavior, and the role of movements' goals and values and resulting value conflict with the larger society were key topics (besides Turner and Killian, 1972, see Smelser, 1962). But about this time the study of 'social movements' as a distinct phenomenon, spurred by the Civil Rights, Anti-Vietnam, Student Power, and Feminist movements (among others), was gaining momentum and an intellectual revolution occurred via a series of new theoretical perspectives. In fairly quick succession resource mobilization, political opportunities and opportunity structure, and framing processes emerged and became leading theoretical perspectives on social movements, especially in the USA (McAdam et al., 1996). The first two in particular gave more attention to 'counter-movements', or organized efforts to oppose the goals of social movements (although Turner and Killian, 1972 did discuss them briefly), and what I was analyzing in the chapter were preliminary efforts to mount an 'anti-environmental counter-movement'.

Opposition to environmentalism was scattered and often led by the business community, and had not yet congealed into a counter-movement, in the early 1970s. The first sign of *organized* opposition, the Western states-based 'Sagebrush Revolution' aimed at opening up public lands for private resource use, was just emerging and only developed an organizational base in the late 1970s. It was followed in the late 1980s by its broader but still Western-based successor—the 'Wise Use Movement'—promoting resource use over preservation (Switzer, 1997). Thus, the rich literature on counter-movements, stimulated by McCarthy and Zald's resource mobilization theory (1977) and various strands of political opportunity theory (e.g., McAdam, 1982), and maturing into a full-fledged theory of counter-movements with Meyer and Staggenborg (1996; also see their chapter in this volume, which updates their theory), was not yet available. The latter theory clarifies why a range of efforts—even if not highly organized—to counter the environmental movement were emerging, as opposition is likely to appear when a social movement shows signs of success, its goals are perceived as a threat, and political allies are available to assist with mobilizing efforts against it (Meyer and Staggenborg, 1996). The first two were quickly apparent in the early 1970s, while the third evolved more slowly (with backing from corporations and many Republicans) but became a major factor with the election of Ronald Reagan in 1980.

The third theoretical perspective, framing processes (e.g. Snow et al., 1986), would have been even more useful in writing the chapter, since I was basically analyzing how opponents of the environmental movement were trying to portray or frame it as a major threat to cherished American values (as noted in the conclusion). This was early evidence of an emerging 'framing contest' that in retrospect we know is typical of social movements and their opponents (McAdam et al., 1996). Environmentalists framed their goals as solving environmental problems in order to protect environmental quality and a habitable environment, while their opposition framed these goals as threats to individual rights, private property, a laissez-faire economy, economic growth and progress—values traditionally important to Americans. We have witnessed numerous permutations of these framing contests in the ensuing decades, especially as global-level problems (most notably human-caused climate change) have emerged. Efforts to ameliorate them have been labeled as threats to the above-noted values, plus national sovereignty and the 'American way of life' writ large, by the Conservative Movement (Rowell, 1996; also see Helvarg, 1994). By the 1990s the Conservative Movement became—with the backing of corporate America—the primary force (followed by the Republican Party) behind anti-environmentalism (Jacques et al., 2008; McCright and Dunlap, 2000).

What I did not foresee in 1976, and which few if any social scientists recognized, was the depth and breadth of the 'conservative revolution' that was about to bring fundamental changes to the US (and many other nations). Numerous conservative think tanks, most notably the Heritage Foundation, were established in the 1970s and 1980s in response to the progressive movements of the 1960s and 1970s. These social movement organizations and the broader Conservative Movement served as a general or umbrella counter-movement (Lo, 1982), spawning efforts to combat not only environmental regulations but welfare programs, affirmative action, women's rights and other progressive causes (Stefancic and Delgado, 1996). Rather than just renewing historical strands of conservative and right-wing thinking in the US, this new conservatism also had roots in European 'neo-liberalism' (formulated by Friedrich Hayek, Ludwig von Mises and others) that was imported to the US, the UK and other nations by intellectual entrepreneurs and their wealthy supporters and planted in think tanks and many universities (Jones, 2012). Neo-liberal (or free-market) thinking came to the fore with Reagan in the US and Thatcher in the UK, both of whom enacted neo-liberal policies such as tax cuts, deregulation and privatization along with major reductions in welfare and other social programs designed to help disadvantaged sectors of society (Hoover, 1987).

This ideologically based (in neo-liberal, free-market ideology) strand of conservatism was joined with a wide range of other socio-cultural causes such as opposition to abortion and gay rights pushed by the Religious Right and other interests to create a broader and more powerful, if less ideologically coherent, Conservative Movement (Diamond, 1995). It was helped immensely by the growth of talk radio (after the 'fairness doctrine' was abolished toward the end of the Reagan Administration), birth of Fox News and then right-wing websites like Breitbart (Jamieson and Cappella, 2008). Conservative commentators such as Rush Limbaugh attacked progressives and their causes viciously, and a key indicator of their success is that their frequently used pejorative labels like 'eco-freaks' and 'environazis' diffused into the larger society (Rowell, 1996), turning 'environmentalist' from a positive term into a negative one in many sectors (just as they have done with feminism, by popularizing slurs like 'feminazis'). A good indicator of their success is reflected in Gallup trend data on an item asking, 'Do you consider yourself an environmentalist or not?' In three polls conducted between 1989 and 1991 an average of 76 percent of US adults said 'yes', but the trend turned downward throughout the 1990s (when the conservative movement made anti-environmentalism a key element of its agenda and conservative media were becoming more influential) and stood at only 42 percent in 2016 (Jones, 2018). A more significant impact of the conservative assault on environmentalism has been a huge increase in political polarization over environmental protection policies, among both political elites (e.g., members of Congress) and the general public, with Republicans and conservatives becoming less supportive and increasingly opposed to such policies—resulting in a major chasm between the two political camps (McCright et al., 2014).

In short, anti-environmentalism has become a far more powerful force, rooted in a neo-liberal ideology that is hostile to environmental protection and other efforts that impinge upon individual and corporate 'rights' (Antonio and Brulle, 2011), than I could have foreseen in the mid-1970s. In fact, in an era of hegemonic neo-liberalism (Brown, 2015), and joined by the recent faux-populist rage at government in general fomented by politicians like Trump, anti-environmentalism and resulting political polarization make the development, implementation and enforcement of environmental regulations nearly impossible in the US (Hejny, 2018). Anti-environmentalism is also more complex and diverse, especially across local, regional and national contexts, as the chapters in this volume illustrate. Nonetheless, I believe that the following chapter can offer some valuable insights to the evolution of the US environmental movement and its opposition over the past four-plus decades, as well as to the spread of anti-environmentalism to many other nations (Rowell, 1996; also see Chapter 5 by Ocelík in this volume).

After focusing on the goals (or values) and major strategies of early environmentalism, I developed a typology (in Figure 6.1 of the chapter) consisting of a 'major goal' dimension (normative change versus value change) and 'predominant strategy' dimension (personal transformation versus societal manipulation).[1] I think the typology, which results in four 'ideal types' of environmentalists—meliorists, reformists, alternativists and transformationists—remains useful for analyzing environmentalism and its evolution over the years.[2] Meliorists seek normative change via personal transformation, like energy conservation and green consumption, while reformists try to change social norms via societal manipulation such as supporting pro-environmental politicians, lobbying for new regulations and pressuring corporations to replace harmful products. Alternativists also emphasize personal transformation but in pursuit of deeper value change, and engage in voluntary simplicity lifestyles, living 'off the grid' and getting back to nature. Finally, transformationists aim for value change via societal manipulation, pursuing societal changes like transitioning from fossil fuels to a renewable energy-based and sustainable society via legislation, taxes, boycotts, protests, and so on.

In 1976 I suggested that the environmental movement was shifting from an emphasis on normative to value change as its fundamental goal, and from personal transformation to societal manipulation as its primary strategy, and I still think that was the case. However, the election of Ronald Reagan was a huge negative shift in the political opportunity structure (POS) from the generally pro-environmental Jimmy Carter administration, which had institutionalized environmentalism via its appointment of numerous environmental leaders to administrative positions but was hampered by energy and economic problems (Layzer, 2012). Reagan's reversal led the movement to renew an emphasis on lobbying, legal action, mobilizing public opinion and other efforts to protect environmental regulations—a strong reformist orientation that helped curtail Reagan's and Bush Sr's anti-environmental agendas to some degree (Layzer, 2012; Turner and Isenberg, 2018). Environmentalism built momentum throughout the 1980s by emphasizing the Reagan Administration's threat to environmental protection (Dunlap, 1987), and was strengthened considerably by the growth of local, grass-roots and environmental justice groups that added more diversity to the movement (Dunlap and Mertig, 1992). At the national level 'green consumerism' and other meliorist actions once again became popular (with corporate encouragement), leading to large celebrations of the 20th Earth Day and an all-time high in the public's expression of pro-environmental views during 1990 and 1991 (Dunlap, 1992).

The Reagan and Bush Sr administrations' anti-environmental stances demonstrated the dramatic effect that changes in the POS have had on the environmental movement—in this case stimulating more activism and public support for environmental protection, but by no means successfully curtailing the two administrations' weakening enforcement of existing environmental regulations and opposition to enacting new ones (Layzer, 2012; Turner and Isenberg, 2018). The next Republican Administration, Bush Jr, instituted far more aggressive efforts to undermine environmental protection programs, but due to 9/11 and the resulting national focus on terrorism, environmentalists had less success in countering them (Layzer, 2012). And, of course, the Trump Administration's disregard and outright hostility toward environmental protection (especially climate change mitigation) has made the Reagan/Bush Sr and even Bush Jr efforts seem modest in comparison (Turner and Isenberg, 2018)—but with little effective push-back from environmentalists (due to the growing de-legitimization of environmentalists noted earlier). This overall trend reflects the transition of the Republican Party from a conservative to a truly right-wing party, with outright antipathy toward environmental regulations and environmental protection writ large (Mann and Ornstein, 2016; Chinoy, 2019).

Unfortunately, the two 'positive' shifts in the POS brought about by the Clinton/Gore and Obama Administrations did not come close to counteracting the negative impacts of their respective Reagan/Bush Sr and Bush Jr predecessors. Clinton was committed to economic growth and largely accepted the growing neo-liberal emphasis on de-regulation to help foster it, leading his administration to adopt a 'green growth' strategy. This, in conjunction with increased Congressional opposition following the 1994 GOP capture of the House of Representatives, led Clinton to compromise his (and his VP Al Gore's) pro-environmental agenda (Nie, 1997; Layzer, 2012). Later, the Obama Administration got off to a disappointing start in the environmental realm, partly attributed to his Chief of Staff Rahm Emanuel's dismissal of the political importance of environmental and climate-change issues early on (Kincaid and Roberts, 2013), and then was hampered by intensified Republican opposition in Congress following large Democratic losses in the 2010 election. While Obama did eventually take many pro-environmental actions later in his administration, especially concerning climate change, Republican control of Congress necessitated relying on Executive Actions—many of which were quickly dismantled by the Trump Administration (Turner and Isenberg, 2018).

I have noted these shifts in the POS because they have been major factors affecting the environmental movement and its opposition over the past four decades. Of special importance is that the Republican Party has become a crucial component of the anti-environmental counter-movement, ensuring that the latter's concerns are institutionalized within the highest levels of government when they are in power (Dunlap and McCright, 2015; Hejny, 2018), while environmentalists are pushed out (and do not regain insider status effectively in recent Democratic administrations). Furthermore, Republican control of one or both houses of Congress has put a huge damper on environmental legislation, with their proposals being to weaken or end current regulations rather than strengthen or update them—continually putting environmentalists and Democrats on the defensive (Layzer, 2012; Turner and Isenberg, 2018).[3]

These increasingly dramatic shifts in the POS and Republicans' embrace of anti-environmentalism have clearly affected the goals and strategies of environmentalists over the decades. In addition, the growth of environmental justice and other grassroots campaigns from local to global levels and the recent birth of a youth-driven 'climate movement' have made contemporary environmentalism far more diverse than in the early 1970s when the movement was dominated by major national organizations like the Sierra Club (Mitchell et al., 1992). All of this makes it impossible to trace the evolving goals and strategies of environmentalists in a short space; indeed it would warrant book-length treatment. So let me just highlight a few highly significant changes to demonstrate the continuing utility of the typology presented in the following chapter.

Early efforts to bring about deep value change with a steady-state or sustainable society via structural changes requiring societal manipulation strategies lost momentum during the Reagan years with his rejection of any notion of 'limits' on humans and economic-driven growth specifically (Dunlap and McCright, 2015). But over the years it has resurfaced in a variety of permutations. Perhaps most visible at present is the 'Green New Deal' being pushed by progressive Democrats and environmentalists (Galvin and Healey, 2020), along with widespread endorsement of the need for 'radical change' in our current economic system among young climate change activists (Beer, 2020). These 'transformationists' are clearly pushing for a major value change and accompanying social-structural changes. Deep value change is also the goal of a variety of alternativists, from serious efforts to achieve simpler, self-reliant lifestyles to establishing a 'new economy' (both of which have a strong personal transformation orientation) (Schor and Thompson, 2014).

Of course, those content with normative change continue to be active, including reformists such as many environmental organizations—most notably the League of Conservation Voters—supporting pro-environmental candidates and lobbying Congress and state legislatures, boycotting harmful products and targeting corporations with poor environmental records, and much more. Likewise, various forms of green consumption continue to be very popular as meliorists shop for green products and make modest changes in lifestyle such as trying to conserve energy and shifting to renewable energy when possible. While some think these activities may provide a 'gateway' for meliorists to start engaging in more reformist activities like becoming active in environmental organizations and taking political actions, others suggest green consumerism may discourage activism (Szasz, 2007).

I hope these brief observations illustrate the continuing utility of the typology, and want to close by suggesting how it could be used in future research—as well as its critical limitation in today's world. One could clearly provide a more detailed analysis of the evolution of the entire US environmental movement over the past half century via the typology, but it would be much more manageable for purposes such as these: (1) examining the goals and strategies of major strands of environmentalism such as the Environmental Justice movement or the recent climate change movement over time; (2) comparing one or more of these strands with those of the mainstream national organizations; (3) comparing two or more specific organizations within differing strands; and (4) making cross-national comparisons along any of the above lines.

In addition, it should be helpful in tracking changes in anti-environmentalism, as we know that counter-movements alter strategies and modify goals in response to shifts within the movement they are opposing. Depending on the environmental reform proposal being put forth, who is supporting it, and how far it has progressed in the political arena, anti-environmentalists may employ PR campaigns, mobilize astroturf and front groups, engage in political lobbying, constantly attack evidence presented by its sponsors, and use many more modes of obstruction (Brulle and Aronczyk, 2019). Should environmentalists push truly transformative efforts like the Green New Deal, they are likely to encounter opposition from a wide range of actors using the full repertoire of strategies and tactics developed over decades (Seidman, 2019).

These shifts in strategies and tactics are often most readily visible in the evolution of framing contests, as anti-environmentalists quickly shift their rhetoric in reaction to changes in environmentalists' strategies and goals, and both movements shift emphases in response to changes in the political opportunity structure. In terms of the latter, the fortunes of the two movements have been affected by the embracement of hegemonic neo-liberalism throughout much of the world (negatively for environmentalism, positively for anti-environmentalism), but with considerable variation among nations, thus calling for more cross-national comparisons of its effects.

At the same time, it is important to recognize that anti-environmentalism has become so strong and often institutionalized in much of the 'developed' world and especially within 'less-developed nations', that tactics like framing environmentalism negatively have increasingly escalated into outright suppression—often by violent means. In the US, for example, the federal government sometimes labels environmental activists as 'eco-terrorists' posing a significant domestic threat, and joins forces with local and state law enforcement agencies and corporate security forces to violently suppress activists protesting against projects like the Dakota Access Pipeline running near the Standing Rock Sioux Reservation in North Dakota (Hasler et al., 2019). Also, instances of violent repression (including murders) of grassroots environmentalists worldwide, particularly in Latin American and Asia, are occurring with alarming frequency as a result of their opposition to profit-driven ecological destruction that threatens their livelihoods, lifestyles and basic survival (Poulos and Haddad, 2016; Rasch, 2017). Although such violent suppression of environmentalists is not new (Helvarg, 1994; Rowell, 1996), it appears to be ever more common in a world driven by the quest for endless growth above all else (Lynch et al., 2018)—something that I and other commentators on the Environmental Movement certainly did not foresee in the early 1970s.

NOTES

1. I explain in the chapter that these labels were used in order to be compatible with the perspectives I was drawing on, but in retrospect wish I had used 'power vs. participation' as labels for the two primary strategies and perhaps 'normative vs. structural change' as labels for the two basic goals since these terms might be more descriptive and easily understood.
2. It is obviously possible to distinguish among a greater variety of environmentalists (see, e.g, Schnaiberg and Gould, 1994), especially as the movement has become increasingly diversified, but these four were adequate for capturing major differences in goals and strategies in combination.
3. This is most apparent in the case of climate change, where the GOP has become a central cog in the 'denial machine' (Dunlap and McCright, 2015).

REFERENCES FOR PREFACE

Antonio, R.J. and Brulle, R.J. (2011) The unbearable lightness of politics: Climate change denial and political polarization. *Sociological Quarterly*. **52**, pp. 195–202.
Beer, C.T. (2020) 'Systems change not climate change': Support for a radical shift away from capitalism at mainstream U.S. climate change protest events. *Sociological Quarterly*. Available from DOI: 10.1080/00380253.2020.1842141.
Brown, W. (2015) *Undoing the Demos: Neoliberalism's Stealth Revolution*. Brooklyn, NY: Zone Books.
Brulle, R.J. and Aronczyk, M. (2019) Organized opposition to climate change action in the United States. In: Kalfagianni, A., Fuchs, D. and Hayden, A. (eds) *Routledge Handbook of Global Sustainability Governance*. New York, NY: Routledge, pp. 218–29.
Catton, W.R. and Dunlap, R.E. (1978) Environmental sociology: A new paradigm. *The American Sociologist*. **13**, pp. 41–9.
Catton, W.R. and Dunlap, R.E. (1980) A new ecological paradigm for post-exuberant sociology. *American Behavioral Scientist*. **24**, pp. 15–47.
Chinoy, S. (2019) What happened to America's political center of gravity? *New York Times*. Available from: https://www.nytimes.com/interactive/2019/06/26/opinion/sunday/republican-platform-far-right.html.
Diamond, S. (1995) *Roads to Dominion: Right-wing Movements and Political Power in the United States*. New York, NY: Guilford Press.
Dunlap, R.E. (1987) Polls, pollution, and politics revisited: Public opinion on the environment in the Reagan era. *Environment*. **29**(July/August), 6–11, pp. 32–7.
Dunlap, R.E. (1992) Trends in public opinion toward environmental issues, 1965–1990. In Dunlap, R.E. and Mertig, A.G. (eds) *American Environmentalism: The U.S. Environmental Movement, 1970–1990*. Washington, DC: Taylor and Francis, pp. 89–116.
Dunlap, R.E. and Gale, R.P. (1974) Party membership and environmental politics: A legislative roll-call analysis. *Social Science Quarterly*. **55**, pp. 670–90.

Dunlap, R.E. and Mertig, A.G. (eds) (1992) *American Environmentalism: The U.S. Environmental Movement, 1970–1990*. Washington, DC: Taylor and Francis.

Dunlap, R.E. and McCright, A.M. (2015) Challenging climate change: The denial countermovement. In Dunlap, R.E. and Brulle, R.J. (eds) *Climate Change and Society: Sociological Perspectives*. New York, NY: Oxford University Press, pp. 300–332.

Dunlap, R.E. and Van Liere, K.D. (1978) The 'new environmental paradigm': A proposed measuring instrument and preliminary results. *Journal of Environmental Education*. **9**(4), pp. 10–19.

Dunlap, R.E. and Van Liere, K.D. (1984) Commitment to the dominant social paradigm and concern for environmental quality. *Social Science Quarterly*. **65**, pp. 1013–28.

Galvin, R. and Healey, N. (2020) The green new deal in the United States. *Energy Research & Social Science*. **67**. Available from DOI: 10.1016/j.erss.2020.101529.

Hasler, O., Walters, R. and White, R. (2019) In and against the state: The dynamics of environmental activism. *Critical Criminology*. **28**, pp. 517–31.

Hejny. J. (2018) The Trump Administration and environmental policy: Reagan redux. *Journal of Environmental Studies and Sciences*. **8**, pp. 197–211.

Helvarg, D. (1994) *The War Against the Greens*. San Francisco, CA: Sierra Club Books.

Hoover, K.R. (1987) The rise of conservative capitalism: Ideological tensions within the Reagan and Thatcher governments. *Comparative Studies in Society and History*. **29**, pp. 245–68.

Jacques, P.J., Dunlap, R.E. and Freeman, M. (2008) The organization of denial: Conservative think tanks and environmental scepticism. *Environmental Politics*. **17**, pp. 349–85.

Jamieson, K.H. and Cappella, J.N. (2008) *Echo Chamber: Rush Limbaugh and the Conservative Media Establishment*. New York, NY: Oxford University Press.

Jones, D.S. (2012) *Masters of the Universe: Hayek, Friedman, and the Birth of Neoliberal Politics*. Princeton, NJ: Princeton University Press.

Jones, J.M. (2018) Confidence in higher education down since 2015. *Gallup Poll*. Available from: https://news.gallup.com/opinion/gallup/242441/confidence-higher-education-down-2015.aspx?version=print.

Kincaid, G. and Roberts, J.T. (2013) No talk, some walk: Obama Administration's first-term rhetoric on climate change and US international climate budget commitments. *Global Environmental Politics*. **13**(4), pp. 41–60.

Layzer, J.A. (2012) *Open for Business: Conservatives' Opposition to Environmental Regulation*. Cambridge, MA: MIT Press.

Lo, C.Y.H. (1982) Countermovements and conservative movements in the contemporary U.S. *Annual Review of Sociology*. **8**, pp. 107–34.

Lynch, M., Stretesky, P.B. and Long, M.A. (2018) Green criminology and native peoples: The treadmill of production and the killing of indigenous environmental activists. *Theoretical Criminology*. **22**(3), pp. 318–41.

Mann, T.E. and Ornstein, N.J. (2016 [2012]) *It's Even Worse Than It Was* (new and expanded edn). New York: Basic Books.

McAdam, D. (1982) *Political Process and the Development of Black Insurgency, 1930–1970*. Chicago, IL: University of Chicago Press.

McAdam, D., McCarthy, J.D. and Zald, M.N. (eds) (1996) *Comparative Perspectives on Social Movements*. Cambridge: Cambridge University Press.

McCarthy, J.D. and Zald, M.N. (1977) Resource mobilization and social movements: A partial theory. *American Journal of Sociology*. **86**, pp. 1214–41.

McCright, A.M. and Dunlap, R.E. (2000) Challenging global warming as a social problem: An analysis of the conservative movement's counter claims. *Social Problems*. **47**, pp. 499–522.

McCright, A.M., Dunlap, R.E. and Xiao, C. (2014) Political polarization on support for government spending on environmental protection in the USA, 1974–2012. *Social Science Research*. **48**, pp. 251–60.

Meyer, D.S. and Staggenborg, S. (1996) Movements, countermovements, and the structure of political opportunity. *American Journal of Sociology*. **101**, pp. 1628–60.

Mitchell, R.C., Mertig, A.G. and Dunlap, R.E. (1992) Twenty years of environmental mobilization: Trends among national environmental organizations. In Dunlap, R.E. and Mertig, A.G. (eds)

American Environmentalism: The U.S. Environmental Movement, 1970–1990. Washington, DC: Taylor and Francis, pp. 11–26.

Nie, M.A. (1997) 'It's the environment, stupid!' Clinton and the environment. *Presidential Studies Quarterly*. **72**, pp. 39–51.

Poulos, H.M. and Haddad, M.A. (2016) Violent repression of environmental protests. *SpringerPlus*. **5**, p. 230. Available from DOI: 10.1186/s40064-016-1816-2.

Rasch, E.D. (2017) Citizens, criminalization and violence in natural resource conflicts in Latin America. *European Review of Latin American and Caribbean Studies*. **103**, p. 1310142.

Rowell, A. (1996) *Green Backlash: Global Subversion of the Environmental Movement*. London, UK and New York, NY, USA: Routledge.

Schnaiberg, A and Gould, K.A. (1994) *Environment and Society: The Enduring Conflict*. New York, NY: St. Martin's.

Schor, J.B. and Thompson, C.C. (eds) (2014) *Sustainable Lifestyles and the Quest for Plentitude*. New Haven, CT: Yale University Press.

Seidman, D. (2019) *The Anti-new Deal Coalition*. Buffalo, NY: Public Accountability Coalition. Available from: https://public-accountability.org/report/the-anti-green-new-deal-coalition/.

Smelser, N.J. (1962) *Collective Behavior*. New York, NY: Free Press.

Snow, D.A., Rochford, B., Worden, S.K. and Benford, R.D. (1986) Frame alignment processes, micro-mobilization, and movement participation. *American Sociological Review*. **51**, pp. 464–81.

Stefancic, J. and Delgado, R. (1996) *No Mercy: How Conservative Think Tanks and Foundations Changed America's Social Agenda*. Philadelphia, PA: Temple University Press.

Switzer, J.V. (1997) *Green Backlash: The History and Politics of Environmental Opposition in the U.S.* Boulder, CO: Lynne Rienner Publishers.

Szasz, A. (2007) *Shopping Our Way to Safety*. Minneapolis, MN: University of Minnesota Press.

Turner, J.M. and Isenberg, A.C. (2018) *The Republican Reversal: Conservatives and the Environment from Nixon to Trump*. Cambridge, MA: MIT Press.

Turner, R.H. and Killian, L.M. (1972) *Collective Behavior*. 2nd edn. Englewood Cliffs, NJ: Prentice-Hall.

UNDERSTANDING OPPOSITION TO THE ENVIRONMENTAL MOVEMENT: THE IMPORTANCE OF DOMINANT AMERICAN VALUES

When the Environmental Movement dramatically emerged upon the national scene with the celebration of the first Earth Day (22 April 1970),[1] there was widespread belief that it would quickly succeed in achieving its goal of 'environmental quality'. Surely, it was argued, no one could be opposed to cleaning up the environment, for 'Polluted air and reeking rivers ... affect everyone' (Janssen, 1970, p. 54). So 'consensual' was the issue of 'saving the environment' that one commentator argued, 'Alarm over the environment has created a kind of "new politics" that transcends traditional party or ideological leanings. Even members of the John Birch Society and the S.D.S. [Students for a Democratic Society] can agree that clean air and water are desirable' (Main, 1971, p. 312). Such views gave credence to optimistic projections that, once informed of the seriousness of the environmental threat, Americans would take prompt and meaningful actions to solve environmental problems (see, e.g., Jordan and Deans, 1970, p. 59).

There is considerable evidence that the public quickly came to define environmental problems as serious and profess support for their solution (see, e.g., Albrecht and Mauss, 1975, pp. 567–73; Erskine, 1972), and politicians such as President Richard Nixon eagerly jumped aboard the 'environmental bandwagon'. However, the initial sense of optimism concerning the solution of our environmental problems faded rather rapidly. Quick solutions to the problems have not been forthcoming, and despite an impressive amount of citizen and government action as well as undeniable instances of air and water pollution abatement, it appears that the overall magnitude of environmental degradation continues to increase (see, e.g., National Wildlife Federation, 1976). While a variety of factors have contributed to our society's failure to make significant progress in halting environmental abuse,[2] a crucial factor is that the original 'consensus' surrounding the issue of protecting the environment has rapidly disappeared. Not only has public support for environmental quality declined significantly (see Buttel, 1975; Dunlap and Dillman, 1976), but a substantial amount of organized opposition to the Environmental Movement has developed (see, e.g., Albrecht, 1972; Morrison, 1973). The basic goal of this paper is to contribute to a fuller understanding of the demise of environmental quality as a consensus issue—specifically, the highly interrelated decline in public support for and rise of organized opposition to environmental reforms.[3]

Several analysts have recently called attention to the Environmental Movement's declining support and rising opposition, and their explanations of these phenomena have generally stressed the importance of economic factors—that is, the 'costs' of achieving environmental quality. For example, pollution control is expensive, and the costs must be borne either by industry or by consumers. Likewise, environmental regulations occasionally threaten existing industries and jobs, and may also thwart the development of new industries and employment opportunities. Further, environmental protection may entail shifts in limited governmental resources, thus diverting funds from other programs. Finally, the increasingly mentioned necessity of slowing down economic growth in order to effectively combat environmental degradation (e.g., Daly, 1973; Meadows et al., 1972) may pose the most severe cost of all, since traditionally such growth has resulted in material benefits for nearly all segments of our society. Economic factors such as these have been used to explain both the declining support for environmental protection among the general public,[4] and the increased hostility and opposition to environmentalists from numerous segments of society including industrialists, communities and regions seeking economic 'development', politicians, and blue collar workers and unions (e.g., Albrecht, 1972; Buttel, 1975; Kohl, 1975; Morrison, 1973; and Schnaiberg, 1973, pp. 617–21).

While analyses emphasizing the role of economic self-interest are crucial to understanding reactions to the Environmental Movement, they are not sufficient.[5] Specifically, although the growing opposition to the movement can be partially understood as a result of threatened economic interests (in the broadest sense of the term), there is another factor that has contributed significantly, although perhaps not equally, to the rise of such opposition. This factor is the conflict between the basic goal of the Environmental Movement—the achievement and maintenance of environmental quality—and the dominant value system of our society. I will argue that the increasing opposition to the once-consensual (or so it seemed to many) issue of 'saving the environment' can be attributed, at least in part, to the fact that environmental quality has never been an important value in our society, and further, to growing awareness that the achievement of environmental quality poses a threat to many of our society's most cherished values.

ENVIRONMENTAL QUALITY AND DOMINANT AMERICAN VALUES

Several students of social movements (see, e.g., Killian, 1964; King, 1956; Turner and Killian, 1972) have noted the importance of the degree of congruence between the goals of a social movement (the values it seeks to implement) and the values of the larger society. It is generally agreed that—other things being equal—the greater the congruence between the two, the less opposition a social movement will evoke and the greater its probability of success in achieving its goals. As Turner and Killian (1972, p. 258) put it:

> every movement is viewed in the society either as generally consistent with, or fundamentally antagonistic to, the established value scheme. How it is viewed will determine the type and tactics of opposition with which it is confronted, the circumstances under which it recruits members, the degree to which it can operate openly through legitimate means, and many other features.

My thesis is that in recent years the Environmental Movement has come to be defined increasingly as 'fundamentally antagonistic' to the dominant value system in our society, and that this accounts for a good deal of its opposition. To support this thesis I need to examine briefly both the values espoused by the Environmental Movement, as well as the values constituting the dominant American value system.

Not surprisingly, it is difficult to explicate the basic goal (the ultimate value it seeks to implement)[6] of the contemporary Environmental Movement, for social movements are often not explicit about the goals-values they seek to implement (Killian, 1964, p. 434; Turner and Killian, 1972, p. 269). However, I suggest the following comes close to capturing the basic goal of the Environmental Movement: to maintain, and achieve where necessary, a natural environment that adequately supports existing biological life and provides a high quality of life for human beings. Thus, environmentalists often speak or write of such goals as the following: 'preserving the integrity of ecosystems', 'maintaining a habitable environment', 'respecting the rights of nature' and 'preserving the beauty of the natural environment'.[7] How does this emphasis placed on environmental quality fit with dominant American values?

Specifying clearly the dominant values in a society is difficult. However, in recent years a number of scholars have endeavored to determine those values that are given primacy in our society, and provide cultural guidelines for evaluating and justifying behavior[8] (see Gabriel, 1974; Geiger, 1974; Rokeach, 1973; Williams, 1967). Despite the use of differing theoretical perspectives and research techniques, these scholars are nearly unanimous in asserting the following as important American values: personal freedom, individual rights, democracy, equality (or at least equal opportunity), achievement, success, material comfort and progress. Also frequently mentioned, although less unanimously, are free enterprise, private property, nationalism, and scientific and technological development. One searches their writings in vain for mentions of anything analogous to 'environmental quality' as an important American value. The closest approximation to be found is 'A World of Beauty', included by Rokeach in his list of 'terminal values'. It, however, is ranked quite low (15th out of 18 such values) in two national surveys of the US population (Rokeach, 1973, 1974).[9] In short, available evidence indicates that environmental quality is given low priority (relative to other values) within our society.

Furthermore, not only is environmental quality absent among our society's dominant values, but many analysts view the latter as directly contributing to environmental degradation. 'At the root of the environmental crisis ... are the basic values which have built our society' (Swan, 1971, p. 225) is a representative statement of this viewpoint. In an effort to explain the origins of our environmental problems, writer after writer points an accusing finger at our society's emphasis on progress and growth, materialism, individual (versus societal) rights, private property, laissez-faire and technological development (see, e.g., Caldwell, 1970; Campbell and Wade, 1972; Udall, 1964; Whisenhunt, 1974). Such values, it is argued, either directly contribute to environmental degradation, or make it difficult to combat it effectively. For example, the emphasis on growth and material comfort clearly encourages environmental abuse, while the primacy placed on individual rights, private property and a laissez-faire economy often impedes effective pollution abatement programs. Thus, besides environmental quality not being one of our society's most important values, many of the latter are held to be inconsistent with achieving and maintaining it.

This inconsistency is crucial for my purpose, and in recent years it has become more and more apparent that efforts to achieve environmental quality pose a direct threat to many of our society's most cherished values. For example, a growing body of literature suggests that in order to achieve and maintain a quality environment it may be necessary to restrict individual freedoms, property rights and free enterprise; emphasize cooperation over individualism; slow down economic growth and thus possibly halt increases in material comfort and threaten opportunities for success; institute more centralized governmental planning with a consequent de-emphasis on political democracy; and finally, sacrifice a significant degree of national sovereignty in order to achieve the international cooperation needed to solve global environmental problems (see, e.g., Daly, 1973; Ehrlich and Ehrlich, 1974; Hardin, 1972; Heilbroner, 1974; Meadows et al., 1972; Ophuls, 1976; Mesarovic and Pestel, 1974; Schumacher, 1973).

There can be little doubt that such diagnoses of our environmental problems, and proposals for alleviating them, are viewed by some as a threat to cherished American values. It is hardly surprising, then, that the increased attention given to such analyses and proposals has spawned increased opposition to the Environmental Movement. While the 'economy versus environment' and 'payrolls versus pollution' arguments are still frequently used, opponents of the Environmental Movement appear to be making increasing use of the fact that environmentalism represents a threat to traditional values. Especially in the mass media (ranging from paid advertisements to letters-to-the-editor) one encounters a growing number of charges that environmentalists, environmental regulations, and governmental agencies charged with protecting environmental quality represent threats to 'progress', 'free enterprise', 'private property', 'Constitutional rights', a 'high standard of living', 'the American way of life' and so on.[10] In short, I am arguing that growing awareness of these perceived threats has contributed significantly to the increased opposition to environmentalism in recent years.[11] Clearly threatened values, as well as threatened economic interests, need to be taken into account in order to understand opposition to the Environmental Movement.

Whatever their relative contributions, there seems little doubt that the combination of threatened values and economic costs posed by the Environmental Movement has caused it to evolve, in a few short years, from a consensual to a conflictual social movement. To clarify this change, and in particular the importance of value conflict in generating the change, I turn to an examination of the evolving Environmental Movement from the perspective of traditional social movement typologies. Such typologies are useful in clarifying the basis of the movement's opposition and provide insights into the likely evolution of the Environmental Movement and its opposition.

THE CHANGING ENVIRONMENTAL MOVEMENT

There are a number of social movement typologies that can be applied to the Environmental Movement, allowing us to go beyond simply noting that it has changed from a 'consensual' to a 'conflictual' movement. In particular, three classic typologies appear well suited for describing the changing Environmental Movement—especially in terms of its challenge to dominant societal values. The first typology consists of the traditional distinction between 'reform' and 'revolutionary' movements. As noted by Turner and Killian (1972, p. 257), 'The revolutionary movement is said to challenge the fundamental values of a society, whereas the reform movement seeks modifications within the existing value scheme.'

Although quite popular, Turner and Killian suggest that this typology is difficult to use, due to the difficulty of an investigator accurately judging 'the ultimate relation' between the values of a social movement and those of the larger society. Consequently, Turner and Killian (1972, p. 258) propose an alternative typology based solely on public perception of a movement's relationship to societal values. A 'respectable movement' is one that is viewed as 'generally consistent with' the established value scheme, whereas a 'revolutionary movement' (I prefer to use the term 'radical' in order to distinguish between this and the above typology) is one that is viewed as 'fundamentally antagonistic' to societal values.[12] Finally, there is Smelser's (1962) distinction between 'norm-oriented' and 'value-oriented' social movements, the former attempting to achieve their goals through the creation of new norms (e.g., new rules, laws or regulatory agencies), and the latter requiring change in basic societal values to achieve their goal of a new social order. These three typologies are quite similar in fundamental respects, and it is therefore not surprising that they yield compatible views of the changing nature of the Environmental Movement.

Changing Goals of the Environmental Movement: From Normative Change to Value Change

On the basis of my earlier discussion of the lack of congruence between the basic goal of the Environmental Movement and dominant American values, and growing awareness of this fact, the following should come as no surprise: I see the Environmental Movement increasingly shifting from 'reform' to 'revolutionary' in character; increasingly viewed as less 'respectable' and as more 'radical'; and increasingly becoming less 'norm-oriented' and more 'value-oriented' in nature. In order to further substantiate these claims, I briefly examine some changes experienced by the movement in recent years specifically from the perspective of Smelser's norm-oriented versus value-oriented typology, the most theoretically grounded (in Parson's general theory of action) of the three.

Smelser (1962, p. 109) sees participants in a norm-oriented movement as basically seeking 'the restoration, protection, modification, or creation of social norms. More particularly, they may demand a rule, law, or regulatory agency designed to control the inadequate, ineffective or irresponsible behavior of individuals.' This would seem to be an apt description of the major thrust of the Environmental Movement at the time of the first Earth Day (22 April 1970). It was widely believed that with new laws designed to protect the environment, and governmental agencies to enforce them, the goal of environmental quality could be achieved. However, despite considerable success at the normative level (e.g., the passage of environmental legislation and the establishment of environmental agencies at various levels of government—see, for example, Albrecht and Mauss, 1975, pp. 599–605), some environmentalists quickly came to realize that such accomplishments were insufficient to halt environmental deterioration—because the laws and regulations were either inadequate or poorly enforced (e.g., Rathlesberger, 1972).

Although progress seems to have been made in abating air pollution in the US in recent years, problems such as water pollution, noise pollution, solid waste disposal and loss of wildlife habitat continue to worsen (see, e.g., National Wildlife Federation, 1976). Further, the increased attention given to environmental issues throughout society has led to the discovery of heretofore neglected issues—such as the possibly carcinogenic effects of chemical pollutants, the possible threat of aerosols to the earth's protective layer of ozone and the rapid depletion of available energy sources. The near-sudden development of numerous such ominous problems (and growing recognition of their complexity) has no doubt played a crucial role in convincing environmentalists that mere laws and regulations are insufficient to halt environmental deterioration. As a consequence, goals entailing more fundamental changes are increasingly put forth, and we now hear calls for 'no growth', 'basic change in lifestyle', 'zero population growth' and the achievement of a 'steady-state' society.[13] In short, a growing number of environmentalists are calling for fundamental changes in basic societal values (as discussed at length earlier). Indeed, Smelser's (1962, p. 120) definition of a value-oriented movement, offered well over a decade ago, sounds as if it were a description of the contemporary Environmental Movement, for such a movement 'envisions a modification of those conceptions concerning "nature, man's place in it, man's relation to man, and the desirable and non-desirable as they may relate to man–environment and inter-human relations."'

As the Environmental Movement has become more value-oriented by seeking to alter basic societal values, it has understandably taken on more of a 'revolutionary' cast and consequently has come to be viewed as somewhat more 'radical' in nature.[14] Certainly this helps account for its growing opposition and declining support among the general public, as it has become increasingly acceptable to oppose 'environmental extremism' and deny support to 'radical' environmental proposals. Further, these changes have also had an effect on the basic strategies of the Environmental Movement, which in turn have influenced its opposition.

Changing Strategies in the Environmental Movement

Social movements vary not only in terms of the degree to which their goals represent a threat to societal values, but also in terms of the basic strategies they employ in an effort to achieve their goals. Furthermore, there appears to be some correspondence between the degree to which a movement's goals challenge societal values, and the primary strategy the movement uses to attain its goals. I will examine the relationship between goals and strategies in the context of the contemporary Environmental Movement, but first need to discuss a traditional typology of social movement strategies, and apply it to the changing Environmental Movement.

As Killian (1964, p. 448) notes, 'the strategy of a social movement may take either of two general directions—societal manipulation or personal transformation'.[15] The former strategy depends on the direct exercise of power in order to achieve the movement's goals, and may encompass a wide range of specific tactics from very mild to quite extreme (e.g., lobbying for new legislation, boycotts, strikes and military coups). In contrast, the latter strategy 'seeks success through widespread conversion of individuals' (Killian, 1964, p. 449), and rests on the premise that once a sufficient proportion of individuals are 'converted' to the movement's values, basic institutional change will follow. In other words, it is assumed that after a sufficient number of people have internalized the 'proper' values, and altered their behavior accordingly, the desired institutional change will occur. The 'personal transformation' strategy is generally used by religious movements, and Reich's (1970) well-known optimism concerning the eventual ascendance of 'Con III' rested on the presumed efficacy of such a strategy.

Killian (1964, p. 451) notes that social movements typically employ some combination of these two basic strategies, although one will typically be predominant at any given point, and the relative emphasis placed on one or the other may shift over time. The early Environmental Movement (approximately 1969 to 1971) clearly employed both strategies to a significant degree: The 'societal manipulation' strategy was reflected in such tactics as lobbying for environmental laws and regulatory agencies, taking legal action against polluters, and working for the election of 'pro-environmental' politicians. Less frequently used tactics such as economic boycotts, demonstrations and occasional acts of 'ecotage' against polluters also reflected this strategy (see Gale, 1972; Morrison et al., 1972). On the other hand, tactics based on the 'personal transformation' strategy were also widely used, as witness the popularity of anti-litter campaigns, recycling efforts, the purchase of 'environmentally safe' products (such as low-phosphate detergents), the substitution of walking, bicycling and car-pooling for traditional driving habits, and the entire 'environmental education' thrust. Such personal transformation tactics ranged from very mild (e.g., putting bricks in toilet tanks to lessen water usage) to fairly extreme (e.g., joining a 'back-to-nature' commune).

Despite the obvious mixture of strategies employed by the early Environmental Movement, my sense is that the 'personal transformation' strategy was somewhat more popular, especially among the newer converts and more peripheral members (see Mauss, 1975, pp. 47–8 and Wilson, 1973, p. 306 for discussions of categories of membership). This is reflected in the widespread acceptance of 'pollution is a people problem', a view nicely captured by Pogo's diagnosis that, 'We have met the enemy, and he is us.' That the personal transformation strategy was so popular is not surprising, for Turner and Killian (1972, p. 275) suggest that it will predominate when: (1) people believe 'widespread self-improvement is possible'; (2) people assume that 'the societal order will reflect the integrity and character of individual men'; and (3) 'people can take some responsibility upon themselves for their present unsatisfactory condition.' At the time of the first Earth Day, I believe that there was widespread acceptance of the view that individuals could modify their environmentally abusive behaviors, that such behavioral change would ultimately influence the social order, and—as noted above—that *individuals* were indeed responsible for environmental deterioration.

However, it appears that in the past few years the Environmental Movement has increasingly shifted its emphasis more toward a 'societal manipulation' strategy, with the use of consequent 'power' tactics. A number of factors, in addition to growing rejection of the above beliefs,[16] seem to have contributed to this change. First, and perhaps most obvious, was recognition that many individuals (as well as corporations and governments) would not voluntarily halt environmentally abusive practices—due to the costs involved (Morrison, 1973, p. 74).[17] Two other relevant factors are suggested by Turner and Killian (1972), who argue that movements will shift toward societal manipulation strategies 'when they have achieved some success and added persons of influence to their membership' (p. 275) and 'when there is pressure for a more immediate solution of social problems than the gradual process of winning men's souls can promise' (p. 276). Both factors fit the Environmental Movement's recent history, as on the one hand it achieved considerable success in terms of increased membership, institutionalization of laws and regulatory agencies, and support from public officials and scientists (Morrison, 1973; Schnaiberg, 1973) and—as noted earlier—it has increasingly pointed to the existence of problems requiring 'immediate' solutions and the possibility of imminent 'eco-catastrophes'.

A final factor influencing a shift toward a societal manipulation strategy, and the most important in my view, is Killian's (1964, p. 450) observation that the greater the threat to traditional societal values posed by a social movement, the more difficulty the movement encounters in converting large numbers of individuals to its goals and thus the greater reliance placed on the exercise of 'power' to achieve these goals. As I discussed in detail earlier, the Environmental Movement has increasingly become viewed as a threat to many of our society's most important values; consequently, I suspect that a growing number of people are becoming hesitant about being labeled 'environmentalists'. This tends to make it more difficult for the movement to convert people, and thus naturally leads to a greater reliance on the direct exercise of power to achieve goals.[18] Therefore, there appears to be increased emphasis on law suits, lobbying for new and stronger environmental regulations, and the election of pro-environmental government officials.[19]

The Interaction between Values, Strategies and Opposition

When considering the above changes in the Environmental Movement, it must be kept in mind that its opponents have been actively engaged in efforts to label it as a threat to such values as individual rights, progress, private property rights, and so on (as well as economic interests), and this has created a truly interactive process. Thus, the more radical a movement is portrayed and perceived, the more difficulty it will have in successfully using a personal transformation strategy dependent on widespread conversion, and therefore the more likely it will come to rely on a societal manipulation strategy. The use of consequent power tactics, however, is likely to reinforce the radical image of the movement, and is especially likely to provoke an escalation of opposition (including a greater effort to label it as radical).

In short, although the processes are complex and interactive, there seems to be some correspondence between the strategy (and consequent tactics) employed by a social movement, and the extent to which the movement's goals are viewed as incompatible with the value systems of the larger society. There seem to be reciprocal tendencies which compel a radical, revolutionary or value-oriented movement to rely more heavily on societal manipulation than personal transformation. Such tendencies appear to have occurred in the case of the Environmental Movement in recent years, as it has become both more value-oriented and thus somewhat more radical and revolutionary and more committed to the strategy of societal manipulation and power tactics.

It should be apparent that I have been focusing on changes in the Environmental Movement along two dimensions: predominant strategy and degree of threat to the dominant value system. In an effort to sum up, as well as clarify, the foregoing discussion, I will employ a final typology—one that allows both of the foregoing dimensions to be considered simultaneously.

Mapping the Changing Environmental Movement

A decade ago the anthropologist David Aberle (1966) presented an innovative typology for classifying social movements, or shifts in particular movements over time, which consists of two dimensions quite similar to those I have been discussing. In his words (1966, p. 316):

> Social movements may be classified by reference to two dimensions. One is the dimension of the locus of the change sought. The other is the dimension of the amount of change sought. As to locus, a movement may aim to change individuals or some supra-individual system—the economic order, the technological order, the political order. As to amount of change, movements may aim at total or partial change.

By cross-classifying these two dimensions he produced a classification of four basic types of social movements: *Transformative* (total change at the supra-individual level), *Redemptive* (total change at the individual level), *Reformative* (partial change at the supra-individual level) and *Alternative* (partial change at the individual level).

With a few minor modifications, the two dimensions in Aberle's typology become consistent with the unidimensional typologies I have used previously—and thus more clearly map the previously discussed changes the Environmental Movement has experienced in recent years. First, rather than speaking of amount of change ('total' or 'partial'), I will distinguish between the basic goal of a movement: value change or normative change (reform versus revolutionary or respectable versus radical could also be substituted for this dimension). Second, I will substitute predominant strategy ('societal manipulation' versus 'personal transformation') for locus of change ('supra-individual' versus 'individual'), for the meanings are almost identical. Finally, in an effort to use terminology appropriate for describing the variety of participants in the Environmental Movement, I will use somewhat different terms than Aberle to describe the incumbents of the four cells resulting from a cross-classification of the above two dimensions.

The adaption of Aberle's typology is presented in Figure 6.1, which allows me to classify different types of environmentalists and, since the relative proportions have shifted over time, to 'map' changes in the predominant nature of the movement in recent years. Besides labeling the incumbents of each cell, I have also noted some of the major strategies or goals characteristic of the various types of environmentalists and, finally, indicated (with arrows) what I see as the major directions of movement between cells—thus accounting for the earlier-discussed changes in the Environmental Movement.

Focusing first on the two bottom cells, we find the 'reformists' and the 'meliorists',[20] both of whom are primarily concerned with normative change. The former tend to emphasize the development and implementation of formal norms such as environmental laws and regulations via lobbying, initiatives and referenda, election of 'pro-environmental' officials, and the use of law suits. In addition, they may occasionally try to sanction—via letter-writing campaigns, boycotts, etc.—what they perceive as 'anti-environmental' activities by industries and government. All of their efforts can be seen as attempts to 'reform' environmentally abusive behaviors and practices. In contrast, meliorists are primarily concerned with the development of informal behavioral norms—that is, by setting personal examples they seek to prompt such behaviors as energy conservation, purchasing environmentally sound products, and recycling home waste and used products. Thus, they are truly attempting to 'ameliorate' environmental degradation. Keeping in mind that any given individual might be classified into both categories,[21] the 'ideal type' reformist would be a member of one of the multitude of formal environmental organizations. In contrast, meliorists would be likely to include such heterogeneous groups as students working on recycling projects, members of civic groups mobilized for 'clean-up campaigns' and concerned individuals who want 'to do something' about environmental problems.

My impression is that the proportion of reformists to meliorists has increased since 1970. On the one hand, I suspect this is due to the 'conversion' of some meliorists to the reformist camp, either because (as noted earlier) they came to realize that personal transformation strategies stressing voluntary actions are insufficient, or because their ameliorative activities such as recycling brought them into contact with individuals who recruited them to reformist organizations.[22] On the other hand, meliorists were probably the most likely to abandon the Environmental Movement, due to their minimal commitment to its goals and also to their lack of organizational involvement (see Wilson, 1973: Chapters 8 and 9 on the importance of the latter).

The crucial shift I have been discussing in this paper, however, is upward from a concern with normative change to the goal of value change. This leads us to a consideration of the two upper cells—the incumbents of which I have termed 'transformationists' and 'alternativists'. The latter term appears especially appropriate for a key component of this cell—those individuals who have forsaken modern, urban life for 'back-to-nature' living (often based on the use of 'appropriate technology'—see Schumacher, 1973), as they are attempting to create an 'alternative' life style. This segment of the Environmental Movement is clearly related to the 'cultural revolution' portion of the Youth Movement of the Sixties, as many 'Hippies' participated in the retreat to nature. Also, I suspect that a number of disillusioned 'reformists' have taken up such a lifestyle. However, the term also applies to those who seek to inculcate, often via widespread environmental education (see, e.g., Swan, 1971), a new 'environmental ethic' among the public—as a society guided by such an ethic would certainly differ from our current society (see, e.g., Nash, 1974). Both types of alternativists appear to draw heavily on the philosophical tradition of 'Transcendentalism' with its emphasis on nature worship (Fleming, 1972), and clearly reject many dominant American values.

The final cell contains the 'transformationists', those who seek to transform our present social order into a fundamentally different one—perhaps best captured by the 'Steady-State

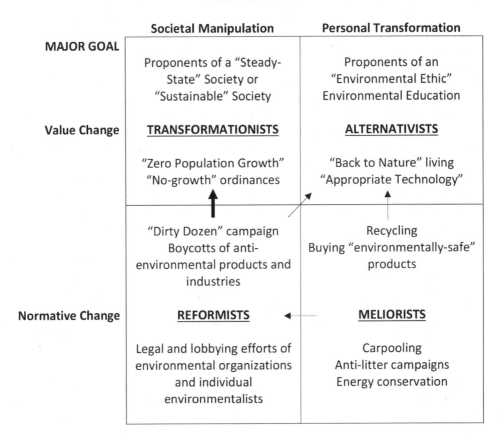

Note: Arrows indicate hypothesized major (solid line) and minor (dotted line) directions of shifts from 1970 to the present.
Source: Adapted from Aberle (1966), Smelser (1962) and Turner and Killian (1972).

Figure 6.1   *A typology for mapping the changing environmental movement*

Society' concept (see Daly, 1973; Ophuls, 1976). Such a society would require a change in most of our dominant values and institutions, and its proponents are (in my view) the 'cutting edge' of the Environmental Movement. Although small in number, the ideology they are developing appears to be filtering down to a growing number of reformists. Moderate indications of their success so far are that fundamental values such as growth and progress have been challenged by attempts to institute 'no-growth' ordinances in some communities and by numerous efforts (often successful) to halt the construction of both nuclear and non-nuclear power plants. Likewise, both growth and individual rights are challenged by proponents of 'zero population growth', who seek to limit population growth, even if it means restricting the rights of parents to determine the number of children they may have.

It is the combination of putting forth policies that represent a severe challenge to traditional American values, and actively pushing for their implementation—in the form of lobbying, initiatives and referenda, and testifying before Congress (see Committee on Merchant Marine and Fisheries, 1973)—which makes the transformationists the greatest threat to the status quo. Individuals living in the backwoods, or academicians issuing calls for an environmental ethic, are generally tolerable—for only when they can successfully convert large numbers of people do they pose a serious threat. In contrast, individuals actively engaged in the political process, and calling for a fundamental transformation of contemporary society, represent a significant threat to the status quo. Thus, to reiterate my major point, as the Environmental Movement has gradually begun to call for value (rather than just normative) change, and as it has consequently relied more on a 'societal manipulation' strategy, it has understandably encountered increased opposition.

CONCLUDING REMARKS

I begin the concluding remarks with a caveat: to understand opposition to the Environmental Movement one must consider both social-structural as well as social-psychological factors. Thus, the basic thrust of the foregoing analysis has been (at least implicitly) at the social-psychological level. In other words, I have implied that a growing number of Americans apparently realize that the goal of environmental quality, and especially the policies needed to achieve it, represent a threat to many of their cherished values. I believe that this is in fact the case, and there are attitudinal data (see note 11) that lend support to the contention. However, I must stress that this value-conflict is often actively engendered by the opponents of the Environmental Movement—especially those whose positions in the social structure provide them with considerable influence (e.g., industrialists, politicians and union officials). Such opponents make use (likely unknowingly) of fairly well-established social-psychological processes: by defining an 'attitude object' such as land-use planning as negatively affecting a strongly held value such as private property rights, they are likely to be successful in creating negative attitudes toward the former (see, e.g., Rosenberg, 1966). Thus, it is not only the more explicit articulation of radical goals by environmentalists, but this active definitional effort by their opponents, which has led to increased opposition to the Environmental Movement.

In recent years students of power have come to realize the important role that societal values, and especially their manipulation by individuals in positions of power, play in preserving the status quo (see, e.g., Bachrach and Baratz, 1970; McFarland, 1969). Defenders of the status quo can legitimate their actions by defining them as attempts to preserve traditional values (even if they are motivated primarily by economic interests), and at the same time de-legitimate challengers to the status quo by picturing them as threats to these values. Furthermore, even in the absence of such active opposition, challengers to the status quo (such as the Environmental Movement) will find that traditional values pose a severe obstacle—simply because their existence 'is seen as "right", "natural", a "way of life"' (McFarland, 1969, p. 79). Thus, values such as property rights, personal freedom, progress and growth may be so integrated into a society that many of its members will find it inconceivable that opposing values should be given serious consideration.

In sum, by increasingly pointing to problems and proposing solutions that require fundamental change in societal values, the Environmental Movement will inevitably encounter escalating opposition—including the multi-faceted power of the 'status-quo'. Of course, movements seeking to 'transform' societies have never faced an easy task, and environmentalists are coming to recognize this fact.

NOTES

1. It's more accurate to say that the movement emerged during the late 1960s as it evolved from the earlier Conservation Movement, but Earth Day established 'environmentalism' as a major and highly visible social movement. For explanations of the rise of the Environmental Movement, which stress in varying degrees its link with the earlier Conservation Movement, see Albrecht and Mauss (1975); Fleming (1972); Gale (1972); Morrison et al. (1972); and Schnaiberg (1973).
2. The policy-making and policy-implementing processes are replete with barriers to rapid and significant reform, as noted in Bachrach and Baratz (1970).
3. See Hornback and Morrison (1975) and Turner and Killian (1972) on the inter-relationships between social movements, their opposition and public opinion.
4. Another factor contributing to the decline in public concern is that social problems (which environmental quality became by 1970) often have a 'natural history' in which the initial stage of widespread concern inevitably dissipates (see Dunlap and Dillman, 1976) and the references therein). However, such a model does not account for the rise of organized opposition to a social movement, the major focus of this paper.
5. I should note that two analysts who have stressed the role of economic costs in giving rise to opposition to the Environmental Movement have also touched on factors similar to those I will discuss: Albrecht (1972, p. 2) mentions the movement's threat to the 'American ethic of growth' while Morrison (1973, p. 74) expands the concept of costs to include 'autonomy and freedom in decision making'. Also, Sills (1975) provides a very informative discussion of a wide range of criticisms of the Environmental Movement that do not stem from threatened economic interests; however, while complementary, our analysis differs considerably from his.
6. Following Turner and Killian, I equate the 'goals' of a social movement with the 'values' it seeks to implement. Such goals (values) are expressed through a movement's 'ideology' (see Killian, 1964, p. 434; Turner and Killian, 1972, p. 269).
7. Interested readers should consult such environmentalist periodicals as *Environmental Action*, *Environment Action Bulletin*, *Environment* and *The Ecologist*, as well as the publications of environmental organizations such as the *Sierra Club Bulletin*, *National Wildlife*, *Audubon*, *Conservation Foundation Letter*, *Not Man Apart*, and *The Living Wilderness*. For a good listing of the latter organizations, see the National Wildlife Federation's *Conservation Directory*, which is periodically updated.
8. I will follow Williams (1967, p. 23), and 'define values as those conceptions of desirable states of affairs that are utilized in selective conduct as criteria for preference or choice or as justifications for proposed or actual behavior.' I realize that there is not uniform acceptance of 'dominant' American values among all segments of society. However, I believe that the values I list as dominant American values are given primacy by a majority of Americans, and provide widely accepted guidelines for evaluating and justifying behavior in our society (see the data in Christenson and Yang, 1976).
9. This finding tends to validate the absence of Transcendentalist values such as 'natural beauty', 'love of nature' and 'living in harmony with nature' from the above list. Although a viable philosophical tradition, Transcendentalism has apparently not permeated the culture of our society to a significant degree (see Fleming, 1972).
10. A good example of anti-environmental forces appealing to such values has occurred in Northern California, where the 'Straight Arrow Coalition' was formed out of resentment toward various governmental regulations (especially the requirement of 'environmental impact reports' for logging operations). The Coalition's 'Statement of Purposes and Objectives' states that, 'the few have robbed the many of their jobs, their incomes, their pensions, their land, their constitutional rights and their dignity ... all under the guise of environmental protection and protecting the "little guy from himself".' It goes on to state that, 'Governmental intervention in the private lives of its citizens

must not be allowed to continue. Straight Arrow will fight for personal freedom as outlined in the Bill of Rights.' Thanks to William Devall for bringing information on the S.A.C. to my attention.
11. For example, numerous studies have found a negative association between environmental concern and political conservatism, presumably because the latter reflects a greater commitment to individualism, laissez-faire, private property rights, free enterprise, and so on (see Dunlap, 1975a). Also, a modest negative association has been found between 'pro-growth' attitudes and environmental concern (Buttel and Flinn, 1976).
12. I tend to agree with Wilson (1973, p. 22) that the second typology really does not solve the problem of observer bias, for the observer must still judge the degree to which a movement is viewed as 'respectable' or 'radical'. Also, I should note that Turner and Killian (1972, p. 258) include a third type of movement, the 'peculiar' movement, in between respectable and revolutionary (radical) movements. However, for our purposes it can be ignored.
13. In addition to the sources cited earlier, the periodicals cited in note 7 should be consulted.
14. Needless to say, I am not arguing that at present it is a revolutionary movement, nor that environmentalists are generally viewed as extremely 'radical'. Nonetheless, things are clearly moving in these directions, and environmentalism is no longer simply a 'reform' movement or, in many circles, a 'respectable' movement. The fact that environmentalists have been relatively successful in avoiding the 'radical' label thus far is largely attributable to their predominately white, upper-middle-class composition (Dunlap, 1975b), and location in important institutions such as universities and government agencies (Morrison, 1973).
15. In their use of this typology to examine the changing strategy of the Environmental Movement, Morrison et al. (1972, p. 264) refer to 'power' versus 'participation' strategies. While the source they cite (Killian, 1964, pp. 448–9) is somewhat ambiguous, Turner and Killian (1972, pp. 256–7 and pp. 274–5) clearly do not equate 'societal manipulation versus personal transformation' strategies with the 'power orientations, participation orientations and value orientations' of social movements. They treat the latter as akin to 'functional imperatives', in that every movement (if it is to succeed) must achieve a degree of power, maintain the participation of members and retain its values or goals. While I find the terminology Morrison and his colleagues used to describe the two strategies intuitively appealing, I will stick with 'societal manipulation versus personal transformation' in order to be consistent with Turner and Killian. Nonetheless, readers are warned that when I discuss 'tactics' (the specific actions used on behalf of the guiding strategy), I will occasionally feel compelled to term a specific tactic as the use of 'power'—as the term is commonly understood.
16. Some direct evidence of such changes has been documented by Bartell and St George (1974) in a trend study of Sierra Club members. Within a period of one year (1971 to 1972) they found a significant decline in members' 'trust in system responsiveness', and a consequent shift toward greater endorsement of more militant tactics.
17. This problem is compounded by the fact that most goals of the Environmental Movement such as clean air and water are what economists term 'public goods'—that is, once they are attained they become available to everyone, including those who did not contribute to their attainment. The nature of public goods makes it difficult to mount effective 'collective action' on their behalf, as individuals are generally unwilling to bear the costs involved given knowledge that others may come to enjoy the same benefits without paying any costs. The problematic nature of 'collective action' to achieve public goods has been explicated by Olson (1968), and underlies Hardin's (1972) 'tragedy of the commons'. To the extent that environmentalists come to understand the logic of collective action, and the problematic nature of relying on voluntary action to achieve public goods, we can expect them to place even greater emphasis on 'societal manipulation' strategies such as lobbying for laws which require compliance.
18. Some of the shift toward 'societal manipulation' is no doubt due to the loss of 'peripheral' members, who I earlier argued were more likely to rely on the 'personal transformation' strategy. However, I doubt that their loss is sufficient to account for all of the shift, and refer the reader to the study cited in note 16. It is also worth noting at this point that Turner (1970, p. 149) argues that the tactic of 'persuasion' (as opposed to 'bargaining' or 'coercion') depends upon identifying 'the proposed course of action with values held by the target group' (i.e., the larger society). To the extent that a movement cannot identify its goals with societal values, the more likely it will have to use bargaining or coercion rather than persuasion.

19. The best example of the latter tactic is the biannual 'Dirty Dozen Campaign' conducted by Environmental Action. Since 1970 this organization has chosen twelve members of Congress with very poor voting records on environmental measures, and who do not appear to be unbeatable, and labeled them the 'Dirty Dozen'. In addition to 'exposing' their poor voting records, Environmental Action directly aids (financially and otherwise) their opponents. Thus far the campaigns appear to have been relatively successful—see the summary of the 1970, 1972 and 1974 campaign results in Redburn and Baldwin (1975).
20. This term is borrowed from Schnaiberg (1973, pp. 611–16), who classified environmentalists into four categories: 'cosmetologists', 'meliorists', 'reformists' and 'radicals'. In terms of our typology, his first two categories would be included in our 'meliorist' cell, his 'reformists' would be identical to ours, while his 'radicals' would be divided into our 'transformationists' and 'alternativists' cells.
21. Actually, while I would expect many reformists to also engage in melioristic activities, the opposite is not the case. Likewise, many transformationists might engage in alternativist activities, but not vice versa. In other words, I suspect that many individuals committed to a societal manipulation strategy will often have a personal life-style similar to those who limit themselves to the personal transformation strategy.
22. Students of social movements are increasingly stressing the importance of personal contact in the recruitment of individuals into social movements—especially formal movement organizations (see, for example, Wilson, 1973, pp. 131–3).

REFERENCES

Aberle, D.F. (1966) *The Peyote Religion among the Navaho*. Chicago, IL: Aldine.
Albrecht, S.L. (1972) Environmental social movements and counter-movements: An overview and an illustration. *Journal of Voluntary Action Research*. **1**(October), pp. 2–11.
Albrecht, S.L. and Mauss, A.L. (1975) The environment as a social problem. In: Mauss, A.L. (ed.) *Social Problems as Social Movements*. Philadelphia, PA: J.B. Lippincott, pp. 556–605.
Bachrach, P. and Baratz, M.S. (1970) *Power and Poverty: Theory and Practice*. New York, NY: Oxford University Press.
Bartell, T. and St. George, A. (1974) A trend analysis of environmentalists' organizational commitment, tactic advocacy, and perceptions of government. *Journal of Voluntary Action Research*. **3**(July/October), pp. 41–6.
Buttel, F.H. (1975) The environmental movement: Consensus, conflict, and change. *Journal of Environmental Education*. **7** (Fall), pp. 53–63.
Buttel, F.H. and Flinn, W.L. (1976) Economic growth versus the environment: Survey evidence. *Social Science Quarterly*. **57**(September), pp. 410–20.
Caldwell, L.K. (1970) Authority and responsibility for environmental administration. *The Annals of the American Academy of Political and Social Science*. **389**(May), pp. 107–15.
Campbell, R.R. and Wade, J.L. (1972) Value systems. In: Campbell, R.R. and Wade, J.L. (eds) *Society and the Environment: The Coming Collision*. Boston, MA: Allyn & Bacon, pp. 337–45.
Christenson, J.A. and Yang, C. (1976) Dominant values in American society: An exploratory analysis. Sociology and Social Research. **60**(July), pp. 461–73.
Committee on Merchant Marine and Fisheries (1973) *Growth and its Implications for the Future, Part 3*. Hearing Appendix for the Subcommittee on Fisheries and Wildlife Conservation and the Environment, 93rd Congress, Serial No. 93-29. Washington, DC: U.S. Government Printing Office.
Daly, H.E. (ed.) (1973) *Toward a Steady-State Economy*. San Francisco, CA: W.H. Freeman.
Dunlap, R.E. (1975a) The impact of political orientation on environmental attitudes and actions. *Environment and Behavior*. **7**(December), pp. 428–54.
Dunlap, R.E. (1975b) The socioeconomic basis of the environmental movement: Old data, new data, and implications for the movement's future. Paper presented at the Annual Meetings of the American Sociological Association, August, San Francisco.
Dunlap, R.E. and Dillman, D.A. (1976) Decline in public support for environmental protection: Evidence from a 1970–1974 panel study. *Rural Sociology*. **41**(Fall), pp. 382–90.

Ehrlich, P.R. and Ehrlich, A.H. (1974) *The End of Affluence.* New York, NY: Ballantine Books.
Erskine, H. (1972) The polls: Pollution and industry. *Public Opinion Quarterly.* **36**(2), pp. 263–80.
Fleming, D. (1972) Roots of the new conservation movement. *Perspectives in American History.* **6**, pp. 7–91.
Gabriel, R.H. (1974) *American Values: Continuity and Change.* Westport, CT: Greenwood Press.
Gale, R.P. (1972) From sit-in to hike-in: A comparison of the civil rights and environmental movements. In: Burch, W.R., Cheek, N.H. and Taylor, L. (eds) *Social Behavior, Natural Resources, and the Environment.* New York, NY: Harper & Row, pp. 280–305.
Geiger, H.K. (1974) *American Values through the Eyes of Expert Observers.* Unpublished manuscript. Department of Sociology, University of Wisconsin, Madison.
Hardin, G. (1972) *Explaining New Ethics for Survival.* New York, NY: Viking Press.
Heilbroner, R.L. (1974) *An Inquiry into the Human Prospect.* New York, NY: W.W. Morton.
Hornback, K.E. and Morrison, D.E. (1975) *The Role of Public Opinion on Social Movement Evolution.* Paper presented at the Annual Meeting of the American Sociological Association, August, San Francisco.
Janssen, P.R. (1970) The age of ecology. In Mitchell, J.G. and Stallings, C.L. (eds) *Ecotactics: The Sierra Club Handbook for Environmental Activists.* New York, NY: Pocket Books, pp. 183–92.
Jordan, P.A. and Deans, R.L. (1970) Freedom and responsibility: An environmental dilemma. In: Mergen, F. (ed.) *Man and His Environment: The Ecological Limits of Optimism.* New Haven, CT: Yale University School of Forestry, Bulletin No. 76, pp. 55–77.
Killian, L.M. (1964) Social movements. In: Faris, R.E.L. (ed.) *Handbook of Modern Sociology.* Chicago, IL: Rand McNally, pp. 426–55.
King, C.W. (1956) *Social Movements in the United States.* New York, NY: Random House.
Kohl, D.H. (1975) The environmental movement: What might it be? *Natural Resources Journal.* **15**(April), pp. 327–51.
Main, J. (1971) Conservationists at the barricades. In: Frakes, G.E. and Solberg, C.B. (eds) *Pollution Papers.* New York, NY: Appleton-Century-Crofts, pp. 311–23.
Mauss, A.L. (1975) *Social Problems as Social Movements.* Philadelphia, PA: J.B. Lippincott.
McFarland, A.S. (1969) *Power and Leadership in Pluralist Systems.* Stanford, CA: Stanford University Press.
Meadows, D.H., Meadows, D.L., Randers, J. and Behrens III, W.W. (1972) *The Limits to Growth.* New York, NY: Universe Books.
Mesarovic, M. and Pestel, E. (1974) *Mankind at the Turning Point: The Second Report to The Club of Rome.* New York, NY: E.P. Dutton.
Morrison, D.E. (1973) The environmental movement: Conflict dynamics. *Journal of Voluntary Action Research.* **2**(Spring), pp. 74–85.
Morrison, D.E., Hornback, K.E. and Warner, W.K. (1972) The environmental movement: Some preliminary observations and predictions. In: Burch, W.R., Cheek, N.H. and Taylor, L. (eds) *Social Behavior, Natural Resources and the Environment.* New York, NY: Harper & Row, pp. 259–79.
Nash, R. (1974) Environment ethics. In: Clarke, R.O. and List, P.C. (eds) *Environmental Spectrum.* New York, NY: Van Nostrand, pp. 142–51.
National Wildlife Federation (1976) 76 EQ Index. Reprinted from *National Wildlife* (February–March).
Olson, M. (1968) *The Logic of Collective Action: Public Goods and the Theory of Groups.* New York, NY: Schocken.
Ophuls, W. (1976) *Ecology and the Politics of Scarcity: Prologue to a Political Theory of the Steady-State.* San Francisco, CA: W.H. Freeman.
Rathlesberger, J. (ed.) (1972) *Nixon and the Environment: The Politics of Devastation.* New York, NY: Village Voice/Taurus Communications.
Redburn, T. and Baldwin, D. (1975) Introducing the clean-up Congress act. *Environmental Action.* **7**(December 20), pp. 12–14.
Reich, C.A. (1970) *The Greening of America.* New York, NY: Random House.
Rokeach, M. (1973) *The Nature of Human Values.* New York, NY: The Free Press.
Rokeach, M. (1974) Change and stability in American value systems, 1968–1971. *Public Opinion Quarterly.* **38**(Summer), pp. 222–38.

Rosenberg, M.J. (1966) Cognitive structure and attitudinal affect. In: Proshansky, H. and Seldenberg, B. (eds) *Basic Studies in Social Psychology*. New York, NY: Holt, Rinehart and Winston, pp. 149–56.

Schnaiberg, A. (1973) Politics, participation, and pollution: The environmental movement. In: Walton, J. and Carns, D. (eds) *Cities in Change: A Reader on Urban Sociology*. Boston, MA: Allyn & Bacon, pp. 605–27.

Schumacher, E.F. (1973) *Small is Beautiful: Economics as if People Mattered*. New York, NY: Harper & Row.

Sills, D. (1975) The environmental movement and its critics. *Human Ecology*. **3**(1), pp. 1–41.

Smelser, N.J. (1962) *Collective Behavior*. New York, NY: Free Press.

Swan, J.A. (1971) Environmental education: One approach to resolving the environmental crisis. *Environment and Behavior*. **3**(September), pp. 223–9.

Turner, R.H. (1970) Determinants of social movement strategies. In: Shibutani, T. (ed.) *Human Nature and Collective Behavior: Papers in Honor of Herbert Blumer*. Englewood Cliffs, NJ: Prentice-Hall, pp. 145–64.

Turner, R.H. and Killan, L.M. (1972) *Collective Behavior*. 2nd edn. Englewood Cliffs, NJ: Prentice-Hall.

Udall, S.L. (1964) *The Quiet Crisis*. New York, NY: Avon Books.

Whisenhunt, D.W. (1974) *The Environment and the American Experience*. Port Washington, NY: Kennikat Press.

Williams, R.P. (1967) Individual and group values. *The Annals of the American Academy of Political and Social Science*. **371**(May), pp. 20–37.

Wilson, J. (1973) *Introduction to Social Movements*. New York, NY: Basic Books.

7. The effect of public opinion on environmental policy in the face of the environmental countermovement

Kerry Ard, Tiffany Williams and Paige Kelly

INTRODUCTION

Who shapes environmental policy in America? Social scientists have long been concerned with whose interests are represented in the policy-making processes. An ideal democratic society is one in which elected officials are responsive to public opinion. However, scholars have argued that the power of public opinion has been eroded with the rise of the political mobilization of the business class in the 1980s and 1990s (Mills, 1956; Vogel, 1989; Domhoff, 2002). This is of interest to environmental policy scholars who have found in recent decades there has been a coalescing of industrial interests in opposition to environmental protection measures (McCright and Dunlap, 2003; 2010; Brulle, 2013). This raises the question of whether this movement has shifted the relative importance of industrial voices in the environmental policy making process versus public concern. As some scholars argue, '[m]ore power for organized interests almost necessarily means less power for the general public' (Burstein, 2014, p. 3). Yet there has been very limited research that considers both how public opinion and industry influence environmental policy-making. Vandeweerdt et al. (2016) provides one of the few examples, finding a positive robust relationship between public opinion and congressional voting on four bills related to cap and trade of greenhouse gases, even when controlling for campaign contributions from industries considered at odds with these policies. Yet this study is limited to a small number of bills over a short time frame, and with the rising political mobilization of the business class, scholars are increasingly arguing that, '[b]usiness interests disproportionately influence U.S. policy' (Banerjee and Murray, 2020).

The question of whether business or the public is more influential on environmental policy is important considering the differing positions between these interest groups on environmental issues. Research has consistently shown the US public has high levels of concern about environmental issues, with more than half the population on average expressing high levels of concern (McCright and Dunlap, 2011b). In January 2020, the Pew Research Center for the first time in two decades reported, 'nearly as many Americans say protecting the environment should be a top policy priority (64%) as say this about strengthening the economy (67%)' (Pew, 2020). However, social scientists have argued that the success of the consumer and environmental movements of the 1960s through the 1970s led to a backlash among the conservative business class (Layzer, 2012; Blumenthal, 1986). In the realm of environmental policy, these issues came to the fore during climate change negotiations in the late 1990s, prompting the term the Climate Change Counter Movement (CCCM) to describe the coordinated effort by certain businesses to lobby against environmental protective measures that run counter to their perceived economic interests (Dunlap and McCright, 2015; McCright and Dunlap, 2003;

2010; Brulle, 2013). A significant mechanism for groups lobbying, or seeking to influence politicians' positions or voting, is through political action committees (PACs) donations. PACs are formed to represent the interests of businesses, labor or other ideological groups, by collecting and aggregating donations with the purpose of raising and spending money to elect or defeat political candidates.

Scholarship on the CCCM has grown substantially over recent years with robust evidence of a strengthening industry-led movement to lobby against environmentally friendly policy. For example, Ard et al. (2017) found donations by CCCM PACs increased dramatically from 1990 to 2010. Every increase in 10 000 USD donated to a Congressional representative by a CCCM PAC increased the propensity of a Congressional member to vote against environmental protection by 2 percent (Ard et al., 2017). Similarly, Brulle (2013) linked funding records of 91 organizations that promote climate change skepticism with 140 donor foundations. This study found that a few major corporations, primarily ExxonMobil and Koch Enterprises, played a major role in funding these climate skeptic organizations and showed, 'evidence of a trend toward concealing the sources of CCCM funding through the use of donor directed philanthropies.' In a follow-up study, Brulle (2018, p. 300) examined lobbying reports from the Center for Responsive Politics, finding that lobbying on climate change varied from 2 to 9 percent of total lobbying from the 107th to the 114th Congresses and increased when the 'Democratic Party controlled both houses, as well as the Executive Branch, and moved to fulfill its promise of passing climate legislation.'

While there has been a good deal of work examining industrial lobbying efforts on environmental legislation, there has been less work examining if these newly bolstered lobbying efforts have dampened the impact of public opinion on policy-makers in comparison. This chapter seeks to address this gap in the literature, by directly examining the relative influence of constituents' concerns versus industry PAC donations on Congressional representatives' environmental voting. To do so, we ask three questions: (1) To what extent do different industries' PAC contributions effect representatives' proclivity to vote for or against environmental policies; (2) To what extent does public concern towards environmental issues, among representatives' constituents, influence those representatives' environmental voting; and (3) What is the relative influence of industries' PAC donations and public concern on representatives' support for environmental policies? The purpose of this study is to address the extent to which constituents' environmental concerns influence the environmental voting behavior of their Congressional representatives relative to the influence of industries' PAC donations. In doing so, we offer insight into whether Congressional members are more responsive to their constituents' preferences and concerns, or whether they are increasingly responsive to PACs' interests.

We begin this chapter by reviewing the various theories on the role of public opinion and interest groups' influence on policy formation, as well as the history of the drivers of policy-making. Next, we review the extant literature on factors known to shape environmental policy-making: industrial donations made via PACs, public opinion and representatives' demographic characteristics. We then provide primary empirical analyses of how these various factors influence congressional members' environmental voting from 1990 to 2010. We conclude with a discussion of our findings as well as the implications of this work for future research on environmental policy-making.

POLICY FORMATION THEORY AND HISTORY OF INTEREST GROUPS IN POLICY-MAKING

In simplistic terms, much of the research on the drivers of US public policy is focused on the question of *who governs America* (Dahl, 1961; Domhoff, 1990). One perspective emerging from such work focuses on democratic explanations in which all interested parties have equal representation in the political process and influence over policy outcomes. Another perspective emerges from the elitist tradition, which argues that a political process and policy-making are captured by powerful interest groups, particularly businesses (Higley, 2010).

Democratic theory contends that political representatives are accountable to their constituents, and thus, they must enact policies consistent with public opinion if they hope to seek re-election (Burstein and Linton, 2002). Yet gauging public opinion on issues is always a difficult task, especially on issues of low salience where slight word changes in survey questions can greatly alter results (Stimson, 2004). With the advent of public opinion polling, and survey methodology, in the 1930s and 1940s, the possibility arose to understand where the populist stands on policy matters and determine if policy decisions were consistent with these views. In an early study, Page and Shapiro (1983, p. 175) connected policy changes with changes in public opinion on 357 issues from 1935 to 1979 and found 'considerable congruence between changes in preferences and in policy'. However, in a more recent study examining public opinion's influence on policy enacted between 1981 and 2002, Gilens and Page (2014) examined average citizen preferences from general social surveys on 1799 specific pieces of proposed policy. The authors compare these public opinion preferences with policy preferences of major business interests, and those in a top income bracket that they label as 'economic elites', then they examine whether a policy was adopted within four years of the survey, finding, 'when one holds constant net interest-group alignments and the preferences of affluent Americans, it makes very little difference what the public thinks' (Gilens and Page, 2014, p. 572).

The impact of public opinion on policy outcomes takes on a different cast with the rise of the political influence of the American business class in the 1980s and 1990s. In one of the first histories of the relationship between the business class and policy-makers during this period, Vogel (1989) notes the increasing investment companies were making into their political lobbying efforts. In 1970, relatively few Fortune 500 companies had formal lobbying components, but within ten years, 80 percent of these companies had established a division for managing the companies' 'external environment' (Vogel, 1989, p. 195). This increased lobbying effort was in response to the sweeping health and environmental reforms of the 1960s and 1970s. Layzer (2012, p. 50) cites journalists' writing at that time, that never had 'the force of public opinion intruded so emphatically on the business community's patterns of operation,' and 'after decades of reticence, the business community has quietly become the most influential lobby in Washington.' Yet efforts to persuade policy in favor of businesses had to operate within the bounds of public opinion, and public opinion was increasingly on the side of environmental protection.

For industrialists, to lobby against policies preferred by the public required using subtler techniques. One of the major mechanisms that businesses began to employ to influence policy during this time was a new lobbying option that became more readily available in 1974, called political action committees or PACs. PACs are groups organized to raise money to elect and defeat candidates. They were successfully used by labor unions in the 1960s, which allowed them to bundle donations from members of labor unions and administer them as a whole via

PACs. In 1907 the Tillman Act barred corporations and banks from giving money to candidates (Waterhouse, 2013). However, in 1976 in *Buckley v. Valeo* the Supreme Court declared political donations were politically protected speech, a ruling that was extended in 2010 with the *Citizens United v. FEC* case (Waterhouse, 2013). This, along with a series of congressional reforms to campaign finance rules in the mid-1970s, allowed for a '[d]ramatic explosion in corporate-funded political action committees' (Waterhouse, 2013, p. 10). PACs gave industrialists the ability to bundle donations in a way that made specific donations opaque to public scrutiny. Such anonymity became increasingly important for industrialists who might want to lobby against the interests of their consumer base without losing their patronage.

The influence of PACs on policy-making has been well studied. However, the argument that PAC donations are associated with a quid pro quo for legislators' votes has not found support in recent literature (Fowler et al., 2020). In their analysis of PAC donations from 2939 publicly traded firms over 16 years, Fowler et al. (2020) found no evidence that donations were related to increased value of a company after their candidate was elected. However, there are multiple reasons why a corporation would donate via PACs. A large body of research finds support for the argument that donations allow for increased access to policy-makers. In an experiment done by Brodbeck et al. (2013), researchers called offices of members of Congress first presenting themselves as private citizens and then as a registered federal lobbyist. They found that in their role as lobbyists they secured 27 meetings compared to just 7 meetings in the role of individual citizen. In fact, in interviews with PAC managers, Clawson et al. (1998) established that PACs are there to develop a relationship with representatives and their staff – to be their 'go to' friends. As one PAC leader states, bringing in a check to a congressional aide might make them happy, 'because he has to raise $10,000 that week, and you just walked in the door with a $3,000 check and you are a hero today at least, but I think the meaningful relationships are those that develop over time and that have many dimensions to the relationship' (Clawson et al., 1998, p. 85).

DRIVERS OF ENVIRONMENTAL POLICY

Now turning to the more specific literature on environmental policy-making, we emphasize three factors shown to influence the passage of environmental legislation: CCCM industries' PAC donations, public opinion, and representatives' demographic composition. We end by discussing the limitations of the current literature in addressing the extent to which these factors simultaneously shape environmental policy, before turning to our own empirical work to address our research questions.

The role of industrial donations in influencing environmental policy specifically has been studied to a lesser extent and results show varied relationships. For example, at a state level, Hogan (2021) examined four legislative sessions within 22 state legislations, finding that pro-environmental campaign donations significantly impacted Democrat environmental voting but not that of Republicans, and that pro-business contributions had no impact. Similarly, Bishop and Dudley (2017) provide an examination of PAC donations from companies with an interest in the Marcellus Shale during the passage of Pennsylvania's Act 13, a piece of legislation that constrained local communities' ability to restrict hydraulic fracturing industries. The authors found that donations were largely channeled towards those legislators who were in leadership roles and thus offered more political leverage on policy outcomes, concluding that roll-call was likely to be related to campaign contributions but members were 'influenced by longer-term, slowly cultivated relationships with industry' (Bishop and Dudley, 2017, p. 171).

Despite the evidence that the business industry has strong relationships with political representatives, representatives are reliant on the public for re-election and therefore must ostensibly align with public opinion in their legislative voting behavior. Work that has been done examining the role of public opinion on environmental voting outcomes shows a relatively strong linkage between representatives' voting and their constituents' interests. For example, a recent study linked conservative/liberal leanings of a district with roll-call voting on environmental issues across four legislative sessions for 22 states and found the 'general public opinion in a lawmaker's district matters greatly for how he or she votes on environmental issues' (Hogan, 2021, p. 561). Similarly, Anderson (2011) estimated district level concern by membership in environmental organizations, finding a strong relationship between this measure and League of Conservation (LCV) voting scores. Furthermore, this was true for both Democrat and Republican members even when controlling for the underlying political leanings of the district (Anderson, 2011).

If, overall, representatives are responsive to their citizens' environmental concerns it is helpful to understand how stable these opinions are. Overall, research has shown that public opinion on environmental issues, while often of low salience, generally increased throughout the 1980s and 1990s (Dunlap, 1991). Looking at data from 2001 to 2010, McCright and Dunlap (2011b) found that from 2001 to 2008, the percentage of Americans who believe that global warming is currently happening trended upward from 54.3 percent to 60.8 percent in 2008 with a sharp decline to 50.1 percent in 2010. However, polarization among Democrats and Republicans regarding global warming and climate change has generally increased over time (Johnson and Schwadel, 2019; McCright and Dunlap, 2011b), with Republicans less likely than Democrats to support government spending and efforts to combat environmental issues (Konisky et al., 2008). Conservatives are also more likely to be climate change deniers (Schwirplies, 2018) and support counter claims to climate science (McCright and Dunlap, 2000). Conservative White males are more likely to be climate change deniers than other demographics (McCright and Dunlap, 2011a).

The political polarization of environmental issues in the public domain has been hypothesized to be related to efforts by business interests and political elites to undermine public concern about environmental issues (Dunlap et al., 2016). For example, Farrell (2015) analyzed 40 000 communications (i.e. press releases, website articles, policy statements, conference transcripts, published papers, and blog articles) from actors within organizations identified by Brulle (2013) as those donating to organizations promoting climate skepticism. The author found these organizations' media texts were 'meant to polarize the climate change issue' (Farrell 2015, p. 92). In prior work, Brulle et al. (2012) collated 74 public opinion surveys over nine years and linked these trends in opinion with 'elite cues', such as number of Congressional hearings on climate change, press releases on these issues, and roll-call votes on climate change bills. The authors found that when Democrats voted for environmental issues it had no impact on environmental opinions writ large, but when Republicans voted for/against environmental issues it had a significant effect on public opinion in the same direction (Brulle et al., 2012). They also found issuances of Democratic or Republican Party press releases on climate change were related to increases/decreases in public opinion respectively (Brulle et al., 2012).

In addition to political donations and constituents' concern about environmental issues, specific demographic characteristics have been related to environmental concern. While what demographic characteristics are associated with environmental concern is a question of ongoing scholarly interest, there are many indicators that show consistent relationships. For example, research from the past several decades has consistently found that women engage in more private environmentally oriented behaviors such as driving less or recycling more than men (Hunter et al., 2004; McCright and Xiao, 2014). Women are also more supportive than men of government spending to address environmental issues (Konisky et al., 2008) and women tend to express more concern than men regarding health-related environmental issues (Xiao and McCright, 2013).

In addition to gender, race is shown to be consistently related to environmental concern, with Whites more likely to perform public environmental behaviors than non-Whites (Xiao and McCright, 2014). However, in a recent nationally representative survey of the US, 1212 adults, environmental concern amongst non-Whites was consistently underestimated, yet non-Whites were found to be more concerned about environmental issues than Whites (Pearson et al., 2018). Blacks have been found to have a higher level of personal worry than Whites regarding environmental issues such as air and water pollution, which are typically issues of environmental justice. In addition, Blacks were found to have no less concern than Whites on traditional environmental issues, such as quality of the environment in general, species extinction, and loss of tropical rainforests (Lazri and Konisky, 2019).

Research on the relationship between age and education has been less consistent. In a recent analysis of General Social Survey data on spending on the natural environment from 1973 to 2014, it was found that over this time-period age was strongly related to environmental concern, with younger respondents significantly more concerned about environmental issues. While previous work has argued that younger people are associated with higher levels of concern due to birth cohort effects (Guber, 2003; Van Liere and Dunlap, 1980), these authors controlled for cohort and still found a robust relationship between age and concern. Guber (2003) argued that higher levels of education were associated with greater ability to understand complex problems like environmental issues. Greater levels of education have been positively associated with environmental concern, with research showing that House of Representatives 'with a bachelors/associates degree voted the pro-environmental position 25% less often than those with a graduate degree, and representatives with a high school diploma 43% less often than those with a graduate degree' (Ard et al., 2017, p. 1123).

In the following analysis, we control for the demographic variables of Congressional representatives associated with environmental concern and hone in on the relationship between environmental voting and donations from industrial political action committees as well as public opinion on environmental issues at the state level.

DATA AND METHODS

Dependent Variable

Our dependent variable is Congressional voting on environmental protection measures. We obtained 3299 roll-call votes for House of Representatives for every session from the 103rd and 111th Congress. These data were obtained from the League of Conservation Voters

Table 7.1   Descriptive statistics on PAC donations and sociodemographic variables for all representatives and by party from 1990 to 2010

	Republicans	Democrats
Average LCV Score	20%	77%
Percentage of time vote is pro-environment		
Biographical		
Mean Year Born	1946	1944
Sex		
Male	2,036	2,089
Female	183	409
Race		
non-Hispanic White	2,170	1,925
African American	7	381
Hispanic	33	157
Asian	9	35
Education		
High School	143	105
Bachelor's or Associate	744	686
Graduate Degree	1,332	1,707
Regions		
South	850	78
Non-South	1,369	1,714
N	2,219	2,498

(LCV), an environmental advocacy group founded in 1970 that defines which pieces of legislation voted on in Congress are aimed at protecting the natural environment. Like other groups, such as the American Conservative Union, these organizations score a vote as either 'for' or 'against' the issue of importance to them. In the case of the LCV, how each vote reflects on the representative's stance on environmental issues is determined by a group of leaders across 20 environmental organizations. The total number of 'for' votes that a representative cast were tallied and used to calculate the percentages of times a representative voted in the determined pro-environmental direction. Information on the biographic information of representatives (sex, party, race, gender, age, education) was obtained from the Congressional Quarterly Press' Congress Collection. We did not find a significant correlation between representatives' age and LCV and therefore left it out of the remaining analyses. Party Independents, and those who could vote at their own discretion, such as the Speaker of the House, were dropped from the analysis. See Table 7.1 for descriptive statistics for congressional representatives.

Independent Variables

The 2010 *Citizen United* ruling allowed for 'both corporations and unions to spend unlimited funds on electioneering' (La Raja and Schaffner, 2014, p. 102). Due to the considerable modification of the rules of PAC spending by the *Citizens United* case in 2010 (Hansen et al., 2015; La Raja and Schaffner, 2014), we restrict our analysis of donations to the era before this drastic regulation change was implemented to preserve congruity in the lobbying choices and motivations available to corporations. This also allows us to concentrate on the period where the CCCM grew and expanded (Brulle, 2013). Since the *Citizens United* allowed for unprecedented unanimous corporate spending (Hieta, 2017), the results outlined below are likely to be an underestimate of the actual industrial donations in today's political landscape. Even so, between 1990 and 2010 there were 'many ways in which a corporation or union may legally participate in federal election activities' (FEC, 2007, p. ii). For example, a corporation or union can organize a political committee that has the ability to make contributions on their behalf (FEC, 2007). Information disclosed by PACs when they file with the Federal Election Commission (FEC) is used by The Center for Responsive Politics to classify the corporation, trade association, union or other entity that controls the PAC into 13 meta-categories, or sectors that are further broken down into 92 industries. These categories generally fall within the same groupings as the North American Industry Classification Systems (NAICS) but not exactly, as PACs can also be classified as purely ideological, such as those promoting gun rights or abortion issues. Excluded from this analysis are ideological PACs that are unrelated to the subject matter of this research project, such as PACs classified for and against abortion, gun rights and gun control, Pro Israel, general liberal and conservative PACS, and leadership PACs. We did, however, choose to include PACs specified as environmental and human rights organizations, as they have ideologies relevant to this project.

Pairwise correlations were run with representatives' LCV scores with the remaining 70 industries. Those that had no significant relationship with LCV scores at the 0.05 level were discarded. These excluded industries were: Gambling, Civil Servants, Clergy, Construction, Environmental Services/Equipment, Lobbyists, Miscellaneous Agriculture, Communications/Electronics, Live Entertainment, Savings and Loans, Sea Transport, Securities, TV/Movies/Music. Sixty-one industries remained, eight of which we classified as indicative of the CCCM. These were: Oil and Gas (e.g. American Petroleum Institute), Mining, Electric Utilities, Chemical Industry, Steel Production, Waste Management, and Miscellaneous Energy and Manufacturing (e.g. automobile manufacturers, National Association of Manufacturers). The literature has already previously recognized these industries as being a part of the counter-movement working against environmental interests (Vandeweerdt et al., 2016; Brulle, 2013 sup; Layzer, 2012). The remaining 53 industries significantly correlated with LCV were grouped based on their industrial sectors, which we confirmed were generally related to the directionality of their relationship with LCV scores. As a result, we included in our analysis the following industrial sectors: Agriculture, Retail Business (e.g. Chamber of Commerce), Construction, Defense, Health, Ideological, Labor, Communications/Electronics, Finance, Insurance and Real Estate, Lawyers, Natural Resources, Non-Profits and Transportation (e.g. railroads). We chose to keep PACs classified under labor unions (e.g. coal miners' union) separate from industries represented in our CCCM classification as we expect these groups have a more unique set of motivations based around their members' health, unlike other PACs we group under the CCCM who are motivated primarily by economic incentives. Similarly, we keep transportation separate from the CCCM because this industrial sector was generally in support of biofuels (Herrera, 2006), a topic also supported by environmental groups. See Table 7.2 for a complete breakdown of which industries were grouped in each sector.

Donations were adjusted for inflation, making them all equivalent to 2010 dollars, then divided by 10 000 to simplify the interpretation in our statistical models. Table 7.2 breaks down the average amount given by industrial PACs by party. We found that across all industries,

Table 7.2 Average amount from PAC per representative from 1990 to 2010

	Republicans	Democrats
CCCM Industry		
Oil & Gas	$13,894.81	$5,346.37
Mining	$3,035.74	$1,011.30
Electric Utilities	$14,085.40	$10,742.55
Misc Energy	$1,335.87	$1,079.57
Steel Production	$752.47	$654.91
Misc Manufacturing	$6,239.71	$3,468.82
Chemical & Related	$4,290.64	$2,107.54
Waste Management	$692.36	$607.45
Sector		
Agribusiness	$28,337.27	$19,178.88
Retail Business	$27,792.92	$13,763.69
Communications/Electronics	$11,741.50	$8,483.55
Construction	$12,055.41	$5,146.31
Defense	$12,488.89	$9,809.60
Finance, Insurance & Real Estate	$53,284.51	$38,902.95
Health	$40,329.49	$33,988.57
Ideological	$629.45	$3,243.74
Labor	$13,743.06	$103,894.20
Lawyers	$8,634.58	$15,602.57
Natural Resources	$425.23	$110.79
Non-Profits	$396.72	$625.90
Transportation	$20,905.08	$11,244.33

Republicans received on average $634 less than Democrats, due primarily to the large sums of money that Democrats received from labor unions. Removing labor unions from the analysis, Republicans then received $3628 more on average from PACs than Democrats. Republicans received, on average $2746 more than Democrats from CCCM industries in general.

Annual state-level public opinion data on environmental issues were obtained from the General Social Survey (GSS). GSS data is collected annually or biannually in a nationally representative sample since 1972. Since 1973 they have been collecting responses to the question:

> We are faced with many problems in this country, none of which can be solved easily or inexpensively. I'm going to name some of these problems, and for each one I'd like you to name some of these problems, and for each one I'd like you to tell me whether you think we're spending too much money on it, too little money, or about the right amount. Are we spending 'too much', 'too little', or 'about right' amount of money on improving and protecting the environment?

There are other questions asked in the GSS that might be of interest to a study. Yet the question noted above is the only variable consistently asked over the period examined. We focus on the years 1990 to 2010, when the CCCM has been shown to be increasingly investing in their political donations via PACS (Ard et al., 2017). The census tract that a respondent lived in was obtained from restricted GSS data. Weighted responses to the question laid out above was averaged by state with those responding by saying there was 'too little' spending on environmental protection as 1, those 'about right' as 2, and those as 'too much' as 3. Those states (N

= 161) where there were fewer than 30 respondents for the year examined were dropped from the analysis, leaving a total of 347 state-by-year observations.[1]

Analytic Strategy

We model repeated observations on an individual representative's voting over time using mixed model logistic regression (SAS PROC GLIMMIX) to estimate the probability of a pro-environmental roll-call vote. Predictor variables included fixed effects for a representative's race, sex, education, party and if they represent a southern or non-southern state using Census boundary regions. We include a fixed effect for the representatives' state-level average public opinion on environmental spending during a given congressional session. We also included a fixed effect interaction variable between party and congressional session to control for political polarization and covariates for industrial PAC donations. Finally, a random effect for each person, nested within race, sex and education, was included to control for repeated votes by the same subject. We ran sensitivity analyses including a fixed effect for age, as well as the year the representative started in Congress. Neither of these variables were significant and results were virtually identical to those presented here. In addition, we ran LCV as a lagged variable to see if donations from the previous year impacted future LCV and found the results were substantially the same. Finally, public opinion data was interacted with time and not found to be significant, suggesting the relationship between public opinion and LCV was consistent over the period examined.

RESULTS

One of the major questions we seek to address in this chapter is whether public opinion has had any effect on representatives' pro-environmental voting records over the past decades in which CCCM industries' (Oil and Gas, Mining, Electric Utilities, Chemical Industry, Steel Production, Waste Management, and Miscellaneous Energy and Manufacturing) PAC donations activity had increased. Figure 7.1a shows the average public opinion score on national environmental spending across congressional sessions from 1990 to 2010. We can see that while there have been slight modulations in the degree of support over time, on average constituents' environmental opinions fell between 1.4 and 1.5. This indicates that on average constituents believe that the federal government is spending 'too little' or 'about right' on improving or protecting the environment. This is similar to relatively consistent average LCV scores amongst Congress, which average nearly 50 percent of the House casting pro-environmental votes from 1994 to 2010, albeit due to increasing polarization (Figure 7.1b).

To examine the relationship between public opinion, PAC donations, and environmental voting over time we present six models (Table 7.3). Models 1–3 show results with donations aggregated among the eight industries identified as benefiting from the CCCM. Models 4–6 show results with donations disaggregated by the specific industries, which allows for exploration of which CCCM industry groups are leading the trends we see in the first three models. Models 1 and 4 are both run for the full dataset with representatives from both political parties included, whereas the results for Models 2 and 5 are for Democrats alone and Models 3 and 6 are for Republicans alone. All models control for Congress and political polarization;

The effect of public opinion on environmental policy 143

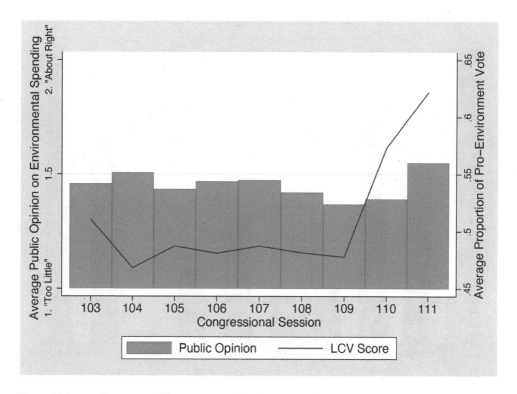

Figure 7.1a   Average public opinion and LCV scores by congress

however, while significant, these estimates are not shown, so as to keep the table uncluttered and focused on the variables of interest.

In the full models, the odds of a Democrat representative voted pro-environment are about 55 times higher than for a Republican representative ($p < 0.001$, Models 1 and 4). Our estimates for public opinion, a main contribution of this chapter, show that as constituents within representatives' states increasingly believe the federal government is spending 'too much' on improving or protecting the environment, the odds of a representative voting pro-environment decrease by 18 percent ($p < 0.05$, Models 1 and 4). When the sample is constrained to only Republican representatives, public opinion is nonsignificant (Models 3 and 6). Yet among Democrat representatives, as constituents within representatives' states increasingly believe the federal government is spending 'too much' on improving or protecting the environment increases, the odds of a Democrat representative voting pro-environment decrease by 25 percent ($p < 0.05$, Model 2).

Our estimates for PAC donations, the other main contribution of this chapter, show the enduring influence of CCCM industries on representatives' pro-environmental voting across political parties and time. To begin, when the eight CCCM industries are aggregated we can see that for every additional $10 000 donation an individual representative received from a CCCM PAC, their probability of voting for the pro-environmental position decreased by 3 percent (Model 1). These effects hold across Democrat and Republican representatives. With every additional $10 000 donation a Democrat or Republican representative received from a CCCM PAC, their likelihood of voting for the pro-environmental position decreased by 4 percent and

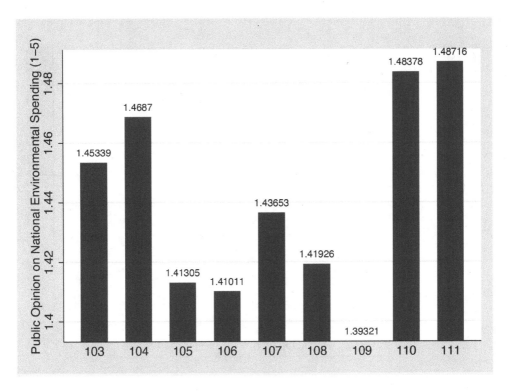

Figure 7.1b   Average public opinion by congressional session

3 percent, respectively (p < 0.01, Models 2 and 3). When we disaggregate the CCCM group into its component industries (Models 4–6), we see which industries' donations are drivers of these associated voting patterns. In the full models (Model 4), every additional $10 000 donation from an Oil and Gas PAC decreased the odds of voting for the pro-environmental position by 6 percent (p < 0.001). Similarly, every additional $10 000 donation from a Utilities PAC decreased the odds of voting for the pro-environmental position by 4 percent. Yet, every additional $10 000 donation from a Chemical Manufacturing PAC increased the odds of voting for the pro-environmental position by 13 percent. These relationships show important differences when parties are separated and compared in Model 5 and 6. Oil and Gas donations are a nonsignificant predictor of Republicans' pro-environmental voting, yet for Democrats every additional $10 000 donation from an Oil and Gas PAC decreased the odds of voting for the pro-environmental position by 9 percent (p < 0.001). Meanwhile, donations from Steel Production industries were not significantly related to environmental voting in the full model or for Republicans (Models 4 and 6), but for every additional $10 000 donation received from Steel Production PACs the probability they would vote pro-environment decreased by 21 percent. Finally, among the CCCM PACs, Republicans' environmental vote was only influenced by Utilities PACs, with every additional $10 000 donation from a Utilities PAC decreasing the odds they would vote pro-environment by 6 percent (p < 0.01, Model 6).

These analyses also illuminate other industries' PAC donations' influence on representatives' pro-environmental voting. For example, ideological groups, which are made up of

Table 7.3   Results from multilevel ordered logistic regression models predicting pro-environmental voting from 1990 to 2010

		Model 1:		Model 2:		Model 3:	
		Odds Ratio	95% Confidence	Odds Ratio	95% Confidence	Odds Ratio	95% Confidence
Party [a]				*Democrats*		*Republicans*	
	Democrat	54.58***	43.0, 69.2				
Public Opinion on Environment		0.82*	0.68, 0.99	0.75*	0.58, 0.98	0.90	0.68, 1.18
PAC Industry/Sector							
CCCM	CCCM	0.97***	0.95, 0.98	0.96***	0.94, 0.98	0.97**	0.95, 0.99
	Oil/Gas						
	Mining						
	Utilities						
	Energy						
	Manufacturing						
	Chemical Manufacturing						
	Steel Production						
	Waste Management						
	Transportation	0.79	0.95, 1.00	0.99	0.95, 1.04	0.94**	0.91, 0.98
	Finance	1.00	0.99, 1.01	1.00	0.99, 1.01	1.00	0.99, 1.01
	Natural Resources	0.99	0.73, 1.34	0.45*	0.49, 1.74	1.28	0.89, 1.82
	Ideological	1.14**	1.04, 1.26	1.07	0.96, 1.20	1.52***	1.25, 1.85
	Lawyers	1.03	0.99, 1.07	1.04	0.99, 1.09	1.00	0.94, 1.07
	Defense	1.02*	1.00, 1.04	1.01	0.98, 1.04	1.02	0.99, 1.05
	Agriculture	0.97***	0.96, 0.98	0.98*	0.97, 1.00	0.96**	0.94, 0.99
	Construction	1.01	0.96, 1.06	0.95	0.88, 1.03	1.01	0.95, 1.08
	Labor Unions	1.02**	1.01, 1.03	1.01**	1.00, 1.02	1.09***	1.07, 1.12
	Communication	1.01	0.98, 1.04	1.04*	1.00, 1.09	0.98	0.94, 1.02
	Health	1.02***	1.01, 1.03	1.04***	1.02, 1.05	1.01	1.00, 1.02
	Non-Profit	0.93	0.77, 1.12	0.90	0.71, 1.13	0.87	0.63, 1.19
	Retail	1.01	0.98, 1.03	0.94**	0.90, 0.98	1.06***	1.02, 1.09
Race [b]							
	African American	1.53*	1.16, 2.01	1.33*	1.03, 1.72	1.55	0.35, 6.79
	Asian	1.49	0.70, 3.15	2.38	0.99, 5.73	0.60	0.16, 2.22
	Hispanic	1.27	0.87, 1.85	1.01	0.69, 1.46	2.27	0.92, 5.59
Sex [c]							
	Female	1.75***	1.41, 2.19	1.75***	1.36, 2.25	1.47*	1.00, 2.17
Education [d]							
	High School	0.63**	0.46, 0.86	0.63*	0.42, 0.96	0.64*	0.41, 0.98
	Bachelors/Associates	0.73***	0.62, 0.87	0.70***	0.57, 0.86	0.83	0.65, 1.05
Region [e]							
	Non-South	2.27***	1.95, 2.64	2.41***	1.99, 2.92	1.95***	1.56, 2.44
Intercept		0.13***	0.09, 0.19	9.43***	5.89, 15.1	0.10***	0.06, 0.16

	Model 4:		Model 5:		Model 6:	
	Odds Ratio	95% Confidence	Odds Ratio	95% Confidence	Odds Ratio	95% Confidence
			Democrats		*Republicans*	
Party [a]						
Democrat	54.69***	43.1, 69.4				
Public Opinion on Environment	0.82*	0.68, 0.99	0.77	0.60, 1.00	0.89	0.68, 1.17
PAC Industry/Sector						
CCCM						
Oil/Gas	0.94***	0.91, 0.97	0.91***	0.86, 0.96	0.97	0.93, 1.02
Mining	0.95	0.85, 1.05	0.94	0.80, 1.11	0.98	0.85, 1.13
Utilities	0.96**	0.94, 0.99	0.98	0.94, 1.01	0.94**	0.90, 0.98
Energy	0.95	0.83, 1.09	0.98	0.82, 1.18	0.93	0.75, 1.15
Manufacturing	1.03	0.97, 1.09	1.07	0.97, 1.18	1.00	0.93, 1.08
Chemical Manufacturing	1.13**	1.05, 1.22	1.11	1.00, 1.23	1.12	0.99, 1.25
Steel Production	0.89	0.77, 1.04	0.79*	0.63, 0.99	0.95	0.77, 1.16
Waste Management	0.92	0.78, 1.09	0.85	0.68, 1.06	0.98	0.76, 1.27
Transportation	0.98	0.95, 1.00	1.00	0.96, 1.04	0.94**	0.90, 0.97
Finance	1.00	0.99, 1.01	1.00	0.99, 1.01	1.00	0.99, 1.01
Natural Resources	1.02	0.74, 1.40	0.46*	0.24, 0.86	1.26	0.87, 1.82
Ideological	1.14**	1.04, 1.26	1.08	0.97, 1.21	1.53***	1.26, 1.87
Lawyers	1.02	0.98, 1.07	1.04	0.99, 1.10	1.00	0.93, 1.06
Defense	1.02	1.00, 1.04	1.01	0.98, 1.04	1.02	0.98, 1.05
Agriculture	0.97***	0.96, 0.98	0.98	0.97, 1.00	0.96**	0.94, 0.98
Construction	1.00	0.95, 1.05	0.95	0.88, 1.03	1.00	0.94, 1.07
Labor Unions	1.02***	1.01, 1.03	1.01*	1.00, 1.02	1.09***	1.07, 1.12
Communication	1.01	0.98, 1.04	1.03	0.98, 1.07	0.98	0.94, 1.02
Health	1.01**	1.01, 1.02	1.03***	1.02, 1.05	1.01	1.00, 1.02
Non-Profit	0.94	0.78, 1.14	0.90	0.71, 1.13	0.88	0.64, 1.21
Retail	1.01	0.98, 1.03	0.93**	0.90, 0.98	1.05**	1.02, 1.09
Race [b]						
African American	1.52**	1.16, 2.00	1.32*	0.60, 1.00	1.59	0.36, 6.98
Asian	1.48	0.70, 3.12	1.09*	1.02, 1.71	0.58	0.15, 2.15
Hispanic	1.29	0.88, 1.88	1.02	0.46, 2.62	2.31	0.94, 5.70
Sex [c]						
Female	1.75***	1.41, 2.19	1.74***	0.70, 1.48	1.47	1.00, 2.17
Education [d]						
High School	0.63**	0.46, 0.86	0.63*	0.42, 0.95	0.65*	0.42, 0.99
Bachelors/Associates	0.74***	0.63, 0.87	0.70***	0.57, 0.86	0.83	0.65, 1.05
Region [e]						
Non-South	2.24***	0.94, 1.27	2.37***	1.95, 2.87	1.94***	1.55, 2.43
Intercept	0.13***	0.09, 0.18	8.85***	5.52, 14.2	0.10***	0.06, 0.16

Notes: Odds Ratios (OR) are the exponentiated coefficients and are interpreted as follows: (1) if OR < 1 then there are lower odds, or; (2) if OR > 1 than there are greater odds of association with the exposure and outcome.
[a] reference category is Republican; [b] reference category is non-Hispanic white; [c] reference category is male; [d] reference category is graduate degree; [e] reference category is South.
*p < 0.05; **p < 0.01; ***p < 0.001

human rights and environmental groups, increased the probability a representative would choose the pro-environmental position by 14 percent (p < 0.01, Models 1 and 4). However, the influence of ideological groups is most pronounced among Republicans, where every additional $10 000 donation from an Ideological PAC increased the odds of voting for the pro-environmental position by approximately 52 percent (p < 0.001, Models 3 and 6). Labor unions appear to have significant and similar effects on voting across party lines. For example, every additional $10 000 donation increased the probability of all representatives taking the pro-environmental position by 2 percent, but only increased the odds for Democrats by 1 percent (Models 2 and 5), yet increased the probability among Republicans by 9 percent (Models 3 and 6). Simultaneously, PAC donations from Health industries appear to only influence Democrats and the full model. For example, every additional $10 000 donation from Health PACs increased the probability of all representatives taking the pro-environmental position by 1–2 percent (Models 1 and 4), whereas it increases the odds for Democrats by 3–4 percent (Models 2 and 5), and had no effect on Republicans' voting. Yet, Republican representatives alone were more likely to take pro-environmental position because of additional donations from Retail PACs (Models 3 and 6). In fact, Democrats were less likely to take the pro-environmental position as a result of additional donations from Retail PACs (Models 2 and 5), and the full model had a nonsignificant relationship with Retail PACs' donations. Finally, Transportation, Agriculture and Natural Resource PACs had significant but varied effects across party lines. For example, every additional $10 000 donation from a Transportation PAC decreased the probability of Republican representatives taking the pro-environmental position by 6 percent (Models 3 and 6) but had no effect on environmental voting for all representatives and Democrats. Agriculture PAC donations were associated with decreased odds of the full sample and Republicans taking the pro-environmental position by 3 and 4 percent, respectively. Meanwhile, Natural Resource donations were only associated with Democrats' pro-environmental voting, such that every additional $10 000 donation decreased the probability of Democrats taking the pro-environmental position by 54 percent (Model 2).

Moving onto representatives' demographics effect on pro-environmental voting, African American representatives are 53 percent more likely to have voted pro-environment relative to White representatives (p < 0.01), and there are no significant differences between non-Hispanic White, Asian, and Hispanic representatives' pro-environmental voting (p > 0.05). Importantly, African American Democrats are 33 percent more likely to have voted pro-environment relative to White representatives, while there were no significant racial divides in pro-environmental voting among Republican representatives, probably because the sample size is too small for proper estimation. However, gender divides in pro-environment positions were significant and similar across party lines. For example, the odds that a women representative took the pro-environmental stance were 75 percent higher than for their male colleagues in the full models. In the Democrat only models, women took the pro-environmental position 25–26 percent more often than men, and among Republicans women took the pro-environmental position 47 percent more often than men (although significance varied between models). Educational differences among representatives had consistent and similar effects across parties as well. Relative to representatives with a graduate degree, those with a high school degree were 35–37 percent less likely to take the pro-environment position regardless of party identity (Models 1–6). However, the differences among representatives with a bachelors/associates degree relative to those with graduate degrees varied somewhat. For example, all representatives, and only Democrats with bachelors/associates degrees, were between 27–30 percent less likely than representatives with a graduate degree to take the pro-environmental position; however, there were no significant differences among Republicans with a bachelors/associates degree relative to those with a graduate degree in their pro-environmental voting. Finally, representatives with their districts in the South were significantly less likely to take a pro-environmental position regardless of party affiliation. For example, representatives with districts outside of the South took the pro-environmental position 2.2 times more often than those with districts in the South (Models 1 and 4). Among Democrats, representatives with districts outside of the South took the pro-environmental position 2.4 times more often than those with districts in the South (Models 2 and 5), while among Republicans, those not in the South were 94–95 percent more likely to take the pro-environment position than those in the South (Models 3 and 6).

DISCUSSION

Despite the growing importance and interest in environmental policy-making in the US, there remain substantial limitations to scholars' understanding of the relative drivers of legislators' voting on such issues. Explanations of the factors expected to impact environmental voting tend to pit the general public's opinion against businesses' PACs donations. Yet, there remains a dearth of evidence about the relative importance of each of these factors relative to one another and how they vary across time and representatives' political affiliation.

Our analysis documents the importance of representatives' political party, general public opinion, and PACs donations, as they correlate with congressional members' pro-environmental voting stances. Our analyses show that by far the most important predictor of pro-environmental voting among congressional representatives is their political party affiliation. We also show, however, that the influence of public opinion and PACs donations on environmental policy-making varies between Democrats and Republicans. Thus, while public opinion and business interests are believed to be mechanisms through which various interest groups influence congressional representatives' voting stances, the degree to which this is true varies by representatives' political affiliations as well as their demographic characteristics. For example, overall, we find that both constituents' opinions about the importance of pro-environmental spending by the federal government and CCCM PACs donations matter to legislators' voting stance. However, when we examined these relationships by party, public opinion only influences Democrats' voting, while CCCM PACs donations only affected the voting stance of Republicans.

Equally interesting are how differences in the specific industries' PACs donations have varying influence over pro-environmental voting by political parties, as well as the fact that demographic characteristics of representatives vary in meaningful ways by political parties. For example, the oil and gas and steel production industry's PACs donations are shown to reduce pro-environmental voting among Democrats, but have a nonsignificant influence on Republicans, while utility PAC donations have a significant negative influence on pro-environmental voting among Republicans, but no influence over Democrats' voting. Outside of CCCM industries, we see that ideological PACs donations have a large, positive influence on Republicans' pro-environmental voting but no influence on Democrats' voting, while labor unions and communication PACs have a positive effect on Democrats alone.

One of the major limitations of this study, along with most studies examining public opinion on environmental concern, is that the data are limited. Specifically, there is a lack of nationally representative data over time. There have been many efforts to overcome this limitation, such as trying to make questions commensurate across surveys (Brulle et al., 2012), utilizing proxy measures like degree of conservativism (Hogan, 2021), and using algorithms to estimate survey responses (Vandeweerdt et al., 2016). Our efforts to overcome the same limitations were to average survey responses across states. While we preferred this measure due to its potential for straightforward interpretation, it did constrain us to those states that had enough respondents to be representative, that is, dropping those with fewer than 30 observations (Scherbaum and Ferreter, 2011). While survey weights developed by the National Opinion Research Center were applied to make response representative, more data is almost always better. Efforts should be made to develop, and make accessible, robust, nationally representative, longitudinal survey instruments that future research can utilize.

This study also makes a few assumptions that future work should endeavor to test, such as the independent nature presumed between PAC donations and public opinion. Although we found no significant interaction between these variables, PACs do spend their funds on advertising, which might influence public opinion in a way our study was unable to test. While previous work has shown a significant relationship between media coverage and environmental concern (Brulle et al., 2012) they also noted the impact of television coverage does not last longer than a month. In this study, we assumed the long-term nature of our study would smooth out the effects of media, but future work should attempt to capture these effects.

While this study provides important insights into the role of interest groups in environmental policy-making, the balancing act of keeping all voices and interests equal in the policy process is a never-ending process. Where the US lies on this continuum varies across time, policy issue, and where in the political process these groups are interacting with policy-makers (Wlezien, 1995; Bevan and Rasmussen, 2020). While we took a bird's-eye view of these processes, by looking over time at a national level, there are many more perspectives from which these relationships could be examined, for example, narrowing in on specific pieces of legislation and trying to relate these to specific industries as was done at the state level by Bishop and Dudley (2017) who examined legislation in Pennsylvania on hydraulic fracturing. Additionally, narrowing in on specific survey questions related to pieces of legislation would be enlightening. While scholars have done this type of work with several different types of policies (Gilens and Page, 2014) this has yet to be done on issues related to the environment.

The dynamics of movements and their countermovements, and their impact on policy outcomes, argue for the importance of understanding the political opportunities that social movements work within; the state can 'repress or facilitate collective action by altering the relative costs of particular tactics' (Meyer and Staggenborg, 1996, p. 1633; Soule and Olzak, 2004; Giugni, 1998). The US government has facilitated action by industry by granting personhood and adjudicating donations to political candidates as protected free speech. The analyses presented here support the argument that the climate change countermovement has utilized these expanding political opportunities presented by the US government to allow for donations from industry to be channeled towards legislators as a catalyst for mobilization (Soule et al., 1999). Scholars of the CCCM should seek out those political opportunities which have allowed for these movements to gain influence in the policy process over time. This is likely to vary over time and across country. How do these relationships hold across contexts?

Scholars of American democracy have long noted that government responsiveness to public opinion is a corner stone of its health (Burstein, 2014). Yet what weight do citizens' voices have in comparison with others? Should those industries that are likely to be impacted by legislation have a greater say? As it currently stands, we find no evidence that the influence of public opinion on Congressional members' LCV scores changed over time. However, we did find that respondents' environmental voting was more strongly correlated to PAC donations, particularly from CCCM industries, than their state constituents' opinion on environmental issues. As political scholars back to Plato have argued, democracy only works when its citizens participate. One could say that businesses began to take an active role with their increased political lobbying in the 1980s and 1990s. This raises the question of whether other interests will have the ability to increase their participation in step with these efforts.

NOTE

1. All states had years they were not in the analysis with the exception of the following states: California, Idaho, Iowa, Michigan, New Hampshire, New York, North Carolina, Pennsylvania, Texas, Virginia and Washington. Those states that were dropped from the analysis were dropped an average of four times with a max of ten times for Kentucky, nine times for Delaware and eight times for Connecticut, South Carolina and Oregon. A t-test of the state mean GSS scores that were dropped from the analysis due to small sample size did not show any statistically significant differences to those that were left in the model.

REFERENCES

Anderson, S.E. (2011) Complex constituencies: Intense environmentalists and representation. *Environmental Politics*. **20**(4), pp. 547–65.

Ard, K., Garcia, N. and Kelly, P. (2017) Another avenue of action: An examination of climate change countermovement industries' use of PAC donations and their relationship to Congressional voting over time. *Environmental Politics*. **26**(6), pp. 1107–31.

Banerjee, T. and Murray, J. (2020) Class dominance or fracturing? Sources of broad interest in lobbying by Fortune 500 corporations. *Sociological Perspectives*, pp. 1–19.

Bevan, S. and Rasmussen, A. (2020) When does government listen to the public? Voluntary associations and dynamic agenda representation in the United States. *Policy Studies Journal*. **48**(1), pp. 111–32.

Bishop, B.H. and Dudley, M.R. (2017) The role of constituency, party, and industry in Pennsylvania's Act 13. *State Politics and Policy Quarterly*. **17**(2), pp. 154–79.

Blumenthal, S. (1986) *The Rise of the Counter-establishment*. New York, NY: Union Square Press.

Brodbeck, J., Harrigan, M.T. and Smith, D.A. (2013) Citizen and lobbyist access to Members of Congress: Who gets and who gives? *Interest Groups & Advocacy*. **2**(3), pp. 323–42.

Brulle, R.J. (2013) Institutionalizing delay: Foundation funding and the creation of U.S. climate change counter-movement organizations. *Climatic Change*. **122**(4), pp. 681–94.

Brulle, R.J. (2018) The climate lobby: A sectoral analysis of lobbying spending on climate change in the USA, 2000 to 2016. *Climatic Change*. **149**(3–4), pp. 289–303.

Brulle, R.J., Carmichael, J. and Jenkins, J.C. (2012) Shifting public opinion on climate change: An empirical assessment of factors influencing concern over climate change in the U.S., 2002–2010. *Climatic Change*. **114**(2), pp. 169–88. Available from DOI: 10.1007/s10584-012-0403-y.

Burstein, P. (2014) *American Public Opinion, Advocacy, and Policy in Congress*. New York, NY: Cambridge University Press.

Burstein, P. and Linton, A. (2002) The impact of political parties, interest groups, and social movement organizations on public policy. *Social Forces*. **81**(2), pp. 381–408.

Clawson, D., Neustadtl, A. and Weller, M. (1998). *Dollars and Votes: How Business Campaign Contributions Subvert Democracy*. Philadelphia, PA: Temple University Press.

Dahl, R.A. (1961) *Who Governs? Democracy and Power in an American City*. New Haven, CT: Yale University Press.

Domhoff, G.W. (1990) *The Power Elite and the State: How Policy is Made in America*. Hawthorne, NY: Aldine de Gruyter.

Domhoff, G.W. (2002) *Who Rules America?* 4th edn. New York, NY: McGraw-Hill.

Dunlap, R.E. (1991) Trends in public opinion toward environmental issues: 1965–1990. *Society and Natural Resources*. **4**(3), pp. 285–312.

Dunlap, R.E. and McCright, A.M. (2015) Challenging climate change: The denial countermovement. In: Dunlap, R. and Brulle, R. (eds) *Climate Change and Society: Sociological Perspectives*. New York, NY: Oxford University Press, pp. 300–333.

Dunlap, R.E., McCright, A.M. and Yarosh, J.H. (2016) The political divide on climate change: Partisan polarization widens in the U.S. *Environment: Science and Policy for Sustainable Development*. **58**(5), pp. 4–23. Available from DOI: 10.1080/00139157.2016.1208995.

Farrell, J. (2015) Corporate funding and ideological polarization about climate change. *Proceedings of the National Academy of Sciences*. **113**(1), pp. 92–7.

Federal Election Commission (FEC) (2007) Corporations and labor organizations. *Federal Election Commission* (online). Available from: http://classic.fec.gov/pdf/colagui.pdf. (accessed 17 August 2017).

Fowler, A., Garro, H. and Spenkuch, J.L. (2020) Quid pro quo? Corporate returns to campaign contributions. *The Journal of Politics*. **82**(3), pp. 844–58. Available from DOI: 10.1086/707307.

Gilens, M. and Page, B.I. (2014) Testing theories of American politics: Elites, interest groups, and average citizens. *Perspectives on Politics*. **12**(3), pp. 564–81.

Giugni, M.G. (1998) Was it worth the effort? The outcomes and consequences of social movements. *Annual Review of Sociology*. **24**, pp. 371–93.

Guber, D. (2003) *The Grassroots of a Green Revolution: Polling America on the Environment*. Boston, MA: MIT Press.

Hansen, W.L., Rocca, M.S. and Ortiz, B.L. (2015) The effects of citizens united on corporate spending in the 2012 presidential election. *The Journal of Politics*. **77**(2), pp. 535–45.

Herrera, S. (2006) Bonkers about biofuels. *Nature Biotechnology*. **24**(7), pp. 755–60. Available from DOI: 10.1038/nbt0706-755.

Hieta, E. (2017) The business of electing a President. *European Journal of American Studies*. **12**(2). Available from DOI: 10.4000/ejas.12123.

Higley, J. (2010) Elite theory and elites. In: Kevin, L.T. and Craig, J.J. (eds) *Handbook of Politics: State and Society in Global Perspective*. New York, NY, USA and London, UK: Springer, pp. 161–76.

Hogan, R.E. (2021) Legislative voting and environmental policymaking in the American states. *Environmental Politics*. **30**(4), pp. 559–78.

Hunter, L.M., Hatch, A. and Johnson, A. (2004) Cross-national gender variation in environmental behaviors. *Social Science Quarterly*. **85**(3), pp. 677–94.

Johnson, E.W. and Schwadel, P. (2019) Political polarization and long-term change in public support for environmental spending. *Social Forces*. **98**(2), pp. 913–39.

Konisky, D.M., Milyo, J. and Richardson, L.E. (2008) Environmental policy attitudes: Issues, geographical scale, and political trust. *Social Science Quarterly*. **89**(5), pp. 1066–85.

La Raja, R. and Schaffner, B. (2014) The effects of campaign finance spending bans on electoral outcomes: Evidence from the states about the potential impact of citizens united v. FEC. *Electoral Studies*. 33, pp. 102–14.

Layzer, J. (2012) *Open for Business: Conservatives' Opposition to Environmental Regulation*. Cambridge, MA: MIT Press.

Lazri, A.M. and Konisky, D.M. (2019) Environmental attitudes across race and ethnicity. *Social Science Quarterly*. **100**(4), pp. 1039–55.

McCright, A.M. and Dunlap, R.E. (2000) Challenging global warming as a social problem: An analysis of the conservative movement's counter-claims. *Social Problems*. **47**(4), pp. 499–522. Available from DOI: 10.2307/3097132.

McCright, A.M. and Dunlap, R.E. (2003) Defeating Kyoto: The conservative movement's impact on U.S. Climate. *Social Problems*. **50**(3), pp. 348–73.

McCright, A.M. and Dunlap, R.E. (2010) Anti-reflexivity. *Theory, Culture & Society*. **27**(2–3), pp. 100–133. Available from DOI: 10.1177/0263276409356001.

McCright, A.M. and Dunlap, R.E. (2011a) Cool dudes: The denial of climate change among conservative white males in the United States. *Global Environmental Change*. **21**(4), pp. 1163–72.

McCright, A.M. and Dunlap, R.E. (2011b) The politicization of climate change and polarization in the American public's views of global warming, 2001–2010. *Sociological Quarterly*. **52**(2), pp. 155–94.

McCright, A.M. and Xiao, C. (2014) Gender and environmental concern: Insights from recent work and for future research. *Society & Natural Resources*. **27**(10), pp. 1109–13.

Meyer, D. and Staggenborg, S. (1996) Movements, countermovements, and the structure of political opportunity. *The American Journal of Sociology*. **101**(6), pp. 1628–60.

Mills, C.W. (1956) *The Power Elite*. New York, NY: Oxford University Press.

Page, B.I. and Shapiro, R.Y. (1983) Effects of public opinion on policy. *American Political Science Review*. **77**(1), pp. 175–90.

Pearson, A.R., Schuldt, J.P., Romero-Canyas, R., Ballew, M.T. and Larson-Konar, D. (2018) Diverse segments of the US public underestimate the environmental concerns of minority and low-income Americans. *Proceedings of the National Academy of Sciences*. **115**(49), pp. 12429–34. Available from DOI: 10.1073/pnas.1804698115.

Pew Research Center (2020) As economic concerns recede, environmental protection rises on the public's policy agenda. *Pew Research Center* (online). Available from: https://www.pewresearch.org/politics/2020/02/13/as-economic-concerns-recede-environmental-protection-rises-on-the-publics-policy-agenda/ (accessed July 2020).

Scherbaum, C.A. and Ferreter, J.M. (2011) Estimating statistical power and required sample sizes for organizational research using multilevel modeling. In: Vogt, W.P. (ed.) *SAGE Quantitative Research Methods*. London: Sage. pp. 348–67.

Schwirplies, C. (2018) Citizens' acceptance of climate change adaptation and mitigation: A survey in China, Germany, and the U.S. *Ecological Economics*. **145**, pp. 308–22.

Soule, S.A. and Olzak, S. (2004) When do movements matter? The politics of contingency and the Equal Rights Amendment. *American Sociological Review*. **69**(4), pp. 473–97.

Soule, S., McAdam, D., McCarthy, J. and Su, Y. (1999) Protest events: Cause or consequence of state action? The U.S. women's movement and federal congressional activities, 1956–1979. *Mobilization: An International Quarterly*. **4**(2), pp. 239–56.

Stimson, J. (2004) *Tides of Consent*. New York, NY: Cambridge University Press.

Van Liere, K.D. and Dunlap, R.E. (1980) The social bases of environmental concern: A review of hypotheses, explanations and empirical evidence. *Public Opinion Quarterly*. **44**(2), pp. 181–97.

Vandeweerdt, C., Kerremans, B. and Cohn, A. (2016) Climate voting in the US Congress: The power of public concern. *Environmental Politics*. **25**(2), pp. 268–88.

Vogel, D. (1989) *Fluctuating Fortunes: The Political Power of Business in America*. New York, NY: Basic Books.

Waterhouse, B.C. (2013) *Lobbying America: The Politics of Business from Nixon to NAFTA*. Princeton, NJ: Princeton University Press.

Wlezien, C. (1995) The public as thermostat: Dynamics of preferences for spending. *American Journal of Political Science*. **39**(4), pp. 981–1000.

Xiao, C. and McCright, A.M. (2013) Gender differences in environmental concern: Revisiting the institutional trust hypothesis in the USA. *Environment and Behavior*. **47**(1), pp. 17–37.

Xiao, C. and McCright, A.M. (2014) A test of the biographical availability argument for gender differences in environmental behaviors. *Environment and Behavior*. **46**(2), pp. 241–63. Available from DOI: 10.1177/0013916512453991.

8. Anti-environment, or pro-livelihood? Dissecting environmental conflict and its key drivers in Northern New South Wales

Vanessa Bible

Across the globe, environmental campaigns are rarely witnessed in isolation from the anti-environmental diatribe so frequently aimed at conservationists and activists, sensationalised by media, marring relations, and souring any efforts of negotiation and peaceful, collaborative resolution. But to take a closer look, all is not as it might seem. While industrial, commercial and political interests play a key role in driving conflict over environmental issues, the average person on the ground is often caught in the crossfire between environmental concerns and the mantra of 'jobs and growth'. In Australia, there has been a growing acknowledgement over the past few decades that individuals who work in extractive industries are not as 'anti-environmental' as they have been accused of. Many resource extraction workers who display a negative attitude towards 'greenies', such as those employed in forestry and agriculture, are not so much motivated by ecophobia, but rather by a deep and understandable fear of loss of livelihood. Such fear may be manipulated by true anti-environmentalism at higher levels, but a wealth of evidence can be drawn from Australian environmental campaigns that demonstrates the average worker does not have a vendetta against nature.

This chapter provides a brief history of some of Australia's key environmental campaigns in the Northern Rivers region of New South Wales, investigating the nature of the tension that has arisen. Drawing on the disciplines of both history and peace studies, this historical case study has arisen from research conducted in the region that investigates the relationship between environmental attitudes, ecological violence and conflict, and peacebuilding. The research methodology consisted primarily of documentary analysis, historical-comparative analysis, and oral history. Documentary analysis of archival sources including newspaper articles, government correspondence, and the archives of environmental organisations illuminated the changing nature of attitudes over time. Twenty-five oral history interviews were conducted with environmentalists, farmers and other local community members throughout the region, in order to directly interrogate the individual's subjective experience of the natural environment. As Leena Rossi (2011, p. 153) explains, oral history is 'irreplaceable' as an environmental history method, as 'every person has a relationship with his/her environment that is worth studying', and oral history allows for a deeper exploration of this connection between people and place.

It was as a result of this research that a unique and unexpected narrative emerged. This chapter will present this narrative. What is apparent, on deeper investigation, is that so-called anti-environmentalism at the grassroots level is rarely based on a blatant disregard for the natural environment. Such tension much more frequently arises as a result of fundamental misunderstandings of values and motivations, and one of the most significant drivers of conflict has been the issue of belonging – the question of who has the right to speak for this place, this forest, or this rural settlement. When generations of families have lived off the land, an 'outside' influence that threatens their livelihoods can understandably spark outrage and indignation. Furthermore, in some cases, these supposed anti-environmentalists possess very strong connections to the local environment and even a reverence for the natural environment on which they depend. Such understandings have been gradually transforming the landscape of the Australian environment movement, now encompassing a broad social base united against issues such as invasive and destructive coal and gas mining. These new movements bring traditional 'enemies' together, and today it is not uncommon to see Indigenous Elders, farmers, and environmentalists standing side by side on the frontline at environmental protests and blockades.

SETTING THE CONTEXT: THE COLONIAL LANDSCAPE

Since the beginning of the British occupation of Aboriginal lands in 1788, European colonists distinguished themselves 'among all nations by knocking (the) hell out of the place so rapidly' (Brouwer, 1979, p. 15). Australian environmental historian Tom Griffiths (1997, p. 4) makes the insightful point that it is an unfortunate coincidence of timing that Australia 'experienced colonization and industrialization almost coincidentally, a compressed, double revolution'. As a consequence, the Australian landscape was altered rapidly and dramatically in the march towards 'progress', settlement and development. This occurred throughout much of coastal Australia; however, the devastating ecological impacts experienced throughout the country were not seen in Northern New South Wales (NSW) for several decades after the initial British invasion.

The Northern Rivers Region, located in coastal Northern NSW, and the verdant green forest that once stood upon the landscape, was first sighted by Captain James Cook and botanist Joseph Banks during their journey up the east coast of Australia in 1770 (Beaglehole, 1964, p. 317). Cook's crew assumed correctly that the land could be remarkably productive; the region was known to its Indigenous inhabitants as Bundjalung Country, and at its heart stood Wollumbin, the remnants of an ancient Gondwanan shield volcano responsible for the fertile lands created as a result of its eruption some twenty million years previously. When James Henry Rous and Governor Darling sailed down the coast from Moreton Bay (in the colony of Queensland) in 1827, again the European eye noted the fertile qualities of the land and hypothesised that there must be significant water resources in the region, standing in contrast with the withered brown drought-affected landscape in the south of New South Wales (Daley, 2011[1966], p. 9). While the fabled river was known to exist, the Richmond River mouth did not easily yield the secret of its location, and it was not until 1828 that Rous found the Richmond estuary guarded by a treacherous sandbar. On 26 August 1828, Rous anchored at what was then known as Bullenah, before the estuary of the river he named Richmond (Ryan, 1979, p. 9).

Just as the secrecy of the river's location protected the landscape from the environmental impacts of colonisation, so too did the mighty tangle of forest. The 'Big Scrub', named as such because the ancient Gondwanan rainforest was considered to be little more than an inconvenient obstacle in the path of 'improvement', covered an area of 700 square kilometres, with forest so dense that the Richmond and her tributaries offered the only access inland for the European colonists (Garbutt, 2010, p. 33). The forest did, however, have one significant redeeming feature, encapsulated in the epithet for *Toona ciliata*, or Australian red cedar – 'red gold'. Itinerant workers, often living in complete isolation, sought the wealth that cedar could provide (and perhaps the adventure) (Cousins, 1933, p. 38; Hoff, 2006, p. 17). The cedar-getters gradually spread from the banks of major waterways to minor tributaries and inland in their quest for wealth. In 1843, timber-cutter camps were established at Lismore, Bexhill and Terania (Hurley, 1948, p. 199). As they advanced into the forest, the clearings left behind them were filled with squatters who sought a second source of wealth: fertile soil.

The existing grasslands, carved out of the rainforest by the Bundjalung people, were among the first pieces of land to be settled (Cousins, 1933, p. 35). The European-made clearings followed. Widespread clearing was at this stage more unusual than selective harvesting given the legal restrictions surrounding settlement, but the John Robertson Land Acts of 1861 would signal another change of direction for the fate of the forests. The land acts, designed to encourage an agriculture-based economy, allowed selectors to claim a plot of land on the condition that they clear it, build on it and cultivate it (Waterhouse, 2006, p. 65). Clearing produced far more timber than the settlers could use, and so it was usually piled up and burnt (Henderson, n.d.). The virgin soil, fertilised by the ash of the Big Scrub, proved to be remarkably productive farmland and was put to cultivation.

The frenzied expansion of agricultural and natural resource-based industries continued, carving their way further into the Big Scrub. Sugar was a lucrative industry in the late 1860s, and the Richmond proved to be ideally suited to the crop, at least temporarily. During the 1870s, rarer timbers such as hoop pine were sought, and Bolton (1981, p. 40) estimates that for each year of the early 1870s, more than 1 676 000 metres of pine and ash and 1 066 000 metres of cedar were hewn out of the forest. Ever deeper into the forest the cedar cutters ventured, and by the late 1880s the last bastions of precious timbers were sought out.

When Oliver Fry, Commissioner of Crown Lands, proclaimed in 1847 (p. 542) that the Richmond possessed 'deep, rich soil – the best possible land', he could not have known that rainforest soil only has a nutrient-dense top layer, relying on its vegetation to keep it fertile and to prevent the erosion of nutrients. The soil was becoming 'exhausted' by the heavy demands placed upon it, particularly from sugarcane, and so again the Richmond settlers changed direction in their pursuit of profit (Gollan, 1938, p. 72). It was dairying, more than any other industry thus far, that would bring great economic wealth to the region. From the 1890s and well into the new century, the region became a centre for the record-breaking dairying industry, which some claim was 'without par' (Cousins, 1933, pp. 63–4; McCaffrey, c.1958, p. 37).

During the 1900s the clearing of the Scrub continued, as timber-getters sought out the last of the cedar as well as the giant hardwoods on the highest peaks and ridges of the Nightcap Range. Manning Clark (1976, p. 69) writes that by the early 1900s, most of the trees were gone, and 'from end to end, the Big Scrub was destroyed, some of the land being wanted for sugar cane, some for dairying, but eventually practically all the land ... was used for dairying.' The next industry boom followed; from the 1920s, banana plantations could be found growing on the sides of the cleared hills and mountains (Ryan, 1998, p. 1). These successful industries – timber, dairying and bananas, would face serious economic decline by mid-century, leaving behind a radically altered and environmentally degraded landscape. The region had endured swift and widespread environmental change, likely more so than during any other period since the eruption of the Tweed shield volcano created the very environmental conditions that were so heavily exploited.

On the surface, this overview of the development of the region fits the dominant narrative of anti-environmentalism: short-term natural resource exploitation and economic profit with no real awareness of the long-term impacts is completely justified if jobs are created, and human livelihoods are sustained. However, while such a mentality has often driven big business and political interests, there is plenty of evidence to suggest that the average worker holds a much more complex set of values and attitudes towards the natural environment, and there is a real danger in assuming that those whose livelihoods depend on natural resources are anti-environmental. Running alongside the history presented above is an alternative and little-known history of place attachment, conservation efforts, and a true respect for the natural environment.

A DIFFERENT STORY: RECONSIDERING THE NORTHERN RIVERS

Just as the Big Scrub and the resource wealth it provided was central to the story of the colonisation of the region, responses to its clearing were at the heart of growing conservationist concerns. Despite the dominance of a resource extraction mentality and the overwhelming influence this exerted over the relationship between people and environment, from the start of European settlement there also existed some appreciation for the natural beauty of the region and a growing concern over the fate of the forest.

Tim Bonyhady, in his influential work *The Colonial Earth* (2000), argues that significant numbers of early Australian settlers held genuine environmental concerns. Contrary to the common view that the first colonists were oblivious to environmental impacts, Bonyhady (2000, p. 3) argues that, 'while many colonists were alienated by their new environment, others delighted in it.' Although in the minority, such colonists were perhaps influenced by subtler Western paradigm shifts, and would help other Australians come to terms with what belonging in this new place meant. From the early nineteenth century, the natural sciences started to attract interest and gain prominence, and the field of biology came into being in the early 1800s with the publication of *Biologie, Oder Philosophie der lebenden Natur* by Gottfried Reinhold Treviranus, who established the science as the study of 'the doctrine of life' (Richards, 2002, p. 4). Scholars such as Finney (1993), Moyal (1993) and Christoff (2000) argue that scientists and naturalists were at the forefront of the earliest attempts to seek an understanding of the Australian environment. Scientists made efforts to establish a uniquely Australian school of natural science, and in 1821 the Philosophical Society of Australasia was formed. Minutes of the first meeting reveal the organisation's motivations: 'Nature had been leading us through a mazy dance of intellectual speculation only to laugh at us at last in this fifth continent' (Philosophical Society of Australasia, 1821). Curious about the scientific wonders offered by their new surroundings, scientists set out to document and understand this new land 'where the laws of nature seemed reversed' (Moyal, 1993, p. 70).

In 1866 the *Game Protection Act* was introduced in response to dwindling numbers of previously abundant species, as well as a result of social pressure to reduce levels of animal cruelty (Christoff, 2000, p. 209). In the same year, Australia's first nature reserve was established at Fish River Caves, now known as the Jenolan Caves (Hall, 1992, p. 91). Bonyhady argues that in the second half of the nineteenth century, increasing numbers of settlers described the Australian environment as a 'heritage' and a 'national estate'. Again, contrary to popular narrative, Bonyhady (2000, p. 9) argues that 'the settler's attachment to the colonial landscape was matched by the desire to preserve it. The protection of the continent's native fauna and flora, pollution of its rivers, degradation of its pastoral lands ... preservation of beauty spots ... were all major issues of the colonial era.' As the population increased, so too did the number of settlers who rejoiced in the Australian environment, and naturalists enthusiastically collected specimens of all kinds (Finney, 1993, p. xi).

In the Northern Rivers, Lismore Station owner William Wilson made a hobby of collecting 'geological specimens, stones, fossils, minerals and (petrifications)' from around the family homestead, and at one point sent a sample of his collections to the United States for exhibition (Dawson, 1938, p. 32). Indicating an obvious interest in his surroundings, Wilson was not alone in his appreciation for the local natural environment. James Ainsworth was one of the first settlers in the region. He recalled that in 1847, the river at Ballina was 'just as nature had planted it. Forest and scrub crowded unbrokenly to the water's edges on each side, offering a foliage that was unsurpassed in its semi-tropical beauty' (Hoff, 2006, p. 15).

AN INDIGENOUS LANDSCAPE

In 1863, cedar-getter Joshua Bray ventured to the south side of Wollumbin with Grasshopper, a Bundjalung man, and remarked:

> Some of the scenery was wildly grand. I sat down for half an hour to admire the Magnificent Panorama that lay stretched around me. All away to the West rose tier after tier of mountains grouped in every variety of majestic outline, and almost above me was Walumban ... Here and there were mingled glimpses of the Tweed River its glassey surface green and over-hanging verdue, adding beauty to the scene. To the north and south were black-looking forests and mountains, it was really grand, and altogether calculated to impress one with an idea of vastness, and absorb every other feeling in an overpowering feeling of awe (cited in Hoff, 2006, p. 13).

Hoff (2006, p. 13) theorises that Bray may well have been the first white man to ever see the sacred mountain up close, only permitted to do so as a guest of the Bundjalung. Bray's description differs markedly from other European interpretations of the landscape. It reveals a sense of wonder and respect, with trees considered for their beauty rather than their resource value. Perhaps Bray, seeing the landscape from an Aboriginal perspective, was able to gain a different understanding of the environment. This seems very possible, given that other locals who had a positive relationship with the Bundjalung people also shared a reverence for the land.

The story of the remarkable Ogilvie/Bundock family is unique in the colonial history of the region. Edward Ogilvie initially established a run to the south of the Big Scrub in 1840, adopting the Aboriginal place name of Yulgilbar and learning the local Bundjalung language. Ogilvie 'allowed' the local Aboriginal people to hunt on the property and made efforts to maintain a positive relationship with the Bundjalung people (Farwell, 1973). Captivated by the beauty of the region, he also claimed land further north, again giving it the Bundjalung name for the place: 'Wiangaree' (Keane, 1956, p. 9). Ogilvie's nephew would later write of his uncle's first impressions of Wiangaree at sunset, recounting, 'he said that as he looked at it he thought it was the most beautiful sight he had ever seen in his life' (Bundock, 1922). Ogilvie's sister Mary and her husband, William Bundock, took up residence in 1846 (Daley 2011[1966], p. 88). Like her brother, Mary expressed an extreme fondness for the land. She described the

Richmond River as 'a beautiful stream of clear water running over clean sand and pebbles, an ideal of beauty and purity not surpassed anywhere' (Watson, 2014, p. 195), and regretted her decision to introduce non-native water hyacinth to the natural lagoon on the property (Mears, 1985, p. 76).

Edward and Mary had grown up in the Hunter Valley, a few hundred kilometres to the south, where they had a close relationship with the local Aboriginal people, the Wonnarua. Mary encouraged her children to do likewise, and the Bundock children grew up speaking the local Bundjalung dialect and learning Aboriginal cultural values (Hoff, 2006, pp. 262–3; Mears, 1985, p. 76). Mary's daughter, also known as Mary Bundock, gained an intimate understanding of the local environment, its topography and the healing properties of its native vegetation from Bundjalung Elders, bringing her knowledge of bush medicine to Aboriginal and white people alike (Bundock, 1922). Both mother and daughter were known as painters, producing landscape portraits of the local environment, and Miss Mary published articles on the culture of the Bundjalung people (Bundock, 1978[1898], pp. 261–6). Hoff (2006, p. 262) makes the link between the relationship with the Bundjalung and a connection with the natural environment, claiming of Mary: '[H]er life is a paradigm of what settlers could learn and enjoy from their friendships with local Bundjalung clanspeople. Mary's extended family formed a deep emotional attachment to the pastoral lease at Wyangarie.' The Ogilvie/Bundock family was seemingly ahead of its time in terms of their relationship both with the Bundjalung people and with the natural environment. While they were a prominent family who profited greatly from the natural resources of the region, it is difficult to ascribe anti-environmental values to them.

SETTLING IN

As early as 1872 the tourism potential of the region was recognised when a visitor to the Border Ranges (the mountain range that sits on the northern border of NSW) remarked that the forest 'should be shown to the Sydney tourist' (Quartpot and Ruby Creeks Revisited, 1872, p. 2). The first three decades of the twentieth century saw the publication of a significant number of tourist guides, their content demonstrating environmental attitudes in transition. Kijas (2003, p. 21) argues that many of these guides focus on the loss of the Big Scrub, and while they contain 'exuberant' proclamations of the white man's triumph over nature, they also reveal 'more ambivalent tones concerned at the extent of destruction of the brush'. This sentiment was echoed by those who had profited from the forests as well; just fifty years after the European discovery of red cedar in the region, cedar-getter Charles Jarrett (1894, p. 8) exclaimed, 'now extinct is the echo, destroyed the beautiful foliage, exterminated are near all the graceful cabbage tree palms, torn down and burnt the clinging beautiful flower-bearing vines and tendrils.'

Kijas (2003, p. 28) argues that in the early twentieth century there were two competing notions of resource value in the region, one favouring farming and the other, logging. The latter proved to exert a strong influence, and government policy changes would significantly impact upon the future of the region. In 1908, the New South Wales Parliament established a Royal Commission of Inquiry into Forestry – professional forestry bodies were established, and 67 state forests were declared in the 'upper north-east region' between 1913 and 1920 (Kijas, 2003, p. 28). The New South Wales *Forestry Act* was introduced in 1916, tasked with the 'dedication, reservation, control and use of State forests, timber reserves, and Crown lands for forestry and other purposes'. With this Act, the Forestry Commission was established, and professional foresters would in time consider themselves to be Australia's 'first conservationists' (Howard, 2004, p. 20).

In a legislative sense, perhaps they were. Aboriginal Australians were, and continue to be, the country's first environmentalists, but the Forestry Commission were tasked with the job of *conserving*. In the literal sense of the word, they were to protect the forests and their resource value for later, so that forests could continue to serve human interests. Regardless of the intent, the Act undoubtedly slowed the rate of forest clearing, and also paved the way for the introduction of further environmental legislation such as the *Wildflowers and Native Plants Protection Act*, introduced in New South Wales in 1927 (Bolton, 1999, p. 31). With precious little of the Big Scrub left, Whian Whian had been declared a state forest in 1914, and in the 1920s a forestry camp and plant nursery were built at Rummery Park, deep in a patch of remnant Scrub. The camp provided accommodation for foresters during the work week, and the nursery facilitated the botanical education of employees and regeneration of cleared forest (Commonwealth of Australia and State of New South Wales, 2000, p. 5).

Government policy did not necessarily align with the evolving attitudes of conservation-minded citizens and local concerns. Bolton argues that the appointed 'Conservators of Forests' struggled to convince politicians of the need for environmental stewardship (Bolton, 1999, p. 31). In the village of Alstonville in 1920, local councillors made the decision to prevent the felling of black bean trees in a town park, instead seeking knowledge of the local species and recommending that 'a black bean pod and a wild passion vine be sent to the Government Botanist for his opinion as to whether some are dangerous to animals eating them' (Tintenbar Shire Council, 1920, p. 7). A decade earlier, clergyman James Green had felt particularly passionate about the clearing of the Big Scrub; in contrast with the praise so often given to pioneers for their hard labour, Green (1910, pp. 175–9) accused the cedar-getters of a destructive and myopic attitude, arguing:

> It is to be feared that the pioneer thought too little of the beauty ... *He* thought only of the cedar ... beautiful as the country is with its settled air of pastoral prosperity, the old onrider now looks to the past for his visions of beauty ... Something is lost. Mistakes have been made. Civilisation has been cruel, ruthless, and even foolish, for this land ought to have been the paradise of the continent.

Green's words are highly critical and remarkably different from the prevailing attitudes of the time, demonstrating the depth of passion involved in the evolving conservation ethic. Walker (1991, pp. 27–8) argues that by the interwar period, campaigners had 'developed an ecological consciousness'. In and around Sydney, conservationists such as Myles Dunphy passionately campaigned for the establishment of more National Parks and promoted a different mode of engaging with the natural environment, establishing bushwalkers clubs from the 1920s (Borschmann, 1999, pp. 226–9; Meredith, 1999). These organisations were to become vehicles for grassroots environmental campaigning, with public environmental advocacy marking another shift in Australian environmental attitudes.

In the 1930s the farming communities of the Alstonville area came together to campaign for the conservation of Lumley Park, in what appears to be the first instance of citizen-initiated rainforest regeneration in Australia. They considered the three acres of forest to be worthy of preservation as it was representative of how the local environment looked prior to white settlement (Lymburner, 2004, p. 7). In 1934, the park was declared a 'Preserve for Native

Trees', and weeding and regeneration work commenced. A report to the National Parks and Wildlife Service asserts that this was likely to have been the first rainforest regeneration site in Australia (Hunter, 1997). Seeds of rainforest species were collected from the local area and cultivated. Other Big Scrub remnants were also considered worthy of preservation during this time, although not attracting the same level of community enthusiasm or regeneration efforts as Lumley Park. Booyong Reserve, south of Bangalow, was gazetted as a flora and fauna reserve by Byron Shire Council in 1931, and a committee was established to oversee its management (Byron Shire Council, n.d.). There is also evidence that local landholders chose to preserve significant stands of Scrub on their own private property (Green, 1910, pp. 178–9; New South Wales National Parks and Wildlife Service, 1997, p. 5), further demonstrating that we should never assume that farmers have been mindless environmental vandals.

THE BORDER RANGES

Hutton and Connors (1999, p. 149) argue that, with the mechanisation of the forestry industry from the 1950s, forestry commissions throughout Australia were 'captured by the industry they were supposed to be regulating, [and] rapid changes in technology, industry organisation and forestry policy were ensuring that vast changes were occurring' in the forests, blurring the line between government and industry. In the Big Scrub, chainsaws, trucks and tractors 'marked new patterns on the forest landscape' (Dargavel, 1994, p. 90). Increased efficiency led to the centralisation of local sawmills, reducing the time that loggers and sawmillers spent in the forests (Watson, 1990, p. 3). Watson (1990, p. xvii) argues that with this change, the 'north coast hardwood mills ... went from family businesses into modern corporations', and modern machinery resulted in a more 'impersonal, mass-production management method.' This mechanisation arguably damaged the relationship between forester and forest – in addition to spending less time in the forest itself, loggers no longer required as much intimate knowledge of the forests when logs were sawed through much faster, and forests were traversed by motor vehicle.

In the Border Ranges, John Lever, a generational logger, had been working in the forests since the age of 14 – a '[s]elf-taught botanist, engineer and surveyor, his life ha[d] been a close communion with nature' (Brown, 1976, p. 14). Lever's ecological knowledge had been acquired experientially, informed by the forest itself, and he had walked extensively and spent many nights deep within the forest (Chick, 1976, p. 16). Lever's relationship to the natural environment was one of intimacy and respect; contrary to the reputation of foresters, he lobbied the Forestry Commission to spare the large, rare timber, and in 1948, Lever and two friends nominated the forest to become a National Park (Kendell and Buivids, 1987, p. 28). Lever's campaign 'came to an abrupt end' in 1952 when the Premier 'refused to even consider their proposal' (Brown, 1976, p. 14). While this place-based, ecologically informed style of conservation was gaining strength, 'official' conservation, as dictated by the top-down powers of government and policy, was shifting closer towards anti-environmental values.

This change in the attitude of the forestry industry is evidenced by the dismay displayed by some foresters, who lamented that the industry was not what it used to be. Just as Lever had passionately opposed the destruction of the forest 'patriarchs', so too did other foresters start to question the wisdom of the 'captured' Forestry Commission (Hutton and Connors, 1999, p. 202). Alex Floyd, who would become one of Australia's foremost rainforest botanists, started his career with the Forestry Commission in 1951 and was assigned to the forests of the North Coast in 1956. He recalls:

> [t]he definition of conservation in those days was the wise use of natural resources. Those were the words. That was conservation. It meant that we weren't wasteful of timber ... we weren't looking towards conserving some areas in their natural state as such ... The problem of course was that you had commitments to sell this timber to various people. You could come up with ideas but if they were more expensive and if they reduced the amount of timber available for harvesting, then you were creating problems (Floyd, cited in Borschmann, 1999, p. 100).

Floyd also recalls the impressive knowledge of local forester Harold Hayes, who lived in the forests and whose knowledge came from his direct experience of place. Hayes had a deep reverence for the forests that sustained his livelihood, and Floyd recollects that Hayes did not need to look upwards – he could distinguish trees from among 300 species simply by the bark, such was his intimate forest knowledge (Borschmann, 1999, p. 100). Another of his methods was to cut into a tree and to examine the colour, smell it, or taste it, creating what environmental humanist Stacy Alaimo (2010) refers to as a transcorporeal experience of nature. One of the key elements of Alaimo's concept describes the process by which external elements of nature enter the human body, in Hayes' case, through smell and taste, creating a purely interconnected experience in which the boundaries between the corporeal and elemental nature are diffused. Only an intimate relationship with and understanding of the forest could facilitate a transcorporeal experience, altering one's very sense of self through a direct experience of nature.

In the Border Ranges, the National Park campaign started by John Lever in 1948 was reignited in 1969, now stronger with the weight of over twenty years of conservationist knowledge and experience. Lever again proposed the creation of a National Park. Again the proposal was ignored, and the Forestry Commission continued carving up the forest into allocations for local timber mills – the campaign to save the forest would become a conflict between forestry and conservation interests (Monroe and Stephens, 1976, p. 1). Adding to the forestry industry's argument was the decline in agricultural productivity in the region, which by this stage was resulting in negative population growth, increasing the pressure to maintain more economically viable industries such as logging (Standen, 1976, pp. 67–78; Monroe, 1976, pp. 79–81). Furthermore, conservationists were up against a primary industry-dependent population. While the average number of workers in agriculture, forestry and fishing in NSW in 1971 stood at 5.9 per cent, in the Richmond-Tweed the figure stood at 22.5 per cent (Standen, 1976, p. 68). The relationship between locals and the natural environment was, for many, one of economic dependence, and challenging this relationship caused anger and conflict. But while the way in which the opposing sides related to the environment differed radically and were often based on contrasting views of the environment, both sides nonetheless had a passionate connection to the forests.

It was not a simple matter of conservation interests clashing with primary industry. The campaign for the Border Ranges had been initiated by a logger, and was further advanced by a farmer, highlighting the way in which connections to the natural environment can look very different depending on one's perspective. Jim Gasteen, a cattle farmer, had been trying to raise awareness of the environmental consequences of land clearing since the early 1960s (Lines, 2006, p. 150). When Gasteen noticed that the orchids which grew high on the trees at the back of his property were disappearing, he was dismayed to discover the cause – 'the

Forestry cut the trees down for them! As a result we became upset' (cited in Somerville, 2005, pp. 14–15). Gasteen soon learned of the Forestry Commission's plans to construct a road to the top of the Border Ranges to assist logging operations: 'I prickled like an old scrub pig with the dogs behind him and immediately started an all-out effort to halt the road' (cited in Kendell and Buivids, 1987, p. 31). 'Honorary Ranger' with the National Parks and Wildlife Service, Russ Maslen was also dismayed and in 1972 with three other members, he formed the Border Ranges Preservation Society, which drew together environmentalists, loggers and farmers. Demonstrating a desire for intergenerational justice, a local logger pleaded:

> Go and stand on the end of the Pinnacle … Because if you don't do that, I don't think you've lived. That you've got to go up there and walk through that forest … that's what the Border Ranges is there for. It's for those things to be available for my kids and their kids and their kid's kids (cited in Watson, 1990, p. 81).

While the NSW Government rejected the National Park proposal in 1976, the campaign had transformed the relationship between the people and the environment they fought so hard to protect, and the Border Ranges campaign helped teach the rest of Australia what rainforest was. The forest would be declared a National Park from 1979, but only as a result of the efforts of an entirely new style of environmentalism that at its core, fundamentally challenges widespread assumptions that those whose livelihoods are derived from the land are inherently anti-environmental.

TERANIA CREEK

At the same time that the Border Ranges campaign was unfolding, a radically different campaign was underway just 30 kilometres away that would actively drive wedges between local loggers and environmentalists. At Terania Creek in 1979, the first known successful forest blockade in history occurred (Bible, 2018). One of the last remnant patches of the original Big Scrub was under threat, and a collective of new settlers comprised nearly entirely of counter-culturalists stood up to defend the forest. In the wake of industry decline from the 1950s onwards, many alternative lifestylers and self-identified hippies had made the region a haven for environmental values, transforming the region into the largest concentration of counter-cultural communities in the Southern Hemisphere. When this ecologically conscious community learned that the forest was under threat, an unsuccessful five-year campaign initiated in 1974 spontaneously erupted into a direct action blockade that lasted four weeks. The NSW Government ordered a stop to the logging, and after a lengthy inquiry and further blockades of neighbouring forests, rainforest logging was banned in NSW in 1982 (Bible, 2018).

The protest led to bitter disputes between protesters, the forestry industry, and communities that were dependent on logging (Turvey, 2006; Watson, 1990). However, the conflict that erupted between the old logging communities and new settlers cannot be conveniently categorised as a clash of environmental vs. anti-environmental values. As the history reveals, conservation efforts in the region were often *initiated* by these primary industry-dependent communities. The key drivers appear to be the threat of loss of livelihood, and perhaps even more so, the competing notions of belonging in the region. These two drivers are closely related, as it was the new settlers that threatened to undermine local jobs. The loggers felt driven out of the forests that had provided them and their families with their livelihoods, made worse by the fact that many of the protesters were new to the region and therefore not considered local – it was not their (literal) place to have such a powerful say over the fate of the forests.

Local newspaper, *The Northern Star*, was particularly critical of the protesters, and it had featured a high volume of negative stories about the radical 'non-locals' since the counter-cultural influx in the early 1970s (Martin and Ellis, 2003). Associated Country Sawmillers of NSW published advertisements in the paper, harking back to the era of wise-use conservation and proclaiming themselves to be the 'true conservationists'. An editorial piece named 'First Here, and we'll be the last to leave' (1979, p. 24) remarked, 'If groups such as those at Terania Creek were allowed to go unchecked chaos would be upon us, and the economy ruined', demonstrating a close relationship between the notions of local-ness, and economic stability.

It could be argued that environmental conflict is rarely about anti-environmentalism, and is far more often situated in the tension between various environmental concerns and economic growth and 'development', and forestry workers and farmers have too often been unfairly placed on the wrong side. Terania protester Nan Nicholson (2012) recalls,

> the local sawmiller at Nimbin was a plant nut, he grew rainforest plants. Barry Walker ... he was fantastic. And all the loggers I've got into deep conversations with, they say the same thing as us, that we're running out of timber and we're flogging the place, but what can we do, we need to stay alive, and that's all reasonable. In the end we're all on the same side. It's the big bureaucracies and the big governments that everybody hates.

Speaking from an industry perspective, former forest ranger Robert Kooyman concurs, explaining that he has spoken to 'many, many' logging operators, marketing foremen and other forest workers who have revealed that they regret the damage done to the forests. He concludes, 'if you get a bushman, they also have a love of the bush. Most times it is economic pressures that drive people to become so bloody minded' (cited in Borschmann, 1999, p. 91). Russell Kelly (2003) argues that there were actually a significant number of local residents who had been 'quietly arguing' with authorities over environmental concerns, and they were consequently empowered by the arrival of the new settlers who were willing to speak out in less-than-quiet ways. An *ABC Radio* programme also recalls the attitudes of long-term locals, stating that 'the Stewarts and Nowlans were relaxed about the "hippies" stopping the logging' because the *loggers* were the 'outsiders' coming to destroy the valley (McGee, 2014).

Despite their resentment towards the loggers' activities, the protesters at Terania Creek did not hold the same level of resentment towards the loggers themselves. Nan Nicholson (2010) recalls:

> I find with all these people, when I'm in a sort of confrontational situation with loggers or police ... mostly they're not listened to nearly enough, so if you're actually willing to be quiet and listen to what they want to say, you can get a long way. More often what you find is you both have a similar point of view. And I've spoken to many loggers who have said "We're just the meat in the sandwich. We know this stuff won't last but I've got a family to maintain, so I've gotta keep logging this. But I know it sucks...". I have a lot of sympathy for these people. And mostly when you talk to just about anyone, including the most vehement opposition, you can see their point of view is pretty much similar to your own in lots of ways, same sort of elements that are important for each person.

Despite the common assumption that environmentalists will always be on the opposing side of farmers, loggers and others whose livelihoods are tied to the land, it is critically important to acknowledge that expressions of belonging and place attachment can vary widely, and often, those perceived to be at odds with environmental concerns are not necessarily the 'enemy'.

FARMERS AND MINING

Leigh Shearman is a dairy farmer in the Northern Rivers. A generational farmer, Shearman (2012) expresses a deep connection to her property, and despite living her whole life in the Northern Rivers, her sense of belonging is to the local land itself and to the practice of farming rather than to the region. Well aware of the criticism that farmers often attract from environmentalists, she is sensitive to claims that farmers are anti-environmental, and demonstrates surprise and gratitude at the acknowledgement that farmers have a deep understanding of and reverence for the environment. Shearman (2012) explains:

> Farmers know the balance between the land, between trees for shade for animals, between keeping the banks healthy, so ... you don't lose half your farm to erosion, and so that cows don't slip down a steep bank and all of that ... yes they might have taken away the Big Scrub, and that was probably the wrong thing to do. But in their time, that was what they had to do, to actually make a living ... You get a lot more farmers now that care for the land properly, and that are environmentalists than ever before, than *ever* before [emphasis added].

Shearman's land ethic runs more deeply than merely safeguarding her land for economic profit, and her relationship with the natural environment is one of deep understanding. 'It takes years to learn what a lot of farmers know. Because they've grown up with it. And we don't realise the knowledge we've got ... to look after the land. It's in us and it's in our blood' (Shearman, 2012). Shearman (2012) also expresses a desire to protect the land for future generations, demonstrating a strong sense of intergenerational justice.

Ted Hodinott (2014), a local hobby farmer, also remarks:

> I think farmers really are the penultimate environmentalists. I think you talk to any farmer ... they would all consider themselves environmentalists because they're doing things that are sustainable ... That nexus between greenie and farmer, environmentalist, there's a play on juggling different terminologies. But all farmers, I think if they've got the best interests in passing it on to future generations, they're environmentalists ...

Dismantling stereotypes, Meg Neilsen is another Northern Rivers farmer and a National Party voter (traditionally the political party of choice for conservative country voters). Neilsen (2014) enthuses about the abundance of native wildlife on her cattle property and her love for all species. She remarks:

> I'd say in the last 10 years I've really got to feel more at home with nature, more at home here ... That's my real connection I think and that's where I really feel at home – more so with wildlife and nature than with people ... I think it's that stewardship of the land. I think it's an extension of caring for something ... caring for the life. I mean, I love the cows – I love them. And to make their lives as good as I possibly can and look after the pastures ... look after the trees, that's just so important (Neilsen, 2014).

These farmers, alongside an alliance of many other local farmers, Bundjalung elders, environmentalists, and the 'mainstream' community were at the heart of a powerful anti-unconventional gas movement in the region. In May 2012, an anti-gas mining rally in Lismore drew a crowd of 7000 people (in a city of less than 30 000). Shearman (2012) explains the significance of the broad-based event:

> to get 7,000 people walking against CSG [coal seam gas] in a rally in Lismore, and I can assure you that if 10% of them were radicals, that would be an exaggeration. They were farmers in their sixties and seventies that have never done anything like that ever before in their life, and they felt strong enough that they did that.

Despite overwhelming community opposition, gas companies proceeded with unconventional gas drilling projects in the region. In 2012 and 2013, residents of the Northern Rivers mounted blockades against the drilling of gas wells at Doubtful Creek and Glenugie, but were unsuccessful. In early 2014, however, when it became apparent that a significant gas fracking project was planned for farmland at Bentley, 14 kilometres from Lismore, an immediate and spontaneous blockade was established.

The Bentley Blockade lasted until May 2014, attracting thousands of people who held constant vigil at the proposed mine site. As a direct result of the blockade, the project was halted, and the gas company's licence was bought back by the NSW Government under pressure from the community. While there were high numbers of local members of the alternative community at the site, at the frontlines alongside the Indigenous Elders were the farmers. A delegation of ten locals met with NSW Minister for Resources and Energy Anthony Roberts. Kim Curtis (2014) recalls her defensive reaction to assumptions that the blockade was 'full of ferals':

> after he spoke to us, I think he was humbled a bit. Because he didn't realise, it's not ferals, there were ten of us. Ten farmers, from around here. And I said to him, and even if it was ferals, so what? I love them. They're protecting our [land] – so what? What have you got against them?

Historically there has been tension between farmers and environmentalists in Australia, but Curtis' declaration demonstrates that these local farmers were not anti-environmental, nor anti-environmental*ist*. This was further demonstrated when the electorate of Ballina elected a Greens representative to the NSW State Parliament in 2015, marking the first time a Greens MP has claimed a seat in any regional Australian electorate (Alcorn, 2015). Many of today's environmental issues are now mainstream issues that cut across old battle lines, uniting those with traditionally opposing views, and helping to unravel the old narrative that those whose livelihoods are sourced from the environment are somehow inherently anti-environmental.

CONSIDERATIONS

Shearman's comment that today there are more environmentally minded farmers 'than ever before' is due in no small part to advances in environmental knowledge and the influence of environmentalist concerns. Many farmers have indeed come a long way in acknowledging the mistakes of the past. Just as a significant number of loggers look back with regret on the ecologically violent practices upon which their livelihoods depended, so too are farmers reflecting upon old methods. Irrigators are considered to be among the most anti-environmental of all Australian farmers, accused of consuming precious water while towns run dry in the Murray

Darling Basin, yet Tim Duddy of the NSW Irrigators Council feels that if he had his time again, there are some things he would 'never ever' repeat (Duddy, 2013).

Environmental campaigns in the Northern Rivers provide strong evidence that despite common perceptions, environmental conflict is not as simplistic a matter as 'greenies' vs. primary industries. The Border Ranges campaign for example had been initiated by a logger, and was advanced by a local grazier, challenging assumptions about the way in which loggers and farmers relate to the land. This is a significant detail, and increasingly, academics are acknowledging the deep ties that *can* (but do not necessarily *always*) exist between loggers and farmers and the natural environment, which frequently include an empirical understanding of seasons, cycles, soils and other knowledge required when working closely with the land. As Garbutt (2011, p. 218) argues, we cannot and should not attempt to 'assimilate different forms of belonging onto the one plane.' While the expressions of belonging may differ, the common ground is a deep connection to place and environment, and the environment movement in Australia is increasingly inclusive of a much broader social base than in the past.

While it must be acknowledged that the Northern Rivers story is unique, and the power and influence of the activism emanating from the region is unparalleled throughout Australia (Bible, 2018), similar stories that challenge the apparent anti-environmentalism of farmers in particular are emerging from beyond the region. The Lock the Gate Alliance (LTG) for example, established in 2010, has played a major role in the uniting of farmers and environmentalists against the environmentally destructive impacts of the fossil fuel industry on agricultural land. Originating in the gas fields of Queensland (QLD) and growing to encompass and support localised anti-coal mining groups, the now Australia-wide alliance gives voice to a united movement. So strong are the environmental concerns, that increasingly farmers have been engaging in direct action tactics, previously the realm of radical activists alone. A rural newspaper reports: '[w]hen conservative rural people take law-breaking lessons from seasoned environmental activists, some ancient order of things has been overturned ... Non-violent direct action isn't new, Mr Phillips observed, pointing to the examples of Jesus and Gandhi. But it's a concept that's very fresh to Australian farming communities' (Cawood, 2013).

This phenomenon is not restricted to LTG members and supporters – the growing alliances between farmer and environmentalist can be seen in a number of ways, from wheat farmers running as Greens candidates in elections, to a farmer prioritising the rights of koalas and Aboriginal heritage concerns over the loss of his own livelihood in his reasons for speaking out against a coalmine on the Liverpool Plains, in the heart of central NSW (Clifford, 2013; Fisher, 2015). Farmers are also on the frontlines of climate change campaigning; an advocacy group called Farmers for Climate Action (2019) recently conducted a survey of 1300 farmers, and they found that 88 per cent want to see more effective political action on climate change.

Furthermore, this phenomenon is certainly not unique to Australia, and it is probably the case that wider research will illuminate the many and varied complex relationships between those working in primary industries and their relationship to the natural environment. Rhoda Wilkie's work on 'human–livestock relations in northeast Scotland' (2005) reveals that cattle farmers often establish emotional connections with livestock, and interestingly, those with greater levels of socio-economic privilege are more likely to be able to afford the luxury of indulging these connections. This creates parallels with the Australian examples discussed, demonstrating again that so-called anti-environmental attitudes are driven by economic need. Similarly, Colter Ellis' (2014) work reveals that cattle farmers in the United States develop emotional bonds with their cattle, and farmers find themselves having to actively emotionally distance themselves from livestock in order to view them as commodities rather than sentient beings. In both cases, there is tension between the need for a stable livelihood, and a natural inclination towards establishing bonds with more-than-human species.

Of course, this argument does not make the claim that there are no anti-environmental loggers or farmers. There most certainly are; however, it would appear that the old, deeply entrenched battlelines have shifted, and today the anti-environmental attitudes more often than not come from the large-scale primary producers who are well supported by big business and political interests. The true anti-environmentalists are those who deliberately use the 'jobs vs. the environment' rhetoric, as if the two are mutually exclusive, in order to increase profits or win elections. The 2019 federal election result in Australia demonstrates the power that anti-environmental rhetoric can have; the election was arguably won in QLD on the promise of 'jobs and growth' generated from the Adani coalmine, despite the fact that the actual number of jobs that the project will create have been deliberately and grossly overstated (Cox, 2019). Environmentalists need to reassess who the anti-environmentalists really are – not those who take up the limited number of jobs that Adani will offer, but rather, those who convinced these few, soon-to-be well-paid individuals that environmentalists are their enemy. The role that the media plays in shaping public opinion around environmental issues also requires more focus, as highlighted by Lester and Hutchins (2012, 2013).

In Australia there is great hostility between small farmers and large agribusiness, most notably seen in relation to Cubbie Station, the largest irrigation property in the Southern Hemisphere. The station sits at the top of the vitally important Murray Darling Basin, and many farmers feel that it is directly responsible for preventing huge volumes of water from entering the river system that runs through five of Australia's eight states and territories (Davies et al., 2018). It should also be noted that farmers who campaign for the protection of agricultural lands could be considered to be merely protecting their own economic interests. While this may be so, it does not automatically make these farmers anti-environmental, but simply pro-livelihood, and today many farmers are aware that a healthy environment equates to a healthy income.

If history seeks to illuminate the past in order to help us to understand the present, then environmental history can provide powerful insights into the changing nature of human–nature relationships over time. Historians seek to interpret and re-interpret the past, uncovering previously hidden narratives. Any investigation of anti-environmentalism can benefit from a consideration of historical trends, and potentially, an uncovering of stories that run counter to the dominant narrative. This also suggests to researchers of anti-environmentalism that the rich methodologies of the environmental humanities offer potentially untapped avenues of inquiry.

Upon dissecting the drivers of environmental conflict, key understandings emerge. To advance environmentalism we need to understand the issues, and how conflicts arise. Environmentalists should never make assumptions about people whose livelihoods depend on primary industries. Reaching beyond the apparent divide and establishing common ground strengthens environment movements as new alliances are formed. Similarly, caring for one's livelihood does not make an individual anti-environmental, even if intensive conflict and emotional anger manifests – this is an understandable response to threats of job loss. And lastly, feelings of belonging and competing notions of localness should not be underestimated. As Elaine Stratford (2009) argues, it is the threat of loss of place, more than any other factor, that most influences environmental politics. Environmental movements that acknowledge these truths are built upon broader bases, and can more readily campaign against the real anti-environmental forces of big business and dirty politics.

REFERENCES

Alaimo, S. (2010) *Bodily Natures: Science, Environment and the Material Self*. Bloomington, IN: Indiana University Press.

Alcorn, G. (2015) In vast swaths of rural New South Wales, there's only one election issue: Coal seam gas. *The Guardian*. Available from: www.theguardian.com/australia-news/2015/mar/26/in-vast-swaths-of-rural-new-south-wales-theres-only-one-election-issue-coal-seam-gas (accessed 26 March 2015).

Associated Country Sawmillers of New South Wales (NSW) (1979) First here, and we'll be the last to leave [editorial]. *Northern Star*. 15 August, p. 24.

Beaglehole, J.C. (ed.) (1964) *The Journals of Captain James Cook on His Voyages of Discovery, vol. 1: The Voyage of the Endeavour 1768–1771*. Cambridge: Cambridge University Press.

Bible, V. (2018) *Terania Creek and the Forging of Modern Environmental Activism*. Cham: Palgrave.

Bolton, G. (1981) *Spoils and Spoilers: Australians Make Their Environment 1788–1980*. North Sydney: Allen & Unwin.

Bolton, G. (1999) A gum leaf in the billy: The bush shapes Australia. In Borschmann, G. (ed.) *The People's Forest: A Living History of the Australian Bush*. Blackheath: The People's Forest Press, pp. 29–35.

Bonyhady, T. (2000) *The Colonial Earth*. Carlton: Miegunyah Press.

Borschmann, G. (ed.) (1999) *The People's Forest: A Living History of the Australian Bush*. Blackheath: The People's Forest Press.

Brouwer, S. (ed.) (1979) *The Message of Terania*. Lismore: Terania Media.

Brown, J. (1976) A Society to Fight Fire with Fire. *Habitat*. 4(3), p. 14.

Bundock, C.W. (1922) Old Wyangarie Station – Days when food was short. *Casino & Kyogle Courier*. Diamond Jubilee Supplement.

Bundock, M. (1978[1898]) Notes on the Richmond Blacks. In: McBryde, I. (ed.) *Records of Times Past: Ethnohistorical Essays on the Culture and Ecology of the New England Tribes*. Canberra: Australian Institute of Aboriginal Studies, pp. 261–6.

Byron Shire Council (n.d.) Booyong Reserve for public recreation and preservation of native flora and fauna. Informational sign, Booyong Reserve. Sighted by author 31 December 2015.

Cawood, M. (2013) Rural activism rising. *The Land*. Available from: www.theland.com.au/news/agriculture/general/news/rural-activism-rising/2670203.aspx (accessed 12 September 2013).

Chick, B. (1976) Campaign after campaign. *Habitat*. 4(3), p. 16.

Christoff, P. (2000) Environmental citizenship. In: Hudson, W. and Kane, J. (eds) *Rethinking Australian Citizenship*. Melbourne: Cambridge University Press, pp. 200–214.

Clark, M. (1976) *A Discovery of Australia*. 1976 Boyer Lectures. Sydney: ABC.

Clifford, C. (2013) Penny Blatchford nominates as Greens candidate for Senate. *ABC News*. Available from: www.abc.net.au/news/2013-08-13/penny-blatchford-nominates-as-greens27-candidate-for-senate/4882126 (accessed 21 February 2016).

Commonwealth of Australia & State of New South Wales (2000) *Regional Forest Agreement for North East New South Wales*. Sydney.

Cousins, A. (1933) *The Northern Rivers of New South Wales*. Sydney: Shakespeare Head Press.

Cox, L. (2019) Adani jobs explained: Why there are new questions over Carmichael mine. *The Guardian*. Available from: https://www.theguardian.com/environment/2019/jun/05/adani-jobs-explained-why-there-are-new-questions-over-carmichael-mine (accessed 27 June 2019).

Curtis, K. (2014) Interviewed by: Bible, V. (digital recording). Bentley, 18 April. In author's possession.

Daley, L.T. (2011[1966]) *Men and a River: Richmond River District 1828–1895*. 2nd edn. Lismore: Richmond River Historical Society.

Dargavel, J. (1994) Constructing Australia's forests in the image of capital. In: Dovers, S. (ed.) *Australian Environmental History: Essays and Cases*. Melbourne: Oxford University Press, pp. 80–99.

Davies, A., Bowers, M., Ball, A. and Evershed, N. (2018) Murray-Darling: When the river runs dry. *The Guardian*. Available from: https://www.theguardian.com/environment/ng-interactive/2018/apr/05/murray-darling-when-the-river-runs-dry (accessed 28 June 2018).

Dawson, R.L. (1938) Pioneer squatters, Richmond River: Some recollections and character sketches. *Richmond River Historical Society Journal*. 1, pp. 27–37.

Duddy, T. (2013) Mining and farmland protection. Paper presented at the Mining in a Sustainable World: Environmental, Social and Political Economical Issues Conference, University of New England, 13–15 October, Armidale.

Ellis, C. (2014) Boundary labour and the production of emotionless commodities: The case of beef production in the United States. *The Sociological Quarterly*. **55**(1), pp. 92–118.

Farmers for Climate Action (2019) Our work. *Farmers for Climate Action*. Available from: https://www.farmersforclimateaction.org.au/our_work (accessed 27 June 2019).

Farwell, G. (1973) *Squatter's Castle: The Story of a Pastoral Dynasty, Life and Times of Edward David Stewart Ogilvie*. Melbourne: Lansdowne Press.

Finney, C.M. (1993) *Paradise Revealed: Natural History in Nineteenth-Century Australia*. Melbourne: Museum of Victoria.

Fisher, T. (2015) Liverpool Plains rally against the Shenhua coal mine (in-person conversation) (personal communication, 15 February 2015).

Fry, O. (1847) *Commissioner of Crown Lands to Select Committee on the Minimum Upset Price of Land, 16 August, 1847*. Votes and Proceedings of the Legislative Council of New South Wales, vol. 2, p. 542.

Garbutt, R. (2010) The clearing: Heidegger's Lichtung and the Big Scrub. *Cultural Studies Review*. **16**(1), pp. 27–42.

Garbutt, R. (2011) *The Locals: Identity, Place and Belonging in Australia and Beyond*. Cultural Identity Studies vol. 22. Bern: Peter Lang.

Gollan, J. (1938) The agricultural and pastoral developments of the Mid-Richmond. *Richmond River Historical Society Journal*. **1**, pp. 69–74.

Green, J. (1910) *The Lost Echo: The Story of the Richmond*. Sydney: NSW Bookstall.

Griffiths, T. (1997) Introduction: Ecology and empire: Towards an Australian history of the world. In: Griffiths, T. and Robin, L. (eds) *Ecology and Empire: Environmental History of Settler Societies*. Carlton South: Melbourne University Press, pp. 1–16.

Hall, C.M. (1992) *From Wasteland to World Heritage: Preserving Australia's Wilderness*. Carlton: Melbourne University Press.

Henderson, M. (n.d.) *Our Heritage: Archive*. Lismore: Richmond River Historical Society.

Hodinott, T. (2014) Interviewed by Bible, V. (digital recording). Bentley, 19 April. In author's possession.

Hoff, J. (2006), *Bundjalung Jugun: Bundjalung Country*. Lismore: Richmond River Historical Society.

Howard, A. (2004) I'm a forestry professional too! *The Forester*. **46**(2), p. 20.

Hunter, R.J. (1997) A review of rainforest restoration in nature reserves in Lismore district. Lismore: unpublished report to the New South Wales National Parks and Wildlife Service.

Hurley, P.J. (1948) *Red Cedar: The Story of the North Coast*. Sydney: Dymocks Book Arcade.

Hutton, D. and Connors, L. (1999) *A History of the Australian Environment Movement*. Melbourne: Cambridge University Press.

Jarrett, C. (1894) The pioneers. *Ballina Pilot*, p. 8.

Keane, E. (1956) *Kyogle, New South Wales: 1839–1956*. Sydney: Oswald Ziegler.

Kelly, R. (2003) The mediated forest: Who speaks for the trees? In: Wilson, H. (ed.) *Belonging in the Rainbow Region Cultural Perspectives on the NSW North Coast*. Lismore: Southern Cross University Press, pp. 101–20.

Kendell, J. and Buivids, E. (1987) *Earth First*, Sydney: ABC Books.

Kijas, J. (2003) From obscurity into the fierce light of amazing popularity. In: Wilson, H. (ed.) *Belonging in the Rainbow Region Cultural Perspectives on the NSW North Coast*. Lismore: Southern Cross University Press, pp. 21–40.

Lester, L. and Hutchins, B. (2012) The power of the unseen: Environmental conflict, the media and invisibility. *Media Culture and Society*. **34**(7), pp. 847–63.

Lester, L. and Hutchins, B. (eds) (2013) *Environmental Conflict and the Media*. New York, NY: Peter Lang.

Lines, W.J. (2006) *Patriots: Defending Australia's Natural Heritage*. St Lucia, Brisbane: University of Queensland Press.

Lymburner, S. (2004) *Lumley Park: Vegetation Management Plan*. Report to Ballina Shire Council, Ballina.

Martin, F. and Ellis, R. (2003) Dropping in, not dropping out. In: Wilson, H. (ed.) *Belonging in the Rainbow Region Cultural Perspectives on the NSW North Coast*. Lismore: Southern Cross University Press, pp. 179–205.

McCaffrey, F. (c.1958) First century of dairying in NSW. In: *The Notebooks of Gainsford McCurdy, Settlement of the Richmond River*. Lismore: Gainsford McCurdy, Richmond River Historical Society Archives.

McGee, T. (2014) Reconsidering Nimbin 40 years after the Aquarius Festival. *Ockham's Razor, ABC Radio* (transcript online). Available from: www.abc.net.au/radionational/programs/ockhamsrazor/5431260 (accessed 10 May 2014).

Mears, P. (1985) *Women Down the Valley*. Lismore, Australia: NSW Department of Education, North Coast Region.

Meredith, P. (1999) *Myles and Milo*. St Leonards: Allen & Unwin.

Monroe, R. (1976) The border ranges – A land use conflict. In: Monroe, R. and Stephens, N.C. (eds) *The Border Ranges: A Land Use Conflict in Regional Perspective*. St Lucia, Brisbane: Royal Society of Queensland, pp. 79–81.

Monroe, R. and Stephens, N.C. (eds) (1976) *The Border Ranges: A Land Use Conflict in Regional Perspective*. St Lucia, Brisbane: Royal Society of Queensland.

Moyal, A. (1993) *A Bright and Savage Land: Scientists in Colonial Australia*. Sydney: Penguin.

Neilsen, M. (2014) Interviewed by Bible, V. (digital recording) Bentley, 18 April. In author's possession.

New South Wales National Parks and Wildlife Service (1997) *Big Scrub Nature Reserves: Plan of Management*. Lismore, Australia: NSW National Parks and Wildlife Service.

Nicholson, N. (2010) Interviewed by Bible, V. (digital recording) Terania Creek, 7 March. In author's possession.

Nicholson, N. (2012) Interview by Bible, V. (digital recording) Terania Creek, 5 May. In author's possession.

Philosophical Society of Australasia (1821) Minute Book. 27 June, Location SZ1007. Sydney: Mitchell Library archives.

Quartpot and Ruby Creeks Revisited (1872) *Armidale Express and New England General Advertiser*. 9 November, p. 2.

Richards, R.J. (2002) *The Romantic Conception of Life: Science and Philosophy in the Age of Goethe*. Chicago, IL: University of Chicago Press.

Rossi, L. (2011) Oral history and individual environmental experiences. In: Myllyntaus, T. (ed.) *Thinking through the Environment: Green Approaches to Global History*. Cambridge: White Horse Press, pp. 135–55.

Ryan, M. (1979) *Lismore: The Story of a North Coast City*. Milson's Point: The Currawong Press.

Ryan, M. (1998) *Days and Ways of Old Time Nimbin*. Nimbin: Nimbin Chamber of Commerce.

Shearman, L. (2012) Interviewed by Bible, V. (digital recording). Goolmangar, 13 June. In author's possession.

Somerville, J. (2005) *Saving the Rainforest: The NSW Campaign 1973–1984*. Narrabeen: J.G. Somerville.

Standen, P. (1976) A planning perspective – The New South Wales position. In: Monroe, R. and Stephens, N.C. (eds) *The Border Ranges: A Land Use Conflict in Regional Perspective*. St Lucia, Brisbane: Royal Society of Queensland, pp. 67–78.

Stratford, E. (2009) Belonging as a resource: The case of Ralph's Bay, Tasmania, and the local politics of place. *Environment and Planning*. **41**, pp. 796–810.

Tintenbar Shire Council (1920) Correspondence. *Northern Star*. 16 November, p. 7.

Turvey, N. (2006) *Terania Creek: Rainforest Wars*. Brisbane: Glass House Books.

Walker, R. (1991) Fauna and flora protection in New South Wales, 1866–1948. *Journal of Australian Studies*. **28**, pp. 17–28.

Waterhouse, R. (2006) Agrarian ideals and pastoral realities: The use and misuse of land in rural Australia. In: Crotty, M. and Roberts, D.A. (eds) *The Great Mistakes of Australian History*. Sydney: University of New South Wales Press, pp. 64–78.
Watson, D. (2014) *The Bush: Travels in the Heart of Australia*. Melbourne: Hamish & Hamilton.
Watson, I. (1990) *Fighting over the Forests*. Sydney: Allen & Unwin.
Wilkie, R. (2005) Sentient commodities and productive paradoxes: The ambiguous nature of human–livestock relations in Northeast Scotland. *Journal of Rural Studies*. **21**, pp. 213–30.

PART V

SOCIAL NETWORKS AND ANTI-ENVIRONMENTALISM

9. Climate change counter movement organisations: an international deviant network?

Ruth E. McKie

INTRODUCTION

The growing urgency to address human-caused climate change presents a significant challenge to the global capitalist fossil fuel economy (Cherp et al., 2016). The global capitalist economy has grown powered by fossil fuels that are extracted from the earth and converted into energy. However, this fossil fuel economy has become central in the destruction of the environment (Lynch, 2016). Since the rise of industrial capitalism and as it continues today, it has caused significant ecological disorganisation (Stretesky et al., 2013). One impact of the industrial process has been the rise in CO_2 emissions and the resulting contribution towards the rise in temperatures of the earth's atmosphere (Lynch et al., 2013). For the capitalist or the owners of the means of production (i.e. fossil fuel industry), this ecological destruction has been vital to economic growth and the accumulation of profit (Foster et al., 2010). Thus, under the logic of capitalism, this pursuit of power and profit requires continuous ecological destruction if economic growth is to be protected (see also, Magdoff and Foster, 2011).

In response to the consensus that human-caused climate change presents significant risks to the ecosystem, international and domestic governmental agencies and private firms have implemented governance strategies such as the United Nations Framework Convention on Climate Change (UNFCCC) to reduce the consumption of heavily polluting natural resources, challenging the conventional norm of abundant natural resources that has historically supported this fossil fuel economy.

Social scientists have documented the extensive operations of the Climate Change Counter Movement (CCCM) (e.g. Boussalis and Coan, 2016; Brulle, 2014; Dunlap and McCright, 2015) that operates to protect against a shift from a fossil fuel economy. The CCCM operates as one component of the anti-environmental movement. Broadly, anti-environmentalism refers to the responses of industry actors – including those in the fossil fuel industry – that have created and driven a narrative pitting protection of the environment against the benefits of economic growth (Brick, 1995). These CCCM organisations were originally associated with the 'Wise Use' Movement in the US, which purposely emerged to attack environmentalists and environmentalism (Jacobs, 1995). The Wise Use Movement messaging emphasised that there was a trade-off between environmental and economic interests (Gemenis et al., 2012). The environment was positioned as part of a series of policies pitted in opposition to the economy. CCCM organisations played a role in facilitating this discussion that climate change remains something that can be part of a cost–benefit analysis rather than a single policy issue itself.

The CCCM has historically operated in the United States (US) (e.g. Boussalis and Coan, 2016; Brulle, 2014; Dunlap and McCright, 2015). Members have produced pseudo-scientific reports, held conferences, lobbied in governments and made regular media appearances (Dunlap and Jacques, 2013) in efforts to distort the realities of climate change aiming to pursue support or in this case non-support for urgent action on human-caused climate change. While remaining dominant in the US, CCCM organisations have emerged and operate in other parts of the world (Dunlap and McCright, 2015; Fischer and Plehwe, 2017; Plehwe, 2014). Here, I expand this international investigation into the CCCM and ask the question: Is the CCCM an International Deviant Network? To do this, I first explore the international scope of the CCCM. Second, I identify a new theoretically innovative approach to examine the movement using criminological theory (McKie, 2018a, 2018b). I apply the traditional criminological theory 'Techniques of Neutralization' (Sykes and Matza, 1957) to organise the diversity of scepticism presented in the messages of CCCM organisations. Finally, I illustrate the limited geographical differences in the application of these messages across countries, offering a preliminary diagnosis on why this may be the case.

THE INTERNATIONAL CLIMATE CHANGE COUNTER MOVEMENT NETWORK

CCCM organisations engage in a form of knowledge production, providing a venue for those wishing to sustain a fossil fuel-based status quo, and to debate different views about how best to overcome capitalism's environmental harms (Sapinski, 2015). They disseminate knowledge aiming to legitimise a certain type of fossil fuel-based, capitalist, economic governance while delegitimising others to protect an economic system challenged by certain forms of climate governance (see also, Dunlap and Brulle, 2015). These messages serve to construct doubt amongst the public and politicians in an era where attitudes continue to change and respond more favourably to environmental protection (e.g. Anderson et al., 2017).

McCright and Dunlap (2000, 2003, 2010, 2017) have outlined the operation and impacts of the US CCCM. In 2015, they emphasised the growing urgency to address the international CCCM, stating, 'we need more studies in other nations, and especially cross-national comparisons, as undoubtedly the sources and nature of denial vary across national contexts' (Dunlap and McCright, 2015, p. 319). They add that more attention must be paid to the 'international coordination of denial activities, beyond the roles of key actors from the US, UK, and Canada in stimulating denial organisations abroad' (p. 319).

Responding to the calls to examine the international scope of the movement, Figure 9.1 maps 465 CCCM organisations located across 53 countries between 1950 and 2016 derived from a coding scheme used by McKie (2018a).[1] For the purposes of this chapter, the CCCM includes conservative think tanks (CTTs), front groups, trade and professional associations, coalitions, and philanthropic foundations. While there is variation in the characteristics of CCCM organisations in different countries, they do operate in different parts of the world (see also, Fischer and Plehwe, 2017; Plehwe, 2014; Harkinson, 2009; Hamilton, 2010).

Unsurprisingly, most CCCM organisations have operated and continue to do so in the US (N = 319). Nonetheless, while there are fewer organisations in other parts of the world, these organisations have and do still operate. Some have emerged in other developed or economically wealthy nations including the United Kingdom (UK) (N = 17), Canada (N = 16), Australia (N = 12). Others have emerged in developing nations or those with a growing economy, including Peru (N = 5), Brazil (N = 5), Chile (N = 2), Nigeria (N = 3) and Ghana (N = 1). This international

Climate change counter movement organisations 175

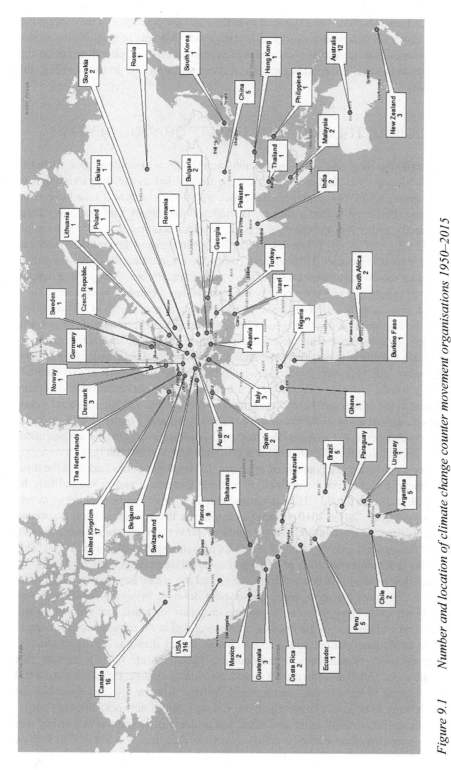

Figure 9.1 Number and location of climate change counter movement organisations 1950–2015

network of CCCM organisations has expanded over time and the operation of these organisations in other countries is deservedly worthy of investigation. One way to examine the modus operandi of these organisations across countries is to examine this geographic distribution and the messaging strategies that different organisations adopt and why. To do this, I turn to the field of criminology.

CRIMINOLOGICAL THEORY AND CLIMATE CHANGE DENIAL

Criminologists examine the causes, the implications and the prevention strategies related to crime and criminal activity. Criminal activity can be understood as the direct violation of criminal law (Canton, 2017). These laws are built upon a series of norms and values (i.e. what is right and wrong) that exist within a society. Deviancy is an activity that may not violate criminal law directly; rather it is an activity that is not considered moral or to follow the traditional norms and values of society (Quinney, 1965). Both criminal and deviant behaviour can be thought of as a social construct (Hillyard and Tombs, 2007), constructed under the values and norms within a society dependent on time, place and space (Polizzi, 2016). For example, what is considered criminal in one country may not be considered criminal in another.

Going further, something that is considered harmful or causes some form of victimisation, may in fact not be criminalised or perceived as deviant because of the nature of the political economic system. That is, those who are more powerful in the social structures of society under a capitalistic economic system have the means and power to define what is considered criminal and deviant (e.g. Quinney, 1965; Sutherland, 1945). This means that crimes committed by the most powerful in society may not be punished and/or may not be considered a crime. To draw attention to the crimes and harms committed by those often with higher social status, researchers have adopted a social harms perspective (Hillyard and Tombs, 2007). A social harms perspective then refers to those acts that may not be defined as criminal or deviant under traditional law, yet that do cause significant harm (Hillyard and Tombs, 2007).

Most environmental harms are committed by or are the result of actions taken by the most powerful in society, but may not be defined as criminal under law and/or are unlikely be prosecuted (e.g. Lynch et al., 2013). Human-caused climate change can be thought of as one example (e.g. Lynch et al., 2013, 2010). Scientists emphasise the ecological harm associated with the production and consumption of fossil fuels. However, the economic infrastructure requires the continuous extraction of fossil fuels in its pursuit of profit (Altvater, 2007). This economic pursuit is accompanied by a political and social divide between the owners of the means of production or the most powerful in society and the wider population. Those with power are those that construct these legal frameworks defining behaviour or activities as environmentally harmful. Thus, they can negate the criticisms of fossil fuel production and consumption as harmful because of their positions of power within the criminal justice system.

The problem of climate change and climate change denial then can be understood as somehow harmful with criminogenic consequences. Lynch et al. (2010) contend that state-based policies, or lack thereof in the US to address climate change, indicate a purposeful undermining of action to remedy climate change. Similarly, Kramer (2013) argues that the lack of US legislation to address climate change is the outcome of networks between corporate actors, lobbying firms, think tanks and other stakeholders in environmental policy that have negatively impacted climate change action. Likewise, Ruggiero and South (2013) draw attention to industries such as oil and coal companies that use their money to influence environmental regulation. They add that there are groups (CCCM organisations) with significant power to influence environmental policies and regulations that cast doubt on climate science.

Taking a criminological approach that highlights corporate and (political) states' role in failing to address the problem of climate change seriously, provides a point of reference to frame these practices as deviant. Thus, I contend that these organisations can be considered an international deviant network. This is because, in the context of climate change, it is morally right to support the scientific evidence on human-caused climate change. Positions that deny or that are sceptical about human-caused climate change 'deviate' from the accepted norms and values of a society. Moreover, this is not simply a single individual denying climate change. Not unlike an organised crime gang, there is a group of actors that operate across countries violating a series of norms and values in the pursuit of profit.

To help further support this argument, I draw a theoretical link between CCCM organisations and neutralisation theory (Sykes and Matza, 1957). Sykes and Matza posited that a juvenile delinquent will operationalise one or more 'techniques of neutralisation' to justify their deviance. A delinquent employs these techniques to shape attitudes, convincing others that their behaviour should not be criminalised. A person committing a deviant act adheres to conventional norms, but they may use one or more neutralisation techniques to justify violations of these conventional norms. In doing so, (1) they are able to justify their continued deviant practices; and (2) they mitigate any potential negative feelings or dissonance as they recognise their practices are harmful.

The five techniques of neutralisation originally derived by Sykes and Matza (1957) were:

1. *Denial of Responsibility* contends that the deviant is accidental and/or the deviant was a victim of their environment and therefore unable to control their actions.
2. *Denial of Injury or Harm* asserts that an act will not injure or significantly injure someone or something; and/or there are likely positive impacts resulting from this behaviour.
3. *Denial of Victim* on the one hand claims the victim is deserving. On the other, it describes a person's failure to activate their internal moral reasoning because the victim may be 'physically absent, unknown, or a vague abstraction' (p.668).
4. *Condemnation of the Condemner* shifts the criticisms of a deviant act to those condemning that person's actions, thereby rejecting the higher status of the condemners.
5. *Appeal to Higher Loyalties* proposes that the deviant act was necessary and imitates a sacrifice to satisfy the requirements of an intimate social group.

Over time, researchers have expanded the number of these techniques, applying them to a variety of criminal and non-criminal behaviours. One important contribution is the application of the theory to the study of social harms (Hillyard and Tombs, 2004).

I argue that on behalf of fossil fuel interest groups (see also Brulle, 2014), CCCM use neutralisation techniques to frame the argument that action on climate change is debatable. This is an effort to resist challenges to a fossil fuel-based economic system that is challenged by international efforts to adapt and mitigate climate change. That is, Western capitalism has relied on fossil fuel intensive production, which has historic negative ecological impacts (Foster et al., 2010; Stretesky et al., 2013). This inevitably influences policy decisions to address climate change because of its direct links with industrial processes and the accumulation of capital, leading to actors such as CCCM organisations attempting to defuse significant action to remedy climate change (see also McKie, 2018a).

More specifically, neutralisation techniques provide an alternative way to categorise messages used by CCCM organisations. This is because the impacts of convincing the public and/or politicians to resist or undermine climate action may contribute to a lack of support for action to remedy this problem. Inadvertently, then, this may lead to a failure to address the harms caused by climate change and contribute to further environmental harm.

CLIMATE CHANGE COUNTER MOVEMENT NEUTRALISATION TECHNIQUES

Table 9.1 presents variants of these techniques of neutralisation derived from Sykes and Matza's originals. This prior coding scheme was used to examine the diversity of scepticism in a content analysis of 417 documents produced by CCCM organisations in 2015 (see McKie, 2018a for further information). The first six techniques were originally proposed and derived by combining broader knowledge on neutralisation theory and the CCCM. The final technique, Justification by Comparison (JBC), emerged from the analysis. The technique JBC was previously identified by Thompson and Harred (1992) in their study on topless dancing.

Table 9.2 provides the frequency of organisations adopting each neutralisation technique found in the data described above and an example. Variants of COC were the most common technique (N = 268) where CCCM organisations have criticised and demonised environmentalists, climate scientists and/or climate change policy. For instance, the Canadian-based Montreal Economic Institute contended, 'There is a certain fringe of the environmentalist movement whose members have almost nothing good to say about their fellow men and women. If not for humans, they sometimes explicitly argue, the Earth would be a wonderful place' (2015). Similarly, the Austrian based Hayek Institute stated, 'It is the propaganda around the world that has produced fear of the "global climate", the "climate catastrophe" and "climate change"' (2015).

The second most common technique was AHL (N = 159), where organisations contend that economic progress and development is more important than preventing climate change. Rather than imposing environmental regulations and alternative renewable energy resources, it is more important that the world continue economic and social development via the use of fossil fuels, particularly to protect the interests of developing nations. For example, the UK-based Clexit argued, 'For developing countries, the Paris Treaty would deny them the benefits of reliable low-cost hydrocarbon energy … thus prolonging and increasing their dependency on international handouts' (2015). Similarly, the US-based International Climate Science Coalition applied AHL, stating, 'so-called new renewable energy technologies are extremely expensive and rely on huge subsidies. To use such intermittent and diffuse power sources requires that the consumer pays between three and ten times the price of power from conventional sources' (2015).

The frequency of organisations adopting the pseudo-scientific techniques DOR (N = 115), DOI1 (N = 83) and DOI2 (N = 51) was far less compared to the COC and AHL techniques. In the Netherlands, the Planck Foundation employed DOR, stating, 'climate change is of all times' (2015). The Canadian-based Mannkal Economic Foundation adopted DOI1, stating, 'Man-made CO_2 emissions throughout human history constitute less than 0.00022 percent of the total naturally emitted from the mantle of the earth during geological history' (2015). The technique DOI2 represents messages that declare positive outcomes from climate changes.

Table 9.1 Climate change counter movement neutralisation techniques

Name	Abbreviation	Original Technique	Climate Change Counter Movement Neutralisation Techniques
Denial of Responsibility	DOR	Denial of Responsibility is used to contend that the deviant or criminal act is accidental and/or fell victim to their social environment unable to control their actions	Climate change is happening, but humans are not the cause
Denial of Injury	DOI1	Denial of Injury 1 asserts an act will not injure or significantly injure someone or something; and/or	(DOI1) There is no significant harm caused by human action
	DOI2	Denial of Injury 2 asserts there are likely positive impacts from this behaviour	(DOI2) There may even been some benefits
Denial of Victim	DOV	Denial of Victim on the one hand juxtaposes victim and offender as the deviant becomes the condemner and law enforcer	There is no climate change or climate change victims
Condemnation of the Condemner	COC	Condemnation of the Condemner shifts negative opinions or criticisms of a deviant to those condemning that person's actions, thereby rejecting the higher status of the condemners	Climate change research is misrepresented by scientists, and manipulated by media, politicians and environmentalists
Appeal to Higher Loyalties	AHL	Appeal to Higher Loyalties imitates a sacrifice to satisfy the requirements of an intimate social group	Economic progress and development are more important than preventing climate change
Justification by Comparison	JBC	Justification by Comparison argues other crimes or deviant activities are more significant and harmful than the one committed by the individual	Other policy issues are more important to address comparative to climate change

Table 9.2 Frequency of climate change counter movement organisations adopting a neutralisation techniques and examples

Technique of Neutralisation	Freq	Example (Organisation Name, Location)
DOR	115	'Climate change is of all times (Greenland used to be green, so climate change has driving factors other than man made CO_2)' (Planck Foundation, The Netherlands).
DOI1	83	'Man-made CO_2 emissions throughout human history constitute less than 0.00022 percent of the total naturally emitted from the mantle of the earth during geological history.' (Mannkal Economic Foundation, Canada).
DOI2	51	'The evidence is overwhelming that rising atmospheric CO_2 levels will continue to help plants thrive, leading to greater biodiversity, shrinking deserts, expanding habitat for wildlife, and more food for a growing human population …'. (Heartland Institute, US).
DOV	10	'[Higher CO_2 concentrations and rising temperatures are causing] no harm to the global environment or to human health'(Capitol Resource Institute, US).
COC	268	'The assertion of a "man-made climate change" is not justified as a science and therefore a fraud against the population'(European Institute for Climate and Energy, Germany).
AHL	159	'So-called new renewable energy technologies are extremely expensive and rely on huge subsidies. To use such intermittent and diffuse power sources requires that the consumer pays between three and ten times the price of power from conventional sources (coal, oil, natural gas, hydro and nuclear)' (International Climate Science Coalition, US).
JBC	29	'[J]ust as developing countries are not expected to do as much as developed countries to curb emissions, New Zealand's actions should be less ambitious than Australia's because it is a wealthier country …'. (New Zealand Initiative, 2015).

For example, the Heartland Institute stated, 'the evidence is overwhelming that rising atmospheric CO_2 levels will continue to help plants thrive leading to greater biodiversity, shrinking deserts, expanding habitat for wildlife and more food for a growing human population' (2015).

DOV (N = 10) and JBC (N = 29) were the least common techniques. Examples include the Capitol Resource Institute, who stated, 'The Institute maintains that higher CO_2 concentrations and rising temperatures are causing "no harm to the global environment or to human health"' (2015). The New Zealand Initiative employed JBC, stating, 'just as developing countries are not expected to do as much as developed countries to curb emissions, New Zealand's actions should be less ambitious than Australia's because it is a wealthier country' (2015). Similarly, the US branch of the Committee for a Constructive Tomorrow stated, 'Even drastic reductions in US CO_2 emissions will mean nothing globally, because China, India and other developing nations are now emitting far more CO_2 than the US could eliminate even by shutting down its economy' (2015).

Like much of the neutralisation theory literature (see Maruna and Copes, 2005), often CCCM organisations adopt multiple techniques. An example here includes the US-based Citizens for Government Waste (2016), which combined DOR, DOI1, DOI2, COC and AHL:

> more and more scientists are speaking out, declaring that most global warming is not man-made [DOI1] but a natural and cyclic occurrence [DOR] and that CO_2 is not a pollutant, but a gas that is necessary for life on earth [DOI2]. Before taxpayers send hundreds of billions of their dollars to government bureaucrats and politicians that want to control their activities and redistribute their wealth to politically-favoured policies [COC], there should be a debate on whether CO_2 and global warming warrant such a drastic and expensive response [AHL].

Similarly, the US-based Education Action Group Foundation (2015) combined DOR, DOI1, COC and AHL:

> Following are some basic facts about global warming that are in direct contrast to the spoon-fed pabulum that is being force-fed as undisputed fact through the mainstream media and our government-sanctioned educational system [COC] ...There is no scientific consensus on the human role in climate change ... Future warming due to human greenhouse gas emissions will be much less than the United Nations forecasts [DOI1] ... CO_2 has not caused weather to become more extreme, polar ice and sea ice to melt, or sea level rise to accelerate [DOR] ... Reducing CO_2 emissions is extremely expensive and won't affect the weather ... Public policies should aim at fostering economic growth to adapt to natural climate change [AHL].

The multiple use of neutralisation techniques aims to appeal to different groups of people who may respond more favourably to some techniques than others. It signifies the importance of a systematic and organised campaign by CCCM organisations to reach those that might show a more favourable response to certain arguments than others. Incorporating several forms of messaging infuses further doubt by fuelling alternative opposing opinions on the consensus in a process. This conclusion aligns with the previous findings of Boussalis and Coan (2016), who highlight the prevalence of multifaceted arguments to construct a narrative of denial, thus creating doubt and confusion over specific issues and their subsequent response to reach a diverse audience.

It is important to note the limitations of this categorisation. Here, I divided the messages used by the CCCM into seven groups. However, as the movement evolves it may be that the number of defined techniques is insufficient and/or they may diversify. Thus, while this

Table 9.3 The frequency and percentage of organisations adopting a technique by continent

	DOR Freq (%)	DOI1 Freq (%)	DOI2 Freq (%)	DOV Freq (%)	AHL Freq (%)	COC Freq (%)	JBC Freq (%)
Europe (N = 20)	13 (11.5%)	10 (12.8%)	6 (11.8%)	0 (0%)	28 (17.8%)	37 (14.2%)	3 (10.7%)
North America (N = 2)	83 (73.5%)	56 (71.8%)	39 (76.5%)	9 (100%)	108 (68.7%)	188 (72.1%)	23 (82.1)
South America (N = 10)	5 (4.4%)	5 (6.4%)	0 (0%)	0 (0%)	10 (6.4%)	17 (6.5%)	1 (3.6%)
Africa (N = 2)	2 (1.8%)	2 (2.6%)	0 (0%)	0 (0%)	2 (1.3%)	3 (1.1%)	0 (0%)
Oceania (N =2)	5 (4.4%)	3 (3.8%)	3 (5.9%)	0 (0%)	7 (4.5%)	11 (4.2%)	1 (3.6%)
Asia (N = 7)	5 (4.4%)	2 (2.6%)	2 (3.8%)	0 (0%)	2 (1.3%)	4 (1.5%)	0 (0%)
Russia (N=1)	0 (0%)	0 (0%)	1 (2%)	0 (0%)	0 (0%)	1 (0.4%)	0 (0%)
Total Number of Techniques	113 (100%)	78 (100%)	51 (100%)	9 (100%)	157 (100%)	261 (100%)	28 (100%)

coding scheme has provided information at one point in time to help understand the messages adopted by CCCM, that is not to say they may not morph, change or increase. Nonetheless, the point remains that this criminological framework provides the starting point to label the actions of the CCCM as in some way harmful.

Further exploration helps consider any geographic variation in these techniques. Table 9.3 provides the frequency and percentage of organisations using each technique across each continent in 2015. Note, I separate Russia, noting its placement across two continents. 'N' represents the number of countries in the sample that had at least one operating CCCM. Additionally, in Table 9.4, I present the frequency and percentage of organisations adopting a technique by continent excluding the US. This is because we often treat the US as an outlier with significantly higher number of CCCM organisations.

There are several interesting observations about the geographic distribution of each technique. The most poignant is the observable lack of variation across countries in the use of the COC technique. As a reminder, the COC technique refers to the demonisation and criticism of climate scientists, environmentalists, the media and politicians. Even when US observations are removed from the sample, the COC technique remains the most common technique used by organisations across countries. Consistently adopting this technique directly targets political decision makers and those carrying out scientific research, creating a political hostile message. This conclusion parallels the CCCM literature, including McCright and Dunlap (2000), who suggest that criticism of scientists, environmentalists and policymakers is a tool used by sceptics to discourage climate action across the world.

There is little geographic variation in the adoption of AHL where organisations suppose that social and economic development – from fossil fuels – is more important than addressing climate change. Organisations across both low- and high-income nations in the sample employ this technique. There are two points to make on this observation drawing on wider contextual

Table 9.4 The frequency and percentage of organisations adopting a technique by continent excluding the US

	DOR Freq (%)	DOI1 Freq (%)	DOI2 Freq (%)	DOV Freq (%)	AHL Freq (%)	COC Freq (%)	JBC Freq (%)
Europe (N = 20)	13 (35.2%)	10 (40%)	6 (46.2%)	0 (0%)	28 (50%)	37 (45.1%)	3 (60%)
North America (excluding US) (N = 1)	7 (18.9%)	3 (12%)	1 (7.7%)	1 (100%)	7 (12.5%)	9 (11%)	0 (0%)
South America (N = 10)	5 (13.5%)	5 (20%)	0 (0%)	0 (0%)	10 (17.9%)	17 (20.7%)	1 (20%)
Africa (N = 2)	2 (5.4%)	2 (8%)	0 (0%)	0 (0%)	2 (3.6%)	3 (3.7%)	0 (0%)
Oceania (N = 2)	5 (13.5%)	3 (12%)	3 (23.1%)	0 (0%)	7 (12.4%)	11 (13.4%)	1 (20%)
Asia (N = 7)	5 (13.5%)	2 (8%)	2 (15.4%)	0 (0%)	2 (3.6%)	4 (4.9%)	0 (0%)
Russia (N = 1)	0 (0%)	0 (0%)	1 (7.6%)	0 (0%)	0 (0%)	1 (1.2%)	0 (0%)
Total Number of Techniques	37 (100%)	25 (100%)	13 (100%)	1 (100%)	56 (100%)	82 (100%)	5 (100%)

knowledge. First, this observation loosely suggests that messaging may take the form of appealing to higher loyalties in some of the low-income countries such as Peru, Nigeria and Brazil. Compared to the frequency of other techniques, more CCCM organisations in many of these low-income countries use the argument that social and economic development is more important than addressing climate change in certain countries compared to others. I can speculate that CCCM organisations may well emerge to resist domestic and international policy that imposes boundaries of the potential for economic growth in some of these low-income countries. This conclusion reflects evidence on the industries driving economic development amongst lower-income nations, where in the sample, much of their GDP growth is from natural resource production and exportation (Muradian et al., 2012).

Second, organisations in higher-income nations also employ this technique. This may reflect the interests of high-income countries that reap the benefits of an environmentally harmful capitalist economic system that often has disproportional impacts on low-income countries, driving the employment of this technique (McKie, 2018a). It may be the case that in economically powerful nations (such as the US, UK and Canada), that benefit most from climate inaction, countermovement organisations disguise a concern for low-income nations. At the heart of this message, however, is protecting the interests of the fossil fuel industry with bases in these countries to delegitimise regulatory and political action. In other words, the dissemination of messages to protect global fossil fuel-based capitalism is important for developed nations such as the US, to effect politics across countries. In doing so, rich nations continue to experience a type of lifestyle based on ecologically harmful over-production and consumption (Altvater, 2009), while also not directly experiencing the significant environmental harm associated with this resource extraction (Roberts and Parks, 2009).[2] Instead, this burden is placed upon low-income and/or developing nations.

A final point on geographic variation considers the science-oriented techniques: DOR, DOI1, DOI2 and DOV. While used far less in comparison to other techniques, CCCM organisations across low- and higher-income nations adopt these techniques, indicating no initial observational geographic differences. It may be the case that this message transference of pseudo-scientific techniques is simply another way to disorganise public knowledge of the clear evidence on human-caused climate change. Joining various types of pseudo-scientific perspectives on climate change serves to reinforce this idea that the evidence is still unsubstantiated. 'The era of science denial is not over' (Boussalis and Coan, 2016, p. 89) and movements are still using these techniques that present 'alternative facts' to support their position that climate change is up to date and/or action is unnecessary.

The concept of policy diffusion (Strang and Meyer, 1993) may be useful to explore the observable lack of geographic variation in the messages adopted by organisations across countries. Diffusion here refers to the decision taken by one government on a policy issue that is shaped or influenced by others (Shipan and Volden, 2008). Meyer et al. (1997) proposed that, within the arena of policymaking, there is a form of statelessness, whereby international policy decision making is communicated across countries. It is via economic, political and societal interlinkages between nation states that offer channels for the transfer of policy ideas (Tews et al., 2003).

Dunlap and McCright (2015) argue that CCCM organisations are shifting beyond the US, spreading their messages to resist actions to address climate change. The lack of geographic variation in the message adopted by CCCM organisations may indicate a form of diffusion. CCCM organisations are operating as an international advocacy organisation (Dunlap and McCright, 2015) or policy project promoting a specific response, or lack thereof, to climate change (see also Carroll and Sapinski, 2010; Sapinski, 2016). The ideological positioning of these organisations is likely to be a predictor of its receptivity to external forces to engage in this policy project and adopt a similar perspective towards climate change. This means the level of analysis must change from a country level to an organisational level to establish if this may explain some differences in messages across countries.

At an organisational level, the ideological beliefs of an organisation may increase or decrease the likelihood of adopting similar policy positions proposed by organisational actors in different countries (Gilardi, 2010). Evidenced across the literature, CCCM organisations are predisposed to adopting a neoliberal and/or libertarian ideology (e.g. Dunlap and McCright, 2015). Organisations across countries that follow this ideological trend may be more likely to adopt a position of climate change denial. Out of 465 organisations, 388 openly identify and promote either (1) market-based forms of policy and/or (2) adopt a neoliberal ideological or libertarian philosophy often associated with the political right and climate change denial. It is clear then that one of the driving principles within these organisations is to protect characteristics of a neoliberal economic market. This is like the conclusions of Fischer and Plehwe (2017), who explored the neoliberalisation of think tanks across Latin America. While further multivariate analysis would provide more insight into variation at an organisational level, these preliminary results indicate some reasons as to why organisations may adopt messages, not based on country-level factors, but on an organisational level. Therefore, a lack of geographic variation may be attributed to an organisational level dynamic to the movement. Messaging about climate change instead may be explained more as the consequence of a joint security response (Sapinski, 2016). When threats to the status quo expand and put pressure on those wishing to maintain it, organisations across countries will collectively adopt similar messaging to adjust to the impacts of the threat influenced by their ideological culture.

Furthermore, this observational lack of geographic variation may reflect the influence of US CCCM organisations playing a dominant role in the diffusion of anti-reflexive thought to prevent a shift from a global capitalist fossil fuel-based economy (McCright and Dunlap, 2010). This means the arguments adopted by dominant CCCM organisations in the US may have spread across countries. Certain individual actors in the US CCCM lead the disinformation campaign across countries; 58.1 percent of CCCM organisations in this sample across 32 countries do promote or reference research by one or more of the Heartland Institute's Global Warming Experts. The list comprises well-known climate sceptics that have questioned the scientific consensus, and/or that have criticised environmentalists, climate scientists and environmental policymaking. For instance, climate sceptic Willie Soon is a research fellow at the US-based Heartland Institute, Science and Environmental Policy Project, and the George C. Marshall Institute. He has produced research and written op eds for the Canadian Fraser Institute, was a founding member of the UK-based CCCM Clexit, and his work is cited by several CCCM organisations in other countries including Fake Climate (Brazil) and Fundacion Atlas (Argentina). Ultimately, this group of contrarians may be employed by or have their work cited by CCCM organisations, signalling a diffusion of positions on climate change that may well be dominated by the interests of US-based actors. In other words, CCCM organisations use the work of contrarian scientists directly or indirectly to legitimise their oppositional positions, operating across countries, indicating a concentrated effort partly influenced by this specific group of actors.

However, this notion of diffusion, particularly in the interests of the US and its influence on international climate action, may be challenged. Progress on international and domestic environmental and climate agreements has continued despite the US remaining an outlier (McCright and Dunlap, 2017). For instance, across Latin America, several individual countries have imposed and set the pace for environmental taxes (O'Toole, 2017). Chile and Mexico have launched a tax inititive in 2018 to manage individual and organisational level pollution, compensating for human pressures on the environment (see also Arlinghaus and Van Dender, 2017). Nevertheless, several policy decisions from other countries on resource extraction activities pose a question on significant environmental progress, signalling that the messages adopted by the CCCM are still consistent with certain policy developments. For example, India continues to be one of the strongest growing economies (International Monetary Fund, 2017) but relies heavily on crude oil imports for its primary energy source (Abdi, 2018), meaning it continues to produce environmentally harmful impacts. Moreover, fossil fuel subsidies remain high across larger developed countries and regions such as China, Russia, the European Union, India and Japan (Coady et al., 2017), again indicating continuing and expanding harm to the environment.

While only anecdotal, this diagnosis suggests the potential diffusion of arguments and policies proposals to (1) continue subsidising and expanding the fossil fuel economy; (2) offer free market forms of environmentalism (see also Sapinski, 2016); and (3) minimise action to address climate change based on the concerns that the economy and social and economic development will suffer if climate action is pursued. Thus, similar justifications emerging within the discourse and actions of the governance systems in other countries indicate forms of diffusion of messaging and arguments adopted in policy that may in fact decrease attention to, or minimize significant action to address climate change.

THE CLIMATE CHANGE COUNTER MOVEMENT: AN INTERNATIONAL DEVIANT NETWORK?

In short, there are three key conclusions drawn from this chapter. First, there is an operational international CCCM. While skewed to the US, CCCM organisations are spread across several continents. This supports the point made by Carroll and Sapinski (2010), who argue that the CCCM forms a specific policy network operating across countries to impact domestic level and international legislation on climate change. Furthermore, this corresponds with Dunlap and McCright's (2015) point: 'climate change denial is firmly rooted in nations with very strong commitments to neoliberalism and a powerful fossil fuel industry' (p. 319). The world economy is structured around a neoliberal global capitalist economic structure. Central to continued market expansion is the protection of fossil fuels, and ultimately in the view of those most powerful – including the fossil fuel lobby – they must operationalise strategies to protect this structure that allows them to maintain these positions of power. The CCCM, then, is operating as a global advocacy network to increase opposition to international climate change action.

Second, these messages are diverse, and preliminary observations indicate little geographic variation in the use of these techniques by organisations across countries. Again, this lack of geographic variation could be attributed to a larger policy project built up of several organisations that are interconnected in a political project to stimulate support for climate inaction. On the surface, this lack of geographic variation may in part be constructed using a cohesive messaging strategy consistent with CCCM organisations across countries.

Finally, I offered a new conceptualisation to answer the question: is the CCCM an 'International Deviant Network'? Here, I have used Sykes and Matza's neutralisation theory as an avenue to illustrate how the messages adopted by CCCM organisations can be employed or looked at in terms of a deviance lens. That is, CCCM organisations use a set of neutralisation techniques to construct doubt and frame the argument that climate science is up for debate. In doing so, it skews the lens through which the public and political actors come to understand the severity of climate change and support for the subsequent response. As a result, the framing of doubt may in fact minimise or forestall climate action (see also Walters, 2018). While CCCM organisations may not be violating criminal law, their actions, including messaging that may be adopted by the public and the subsequent inaction on climate change that results is essentially harmful and therefore deviant. Thus, the CCCM operates as an international deviant network.

Under this assessment, what are the next steps for research? First, research needs to continue to examine how the movement will evolve. More recently, we have seen the CCCM continue to operate and expand its discourse in mainstream politics. For example, under a Donald Trump presidency, the media narrative has given a further platform where one of the leaders of the 'free world' continues to deny and present sceptic views and positions about climate change (De Pryck and Gemenne, 2017). These positions are echoed either in spoken discourse (online and offline) and/or via policies by other international authoritative figures including Jair Bolsonaro, Brazilian president since 2019, and Australian Prime Minister Scott Morrison since 2018. This is despite evidence of clear environmental challenges emerging in their own countries reportedly linked to human-caused climate change. Further research must explore if and how there are interconnections between these 'populist' leaders in a 'post truth world'

(Lockwood, 2018) and what may happen as society continues to change in the wake of further climate changes.

Moreover, researchers must continue their work on understanding the impact of denial on public opinion and what are the opportunities to mediate this. Studies have examined the influence of exposure to denial messaging and public opinion on climate change (e.g. McCright, 2011; McCright et al., 2016; Weber and Stern, 2011). These results continue to show that, while there appears to be broad support in the belief of human-caused climate change, how this is implemented into action continues to be limited (Heald, 2017). As Lewondowsky et al. (2017) note, this may be because individuals tend to reject scientific findings when they threaten their core beliefs. While climate denialism is more strongly associated with those on the political right, it is consistent across political orientation. Managing climate science touches 'on people's lifestyle or worldviews, or impinge[s] on corporate interests' (p. 26), thus increasing the likelihood of rejecting science (see also Brulle and Norgaard, 2019). Subsequently, a lack of democratic support or interest to address the climate crisis, especially by richer nations – those with greater economic capacity to reduce fossil fuel consumption, while helping fund social and economic development in low-income nations (International Monetary Fund, 2017) – may be considered harmful by failing to meet the challenges on the ecological system because of human-caused climate change.

Going further, research needs to continue to turn and look at the role of diffusion. More recently the work of Brulle (2014) and Farrell (2016, 2019) have examined the social networks emerging between organisations in the US CCCM. But how do these expand across countries. Are there interrelations between countries whereby the US CCCM is infiltrating other organisations across different parts of the world to influence policy decision making? Or is there an independent shift in different countries as the growing scientific evidence indicates a clear necessary vision that approaches to fossil fuel use and maintaining an economic growth model need to be challenged and transformed (McKie, 2018a)? These questions need to be answered if we are to identify a pathway of evidence-based techniques to counter climate denial that challenges these attitudes outside of the US.

In short, this contribution to the *Handbook of Anti-Environmentalism* has provided one of the first applications of the CCCM through a criminological lens. Moreover, it is one of the first applications to make some cross-national comparisons on the messages adopted by CCCM organisations across countries setting the foundation for further cross-national examination. While it is not without its limitations, the theoretical application has helped to conceptualise the CCCM as an *International Deviant Network*. These organisations do operate across countries as another component/branch of the anti-environmentalism movement more broadly. They use messaging strategies, referred to here as techniques of neutralisation, to undermine climate action and protect the interests of a fossil fuel-based global capitalist economy.

NOTES

1. See McKie (2018a) regarding the identification and coding process of the organisational universe. Twenty-one of the organisations identified in the universe were not operational in 2015 and their data were removed from the content analysis.
2. This argument is drawn from the literature on the Pollution Haven Hypothesis (e.g. Copeland and Taylor, 2004) and the Unequal Ecological Exchange Theory (e.g. Jorgenson, 2009). Evidence

across a variety of studies indicates a relationship between the transference of environmental harms to low-income nations, while richer nations obtain the benefits of related production processes.

REFERENCES

Abdi, B. (2018) India's crude oil import bill rose 28 per cent to $8.1 billion in Feb. Available from: https://energy.economictimes.indiatimes.com/news/oil-and-gas/indias-crude-oil-import-bill-rose-28-per-cent-to-8-1-billion-in-feb/63401693 (accessed 13 June 2018).

Altvater, E. (2007) The social and natural environment of fossil capitalism. *Socialist Register.* **43**, pp. 37–60.

Altvater, E. (2009) Postneoliberalism or postcapitalism? The failure of neoliberalism in the financial market crisis. In Brand, U. (ed.), *Postneoliberalism: A beginning debate. Development Dialogue.* No. 51. pp. 73–88.

Anderson, B., Bhmelt, T. and Ward, H. (2017) Public opinion and environmental policy output: A cross-national analysis of energy policies in Europe. *Environmental Research Letters.* **12**(11). Available from DOI: 10.1088/1748-9326/aa8f80.

Arlinghaus, J. and Van Dender, K. (2017) The environmental tax and subsidy reform in Mexico. OECD Taxation Working Papers, No. 31, Paris: OECD Publishing. Available from DOI: 10.1787/a9204f40-en.

Boussalis, C. and Coan, T.G. (2016) Text mining the signals of climate change doubt. *Global Environmental Change.* **36**, pp. 89–100.

Brick, P. (1995) Determined opposition: The wise use movement challenges environmentalism. *Environment: Science and Policy for Sustainable Development.* **37**(8), pp. 17–42.

Brulle, R.J. (2014) Institutionalising delay: Foundation funding and the creation of US climate change counter-movement organisations. *Climatic Change.* **122**(4), pp. 681–94.

Brulle, R.J. and Norgaard, K.M. (2019) Avoiding cultural trauma: Climate change and social inertia. *Environmental Politics.* **18**(5), pp. 886–908.

Canton, R. (2017) *Why Punish? An Introduction to the Philosophy of Punishment.* London: Palgrave Macmillan.

Capitol Resource Institute (2015) News and views. Available from: https://web.archive.org/web/20150613061153/http://capitolresource.org/news-views (accessed 18 January 2017).

Carroll, W.K and Sapinski, J.P. (2010) The global corporate elite and the transnational policy-planning network, 1996–2006: A structural analysis. *International Sociology.* **24**(4), pp. 501–538.

Cherp, A., Jewell, J., Vinichenko, V., Bauer, N. and De Cian, E. (2016) Global energy security under different climate policies, GDP growth rates and fossil resource availabilities. *Journal of Climatic Change.* **136**(1), pp. 83–94.

Citizens for Government Waste (2016) Pushing back global warming hypothesis. Available from: https://www.cagw.org/thewastewatcher/pushing-back-global-warming-hypothesis (accessed 18 January 2017).

Clexit (2016) Clexit summary and foundation statement. Available from: http://web.archive.org/web/20170918202225/http://clexit.net/wp-content/uploads/2016/07/clexit.pdf (accessed 24 September 2020).

Coady, D., Parry, I., Sears, L. and Shang, B. (2017) How large are global fossil fuel subsidies? *World Development.* **91**, pp. 11–27.

Committee for a Constructive Tomorrow (2015) Climate change. Available from: https://web.archive.org/web/20150906021906/http://www.cfact.org/issues/climate-change/ (accessed 17 January 2017).

Copeland, B.R. and Taylor, M.S. (2004) Trade, growth, and the environment. *Journal of Economic Literature.* **42**(1), pp. 7–71.

De Pryck, K. and Gemenne, F. (2017) The denier-in-chief: Climate change, science and the election of Donald J. Trump. *Law Critique.* Available from DOI:10.1007/s10978-017-9207-6.

Dunlap, R.E. and Brulle, R.J. (2015) *Climate Change and Society: Sociological Perspectives.* Oxford: Oxford University Press.

Dunlap, R.E. and Jacques, P.J. (2013) Climate change denial books and conservative think tanks exploring the connection. *American Behavioural Scientist.* **57**(6), pp. 699–731.

Dunlap, R.E. and McCright, A.M. (2015) Challenging climate change. In: Dunlap, R.E. and Brulle, R.J. (eds) *Climate Change and Society: Sociological Perspectives.* Oxford: Oxford University Press, pp. 300–332.

Education Action Group Foundation (2015) NOPE: Next Generation Science Standards aren't state-driven, either. Available from: https://www.eagnews.org/2015/05/nope-next-generation-science-standards-arent-state-driven-either/ (accessed 18 January 2017).

Farrell, J. (2016) Network structure and influence of the climate change counter-movement. *Nature Climate Change.* **6**, pp. 370–74.

Farrell, J. (2019) The growth of climate change misinformation in US philanthropy: Evidence from natural language processing. *Environmental Research Letters.* **14**(3). Available from DOI: /10.1088/1748-9326/aaf939.

Fischer, K. and Plehwe, D. (2017) Neoliberal think tank networks in Latin America and Europe, strategic replication and cross-national organising. In: Salas-Porras, A. and Murray, G. (eds), *Think Tanks and Global Politics: Key Spaces in the Structure of Power.* New York: Palgrave Macmillan, pp. 159–86.

Foster, J.B., Clark, B. and York, R. (2010) *The Ecological Rift: Capitalism's War on the Earth.* New York, NY: Monthly Review Press.

Gemenis, K., Katsanidou, A. and Vasilopoulou, S. (2012) The politics of anti-environmentalism: Positional issue framing by the European radical right. Paper presented at the PSA Annual Conference, 3–5 April, Belfast.

Gilardi, F. (2010) Who learns from what in policy diffusion processes. *American Journal of Political Science.* **54**(3), pp. 650–66.

Hamilton, C. (2010) Think tanks, oil money and black ops. *ABC News Australia* (online) Available from: http://www.abc.net.au/news/2010-02-24/32974?pfmredir=sm (accessed 30 June 2017).

Harkinson, J. (2009) Climate change deniers without borders. *Mother Jones* (online). Available from: http://www.motherjones.com/environment/2009/12/climate-deniers-atlas-foundation/ (accessed 25 January 2017).

Hayek Institute (2015) Can the G7 leaders put a stop to climate change? Available from: https://web.archive.org/web/20150915162813/http://www.hayek-institut.at/konnen-die-g7-machtigen-dem-klimawandel-einhalt-gebieten.html (accessed 24 September 2020).

Heald, S. (2017) Climate silence, moral disengagement, and self-efficacy: How Albert Bandura's theories inform our climate-change predicament. *Environment: Science and Policy for Sustainable Development.* **59**(6), pp. 4–15. Available from DOI: 10.1080/00139157.2017.1374792.

Heartland Institute (2015) Climate Change. Available from: http://web-old.archive.org/web/20210210180341/https://www.heartland.org/Center-Climate-Environment/ (accessed 20 January 2017).

Hillyard, P. and Tombs, S. (2004) Towards a political economy of harm: States, corporations and the production of inequality. In: Hillyard, P., Pantazis, C., Tombs, S. and Gordon, D. (eds), *Beyond Criminology: Taking Harm Seriously.* London: Pluto Press, pp. 30–54.

Hillyard, P. and Tombs, S. (2007) From "crimes" to social harm? *Crime, Law and Social Change.* **48**(1), pp. 9–25.

International Climate Science Coalition (2015) Core principles. Available from: http://www.climatescienceinternational.org/index.php?option=com_content&view=article&id=121&Itemid=67 (accessed 18 January 2017).

International Monetary Fund (2017) *Seeking Sustainable Growth: Short-Term Recovery, Long-Term Challenges.* Washington, DC: International Monetary Fund.

Jacobs, H.M. (1995) The anti-environmental Wise Use Movement in America. *Land Use Law and Zoning Digest.* **47**(2), pp. 32–71.

Jorgenson, A.K. (2009) Unequal ecological exchange and environmental degradation: A theoretical proposition and cross-national study of deforestation, 1990–2000. *Rural Sociology.* **71**(4), pp. 685–712.

Kramer, R.C. (2013) Carbon in the atmosphere and power in America: Climate change as state-corporate crime. *Journal of Crime and Justice.* **36**(2), pp. 153–70.

Lewandowsky, S., Ecker, U.K.H. and Cook, J. (2017) Beyond misinformation: Understanding and coping with the "post-truth" era. *Journal of Applied Research in Memory and Cognition.* **6**(4), pp. 353–69.

Lockwood, M. (2018) Right wing populism and the climate change agenda: Exploring the linkages, *Environmental Politics.* **27**(4), pp. 712–32.

Lynch, M.J. (2016) A Marxian interpretation of the Environmental Kuznets Curve: Global capitalism and the rise and fall (and rise) of pollution. *Capitalism, Nature, Socialism.* **27**(4), pp. 77–95.

Lynch, M.J., Burns, R.G. and Stretesky, P.B. (2010) Global warming and state-corporate crime: The politicalisation of global warming under the Bush administration. *Crime, Law and Social Change.* **54**(3–4), pp. 213–39.

Lynch, M.J., Long, M.A., Barrett, K.L. and Stretesky, P.B. (2013) Is it a crime to produce ecological disorganisation? Why green criminology and political economy matter in the analysis of global ecological harms. *The British Journal of Criminology.* **53**(6), pp. 997–1016.

Magdoff, F. and Foster, J.B. (2011) *What Every Environmentalist Needs To Know about Capitalism: A Citizen's Guide to Capitalism and the Environment.* New York, NY: The Monthly Review Press.

Mannkal Economic Foundation (2015) Environment. Available at: http://web-old.archive.org/web/20151016201623/http://www.mannkal.org/environment.php (accessed 17 January 2017).

Maruna, S. and Copes, H. (2005) What have we learned from five decades of neutralization research? *Crime and Justice.* **32**, pp. 221–320. Available from DOI: 10.1086/655355.

McCright, A.M. (2011) Political orientation moderates American beliefs and concern about climate change. *Climatic Change.* **104**(2), pp. 243–53.

McCright, A.M. and Dunlap, R.E. (2000) Challenging global warming as a social problem: An analysis of the Conservative movement's counter-claims. *Social Problems.* **47**(4), pp. 499–522.

McCright, A.M. and Dunlap, R.E. (2003) Defeating Kyoto: The conservative movement's impact on US climate change policy. *Social Problems.* **50**(3), pp. 348–73.

McCright, A.M. and Dunlap, R.E. (2010) Anti-reflexivity. *Theory, Culture and Society.* **27**(2–3), pp. 100–133.

McCright, A.M. and Dunlap, R.E. (2017) Combatting misinformation requires recognising its types and the factors that facilitate its spread and resonance. *Journal of Applied Research in Memory and Cognition.* **6**(4), pp. 389–96.

McCright, A.M., Charters, M., Dentzman, K. and Dietz, T. (2016) Examining the effectiveness of climate change frames in the face of a climate change denial counter-frame. *Topics in cognitive science.* **8**(1), pp. 76–97. Available from DOI: 10.1111/tops.1217.

McKie, R.E. (2018a) *Rebranding the Climate Change Counter Movement through a Criminological and Political Economic Lens.* Ph.D. Northumbria University. Available from: http://nrl.northumbria.ac.uk/33466/.

McKie, R.E. (2018b) Climate change counter movement neutralization techniques: A typology to examine the climate change counter movement. *Sociological Inquiry.* **89**(2), pp. 288–316.

Meyer, J.W., Boli, J., Thomas, G.M. and Ramirez, F.O. (1997) World society and the nation-state. *American Journal of Sociology.* **103**(1), pp. 141–81.

Montreal Economic Institute (2015) Resourceful Earth Day (celebrate freedom, innovation). Available from: https://www.iedm.org/53014-resourceful-earth-day-celebrate-freedom-innovation/ (accessed 24 September 2020).

Muradian, R., Walter, M. and Martinez-Alier, J. (2012) Hegemonic transitions and global shifts in social metabolism: Implications for resource-rich countries. Introduction to the special section. *Global Environmental Change.* **22**(3), pp. 559–67.

New Zealand Initiative (2015) Economic growth. Available from: http://nzinitiative.org.nz/Research/Economic_Growth.html (accessed 17 January 2018).

O'Toole, G. (2017) Latin America sets the pace on environmental taxes. Global Government Forum. Available from: https://www.globalgovernmentforum.com/latin-america-sets-pace-environmental-taxes/ (accessed 24 January 2018).

Planck Foundation (2015) Homepage. Available from: https://web.archive.org/web/20151230114306/http://www.planck.org/ (accessed 17 January 2017).

Plehwe, D. (2014) Think tank networks and the knowledge–interest nexus: The case of climate change. *Critical Policy Studies.* **8**(1), pp. 101–15. Available from DOI: 10.1080/19460171.2014.883859.

Polizzi, D. (2016) *A Philosophy of the Social Construction of Crime.* Bristol: Policy Press.

Quinney, R. (1965) Is criminal behaviour deviant behaviour? *British Journal of Criminology.* **5**(1), pp. 132–42.

Roberts, J.T. and Parks, B.C. (2009) Ecologically unequal exchange, ecological debt, and climate justice: The history and implications of three related ideas for a new social movement. *International Journal of Comparative Sociology*. **50**(3–4), pp. 385–409.

Ruggiero, V. and South, N (2013) Green criminology and crimes of the economy: Theory, research and praxis. *Critical Criminology.* **21**, pp. 359–73.

Sapinski, J.P. (2015) Climate capitalism and the global corporate elite. *Environmental Sociology*. **1**(4), pp. 268–79.

Sapinski, J.P. (2016) Constructing climate capitalism: Corporate power and the global climate policy-planning network. *Global Networks*. **16**(1), pp. 89–111.

Shipan, C.R. and Volden, C. (2008) The mechanisms of policy diffusion. *American Journal of Political Science*. **52**(4), pp. 840–57.

Strang, D. and Meyer, J.W. (1993) Institutional conditions for diffusion. *Theory and Society*. **22**(4), pp. 487–511.

Stretesky, P.B., Long, M.A. and Lynch, M.J. (2013) *The Treadmill of Crime: Political Economy and Green Criminology*. Abingdon: Routledge Publications.

Sutherland, E.H. (1945) Is white collar crime a crime? *American Sociological Review*. **10**(2), pp. 132–9.

Sykes, G. and Matza, D. (1957) Techniques of neutralization. *American Sociological Review*. **22**(6), pp. 664–70.

Tews, K., Busch, P. and Jorgens, H. (2003) The diffusion of new environmental policy instruments. *European Journal of Political Research*. **42**(4), pp. 569–600.

Thompson, W.E. and Harred, J.L. (1992) Topless dancers: Managing stigma in a deviant occupation. *Deviant Behaviour*. **13**(3), pp. 291–311.

Walters, R. (2018) Climate change denial: "Making ignorance great again". In Barton, A. and Davis, H. (eds) *Ignorance, Power and Harm: Critical Criminological Perspectives*. Cham: Palgrave Macmillan, pp. 163–87. Available from DOI:10.1007/978-3-319-97343-2_8.

Weber, E.U. and Stern, P.C. (2011) Public understanding of climate change in the United States. *American Psychologists*. **66**(4), pp. 315–28.

10. Fossil networks and dirty power: the politics of decarbonisation in Australia

Adam Lucas

INTRODUCTION

Sharon Beder noted twenty years ago that anti-environmentalism is a direct 'response to the rise of environmental awareness in the late 1960s and early 1970s' (Beder, 2001). As the environmental movement has grown significantly in power and influence since that time, those firms with substantial interests in avoiding liability for environmental damage and disruption understandably perceive it as a serious threat to their survival. Anti-environmentalism thus represents 'a backlash against the success of environmentalists in raising public concern and pressuring governments to protect the environment' (Beder, 2001; cf. Jacques et al., 2008).

Learning from the successes of their opponents, the corporations involved in anti-environmental activities first adopted and subsequently supercharged the strategies of public-interest advocacy organizations in the 1970s. During the 1980s, they proceeded to build international coalitions and alliances with firms that shared a common interest in opposing environmental regulations. Since that time, a multi-scalar network of interest coalitions consisting most prominently of transnational firms in the fossil fuel, mining, transport, automotive and metals processing sectors have been largely successful in shaping many governments' decision-making processes via lobbying and political donations (Coen and Richardson, 2009; Ward, 2009; Vidal et al., 2011; Mayer, 2017; Farrell, 2016, 2019; Brulle, 2018; Doreian and Mrvar, Chapter 12 in this volume). They have simultaneously sought to favourably influence public opinion using advertising, sponsorships, front groups and think tanks (Beder, 1997; Hager and Burton, 2000; Pearse, 2007; Pooley, 2010). These activities have become so pervasive with regard to climate change and energy politics in the United States that they have been dubbed the 'climate change counter movement' (McCright and Dunlap, 2010; Brulle, 2014; Staggenborg and Meyer, Chapter 2 in this volume) and more recently, the 'climate misinformation movement' (Farrell, 2019).

Recent detailed empirical studies have provided important insights into the composition of the climate change counter movement (C3M) in the US, including the geographical and sectoral locations of key players, the institutions through which it operates, and its political orientations, revenue streams and public relations strategies (Brulle et al., 2012; Farrell, 2015; Hornsey et al., 2018). The same political dynamics have been identified in Australia (Hamilton, 2007; Pearse, 2007; Pearse et al., 2013; Taylor, 2014), and in Canada (Carroll et al., Chapter 11 in this volume; Doreian and Mrvar, Chapter 12 in this volume; Ali, Chapter 13 in this volume). Although the political and financial connections between the movements in fossil-fuel-rich Australia and the US are documented (Pearse, 2007, pp. 211–18; Readfern, 2017, 2018a, 2018b, 2018c), and are also apparent in Canada (as the work of several authors in this volume attests), there are some covert elements of the movement that normally remain hidden and which have consequently not received much scholarly attention.

If climate change denialism can be thought of as the 'outward facing', propaganda arm of fossil capital's power structure (Malm, 2015; Sapinski, 2015; Carroll et al., Chapter 11 in this volume), the Machiavellian strategies to which this chapter seeks to draw attention can be thought of as 'insurgent infiltrations' of liberal democratic processes of governance (analogous to hostile takeovers) that can usually be inferred only from other evidence. As a resource-rich advanced capitalist society, Australia has proven to be an attractive target for powerful commercial and industrial interests to capture key institutions of governance and regulation, including its major political parties and bureaucratic elites. Recent research compiling the findings of environmental non-governmental organizations (NGOs), investigative journalists, progressive think tanks and academics into the employment histories of senior officials in key energy, resource and finance portfolios in Australia demonstrates the intensification of a strategy that has been employed by major corporations to institutionalize their influence throughout government decision-making over many decades (Lucas and Rosenzveig, 2018; Lucas, 2018, 2021; Michael West Media, 2021). This strategy, commonly known as 'the revolving door', enables the normalisation of back-room deals, nepotistic appointments, undeclared conflicts of interest, secret meetings, unauthorised and illegal programmes, and unethical and corrupt payments and inducements. As one of the less well-examined strategies used by the C3M to ensure that the voices of its sponsors have covert, as well as overt, support for their interests within government, it requires further scrutiny, theorizing and opposition.

Recent work in critical political economy, post-positivist policy analysis, science and technology studies, and environmental sociology provides useful concepts and methodologies for understanding how these covert networks operate, although more research remains to be done to demonstrate just how extensive and damaging their influence has become. The analysis that follows contributes to these efforts by attempting to demonstrate that the Australian state displays all the features of having been captured by fossil fuel interests, and that discursive approaches can only take us so far in understanding how the fossil fuel and resource extraction industries currently operate to maintain their incumbency. Consequently, some new conceptual and methodological tools are suggested to improve that understanding. The chapter begins with an outline of the Promethean narrative and some of the more obvious examples of how it has been manifested in networks of overt and covert corporate influence of government decision-making over the last decade. It then explores the various ways in which these largely covert networks of compliance, influence and persuasion operate between the public and private sectors. The development of Australia's electricity sector over the last few decades is provided as a case study in the covert bipartisan support by key politicians and staffers for mismanagement, market distortions and price gouging by dominant players in the industry. This is followed by a discussion of the kind of concepts and methodologies that can best be used to study covert forms of policy-making, and the extent to which it can be concluded that Machiavellian politics has dominated climate change and energy policy-making in Australia over the last few decades. The chapter concludes by suggesting key areas for legislative and regulatory reform.

THE PROMETHEAN NARRATIVE: 'QUARRY AUSTRALIA'

Bipartisan support for the exploitation of Australia's mineral and energy resources has long been a feature of the resource management policies of its major political parties. The consensus between the Labor, Liberal and National parties has been so strong that the country acquired the epithet of 'Quarry Australia' in the early 1980s (Birrell et al., 1982). Australia's political elites have generally been far more comfortable capitalizing on the country's mineral, energy and agricultural wealth than engaging in the more difficult task of developing a sustainable basis for its resource, manufacturing and service sectors (cf. Pearse, 2009; Parr, 2020). Since the early 1990s, a core principle of Australia's major political parties has been to prevent the introduction of any policy measures that 'have net adverse economic impacts nationally or on Australia's trade competitiveness' (Ray, 1994). However, the incorporation of any adverse impacts from what economists euphemistically call 'social and environmental externalities' remains an extraordinarily uncommon practice.

Due to the cavalier way in which it has operated for decades, the mining industry has been a focus of environmental controversy in Australia since at least the early 1970s, as has the Promethean narrative that informs its activities (Green, 1998; Dryzek, 2005; cf. Fremaux and Barry, 2018). But the country's major role in the political economy of fossil energy production has only become a focus of significant controversy over the last decade or so. The extraction of fossil fuels in Australia generates hundreds of billions of dollars in annual export revenue – $252 billion in 2019 – and tens of billions in profits for the companies concerned (DISER, 2020; West, 2020). These extraordinary profits are only achievable because the social, ecological and geological costs that the fossil fuel industry proliferates are 'externalized' (Hamilton, 2007; Pearse, 2007, 2009; Pearse et al., 2013; Hibbins, 2016). Growing public awareness of these negative social and environmental externalities, including human rights abuses, fugitive emissions, particulate pollution, and groundwater and soil contamination, has undermined the progressivist narrative favoured by Australia's political and industrial elites and the generally favourable public perception of their contribution to society (Higginbothom et al., 2010; Soos, 2018).

The corporations that dominate mining and resource extraction in Australia and the conservative political interests that support them have been very effective in countering the efforts of environmentalists to hold them to account for their extensive and frequent transgressions of social norms and federal and state laws. The senior executives of fossil fuel companies are acutely aware that the politics of climate change presents the industry with an existential threat. Consequently, they have been prepared to do whatever it takes to ensure their interests remain part of the dominant narrative motivating Australian political and economic life.

Their primary focus has been the institutionalisation of their political and financial interests across multiple domains of governance. Not only do they have a strong financial incentive to maintain close relations with Australia's incumbent political parties, that is, the Labor, Liberal and National parties, they have ample resources at their disposal to entrench those relationships (Wood et al., 2018). They have arguably been instrumental in undermining democratic norms and the economic health of the nation by weakening environmental regulations and strengthening anti-protest laws (Wahlquist, 2019), instigating the removal of two insufficiently compliant prime ministers, that is, Kevin Rudd and Malcolm Turnbull (Taylor, 2014; Jackson, 2018; Sengupta, 2018), and normalizing aggressive tax avoidance and profit shifting (West, 2014, 2016a, 2017a, 2017b; Bagshaw, 2018).

As I will attempt to demonstrate here, in their efforts to defend the Promethean narrative and their offshoring of massive profits, the fossil fuel and resource extraction industries have been engaged in constructing extensive networks of like-minded former and current politicians, political staffers and senior bureaucrats from whom they can extract sensitive information and political favours. These ideologically compliant individuals routinely move between public office and the private sector in the role of lobbyists, advisors, consultants and executives. In the case of former public officials, they are employed by the very same businesses and industries for which they were responsible while in public office. Not only can they be accused, therefore, of engaging in activities that directly conflict with their former roles, their probity while in public office is also open to serious question.

Networked forms of political influence have become ubiquitous throughout the world over the last few decades, affecting every area of government business in which significant amounts of revenue are routinely generated and expended, including building and construction, finance and banking, transport and logistics, gaming and racing, health and aged care, pharmaceuticals, defence and telecommunications (Vidal et al., 2011; Brookes and Hughes, 2016; Murray and Frijters, 2017). However, there are very few jurisdictions in which any significant attempts have been made to curb such activities, and Australia is no exception. While more empirical work needs to be done to establish the extent of these covert networks across different areas of governance in different countries, there is prima facie evidence that they are particularly pervasive between the fossil fuel and resource extraction industries and government agencies with direct responsibility for oversight of those industries (Mayer, 2017; Bartlett Quintanilla and Cummins-Tripodi, 2018; Lucas, 2018; Wood et al., 2018). Critical examination of the failure by governments to achieve social and environmental goals to which they have publicly committed cannot, therefore, simply restrict itself to analysing politicians' public statements and official government documents.

OVERT AND COVERT INFLUENCES ON POLICY-MAKING IN THE AUSTRALIAN ENERGY SECTOR

There is now a substantial body of research demonstrating how fossil fuel and other carbon-intensive industries have successfully enlisted hundreds, if not thousands, of serving and former politicians, political staffers and bureaucrats in the major fossil-fuel exporting nations of Australia, the United States and Canada to assist them in their campaigns of 'total information management' (Brulle et al., 2012; Farrell, 2015; Hornsey et al., 2018; Hamilton, 2007; Pearse, 2007; Pearse et al., 2013; Taylor, 2014; Readfern, 2017, 2018a, 2018b, 2018c; Lucas, 2018, 2021; Carroll et al., Chapter 11 in this volume; Doreian and Mrvar, Chapter 12 in this volume; Ali, Chapter 13 in this volume). As most of these activities are not illegal, but are nevertheless fundamentally anti-democratic and against the public interest, far more scholarly attention needs to be paid to how these covert networks are built and operate. That requires a focus upon identifying the kinds of individuals and organisations that compose them, and the institutional structures through which they are enabled to act. Important insights about how these networks operate in Australia can be gained by compiling the evidence accumulated by other academics, activists, researchers and journalists, and subsequently refining and extending their analyses.

One recent study that examined the extent to which powerful corporate interests have distorted public policy and decision-making with respect to the mining industry in Queensland was conducted by climate activists Hannah Aulby and Mark Ogge (2016) for the Australia Institute and the Australian Conservation Foundation. Their exposé, *Greasing the Wheels*, provides extensive documentation of how mining companies use a range of legal and semi-legal vehicles to garner influence over decision-makers. These include lucrative lobbying, directorial and advisory positions for retired public officials in the very same companies they were responsible for regulating prior to leaving public office, along with third party fundraising mechanisms, private meetings and personal gifts. They point out that the public accountability issues raised by the 'revolving door' include concerns that public officials' decision-making will be affected by perceptions of their future employment prospects in the private sector, that sensitive information acquired in public office will be conveyed to their private sector employers, and that those individuals re-entering the public from the private sector may provide preferential treatment to their former private sector employers, including the secondment and promotion of like-minded individuals from inside and outside government (Aulby and Ogge, 2016, p. 36).

The role of lobbying and lobbyists cannot be underestimated in this context. Estimates of how much money was spent on lobbying by peak bodies and advocacy groups in Australia between 2015 and 2016 range from $400 million to $700 million (Ireland, 2019). Based on his analysis of the financial statements of twenty of Australia's major business lobbies, investigative journalist Michael West found almost $2 billion had been spent by these firms on lobbying between 2014 and 2017 (West, 2017b). Research on lobbying in the US from more than ten years ago found that, for every US$1 spent, the return on investment can be as high as US$220 (Alexander et al., 2009). Another study by US economists from five years ago found that 65 percent of Australia's billionaires owe their wealth to political favours, comparable to India at 66 percent and Indonesia at 64 percent. By way of contrast, only 1 percent of US billionaires were found to be so connected, and none of the billionaires in the UK, Singapore, Switzerland, Sweden, the Netherlands or Hong Kong (Bagchi and Svejnar, 2015). Over the last few decades, Australia has also become one of the least diverse economies in the OECD, now ranking 87th out of 133 countries, even though it is the eighth richest economy per capita (Atlas, 2021).

Drawing on the work of other academics, investigative journalists, non-government organisations and searches of grey literature, it is possible to construct a relatively comprehensive picture of how the fossil fuel and mining industries have managed to create and maintain an extensive network of lobbyists and 'political service personnel' over many years. These people have occupied or continue to occupy key positions in the major political parties and government, and consist largely of former Labor, Liberal and National party politicians and their staffers. Many of these individuals are subsequently employed, or were previously employed, by lobbying firms and PR companies to promote the value of the industry to politicians across the political spectrum. Perhaps unsurprisingly, these lobbying efforts focus on cabinet ministers and their staffers, but an even larger number of the individuals identified work directly for the firms concerned or their peak industry bodies (Lucas, 2018, 2021; Lucas and Rosenzveig, 2018).

Examples of the influence exerted by these corporations and their peak industry bodies extend from polluting industry executives crafting and drafting climate change and energy policies for the Howard Government (Pearse, 2007, pp. 228–38; Pearse, 2009, pp. 31–45), to government secondments of industry operatives who help shape industry-favourable policies, regulations and infrastructure projects. Attractive offers of remuneration for former senior bureaucrats, political staffers and ministers who have demonstrated their loyalty and commitment while in public office take the form of directorial, paid consultancy and advisory positions (Pearse, 2007; Lucas, 2018, 2021). I have previously described this latter phenomenon as a 'golden escalator' rather than a 'revolving door', because it involves no 'backwards and forwards' movements between the public and private sectors. By way of contrast, many ministerial staffers move in and out of public office with dizzying regularity and remain largely unregulated in their activities. Drawing on the information contained in newspaper and magazine articles, NGO reports, media releases and corporate websites, more than 200 examples of the second and third phenomena have been compiled into a database. This material has provided the basis for an ongoing research project with Michael West Media (Lucas and Rosenzveig, 2018; Michael West Media, 2021), some of which is reproduced in Figure 10.1 and discussed in more detail below. The next phase of this research will include direct comparison of employment movements by these individuals and periods during which key government policy and infrastructure decisions were being made.

It is important to note that the pernicious nature of these networks of influence is not mere speculation. In its preliminary investigations into lobbying in Australia's wealthiest and most populous state, New South Wales (NSW) in 2010, the Independent Commission Against Corruption (ICAC) found that, of 272 individual lobbyists registered in the state, 23 were former state or federal MPs, and 112 were former staffers and advisors. In other words, half of the lobbyists had once worked in government, and many of them had worked in the energy, mining and infrastructure portfolios. Of the 23 former politicians, 17 had connections with the Australian Labor Party (ICAC, 2010). At that time, Labor had been in government since 1995.

After it made these findings, ICAC pursued a series of high-level misconduct cases against former and sitting senior ministers in both Labor and the Coalition, and subsequently exposed their preparedness to act either improperly or corruptly to further their own and the fossil fuel industry's interests. Twenty-three state and federal politicians from the Labor, Liberal and National parties were forced to resign from parliament or from executive positions between May 2013 and December 2015 in relation to allegations of misconduct or corruption. While most were in relation to abuses of parliamentary entitlements, almost one-third of them were involved in questionable or corrupt behaviour related to fossil fuel interests. Three of these politicians were from Labor and four from the Liberals (Austin, 2015).

With respect to the ICAC hearings in New South Wales, it is apparent from the public record of their actions as ministers and their statements in the media, to constituents and parliamentarians, that all of the roughly thirty state politicians involved were engaged in the kinds of activities outlined by Aulby and Ogge above. All of them played key roles in propping up fossil fuel investment and discouraging renewable energy development. However, rather than heeding ICAC's findings and supporting further anti-corruption reforms, the NSW Coalition Government responded to ICAC's successful prosecutions by reducing its budget and investigatory powers (Warhurst, 2017). According to the Centre for Public Integrity, since 2010 there have been funding cuts in the order of $1.4 billion to Australia's accountability institutions by successive state and federal governments: a 30 per cent cut in real terms (Centre for Public Integrity, 2020b). These cuts, along with the major parties' ongoing failure to implement a national integrity commission with wide-ranging investigative and prosecutory powers, are perhaps the most damning indictment of Australia's current political leadership.

It is clear from these cases and many others documented by the author that a significant number of senior politicians who have supported incumbent polluting interests by seeking to delay, compromise or overturn emission reduction measures have been financially rewarded for their troubles through lucrative paid positions as board members, executives, partners, lobbyists and advisors upon their retirement from politics (Lucas and Rosenzveig, 2018; Lucas,

2018, 2021; Michael West Media, 2021), or by securing corrupt payments and other financial benefits while in office.[1]

What is of equal concern is the fact that political party donations from these entities and 'jobs for the boys' for politicians and senior bureaucrats within these industries after retirement are not only poorly regulated or totally unregulated (Bagshaw, 2017; Wood et al., 2018), they have become so commonplace and normalized in recent times that it is possible to point without any effort to former deputy prime ministers, state premiers, senior ministers and top bureaucrats who have accepted such roles. The lack of transparency concerning political donations in Australia is well illustrated by the fact that federal political donation laws are so lax that the sources of more than half of the private incomes of the Liberal and Labor parties during the 2013 election could not be traced (Edwards, 2017). In the 2018–19 financial year, the major parties received more than $100 million in political donations that remain hidden from public view, and more than $1 billion in undisclosed income since 1999 (Centre for Public Integrity, 2020a).

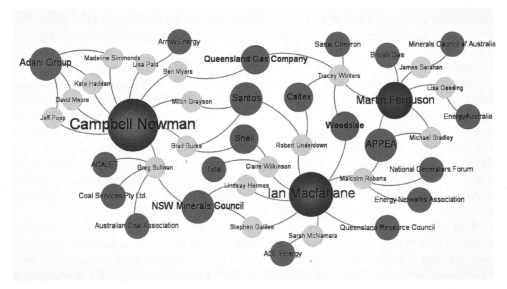

Note: The size of each agent's circle correlates to the number of connections with other agents, not all of which are represented here.

Figure 10.1 Employment relationships between senior politicians (dark grey), political service personnel (light grey), and fossil energy companies and their peak bodies (medium grey)

Figure 10.1 utilizes Gephi social network software to represent just some of these connections covering the ten-year period from 2008 to 2018. It represents the employment relationships between three former senior politicians, that is, Martin Ferguson from the Australian Labor Party (ALP), Ian Macfarlane from the Liberal Party and Campbell Newman from the Liberal National Party (LNP), and those of their staffers with employment histories in fossil energy corporations. The latter have been dubbed 'political service personnel' to indicate their ambiguous allegiances. All of the latter individuals worked for fossil fuel companies or peak industry bodies before and after working as political staffers. All three of the senior politicians took up positions as advisors or executives in the corporate sector within months of their retirement from politics, hence the appellation of 'golden escalator' rather than 'revolving door' to describe such career moves. Both Ferguson and Macfarlane took up positions with fossil fuel and mining interests that they had only recently been responsible for regulating.

Martin Ferguson was the ALP's Federal Minister for Resources and Energy between November 2007 and March 2013. During his time in Federal Cabinet, he was instrumental in delaying the introduction of any meaningful federal policy on renewables, and oversaw a massive expansion in coal and gas production. In other words, he was a spoiler with respect to climate and energy policy (Macdonald-Smith, 2012). He also employed at least half a dozen staffers with strong links to the fossil fuel industry, some of whom were also connected personally to other cabinet ministers. In the same year he left politics, Ferguson took up two post-political positions in natural resources that were directly related to his portfolio responsibilities, as Non-Executive Board Member of British Gas/BG Group (Andrew, 2016), and as Chairman of the Advisory Council to APPEA (Davies, 2015). APPEA is the Australian Petroleum Producers and Exploration Association, the peak lobby group for the oil and gas industry in Australia. Ferguson's move to BG Group occurred when it was involved in a multi-billion dollar deal to sell its gas assets to Shell: assets that Ferguson had helped secure for BG Group and had also spruiked to China while minister. Ferguson took up the former position only six months after he retired as minister. The lobbying code of conduct requires an 18-month cooling-off period for ex-ministers, which was clearly not enforced in this case (Manning, 2015).

Equally powerful and influential was the Liberal Party's Federal Minister for Industry and Science between September 2013 and September 2015, Ian Macfarlane, who was also Federal Minister for Industry, Tourism and Resources between November 2001 and December 2007. Within a year of leaving politics, he had become the CEO of the Queensland Resources Council, the mining and fossil fuel peak industry body in that state, and a Non-Executive Director of Woodside Petroleum at an undisclosed date (Corbett, 2016). As with Ferguson's breach of ministerial standards, no action was taken to prevent Macfarlane from taking up either appointment. Macfarlane similarly employed at least half a dozen staffers with strong links to the fossil fuel industry while in office. Like Ferguson, he was a notorious spoiler with regard to renewable energy policy and a relentless campaigner for the fossil fuel and mining industries.

These brief examples give only a hint of the connections involved, as well as the tactics of delay, omission, misrepresentation, obfuscation and fabrication that characterize the associated activities. However, when considered in its totality, this evidence indicates that those Australian jurisdictions with rich fossil fuel resources have become victims of corporate state capture. If corporate state capture involves a situation in which 'private interests subvert legitimate channels of political influence and shape the rules of the legislative and institutional game through private payments to public officials' (Innes, 2016; cf. Innes, 2017), it is difficult to come to any other conclusion (Soos, 2018; Lucas, 2020, 2021).

FOSSIL NETWORKS AND DIRTY POWER: A CASE STUDY IN CROSS-PARTY SOLIDARITY

The so-called 'climate wars' over national energy policy in Australia clearly demonstrate how the fossil fuel industry has managed to capture governments led by both the major political parties. Together with powerful mining interests, it has ensured that environmental concerns are rendered mute within government policy. The conventional explanation for the failure of the major political parties to come to some agreement about national energy policy is that it is the outcome of deep ideological divisions between factions within them (e.g. Tranter, 2013). While those divisions undoubtedly exist, they do not explain the failure to act by the major parties when clear instances of malfeasance and illegal behaviour by energy and mining companies have been exposed, nor their seeming inability to acknowledge or recognize the need for significant institutional reforms of the electricity sector. As protecting the interests of dominant corporations appears to be the goal, such protection is not convincingly explained by ideological preferences.

Privatization and re-regulation of state-owned electricity infrastructure from the late 1980s onward has proven to be a major structural impediment to transitioning the Australian energy sector to zero carbon sources (Cahill and Beder, 2005). A poorly implemented privatization process has enabled three companies – AGL, Energy Australia and Origin Energy – to dominate both the generation and the distribution of electricity for Australian energy consumers. These so-called 'gentailers' now provide power to 70 per cent of the retail customers in the National Electricity Market,[2] most of which is generated by fossil-fuel assets that were cheaply acquired from their state-owned predecessors and which are now close to retirement (Parkinson, 2017b). These three companies are also, respectively, the first, second and fifth biggest climate polluters in Australia (ACF, 2016). Their market dominance in the retail sector and significant ownership of generating assets has provided them with abundant opportunities to 'game the system' and maximise their profits (Parkinson, 2017a), but few incentives to improve their renewable generating capacity, energy efficiency, or demand management. All three companies have played a significant role in delaying reform of the regulatory, institutional and political barriers to providing Australia with a greater share of renewable energy. As it is their perspectives that have tended to dominate government policy discussions regarding the role that renewable energy should play in Australia's energy mix, numerous reports by academics, industry players and relevant government departments outlining the various steps required to achieve decarbonization have been comprehensively ignored or denigrated by the gentailers' supporters in government (AER, 2017).

With the current exceptions of South Australia, Victoria and the ACT (Australian Capital Territory), what all of this has meant with respect to substantive outcomes in the Australian energy sector is:

a. an inconsistent regulatory framework that provides obstacles to renewable energy investment;
b. a lack of policy coordination between and within most jurisdictions;
c. inadequate monitoring and oversight processes to modify poorly designed and/or administered policies and programs;
d. a lack of government planning for a large-scale renewable energy transition;

e. a failure to effectively consult with a broad range of stakeholders or to properly integrate a range of political views into policy-making; and
f. an extremely strong tendency to simply reproduce or elaborate upon past practices with respect to major infrastructure investments and other important areas of public policy, regardless of whether those practices have proven effective or successful.

A direct outcome of this situation is that Australia now has some of the highest electricity and gas prices for non-industrial consumers in the world, with household electricity prices having increased by 120 per cent in ten years, and gas prices having doubled over four years (Mountain, 2016; Rolfe, 2016; Robertson, 2018). This has been an ongoing source of political controversy, and has highlighted the failure of the country's major political parties to agree upon a national approach that can alleviate what has come to be known as Australia's 'energy crisis' (Leitch, 2017; Hannam and Latimer, 2018). Most industry analysts agree that reining in the market power of the gentailers and increasing the tax take from fossil fuel extraction are keys to that goal, but neither the Labor nor the Liberal parties have shown any inclination to pursue either course.

Contrary to the very sensible recommendations made by a cross-party senate committee in 2017 concerning the retirement of the country's remaining coal-fired power stations over the next ten to fifteen years (Australian Senate, 2017), the so-called 'hard right' faction of the National and Liberal parties continue to argue that the Federal Government should instead be subsidising the construction of new super-critical coal-fired power stations (Murphy and Knaus, 2019; McCullough, 2019). It was recently revealed that similar views are held by some in Labor ranks: the so-called 'Otis Group' is reportedly a right-wing faction of the Federal ALP that has endorsed the pro-coal arguments normally associated with Coalition politicians and industry spokespeople (Martin, 2020). Cross-party solidarity on the issue of subsidies to the fossil fuel industry is also worthy of brief mention: calls from experts in Australia and overseas to remove what now amounts to US$29 billion in domestic post-tax fossil fuel subsidies (Coady et al., 2019) have been met with patronising rhetoric and derision by the major political parties, and denial of their existence by the industry (Lucas, 2016; Slezak, 2016; Soos, 2018). Once again, neither Labor nor the Coalition have been prepared to publicly acknowledge that fossil fuel subsidies are an issue in Australia, or that they distort the 'market' to which they so often rhetorically appeal. Covert bipartisan support for mismanagement, market distortions and price gouging by dominant players in the industry are strong indicators that political ideology alone cannot explain the lack of attention to these issues by the country's incumbent political parties.

THE LOGIC OF INCUMBENCY: STRUCTURAL BIAS AND 'SOFT CORRUPTION'

A majority of Australians have long supported action on climate change and a renewable energy future for the country (Tranter, 2013; Johnston, 2018). Indeed, popular support for renewable energy has resulted in Australia having the highest per capita penetration of rooftop solar photovoltaic systems in the world (Bruce and MacGill, 2016). Although these levels of support vary across party political affiliations, its largely bipartisan nature has not been reflected in the policy positions adopted by Australia's incumbent political parties. A key argument of this chapter is that, although the country's politicians remain implacably divided on the issue of reducing its reliance on fossil fuels for energy, transport and export revenues, the shared Promethean narrative of the incumbent parties requires them to defend the fossil fuel industry whenever it is subjected to any form of criticism. Dedication to this goal-directed narrative transcends the political ideologies of individuals within the relevant parties. But as we will see, it too is limited in explaining the extent to which the Labor, Liberal and National parties are prepared to turn a blind eye to industry malfeasance.

The standard ripostes by politicians from the incumbent parties to any effort at drawing public attention to the shortcomings of the fossil fuel industry tend to draw on minor variations of one or more of the following arguments:

a. Australia is fortunate to have abundant and cheap fossil fuel resources, which provide it not only with energy security but also with thousands of jobs in dozens of regional and remote communities;
b. the significant export revenues generated by Australia's fossil fuel exports pay for a range of essential services that would not otherwise be funded to the same levels;
c. it is better for the global environment if Australia continues to export its coal because Australian coal burns 'cleaner' than its competitors;
d. anti-coal campaigners are jeopardising economic development in India, China and other developing countries that consume the higher-quality Australian coal (making them less polluted than they would otherwise be);
e. renewable forms of energy are still too expensive and unreliable to deploy at scale in Australia and other parts of the world;
f. long distances between population centres and low urban density in Australian cities requires a high consumption of transport fuels by commuters and goods distributors.

As is well known in policy circles, these kinds of 'boosting and blocking' statements are aimed at elevating audience perceptions of the favoured course of action, and denigrating the disfavoured. Consequently, they play an important role in shaping public opinion, because the public tends to endorse the expressed views of those political elites and advocacy groups that purport to represent their interests (Brulle et al., 2012; Tranter, 2013).

As Australian coal and gas production has grown significantly over the last two decades, so has the revenue that it has generated. In the case of coal, the strongest growth was between 2002 and 2012. In the case of gas, the strongest growth has been between 2008 and the present. Both trends have reinforced a widespread perception amongst politicians and the general public that the fossil fuel industry makes significant contributions to the nation's wealth (Richardson and Denniss, 2011). Although this conveniently overlooks more than $40 billion in annual costs imposed by the industry with respect to the many social and environmental externalities associated with it (Coady et al., 2019; cf. Lucas, 2016; Soos, 2018), as well as the tens of billions of dollars in profits that it continues to offshore (West, 2014, 2016a, 2017a, 2017c), none of these criticisms have gained much traction in the public debate. In order to ensure that this remains the case, the industry reinforces the Promethean narrative in as many ways as possible. This is where the role of a compliant media, public relations firms, think tanks, political donations, lobbyists and 'jobs for the boys' become crucial to the future vitality of the industry and its continued plans for expansion (cf. Beder, 1997; Brulle, 2018; Lucas, 2018, 2021).

Grounded in the demonstrably false assumption that fossil-fuel-generated economic growth is an apolitical force that automatically generates good for all, this particular progress story and the talking points from which it is constituted have their origins in the public relations firms and think tanks hired and funded by the fossil fuel and other carbon-intensive industries (Beder, 1997; Hamilton, 2007; Pearse et al., 2013, Ch. 5). As the same PR firms that work for polluting industries also work for the major political parties (Warhurst, 2007; Ward, 2009; Clennell, 2009), it is understandable that they should draw upon the same talking points to legitimate their shared narrative. The same industries also fund think tanks that provide 'fantasy themes' for the framing of public debate by government and industry; that is, elaborate 'alternative realities' that reinforce the interests of those propounding them, but which have little or no basis in reality (McKewon, 2012). For example, one of the world's biggest coal mining companies, Glencore, recently funded a secret, multi-million-dollar campaign using one of the world's top 'political operatives', the C|T Group, to run their covert (but legal) efforts to boost public and government support for coal in Australia. Earlier incarnations of the same company had undertaken work for both the Coalition and Labor parties (Knaus, 2019). Neither party saw fit to give the Glencore story any attention.

Nonetheless, just as ideology does not explain the incumbent political parties' bipartisan support for the fossil fuel industry, the Promethean narrative does not explain their tacit support for illicit and unethical behaviour by prominent industry players. For example, while it does explain why both of the major parties support the construction of the world's largest coal mine in Queensland's Galilee Basin, it does not explain why they have both studiously avoided any public discussion of the Adani Group's dubious track record on environmental, tax and labour issues (Long, 2016a, 2016b, 2017, 2019; Safi, 2018; Long et al., 2017; The Australia Institute, 2018; Long and Slezak, 2019; Environmental Justice Australia, 2019). A handful of the political connections between Adani and the former LNP Premier of Queensland are documented in Figure 10.1, but are by no means representative of all the relevant connections.

With respect to the massive expansion of Australia's natural gas and coal seam gas industries over the last decade, once again, the Promethean narrative does explain why Labor and the Coalition have enthusiastically supported that expansion. But it does not explain why they have enabled a cartel of five companies to control Australia's gas production (i.e. Royal Dutch Shell, Chevron, Origin Energy, Santos and BP/ExxonMobil), or why they have failed to create a domestic gas reserve to ameliorate the current gas shortage in the eastern states, a shortage produced by their own failure to place any export restrictions on any of these companies (Robertson, 2016, 2018). Nor does their bipartisan endorsement of the Promethean narrative explain why neither of them managed to negotiate any appreciable revenue streams from numerous major oil and gas projects after effectively giving the companies concerned more than a decade of 'tax holidays'. Nor does it explain why neither of them have expressed any desire to have these projects audited or monitored – some of which have been operating for decades – enabling the companies concerned to avoid payments of an estimated $90 billion in taxes and royalties (Aston, 2016a, 2016b, 2016c; Knight, 2016; Hutchens, 2017a, 2017b; Bagshaw, 2018). The silence of both major parties concerning the industry's remarkable ability to avoid paying income tax, transgress environmental and public health laws with impunity, and generally 'get its way' on most issues cannot be explained by simply appealing to a shared development narrative.

In a country where mineral and energy production is dominated by a relatively small number of large multinational corporations, and there are relatively few institutional and legal mechanisms available to hold government functionaries to account for their actions, there appear to be no constraints on the ability of the owners of capital to determine social and environmental outcomes. This is evident from the many years of success experienced by these same corporations in their pursuit of a broadly anti-environmental and anti-democratic agenda in Australia, the United Kingdom, the United States, Canada, and elsewhere. In Australia, their many and varied achievements include the repeal of a national price on carbon, delaying investment in a sustainable energy transition, blocking policies on vehicle emission standards, undermining policies promoting electric vehicles, demonizing efforts to phase out coal exports, and overcoming state-wide moratoria on coal seam gas extraction (Hamilton, 2007; Pearse, 2009; Pearse et al., 2013; Taylor, 2014). With the collusion of the world's major accountancy firms and sympathetic bureaucrats and politicians, they have also managed to judiciously avoid the payment of appropriate taxes and royalties for publicly owned fossil fuel resources (West, 2016b, 2017a; Hutchens, 2017a, 2017b; Bagshaw, 2018; Soos, 2018), and avoided any constraints being placed on their production or exports, including the creation of a domestic gas reserve and an adequate strategic petroleum reserve (Robertson, 2016, 2018; Norman, 2019).

CONCEPTUAL TOOLS TO EXPOSE CORPORATE INFLUENCES ON POLICY-MAKING

One of the great strengths of discursive approaches, and one of the reasons I have partially drawn upon them in this chapter, is that they are capable of identifying hegemonic or dominant discourses, and the ways in which they seek to marginalize and exclude threatening alternatives. However, they are less useful at revealing asymmetries of power in concrete situations and how they function. This is because they tend to underestimate the structural power of dominant corporations to make and control global markets. They also generally overlook the instrumental forms of power that enable dominant corporations to shape tax, investment and regulatory regimes in their favour (Mikler, 2018, pp. 35–50). These forms of power are exercised through networking, lobbying, political donations, revolving door appointments and what the author has elsewhere dubbed the 'golden escalator': activities that require different methodologies to uncover (Lucas, 2018). Attention to these kinds of political dynamics arguably requires recognition of Machiavellian behaviour and sabotage as structurally advantageous strategies for corporations wishing to advance or maintain their interests (Bichler and Nitzan, 2017). In this political context, the grounds for statecraft are cunning and duplicity; decision-making is informed by a cynical disregard for morality and a preoccupation with self-interest and personal gain.

Machiavellian accounts of policy- and decision-making are able to account more plausibly for many of the political outcomes we see from anti-environmental campaigning than standard incrementalist and discursive accounts. Starting from similar assumptions about the nature of contemporary market-oriented societies to those outlined by Charles Lindblom in *Politics and Markets* (1977), critical political economy provides a useful conceptual framework for theorizing industrial capitalism as a historical mode of power in which those groups with the most wealth organize themselves to create the order of their societies (Nitzan and Bichler, 2010). Building on insights developed by Thorstein Veblen (1904), Jonathan Nitzan and Shimshon Bichler's capital as power theory argues that, since the emergence of industrial capitalism, financialization has become the standard methodology by which powerful corporations achieve and maintain political and economic dominance across multiple sectors and jurisdictions; various forms of sabotage characterize their efforts to ensure their competitors and rivals do not succeed (Bichler and Nitzan, 2017). What I have tried to do in this study is identify how such strategies have been operationalized with respect to fossil energy sources.

A focus on the political economy of fossil fuels and the governments, industries and businesses that support and rely upon them reveals just how effective the relevant players have been at dominating markets and party politics by mobilizing and multiplying their allies across multiple geographical regions, political constituencies and industry and business sectors. As in other economic sectors involving different kinds of corporate coalitions aimed at oligarchic control, the pursuit of these coalitions' financial interests is typically geared towards minimizing competition from smaller rivals, preventing technological innovations outside their direct control from threatening their market dominance, and ensuring government policies, regulations and legislation are crafted so as to maintain or enhance their market positions (Unruh, 2002; Nitzan and Bichler, 2010; Di Muzio, 2015). This includes routinely exercising their ability to prevent the introduction of legislation or regulations which limit their market power. In policy analysis, these strategies are described as 'veto powers' (Lindblom, 1979; Atkinson, 2011; cf. Parr, 2020).

To the extent that policy expertise in Australian government circles has been hollowed out as a consequence of neoliberal rhetoric concerning 'small government' and the hiring out of government policy to consultants (Pearse, 2007; West, 2015, 2018), the covert exercise of power by party political factions and their corporate backers has tended to become the norm. Nowhere is this more apparent than with respect to environmental, climate change and energy policy in Australia. Thus, on the one hand, we have the largely covert 'money politics' model of Machiavellian policy-making, whereby powerful corporate interests 'buy-off' key decision-makers through various (legal and illegal) means, and thereby secure policy outcomes which are largely or solely favourable to them (West, 2016a). On the other hand, we have the far more visible post-Machiavellian environment in which a range of policy proposals, most of which are consistent with neoliberal preferences for economic instruments, have been successfully 'sold' by policy-makers to decision-makers (Jones, 2010; Radin, 2000).

It is therefore not credible to assume that the policy-making processes pursued by Australia's major political parties with respect to environmental, climate change and energy policy conform with any kind of rationalist model. Rationalists assume that policy-making is a state-centred process whereby expert-certified information flows in a linear and unproblematic fashion from policy-makers to decision-makers, with rational outcomes emerging as long as rigorous procedures are followed (Bridgman and Davis, 2004; cf. Hajer and Wagenaar, 2003; Fischer, 2003). The Australian experience clearly demonstrates to the contrary that expert-certified advice is often ignored, even when it is provided by relevant government agencies to political decision-makers, and that contradictory and often empirically flawed advice is often preferred by governments through various forms of corporate influence-peddling. Those politicians who favour a continuation of the status quo can simply ignore unpalatable expert knowledge and advice, or 'cherry-pick' and commission expert opinions that reflect or reinforce their predetermined positions. Indeed, if they are unable to elicit the 'appropriate' responses from public servants or recognized experts, they can simply bypass conventional forms of advice and decision-making and implement the wishes of corporate lobbyists and principals (Lindblom and Woodhouse, 1993: Chs. 5 and 8; Haas, 2004). Both strategies have resulted in either policy paralysis or, even worse, the development of financially and technically unsound policies that further entrench a narrow spectrum of incumbent business and industry interests.

Decades of policy failure by successive Australian governments with respect to the politics of decarbonization are a consequence of several interacting factors. The term 'policy failure' is used here in the dual sense of poorly designed, evaluated and implemented policies, as well as policies that are blocked or restricted from being realized (Zittoun, 2015, pp. 245–7). The main contributing factors are:

a. a loss of expertise within government and the contracting out of policy advice;
b. the lack of regulation of political donations and enforcement of existing regulations;
c. the absence of effective policies or legislation relating to post-public service employment;
d. the inconsistent and ineffectual regulations surrounding lobbying; and
e. the reduction of funding and resources provided to government monitoring and regulatory agencies.

As these problems have been orchestrated and exacerbated by Australia's major political parties, systemic policy failure in multiple portfolios cannot be resolved by tinkering with existing policies because they are linked to, and an outcome of, larger political processes. Formal and informal alliances between the executives of oil, coal and gas companies and the country's largest electricity companies and political parties have been established and solidified over many decades. The close coordination of these activities and interests with governments in relation to infrastructure investment, financing and organization has created a large technological system consisting of social and technical elements that are institutionally embedded and consequently extremely resistant to change. Gregory Unruh coined the term 'carbon lock-in' to describe how technological, social and institutional forces in industrialized societies create what he calls 'techno-institutional complexes' that generate policy inertia and prevent the adoption of cost-neutral or even cost-effective policies to tackle anthropogenic climate change (Unruh, 2000, 2002; Unruh and Carrillo-Hermosilla, 2006). Political lock-in is one of the attributes of carbon lock-in, and has been documented as one of the key attributes of industrial clusters in geographic regions that lack commitment to innovation and which block structural change (Hassink, 2010; Hassink et al., 2019).

DISCUSSION

The interrogatory method outlined above has provided some insights into how major energy and resource corporations 'groom' individuals within key governance institutions for the sole purpose of pursuing their mutual political and financial interests. It is especially apparent from the corrosive influence of the fossil fuel industry on Australian politics that it has managed to entrench its power within the country's major political parties and key bureaucracies through the three-fold strategy of political donations, lobbying and 'jobs for the boys'. Inadequate restrictions on such activities have enabled major corporate players to shape government policy- and decision-making in a fundamentally undemocratic fashion. The end result is worse environmental outcomes, whether that is with respect to Australia meeting its international treaty obligations, its national obligations to Indigenous Australians concerning land rights, or the protection and use of environmentally sensitive areas and the country's natural resources.

As these poor outcomes are the consequence of inadequate checks on the executive powers of government, new institutions, laws and regulations need to be created to provide citizens with greater transparency and accountability from elected and appointed officials.

Through a largely covert army of current and former politicians, public administrators, journalists, right-wing think tanks, and public relations and advertising agencies, the fossil fuel and other polluting industries have been able to operationalize and sustain their broader goals of profit maximization and market dominance, with all of the negative social and environmental outcomes 'externalized' to people and the planet. They have managed to increase their political influence and maintain public perceptions of their future viability, if not necessity, while simultaneously reinforcing perceptions that renewable energy technologies will not be a threat to their interests any time soon. The existence of what might be described as a network of 'spoilers', 'laggards', 'megaphones', 'moles' and 'attack dogs' within Australia's major political parties and its key bureaucracies has produced a regulatory and policy culture within state and federal governments that is extremely resistant to, and in some cases, virtually incapable of, implementing any commitments that require long-term planning or any significant deviation from the status quo.

The largely invisible networks of influence that pervade many contemporary governance structures throughout the world are a direct result of the corrosion of democratic norms and the winding back of checks and balances on executive power won by previous generations. These anti-democratic processes could arguably be reversed were all levels of government to adopt proportional systems of political representation. There is abundant evidence going back many decades that 'first past the post' electoral systems favour the interests of the wealthy and powerful (Schattschneider, 1952). If all that is required in such a 'winner takes all' political scenario is to persuade a small minority of swinging voters in marginal electorates to support one's party, there is no incentive for incumbent parties to embrace any kind of policy that might threaten their appeal to such voters, who almost invariably vote out of self-interest. In Australia, these forms of persuasion have recently descended into open pork-barrelling of marginal and so-called 'safe' electorates by incumbent Coalition governments to ensure electoral wins, including funding for bushfire relief.

What we are witnessing, therefore, is the construction of neo-feudal networks of loyalty, patronage and privilege. As the most significant ways in which these networks exercise power are not directly observable through the public statements and actions of their functionaries, it is far more illuminating to understand these networks as directly analogous to the kinds of organizational structures exposed in international crime syndicates. Making proportional representation a political norm across all tiers of government would arguably require politicians and political parties to genuinely engage with and represent the interests of their constituents, rather than their major donors and patrons. Genuine engagement and representation requires in turn experimenting with different models of public participation and deliberation, which are then systematically examined, evaluated and institutionalized should they be found to be effective (Chilvers and Kearns, 2016). By simultaneously focusing upon lobbying, donations and post-public-sector employment and how they shape favourable outcomes for the wealthy and well connected in our societies, those of us who are dedicated to genuine democratic reform may be able to shift public opinion in our favour.

With respect to the issue of political donations, because political parties need the mainstream media to win public support for their policies, the easiest way for them to fund expensive media campaigns is to accept large corporate donations, and to tailor their messages to the 'logic' of media exposure. Both concessions make governments beholden to sectional interests that are by definition inconsistent with the public interest. Given the enormous sums of 'dark money' that have flowed into the coffers of the major political parties over the last decade, and the extent to which advertising dollars have clearly distorted electoral outcomes in Australia and elsewhere, there are sound reasons for political campaigns to be publicly funded. Likewise, it is essential for a functioning democracy that all broadcast, print and social media with audiences above a certain numerical threshold be required to provide dedicated 'column inches' and airtime to the fair representation of all candidates' and parties' policy positions during an election campaign, rather than silencing the voices of those with whom we disagree, as the tech giants have recently begun doing. Suitable models for some of these initiatives can be found in Sweden, Canada, Ireland and other jurisdictions, and can be adapted and modified to other jurisdictions where necessary.

CONCLUSION

This chapter has highlighted the need to conceptualize as abuses of power the kinds of extensive and systematic influence-peddling deployed by local, regional and global corporations to shape government policy- and decision-making in their own interests: what has been traditionally referred to as 'Machiavellian politics'. One of the methodologies that can reveal how Machiavellian politics continues to characterize important aspects of political life in contemporary industrial societies involves detailed examination of the employment histories of key political staffers and decision-makers who have moved between the public and private sectors. The next phase of this research involves examining the records of parliamentary debates, committee hearings, lobbyist registers, policy announcements, press releases and regulatory amendments to determine to what extent these can be correlated with particular personnel histories and the timing of position placements. The ultimate goal will be to identify those placements that correspond with intense periods of policy development in key portfolios; or alternatively, whether they correspond with important decisions concerning large infrastructure projects. Clearly, these kinds of techniques could also be applied to other portfolio areas and national contexts, and are broadly portable, that is, they are adaptable by other researchers concerned with corporate power. The most significant challenge for those of us who are dedicated to ongoing democratic reform in the twenty-first century is to curb the power of the corporate sector over increasingly large domains of human and non-human activity.

ACKNOWLEDGEMENTS

I would like to thank Darrin Durant, Marc Hudson, Vanessa Bowden, Michael West, Sandi Keane, Joel Rosenzveig, Phil Johnstone, Andy Stirling, the late Stewart Williams, and the editors of this volume for their advice and feedback concerning various drafts of this chapter and the associated research.

NOTES

1. A database of the charges and findings against these individuals is available from the author on request.
2. In 2016, the 'Big Three' provided 90 per cent of electricity to NSW customers and 80 per cent of electricity to Victorian customers (Mountain, 2016).

REFERENCES

ACF (Australian Conservation Foundation) (2016) Australia's 10 biggest climate polluters. Australian Conservation Foundation. Melbourne: ACF. Available from: https://apo.org.au/sites/default/files/resource-files/2016-02/apo-nid61899.pdf.

AER (Australian Energy Regulator) (2017) *State of the Energy Market May 2017*. Melbourne: Australian Energy Monitor. Available from: https://www.aer.gov.au/system/files/State%20of%20the%20energy%20market%2C%20May%202017%20%28A3%20format%29_1.pdf.

Alexander, R.M., Mazza, S.W. and Scholz, S. (2009) Measuring rates of return for lobbying expenditures: An empirical case study of tax breaks for multinational corporations. *Journal of Law and Politics*. **25**(401), pp. 401–57.

Andrew, S. (2016) Doing it his way: Martin Ferguson steps out of Labor's shadow. *Thomson Reuters*. Available from: https://insight.thomsonreuters.com.au/legal/posts/martin-ferguson-steps-out-of-labors-shadow.

Aston, H. (2016a) Only 5 percent of oil and gas companies pay resource tax. *Sydney Morning Herald*. Available from: https://www.smh.com.au/politics/federal/only-5-of-oil-and-gas-companies-pay-resource-tax-20161010-grz470.html.

Aston, H. (2016b) Nigerian government takes more in oil and gas revenue than Australia, analysis shows. *Sydney Morning Herald*. Available from: https://www.smh.com.au/politics/federal/nigerian-government-takes-more-in-oil-and-gas-revenue-than-australia-analysis-shows-20161121-gsu81p.html.

Aston, H. (2016c) Fossil fuel giants using questionable deductions to shrink tax bills: Auditor-General. *Sydney Morning Herald*. Available from: https://www.smh.com.au/politics/federal/fossil-fuel-giants-using-questionable-deductions-to-shrink-tax-bills-auditorgeneral-20161128-gszcam.html.

Atkinson, M.M. (2011) Lindblom's lament: Incrementalism and the persistent pull of the status quo. *Policy and Society*. **30**(1), pp. 9–18.

Atlas of Economic Complexity (2021) Australia. Available from: https://atlas.cid.harvard.edu/countries/14/.

Aulby, H. and Ogge, M. (2016) Greasing the wheels: The systematic weaknesses that allow undue influence by mining companies on government – a QLD case study. Canberra: Australian Conservation Foundation/The Australia Institute.

Austin, A. (2015) Corruption and incompetence escalate on Turnbull's watch. *Independent Australia*. Available from: https://independentaustralia.net/politics/politics-display/corruption-and-incompetence-escalate-on-turnbulls-watch,8533.

Australian Senate (2017) Retirement of coal fired power stations: Final report to the Environment and Communications References Committee. Canberra: Parliament House. Available from: https://www.aph.gov.au/Parliamentary_Business/Committees/Senate/Environment_and_Communications/Coal_fired_power_stations/Final_Report.

Bagchi, S. and Svejnar, J. (2015) Does wealth inequality matter for growth? The effect of billionaire wealth, income distribution, and poverty. *Journal of Comparative Economics*. (43), pp. 505–30. Available from: https://ssrn.com/abstract=2363220.

Bagshaw, E. (2017) Political donations are 'an unregulated arms race,' Senate committee told. *The Sydney Morning Herald*. Available from: https://www.smh.com.au/politics/federal/political-donations-are-an-unregulated-arms-race-senate-committee-told-20171102-gzda0o.html.

Bagshaw, E. (2018) 'Staggering': $90 billion lost in resources tax. *The Sydney Morning Herald*. Available from: https://www.smh.com.au/politics/federal/staggering-90-billion-lost-in-resources-tax-20180305-p4z2uv.html.

Bartlett Quintanilla, P. and Cummins-Tripodi, P. (eds) (2018) Revolving doors and the fossil fuel industry: Time to tackle conflicts of interest in climate policy-making. The Greens/EFA Group in the European Parliament. Available from: https://www.greens-efa.eu/files/doc/docs/3d2ec57d6d6aa101bab92f4396c12198.pdf.

Beder, S. (1997) *Global Spin: The Corporate Assault on Environmentalism*. Melbourne: Scribe.

Beder, S. (2001) Anti-environmentalism. In Barry, J. and Frankland, E.G. (eds) *International Encyclopedia of Environmental Politics*. Abingdon: Routledge, pp. 19–22.

Bichler, S. and Nitzan, J. (2017) *Growing through Sabotage: Energizing Hierarchical Power*. Working Papers on Capital as Power No. 2017/02. Available from: https://www.econstor.eu/bitstream/10419/162822/1/20170700_bn_growing_through_sabotage_wpcasp.pdf.

Birrell, R., Hill, D. and Stanley, J. (1982) *Quarry Australia? Social and Environmental Perspectives on Managing the Nation's Resources*. Melbourne: Oxford University Press.

Bridgman, P. and Davis, G. (2004) *The Australian Policy Handbook*. Sydney: Allen & Unwin Australia.

Brookes, R. and Hughes, S. (2016) Public servants, private paydays: How ministers and mandarins make life after government pay – a revolving doors special. *Private Eye*. Available from: https://www.private-eye.co.uk/pictures/special_reports/revolving-doors.pdf.

Bruce, A. and MacGill, I. (2016) FactCheck Q&A: Is Australia the world leader in household solar power? *The Conversation*. Available from: https://theconversation.com/factcheck-qanda-is-australia-the-world-leader-in-household-solar-power-56670.

Brulle, R.J. (2014) Institutionalizing delay: Foundation funding and the creation of U.S. climate change counter-movement organizations. *Climatic Change*. **122**(4), pp. 681–94.

Brulle, R.J. (2018) The climate lobby: A sectoral analysis of lobbying spending on climate change in the USA, 2000–2016. *Climatic Change*. **149**(3), pp. 289–303.

Brulle, R.J., Carmichael, J. and Jenkins, J.C. (2012) Shifting public opinion on climate change: An empirical assessment of factors influencing concern over climate change in the U.S., 2002–2010. *Climatic Change*. **114**(2), pp. 169–88.

Cahill, D. and Beder, S. (2005) Regulating the power shift: The state, capital and electricity privatisation in Australia. *Journal of Australian Political Economy*. **55**, pp. 5–22.

Centre for Public Integrity (2020a) Hidden money in politics: What the AEC disclosures don't tell us. Briefing Paper. Available from: https://publicintegrity.org.au/wp-content/uploads/2020/06/Briefing-paper-Hidden-money-in-politics-2019.pdf.

Centre for Public Integrity (2020b), Accountability deficit: The $1.4 billion funding cut of accountability institutions. Available from: https://publicintegrity.org.au/wp-content/uploads/2020/10/Briefing-Paper-Budget-2019-2020.pdf.

Chilvers, J. and Kearns, M. (eds) (2016) *Remaking Participation: Science, Environment and Emergent Publics*. Abingdon: Taylor & Francis.

Clennell, A. (2009) Slips raise queries on greasing the wheels of power. *The Sydney Morning Herald*. Available from: https://www.smh.com.au/politics/federal/slips-raise-queries-on-greasing-the-wheels-of-power-20091006-gjxe.html.

Coady, D., Parry, I., Le, N.-P. and Shang, B. (2019) Global fossil fuel subsidies remain large: An update based on country-level estimates. IMF Working Paper. International Monetary Fund.

Coen, D. and Richardson, J. (eds) (2009) *Lobbying the European Union: Institutions, Actors and Issues*. New York, NY: Oxford University Press.

Corbett, B. (2016) Ian Macfarlane to helm Queensland Resources Council. *Financial Review*. Available from: https://www.afr.com/rear-window/ian-macfarlane-to-helm-queensland-resources-council-20160925-grnwvg.

Davies, A. (2015) CSG industry hires well-connected staffers. *The Sydney Morning Herald*. Available from: https://www.smh.com.au/national/nsw/csg-industry-hires-wellconnected-staffers-20150515-gh2rg3.html.

DISER (Department of Industry, Science, Energy & Resources) (2020) The Australian resources sector – significance and opportunities. *Australian Government*. Available from: https://www.industry

.gov.au/data-and-publications/australias-national-resources-statement/the-australian-resources-sector-significance-and-opportunities.

Di Muzio, T. (2015) *Carbon Capitalism: Energy, Social Reproduction and World Order*. London: Rowman & Littlefield.

Dryzek, J.S. (2005) *The Politics of the Earth: Environmental Discourses*. Oxford: Oxford University Press.

Edwards, B. (2017) Dark money: The hidden millions in Australia's political finance system. *Inquiry into and report on all aspects of the conduct of the 2016 Federal Election and matters related thereto*. Submission 81 – Supplementary Submission 1. Available from: https://www.aph.gov.au/Parliamentary_Business/Committees/Joint/Electoral_Matters/2016Election/Submissions.

Environmental Justice Australia (2019) *Adani Brief Update: The Adani Group's environmental and human rights record*. Environmental Justice Australia. Available from: https://www.envirojustice.org.au/wp-content/uploads/2019/03/Adani-Brief_update_2019.pdf.

Farrell, J. (2015) Network structure and influence of the climate change counter movement. *Nature Climate Change*. **6**, pp. 370–74.

Farrell, J. (2016) Corporate funding and ideological polarization about climate change. *Proceedings of the National Academy of Sciences*. **113**(1), pp. 92–7.

Farrell, J. (2019) The growth of climate change misinformation in US philanthropy: Evidence from natural language processing. *Environmental Research Letters*. **14**, 034013.

Fischer, F. (2003) *Reframing Public Policy: Discursive Politics and Deliberative Practices*. Oxford: Oxford University Press.

Fremaux, A. and Barry, J. (2018) The 'good anthropocene' and green political theory: Rethinking environmentalism, resisting ecomodernism. In: Biermann, F. and Lovbrand, E. (eds) *Anthropocene Encounters: New Directions in Green Political Thinking*. Cambridge: Cambridge University Press, pp. 171–90.

Green, J. (1998) Australia's anti-nuclear movement: A short history. *Green Left Online*. Available from: https://web.archive.org/web/20080405221906/http:/www.greenleft.org.au/1998/330/20531.

Haas, P. (2004) When does power listen to truth? A constructivist approach to the policy process. *Journal of European Public Policy*. **11**(4), pp. 569–92.

Hager, N. and Burton, B. (2000) *Secrets and Lies: The Anatomy of an Environmental PR Campaign*. Munroe, ME: Common Courage Press.

Hajer, M.A. and Wagenaar, H. (2003) *Deliberative Policy Analysis: Understanding Governance in the Network Society*. Cambridge: Cambridge University Press.

Hamilton, C. (2007) *Scorcher: The Dirty Politics of Climate Change*. Melbourne: Black Inc/Agenda.

Hannam, P. and Latimer, C. (2018) Tomago Aluminium warns of 'energy crisis' as power supply falters. *The Sydney Morning Herald*. Available from: https://www.smh.com.au/business/markets/tomago-aluminium-warns-of-energy-crisis-as-power-supply-falters-20180608-p4zkbw.html.

Hassink, R. (2010) Locked in decline? On the role of regional lock-ins in old industrial areas. In: Boschma, R. and Martin, R. (eds) *Handbook of Evolutionary Economic Geography*. Cheltenham, UK and Northampton, MA, USA: Edward Elgar Publishing, pp. 450–68.

Hassink, R., Isaksen, A. and Trippl, M. (2019) Towards a comprehensive understanding of new regional industrial path development. *Regional Studies*. **53**(1), pp. 1636–45. Available from DOI: 10.1080/00343404.2019.1566704.

Hibbins, M. (2016) Multinational sham: How Australia was hoodwinked. *Michael West Media*. Available from: https://www.michaelwest.com.au/sham-how-multinationals-duped-us/.

Higginbothom, N., Freeman, S., Connor, L. and Albrecht, G. (2010) Environmental injustice and air pollution in coal affected communities, Hunter Valley, Australia. *Health and Place*. **16**(2), pp. 259–66.

Hornsey, M.J., Harris, E.A. and Fielding, K.S. (2018) Relationships among conspiratorial beliefs, conservatism and climate scepticism across nations. *Nature Climate Change*. **8**, pp. 614–20.

Hutchens, G. (2017a) Australia must charge royalties on natural gas or lose billions, says expert. *The Guardian*. Available from: https://www.theguardian.com/business/2017/feb/09/australia-must-charge-royalties-on-natural-gas-or-lose-billions-says-expert.

Hutchens, G. (2017b) Senate told current tax on oil and gas projects cannot change but future deals should. *The Guardian*. Available from: https://www.theguardian.com/business/2017/jul/03/senate-told-current-tax-on-oil-and-gas-projects-cannot-change-but-future-deals-should.

ICAC (Independent Commission Against Corruption) (2010) Lobbying in NSW: An issues paper on the nature and management of lobbying in NSW. Sydney: Independent Commission Against Corruption. Available from: http://infrastructure.org.au/wp-content/uploads/2017/06/SUB_ICAC_Lobbying_FINAL_050710.pdf.

Innes, A. (2016) Corporate state capture in open societies: The emergence of corporate brokerage party systems. *East European Politics and Societies*. **30**(3), pp. 594–620. Available from: http://eprints.lse.ac.uk/65167/1/Innes_Corporate%20Brokerage%20Party.pdf.

Innes, A. (2017) Draining the swamp: Understanding the crisis in mainstream politics as a crisis of the state. *Slavic Review*. **76**(S1), pp. S30–S38. Available from: DOI: 10.2307/26564943.

Ireland, J. (2019) Backstage in Canberra: Who is lobbying our MPs? *The Sydney Morning Herald*. Available from: https://www.smh.com.au/politics/federal/backstage-in-canberra-who-is-lobbying-our-mps-20190925-p52up4.html.

Jackson, E. (2018) Turnbull just showed what happens when 'ideology and idiocy' take charge of energy policy. *The Guardian*. Available from: https://www.theguardian.com/australia-news/2018/aug/20/malcolm-turnbulls-emissions-backflip-sends-signal-that-climate-change-is-not-real.

Jacques, P.J., Dunlap, R.E. and Freeman, M. (2008) The organisation of denial: Conservative think tanks and environmental scepticism. *Environmental Politics*. **17**(3), pp. 349–85. Available from: DOI: 10.1080/09644010802055576.

Johnston, W. (2018) Two million PV systems – solar a political power. *PV Magazine*. Available from: https://www.pv-magazine-australia.com/2018/12/04/2-million-pv-systems-solar-a-political-power/.

Jones, S. (2010) The national renewable energy target: An example of post-Machiavellian policy-making. *The Australian Journal of Public Administration*. **69**(2), pp. 165–77.

Knaus, C. (2019) 'National disgrace': Glencore coal campaign revelations prompt calls for reform. *The Guardian*. Available from: https://www.theguardian.com/australia-news/2019/mar/08/national-disgrace-glencore-coal-campaign-revelations-prompt-calls-for-reform.

Knight, E. (2016) Big oil, little tax: Why the fossil fuel giants didn't complain about the resource tax. *The Sydney Morning Herald*. Available from: https://www.smh.com.au/business/big-oil-little-tax-why-the-fossil-fuel-giants-didnt-complain-about-the-resource-tax-20161130-gt0rzo.html.

Leitch, D. (2017) Too much power: The real crisis in Australia's energy markets. *Renew Economy*. Available from: https://reneweconomy.com.au/too-much-power-the-real-crisis-in-australias-energy-markets-28663/.

Lindblom, C. (1977) *Politics and Markets: The World's Political-Economic Systems*. New York, NY: Basic Books.

Lindblom, C. (1979) *The Policy-Making Process*. 1st edn. Englewood Cliffs, NJ: Prentice Hall.

Lindblom, C. and Woodhouse, E.T. (1993) *The Policy-Making Process*. 3rd edn. Englewood Cliffs, NJ: Prentice Hall.

Long, S. (2016a) Adani's complex corporate web spreads to tax havens. *ABC News*. Available from: https://www.abc.net.au/news/2016-12-21/adani-corporate-web-spreads-to-tax-havens/8135700.

Long, S. (2016b) Adani companies facing multiple corruption probes. *ABC News*. Available from: https://www.abc.net.au/news/2016-12-22/adani-companies-facing-multiple-corruption-probes/8140100.

Long, S. (2017) The Labor insider turned Adani lobbyist who smoothed the way for the mega mine. *ABC News*. Available from: https://www.abc.net.au/news/2017-11-23/the-labor-insider-who-lobbied-for-adani/9181648.

Long, S. (2019) Corporate collapse waiting to happen: Adani's mine surviving on lifeline from parent company. *ABC News*. Available from: https://www.abc.net.au/news/2019-07-24/adani-carmichael-subsidiary-surviving-on-lifeline-from-parent/11338926.

Long, S. and Slezak, M. (2019) How a damning assessment got turned into approval for Adani's mine. *ABC News*. Available from: https://www.abc.net.au/news/2019-04-11/adani-damning-assessment-turned-into-approval/10990288?nw=0.

Long, S., Harley, W. and Fallon, M. (2017) Adani's tax haven ties to British Virgin Islands revealed. *ABC News*. Available from: https://www.abc.net.au/news/2017-10-02/adanis-tax-haven-ties-to-british-virgin-islands-revealed/9007714.

Lucas, A. (2016) Stranded assets, externalities and carbon risk in the Australian coal industry: The case for contraction in a carbon-constrained world. *Energy Research and Social Science*. **11**, pp. 53–66.

Lucas, A. (2018) Revealed: The extent of job-swapping between public servants and fossil fuel lobbyists. *The Conversation*. Available from: https://theconversation.com/revealed-the-extent-of-job-swapping-between-public-servants-and-fossil-fuel-lobbyists-88695.

Lucas, A. (2020) LobbyLand: Democracy on life support as the revolving door keeps swinging. *Pearls and Irritations*. Available from: https://johnmenadue.com/lobbyland-australias-democracy-on-life-support-as-the-revolving-door-keeps-on-swinging-and-the-scandals-keep-on-rolling/.

Lucas, A. (2021) Investigating networks of corporate influence on government decision-making: The case of Australia's climate change and energy policies. *Energy Research and Social Science*. **81**, 102271.

Lucas, A. and Rosenzveig Holland, J. (2018) Revolving doors: How the fossil fuel lobby has governments ensnared. *Michael West Media*. Available from: https://www.michaelwest.com.au/revolving-doors-how-the-fossil-fuel-lobby-has-governments-ensnared/.

Macdonald-Smith, A. (2012) Greens slam Ferguson on solar projects. *The Australian Financial Review*. Available from: https://www.afr.com/companies/energy/greens-slam-ferguson-on-solar-projects-20120207-i3o7o.

Malm, A. (2015) *Fossil Capital: The Rise of Steam Power and the Roots of Global Warming*. London: Verso.

Manning, P. (2015) Martin Ferguson's revolving door puts energy industry in a spin. *Crikey*. Available from: https://www.crikey.com.au/2014/06/17/martin-fergusons-revolving-door-puts-energy-industry-in-a-spin/.

Martin, S. (2020) Labor denies breakaway pro-coal group points to division on climate policy. *The Guardian*. Available from: https://www.theguardian.com/australia-news/2020/feb/13/labor-denies-breakaway-pro-coal-group-points-to-division-on-climate-policy.

Mayer, J. (2017) *Dark Money: The Hidden History of the Billionaires Behind the Rise of the Radical Right*. New York, NY: Anchor Books.

McCright, A.M. and Dunlap, R.E. (2010) Anti-reflexivity: The American Conservative movement's success in undermining climate science and policy. *Theory, Culture and Society*. **27**(2–3), pp. 100–133.

McCullough, D. (2019) Victorian Libs and Nationals cold on coal. *The Courier*. Available from: https://www.newcastlestar.com.au/story/5948883/victorian-libs-and-nationals-cold-on-coal/.

McKewon, E. (2012) Talking points ammo: The use of neoliberal think tank fantasy themes to delegitimise scientific knowledge of climate change in Australian newspapers. *Journalism Studies*. **13**(2), pp. 277–97.

Michael West Media (2021) Revolving Doors – democracy at risk. *Michael West Media*. Available from: https://www.michaelwest.com.au/revolving-doors/.

Mikler, J. (2018) *The Political Power of Global Corporations*. Cambridge: Polity.

Mountain, B. (2016) *International Comparison of Australia's Household Electricity Prices: A Report Prepared for Consumer Network, One Big Switch*. CME Australia & MarkIntell. Available from: http://cmeaustralia.com.au/wp-content/uploads/2013/09/160708-FINAL-REPORT-OBS-INTERNATIONAL-PRICE-COMPARISON.pdf.

Murphy, K. and Knaus, C. (2019) Liberals attack Queensland Nationals' push for coal-fired power stations. *The Guardian*. Available from: https://www.theguardian.com/australia-news/2019/mar/11/liberals-attack-queensland-nationals-push-for-coal-fired-power-stations.

Murray, C.K. and Frijters, P. (2017) *Game of Mates: How Favours Bleed the Nation*. Lightning Source.

Nitzan, J. and Bichler, S. (2010) *Capital as Power: A Study of Order and Creorder*. Abingdon: Routledge.

Norman, J. (2019) Australia looks to access US fuel reserves to shore up supplies amid Persian Gulf tensions. *ABC News*. Available from: https://www.abc.net.au/news/2019-08-05/australia-looks-to-buy-us-oil-amid-reserve-concerns/11384196.

Parr, B.L. (2020) *Australian Climate Policy and Diplomacy: Government–Industry Discourses*. Abingdon: Routledge.

Parkinson, G. (2017a) Regulators' wake up call: Fossil fuel majors are gaming markets. *Renew Economy*. Available from: https://reneweconomy.com.au/regulators-wake-up-call-fossil-fuel-majors-are-gaming-markets-18995/.

Parkinson, G. (2017b) AGL bought Liddell for nothing – what will it cost Turnbull? *Renew Economy*. Available from: https://reneweconomy.com.au/agl-bought-liddell-for-nothing-what-will-it-cost-turnbull-14579/.

Pearse, G. (2007) *High and Dry: John Howard, Climate Change and the Selling of Australia's Future.* Melbourne: Viking.

Pearse, G. (2009) Quarry vision: Coal, climate change and the end of the resources boom. *Quarterly Essay.* **33**, pp. 1–122.

Pearse, G., McKnight, D. and Burton, B. (2013) *Big Coal: Australia's Dirtiest Habit.* Randwick: University of New South Wales Press.

Pooley, E. (2010) *The Climate War: True Believers, Power Brokers and the Fight to Save the Planet.* New York, NY: Hyperion.

Radin, B. (2000) *Beyond Machiavelli: Policy Analysis Comes of Age.* Washington, DC: Georgetown University Press.

Ray, R. (1994) Government response to the Report of the Senate Standing Committee on Industry, Science and Technology on Gas and Electricity: Combining efficiency and greenhouse. *Parliament of Australia.* Available from: https://parlinfo.aph.gov.au/parlInfo/search/display/display.w3p;db=CHAMBER;id=chamber/hansards/1994-03-17/0087;query=Id:%22chamber/hansards/1994-03-17/0079%22.

Readfearn, G. (2017) Coal lobby's long game puts talking points into leaders' mouths. *The Guardian.* Available from: https://www.theguardian.com/environment/planet-oz/2017/feb/03/coal-lobbys-long-game-puts-talking-points-into-leaders-mouths.

Readfearn, G. (2018a) You don't have to be a climate science denier to join the Monash coal forum, but it helps. *The Guardian.* Available from: https://www.theguardian.com/environment/planet-oz/2018/apr/05/you-dont-have-to-be-a-climate-science-denier-to-join-the-monash-coal-forum-but-it-helps.

Readfearn, G. (2018b) 'It's all about vested interests': Untangling conspiracy, conservatism and climate scepticism. *The Guardian.* Available from: https://www.theguardian.com/environment/planet-oz/2018/may/08/its-all-about-vested-interests-untangling-conspiracy-conservatism-and-climate-scepticism.

Readfearn, G. (2018c) Inside the AEF, the climate denial group hosting Tony Abbott as guest speaker. *The Guardian.* Available from: https://www.theguardian.com/environment/planet-oz/2018/jun/15/inside-the-aef-the-climate-denial-group-hosting-tony-abbott-as-guest-speaker.

Richardson, D. and Denniss, R. (2011) Mining the truth: The rhetoric and reality of the commodities boom. Institute Paper No. 7. Canberra: The Australia Institute. Available from: https://www.tai.org.au/node/1777.

Robertson, B. (2016) IEEFA update: Australia's natural-gas cartel is bleeding Australia. *IEEFA Australia.* Available from: https://ieefa.org/ieefa-update-australias-natural-gas-cartel-bleeding-australia/.

Robertson, B. (2018) A gas cartel run amuck. *IEEFA Australia.* Available from: https://ieefa.org/ieefa-australia-a-gas-cartel-run-amuck/.

Rolfe, J. (2016) Power shock: NSW families pay the highest electricity prices in the world. *The Sunday Telegraph.* Available from: https://www.dailytelegraph.com.au/news/nsw/power-shock-nsw-families-pay-highest-electricity-prices-in-the-world/news-story/75368ed35e0a817d403868636253e616.

Safi, M. (2018) Adani Group files plea in India high court to stall fraud investigation. *The Guardian.* Available from: https://www.theguardian.com/business/2018/aug/29/adani-group-india-dri-investigation-plea.

Sapinski, J.P. (2015) Climate capitalism and the global corporate elite network. *Environmental Sociology.* **1**(4), pp. 268–79.

Schattschneider, E.E. (1952) Political parties and the public interest. *The Annals of the American Academy of Political and Social Science.* **280**(1), pp. 18–26.

Sengupta, S. (2018) Climate change policy toppled Australia's leader. Here's what it means for others. *The New York Times.* Available from: https://www.nytimes.com/2018/08/24/climate/australia-climate-change.html.

Slezak, M. (2016) Australia's coal-fired power stations 'will need to shut at rate of one a year', hearing told. *The Guardian.* Available from: https://www.theguardian.com/environment/2016/nov/09/australias-coal-fired-power-stations-will-need-to-shut-at-rate-of-one-a-year-hearing-told.

Soos, P. (2018) As planet cooks, Coalition cooks the books on fossil fuel subsidies. *Michael West Media.* Available from: https://www.michaelwest.com.au/as-planet-cooks-coalition-cooks-the-books-on-fossil-fuel-subsidies/.

Taylor, M. (2014) *Global Warming and Climate Change: What Australia Knew and Buried ... then Framed a New Reality for the Public.* Canberra: ANU Press.

The Australia Institute (2018) FOI reveals government found Adani 'may have been negligent' in approval process. Available from: https://australiainstitute.org.au/post/foi-reveals-government-found-adani-may-have-been-negligent-in-approval-process/.

Tranter, B. (2013) The great divide: Political candidate and voter polarisation over global warming in Australia. *Australian Journal of Politics and History.* **59**(3), pp. 397–413.

Unruh, G.C. (2000) Understanding carbon lock-in. *Energy Policy.* **28**(12), pp. 817–30.

Unruh, G.C. (2002) Escaping carbon lock-in. *Energy Policy.* **30**(4), pp. 317–25.

Unruh, G.C. and Carrillo-Hermosilla, J. (2006) Globalizing carbon lock-in. *Energy Policy.* **34**(10), pp. 1185–97.

Veblen, T. (1904) *The Theory of Business Enterprise.* New Brunswick, NJ: Transaction Books.

Vidal, J.B., Draca, M. and Fons-Rosen, C. (2011) 'Revolving door' lobbyists: The value of political connections in Washington. *Vox-EU-CEPR.* Available from: https://voxeu.org/article/political-scandal-and-value-connections-insights-britain-and-us.

Wahlquist, C. (2019) 'Incredibly worrying': Legal fight looms around Australia over clampdown on protest. *The Guardian.* Available from: https://www.theguardian.com/world/2019/oct/06/incredibly-worrying-legal-fight-looms-around-australia-over-clampdown-on-protest.

Ward, I. (2009) Lobbying as a public affair: PR and politics in Australia, paper presented for the *ANZCA09 Communication, Creativity and Global Citizenship Conference*, 8–10 July, Brisbane.

Warhurst, J. (2007) *Behind Closed Doors: Politics, Scandals and the Lobbying Industry.* Sydney: UNSW Press.

Warhurst, J. (2017) We need a royal commission into the corruption and decay of Australian politics. *The Canberra Times.* Available from: https://www.canberratimes.com.au/story/6031956/we-need-a-royal-commission-into-the-corruption-and-decay-of-australian-politics/.

West, M. (2014) Glencore tax bill on $15b income: Zip, zilch, zero. *The Sydney Morning Herald.* Available from: https://www.smh.com.au/business/glencore-tax-bill-on-15b-income-zip-zilch-zero-20140626-3awg0.html.

West, M. (2015) Watching the watchdog: Secondments spell trouble at ASIC. *The Sydney Morning Herald.* Available from: https://www.smh.com.au/business/banking-and-finance/watching-the-watchdog-secondments-spell-trouble-at-asic-20150224-13n6xb.html.

West, M. (2016a) How business lobbyists trump your vote. *Michael West Media.* Available from: https://www.michaelwest.com.au/how-business-lobbyists-trump-your-vote/.

West, M. (2016b) Too slick: Oil major BP misleads Parliament. *Michael West Media.* Available from: https://www.michaelwest.com.au/too-slick-oil-major-bp-misleads-parliament/.

West, M. (2017a) Chevron: A game-changer for multinational tax avoiders. *Michael West Media.* Available from: https://theconversation.com/chevron-a-game-changer-for-multinational-tax-avoiders-76587.

West, M. (2017b) Corporate lobbying a billion dollar business. *Michael West Media.* Available from: https://www.michaelwest.com.au/corporate-lobbying-a-billion-dollar-business/.

West, M. (2017c) Charge tax shark Exxon with contempt of Parliament. *Michael West Media.* Available from: https://www.michaelwest.com.au/charge-tax-shark-exxon-contempt-parliament/.

West, M. (2018) Discovered: Matthias Cormann's billion-dollar black hole. *Michael West Media.* Available from: https://www.michaelwest.com.au/discovered-matthias-cormanns-billion-dollar-black-hole/.

West, M. (2020) Australia's top 40 tax dodgers 2020: Fossil fuels dominate once more. *Michael West Media.* Available from: https://www.michaelwest.com.au/australias-top-40-tax-dodgers-2020-fossil-fuels-dominate-once-more/.

Wood, D., Griffiths, K. and Chivers, C. (2018) Who's in the room? Access and influence in Australian politics. Melbourne: Grattan Institute. Available from: https://grattan.edu.au/wp-content/uploads/2018/09/908-Who-s-in-the-room-Access-and-influence-in-Australian-politics.pdf.

Zittoun, P. (2015) Analysing policy failure as an argumentative strategy in policy-making: A pragmatist perspective. *Public Policy and Administration.* **30**(3–4), pp. 243–60.

11. Regime of obstruction: fossil capitalism and the many facets of climate denial in Canada

William K. Carroll, Shannon Daub and Shane Gunster

Climate-change denialism comprises perhaps the most fateful current within anti-environmentalism today. Driven by corporate priorities in extracting and burning the buried sunshine that still powers 80 per cent of the global economy, denialism has been evolving, as signs of climate breakdown proliferate and impact human lives worldwide. A decade ago, Charles Derber characterized the 'denial regime' as 'a triangle of three intertwined groups': big carbon, its political allies and 'the intelligentsia of Doubting Thomases' in civil society – including think-tanks, media, and other agencies (2010, p. 75). He went on to observe that a process of regime change was underway – a shift from stage 1 denialism (the denial of anthropogenic climate change) to a stage 2 regime, involving many of the same players and proposing 'lines of action that appear to be credible responses to the truth now officially acknowledged but do not run the risk of hurting big oil and coal companies or toppling the entire capitalist applecart' (ibid., p. 82).

As a major producer, exporter and consumer of fossil fuels, whose federal government fashions itself as a climate leader yet strongly supports continued growth of the carbon-extractive sector, Canada presents an interesting case: a climate laggard masquerading as a climate leader. Canada boasts the world's third largest proven oil reserve (most of it in Alberta's tar sands),[1] and is ranked fourth in the world as a producer of natural gas.[2] Its per capita CO_2 emissions are slightly below those of Saudi Arabia and Australia (the world 'leaders') and slightly above those of the United States, according to the Union of Concerned Scientists.[3] These facts have not gone unnoticed by the global climate justice movement. In 2011, alongside the COP negotiations in Durban, the Climate Action Network designated Canada 'Fossil of the Year', for the fifth consecutive year.[4] Canada has continued to receive such 'dishonours', including a Lifetime Unachievement Fossil citation in 2013[5] and a Fossil of the Day award in 2017.[6] Yet the pro-fossil fuel policies that have earned this international notoriety are at odds with mainstream Canadian public opinion. A 2019 survey of Canadians found that 58 per cent agreed with the statement, 'the climate emergency requires that our governments adopt a wartime-scale response, making major investments to retool our economy, and mobilizing everyone in society to transition off fossil fuels to renewable energy' (Klein, 2020). Clearly, the mechanisms through which an effective 'denial regime' has been maintained in Canada bear close scrutiny, and may have relevance to other countries where the fossil fuel sector is entrenched.

This chapter draws upon research we have been conducting since 2015 within the Corporate Mapping Project (CMP) – an interdisciplinary research and knowledge-mobilization effort focused on how corporate power is organized in and around Canada's carbon-extractive sector.[7] Our project brings together academic and community-based researchers, investigative journalists, policy analysts and activists. We have examined both the *internal organization* of corporate power – how fossil-fuel corporations function, their ownership and finance relations, the commodity chains in which they are embedded – and the *multifaceted reach* of corporate power into civil and political society.

Our findings accord with Derber's analysis. In both its internal organization and its cultural and political reach, fossil capitalism[8] in Canada comprises a *regime of obstruction* incorporating aspects of stage 1 and stage 2 denialism, and committed at best to a very slow transition that averts the stranding of fixed-capital assets while opening space for corporations that dominate the fossil sector to gain control of emerging alternative energy systems, as they have been striving to achieve in Germany for instance (Paul, 2018, p. 4).

Corporate reach is, at its core, geared toward protecting investments and profit streams, opening new fields for investment, and minimizing intrusions into profit, such as taxes, regulations and unions. This entails different strategic communications in different contexts, from tactical manoeuvres to secure a specific objective (e.g., the green light for a new pipeline project) to the long game of cultivating a pro-business political and popular culture.

In this chapter we draw on findings from the CMP to examine the dynamics and underlying ideological commitments of climate denial in Canada to illuminate some of the key ways in which corporate power's reach from the fossil-fuel sector has been able to maintain business-as-usual and deny the imperative for climate action, despite growing concerns in the general public about climate breakdown. We begin with a look at the corporate power structure that organizes leading capitalists and their advisors into a corporate community whose elite ties and lobbying practices reach into institutions of civil society and the state. We then turn to the realm of climate denial discourse, taking up Derber's phases but understanding them as distinct modes of denial – which we call 'traditional' and 'new' denialism[9] – that operate simultaneously in the highly contested realm of climate policy and politics. We examine in turn the new mode of climate denial favoured by progressive neoliberals, and the traditional mode, which we argue is manifested today primarily via 'extractive populism'.

CANADA'S FOSSIL FUEL LANDSCAPE

Within Canada's vast and diverse geography, the province of Alberta has been the epicentre of climate-change denialism, particularly of the traditional variety. According to the 2019 survey mentioned earlier, 42 per cent of Canadians consider climate change to be an emergency, but only 27 per cent of Albertans do. And while half of Canadians support phasing out the extraction and export of fossil fuels over the next two to three decades, only 29 per cent of Albertans hold this viewpoint, with 45 per cent opposed to such a wind-down (Klein, 2020). Richly endowed with oil, gas and coal and home to the tar sands that are 'on track to eat up more than half of Canada's carbon emissions budget within the next decade' (Lucas, 2021, p. 20), Alberta has become an affluent region (its 2015 median household income was 31 per cent higher than the national average).[10] But that affluence is increasingly threatened by low oil prices and profit rates and concerns about future demand for bitumen – a low-quality, heavy oil that is both costly and carbon-intensive to upgrade and refine, and that has been the target of extensive environmental and divestment campaigns. In recent years, transnational carbon majors like Shell and ConocoPhillips have exited the tar sands and some international financial institutions have announced divestment plans (Hussey and Pineault, 2017; Flavelle, 2020).

Yet if Alberta has served as an epicentre for fossil capital[11] and climate-change denialism, the regime of obstruction entails much more than Alberta-based business interests.

Other Canadian provinces, notably Saskatchewan, Newfoundland and Labrador, and British Columbia, have also embraced accumulation strategies of intensive carbon extraction involving massive infrastructure projects supported by policies offering various direct and indirect subsidies to the fossil-fuel industry. Moreover, Canada's banks and other institutional investors have been heavily committed to funding big carbon; indeed, according to research by the Rainforest Action Network, they rank among the leading financial enablers of the fossil-fuel industry worldwide (RAN, 2020). Importantly, the regime extends into the cultural and political fields, as a bid for hegemony – to win hearts and minds by presenting the fossil-capital interest in carbon extraction as integral to the prosperity and welfare of Canadians.

As it connects the practices and interests of fossil capital with organizations and agencies in political and civil society, the regime of obstruction is multiscalar. It extends from the everyday to the global, from an industry-friendly curriculum in Saskatchewan classrooms (Eaton and Day, 2019) to transnational corporate-policy networks that have evolved from traditional denial to 'climate capitalism', advocating an incremental passage to ecologically modernized production, averting stranded assets while allowing fossil capital to expand control of replacement energy sources (Sapinski, 2016, p. 106). At each level, the regime combines business practices that reproduce the dominance of fossil fuels as an energy source with political-cultural practices that recruit popular support for fossil capitalism as a way of life requiring only minor adjustments via technological innovation and market-based incentives.

THE FOSSIL-CAPITAL POWER STRUCTURE

Extensive research over the course of the twentieth century and now into the first decades of the twenty-first, has documented, in each advanced capitalist society and also transnationally, networked power structures consisting of elite, extra-market relations that create the basis for 'corporate communities' (Domhoff, 1980; Domhoff et al., 2017; cf. Doreian and Mrvar, Chapter 12, this volume). Of particular interest have been the interlocking directorates and executives through which directors and top executives of one corporation hold such positions in other corporations. These interlocks furnish a structural basis for communication, coordination and social cohesion, enabling the corporate community to define and pursue its common interests in maintaining business-as-usual (Brownlee, 2005; Sapinski and Carroll, 2018), which in Canada's case means an oversized fossil-fuel sector.

Carroll (2017) has shown how a fossil-capital elite, based primarily in Calgary, Alberta (home to most Canadian fossil-capital head offices), forms a highly integrated community that is nested within the broader corporate elite. The extensive interlocking within the fossil-capital sector creates a very dense network that is reinforced by memberships in the Canadian Association of Petroleum Producers and other industry associations. This local network is linked into the national network (and beyond) through the directors and executives of the carbon majors – the largest corporations in the sector, which claim the lion's share of revenues and profits. In particular, a plethora of interlocks connects the fossil-fuel sector to financial institutions based mainly in Toronto, which own substantial shares in the former and are its key funders (Carroll and Huijzer, 2018; RAN, 2020). The Calgary–Toronto axis is complemented by many elite ties between financial institutions and other sectors, and among those other sectors, creating a cohesive national corporate community, a structure of communication, alliances and alignments in which fossil-fuel corporations are well positioned.

From this base, the fossil-capital power structure extends into various organizations within civil society. The CMP has mapped these elite relations as they reach into the governance of industry associations and wider business advocacy organizations like the Business Council of Canada, policy-planning organizations that produce analysis and commentary from a standpoint aligned with corporate interests, and universities and research institutes often hosted by universities (Carroll et al., 2018). Network analysis revealed a configuration in which directors of fossil-capital corporations participate in governance of all these key knowledge-producing organizations, affording them reach into several strategically important segments of the public sphere. As industry groups integrate the network on a sectoral basis, research institutes and post-secondaries form a '*carbon-centred scientific-industrial complex*' (Carroll et al., 2018, p. 439) pressing technical knowledge into the service of accumulation, often under the cover of 'greening' carbon extraction. Business councils and think-tanks are crucial sites in cementing a national influence network. Canada's leading financial companies were also found to interlock with fossil-fuel corporations, policy-planning organizations and business councils, indicating that fossil-capitalists and financial capitalists collaborate in governing the hegemonic institutions within which a business consensus on policy is hammered out.

We concluded, 'The network offers pathways into the production of knowledge, culture and identity, and opportunities to align carbon-capitalist interests with discourses of national interest' (Carroll et al., 2018, p. 444). The architecture of new denialism combines three structural features of corporate power: elite *cohesion* (an integrated corporate community), elite *closure* (exclusion of non-corporate interests such as labour and ENGOs from the elite network) and a rich *organizational ecology* linking fossil-capital proponents into other fields. It thereby offers 'the strategic advantage of diversity'. Fossil capital speaks not through a megaphone but in many voices and from many sites beyond its base in capital accumulation (Carroll et al., 2018, p. 447).

Lobbying is another relation through which the obstructive power of fossil capital is wielded. Robert Brulle (2018, p. 302) points out that 'control over the nature and flow of information to government decision-makers can be significantly altered by the lobbying process, and creates a situation of systematically distorted communication' – with all the harmful impacts to democracy that implies. In a third study of the fossil-capital power structure CMP researchers examined the lobbying network at the federal level, tracing all meetings between fossil-fuel corporations and government officials (both elected and appointed) between 2011 and early 2018 (Graham et al., 2020). This time period included the last few years of an ardently pro-fossil capital Conservative government led by Stephen Harper and the first few years of a Liberal government led by Justin Trudeau and ostensibly committed to addressing the climate crisis. Over the entire period we found 11 452 fossil-capital lobbying contacts with government officials, amounting to just over six contacts per working day. Reflecting the concentration of fossil capital and the key role of industry associations expressing fractional interests of specific sectors, most of the contacts involved a handful of large corporations and such industry associations as Canadian Association of Petroleum Producers and the Mining Association of Canada. Similarly, just a handful of state organizations and officials were the targets of most lobbying, creating 'a "small world" of intense interaction among relatively few lobbyists/firms and the designated public office holders in select centres of state power, who are their targets (Graham et al., 2020). There was no decrease in lobbying with the change of government in 2015, despite the new government's avowal of climate leadership as a top priority.[12]

Despite a changing cast of characters, mapping the lobbying network revealed remarkable continuity in the stable communicative ties through which the fossil-fuel industry participates in shaping federal policy – a pattern Taft, reporting on the situation in Alberta, has termed 'oil's deep state': 'a hybrid public–private state-within-a-state that pursues its agenda regardless of the public interest' (2017, p. 18). Our findings echoed Urquhart's (2018) observation that the 'institutional legacy' of industry-friendly regulations and institutions is strongly resilient in the face of electoral change.[13]

These various analyses of the fossil-capital power structure map the relatively enduring structures within a regime of obstruction that, as in Australia (Lucas, Chapter 10, this volume), is grounded in the dominant economic position of the fossil-fuel industry. Elite integration within the industry, profuse ties that embed it within the broader corporate community, interlocking governance positions extending into think-tanks, business councils, universities and the like, and constant, intensive lobbying all provide pathways through which both the traditional and the new modes of climate denial can be cultivated and disseminated. As part of the Corporate Mapping Project's knowledge-mobilization efforts, an online interactive database, developed in collaboration with the Public Accountability Initiative, allows users to construct their own mappings of these pathways, and identifies as the 'Fossil Power 50'. the most significant carbon emitters (fossil-capital firms), enablers (chiefly financial institutions and captured state regulators) and legitimators (business councils, policy-planning organizations etc.) that comprise the regime of obstruction in Canada.[14]

As illuminating as these structural approaches may be, they are silent as to the actual communicative content that travels along the networked pathways identified through the study of elite interlocks and lobbying. To gain deeper insights on how the regime of obstruction operates, the CMP has focused on communicative agents and practices at key sites in political and civil society, to which we now turn.

A LAGGARD IN LEADER'S CLOTHING: THE NEW CLIMATE DENIAL

Justin Trudeau and the Liberal Party of Canada swept to power in the fall of 2015 amid much optimism about the prospects for renewed environmental leadership. Climate action was a centrepiece of Trudeau's campaign, which promised to rehabilitate Canada's international role during the Paris climate talks, bring in a national price on carbon, phase out fossil fuel subsidies,[15] overhaul the National Energy Board (the country's national energy regulator), invest millions in clean technologies, and ban crude oil tanker traffic on the country's north-west coast. While cagey on the issues of oil sands development and highly contentious proposed new pipelines to export Alberta bitumen, Trudeau's campaign nevertheless provided stark contrast to the approach taken by incumbent Stephen Harper. Harper's Conservative government earned an international reputation for climate obstruction, aggressively pursued fossil fuel extraction with the aim of making Canada an 'energy superpower' (Taber, 2006), and labelled environmental groups a 'threat' to 'Canada's national economic interest' (Oliver, 2012).

Within a year of its election, however, the new Trudeau government approved a major Liquefied Natural Gas (LNG) facility on the west coast, green-lighted two major new oil sands pipelines, and directly acknowledged its intention to continue supporting expanded fossil fuel production. Notwithstanding the accolades Canada received for its role in the Paris climate negotiations, the country's commitment to reduce greenhouse gas (GHG) emissions by 30 per cent below 2005 levels by 2030 is the same target adopted by the blatantly obstructionist Harper government. The target itself has long been viewed as inadequate (for example, see 'Canada', Climate Action Tracker, n.d.), and the measures contained in the Pan-Canadian climate framework are insufficient to meet even this target. The 2019 UN emissions gap report lists Canada as one of six G20 countries that are likely to miss their 2020 reduction targets and as one of seven that 'require further action' in order to meet their 2030 nationally determined contributions (UNEP, 2019, pp. 7–8). Yet the federal government's commitment to expanded oil sands production is so strong that in May 2018 it announced plans to buy the existing Trans Mountain pipeline from Kinder Morgan for CAD 4.5 billion and additionally take over the financing and building of the expansion project.

The deployment of energetic talk of climate leadership and the adoption of GHG reduction policies alongside an expansionary stance on fossil fuel production may appear contradictory, but it is entirely consistent with the 'new' mode of climate denial. This mode of denial has been strategically deployed in recent years in Canada with the aim of rehabilitating the international reputation of Alberta oil sands in order to secure 'social licence' domestically for pipeline projects and internationally for exports of Alberta's heavy crude. While not a brand-new phenomenon per se, this mode of denial has been increasingly favoured by the fossil fuel industry and its political allies in recent years, as public recognition of the urgent need to mitigate climate change grew. However, this mode has received relatively less scholarly attention than what Derber termed stage 1 denial and what we call traditional denial.[16]

Traditional and new denialism have the same ultimate outcome – namely, to delay societal responses that are commensurate with the scale and urgency of the climate crisis. Nevertheless, there are significant differences in the origins and operation of these two modes (see Table 11.1). The organized effort to deny (and/or cast doubt on) the scientific certainty of human-caused climate change began in the late 1980s, as the issue initially captured the attention of policy makers and the public (Dunlap and McCright, 2015; Oreskes and Conway, 2011). Jacques et al. (2008) trace the origins of this effort back further, to the resurgence of the conservative movement in the United States in the 1970s in response to the societal changes and progressive social movements of the 1960s. They document the rise of an 'anti-environmental counter-movement', catalysed by the emergence of environmentalism along with the associated problematization of industrial capitalism's ecological impacts and the adoption of environmental protection policies by governments. This counter-movement promoted what Jacques et al. (2008) call 'environmental skepticism' – an epistemological stance that rejects scientific knowledge about environmental problems and therefore their seriousness; challenges the need for environmental policies; eschews corporate responsibility for environmental problems via regulation or legal liability; and portrays environmental policies 'as threatening Western progress' (ibid.).

The driving force behind the climate denial movement in the United States has been a cluster of conservative think-tanks – allied with fossil fuel corporations and industry groups (along with swaths of the wider corporate sector), and working in tandem with a vast network of conservative front groups, media pundits, bloggers, politicians and contrarian scientists (Jacques et al., 2008; Dunlap and McCright, 2015; McCright and Dunlap, 2003). Powered by funding from conservative foundations and wealthy right-wing elites (Brulle, 2014; Mayer, 2016), the denial counter-movement systematically undermined climate science by 'manufacturing' uncertainty and controversy (Dunlap and McCright, 2015). Jacques (2012, p. 11) argues that the denial movement's efforts have created a 'science trap, where elites and masses cannot differentiate between authentic controversy in scientific literature and manufactured controversy.'

Proponents of the new denialism diverge sharply by accepting the science of climate change and advocating an active policy response. Whereas traditional denialism 'camouflages its true ideological and material objectives' by confusing the public about climate science (Jacques, 2012), new denialism camouflages its objectives by promoting a limited agenda for action that does not threaten capital accumulation by the fossil fuel industry. The championing of modest climate mitigation strategies by institutions and elites is a process Chris Paul Methmann (2010) dubs the 'mainstreaming of climate protection', one that leads to 'paradoxical results' where acceptance of the need for climate protection becomes widespread yet 'climate protection itself changes its meaning and becomes ambiguous.' In making the meaning of climate action ambiguous, new denialism allows industry and governments to create the illusion of action – whether through the adoption of voluntary emissions reduction measures or incremental policy action.

Drawing on the work of Kari Norgaard (2006, 2011), who has studied how everyday people participate in the 'social organization' of climate denial, Jacques (2012) notes that denial can function as a psychological strategy of self-protection in the face of the existential threat of climate change. In a similar vein, the comforting illusion of action may function to neutralize demand for more ambitious climate mitigation requiring deeper social transformations. In other words, new denialism creates a policy trap, in which the public struggles to differentiate between effective policy responses that match the scale and severity of climate change and inadequate solutions that sound good but do little to address the problem.

New denialism also diverges from the traditional mode in organization and ideological orientation. The traditional climate denial movement is an 'extension' of the American conservative movement (Brulle, 2014), though it reaches into and has counterparts in other 'developed' fossil-fuel-producing countries like Canada and Australia (Dunlap and McCright, 2015). Whereas 'political conservatism is the hegemonic glue that binds' the climate denial movement together (Dunlap and McCright, 2010), new denialism is more disparate and cannot really be characterized as a movement per se, though it is more generally aligned with liberal ideology and its proponents. Traditional denialism espouses the 'exemptionalist paradigm'– the belief that human ingenuity and technology exempt capitalist industrial society from the constraints of ecological limits (Dunlap and McCright, 2015; Catton and Dunlap, 1980). New denialism is instead rooted in the 'new exemptionalism' of policy discourses of ecological modernization (Foster, 2012; Blue et al., 2018), which attempt to reconcile the contradictions between industrial capitalist economies and the environmental damage they cause. In this paradigm, climate change is understood as a serious problem that must be addressed, but primarily via technological and market-based fixes (e.g. carbon capture and storage, carbon pricing), while leaving corporate power largely intact. Adherence to ecological modernization is typical of contemporary liberal political movements, as well as more progressive strains of conservativism in Canada.

Given Canada's similar-yet-different political culture vis-à-vis the United States, it is not surprising that new denialism has played a particularly strong role in the country's history of engagement with climate change. As Young and Coutinho (2013) remind us, it was Prime Minister Brian Mulroney's government that made Canada one of the first countries to commit

Table 11.1   Traditional and new denialism compared

Traditional climate denialism	New climate denialism
Rejects or casts doubt on science of climate change	Accepts science of climate change
Manufactures uncertainty and controversy about climate science (Dunlap and McCright, 2015)	Manufactures confusion about the nature and extent of the policy/societal response needed, allowing for the illusion of action
Fights mandatory GHG reductions and other climate policies	Accepts and advocates for mandatory or voluntary GHG reductions together with market-driven and demand-side policy measures like carbon pricing, provided these don't impinge upon industry profits and assets (with exception of coal phase-out policies)
Reassures people in the face of threat to 'ontological security' (Jacques, 2012)	Reassures people in the face of transformative societal changes that feel uncertain, unimaginable or threatening
Promoted especially by right-wing think-tanks, along with other conservative movement actors	Promoted directly by fossil fuel corporations and governments, along with actors from a variety of movements/ideological positions
Climate change science = 'an imminent critique of industrial power, Western modernity and the ideals of Western progress' – an 'ontological threat to Western modernity' (Jacques, 2012, p. 11)	Meaningful/adequate climate change action = a challenge to Western modernity and carboniferous capitalism AND Indigenous worldviews, rights and title accepted in principle but denied in practice if they hinder business-as-usual.
Adheres to 'Human Exemptionalist Paradigm' (Foster, 2012; Dunlap and McCright, 2015)	Adheres to 'New Exemptionalism' and ecological modernization theory (Foster, 2012)

to GHG reductions in 1988. Even so, the negotiation of the United Nations Framework Convention on Climate Change in the early 1990s and subsequent Kyoto Protocol in 1997 triggered a backlash from the country's corporate elite, building to a crescendo of opposition as the federal government moved slowly towards formal ratification of the Kyoto Accord. The opposition movement was led by an informal coalition of powerful business groups – the Business Council of Canada, the Canadian Manufacturers and Exporters Association, the Canadian Chamber of Commerce, and the Canadian Association of Petroleum Producers (Macdonald, 2007). Together they challenged the need for action and the scale of GHG reductions Canada's Kyoto commitment entailed, relying especially on exaggerated claims about 'catastrophic consequences' and casting doubt on the 'certainty' of climate science (Canadian Manufacturers and Exporters, 2002; Chase, 2002; Marshall, 2002). The federal Liberal government of then-Prime Minister Jean Chretien did ultimately ratify the Accord in 2002, but proceeded to do little else. Indeed, given decades of lip service to targets but little concrete action by either Liberal or Conservative governments (Lee, 2017; Simpson et al., 2008), one could argue that Canada has pioneered the new denialism.

The new denialism has emerged as a strategic effort to proactively define the solutions to climate change in a manner that mitigates the threat of action to protect both the interests of producer industries and governments, and the larger economic regime. As we have discussed, the new denialism's roots stretch back to the 1990s, but we suggest that as the impacts of climate change worsen and become more visible to larger numbers of people, it is becoming an increasingly popular mode of obstruction. The 'new' and 'traditional' modes of climate denial are not, however, ultimately at odds, nor do we see evidence to suggest traditional denial efforts are disappearing. Instead, these modes reinforce each other and structure climate politics around an apparent divide between the reactionary conservative–populist forces of outright denial on one side, and a more progressive-leaning incremental agenda for action on the other. In Canada, traditional denial increasingly finds expression in extractive populism, which has arisen as a response to the perceived threat of even the modest incremental policies favoured by new denial proponents.

WHAT'S OLD IS NEW AGAIN: EXTRACTIVE POPULISM AND THE CONSERVATIVE DENIAL MOVEMENT

As the 'grand bargain' championed by Trudeau and former Alberta Premier Rachel Notley – in which support for a modest carbon tax would provide 'social licence' for new pipelines and tar sands expansion – has progressively unravelled (Gutstein, 2018), the Canadian conservative movement and fossil fuel industry advocates have increasingly sought to shore up support for extractivism through a populist storyline built upon three core claims: first, defining extractivism as an unequivocal national/public good; second, warning that this national/public good is under attack; and, third, asserting that political mobilization is necessary to defend it (Gunster, 2019).

Extractive populism rests upon the idea that extractivism – defined broadly as the extraction, refining, transportation and export of resources such as oil, natural gas and coal – constitutes the core of the Canadian economy, and provides a wide range of benefits to *everyone* in the country. A robust and healthy extractive sector is positioned as an essential public good, generating high-paying jobs for workers, opportunities for businesses, and revenues for governments and public services (Barney, 2017).

As noted earlier in this chapter, this claim is hardly unique to extractive populism – indeed, framing the fossil fuel industries as essential to Canadian prosperity is also a cornerstone of the new denialism, championed by 'progressive' politicians such as Trudeau and Notley. 'We're in this together,' noted the former Alberta NDP government's 2018 'Keep Canada Working' campaign, a CAD 23 million effort to persuade the Canadian public about the virtues of the Trans Mountain Expansion Project (Carney, 2019). 'We all have a stake in getting the pipeline expanded. As citizens we'll benefit from the jobs and increased revenue it will bring. And as owners of the pipeline, we'll profit from our investment. That's why all Canadians need to work together to get it built' (www.keepcanadaworking.ca).

Fossil fuels are also actively promoted as enabling the comforts, the convenience – indeed, the very possibility of 'modern life' as we know and enjoy it. As Matt Huber explains, the petroleum industry has actively sought to position its products (and itself) at the core of a modern way of life, constitutive of neo-liberal visions of freedom, prosperity and the good life anchored in lived practices around the home and the automobile (Huber, 2012). Such an 'energy lifeworld' discourse has become prominent in recent advertising from major oil and pipeline companies, as they seek to remind consumers of their dependence upon and entanglement with fossil fuels and, by extension, the corporations that supply them (e.g. Enbridge's 'Life Takes Energy' campaign).

The most noteworthy feature of Canadian extractive populism is its reliance upon nationalism and national identity (Barney, 2017; Aronczyk, 2017), a rhetorical strategy we have elsewhere described as *symbolic nationalization* (Gunster and Saurette, 2014). The origins of Canadian extractive populism can be traced back to the conflict between the Alberta and federal governments around the National Energy Program (NEP), a very mild form of nationalization advanced by the Canadian government in the late 1970s/early 1980s that promised 'Canadian oil for Canadians' (cited in Gutstein, 2018, p. 14). While the programme was widely popular with the Canadian public (especially efforts to 'Canadianize' the industry), it was vigorously opposed by the Alberta government and the oil and gas sector, and aroused widespread outrage among Albertans who perceived the NEP as little more than an attempt to steal economic rents and regulatory authority over a resource that properly belonged to Alberta.

The rapid expansion of the tar sands – especially from the mid-1990s under a neo-liberal development regime championed by Alberta Premier Ralph Klein (Steward, 2017) – generated significant legitimation challenges for industry and government (Davidson and Gismondi, 2011), including: increasing national and international attention to negative local ecological impacts, community health impacts, inadequate and ineffective monitoring, steep emissions growth, disproportionate flow of economic benefits to large corporations and foreign shareholders, vulnerability to boom-and-bust economic cycles, and the violation of constitutionally protected treaty rights (Adkin, 2016). At the same time, industry and the Alberta government were increasingly desperate for pipelines to expand export capacity to US and international markets, as well as more robust coordination among federal and provincial governments to support of energy and resource development (Gutstein, 2018).

Symbolic nationalization offered an ideal strategy of legitimation, enabling the re-presentation of a private, capitalist, corporate-driven enterprise *as if it had been nationalized*, as if it were a public enterprise designed to serve the common good. Over the past decade, industry and government have recognized the rhetorical value of repositioning the sector – and especially the tar sands – as a national treasure (Turner, 2012). Symbolic (rather than real) forms of nationalization were marshalled to win Canadians over to a vision of oil and gas anchoring prosperity for everyone. Wrapped in the flag, the capitalist and narrowly regional logic of the oil and gas industry – that elevates the profits of (often international) shareholders and the regional interests of Alberta ahead of the public good – recedes from view, and extractivism becomes instead positioned as a constitutive part of what makes 'us' Canadian (Barney, 2017; Gunster et al., 2020).

The second core claim of extractive populism is that the public/national benefits of extractivism are threatened by a small, but highly vocal and surprisingly powerful constellation of political forces. Scapegoating external enemies has a long and diverse pedigree in the context of prairie populism and, more specifically, the evolution of 'Western alienation' (Laycock, 2001). As extractivism was symbolically nationalized, however, the storyline about who and what posed a threat necessarily had to evolve. If extractivism was a national public good, then the villainization of an overbearing central government, intent upon plundering provincial resources no longer made sense. This was especially true with the 2006 electoral victory of Stephen Harper's Conservative party. As Prime Minister, Harper helped pioneer a new narrative in which the meaning and identity of 'Canada' was redefined: 'liberal' values and programmes such as multi-culturalism, diversity, peacekeeping and public health-care were out, displaced by an emphasis upon the country's British (colonial) heritage, military accomplishments and, above all, a long and proud history of resource development (Gutstein, 2014). In the wake of a rather stark decline in the Canadian manufacturing sector (most heavily concentrated in Ontario), the Harper government aggressively promoted resource development – and especially the rapid expansion of tar sands mining – as the new core of the Canadian economy, enabling a new era of commodity-based, export-driven economic growth (Fast, 2014). The Conservatives undertook a wide variety of domestic and international initiatives to support the fossil fuel industry, including an extensive overhaul of environmental legislation and policy, suppression and cutbacks to public impact science, and obstruction of international efforts to negotiate a global climate treaty (Turner, 2013). The public centrepiece of such efforts, however, was the federal government's aggressive, multi-faceted promotion of new pipelines.

These promotional efforts, however, were stymied by the success of pipeline opponents in mobilizing public opposition to pipeline projects (Neubauer and Gunster, 2019). In January 2012, the Harper government lashed out at their opponents with an infamous 'open letter' attacking 'environmental and other radical groups' for their alleged attempts to 'stop any major project no matter what the cost to Canadian families in lost jobs and economic growth' (Oliver, 2012). The letter condemned pipeline opponents for threatening to 'hijack our regulatory system to achieve their radical ideological agenda', 'stacking public hearings with bodies to ensure that delays kill good projects' and using 'funding from special interests to undermine Canada's national economic interest'. This basic storyline of 'foreign-funded radicals' had been circulating for decades in Alberta (Gunster and Saurette, 2014), but what was novel was the identification of Canada and Canadians as the victim – a capstone of concerted efforts by conservative politicians, think-tanks, commercial media and the fossil fuel industry to locate narrow, corporate interests at the core of the 'national interest'.

In a systematic review of several pro-oil social media groups (e.g. *Oil Sands Action*, *Oil Sands Strong*, *Canada's Energy Citizens*, *Oil Respect*) conducted over 2016, the demonization of opponents was identified as one of the top two frames prioritized in industry supporter communications (the other being the representation of extractivism as a national/public good) (Gunster et al., 2020). The most popular objects of ridicule are so-called eco-celebrities such as Leonardo DiCaprio because they provide such an effective condensation of the negative clichés about environmentalists, enabling the framing of industry criticism as driven by wealthy, foreign, liberal, hypocritical, fear-mongering elites that do not know anything about Canada, or oil and gas development in this country. Local activists and groups are routinely positioned as 'paid protesters' who do the bidding of wealthy US puppet-masters, thereby reinforcing perceptions that opposition to tar sands and pipelines is a foreign import, and *fundamentally anti-Canadian*. Such claims are especially toxic in a social media environment in which sensationalized, exaggerated and inflammatory assertions spread like wildfire, and enable and encourage the episodic swarming and abuse of individual activists, especially women (O'Neill, 2019) and Indigenous leaders. Narratives that position environmentalists as traitors to their country – actively working to undermine the livelihoods of Canadian families – provide moral licence for vicious, hate-filled attacks upon activists and environmental groups.[17]

The third core claim of extractive populism is that ordinary Canadians must become politically engaged in order to defend extractivism. The emphasis upon political mobilization can be traced to industry's perception that pipeline opponents had become effective campaigners in using social media to deliver values-driven, emotional appeals to mobilize small but motivated constituencies to become active participants in public debates (Coyne, 2015). Traditional tools of corporate influence – especially big-budget, mass-market ad campaigns – were increasingly perceived as outdated and ineffective. In response, industry and its supporters sought to emulate the mobilization strategies of their opponents by targeting and activating those constituencies most likely to support their agenda, such as industry workers, resource-dependent communities, and conservative-minded citizens.

In 2014, for example, the Canadian Association of Petroleum Producers launched 'Canada's Energy Citizens' (CEC), a hybrid marketing and engagement strategy designed to showcase public support for the industry and encourage ordinary Canadians – especially employees and their families – to become vocal industry advocates (Wood, 2018). As Christina Pilarski, the lobby group's campaign manager noted, 'We know the support is out there ... We've made some good progress in identifying that support. The next step is to build relationships with our supporters, and to inspire them to become visible and vocal champions for industry' (cited in Stanfield, 2015, p. 10). Such efforts are commonly dismissed as 'astroturfing', a pejorative label implying the simulation of 'grassroots' advocacy through top-down corporate public relations initiatives with minimal linkages to real communities or people. Without question, corporate resources, strategies and coordination are essential in explaining the origins, evolution and amplification of extractive populism (Gutstein, 2018; Taft, 2017). But simply dismissing all expressions of industry support as astroturfing risks underestimating the extent to which extractive populism genuinely resonates with aspects of the worldviews and experiences of particular communities, especially those with significant ties to the extractive industries (Hochschild, 2017).

Instead, Edward Walker's (2014) conception of *subsidized publics* provides a more useful framework for analysing this type of corporate-led civic engagement. Subsidized publics arise from the use of corporate and industry resources to catalyse and refine the participation of specific groups within the public sphere, thereby giving them a coherence, focus and elevated profile that they would not have had on their own. Such publics frequently serve as a form of elite legitimation, exacerbating existing political inequalities between those groups favoured with such subsidies and those who lack such political sponsorship. But such legitimation proceeds via an active cultural and ideological struggle to articulate corporate and popular interests, rather than through the orchestration of democratic simulacra that conjure mass sentiments out of thin air.

Advocates and supporters have also been developing their own social media campaigns and profile to defend and promote the oil and gas industry (Gunster et al., 2020). Over the past several years, two groups headed by Cody Battershill – *Oil Sands Action* and *Canada Action* – have attracted hundreds of thousands of followers on Facebook, Twitter and other platforms. The Calgary realtor described his activism as emerging out of a frustration with the anti-oil messaging of environmental groups, as well as his perception that 'industry's own efforts have been hampered by too little coordination, too many unchallenged claims, and industry leaders censoring themselves from what needed to be said' (Cattaneo, 2015). Battershill's groups have become increasingly proactive in mobilizing supporters: readers are asked to contact elected officials to express support for projects, write letters to the editor, call in to talk shows, attend rallies and participate in public hearings and assessments (Gunster et al., 2020). Supporters, then, are addressed not simply as individuals who benefit from industry or support resource development, but as members of a collective movement whose actions (or inaction) will determine the future of their community. Such campaigns, then, aim to redefine extractivism itself as a popular, democratic project, reflective of the will of the people (and not corporate power, special interests or even an economic/technological logic).

EPILOGUE

This chapter was written not long before the coronavirus pandemic swept across the world early in 2020, leading to an oil price collapse that has (as of May 2020) seen US and Canadian oil prices plunge below zero. The previous oil price crash in 2014–15 significantly altered the political economy of fossil fuels in Canada, leading to industry restructuring, consolidation and long-term job losses alongside increased production (Hussey, 2020). It is too early to know how the current crisis will again reshape the landscape of fossil power, though the Canadian Association of Petroleum Producers was quick to lobby for a massive bailout package along with a laundry list of requests including suspension of pollution monitoring requirements, a stop to climate policies, delaying plans for laws that would protect Indigenous rights, and exemption from requirements to report lobbying activity (Marshall, 2020). While the full bailout demanded by industry has not, as yet, materialized, the Canadian Association of Petroleum Producers and the federal government have established a 'COVID-19 Market Crisis Joint Working Group'. Undoubtedly we will see an entrenchment of efforts to further prop up a weakened industry with public subsidies and obstruct climate action, but popular mobilization for a green and just recovery from the pandemic is also underway.

The realm of Canadian popular climate politics and discourse may also be transformed by the all too familiar spectacle of denial of medical and epidemiological evidence and expertise about the coronavirus in the US and its terrible consequences – fuelled it would seem by the same ideologically driven mistrust of science (and even many of the same 'merchants' of doubt – see Holden, 2020) that climate denial is built upon. The US experience is in sharp contrast to the comparatively measured response by the Canadian public and elected leaders, who quickly entered a period of policy and politics shaped by public health imperatives and best-available scientific evidence, with public health officials clearly at the helm of most provincial and federal decision-making. As with the oil price collapse, it is too soon to know *how* these events will transform the politics of fossil capitalism and denial efforts in Canada and globally, but surely they will.

Our work suggests that future research upon the elite networks, rhetorical tactics and legitimation strategies of the fossil fuel industry must be attentive to two key questions: first, how does the diversity of such approaches enable the (temporary) assembly of ideologically diverse coalitions – spanning, for example, 'liberals' such as Prime Minister Trudeau to conservative reactionaries such as the former US President, Donald Trump – in support of the ongoing expansion of oil and gas development; second, what are the internal contradictions and divisions of such coalitions, and how can they be intensified and leveraged by pro-climate discourse, advocacy and activism to create openings and opportunities to not only challenge the legitimacy fossil fuel industry itself, but also to drive a wedge between that industry and other elements of capitalist political economy (especially finance capital). The ferocity with which pro-oil forces have moved against their critics is deeply troubling – an affront to democracy as well as the basic conditions of life on this planet – but it may also reflect the underlying fragility and brittle character of carbon capitalism.

NOTES

1. See: https://www.nrcan.gc.ca/energy/energy-sources-distribution/crude-oil/oil-resources/18085.

2. See: https://www.nrcan.gc.ca/science-data/data-analysis/energy-data-analysis/energy-facts/natural-gas-facts/20067.
3. See: https://www.ucsusa.org/resources/each-countrys-share-co2-emissions.
4. See: https://www.equiterre.org/en/communique/canada-wins-fossil-of-the-year-award-in-durban-%E2%80%93-our-5th-colossal-fossil-in-a-row.
5. See: https://climateactionnetwork.ca/2013/11/22/canada-wins-lifetime-unachievement-fossil-award-at-warsaw-climate-talks/.
6. See: https://theenergymix.com/2017/11/13/canada-shares-fossil-of-the-day-award-on-loss-and-damage-finance/.
7. The CMP has published extensively via public-facing reports, studies and commentaries (available at https://www.corporatemapping.ca/), as well as academic journal articles and books. This chapter draws on previously published work by all three authors, in particular Carroll (2017) and (2020), Carroll et al. (2018), Daub et al. (2020) and Gunster (2019).
8. By fossil capitalism we mean a form of capitalism 'predicated on the growing consumption of fossil fuels, and therefore generating a sustained growth in emissions of carbon dioxide' (Malm, 2016, p. 11). Fossil capitalism highlights capitalism's 'inherent and unavoidable dependence on fossil fuels' (Altvater, 2006, p. 39), but also, in the case of Canada, the skewing of industrial production toward carbon extraction, given Canada's relatively rich endowment of oil, gas and coal.
9. The idea of 'the new climate denialism' was initially outlined by Seth Klein and Shannon Daub (2016). Our colleague Marc Lee (2015) has earlier called the approach 'all of the above' policy making.
10. See: https://www12.statcan.gc.ca/census-recensement/2016/dp-pd/hlt-fst/inc-rev/Table.cfm?Lang=Eng&T=101&S=99&O=A.
11. Following a commodity-chain approach, by fossil capital we mean industrial sectors in which carbon energy is extracted, transported, refined and consumed in the production of electricity.
12. See, for example, https://www.treatyalliance.org/. First Nations have also launched numerous court challenges against tar sands pipeline projects, in particular the Trans Mountain pipeline expansion project. For example, see: https://aptnnews.ca/2020/04/07/group-of-first-nations-want-to-launch-fight-of-trans-mountain-pipeline-approval/.
13. A study of fossil-capital lobbying in the province of British Columbia using the same methodology reached similar conclusions (Graham, 2017; Graham et al., 2017).
14. See: https://www.corporatemapping.ca/. The Public Accountability Initiative maintains the interactive online database LittleSis, with which our database is integrated. See: https://littlesis.org/.
15. This commitment was in fact to implement a pledge made in 2009 by Prime Minister Stephen Harper.
16. In addition to Derber, notable exceptions include Young and Coutinho (2013); Bonds (2016); Levy and Spicer (2013); and Methmann (2010).
17. These narratives were complemented and amplified, particularly during the Harper years (2006–2015), by state-based 'discursive obstruction' framing environmentalists as 'folk devils' (Ali, Chapter 13 in this volume).

REFERENCES

Adkin, L. (ed.) (2016) *First World Petro-Politics: The Political Ecology and Governance of Alberta*. Toronto: University of Toronto Press.

Altvater, E. (2006) The social and natural environment of fossil capitalism. In: Panitch, L. and Leys, C. (eds) *Socialist Register 2007: Coming to Terms with Nature*. London: Merlin Press, pp. 37–59.

Aroncyzk, M. (2017) Raw materials: Natural resources, technological discourse, and the making of Canadian nationalism. In: Zubrzycki, G. (ed.) *National Matters: Materiality, Culture and Nationalism*. Stanford, CA: Stanford University Press, pp. 58–82.

Barney, D. (2017) Who we are and what we do: Canada as pipeline nation. In: Wilson, S., Carlson, A. and Szeman, I. (eds) *Petrocultures: Oil, Politics, Culture*. Kingston, ON: McGill-Queen's University Press.

Blue, G., Daub, S., Yunker, Z. and Rajewicz, L. (2018) In the corporate interest: Fossil fuel industry input into Alberta and British Columbia's climate leadership plans. *Canadian Journal of Communication.* **43**(1), pp. 93–110. Available from DOI: 10.22230/cjc.2018v43n1a3309.

Bonds, E. (2016) Beyond denialism: Think tank approaches to climate change. *Sociology Compass.* **10**(4), pp. 306–17.

Brownlee, J. (2005) *Ruling Canada: Corporate Cohesion and Democracy.* Halifax: Fernwood Publishing.

Brulle, R.J. (2014) Institutionalizing delay: Foundation funding and the creation of U.S. climate change counter-movement organizations. *Climatic Change.* **122**(4), pp. 681–94. Available from DOI: 10.1007/s10584-013-1018-7.

Brulle, R.J. (2018) The climate lobby: A sectoral analysis of lobbying spending on climate change in the USA, 2000 to 2016. *Climatic Change.* **149**(3), pp. 289–303.

Canadian Manufacturers and Exporters (2002) *Pain Without Gain: Canada and the Kyoto Accord.* Ottawa: Canadian Manufacturers and Exporters.

Carney, B. (2019) Alberta has spent $23 million calling BC an enemy of Canada. *The Tyee.* Available from: https://thetyee.ca/News/2019/01/15/Alberta-Spent-23-Million-BC-Enemy-Canada/ (accessed 29 April 2020).

Carroll, W.K. (2017) Canada's carbon-capital elite: A tangled web of corporate power. *Canadian Journal of Sociology.* **42**, pp. 225–60.

Carroll, W.K. (2020) Fossil capitalism, climate capitalism, energy democracy: The struggle for hegemony in an era of climate crisis. *Socialist Studies.* **14**(1), pp. 1–26.

Carroll, W.K. and Huijzer, M.J. (2018) *Who Owns Canada's Fossil-Fuel Sector? Mapping the Network of Ownership & Control.* Canadian Centre for Policy Alternatives.

Carroll, W.K., Graham, N., Lang, M., McCartney, K. and Yunker, Z. (2018) The corporate elite and the architecture of climate change denial: A network analysis of carbon capital's reach into civil society. *Canadian Review of Sociology.* **55**(3), pp. 425–50.

Cattaneo, C. (2015) Oilsands at the crossroads. *National Post.* 26 September, FP8.

Catton, W.R. and Dunlap, R.E. (1980) A new ecological paradigm for post-exuberant sociology. *American Behavioral Scientist.* **24**(1), pp. 15–47.

Chase, S. (2002) Ratifying Kyoto estimated to cost up to 450,000 jobs. *The Globe and Mail.* Available from: https://www.theglobeandmail.com/report-on-business/ratifying-kyoto-estimated-to-cost-up-to-450000-jobs/article18286832/ (accessed 29 April 2020).

Climate Action Tracker (n.d.) Canada. Available from: https://climateactiontracker.org/countries/canada/ (accessed 5 December 2018).

Coyne, T. (2015) How social media is changing the debate on energy infrastructure projects. *Todd Coyne.* Available from: https://toddcoyne.wordpress.com/2015/02/02/how-social-media-is-changing-the-debate-on-energy-infrastructure-projects/.

Daub, S., Blue, G., Rajewicz, L. and Yunker, Z. (2020) Episodes in the new climate denialism. In: Carroll, W.K. (ed.) *Regime of Obstruction: How Corporate Power Blocks Energy Democracy.* Edmonton, AB: Athabasca University Press, ch. 9.

Davidson, D. and Gismondi, M. (2011) *Challenging Legitimacy at the Precipice of Energy Calamity.* New York, NY: Springer Science and Business Media.

Derber, C. (2010) *Greed to Green: Solving Climate Change and Remaking the Economy.* Boulder, CO: Paradigm Publishers.

Domhoff, G.W. (ed.) (1980) *Power Structure Research.* Beverly Hills, CA: Sage Publications.

Domhoff, G.W., Campbell, J.L., Cox, R.W., Lachmann, R.W., Lo, C.Y.H., Mintz, B., Peschek, J.G. et al. (2017) *Studying the Power Elite: Fifty Years of Who Rules America?* New York, NY: Routledge.

Dunlap, R.E. and McCright, A.M. (2010) Climate change denial: Sources, actors and strategies. In: Lever-Tracey, C. (ed.) *Routledge Handbook of Climate Change and Society.* Abingdon: Routledge, pp. 240–59.

Dunlap, R.E. and McCright, A.M. (2015) Challenging climate change: The denial countermovement. In: Brulle, R. and Dunlap, R.E. (eds) *Climate Change and Society: Sociological Perspectives.* New York, NY: Oxford University Press, pp. 300–332.

Eaton, E.M. and Day, N.A. (2019) Petro-pedagogy: Fossil fuel interests and the obstruction of climate justice in public education. *Environmental Education Research.* **26**(4), pp. 457–73. Available from DOI: 10.1080/13504622.2019.1650164.

Fast, T. (2014) Stapled to the front door: Neoliberal extractivism in Canada. *Studies in Political Economy*. **94**(1), pp. 31–60.
Flavelle, C. (2020) Global financial giants swear off funding an especially dirty fuel. *The New York Times*. Available from: https://www.nytimes.com/2020/02/12/climate/blackrock-oil-sands-alberta-financing.html (accessed 29 April 2020).
Foster, J.B. (2012) The planetary rift and the new human exemptionalism: A political-economic critique of ecological modernization theory. *Organization and Environment*. **25**(3), pp. 211–37. Available from DOI: 10.1177/1086026612459964.
Graham, N. (2017) State-capital nexus and the making of BC shale and liquefied natural gas. *BC Studies*. (194), pp. 11–38.
Graham, N., Daub, S. and Carroll, B. (2017) Mapping political influence: Political donations and lobbying by the fossil fuel industry in BC. *Corporate Mapping Project*. Available from: http://www.corporatemapping.ca/bc-influence/ (accessed 29 April 2020).
Graham, N., Carroll, B. and Chen, D. (2020) Carbon capital's political reach: A network analysis of federal lobbying by the fossil fuel industry from Harper to Trudeau. *Canadian Political Science Review*. **14**(1), pp 1–31.
Gunster, S. (2019) Extractive populism and the future of Canada. *The Monitor*. **26**(2), pp. 13–15. Available from: https://www.policyalternatives.ca/publications/monitor/extractive-populism-and-future-canada.
Gunster, S. and Saurette, P. (2014) Storylines in the sands: News, narrative and ideology in the *Calgary Herald*. *Canadian Journal of Communication*. **39**(4), pp. 333–59.
Gunster, S., Neubauer, R., Bermingham, J. and Massie, A. (2020) 'Our oil': Extractive populism in Canadian social media. In: Carroll, W.K. (ed.) *Regime of Obstruction: How Corporate Power Blocks Energy Democracy*. Edmonton AB: Athabasca University Press, pp. 197–224.
Gutstein, D. (2014) *Harperism: How Stephen Harper and His Think Tank Colleagues Have Transformed Canada*. Toronto: James Lorimer and Company.
Gutstein, D. (2018) *The Big Stall: How Big Oil and Think Tanks are Blocking Action on Climate Change in Canada*. Toronto: James Lorimer and Company.
Hochschild, A. (2017) *Strangers in Their Own Land: Anger and Mourning on the American Right*. New York, NY: The New Press.
Holden, E. (2020) Climate science deniers at forefront of downplaying coronavirus pandemic. *The Guardian*. Available from: https://www.theguardian.com/world/2020/apr/25/climate-science-deniers-downplaying-coronavirus-pandemic/.
Huber, M. (2012) Refined politics: Petroleum products, neoliberalism, and the ecology of the entrepreneurial life. *Journal of American Studies*. **46**(2), pp. 295–312.
Hussey, I. (2020) *The Future of Alberta's Oil Sands Industry: More Production, Less Capital, Fewer Jobs*. Edmonton: Parkland Institute. https://www.corporatemapping.ca/wp-content/uploads/2020/03/Future-of-Oil-Sands-FINAL.pdf.
Hussey, I. and Pineault, E. (2017) Restructuring in Alberta's oil industry. *Corporate Mapping Project blog*. Available from: https://www.corporatemapping.ca/restructuring-in-albertas-oil-industry-internationals-pull-out-domestic-majors-double-down/ (accessed 29 April 2020).
Jacques, P.J. (2012) A general theory of climate denial. *Global Environmental Politics*. **12**(2), pp. 9–17. Available from DOI: 10.1162/GLEP_a_00105.
Jacques, P.J., Dunlap, R.E. and Freeman, M. (2008) The organisation of denial: Conservative think tanks and environmental scepticism. *Environmental Politics*. **17**(3), pp. 349–85. Available from DOI: 10.1080/09644010802055576.
Klein, S. (2020) *A Good War: Mobilizing Canada for the Climate Emergency*. Toronto: Lorimer (in press).
Klein, S. and Daub, S. (2016) The new climate denialism: Time for an intervention. Available from: https://www.corporatemapping.ca/the-new-climate-denialism-time-for-an-intervention/ (accessed 29 April 2020).
Laycock, D. (2001) *The New Right and Democracy in Canada: Understanding Reform and the Canadian Alliance*. Oxford: Oxford University Press.

Lee, M. (2015) Real test of Paris climate agreement will be how markets and regulators react. *Policy Note blog.* https://www.policynote.ca/real-test-of-paris-climate-agreement-will-be-how-markets-and-regulators-react/ (accessed 29 April 2020).

Lee, M. (2017) *Extracted Carbon: Re-examining Canada's Contribution to Climate Change through Fossil Fuel Exports.* Ottawa: Canadian Centre for Policy Alternatives. Available from: https://www.policyalternatives.ca/publications/reports/extracted-carbon.

Levy, D.L. and Spicer, A. (2013) Contested imaginaries and the cultural political economy of climate change. *Organization.* **20**(5), pp. 659–78. Available from DOI: 10.1177/1350508413489816.

Macdonald, D. (2007) *Business and Environmental Politics in Canada.* Toronto: University of Toronto Press.

Malm, A. (2016) *Fossil Capital: The Rise of Steam Power and the Roots of Global Warming.* London, UK and Brooklyn, NY, USA: Verso.

Marshall, D. (2002) *Making Kyoto Work: A Transition Strategy for Canadian Energy Workers.* Ottawa: Canadian Centre for Policy Alternatives. https://www.policyalternatives.ca/publications/reports/making-kyoto-work.

Marshall, D. (2020) We have the oil lobby's secret list of COVID demands – if approved, they would set environmental protection back decades. *Environmental Defence.* Available from: https://environmentaldefence.ca/2020/04/17/capp_covid_memo/ (accessed 4 May 2020).

Mayer, J. (2016) *Dark Money: The Hidden History of the Billionaires Behind the Rise of the Radical Right.* New York, NY: Penguin Random House.

McCright, A.M. and Dunlap, R.E. (2003) Defeating Kyoto: The conservative movement's impact on U.S. climate change policy. *Social Problems.* **50**(3), pp. 348–73. Available from DOI: 10.1525/sp.2003.50.3.348.

Methmann, C.P. (2010) 'Climate Protection' as empty signifier: A discourse theoretical perspective on climate mainstreaming in world politics. *Millennium.* **39**(2), pp. 345–72. Available from DOI: 10.1177/0305829810383606.

Neubauer, R. and Gunster, S. (2019) Enemies at the Gateway: Regional populist discourse and the fight against oil pipelines on Canada's west coast. *Frontiers in Communication.* **4**, pp. 1–14.

Norgaard, K.M. (2006) 'We don't really want to know': Environmental justice and socially organized denial of global warming in Norway. *Organization and Environment.* **19**(3), pp. 347–70.

Norgaard, K.M. (2011) *Living in Denial: Climate Change, Emotions, and Everyday Life.* Cambridge, MA: MIT Press.

Oliver, J. (2012) An open letter from Natural Resources Minister Joe Oliver. *The Globe and Mail.* Available from: https://www.theglobeandmail.com/news/politics/an-open-letter-from-natural-resources-minister-joe-oliver/article4085663/ (accessed 29 April 2020).

O'Neill, J. (2019) The campaign to silence Tzeporah Berman. *National Observer.* Available from: https://www.nationalobserver.com/2019/08/06/news/campaign-silence-tzeporah-berman (accessed 29 April 2020).

Oreskes, N. and Conway, E.M. (2011) *Merchants of Doubt: How a Handful of Scientists Obscured the Truth on Issues from Tobacco Smoke to Global Warming.* New York, NY: Bloomsbury.

Paul, F.C. (2018) Deep entanglements: History, space and (energy) struggle in the German Energiewende. *Geoforum.* **91**, pp. 1–9.

Rainforest Action Network (2020) *Banking on Climate Change: Fossil Fuel Finance Report 2020.* Available from: https://www.ran.org/publications/banking-on-climate-change-fossil-fuel-finance-report-2020 (accessed 29 April 2020).

Sapinski, J-P. (2016) Constructing climate capitalism: Corporate power and the global climate policy-planning network. *Global Networks.* **16**, pp. 89–111.

Sapinski, J-P. and Carroll, W.K. (2018) Interlocking directorates and corporate networks. In: Nölke, A. and May, C. (eds) *Handbook of the International Political Economy of the Corporation.* Cheltenham, UK and Northampton, MA, USA: Edward Elgar Publishing, pp. 45–60. Available from DOI: 10.4337/9781785362538.00009.

Simpson, J., Jaccard, M.K. and Rivers, N. (2008) *Hot Air: Meeting Canada's Climate Change Challenge.* Toronto: Emblem.

Stanfield, C. (2015) From passive endorsement to active engagement. *Context: CAPP's member magazine.* **3**(2), pp. 8–11.

Steward, G. (2017) *Betting on Bitumen: Alberta's Energy Policies from Lougheed to Klein*. Vancouver: Canadian Centre for Policy Alternatives.

Taber, J. (2006) PM brands Canada an 'Energy Superpower'. *The Globe and Mail*. Available from https://www.theglobeandmail.com/news/world/pm-brands-canada-an-energy-superpower/article1105875/ (accessed 29 April 2020).

Taft, K. (2017) *Oil's Deep State: How the Petroleum Industry Undermines Democracy and Stops Action on Global Warming*. Toronto: James Lorimer and Company.

Turner, C. (2012) The oil sands PR war. *Marketing Magazine*. Available from: http://marketingmag.ca/advertising/the-oil-sands-pr-war-58235/ (accessed 29 April 2020).

Turner, C. (2013) *The War on Science: Muzzled Scientists and Wilful Blindness in Stephen Harper's Canada*. Vancouver: Greystone Books.

UNEP (United Nations Environment Programme) (2019) *Emissions Gap Report 2019*. Nairobi: United Nations Environment Programme. https://wedocs.unep.org/bitstream/handle/20.500.11822/30797/EGR2019.pdf?sequence=1&isAllowed=y (accessed 29 April 2020).

Urquhart, I. (2018) *Costly Fix: Power, Politics, and Nature in the Tar Sands*. Toronto: University of Toronto Press.

Walker, E. (2014) *Grassroots for Hire: Public Affairs Consultants in American Democracy*. Cambridge: Cambridge University Press.

Wood, T. (2018) Energy's citizens: The making of a Canadian petro-public. *Canadian Journal of Communication*. **43**(1), pp. 75–92.

Young, N. and Coutinho, A. (2013) Government, anti-reflexivity, and the construction of public ignorance about climate change: Australia and Canada compared. *Global Environmental Politics*. **13**(2), pp. 89–108.

12. The Koch Brothers and the climate change denial social movement

Patrick Doreian and Andrej Mrvar

INTRODUCTION

This chapter is located in the overlap of multiple intellectual realms. They include: issues related to environmental concerns, especially climate change; a concerted effort to deny the reality of this phenomenon by the Koch Brothers (KB) and their well-organized network of organizations. They have an active agenda for denigrating the widely accepted scientific evidence regarding climate change. This link was made obvious by Leonard (2019a), who recognized that David Koch, now deceased, was the ultimate climate change denier. In one sense, he was prescient, as he recognized that dealing with environmental issues threatened the profitability of Koch Industries, the primary source of the funding for the KB network of libertarian and reactionary allies.

The research project within which this document was created found its inspiration in two books. *Democracy in Chains* (MacLean, 2017) provided a detailed history of the intellectual foundations of an approach dovetailing with the libertarian views of the KBs. This history has a long pedigree going back to the views of John Calhoun, expressed two decades after the founding of the US. The economist James Buchanan, following this tradition, developed a theoretical approach called 'public choice theory'. It focused on how incentives affect governmental action. For his work, he was awarded a Nobel Prize in Economics, which, as far as we can tell, was devoid of any genuine empirical data. Charles Koch found Buchanan's work most useful for fulfilling his 'unrealized dream of liberty, of a capitalism all but free of governmental interference' (MacLean, 2017, p. xxiv). Buchanan spent a long time working at George Mason University (GMU), which has received a huge amount of money from the KBs (especially for 2005–2017). This includes its Foundation receiving close to $86 million, its Institute for Humane Studies receiving close to $35 million and the Mercatus Center receiving almost $9 million from the KBs (Greenpeace, 2014). The latter two units are very prominent in the KB network we have identified.

Dark Money (Mayer, 2017) lays out in great detail the ways in which billionaires, especially the KBs, drove the rise of the radical right in the US and its takeover of the GOP. This is not a new phenomenon. For four decades, the KBs have funded the development of a powerful political movement (Mayer, 2017, p. xviii) aimed at achieving their goal to operate freely without having to deal with intrusive governmental constraints. See also Skocpol and Hertel-Fernandez (2016).

Ours is not the first network study considering the KBs. Skocpol and Hertel-Fernandez (2016) constructed network data for organizations in the KB network and its influence on the GOP as it moved rapidly to the right, including total opposition to any policies attempting to address climate change. Here, we focus on identifying the structure and extent of the KB network. Skocpol and Hertel-Fernandez (2016, p. 4) reveal its 'massive scale, tight integration, ramified organizational reach, and close intertwining with the GOP at all levels'. The KB network identified below is much larger and, perhaps, far more integrated than their analysis suggests.[1] All of the organizations listed in their Appendix A are in the network considered below.

The rest of this chapter has four sections: the Koch brothers' network; climate change denial; the Koch Brothers and climate change denial; and a summary with conclusions.

THE KOCH BROTHERS NETWORK

Both *Democracy in Chains* and *Dark Money* provided lists of units including members of Koch Industries (KI) and their known allies, especially those funded by the KBs. A combined list of these units was assembled from these sources. For each one, its URL was located. All of these items were combined to form an initial list of URLs. The program VOSON, developed by Ackland (2018), is designed to, among other things, identify links between websites. The initial list of URLs was submitted[2] to VOSON to identify web links involving the units identified in *Democracy in Chains* and *Dark Money*. There were 176 such URLs[3] submitted to VOSON. The result of the search was a network with 17,212 units. All of the data analyses that follow were completed using Pajek (Batagelj and Mrvar, 1998).[4]

However, multiple streams of information types flow through the Internet to link URLs. Many of these streams were totally irrelevant for locating the units *truly belonging* to the KB network of units and their allies. These included sports outfits, many lists of the 'top 1000 URLs' (without a specification of the reason for inclusion), units concerned with the construction of methods for designing websites, units simply pointing to websites, again with no rationale for these inclusions, generic web search engines, online libraries (other than those for libertarian causes) and online dictionaries. All of these were removed. Also eliminated were units whose total number of attached links was less than two. The network is a directed network with ties going from one URL to another. The number of attached links for a URL includes those directed to it and those directed from it. The result was a primary network with 1081 units with 5629 ties between units. This is a large network, a reminder of the scope of the KB network of allies.

The websites for each of these units were visited repeatedly to extract textual material declaring their identity, goals and some of the actions taken by them. These were placed into large multiple background files, used to categorize the identified units in terms of their core interests and to extract keywords identifying them. For the first task, the following categories were created: (a) Koch Industries (KI) units; (b) KB allies or likely KB allies; (c) units that could be useful for the KBs, especially business-oriented units but not known as KB allies; (d) units opposed to KB or that were likely KB enemies, many of which were committed environmental groups; (e) units having interests seemingly inconsistent with KB interests; (f) national US news media units; (g) local or regional US news media units; (h) news media units in other countries; (i) all other non-US units; (j) seemingly neutral units but not media; (k) potentially irrelevant units (that may have remained despite the winnowing described above); and (l) US governmental units. The largest three categories are: KB allies (with 466 units); Koch opponents (163 of them) and 63 Koch Industry units, both production units and some of their foundations. Figure 12.1 shows the 'global' network where the vertices are the categories with the units within them placed together.[5]

236 *Handbook of anti-environmentalism*

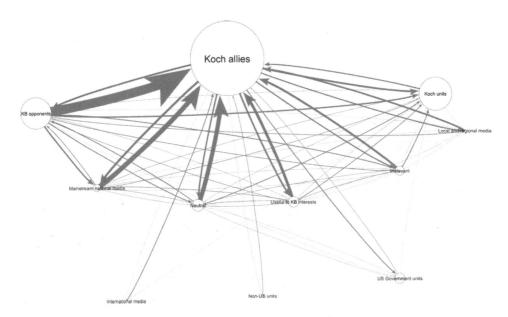

Notes: The size of the vertices reflects the number of units within them. The width of the arcs in the network indicates the number of directed ties between units in the vertices.

Figure 12.1   The global context for the Koch Brothers network

There are reciprocated ties between almost all pairs of vertices in the form of web links, but at quite different levels. The ties going to the Koch allies are larger than those from the Koch allies to the units in other categories. In particular, we note the thickest tie from the KB enemies to the Koch allies. This large number of ties directed at the Koch allies is not, in any way, surprising. The actions of the KBs and their allies are highly likely to provoke their enemies (see below) or trigger otherwise neutral units to become opponents. This is especially the case for climate change denial and blocking efforts to protect the environment.

The Koch allies are remarkably diverse. This is the 'genius' of this created network combining units having distinct ideological interests that, despite differences, are held together. They are willing to support other units with different interests including support of an extremely broad anti-governmental agenda. They include: foundations; financial institutions (including large banks and hedge funds); conservative and libertarian think tanks; research units; colleges and universities (many having departments and programs funded directly by the KBs); organizations engaged in issue advocacy (especially opposing environmental regulation); groups opposed to paying taxes; groups determined to shrink government; Christian organizations and media outlets dedicated to the broad KB cause. The ties from all three other media outlets are stronger towards the Koch allies than the reciprocated ties.

There are many methods for analyzing the overall large identified network from which Figure 12.1 was constructed. The first method we discuss here is the identification of hubs and authorities (Kleinberg, 1999). As a result of this iterative algorithm, each unit in the overall network receives scores measuring the extent to which it is a hub. Similarly, scores measure the extent to which units are authorities. Loosely put, hubs point to authorities and authorities are sources of influential information. While this may appear to be circular as an algorithm, it points to distinctive roles played in this network. We focus here on authorities as they are the primary sources for providing ideas, arguments and funds to other units in the KB network. This cannot be underestimated given the greater influence of the core organizations in the KB network for providing information and arguments to their allies.

The top authorities are: The Cato Institute; The Reason Foundation; The Heritage Foundation; The Foundation for Economic Freedom; The Independent Institute; The Heartland Institute; The Mercatus Center; The Foundation for Individual Rights in Education (FIRE). Most of these have been heavily funded by the Koch Brothers. The Cato Institute is a libertarian think tank headquartered in Washington, DC. It was founded in 1977 by the KBs and heavily funded, and extensively, through channels enabled by them. One of its prominent goals is the downsizing of the national government – if not its elimination. It is also involved in the climate change denial efforts. According to Mayer (2017, p. 106), Charles Koch turned his private foundation into the Cato Institute. It supports total economic freedom for the likes of the Koch brothers. The Reason Foundation[6] is another American libertarian think tank based in Los Angeles, California. It was founded in 1978 and is also funded by the KBs. It strongly supports outsourcing public services to private corporations as a part of a program advocating shrinking the national government (Maclean, 2017, p. 143). No doubt, another motivation is to create additional profit sources for private entities replacing governmental programs. We note that the former Republican administration drive to eliminate the Post Office to replace it with private carriers is consistent with this approach.

The Heritage Foundation, founded in 1973, is a conservative public policy think tank also based in Washington, DC. Its initial funding came from Joseph Coors, an extreme conservative. It promotes public policies based on the principles of free enterprise, limited government, individual freedom, traditional American values and a strong national defense. Some of its funding comes from Koch Family Foundations, along with many conservative donors including Richard Mellon Scaife and the Bradley Foundation, all of which are in the KB network identified by the VOSON web crawl. They were part of a first phase of a concerted effort to form a conservative movement (Skocpol and Hertel-Fernandez, 2016). For reasons of space, we cannot comment on all of the top authorities but, consistent with the topic of this chapter, we consider The Heartland Foundation, which is an American conservative and libertarian public policy think tank. It was founded in 1984 and is a part of the second wave of conservative mobilization (Skocpol and Hertel-Fernandez, 2016). It declares its mission is to discover, develop and promote free-market solutions to social and economic problems. While this sounds benign, the tip off regarding its deeper aims is that it has 'Freedom Rising' under its name. Some of its publications include: attacks on the idea of global warming, promotion of hydraulic fracturing and advocating for free-market environmentalism (in our view, an oxymoron). It is a prominent climate change denier, being especially vitriolic in condemning 'Scandinavian socialism', including all the remarkably constructive environmental policies of these Nordic countries.

Organizations can be characterized by their primary concerns. From the websites of the identified units in the KB network, their statements were used to discern, and code, their primary interests in keywords. The list of keywords that were extracted follows. At face value, many of them sound neutral, even admirable. Yet, many of them are loaded terms for the units in the network of the KB allies and serve as code for meanings other than those usually associated with them in more general contexts. We present them in batches. The first trio is: freedom, liberty and heritage. In this context, freedom appears to mean freedom only for corporate and other economic entities to do what they wish to do. A similar restricted meaning holds for their conception of liberty. MacLean (2017, p. xxviii) describes their conception of liberty as 'the insulation of private property rights from the reach of government'. Heritage appears to mean the heritage of a country dominated by economic interests, a sense of a former proud history and traditional 'family values'.

Another trio of keywords is privatization, free enterprise and free markets. All are critical for the KB and their allies. The second pair of notions is consistent with the central idea of economic actors having the final say as to what occurs in the US. Yet 'free markets', in the classical sense, is not their real objective because of the many efforts made by corporate units to ensure that markets operate to support their dominant economic concerns. They do this through influencing Congress via lobbyists to change the economic rules to favor them. See, for example, Farrell (2016) and Skocpol and Hertel-Fernandez (2016).

The next trio of keywords addresses the core interests of this chapter: climate change, climate change denial and environmental regulation. In this context, Leonard (2019b, p. 553) has described one notable individual, Myron Ebell, a fellow at the Competitive Enterprise Institute (one of the top authorities listed above) and yet another unit funded by the KBs, who was a leading opponent of all regulations trying to reduce carbon emissions and promoted the notion of 'global warming alarmism' (see details of conservative against environmental policymaking in Layzer, 2012). Yet another trio of concerns, as reflected by keywords, is: conservative (promoted), liberal (attacked) and progressive (also attacked). Another set of keywords about the concerns of organizations in this network is: voting, the rule of law and strong defense. Being concerned about all of these, at face value, is valuable and important. But initial perceptions are superficial. On voting, one unit in the KB network is an organization called *True the Vote*. Initially, its website appears to be supportive of inclusiveness, but upon further investigation, their primary concern seemed to be associated with fostering voter suppression, especially regarding voters thought to be more likely to support Democratic candidates. There are other units engaging in similar undertakings including the so-called *Voter Integrity Project*, another misleadingly labeled organization – a hallmark characteristic of units on the right and far right.[7]

A further set of keywords includes taxes, grassroots, gun rights, women's health, American, libertarian and Tea Party. Does anything hold these together? On taxes, corporations avoid paying taxes through multiple devices including offshore accounts.[8] The grassroots notion, especially for the Tea Party, is a complete fiction as it was organized from above with considerable involvement of the KBs. This process, described by some critics using the label 'astroturfing', is a way for sponsors of messages and their organizations to mask their identities while making it seem as though they are mobilized by grassroots participants. Organizations advocating Second Amendment gun rights are prominent in the KB network.

The final set of keywords includes small government (no surprise), limiting government (equally consistent with the notions described above), family values and Christian – both of which are fully consistent with a view stressing a traditional white parochial viewpoint. On reviewing these keywords and the statement on the websites of the KB allies, it is hard to reach any other conclusion about the fundamental aims of the KBs, than that their aims are to: (a) weaken or destroy US democratic institutions, especially the national government (as MacLean (2017, p. xx) puts it, they want to save capitalism from democracy; consistent with this view, Mayer (2017, p. xviii) notes they vilify the very idea of government); (b) obtain complete freedom from governmental regulation, especially regarding having safe workplaces and limited environmental impacts; (c) organize the governing of the US to serve only their interests; and (d) create a network of allies to achieve these goals. For *all of these ambitions*, they have been very successful. This is taken up again in the final two sections.

Yet, there may be additional concerns spread across the KB allies. They include: (a) blocking restrictions on political spending of the rich and corporations; (b) suppressing voting rights (noted above) for people of color, students, the elderly and, perhaps, those having medical problems, if they are thought to oppose Republican policies – plus gerrymandering to favor GOP candidates; (c) obstructing the rights of consumers and workers to sue corporations and force them into arbitration 'courts' fully controlled by the corporations;[9] (d) destroy or weaken unions to depress wages, retirement benefits and health benefits; (e) destroy the social safety net, especially Social Security, worker compensation for injury or health consequences for working in unsafe environments, and job loss benefits; (f) preventing local authorities from passing laws to protect themselves from corporate abuse, especially regarding the environment, a policy promoted by the American Legislative Exchange Council (ALEC) a core ally of the KBs, in our network; and (g) fill Federal courts with ultra-conservative justices.[10]

CLIMATE CHANGE DENIAL

As so much has been written on this topic, we restrict our attention to items informing an assessment of the role of the KBs in sponsoring a significant part of the climate change denial social movement. This includes the *many* relevant actors appearing in the network we have identified. McCright and Dunlap (2003, p. 348) noted the development of a robust consensus about the reality and seriousness of climate change. Their sources include The National Research Council (2001) and the Intergovernmental Panel on Climate Change (2001). The latter is an intergovernmental body of the United Nations. It is dedicated to providing the world with objective, scientific information relevant for understanding the scientific basis of the risks associated with human-induced climate change and all of the human impacts and risks, and possible response options.[11] Subsequent reports from this body present an even bleaker picture regarding climate change and its damaging effects.

McCright and Dunlap (2003, p. 352), following many earlier researchers who informed their document, accepted these researchers' definition of a conservative movement as an 'elite-driven network of private foundations, policy-planning think tanks, and individual intellectuals and activists that directly or indirectly attempt to advance social traditionalism and economic libertarianism on a national level.' They constructed a purposive sample of 14 think tanks. Unsurprisingly, all are in the large KB network we have identified. They document, among other things, a decline in the number of scientists being invited to testify before Congressional committees, fully consistent with the arguments advanced by Skocpol and Hertel-Fernandez (2016). In doing so, they outline the mechanisms for promoted disinformation in these hearings regarding climate change. This attack on scientific evidence regarding the environment had been reinforced by the Trump administration's consistent and systematic attack on science.

Elsasser and Dunlap (2013) push these arguments further in using the 'denial machine' (Begley, 2007), an apt expression for the efforts driven by the KBs and other very wealthy individuals. See also Bardon (2019) for a more extended analysis. Elsasser and Dunlap (2013,

p. 755) write about the multiple challenges to the evidence supporting global warming. The intent of these actions is to attack climate science and, more increasingly, attack scientists, to spread doubt and uncertainty about the reality of humans affecting climate change. The fundamental goal has been to question the need for any governmental policy making regarding the environment.[12] See also Supran and Oreskes (2017) and Dunlap and McCright (2015).

The units identified in the KB network include many in other countries, including some in Canada. Carroll et al. (2018, p. 426) note that corporate interests are designed to protect their investments and profit streams. This is something the KBs recognized a long time ago, as noted by Mayer (2017) and MacLean (2017). The work of Brownlee (2005) reinforces this idea more generally. The mechanisms supporting ultimate corporate control are not confined to the US. The KBs and their allies have an extended international reach, something that is more worrisome. The role of extractive companies in promoting climate change denial cannot be understated. Brulle et al. (2018) examined the spending by oil and gas companies by looking at advertising expenditures of five major oil and gasoline companies. They are ExxonMobil, Shell, ChevronTexaco, British Petroleum, and ConocoPhillips. The first two are in the network we have identified. Brulle et al. (2018) document the rise through most of their time period of such corporate advertising. Carroll et al. (2018) document the link between corporates' elites and climate change denial with a focus on the carbon-capital sector for Canada. Farrell (2016) does the same for the US.

Stepping back slightly, we look at two further sources. Mayer (2017, p. 89) documented the role of a confidential memorandum, sent to the US Chamber of Commerce (in our network, along with many regional and local chambers of commerce), entitled 'Attack on the American Free Enterprise System'. Its author was Lewis Powell, a future conservative Supreme Court Justice. He laid out a battle plan to mobilize organizations to act politically in reaction to this 'attack'. Mayer documents how many foundations funded conservative causes in response and how many other organizations rallied to this call. They became part of an organized conservative network of funders and donors to defend and promote the free enterprise system, but only as they envisioned this concept.

The second source is Oreskes and Conway (2010) who provide an extended examination of corporate entities seeking to obstruct challenges to their behavior, many of which concern the environment. Their detailed studies include the tobacco industry responding to the link between smoking and cancer, the corporate reactions to acid rain damaging ecosystems, the discovery that corporate products (halocarbon refrigerants, solvents, propellants and chlorofluorocarbons, all known as ozone-depleting substances) were damaging the ozone layer in the southern hemisphere and triggering global warming. Oreskes and Conway (2010) document how a key part of the reaction to the knowledge of these connections by scientists was to cast doubt on both scientific findings and the scientists producing them. The title of their book, *Merchants of Doubt*, makes clear what is involved – deception. This is fully consistent with the analysis of Maclean (2017, p. 177) who recognized that 'the game plan' of the libertarians and other conservatives was 'to stop being honest'. This is a trademark characteristic of the KBs and their allies. The funding machine created in response to the Powell memo for conservative causes included the idea of attacking science to defend corporate conduct. It is no surprise that this funding also supports the climate change deniers.

KOCH BROTHERS AND CLIMATE CHANGE DENIAL

The driving force for the KBs opposing all efforts to deal with climate change is clear. Their core business operations involve the processing and selling of fossil fuels. According to Leonard (2019b, pp. 187–90), Koch Industries has been repeatedly fined for environmental violations, repeatedly racking up the 'highest fines' (for increasingly worse detected offenses) that they had to pay. But these fines had minimal impact on the profitability of the places triggering the fines. While being slaps on the wrist, they incurred KB ire. As Leonard (2019b, p. 190) puts it, KI was 'one of the largest, most flagrant violators of environmental laws in the United States during the 1990s.' It did not end there. Mayer (2017, p. 338) reports that in 2012, KI was the number one producer of toxic waste. She reports (2017, p. 155), quoting a representative of The Center for Public Integrity (a unit in the set of KB enemies identified in our network), that the KI's 'pattern of pollution was striking not just for its *egregiousness* but also for its *willfulness*' [emphasis added].

Given the arguments above about the role of oil and gas corporations funding opposition to even having discussions about climate change, we identified the oil, gas and coal organizations and formed a larger network including these units. Many belong to Koch Industries as production facilities and refineries. Also included are oil trade associations and journals supporting the oil and gas industries. We formed this network of 43 units. Then, we formed another network using two steps. The first was done by moving out one step to get the units they cite in the larger network. The second was to include units that were cited in the larger network. The resulting network has 305 units, slightly less than a third of the total number of units.[13] Even so, this is sizeable and makes clear the extent to which the KBs are involved in climate change denial.

The result is shown in Figure 12.2 to reveal the size of just one part of the KB network of allies. We draw the attention of readers to the number of links shown in Figure 12.2.[14] They are many in number. We know that this is a large network. Indeed, this is one of the major points for this chapter. While we know that anti-environmentalism, in all of its forms, can be discussed quite fruitfully in terms of hermetically sealed environmental concepts, devoid of a network context, it is *critically important* to have a deeper understanding and knowledge of the mobilized set of organizations seeking to thwart efforts to protect the environment. Figure 12.2 is presented in the form of two circles of units. The inner circle contains the 43 'oil and gas' units. The outer circle has all of the organizations linked to them in the KB network. Many of the latter are actively involved in climate change denial. Together, they form a formidable force for promoting doubt about the reality of climate change, the role of humans in creating this and all efforts to deal with a problem that is the greatest threat to this planet.

We also extracted two further networks. One is composed of the climate change deniers, the designation for which came from a close reading of their manifestos and mission statements. This network has some isolates, suggesting that they operated alone. When these isolates were removed, the network had 35 units. We did the same for the second network of units supporting climate science and opposing units denying climate change. There were isolates in this network also. When they were removed, 19 opponents remained.[15] We present only one figure in the form of the network formed by 54 units of deniers and their opponents.

The results are shown in Figure 12.3, where the climate change deniers (black circles) are shown on the left and their opponents (gray circles) are on the right.[16] The units with the highest number of ties, indicating greater involvement in climate change denial action, are the

242 *Handbook of anti-environmentalism*

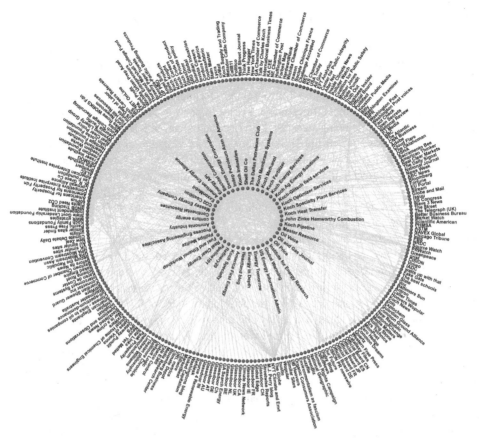

Notes: The extractive units (oil, goal, coal and processing) are in the inner circle. The units linked to them are in the outer circle.

Figure 12.2   *A network involving the extractive industry units and those linked with them*

Heartland Institute and the Cato Institute (both were described above). Another three units are the Competitive Enterprise Institute (one of the top authorities listed above), the Independent Institute and a blog, Watts Up With That? The prominent presence of the last item is a surprise. On the side of the opponents to the climate change deniers, the most prominent units are DESMOG and Polluter Watch (a part of Greenpeace, also in our identified network). Given that the network we identified was the KB network, there may be a bias in this search in that units are identified in relation to the KB network.[17] But the opponents of the climate change deniers appear to have a weakened position. When we drew the network of units identified as opponents to the KBs, we saw that it was fragmented, with many isolates. It appears that units opposing the KBs, and on the left more generally, focus on specific interests of concern to them without seeing the need to collaborate with others. In contrast, the KB network is far more organized in ways incorporating multiple interests in the same network.

The climate change deniers are located mainly on the left of Figure 12.3, while their opponents are located primarily on the right. Of course there are exceptions. For the opponents to the KB allies, DeSmog occupied a prominent place. While we suspect that the number of climate change deniers is far greater than Figure 12.3 suggests, we offer it as an initial portrait.

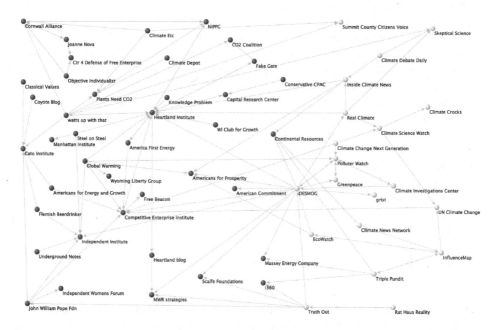

Figure 12.3   The network of climate change deniers and their opponents in the KB network

SUMMARY AND CONCLUSIONS

Dunlap et al. (2016, p. 4) stated that the George W. Bush Administration was widely viewed as the most anti-environmental administration in our nation's history. This assessment is based on two sets of actions: 'denying the significance of human-caused climate change and blocking federal action to deal with it.' What this Bush administration did *utterly pales* in comparison with the actions of the Trump regime and the current GOP. The early career of Vice-President Mike Pence was funded by David Koch before he became Trump's running mate (Mayer, 2017, p. xv). He was an early signatory for 'The Carbon Pledge' introduced by the KB-funded Americans for Prosperity to block 'cap-and-trade efforts'. Also, Mike Pompeo, former Secretary of State, was the Republican congressman who received the most campaign funds from the KBs of all in Congress (Mayer, 2017, p. xv). Both men have long associations with the KBs, fully supporting their political ambitions.

Krugman's (2019) scathing *NYT* op-ed regarding the current GOP called it 'the party that ruined the planet'. He deems their opposition to anything regarding climate change as so extreme that it is 'the world's only major climate-denialist party'. Part of this includes denying the value of science when it does not support their beliefs and policies. He adds that the GOP harasses scientists and attempts to criminalize the conduct of science (see above).[18] This resonates with the treatment of a climate scientist, Michael Mann, who was attacked mercilessly for his work (see Oreskes and Conway (2010, p. 264) and Mayer (2017, p. 245)). As noted above, the fossil fuels industry pours money into funding climate change denial, with the KBs being prominent. Confirming this, Krugman notes that Republicans in the current cycle (2019–2020) received 97 percent of political contributions from the coal industry. Also coming to them was 88 percent of the contributions from oil and gas outfits.

Dunlap et al. (2016, p. 6) and Skocpol and Hertel-Fernandez (2016) document the rightwards movement of the GOP over many years. Mayer (2017, p. 304) stated that following *Citizens United*, a decision rendered by the Supreme Court in 2010, one that opened the floodgates for covert corporate funding of elections, the Kochtopus sprouted a second set of tentacles.[19] But she states that it gave impetus to the KB 'ideological production line', whose extensive scope has been extended further, as documented by the large network of KB allies we have identified. Together, they form a most formidable *network* of organizations supporting an extremist agenda on multiple fronts, including climate change denial, along with hostility towards all efforts to protect the environment. Under the Trump administration, it would have been better to call the Environmental Protection Agency the Environmental Destruction Agency. The Koch Brothers were highly instrumental in affecting this anti-environmental change.

We conclude with an earnest plea, one triggered by the formation of the KB network of allies. It is a fearful and most formidable enemy opposed to dealing with all environmental rescue efforts. By cobbling together an alliance covering multiple interests, they reveal what can be done in an extreme political context. If environmental groups do not form a similar broad alliance and continue, as they appear to do, to focus only on their own separate, but fully legitimate, concerns, they will be swept aside. Pro-environmental reform groups cannot afford to remain in their separate intellectual domains. Nor can they really ignore the brutal fact that there are other frameworks structuring intellectual and pragmatic discourse. Apparently, with far too few exceptions, those with genuine concerns for the environment do not think that the network formed by their opponents merit any attention. If so, their efforts are doomed. We write this while knowing that restricted intellectual frameworks are designed specifically to keep their adherents in a protected safe space where all other interest can be excluded. As a result, we are under no illusions that readers of this chapter will be responsive to these arguments. But if they are, we will treat this a modest success.

NOTES

1. When our research project was started, unfortunately we were unaware of this conference presentation.
2. The analysis was performed by Rob Ackland to generate a Pajek network file for us. We greatly appreciate his generosity in doing this.
3. This is slightly less than the number of URLs in the assembled list as some identified units were defunct at the time of our search and there were some whose URLs could not be located. Also, some required visitors to log in before getting access. However, reading much of the bile in many websites, we opted not to do this.
4. Digital versions of all of the figures presented in this chapter can be downloaded in a zip file from: http://mrvar.fdv.uni-lj.si/SVG/ClimateChanges/ClimateChanges.zip.
5. A digital version of Figure 12.1 can be viewed at: http://mrvar.fdv.uni-lj.si/SVG/ClimateChanges/Figure1.svg.
6. Structurally, it is rather unique. In addition to its top authority status, it is also a prominent hub. This makes it particularly important for the KB network of allies as it both generates information and points to other units providing information.

7. Some of the units have names that are odd. One is the *Independent Women's Forum*, an outfit with many male members, most of whom head Second Amendment gun rights organizations. Another is *Independent Women's Voices*, run by a male at the time of our search! We suspect that the notion of 'independent women' is yet another fiction.
8. Not unrelated to this is FedEx paying no taxes due to the Trump Tax Cut of 2017.
9. This is consistent with the fierce opposition to the creation of the Bureau of Consumer Protection and subsequent Republican attempts to weaken it.
10. This includes the effort of the Senate leader, Mitch McConnell to appoint Justin Walker to the second most important US Appeal Court, based solely on his being a McConnell protégé and extremely conservative. The American Bar Association has declared Walker to be unqualified.
11. This organization has changed the format of its website. At the time of our data collection, one of the climate change denying allies of the KBs had a web format exactly imitating the one for the IPCC to provide allegedly independent 'information' about the science of climate change. It was devoted to attacking the notion and relevance of climate change. It calls itself the Nongovernmental International Panel on Climate Change (NIPCC).
12. Their data source was Townhall, another unit identified in our large network, one that is fully among the Koch allies. The authors report: 'of the 203 columns produced by the 80 different conservatives … *all of them were critical of climate change and/or science.*'
13. When we moved two steps out and two steps in, the result was a network with 949 units, almost all of the identified network. However, such a large network cannot be drawn in a clear fashion.
14. A digital version of Figure 12.2 can be viewed at: http://mrvar.fdv.uni-lj.si/SVG/ClimateChanges/Figure2.svg.
15. When the network of units denying climate change was expanded to include their neighbors, the resulting network had 470 units. When the same was done for their opponents, the resulting network had 195 units.
16. A digital version of Figure 12.3 can be viewed at: http://mrvar.fdv.uni-lj.si/SVG/ClimateChanges/Figure3.svg.
17. A separate search based on the units supporting climate change and opposing climate change deniers may lead to identifying more relevant units.
18. Skocpol and Hertel-Fernandez (2016, p. 1) are clear that this contempt also extends to the social sciences.
19. Since then, we wonder if it has sprouted four more sets of tentacles.

REFERENCES

Ackland, R. (2018) Virtual Observatory for the Study of Online Networks (VOSON) software for collecting and analysing online networks (2004–2018). Available from: https://researchers.anu.edu.au/publications/140076.

Bardon, A. (2019) *The Truth About Denial: Bias and Self-Deception in Science, Politics, and Religion.* Oxford: Oxford University Press.

Batagelj, V. and Mrvar, A. (1998) Pajek – A program for large network analysis. *Connections.* **21**(2), pp. 47–57.

Begley, S. (2007) The truth about denial. *Newsweek.* *150*, 13 August, pp. 20–29.

Brownlee, J. (2005) *Ruling Canada: Corporate Cohesion and Democracy.* Halifax: Fernwood.

Brulle, R.J., Aronczyk, M. and Carmichael, J. (2018) Corporate promotion and climate change: An analysis of key variables affecting advertising spending by major oil companies, 1986–2015. **159**, 87–101. Available from DOI: 10.1007/s10584-019-02582-8.

Carroll, W., Graham, N., Lang, M.K. and Yunker, Z. (2018) The corporate elite and the architecture of climate change denial: A network analysis of carbon capital's reach into civil society. *Canadian Review of Sociology.* **55**(3), pp. 425–50.

Dunlap, R.E. and McCright, A.M. (2015) Challenging climate change: The denial countermovement. In R.E. Dunlap and R.J. Brulle (eds) *Climate Change and Society: Sociological Perspectives.* New York, NY: Oxford University Press.

Dunlap, R.E., McCright, A.M. and Yorosh, J.H. (2016) The political divide on climate change: Partisan polarization widens in the U.S. *Environment*. **58**(5), pp. 4–23.

Elsasser, S.W. and Dunlap, R.E. (2013) Leading voices in the denier choir: Conservative columnist's dismissal of global warming and denigration of climate science. *American Behavioral Scientist*. **57**(6), pp. 754–76.

Farrell, J. (2016) Corporate funding and ideological polarization about climate change. *Proceedings of the National Academy of Science*. **113**(1), pp. 92–7.

Greenpeace (2014) Koch pollution on campus: Academic freedom under assault from Charles Koch's $50 million campaign to infiltrate higher education. *Greenpeace*. Available from: https://www.greenpeace.org/usa/global-warming/climate-deniers/koch-pollution-on-campus/.

Intergovernmental Panel on Climate Change (2001) *IPCC Third Assessment Report: Contributions of IPCC Working Groups*. Geneva: IPCC.

Kleinberg, J.M. (1999) Authoritative sources in a hyperlinked environment. *Journal of the ACM (JACM)* **46**(5), pp. 604–32.

Krugman, P. (2019) The party that ruined the planet: Republican climate change denial is even scarier than Trumpism. *The New York Times*. Available from: https://www.nytimes.com/2019/12/12/opinion/climate-change-republicans.html.

Layzer, J.A. (2012) *Open for Business: Conservatives' Opposition to Environmental Regulation*. Cambridge, MA: MIT Press.

Leonard, C. (2019a) David Koch was the ultimate climate change denier. *The New York Times*. Available from: https://www.nytimes.com/2019/08/23/opinion/sunday/david-koch-climate-change.html.

Leonard, C. (2019b) *Kochland: The Secret History of Koch Industries and Corporate Power in America*. New York, NY: Simon & Schuster.

MacLean, N. (2017) *Democracy in Chains: The Deep History of the Radical Right's Stealth Plan for America*. New York, NY: Penguin Random House.

Mayer, J. (2017) *Dark Money: The Hidden History of the Billionaires Behind the Radical Right*. New York, NY: Anchor Books.

McCright, A.M. and Dunlap, R.E. (2003) Defeating Kyoto: The Conservative movement's impact on U.S. climate change policy. *Social Problems*. **50**(3), pp. 348–73.

National Research Council (2001) *Climate Change Science*. Washington, DC: National Academy Press.

Oreskes, N. and Conway, E.M. (2010) *Merchants of Doubt: How a Handful of Scientists Obscured the Truth on Issues from Tobacco Smoke to Global Warming*. New York, NY: Bloomsbury.

Skocpol, T. and Hertel-Fernandez, A. (2016) The Koch network and the rightward shift in U.S. politics. Paper presented at the Annual Meeting of the Midwest Political Science Association, 7–10 April, Chicago.

Supran, G. and Oreskes, N. (2017) Assessing ExxonMobil's climate change communications (1977–2014). *Environmental Research Letters*. **12**, pp. 1–18.

PART VI

EXTRACTIVE DEVELOPMENT AND ANTI-ENVIRONMENTALISM

13. Neoliberal governance of environmentalism in the post-9/11 security era: the case of pipeline debates in Canada

S. Harris Ali

The main focus of this chapter is to analyse the attempts of the Canadian state under the regime of the former conservative Prime Minister Stephen Harper (2006–2015) to publicly redefine environmental groups as threats to the economy and society. In this context, the following questions may be asked: What were the various discursive strategies adopted by the state to construct this alleged threat and then respond to it? How was the state able to suppress the environmental movement on this basis? In addressing these questions, I focus on how the government used discourses pertaining to national security as justification for an increased surveillance and scrutiny of environmental groups, and discuss the implications this had for environmental groups. As part of this examination, I will discuss how the organizational restructuring in the Canadian intelligence and security assemblage in the aftermath of the 9/11 terrorist attack helped establish the preconditions that facilitated the suppression of environmental groups. In the later sections I discuss the lasting impact of these discursive practices on subsequent governments. Consideration will be given to the environmental policies of current Prime Minister Justin Trudeau, the leader of the centrist Liberal Party elected in November 2015. Throughout the analysis I will also give some attention to the anti-environmentalist stance of US President Donald Trump to illustrate how the Harper Administration's discursive practices prefigured that of US President Trump. The US case will also be used as a point of comparison to the Canadian case to gain further insights. Finally, I will conclude by discussing the implications of this study for analyses that adopt perspectives dealing with moral panics and the suppression of social movements.

Empirical instances to illustrate the discussion will focus on the relationship between the state and the environmental movement in relation to debates pertaining to several high-profile transcontinental pipeline proposals. The data for this were drawn from previously published academic sources as well as investigative journalist accounts from Canadian online and print news sources such as: *The Vancouver Observer*, *The Toronto Star*, *The Globe and Mail*, and the Canadian Broadcasting Corporation (CBC), during the period of 2012 to 2015.

Prime Minister Harper's Conservative government argued that transcontinental pipelines were needed to accommodate a greater volume of oil expected to be extracted from the Alberta oil sands. For the analysis presented here, I will specifically consider the high-profile Keystone XL pipeline proposed by TransCanada Corporation, the Northern Gateway pipeline proposed by Enbridge Inc., as well as the expansion of the Trans Mountain pipeline (originally proposed by the private company Kinder-Morgan Energy Partners). The Keystone XL was to run from the province of Alberta southward through the continental US and terminating at the large-scale oil refineries in the Gulf of Mexico area of Louisiana. The other two pipelines were to run from Alberta westward to the Pacific coast of British Columbia where the oil could then be transported by tanker onward to the Far East.

I follow the orientation of Shriver et al. (2012) as laid out in their investigation of how political and economic elites are able to dominate the discursive arena through the deployment of oppositional frames. According to these authors, much of the current social movement literature focuses on the discursive tactics of activists to discredit the state, while neglecting the other side, namely how the state itself attempts to dominate the discursive field (i.e. to win the 'war of the minds'). In their analysis of the controversies surrounding the siting of a proposed highway bypass in the Czech Republic, Shriver et al. (2012) introduce the notion of 'discursive obstruction'. Discursive obstruction refers to the 'oppositional campaign waged by networks of elite state and private actors who use their power to sway public opinion against movements that challenge elite interests' (Shriver et al., 2012, p. 877). In essence, discursive obstruction involves the construction of a derogatory frame to sway public opinion, thus resulting in the stigmatization and vilification of environmental actors.

The concept of discursive obstruction focuses on the role of oppositional frames, and as such it is consonant with the notion of anti-reflexivity developed by Dunlap and his colleagues. Notably, both perspectives focus on the workings of state-supported counter-movements that attempt to ensure continued capitalist growth in the face of the perceived threat of environmentalism (Dunlap, 2009, 2013; Dunlap and Jacques, 2013; Dunlap and McCright, 2011; Elsasser and Dunlap, 2013; Jacques et al., 2008; McCright and Dunlap, 2003, 2010, 2011). The scope of the anti-reflexivity perspective tends however to be narrower in scope. It emphasizes how strategies that limit environmentalism target the legitimacy of the claims made by environmental scientists, particularly in relation to the existence of anthropogenic climate change and the policies derived thereof. Moreover, analysis that utilizes the anti-reflexivity perspective draws mostly from the US experience. Thus, the research of Dunlap and his colleagues reveals how a US-based coalition of conservative foundations, think-tanks, media outlets and public intellectuals that were financially supported by a number of extremely wealthy conservative families and their foundations and corporations, came to be an influential anti-reflexive force. This well-organized and well-resourced network effectively lobbied for the maintenance of a high-carbon lifestyle and way of life. Notably, a central strategy of the US anti-reflexivity movement was to introduce, develop and perpetuate a discursive frame based on the contrarian position of 'climate change denial' into the policy debate – a frame that today is prominent in President Trump's environmental and industrial policies but is less influential in the Canadian context.

The underlying principle or thrust of the US anti-reflexivity movement – the rejection or apathy towards the reality and seriousness of the ecological crisis – is perhaps to some extent found in Canada, but it also differs in some important respects. It was found that the vast majority (80 per cent) of US Republican Party supporters rejected climate change, while only a smaller majority (59 per cent) of the nearest Canadian political equivalent – supporters of the Conservative party – shared the same position (October 2013 Environics poll cited by Klein, 2014, p. 36). Thus, although the vast majority of Canadian conservatives rejected climate change, they did not do so to the same extent as their US counterparts. Further, 76 per cent of the left-learning New Democratic Party and 60 per cent of the centrist Liberal Party of Canada believed that climate change was real. In comparing the two countries overall, Young and Coutinho (2013) make the argument that the Canadian situation is different from that in the US on several important fronts. First, the types of groups involved in the US anti-reflexivity movement carry less public legitimacy in Canada. Second, surveys revealed that overall, Canadians in the general population were less polarized on climate change issues. This does not mean that anti-reflexivity is absent in Canada. Rather, it implies that anti-reflexivity may simply take on a different form. Thus, Young and Coutinho (2013) contend that the Harper government used tactics that were different from those of the US anti-reflexivity movement but were nevertheless anti-reflexive in orientation. Specifically, the Canadian government never denied the reality of climate change (as was the case in the US), yet did very little in terms of taking real action to address this issue – so the effect was the same in both cases, that is, no progress was made on addressing climate change. As an illustration we can see that the strategy was at play in the Harper government's adoption of intensity-based targets rather than volume-based targets. This government shift in the numerical targets for greenhouse gas emission reductions created the illusion of action or at least of commitment to future action but in essence not really doing anything. Compared to the explicit US denialist strategy, the Canadian government strategy was much less jarring. This tactic of accepting the reality of climate change, while at the same time not doing anything substantial about it, is referred to as the 'acceptance-rejection' strategy (Young and Coutinho, 2013).

I contend that the deployment of environmental policies based on 'acceptance-rejection' is not the whole story; rather the existence of 'acceptance-rejection' must more fully be understood as a result of broader discursive environment. This is because in order for such policies to be adopted, they must first be embedded in a receptive discursive arena, otherwise the acceptance-rejection policies will simply not be able to take hold. In this context, two important dimensions of the broader discursive arena may be considered: (1) the perceived need for increased surveillance and security (i.e. securitization) in a post-9/11 era, and (2) the tacit and unquestioned need to maintain an economy based on the principles of neoliberal market fundamentalism.

OIL SANDS EXTRACTION AND OIL TRANSPORT IN CANADA

At the discursive level, the debates about the proposed pipelines held the promise of serving as entry points for opening up a broader public discussion of future energy development and climate change within Canada and North America (Davidson and Gismondi, 2011). Recognizing the magnitude of the stakes involved in the decisions, numerous First Nations and environmental organizations have mobilized and become engaged in the pipeline debates in various ways, including the adoption of direct-action strategies. The federal government was of course also a main actor in this debate, particularly during the reign of the Conservative government. It was clear that this particular government was interested in foreclosing the potential for that discussion.

Elected in 2006, Prime Minister Stephen Harper of the Conservative Party sought to implement policies that would have natural resource and energy development serve as the chief driver of the national economy (MacNeil, 2014; Way, 2011). Oil sands development was an essential component of this strategy. As such, any activities geared to opposing oil sands development on the basis of environmental, social responsibility or ethical concerns were cavalierly dismissed by the government as obstacles to economic growth. Oil sands extraction is however a particularly carbon-intensive operation, and extraction operations contribute a significant proportion to the country's overall greenhouse gas emissions load (Partington,

2010). In light of this fact, it was evident that a particular focus of the government was to delimit the climate change knowledge base, including the suppression of data related to the monitoring of the environmental impacts of the oil sands extraction activities. For example, various research institutes and libraries housing scientific work on climate change and environmental problems were closed (Owens, 2014), while policies were introduced to make it difficult for government scientists to communicate directly with the media about their research on climate change (see below). Further still, with the passage of an omnibus bill in June 2012, legislative amendments effectively limited the ability of environmental groups to participate in policy-making processes. Thus, citizens and environmental activists interested in giving a written or oral testimony at the NEB hearings on the proposed pipelines were now required to complete a cumbersome ten-page detailed application form, including the submission of a resumé and references (Toledano, 2013).[1] This requirement effectively rendered the process so onerous that only paid lobbyists (such as those from the fossil fuel industry) would be able and willing to put in the time required to comply (Toledano, 2013). In addition to these types of policy actions aimed at directly challenging the ability of activists to mobilize and engage, demobilizing strategies were also indirectly adopted by influencing the discourses used in the public arena. The latter could be discerned in relation to the construction of frames that stigmatized and discredited environmental actors.

ADVERSARIAL FRAMING AS A STRATEGY OF DISCURSIVE OBSTRUCTION

Adversarial framing involves attempts by a social movement group (or in this case, the state) to adopt a broader rhetorical strategy designed to stigmatize those opposed to their claims, thereby undermining the credibility of their opponents (Knight and Greenberg, 2011). Examples of this are seen most vividly in the remarks of Joe Oliver, the Minister of Natural Resources under the Conservative government. In an open letter sent to major North American newspapers, Oliver notes:

> We know that increasing trade will help ensure the financial security of Canadians and their families. Unfortunately, there are environmental and other radical groups that would seek to block this opportunity to diversify our trade. Their goal is to stop any major project no matter what the cost to Canadian families in lost jobs and economic growth. No forest. No mining. No oil. No gas. No more hydro-electric dams ...
>
> These groups threaten to hijack our regulatory system to achieve their radical ideological agenda. They seek to exploit any loophole they can find, stacking public hearings with bodies to ensure that delays kill good projects. They use funding from foreign special interest groups to undermine Canada's national economic interest. They attract jet-setting celebrities with some of the largest personal carbon footprints in the world to lecture Canadians not to develop our natural resources. Finally, if all other avenues have failed, they will take a quintessential American approach: sue everyone and anyone to delay the project even further ...
>
> It [the regulatory system] is broken. It is time to look at it. It is an urgent matter of Canada's national interest. (Government of Canada, 2012)

The statements of the Minister clearly employ an adversarial framing with several insinuations made about the character and intent of all 'environmental and other radical groups'. These include the characterization of environmentalists as anti-trade and selfishly short-sighted and unreasonably obstructionist, and through the reference to 'jet-setting celebrities', and the insinuated allegation that through their association, environmentalists were also hypocrites. Moreover, an underlying theme that can be discerned in the text is the subtle insinuation that environmentalists are unpatriotic, and even anti-Canadian because they 'block the opportunity to diversify our trade ... no matter what the cost to Canadian families in lost jobs and economic growth.' This charge of anti-nationalism is further bolstered by the charge that environmentalists are engaging in the 'quintessential American approach' (i.e. suing). Since, a significant influence in Canadian identity formation is the notion of 'not being American' (Cohen, 2008), the allegation that environmental groups were adopting a 'quintessential American approach' was likely intended to provoke and direct the wrath of many nationalist Canadians against environmentalists.

If unfettered trade and economic growth are cornerstones of the neoliberal program then deregulation is a key facilitating factor in this strategy. Environmentalists, in 'hijacking' the regulatory system in the pursuit of their 'radical ideological agenda', therefore came to be defined as a significant obstacle to the pursuit and achievement of the neoliberal project. The neoliberal project is positively cast by the government as a nationalist enterprise that is not open to question (and hence hegemonic). Environmentalists, as irrational opponents to 'any major project', are in this sense deemed as threats not only to that neoliberal enterprise (which is assumed to be unquestionably necessary for economic survival), but to the Canadian nation-state as a whole. It is with the recognition of such reasoning that we can begin to discern and disentangle the tacit connections being made between two types of ideological framing – that is, one based on a neoliberal agenda and one based on a post-9/11 security frame. The use of such terms and phrases as: 'hijack', 'security', 'radical ideological agenda', 'foreign special interest groups to undermine Canada's national economic interest' and 'It is an urgent matter of Canada's national interests' all point towards the connotation of threat, and therefore the need to take increased national security measures against such threat. If in the aftermath of the 9/11 attacks, security threats were defined exclusively in terms of terrorism, today, more than a decade later, these security risks have become generalized to include many other types of threat that fall under the mantle of a post-9/11 security framing (Hooker and Ali, 2009), including evidently, the threat of environmental groups (McCarthy, 2012).

ENVIRONMENTALISTS AS SECURITY THREATS

The surveillance of environmental groups and other activist groups in North America has existed for some time. For instance, Boykoff (2007) has noted that in 1970 the Federal Bureau of Investigation (FBI) had sent agents to monitor the activities of people involved in the Earth Day rallies across forty cities. What then is new and different today? I would argue that there are two important differences. First, the type of specific rationale adopted by the state to justify their surveillance activities at different historical junctures may vary in accordance with the particular discursive arena present in that period. Thus, Monaghan and Walby observe that although the criminalization and harassment existed in the early period of the environmental movement, 'it was not until the 1990s that discourses of "terrorism" and "extremism" became popular frames for categorizing eco-activists' (2017, p. 55). Today, Canadian security agents regularly define environmentalists as domestic terrorist threats and potential sources of violence (Monaghan and Walby, 2017). Second, the nature of surveillance itself has changed quite profoundly, both from a technical and organizational point of view with advanced digitalization enabling not only more insidious ways of gathering intelligence data, but also for the sharing of such data in ways not possible previously, especially between intelligence and policing agencies – agencies previously prohibited from data sharing. Observers have noted that in the aftermath of terrorist events of 11 September 2001, there has been a dramatic increase in the intensity and centralization of surveillance in Western countries, with a concomitant increase in public funds for policing and security services (Lyon, 2001). Further, since that pivotal moment in history, much greater power is now delegated to police and intelligence services to appropriate data on everyday communications and transactions, phone calls, email and the monitoring of Internet clickstreams. Clearly, the widespread adoption of new and sophisticated digital technologies has increased the scope and ease through which stealth-based monitoring can be conducted and focused upon particular social groups and individuals who are deemed 'suspicious'.

The 9/11 terrorist attacks also ushered in a period of intense organizational restructuring of the intelligence and security agencies in Canada – as delineated in the Canadian Anti-Terrorist Act passed soon after the attacks. The overall purpose of this Act was to respond to the criticism that the Canadian state was not able to 'connect the dots' in its analysis of intelligence because of bureaucratic obstacles and the sequestration of agencies – a situation that was said to be exacerbated because of the prohibition on using foreign security intelligence in domestic law enforcement (Brodeur and Leman-Langlois, 2006). With the passage of the Act, security agencies such as the Communications Security Establishment of Canada (CSEC) and the Canadian Security Service (CSIS) became formally and institutionally linked with law-enforcement agencies, including the Royal Canadian Mounted Police (RCMP) and municipal and regional police agencies as well as private security agencies. In particular, intelligence and monitoring data were now allowed to be shared more broadly through a newly expanded state surveillance network. Such constellations of security and surveillance agencies are referred to as 'fusion-intelligence complexes' or 'fusion centres' (Newkirk, 2010). The emergence of fusion centres may be understood as a novel aspect of contemporary attempts to suppress environmental groups in the post-9/11 era.

The increased attention given to environmental groups as targets of Canadian state surveillance can be traced to the creation of a particular fusion centre known as the Integrated Security Unit (ISU) in 2003. The ISU was originally formed to prevent the potential disruption of several mega-events planned for 2010: the Vancouver Winter Olympics, the G20 meetings in Toronto and G8 meetings in Huntsville, Ontario (Walby and Monaghan, 2011). Then in 2007, the surveillance and monitoring capability of ISU was expanded through the creation of the Integrated Threat Assessment Centre (ITAC). Notably, the ITAC introduced a new classification category for use in its determination of risk potential – Multi-Issue Extremism (MIE). Whereas previous intelligence operations were limited to threats to financial security and terrorism, the introduction of MIEs enabled the security agency CSIS to cast a wider surveillance net that would now include the monitoring of activist groups, Indigenous groups, environmentalists and others who were publicly critical of government policy (Monaghan and Walby, 2012). Another effect of the MIE category was that the term 'extremism' came to be operationalized as a catch-all category that came to encompass any group engaged in civil disobedience and direct action to whatever degree. Consequently, the ITAC began to bundle together an exceptionally broad number of groups, all of whom came to be defined as national security threats. This included several high-profile groups such as People for the

Ethical Treatment of Animals (PETA) and, the most frequently cited group in all the threat assessments analysed, the environmental group Greenpeace (Walby and Monaghan, 2011).

THE SURVEILLANCE OF OIL SANDS PIPELINE OPPONENTS

In 2009, the federal government mandated that the National Energy Board (NEB) and the Canadian Environmental Assessment Agency (CEAA) form a Joint Review Panel to assess the environmental impacts of the proposed Northern Gateway pipeline. As part of its mission, the Panel was to hear public testimony during a series of hearings held in various cities throughout the provinces of British Columbia and Alberta (which the proposed pipeline would traverse). As the hearings themselves became sites of public protest, state actions were taken to secure these sites from the actions of environmental groups who had now become officially defined as a security threat. These groups then became the subjects of state surveillance and monitoring initiatives as police and security agencies sought intelligence on the plans of environmental groups to demonstrate and organize opposition at the Panel hearings. Especially targeted were those groups engaged in issues of environmental protection and democratic rights, such as: Idle No More (an Aboriginal rights group), Leadnow, Dogwood Initiative, the Council of Canadians, the People's Summit, Forest Ethics, Sierra Club, and Eco Society (Alarcon and Millar, 2013).

From a series of email exchanges (comprising 140 pages) from December 2012 to April 2013 between the RCMP, CSIS, the NEB, Trans Canada Corporation, and Enbridge Inc., it was clear that opposition to oil and gas production was perceived as a threat to national security. Thus, in one email letter obtained by Matthew Millar (2013) of the *Vancouver Observer*, Tim O'Neil, the Senior Criminal Intelligence Research Specialist with the Critical Infrastructure Intelligence Team (CIIT) of the RCMP, circulated a memo to the NEB's 'Group Leader of Security' that stated:

> There continues to be sustained opposition to the Canadian petroleum and pipeline industry. Opposition is most notable in British Columbia, with protests focused on the: Enbridge Northern Gateway; Kinder Morgan Trans Mountain pipeline expansion; the increasing use of hydraulic fracturing, and proposed LNG [Liquified Natural Gas] facilities.
>
> Opponents have used a variety of protest actions (directed at the NEB and its members) to draw attention to the oil sands' negative environmental impact, with the ultimate goal of forcing the shutdown of the Canadian petroleum industry. These same groups have broadened their protests to include the pipelines and more recently, the railroad industry, who the opposing groups claim are facilitating the continued development of the Oil Sands.

The level of scrutiny to which environmental and social groups were subjected may be gleaned by considering other email exchanges concerning the NEB Panel hearings. For instance, in one email, under the heading of 'Planned Protests', the same CIIT officer forwarded the following surveillance briefing to members of CSIS, Enbridge and TransCanada Corporation:

> Idle No More (INM). INM is planning to protest by blocking 2100 Enterprise Way, as well at, or around, the Sandman Hotel and Suites Kelowna from 0900 – 1400 hours, 28 Jan 12. This time/date has been chosen to coincide with the ENG JPR [Enbridge Joint Panel Review] hearings.
>
> Leadnow and Dogwood Initiative. On 27 Jan, the Leadnow and Dogwood Initiative will be providing an afternoon workshop and skills training that will provide tools and strategies for community

resistance and solidarity to members of the public. This is intended to foreshadow the Hearings on 28 Jan.

A subsequent surveillance briefing went on to give very specific details of the workshop activities, noting that it was held in a Kelowna church basement and included instructions on how to paint signs and tell stories (CBC News, 2014).

In light of the instances reviewed above, it is quite apparent that the types of surveillance actions taken, as well as the level of state scrutiny adopted, are no longer directed exclusively at terrorist groups, but today such efforts are focused on social justice and environmental groups as well, who have increasingly come under the same category as terrorists. Thus, Monaghan and Walby note:

> Although much of the Canadian security establishment's attention is directed toward potential Islamic threats the categories of CIP [Critical Infrastructure Protection] regularly allow for environmental activists like Greenpeace to be included in conjunction with threats from Al-Qaeda or others with the explicit aim of harming civilian populations. (2017, p. 57)

Publicly defining environmentalists either directly, or indirectly through association, as extremists or terrorists, is part and parcel of the strategy of discursive obstruction and adversarial framing. One consequence of these state-adopted tactics is that by stigmatizing environmentalists they also pave the way for other forms of harassment and persecution, such as singling out environmental groups for targeted financial auditing.

THE AUDITING OF ENVIRONMENTAL GROUPS

In the 2012 Canadian budget, $8 million was allocated to the Canada Revenue Agency for the specific purpose of auditing environmental organizations (Paris, 2012; Millar, 2014). Later the program was expanded to target 60 charities with a dedicated budget of CAD 13.4 million (Linnitt, 2015). The stated justification was that the government wanted assurance that these organizations were abiding by the legal requirement that only 10 per cent of their revenues were being used in political advocacy activities. If the audits uncovered a violation of this regulation, the environmental organization could lose its status as a charity and would not be able to issue tax-credit receipts to donors for their donations. Donations of course constitute a significant source of revenue for many environmental non-governmental organizations and receiving tax-credits represents an important incentive for many potential donors. Thus, the inability to offer this incentive will undoubtedly have a negative impact on the financial resources of environmental groups in a significant way. Two years later in 2014, the audits began and included several high-profile environmental groups such as: the David Suzuki Foundation, Tides Canada, Environmental Defence, the Pembina Foundation, Équiterre and the Ecology Action Centre (Aulakh, 2014).

Aside from allegations that environmental groups were misusing funds, they were also accused of using illegally gained funds. A few months after the 2012 Budget announcement, then Environment Minister Peter Kent made the allegation that environmental groups were 'laundering' foreign funds in Canada (Paris, 2012; CBC, 2012). Specifically, Kent remarked that 'There are allegations – and we have very strong suspicions – that some funds have come into the country improperly to obstruct, not to assist, in the environmental assessment process' (Paris, 2012; CBC, 2012).

It appears that the Canadian government decision to audit environmental groups was influenced by the investigations of the blogger Vivian Krause, who had published some of her findings in the conservative Canadian newspaper *The Financial Post*. In a piece entitled 'U.S. funding for the war on Canadian oil: Tides USA letters reveal $3.2-million in payments over last few months to activist groups and environmental organizations in Canada, US and Europe', Krause (2013) wrote:

> New information contained in U.S. tax returns makes clear that a large percentage of the fuss over the Northern Gateway pipeline has been generated by a single, American organization: ForestEthics, based in San Francisco. In its 2012 tax return, filed with the I.R.S., ForestEthics claims credit for having generated fully 87 per cent of the letters of comment sent to the National Energy Board regarding the Joint Review Panel for the Northern Gateway.

She went on to comment, 'The gist of these initiatives is to foment opposition to pipeline and export infrastructure that is essential for getting Canadian energy to global markets' (Krause, 2013). On a discursive level it is quite evident that Krause adopts a neoliberal frame predicated on unfettered economic development (to be discussed in more detail later). Furthermore, an anti-American sentiment once again informs the adversarial framing discourse, in that it is the source of funding that receives Krause's wrath: US environmental groups.

In the end, targeted audits have significant consequences for the functioning of environmental groups. First, such audits may affect their reputation and credibility in the eyes of the public. As such, the mere suspicion of an alleged minor financial violation (whether founded or not) may result in negative publicity and the stigmatization of the environmental group, which in turn could affect its fund-raising capabilities (in terms of negatively influencing potential donor decisions in the future). The stigmatization may also affect the ability of the environmental organization to expand its membership base as potential recruits become more hesitant to join a stigmatized group. Finally, the audits themselves will draw upon the institutional resources of the environmental organizations as members divert their attention away from day-to-day operations to meeting the logistical demands of the auditors.

Environmental groups argued that these audits were an unfair and illegal practice as the Canada Revenue Agency (CRA) is not allowed to take political direction from the government. Furthermore, critics also observed that high-profile right-wing charitable organizations, such as the Fraser Institute and the CD Howe Institute, who were clearly engaged in political activities, were not selected for the targeted auditing, despite their violation of the CRA rules (Linnitt, 2015). It was also argued by environmental groups that the audits involved requests for detailed accounts of such fundamental social movement activities as the use of social media and calls to action (Fekete, 2014). Indeed, in this light, the gathering of that level of detailed information on activities could be interpreted as another form of intelligence gathering and monitoring. As such, environmental groups argued that the audits were a form of political intimidation especially designed to pressure the groups to not devote their resources to campaigns against the oil sands and pipeline proposals. Intimidation was not only a concern for environmental movement actors, but, as will be discussed now, it was also a concern for government scientists working on environmental issues.

DISCURSIVE OBSTRUCTION THROUGH THE CONTROL OF SCIENTIFIC INFORMATION

It was evident that a particular focus of the Harper government was to delimit the climate change knowledge base, including data related to the monitoring of the environmental impacts of the oil sands extraction activities. Aside from the closing of various research institutes and libraries on climate change and environmental problems mentioned above, policies were also introduced to make it difficult for state scientists to directly communicate to the media about their research on climate change (Learn, 2017).

Due to policy changes introduced by the Harper regime, scientists could not speak to the media without following a new communications protocol. First, the scientist had to contact a special media control centre of the government to gain permission to speak to journalists (Learn, 2017). After that request was submitted, the media centre would then contact the journalists themselves to obtain written questions of what was to be asked of the scientist. The centre would then contact the scientist to obtain written answers. It was at the discretion of the media centre whether to send the written answers directly to the journalist or to change or omit parts of the answers prepared by the scientist (Learn, 2017). The media centre could also delay their response until the journalists' deadline was exceeded.

The government's strategy to limit discussion about climate change and environmental science seemed to be effectual. According to a report by the Professional Institute of the Public Service of Canada (PIPSC), 90 per cent of federal scientists felt they were prevented from speaking openly about their work, while 86 per cent felt they would be reprimanded for criticizing departmental decisions that they felt were detrimental to public interest. It further found that the number of Environment Canada scientists speaking on climate change had decreased by 80 per cent (PIPSC, 2018).

It is interesting to note that the discursive obstruction tactic pertaining to environmental science adopted by the Canadian state was different from that found in the United States. As noted previously, much of the attention of the US anti-reflexivity movement focused on challenging the veracity of the claims of climate change scientists, so as to convince the public that climate change is not real. In the Canadian context, the reality of anthropogenic climate change was largely accepted by the Canadian public, so challenging the claims of scientists was not likely to be successful. In light of this recognition, the alternative tactic adopted by the Canadian state was to disallow scientists from entering the discursive arena altogether. As such, the attempts at discursive obstruction adopted by the Canadian state were not directed exclusively at environmental groups, but also at government scientists. The pursuit of this tactic did not however go unimpeded as public outrage did ensue as awareness about what was happening became apparent. In response, an investigation was launched by the Information Commissioner in April 2013 with the final report released in February 2018 (Chung, 2018; CBC News, 2018; Jones, 2013). The report concluded that the Conservative government did essentially 'muzzle' government scientists in violation of existing laws. Furthermore, the report went on to note that, under the present Trudeau administration, there had been little progress made in terms of addressing those issues. This was corroborated by the follow-up study conducted by PIPSC in spring of 2017, which found that, despite the current Trudeau administration rescinding the communication policy of the previous Conservative government, the effects of the previous administration remained – for example, 53 per cent of the scientists still felt they could not speak freely about their work, while 73 per cent still feared censorship and retaliation if they spoke out. The PIPSC study concluded: 'The message seems clear: undoing 10 years of damage to federal science will take more than a change of government, hopeful mandate letters, or even collective agreement provisions protecting the right of federal scientists to speak.' In what follows we will further explore how, despite a change in government, the discursive obstruction of the Harper administration had an enduring impact in other ways as well.

ANTI-ENVIRONMENTALISM IN THE POST-HARPER ERA

With the election of Prime Minister Justin Trudeau in 2015, there was some optimism that a pro-environment agenda would now be pursued. For some, however, such optimism was short-lived as it became evident that the forthcoming actions and policies of the Trudeau administration did not appear to reflect a strong environmentalist agenda. As discussed above, the Harper regime introduced significant changes to the Canadian legislation pertaining to national security and intelligence gathering and sharing by CSIS. The Trudeau government did attempt to address some of the criticisms of Harper's Anti-Terrorism Act raised by activists. As such, the Trudeau administration introduced amendments that: ensured greater parliamentary oversight and public accountability over the operations of CSIS (by creating a new agency – the National Security and Intelligence Review Agency (NSIRA); introduced less ambiguity surrounding speech restrictions – a serious concern for many activists, and giving a more clearly defined statement of the new powers conferred to CSIS (Harris, 2016). What remained problematic, however, was that information pertaining to lawful direct-action and advocacy activities would still be subject to sharing between intelligence gathering and law enforcement agencies – if they were judged to 'undermine the security of Canada' (Harris, 2016). What comes to be defined as 'undermining security' remained unclear. The direct implication was that Indigenous activists or anti-pipeline protestors would remain subject to intelligence gathering and sharing if their actions were defined as being a threat to Canadian infrastructure. Further, Amnesty International of Canada noted that the amendments did not address the issue that protestors could still be targeted without any official permit or court order (Bronskill, 2015). Thus, despite some changes the practice of surveillance of anti-pipeline activists was still allowed to continue.

The Trudeau administration's record on the pipelines at this point appears mixed overall. On some fronts a pro-environmental stance was adopted. Thus, upon taking office, Prime Minister Trudeau imposed a ban on oil tankers off the coast of British Columbia, effectively disabling the Northern Gateway pipeline proposal from proceeding (Hunter and Tait, 2015). On the other hand, the administration approved two other proposals in 2016 – the expansion of the Kinder Morgan Trans Mountain pipeline and the Enbridge Line 3 (to carry oil from Alberta to Wisconsin). In fact, with regard to the former, after the proponent Kinder Morgan stated that they would pull out of the project due to delays in approval, the federal government purchased the pipeline and held ownership of it as a Crown Corporation. Ironically, after that purchase, the Federal Court rejected the government's approval for the pipeline expansion due to insufficient consultation with First Nations groups as required by federal law (Kane, 2018).

Through an Access to Information Act request, the British Columbia Civil Liberties Association (BCLA) obtained a report that revealed that information gathered by CSIS, as part of ongoing surveillance efforts, led the intelligence agency to conclude that many environmental and Indigenous groups perceived the federal government purchase of Trans Mountain pipeline as a betrayal by the Trudeau government (Bronskill, 2018a).[2] The CSIS report went on to note that this sense of betrayal was leading to a renewed sense of indignation amongst environmental movement actors that could bolster anti-petroleum activism. The report also suggested that this could lead to the possibility of sabotage and violent physical confrontations. These findings and conclusion were shared with private sector oil companies (Bronskill, 2018b). In this light, it was clear that the intensified surveillance and scrutiny of environmental activists that unfolded during the Harper era, as well as the making of the concomitant association of environmental activists as threats to national security and the potential for violence, were continuing under the Trudeau regime.

Finally, in regard to the targeted auditing of environmental groups, it was promised during the 2015 election campaign that the Liberal Party would end the 'political harassment' of charities by 'clarifying the rule governing "political activity"' (Beeby, 2018). However, several years thereafter, a lack of progress remains in terms of reforming the targeted audits initiated by Harper. In fact, although the Trudeau government cancelled the last six audits that were still scheduled to begin, the government allowed those audits already underway to continue. Thus, for example, the group Environmental Defense has been under audit for the last five years, and has spent up to CAD 500 000 in legal fees to appeal the ruling the Canada Revenue Agency that the group loses its charitable registration status (Beeby, 2018). As such, the effects of the ongoing audits are the same as those experienced by environmental groups under the previous regime, they not only contributed to discursive obstruction by stigmatizing environmental groups by publicly calling into question their status as charities, but the mounting of legal challenges to the government audits results in a diminishment of resources that negatively impacted on the everyday functioning of environmental groups.

THE POST-9/11 SECURITIZATION AND NEOLIBERAL GOVERNANCE FRAMES: IMPLICATIONS FOR ADVERSARIAL FRAMING

This chapter has highlighted the relationship between anti-reflexivity and discursive obstruction. By studying this relationship, we are able to gain an understanding of how anti-reflexivity may take different forms, that is, forms that reflect the different discursive arenas and political cultures in which the particular anti-reflexive orientation is embedded. For example, although both Canada and the United States share some common attributes, they nevertheless have pronounced differences in historical trajectories, electoral systems and political cultures. There are of course many important divergences between the two countries, such as Canada having a much more resource (staples)-based economic history; a parliamentary type of polity and a formal representation of left-wing/labour interests to a much greater degree than that found in the United States (see for example Lipset, 1990 on these differences). Consequently, the discursive arena in which environmental groups in the different countries operate will be different, and this will have implications for the types of anti-reflexivity strategies adopted in different nations. Thus, as discussed, anti-reflexivity in the US tended to focus on strategies that questioned the legitimacy of climate science and called into question the reality of climate change itself, whereas in Canada, anti-reflexivity was directed more squarely at environmental groups – who came to be defined as threats to national security. Further, although climate science itself was not questioned in Canada, the Harper regime made it difficult for climate scientists to publicly disseminate their research in this area.

The form that anti-reflexivity took in our Canadian case was based on oppositional framing, where environmentalists were portrayed as 'enemies of the state'. Why was such a portrayal allowed to develop, gain legitimacy, and take hold at this particular point in time? To answer these questions, it is helpful to consider the concept of discursive opportunity structure (Shriver et al., 2012; McCammon et al., 2007). According to this notion, the possibility for a particular interpretive frame to take hold in the public imagination can only occur if that frame is ideologically compatible with the broader discursive environment in which it comes to be embedded (Snow et al., 1986). With this understanding, the discursive opportunity structure does not dictate the particular frame, rather the discursive opportunity structure 'delimits the spaces in which oppositional framing occurs and affects its public character' (Shriver et al., 2012 citing Snow, 2004, pp. 403–404). The important point is the 'fit' between the socially constructed interpretive frame and the broader context. That is, as Noakes and Johnston (2005) observe, the frame must ring true with the broader cultural context; that is, the frame must resonate with the target audience (for instance, a particular block of the voting public or society at large).

With reference to the present case, I have alluded to the idea that the current prevailing 'cultural stock' was one informed by the broader post-9/11 context – a political and cultural backdrop in which much greater political and societal attention is directed towards issues of security, surveillance and vigilance (Lyon, 2001). Indeed, as we have seen, it was this type of broader context that enabled the restructuring of the organizational environment in which the Canadian security establishment now functions (as exemplified for instance by the adoption of intelligence-led policing and the formation of fusion centres). With the emergence of this post-9/11 backdrop, a discursive arena was established in which environmentalists could 'legitimately' be portrayed as security threats, and hence be subject to intensified surveillance, both directly in terms of the monitoring of their day-to-day activities and also in terms of the targeted financial auditing. In other words, the discursive opportunity to define environmentalists as security threats and 'enemies of the state' arose, at least in part, because of the heightened concern about national security and nationalist concerns in the post-9/11 context. Thus, for example, we have reviewed several instances above in relation to how an appeal to Canadian nationalist sentiment and patriotism was being used by various Conservative politicians (i.e. the Minister of Natural Resources, the Environment Minister as well as the Minister of Finance) to negatively influence people's views of environmentalists.[3]

It was noted above that the political opportunity for the oppositional framing of environmentalists was 'in part' due to the influence of the post-9/11 securitization frame. This is because the influence of a second frame may also be discerned – namely one based on neoliberal governance. Neoliberal governance as a frame pertains to the way in which all public issues come to be defined in purely economic terms, stripped of their social basis. Dunford conceptualized neoliberal governance as 'a new governmental mentality that aims to pre-empt, contain, and eliminate threats to corporate profit, including regulatory and safety standards' (2017, p. 71). With neoliberal governance the state attempts to eliminate intolerable threats to the market and public life to ensure political and economic stability, so that there can be continued pursuit of profit. This is why, as Forcese and Roach (2015, p. 23) note, under the Harper regime, terrorism was redefined to include threats to 'Canada's economic or financial stability' or 'interferes with critical infrastructure' – both of which of course have relevance to the way the pipeline debates were framed by the state. Indeed, the development of 'critical infrastructure protection' (CIP) concern has been identified by Monaghan and Walby (2017) as a key discourse that has enabled domestic surveillance within Canada.

In summary, under the influence of the neoliberal governance frame, environmentalists come to be conceived of as a significant threat to the economy as well (and not just a threat to public security in the sense of extremist or terrorist threats). In line with this understanding, it would perhaps be more correct to say that the political opportunity to stigmatize and harass environmental groups came from the convergence of two frames which together opened up a discursive opportunity window to conflate security and economic threats – namely the post-9/11 securitization frame coupled with the neoliberal governance frame.

ENVIRONMENTALISTS AS 'FOLK DEVILS'

One important broader consequence of the opening of the political opportunity window that resulted from convergence of the two frames was that the impetus was created for the emergence of a 'moral panic' and a 'folk devil'. Moral panic refers to a feeling of fear spread amongst a large number of people that some evil threatens the well-being of society (Cohen, 1972). The convergence of feelings of risk or threat with moral disdain is implicit in the notion of moral panic. The folk devil refers to the particular type of individual who is selected out in a scapegoat fashion by the public as the cause of the threat. Such an individual or group therefore becomes the target of moral disdain – a stance that readily resonates with the adversarial framing technique. The folk devil therefore becomes the target of the public's wrath as the moral panic leads to a situation in which pent-up fear bursts out and is directed at that individual or group who are seen as the cause of the social problem. The folk devil represents the identifiable object onto which social fears and anxieties may be projected. Folk devils thus become symbols that are stripped of positive characteristics and endowed with pejorative evaluations. In this connection, Zygmunt Bauman (2016, p. 1) notes that, even though the activities and focus of people appear to be directed towards a particular folk devil, the locus of the panic is the object, its symbolic resonances, not the folk devil itself. In other words, folk devils serve as the ideological embodiment of deeper anxieties, perceived as a 'problem' only in and through social definition and construction. In light of this understanding, the making of environmentalists as folk devils through discursive obstruction and adversarial framing is only one example of a large phenomenon pertaining to the emergence of a whole class of emerging folk devils in the post-911 context – Muslims, refugees, immigrants, asylum seekers, elites, and so on – all of whom represent the specific crystallized sites of a more generalized moral panic. This generalized moral panic may be thought of as predicated upon a heightened sense of risk consciousness that is prevalent and characteristic to life in late modernity (Giddens, 1989, 1990; Beck, 1992), coupled with deep-seated contemporary concerns over economic security and precarity (Hochschild, 2016; Sassen, 2014; Mishra, 2017). The pervasive influence of the conflation of the post-9/11 securitization frame and the neoliberal frame is perhaps what enables anti-environmentalism and anti-reflexivity to endure even with the change in political regime. That is to say, although there was regime change, that change took place within the context of an unchanged, or slow-to-change, discursive arena.

SUPPRESSION OF ENVIRONMENTALISM

Walby and Monaghan (2011, p. 24) note the concept of 'repression' is commonly used in the social movement literature, but they are wary of the usage of this term because it is close in meaning to the idea of 'overt governmental coercion'. For this reason, following Boykoff, they prefer the term 'suppression' – a more general term that refers to the 'process through which the preconditions for dissident action, mobilization, and collective organization are inhibited by either raising their costs or minimising their benefits' (2007, p. 12). For our purposes here, the term 'suppression' is also preferable because it emphasizes the less coercive aspects of social control tactics such as those based on clandestine surveillance practices and harassment that we have reviewed above with respect to pipeline opponents and environmentalists. The processes of state-imposed adversarial framing and discursive obstruction represent means to suppress environmental activism and collective action. This suppression or demobilization may take effect by either raising the costs or minimizing the benefits of mobilization for social movement activists. Demobilization is the process in which social movement actors discontinue the making of contentious claims and disengage from contentious politics (Boykoff, 2007). In this light, Boykoff (2007) has identified several overlapping social mechanisms that facilitate demobilization, including: resource depletion, stigmatization, and intimidation. We see all of these at play in the present case.

As reviewed above, there were several clear instances of the depletion of various types of environmental group resources, including: spending a much greater time in filling out complex forms that became necessary to allow the group to give testimony at NEB hearings on the pipelines; the destruction of databases and archives of environmental research data; repeated tax audits whereby activist groups had to redirect their efforts away from day-to-day operations to meet the demands of government auditors; to pay for legal fees to appeal the loss of charitable status due to the tax audits; and the loss of revenues due to declining donations because of the loss in charitable status. It should be noted that, even if a loss of charitable status did not result, merely being selected out for a targeted audit may have led to suspicion amongst potential donors who may be less reluctant to direct their donations to a stigmatized group – hence the resultant loss in financial resources. Similarly, with the wavering of reputation, volunteers may be reluctant to give their time to such groups, thus depriving the group of vital human resources.

In addition to the indirect forms of stigmatization associated with the audits, stigmatization was more directly and explicitly evident in the various strategies of adversarial framing we have reviewed above. Most vividly this is seen in the remarks of the Conservative Natural Resource Minister, who charged environmentalists as being: selfish, short-sighted, hypocrites, unpatriotic, and extremists. Boykoff notes that the effects of stigmatization are numerous, including 'putting social movements on the defensive, on the ever-unfolding path of self-explanation, justificatory back-tracking, and damage control' (2007, p. 297). For the purposes of the present discussion, one main effect from a discursive perspective is that, under the present post-9/11 political and cultural climate, stigmatization facilitated the process through which the environmentalist was socially constructed as a folk devil and a security threat and hence defined as a legitimate subject of state surveillance and control.

The social mechanism of intimidation may also be identified in our case study. Boykoff notes that intimidation imposes a new logic on social movement activity, forcing actors to consider the consequences of their activities and to reconsider their position and commitment.

One effect of intimidation we have already seen is in terms of the potential for recruitment; volunteers may reconsider their involvement in the group. A second example seen is the reluctance of government scientists to publicly discuss their research findings on climate change and environmental issues.

Lastly, it is useful to put into socio-historical context of developments such as the making of environmentalists into folk devils and the moral panic that ensues, as well as the techniques of suppression discussed above. In an insightful social constructionist analysis of ecoterrorism (particularly the Earth Liberation Front) during the George W. Bush administration in the US from 2001 to 2009, Paul Joosse (2012) observes that corporate and state interests were expressed in such a way that mainstream media coverage normalized discourses of ecoterrorism. Consequently, any legitimate and reasoned environmental claims by these groups were not given any consideration in the media depictions. This may have set the stage for the types of developments we have discussed in the present chapter with respect to the administration of Canadian Prime Minister Stephen Harper. That is, that which was previously applicable to only certain 'extreme' groups now seems to apply to mainstream environmental groups in Canada, and with the same effects – a loss of legitimacy of environmental groups and their message in the eyes of the public.

CONCLUDING REMARKS

This chapter highlights one neglected aspect of the anti-reflexivity movement, namely the use of discourse to justify the state suppression of environmental groups. Anti-reflexivity as a counter-movement is multidimensional. This is perhaps not surprising given that the environmental issues themselves are inherently complex, encompassing many different facets of the social and biophysical world. Thus, political strategies designed to counter environmentalism may select out particular elements of the environmental problematic to focus upon while neglecting others. For instance, in the case of the United States, the discursive context was one in which anti-reflexivity takes a form based on the denial of the reality and science of anthropogenic climate change. In Canada, the context was different for various reasons, but most importantly because the reality of climate change was not questioned to the same degree it was in the United States. This may have influenced the emergence of a different form of anti-reflexivity developing in Canada.

In Canada, state actors directed their anti-reflexivity strategies against environmentalists through a different set of discourses. Notably, discursive obstruction in Canada was based on the adversarial framing of environmentalists as 'folk devils'. This particular framing was made possible because of the convergence of two dominant discourses, namely neoliberal governance and a post-9/11 emphasis on securitization. Neoliberal governance may have particular influence in a country such as Canada, which has historically developed on the basis of natural-resource extraction. Although that dependence may not be as integral to the Canadian economy today as it was in the past, the influence still remains. For example, emphasis on the development of infrastructure (such as the railway) was very important for the transport of natural resources of historical import (e.g. wheat, fish, metal ores, potash, wood, etc.). Today, the pipeline as a form of infrastructure has taken on greater significance for the transport of a particular resource that is now in demand: oil. The development of pipelines-as-infrastructure is clearly influenced by dynamics of neoliberalism that have intensified since the mid-1980s.

And the efforts of the former prime minister to make Canada an 'energy superpower' (Way, 2011; MacNeil, 2014) reflect this neoliberal emphasis. In this context, environmentalists and others opposed to the pipelines are seen as obstacles to neoliberal economic development. For the state to eliminate these perceived obstacles, while retaining legitimacy in the eyes of the public, state actors in Canada made recourse to the post-9/11 securitization discourse – a discourse that rose to prominence and influence with the restructuring of the security assemblage in Canada after 9/11. The securitization discourse enabled the state to redefine environmentalists as 'security' threats who would be subject to surveillance and other forms of suppression. It justified the various suppressive techniques reviewed in this chapter, including making it difficult for environmentalists to participate in the public processes pertaining to environmental policy-formation, the targeted auditing of environmental groups, and the control of scientific information.

NOTES

1. Furthermore, restrictions were put in place on who would be able to speak at these hearings. Specifically, individuals proposing to speak had to demonstrate their stake in the issue, and this was narrowly defined in terms of the pipeline impacts and not concerns about the broader implications of the pipeline for climate change and enabling the expansion of oil sands extraction (Campbell, 2010; Toledano, 2013).
2. The BC Civil Liberties Association argued that such surveillance efforts were illegal, in that CSIS is not legally entitled to collect information about Canadians unless there are reasonable grounds to conclude that the parties put under surveillance are a threat to national security (Bronskill, 2018a).
3. It is interesting to note that the use of patriotic themes to discredit activists is not unique to the Canadian pipeline case. For instance, Cable et al. (2008) found the deployment of a similar strategy in influencing the public's views about activist claims concerning hazardous exposures at the Oak Ridge Nuclear testing site in Tennessee.

REFERENCES

Alarcon, K. and Millar, M. (2013) Harper government under fire for spying on environmental groups. *The Vancouver Observer* (online). Available from: http://www.vancouverobserver.com/environment/harper-government-under-fire-spying-environmental-groups (accessed 12 June 2014).

Aulakh, R. (2014) Audits of environmental charities linked to position on oilsands: The message is, don't talk about oilsands development and its effect on climate change, green groups say. *Toronto Star* (online). Available from: http://www.thestar.com/news/world/2014/02/07/audits_of_environmental_charities_linked_to_position_on_oilsands.html.

Bauman, Z. (2016) *Strangers At Our Door*. Malden, MA: Polity Press.

Beck, U. (1992) *The Risk Society: Towards a New Modernity*. Thousand Oaks, CA: SAGE.

Beeby, D. (2018) CRA loses court challenge to its political-activity audits of charities: Ontario judge's ruling wipes out section of Income Tax Act limiting political activity by charities. *CBC News* (online). Available from: https://www.cbc.ca/news/politics/charity-political-audits-cra-lebouthillier-farha-poverty-environmental-gray-liberal-1.4750295 (accessed 17 June 2019).

Boykoff, J. (2007) Limiting dissent: The mechanisms of state repression. *Social Movement Studies: Journal of Social, Cultural and Political Protest*. 6(3), pp. 281–310.

Brodeur, J.P. and Leman-Langlois, S. (2006) Surveillance-fiction or high policing. In: Haggerty, K. and Ericson, R. (eds) *The New Politics of Surveillance and Visibility*. Toronto: University of Toronto Press, pp. 171–98.

Bronskill, J. (2015) Bill C-51 could be used to target activists: Amnesty International. *The Canadian Press* (online). Available from: https://www.huffingtonpost.ca/2015/03/09/anti-terrorism-bill-could_n_6831898.html.

Bronskill, J. (2018a) Spy service says federal pipeline purchase seen as 'betrayal' by opponents. *The Canadian Press* (online). Available from: https://www.ctvnews.ca/canada/spy-service-says-federal-pipeline-purchase-seen-as-betrayal-by-opponents-1.4164942 (accessed 17 June 2019).

Bronskill, J. (2018b) The B.C. Civil Liberties Association alleges CSIS passed information to oil companies and held secret conferences with these petroleum industry players at its headquarters. *The Canadian Press* (online). Available from: https://vancouversun.com/news/local-news/csis-spying-on-anti-pipeline-activists-feds-try-to-pull-cloak-of-secrecy-over-court-case.

Cable, S., Shriver, T.E. and Mix, T. (2008) Risk society and contested illness: The case of Oak Ridge nuclear workers. *American Sociological Review.* **73**, pp. 380–401.

Campbell, K. (2010) Pipeline assessment needs to include upstream impacts. Available from: http://www.pembina.org/blog/368.

CBC (Canadian Broadcasting Corporation) News (2012) Environmental charities 'laundering' foreign funds, Kent says. *CBC News* (online). Available from: http://www.cbc.ca/news/politics/environmental-charities-laundering-foreign-funds-kent-says-1.1165691 (accessed 31 March 2014).

CBC (Canadian Broadcasting Corporation) News (2014). Alleged CSIS, RCMP spying on Northern Gateway pipeline protesters prompts complaint. *CBC News* (online). Available from: http://www.cbc.ca/m/touch/news/story/1.2526218 (accessed 31 March 2014).

CBC (Canadian Broadcasting Corporation) News (2018) It's official – the Harper government muzzled scientists. Some say it's still happening. *CBC News* (online). Available from: https://www.cbc.ca/news/technology/muzzled-scientists-1.4545562.

Chung, E. (2018) More than half of federal government scientists still feel muzzled, poll finds. *CBC News* (online). Available from: https://www.cbc.ca/news/technology/muzzled-scientists-1.4545562 (accessed 17 June 2019).

Cohen, A. (2008) *The Unfinished Canadian.* Toronto: McClelland & Stewart.

Cohen, S. (1972) *Folk Devils and Moral Panics: The Creation of the Mods and Rockers.* London: MacGibbon and Kee.

Davidson, D.J. and Gismondi, M. (2011) *Challenging Legitimacy at the Precipice of Energy Calamity.* New York, NY: Springer.

Dunford, D.T. (2017) The Lac-Mégantic derailment, corporate regulation, and neoliberal sovereignty. *Canadian Review of Sociology.* **54**(1), pp. 69–86.

Dunlap, R. (2009) Why climate-change skepticism is so prevalent in the USA: The success of conservative think tanks in promoting skepticism via the media. *IOP Conference Series: Earth and Environmental Science.* **6**(53), p. 532010. Available from DOI: 10.1088/1755-1307/6/53/532010.

Dunlap, R.E. (2013) Climate change skepticism and denial: An introduction. *American Behavioral Scientist.* (57), pp. 691–98.

Dunlap, R.E. and Jacques, P.J. (2013) Climate change denial books and Conservative think tanks: Exploring the connection. *American Behavioral Scientist.* (57), pp. 699–731.

Dunlap, R.E. and McCright, A.M. (2011) Organized climate-change denial. In: Dryzek, J.S., Norgaard, R.B. and Schlosberg, D. (eds) *Oxford Handbook of Climate Change and Society.* New York, NY: Oxford University Press, pp. 144–60.

Elsasser, S.W. and Dunlap, R.E. (2013) Leading voices in the denier choir: Conservative columnists' dismissal of global warming and denigration of climate science. *American Behavioral Scientist.* (57), pp. 754–76.

Fekete, J. (2014) The budget will crack down on charities with links to terrorist groups: Jim Flaherty. *National Post* (online). Available from: http://news.nationalpost.com/2014/02/07/budget-will-crack-down-on-charities-with-links-to-terrorists-organized-crime-jim-flaherty/ (accessed 31 March 2014).

Forcese, C. and Roach, K. (2015) Bill C-51 Backgrounder #3: Sharing information and the lost lessons of the Maher Arar experience. Working Paper. University of Toronto Faculty of Law and the University of Ottawa Faculty of Law Working Paper, pp. 1–37.

Giddens, A. (1989) *The Consequences of Modernity.* Stanford, CA: Stanford University Press.

Giddens, A. (1990) *Modernity and Self-Identity: Self and Society in the Late Modern Age.* Stanford, CA: Stanford University Press.

Government of Canada (2012) An open letter from the Honourable Joe Oliver, Minister of Natural Resources. Natural Resources Canada (online). Available from: http://www.nrcan.gc.ca/media-room/news-release/2012/1/1909 (accessed 31 March 2014).

Harris, M. (2016) Canadians aren't up for mass surveillance. *iPolitics*. Available from: https://ipolitics.ca/2016/03/17/canadians-arent-up-for-mass-surveillance/ (accessed 17 June 2019).

Hochschild, A. (2016) *Strangers in Their Own Land: Anger and Mourning on the American Right*. New York, NY: The New Press.

Hooker, C. and Ali, S.H. (2009) SARS and security: Health in the new normal. *Studies in Political Economy*. **84**(1), pp. 101–126.

Hunter, J. and Tait, C. (2015) Why the Northern Gateway pipeline is probably dead. The Globe and Mail. Available from: https://www.theglobeandmail.com/news/british-columbia/why-the-northern-gateway-project-is-probablydead/article27620342/ (accessed 17 June 2019).

Jacques, P., Dunlap, R.E. and Freeman, M. (2008) The organization of denial: Conservative think tanks and environmental scepticism. *Environmental Politics*. **17**(3), pp. 349–85.

Jones, N. (2013) Canada to investigate the muzzling of scientists. *Nature News Blog* (online). Available from: http://blogs.nature.com/news/2013/04/canada-to-investigate-muzzling-of-scientists.html.

Joosse, P. (2012) Elves, environmentalism, and 'eco-terror': Leaderless resistance and media coverage of the Earth Liberation Front. *Crime, Media, Culture*. **8**(1), 7593.

Kane, L. (2018) Court ruling quashes approval of Trans Mountain. *The Canadian Press* (online). Available from: https://www.ctvnews.ca/business/court-ruling-quashes-approval-of-trans-mountain-1.4073752 (accessed 17 June 2019).

Klein, N. (2014) *This Changes Everything: Capitalism vs. The Climate*. Toronto: Alfred A. Knopf.

Knight, G. and Greenberg, J. (2011) Talk of the enemy: Adversarial framing and climate change discourse. *Social Movement Studies*. **10**(4), pp. 323–40.

Krause, V. (2013) U.S. funding for the war on Canadian oil. *National Post* (online). Available from: http://opinion.financialpost.com/2013/11/29/vivian-krause-new-u-s-funding-for-the-war-on-canadian-oil/ (accessed 31 March 2014).

Learn, J. (2017) Canadian scientists explain exactly how their government silenced science. *Smithsonian Magazine*. Available from: https://www.smithsonianmag.com/science-nature/canadian-scientists-open-about-how-their-government-silenced-science-180961942/.

Linnitt, C. (2015) Trudeau instructs minister of national revenue to free charities from political harassment. *The Narwhal*. Available from: https://thenarwhal.ca/trudeau-instructs-minister-finance-free-charities-political-harassment/ (accessed 17 June 2018).

Lipset, S.M. (1990) *Continental Divide: The Values and Institutions of the United States and Canada*. New York, NY: Routledge.

Lyon, D. (2001) Surveillance after September 11. *Sociological Research Online*. **6**(3). Available from: http://www.socresonline.org.uk.ezproxy.library.yorku.ca/6/3/lyon.html.

MacNeil, R. (2014) Canadian environmental policy under Conservative majority rule. *Environmental Politics*. **23**(1), pp. 174–8.

McCammon, H.J., Newman, H.D., Muse, C.S. and Terrell, T.M. (2007) Movement framing and discursive opportunity structures: The political successes of the U.S. women's jury movement. *American Sociological Review*. **72**(5), pp. 725–49.

McCarthy, S. (2012) Ottawa's new anti-terrorism strategy lists eco-extremists as threats. *The Globe and Mail* (online). Available from: http://www.theglobeandmail.com/news/politics/ottawas-new-anti-terrorism-strategy-lists-eco-extremists-as-threats/article533522/ (accessed 12 June 2014).

McCright, A.M. and Dunlap, R.E. (2003) Defeating Kyoto: The Conservative movement's impact on U.S. climate change policy. *Social Problems*. **50**, pp. 348–73.

McCright, A.M. and Dunlap, R.E. (2010) The American Conservative movement's success in undermining climate science and policy. *Theory, Culture & Society*. **27**(2–3), pp. 100–133.

McCright, A.M. and Dunlap, R.E. (2011) The politicization of climate change and polarization in the American public's views of global warming. *Sociological Quarterly*. **52**(2), pp. 155–94.

Millar, M. (2013) Harper government's extensive spying on anti-oilsands groups revealed FOIs. *The Vancouver Observer* (online). Available from: http://www.vancouverobserver.com/print/node/17066 (accessed 31 March 2014).

Millar, M. (2014) Flaherty cites terrorism when asked why CRA is auditing environmental charities. *The Vancouver Observer* (online). Available from: http://www.vancouverobserver.com/news/flaherty-cites-terrorism-when-asked-why-cra-auditing-environmental-charities (accessed 12 June 2014).

Mishra, P. (2017) *Age of Anger: A History of the Present*. New York, NY: Farrar, Straus and Giroux.

Monaghan, J. and Walby, K. (2012) Making up 'terror identities': Security intelligence, Canada's integrated threat assessment centre and social movement suppression. *Policing and Society: An International Journal of Research and Policy*. **22**(2), pp. 133–51.

Monaghan, J. and Walby, K. (2017) Surveillance of environment movements in Canada: Critical infrastructure protection and the petro-security apparatus. *Contemporary Justice Review*. **20**(1), pp. 51–70.

Newkirk, A.B. (2010) The rise of the fusion-intelligence complex: A critique of political surveillance after 9/11. *Surveillance and Society*. **8**(1), pp. 43–60.

Noakes, J.A. and Johnston, H. (2005) Frames of protest: A road map to a perspective. In: Johnston, H. and Noakes, J.A. (eds) *Frames of Protest: Social Movements and the Framing Perspective*. Lanham, MD: Rowman & Littlefield, pp. 1–29.

Owens, B. (2014) Canadian government accused of destroying environmental archives: Researchers fear that valuable documents will disappear as libraries close and merge. *Nature* (online). Available from: http://www.nature.com/news/canadian-government-accused-of-destroying-environmental-archives-1.14539 (accessed 29 April 2014).

Paris, M. (2012) Charities urge Peter Kent to retract 'laundering' accusation. *CBC News* (online). Available from: http://www.cbc.ca/news/politics/charities-urge-peter-kent-to-retract-laundering-accusation-1.1213026 (accessed on 31 March 2014).

Partington, P.J. (2010) The geography of Canada's greenhouse gas emissions. Available from: http://www.pembina.org/blog/337 (accessed 31 March 2014).

Professional Institute of the Public Service of Canada (PIPSC) (2018) Defrosting public science: A survey report on federal government efforts to reverse the effects of the Big Chill. *PIPSC* (online). Available from: https://www.pipsc.ca/sites/default/files/comms/Defrosting-report-e_v4%202_1.pdf (accessed 17 June 2018).

Sassen, S. (2014) *Expulsions: Brutality and Complexity in the Global Economy*. Cambridge, MA: Belknap.

Shriver, T., Adams, A.E. and Cable, S. (2012) Discursive obstruction and elite opposition to environmental activism in the Czech Republic. *Social Forces*. **91**(3), pp. 873–93.

Snow, D.A. (2004) Framing processes, ideology, ad discursive fields. In: Snow, D.A., Soule, S.A. and Kriesi, H. (eds) *The Blackwell Companion to Social Movements*. Malden, MA: Blackwell Publishing, pp. 380–412.

Snow, David A., Rochford, E., Worden, S.K. and Benford, R.D. (1986) Frame alignment processes, micromobilization, and movement participation. *American Sociological Review*. **51**(4), pp. 464–81.

Toledano, M. (2013) How activists shut down the Enbridge Line 9 pipeline hearings. *Vice News*. Available from: https://www.vice.com/en_ca/article/xdm593/how-activists-shut-down-the-enbridge-line-9-pipeline-hearings.

Walby, K. and Monaghan, J. (2011) Private eyes and public order: Policing surveillance in the suppression of animal rights activists in Canada. *Social Movement Studies: Journal of Social, Cultural and Political Protest*. **10**(1), pp. 21–37.

Way, L. (2011) An energy superpower or a super sales pitch? Building the case through an examination of Canadian newspapers coverage of oil sands. *Canadian Political Science Review*. **5**(1), pp. 74–98.

Young, N. and Coutinho, A. (2013) Government, anti-reflexivity, and the construction of public ignorance about climate change: Australia and Canada compared. *Global Environmental Politics*. **13**(2), pp. 89–108.

14. Fashioning anti-environmentalism in Turkey: the campaign against the Bergama movement
Hayriye Özen

INTRODUCTION

Starting in mid-2001, various claims concerning the significant contribution of gold mining to the economic development and national interests of Turkey were voiced by many, including state and non-state actors, journalists, influential columnists, academics, mining professionals, mining corporations, and members of parliament. What prompted these efforts and galvanized these different actors was the success of an environmental protest movement generated in the early 1990s against the attempts of a mining multinational to operate a goldmine in Bergama, a small town in the Aegean region. Being the first environmental movement that managed to mobilize the inhabitants of villages – conventionally the most apolitical segments of society – to expand its support base at the national level, to bring the ecological and social threats of gold mining to the national agenda, and to win court decisions the Bergama movement politicized the issues of environment and gold mining as never before. The authorities were at first in a quandary as to what strategies and tactics to use against this movement, but later initiated a series of counter-steps to this new movement and the serious challenge it posed not only to the operation of the goldmine in Bergama, but to gold mining in general and the related state policies. In alliance with various non-state actors favoring gold mining, the authorities launched a seemingly well-coordinated campaign that effectively countered the effects of the Bergama movement, legitimizing ecologically destructive gold mining operations.

This chapter seeks to shed light both on the formation and on the effects of this anti-environmental campaign conducted against the Bergama movement. Focusing on the discursive struggle waged through this counter-campaign, it demonstrates that the anti-environmentalism of this campaign lies not only in what it says, but also in what it leaves unsaid. On the one hand it engaged in a contest over the meaning of gold mining for Turkey by emphasizing culturally resonant themes and using post-truth techniques, and on the other, the campaign discourse was remarkably silent on environmental issues raised by the Bergama movement. That silence was an integral part of this discourse, which associated gold mining with economic development and national interests and sovereignty, while portraying the protest movement as a foreign plot to prevent gold mining in Turkey. By appealing to the desire for economic development and by fueling nationalist feelings, this discourse proved critical in first removing from the public agenda the environmental claims and concerns of the Bergama movement and, thereby, opening the way to the ecologically destructive gold mining activities, and second, in preparing the ground for the repression of the protests. The effectiveness of this anti-environmental discourse in controlling and quelling the Bergama movement eventually resulted in it becoming one of the state's main, if not the main, techniques used to counter environmental movements, particularly those that manage to gain widespread sympathy and support among the general public.

The empirical data of the study were collected by using both primary and secondary sources. The primary sources included newspaper reports drawn from three national daily newspapers, *Milliyet*, *Hürriyet*, and *Turkish Daily News*, between 1998 and 2003, and a monthly bulletin, Ovacik Bulletin, issued by the mining company between March 2000 and March 2003. The secondary sources were two reports (Cangı, 2002; TMMOB, 2003) and three books (Taşkın, 1998; Hablemitoğlu, 2001; Akdemir, 2011) on the issue. Of the three books, one was written by a protester (Taşkın, 1998), one by a pro-gold mining academic (Hablemitoğlu, 2001), and one by a journalist (Akdemir, 2011).

In the following sections, I first briefly outline the main characteristics of the Turkish context with a view to showing the relationship between the context and environmental issues. Then, after delineating the Bergama movement, I focus on the anti-environmental campaign launched in opposition. I conclude the study by discussing the implications of the Bergama case.

THE TURKISH CONTEXT: ENVIRONMENTAL ISSUES AND POLICIES IN THE NEOLIBERAL ERA

As environmental degradation in Turkey intensified from the 1980s, due to the process of neoliberal transition, that is, the transformation from a heavily protected and state-led economy to a free market one, the number of environmental protests and movements also increased correspondingly. In this transformation, the market and market forces, and foremost among these, foreign capital, were attributed an unprecedented significance for the economic development of the country. Due to its 'obsessive and myopic commitment' to economic development (Özveren and Nas, 2012), the Turkish state provided new sources for the accumulation of capital through those mechanisms such as privatization of public goods, redistribution of state assets, and particularly, commodification of nature and urban spaces, overlooking the environmental problems created by these mechanisms. The issue of the protection of the environment came onto the state agenda in the 1980s, mostly due to external pressures (Adaman and Arsel, 2005). As such, the measures taken in this respect can be considered as mere window-dressing (Somersan, 1993). Neither the establishment of the Ministry of Environment in 1991, nor the enactment of a body of environmental laws and regulations, especially in the European Union accession process, were outcomes of a genuine concern with the environmental consequences of new liberal policies (Ünalan, 2016). In fact, as the advent of the neoliberal journey of the country was marked with a series of economic crises erupting at almost regular intervals in 1991, 1994, 1998/99, 2000 and 2001 (Öniş, 2004, 2010; Şenses, 2012), the issue of the protection of the environmental was further neglected. In an attempt to improve the investment climate for national and foreign investors, many more natural areas and resources were opened up to exploitation by corporations. In order to do this, the environmental legislation was constantly reformulated to advance the interests of business, and furthermore, the implementation of existing laws was insufficiently enforced (Çavdar, 2012).

All these paved the way for the generation of various environmental struggles at many different locales; some were sporadic protests, others were sustained movements. One of the early movements that voiced environmental concerns and posed an enduring and substantial challenge to the neoliberal mining policies emerged against the attempts of a multinational corporation to operate a gold mine in Bergama, a small town in the Aegean region. As detailed in the following, despite emerging in the early 1990s, this movement became highly active and influential until it was marginalized and quelled by the forces of the status quo in the early 2000s (Özen, 2009).

THE BERGAMA MOVEMENT

The environmental protest movement in Bergama was the first of its kind on several counts. A key characteristic was its status as the first mobilization in Turkey against gold mining. As is the case in many other fields, the activities in the gold mining field increased after the neoliberal transformation of the Turkish economy started in 1980. Multinational mining companies in particular were interested in extracting the gold reserves in various parts of the country. Regarding foreign investments as highly valuable for economic development, governmental authorities had no hesitation in granting operation permits to these companies, ignoring ecological and social consequences of such activities. Bergama was among the first places where mining multinationals attempted to start extractive activities. The mobilizations emerged within a short time at the local level after mining operations were announced in Bergama by Eurogold, a joint venture between Poseidon Gold Limited (67 percent) belonging to Australia's Normandy Poseidon, and Canada's and Germany's Metal Mining Corporation (33 percent) (Taşkın, 1998). The Bergama movement was also the first environmental movement that, after emerging at the local level, went on to attract nationwide and even international attention and support. After emerging in the early 1990s through the mobilization of the rural population, it rapidly mobilized the support of environmental groups and non-governmental organizations (NGOs) at both national and international levels (Kadirbeyoğlu, 2001; Özen, 2009). The widespread support that the movement received provided it with the resources to engage in highly effective and innovative collective actions, which included organizing meetings, seminars and panels, mailing letters and submitting petitions to the Turkish Parliament, visiting the Prime Minister, and more importantly, staging a series of public protests not only in Bergama, but also in the cities of İzmir, Ankara and İstanbul. It was also the first local environmental campaign to last for more than 15 years.

As such, the Bergama movement effectively politicized environmental issues related to gold mining, posing a serious challenge to gold mining in Bergama in particular, and in Turkey in general. It produced significant outcomes with regard to environmental issues. One of the most significant achievements of the movement in this respect was the Council of the State's groundbreaking decision concerning the gold mine. In May 1997, the Council of the State ruled that the mining operations in the Bergama area unfairly infringed the local residents' right to a healthy environment, as defined in Article 56 of the Turkish Constitution, and their right to protect their environment, as defined in Article 17 of the Constitution. Appeals by the government and the company failed to change the decision of the Court, which became definite in November 1998.

This, however, was only a short-term victory for the movement. Rather than giving up, the mining company and government started a campaign in a bid to reverse the environmental achievements of the Bergama movement. Thus, as is the case with other anti-environmental counter-movements emerging in reaction to the successes of environmental movements (Austin, 2002; Jacques et al., 2008; Dunlap and McCright, 2015), this campaign emerged in response to the environmental gains of the Bergama movement. Similarly, as demonstrated in what follows, like many other anti-environmental counter-movements, this campaign was the result of the efforts of various economic and political elites.

THE LAUNCH OF THE ANTI-ENVIRONMENTAL CAMPAIGN AGAINST THE BERGAMA MOVEMENT

In no time after the issuance of the final court verdict, the company started the application process for gold mining authorizations anew: it demanded another environmental risk assessment based on its claim of measures taken to remedy environmental problems referred to in the ruling of the Council of State (*Turkish Daily News*, 27 November 1998). In doing this, the company officials announced to the public that they had changed 'a lot of things' in the mine, which now boasted the best safety system in the world (*Turkish Daily News*, 27 November 1998). Upon this re-application, the government commissioned a state-funded scientific council, the Turkish Institute of Scientific and Technical Research (TÜBİTAK), to undertake a detailed risk assessment of the mine (*Hürriyet*, 13 July 2000; TMMOB, 2003). Delivering a report to the government that stated that all the environmental risks referred to by the Council of the State had either been totally eliminated or brought well within acceptable limits after the company's additional safety measures TÜBİTAK suggested that the operation of the company would contribute to the Turkish economy (*Turkish Daily News*, 13 July 2000). On the basis of this report, the undersecretary of the Prime Ministry produced a circular that instructed the related ministries in April 2000 to grant operation permissions to the company. It was underlined in the statement that the prevention of the operation of the mine would block the inflow of foreign investments into the country (*Turkish Daily News*, 14 June 2000). Accordingly, after a number of ministerial decisions to renew operating permits, permission was given for a one-year trial production period. As a result, despite the court orders to the contrary, the company started production on 13 April 2001 (*Hürriyet*, 28 May 2001).

These efforts were followed by a well-coordinated anti-environmental campaign designed to remove obstacles to gold mining by dismissing all environmental objections. The actors that were engaged in this campaign included journalists, influential columnists, TV personalities, academics, politicians, and various governmental and state actors. In response to the discourse of the Bergama movement that underlined the devastating environmental effects of gold mining, through this campaign, a discourse was articulated that put forward economic benefits. This gold mining discourse completely overlooked the environmental concerns and objections of the Bergama movement, focusing instead on justifying the gold mining agenda, and on undermining the Bergama movement. In contrast to earlier efforts that dealt with convincing the locals of the benefits of the operation of the mine in Bergama, this campaign was aimed at the general public. In relation to this, the discourse linked the specific issue of the operation of the goldmine in Bergama into the wider issue of gold mining in Turkey. Initially produced by the company, this discourse was remolded later as additional actors involved in the struggle tried to increase its popular appeal. The gold mining campaign managed, first, to take over the control over the debate on the issue from the Bergama movement, and, then, to shift it in favor of gold mining.

Although it did not explicitly make anti-environmental claims, the gold mining discourse was anti-environmental in its character. As Austin (2002, p. 75) argues, anti-environmentalism refers to 'an assemblage of ideologies and political practices designed to advance capital accumulation and manage the discontents stemming from industrial production and mass consumption'. The following section shows how the campaign managed to promote gold mining at the expense of the natural environment, not only by voicing the arguments for economic development and national well-being, but also by deliberately maintaining silence on environmental issues raised by the Bergama movement.

The Gold Mining Discourse

It would not be an exaggeration to say that the heart and soul of the gold mining discourse emerged, on the one hand, from the association of gold mining with economic development and, on the other, from the spreading of conspiracy theories. As is the case in many other discourses articulated against environmental movements, the gold mining discourse put a heavy emphasis on economic development. By drawing on the themes of development, which, as explained later, resonate strongly with the general public in the Turkish context, it linked the particular issue of the Bergama goldmine operation to broader issues of gold mining, the inflow of foreign capital, and economic development. More precisely, the operation of the mine was depicted as critical for opening the way to gold mining, to the inflow of foreign capital and, thus, to the economic development of Turkey. It is striking to note that, in doing this, the discourse relied on the heavy use of a post-truth rhetoric about the amount of gold reserves in Turkey. As reflected in the words of a company official:

> Turkey must immediately make its decision about gold mining for its future, and the main question is 'will Turkey give permission to mine gold or not?' because more than 6,500 tons of gold are waiting to be extracted, having a value of about $70 billion. This has huge importance for the development of the country, and other things can be discussed only after this main question is answered. (Güçkan, *Turkish Daily News*, 9 December 1999)

These unwarranted and unjustified claims about the gold reserves of Turkey were accompanied by the conspiratorial claims about 'hidden and concealed' truth of the Bergama movement. Conspiracy theories were used to assert that the movement was not what it claimed, that the protesters' real concerns were not the issues related with environment, nature, and pollution and degradation, but these were used to disguise the movement's broader aim of hampering the Turkish nation's economic progress in order to serve the interests of external powers. Specifically, it was stated by the company officials that 'some local politicians cooperate with external forces in order to prevent the development of Turkey' (*Hürriyet*, 20 January 1998), and that 'peasants [of Bergama] were organized or supported by external forces who did not want Turkey to mine its rich gold sources' (*Turkish Daily News*, 22 October 2000; Ovacik Bulletin, 2000a). As to the interests of 'external forces', the charge was made by company officials that the gold supplying countries were trying to prevent the production of gold in Turkey: 'There are numerous external forces supporting the [protesting] peasants ... because gold mining in Bergama will earn Turkey $70 billion and do away with the need to import gold' (*Turkish Daily News*, 22 October 2000). In the monthly bulletin issued by the mining company, it was claimed that the contribution of the mine to the Turkish economy would be $300 billion (Ovacik Bulletin, 2000b). Through these claims, which had no basis in fact (Akdemir, 2011), the Bergama movement was represented not as a grassroots mobilization opposed to the environmentally destructive effects of gold mining, but as the agents of the interests of foreign powers.

By linking gold mining to economic development, the gold mining discourse, no doubt, attempted to appeal to the public desire for economic development and well-being. This was not a difficult task to perform, given that almost all sections of society were experiencing economic hardships due to the continuing deep recession when this campaign was started. However, by articulating the themes of development, the gold mining discourse not only aimed to appeal to economic interests but also tried to mobilize the matrix of meanings associated with the development discourse in the Turkish context in favor of the mine. Economic development was historically conceived in the Turkish context as one of the most, if not the most, important means of ensuring not only the country's progress and strength, but also economic independence and thus, national sovereignty. This perception was originally shaped by the legacies of the Ottoman Empire, and its political problems created by its economic weaknesses and financial dependence on Western European powers (Pamuk, 2012). From its foundation in the early 1920s to date, therefore, Turkey accorded great importance to economic independence, which would be gained through national economic development (Buğra, 1994; Buğra and Savaşkan, 2012). As such, development was depoliticized and became an important component of common national consciousness, and an unquestioned national objective to be achieved through the efforts of the entire nation under the leadership of the state. In other words, by regarding development as a key dimension of national sovereignty, an overwhelming commitment to it was created. By placing a special emphasis on the economic development theme, the gold mining discourse set out to capitalize on this specific meaning of development in the Turkish context.

The gold mining discourse attempted to gain rhetorical force also on the basis of conspiracy theories, which have great capacity to arouse common affects and aspirations in the Turkish context and, therefore, are very effective tools in influencing the general public. The conspiracies focused on foreign plots, a narrative embedded in the collective memory of Turkish society due to the political developments occurring within the last few decades of the Ottoman Empire. Simply put, socio-political disintegration and fragmentation during the nineteenth and early twentieth century, the difficulties experienced after the defeat of the Ottoman Empire in the First World War, and the hostile ambitions of the imperialist powers of the period created deeply embedded suspicions and anxieties particularly concerning the 'outside world' and 'foreign powers'. The suspicions about the outside world and accompanying conspiracy theories were often used in the following periods in the mainstream discourses. As a result, conspiracies formed in the Turkish context, to a considerable extent became a common disposition, a way of thinking and a way of making political analysis (Gürpınar, 2013; Guida, 2008).

Hence, in its bid to justify and legitimate gold mining in the eyes of the general public, the gold mining discourse became highly vocal on development themes and conspiratorial themes. While the company took the lead in the construction of this discourse, re-articulation by other actors, such as journalists, academics and politicians, proved critical in its dissemination and popular appeal, as shown in the following.

Increasing the Appeal of the Gold Mining Discourse

A number of new actors were involved in the gold mining campaign in the second half of 2001 after a new court decision in favor of the Bergama movement. As an outcome of the new litigation process started by the protesters, the Izmir Administrative Court canceled the mining company's operation permits on the basis of the above-mentioned circular of the Prime

Ministry (Cangı, 2002). Following this court order, a newspaper, and a group of journalists, academics, and politicians embarked on a range of seemingly highly coordinated practices to counter the Bergama movement. To be more concrete, these attacks on protestors came from the mainstream newspaper, *Milliyet*, previously supportive of the protesters in the earlier phases of the struggle, journalists and columnists, academics, and two politicians (Erol Al and Hasan Ozgobek) from the Democratic Leftist Party (DSP), a partner of the coalition government of the time.

Following the lead of the company, these actors also focused their efforts on representing gold mining as critically significant for economic development, on the one hand, and demonizing the Bergama movement on the basis of conspiratorial claims, on the other. In doing these, they re-articulated, refined, and elaborated the gold mining discourse originally constituted through the efforts of the mining company. Since they engaged in these efforts at a time of deep economic crisis, as mentioned earlier, these actors placed great emphasis on the extraction of 'the large amounts of gold reserves in Turkey' for economic recovery. It was the two politicians from the ruling DSP who first voiced these arguments. They prepared a report that speculated that there are gold reserves in 580 different locales in Turkey (Akdemir, 2011). Then, a number of first-page news and commentaries in favor of gold mining appeared in *Milliyet*. For instance:

> According to the reports on gold mining that were presented to the Prime Minister, Turkey has the second biggest gold reserves in the world after South Africa ... The scientific reports presented to the Prime Minister show that Turkey can use these reserves to overcome its economic hardships. According to studies, the minimum value of Turkey's gold reserves is about 400 billion dollars ... If all reserves are opened to production, it will create employment opportunity for 25 thousand people. (Bila, *Milliyet*, 30 June 2001)

These claims were accompanied by conspiratorial allegations about the protesters, but this time by clearly pointing to external forces behind the protests. Specifically, it was stated that the Bergama movement was 'supported by German FIAN foundation'. It was also claimed that 'Germany's gold export to Turkey, which is about 800 million dollars a year, is seen as the reason behind the support of German institutions to the protesters' (Bila, *Milliyet*, 30 June 2001). Similar news and commentaries continued to appear in the same newspaper during July and August 2001. For instance, an article that appeared one day after the commentary quoted above stated, 'there are insistent claims about the financial support of Germany to the resistance in Bergama', while another maintained that 'mining engineers and academics believe that it is meaningless to oppose to gold-mining' (*Milliyet*, 1 July 2001). A few days later, another article entitled 'Bergama mine proudly presents' stated that the gold mining company in Bergama had taken all possible safety measures (*Milliyet*, 12 July 2001). The following day another article entitled 'Opinions were changed after the gold production' stated, without evidence, that the protesters had given up resisting and began supporting the mine after they saw the gold produced by the company (*Milliyet*, 13 July 2001). *Milliyet* also widely covered the other actors' pro-mining activities, including the press conferences of the company officials, and that of the 18 academics from the mining departments of different universities with the following first-page headline: 'Turkey will overcome economic crisis through gold mining' (*Milliyet*, 14 July 2001). In the following weeks, more news items appeared underlining how Turkey would use its gold reserves to leap forward in economic development (*Milliyet*, 29 July 2001; *Milliyet*, 24 August 2001).

These endeavors were greatly aided with a book issued in August 2001 (Hablemitoğlu, 2001). Written by an academic and distributed widely free of charge, the book put forth the same claims, reinforced with new conspiratorial claims, nationalist themes, and, more strikingly, the exploitation of religious differences and enmities within Turkish society. Overall, the book closely tied gold mining to 'national interests', while painting the protesters as the 'betrayers' of national interests. In a bid to support the claim about the protesters' 'betrayal', it raised new conspiratorial claims while evoking historical religious enmities.

Specifically, the book detailed the claim that Germany was behind the protests. It contended that the leading protesters, whether 'deliberately or not', worked for Germany and for their own selfish individual interests, receiving financial support from some German foundations active in Turkey to prevent gold mining. It maintained that, as part of a German plan to prevent Turkey from extracting its rich gold reserves, these foundations instigated the leading protesters to mobilize the local population in Bergama against the mine on environmental grounds. Overall, the book's patriotic rhetoric attempted to harness the rich affective range of nationalism, drawing on both positive aspects such as pride and belonging, and negative aspects, such as hatred and fear, in favor of gold mining and against the Bergama movement and the protesters. By portraying Turkey's rich potential for development through the use of its gold reserves and, thereby, its national strength, it aimed to render the mining as a key issue for national interests. In this respect, it also drew an analogy between gold mining and the two 'hot topics' of Turkish nationalism, the Kurdish issue and the Cyprus issue. For instance, referring to a European Parliament's resolution on Turkey, it said:

> If you say with a natural reflex 'I am not an occupying power in Cyprus, I do not give Cyprus' or 'I do not deliberately contribute to the process of establishment of a separate Kurdish state', then you should oppose to the [environmental] demands of European Parliament on thermal power plants and on gold production in Bergama. (Hablemitoğlu, 2001, p. 6)

The book also, as mentioned above, presented the protesters as fronts for foreign powers, that is, as those who act against the national interests. It is also interesting to note in this respect that the book employed this nationalist rhetoric to promote the operation of the multinational gold mining company; all companies, it stated, whether Turkish or foreign, that contribute to the Turkish economy should be welcomed (Hablemitoğlu, 2001).

Moreover, and perhaps more importantly, the book also attempted to exploit the ethno-religious cleavages and conflict between the Sunni majority and Alevi minority in favor of gold mining. On the basis of a selective view of the protesters, it claimed that only Alevi villagers were opposed to the mine. More precisely, the book's distinct ethno-religious bias was seen in the assertion that the German foundations instigated the leading protesters to mobilize the Alevi villages on environmental grounds. This was not an empirically valid claim because only three of the seventeen villages that opposed the mine were Alevi villages. The deliberate misrepresentation of the protesters' religious identities aimed to sway public sympathy by capitalizing on the Sunni majority's deeply embedded prejudices about the Alevi minority.

The book rapidly brought the gold mining issue onto the public agenda. Based on these allegations, TV programs were made, and headlines appeared on the front pages of almost all daily newspapers (Özen, 2009). Several influential columnists drew on the claims to justify views in favor of gold mining. For instance, criticizing a court order issued in favor of the protesters, a columnist stated:

Whatever its reason, the protests hinder the use of our natural resources which could change the fate of Turkey. As you can guess, I am talking about the [theater] play being staged [by the Bergama movement] for 13 years ... The peasants, who probably know nothing about the concept of environment, engage in protests for protecting environment. They come to Ankara and stage protests to resist imperialism, a term they, perhaps, have never heard of before. And [they assume that] the people of this country are stupid enough to believe that all these are nothing but 'an innocent peasant reaction'. (Ekşi, *Hürriyet*, 18 October 2002)

In another article, the same columnist, implicitly approving the violation of the rule of law by the government, claimed that there was no country in the world that, despite having existing gold reserves, does not produce more gold (Ekşi, *Hürriyet*, 19 October 2002). Similar arguments and claims were expressed by a number of other influential columnists. Following all these, the same claims were publicly expressed by many state authorities to strengthen their support for the mining company. It is striking to note for example that a military official, the then air force commander, clearly stated the same claims when answering journalists' questions about missions in Afghanistan: 'You should look at Turkey. We have the richest gold reserves in the world. But they cannot be extracted because of Germany' (*Star*, 2 October 2001). Another telling example is the visit by a group of high-ranking military officials to the company to present a plaque showing their gratitude for its service to Turkey (*Cumhuriyet*, 28 October 2002).

Thus, the campaign against the Bergama became overly focused on the economic benefits of gold mining and on the protesters' betrayal and treachery of the country. It was, however, curiously silent on the environmental issues leading to the mobilization of the Bergama protesters. It is to this silence that now I turn.

The Silence of the Gold Mining Discourse on Environmental Issues

In attacking environmental movements, anti-environmental counter-movements often adopt the tactic of undermining the environmental claims of these movements (see Boynton, 2015; Dunlap and McCright, 2015; Ferguson, 2009; McCright and Dunlap, 2000, 2003). They promote 'environmental skepticism' by raising questions and doubts about the seriousness and the scale of environmental problems (Jacques et al., 2008, p. 351). Moreover, they prioritize economic growth and development over environment (see Lomborg, 2001). In relation to this, they often rely on constructing binary arguments and dichotomies by 'counter-posing "jobs" versus "nature", "people" versus "planet", "growth" versus the "environment" and so on' (White et al., 2007, p. 135).

Unlike other environmental counter-movements, the campaign against the Bergama movement did not directly confront the environmental claims of the protesters. It neither disputed the seriousness of environmental claims of the Bergama movement, nor accused the protesters of raising unnecessary and unjustified environmental issues. In fact, the gold mining discourse articulated through the campaign against the Bergama movement hardly voiced environmental issues or even mentioned the environment. Instead of trying to downplay the seriousness of the environmental problems, this discourse exaggerated the economic benefits of gold mining. Accordingly, the diverse criticisms made of the Bergama movement by the different actors of the pro-gold mining campaign focused mainly on the negative effects of the movement on economic development, and on the hidden and malicious aims of the leading protesters. In doing this, rather than counter-pose 'development' versus 'environment', they claimed that 'development' was blocked by those who used the environment as a pretext to hide their real aims.

This deliberate silence on environmental issues was strategic. It was an integral part of the gold mining discourse or, more precisely, an integral part of the strategies underlying this discourse and, as such, it conveyed certain messages. As argued by Foucault (1978, p. 27), silence is 'less the absolute limit of discourse, the other side from which it is separated by a strict boundary, than an element that functions alongside the things said, with them and in relation to them within over-all strategies.' In order to grasp the meaning of the silence of the pro-gold mining discourse on ecological/environmental issues, therefore, we should consider it in addition to the voiced discourse. Taking both into account, it can be said that gold mining discourse functioned in two specific ways. One is that by usurping the public space with the significance and indispensability of gold mining for economic development, but ignoring the environmental cost of such development, it dictated which issue would and which would not form the agenda of the state or the public concerning gold mining. In other words, by bringing economic development to the forefront, it infused gold mining with economic gains, but not with environmental problems. The other function of the discourse was that it became possible to construct the Bergama movement as a foreign conspiracy and treason only through the silence over the movement's genuinely pro-environment nature.

Hence, by adopting the strategy of silence, the anti-environmental campaign aimed at rendering invisible both the environmental issues voiced by the Bergama movement and the environmental character of this movement. This strategic silence, in this sense, is similar to Lester and Hutchins' (2012, p. 851) concept of 'strategic invisibility'. Examining an environmental conflict in Tasmania, Lester and Hutchins argue that major participants in such conflicts may deliberately remain invisible and keep environmental issues out of sight in order to minimize the effects of the media and others on the definition of environmental risks and problems. Both strategies, thus, are based on 'instrumental logic of containment' (Lester and Hutchins, 2012, p. 859) and, accordingly, are intended to control the meanings attributed to the environment and environmental issues. Remaining silent or invisible, as Lester and Hutchins (2012) also emphasize, is both the instrument and effect of power. Therefore, depending on who uses them against whom, these strategies may create highly significant outcomes. In the Tasmanian case, the concerted efforts to maintain the invisibility of all parties involved in the environmental conflict reduced the influence of the media over the process of negotiations between these parties. In contrast in the Bergama case, the pro-gold mining groups' silence on environmental issues and on the environmental character of the movement made repression possible without igniting a serious public reaction.

Repression of the Bergama Movement

The representation of the Bergama movement not as an environmental movement against gold mining, but, rather, as a particular instance of an overall plan and plot against Turkey, enabled the authorities to define and treat it as a national security issue and, on the basis of this, to introduce a series of repressive measures. In this regard, the allegations of the collaboration with German foundations were used as grounds for placing the Bergama movement on the agenda of the National Security Council, a state institution dealing with security issues. Almost simultaneously, it was also brought to the Turkish parliament's agenda by one of the above-mentioned Members of Parliament, who demanded an investigation on the activities of German foundations in Turkey (*Hürriyet*, 29 September 2001).

Eventually, the chief prosecutor of Ankara State Security Court started an investigation into both the German foundations and the leading protesters for engaging in activities threatening state security. Following the investigation, the prosecutor brought the case to the State Security Court, preparing an indictment in which the German foundations were charged with engaging in clandestine activities and espionage to undermine the Turkish state, while the leading protesters were charged with spying for Germany and receiving money from German foundations (*Turkish Daily News*, 31 October 2002). Presenting the claims in Hablemitoğlu's book as evidence for all these allegations, the prosecutor accused the protesters with the charge of 'secret plots against the security of the state' under Article 171 of the Turkish Penal Code (*Turkish Daily News*, 31 January 2003). What is noteworthy here is that the activities described in this article were defined in the Anti-Terror Law among the terrorist offenses. In the meantime, there was a harsher response of social control agencies to the Bergama protests, even though these had become considerably more moderate than the ones staged in the 1990s (*Hürriyet*, 27 May 2001; 26 March 2002; 3 July 2002). The police responses to the public protests of the Bergama movement together with the long series of trials in the State Security Court were widely covered by national media. All these strategies proved highly influential in decreasing public sympathy for the Bergama movement. Although the State Security Court eventually acquitted the protesters, there was no substantial change in public opinion, which had been shaped through the allegations of the actors of the gold mining campaign.

Anti-Environmental Effects of the Campaign

The campaign achieved its aim of radically altering the whole context of the gold mining debate that the Bergama movement had started. By speculating about the gold reserves in Turkey and, in relation to this, by associating gold mining with economic development, it was able to shift the debate in its favor. As this campaign made its appearance in 2001, at a time of deep economic crisis, the emphasis on the economic development resonated with the general public. The speculations about the extent of the gold reserves made the claims about the German plot more plausible. However, it was particularly the claims about the covert collaboration of the leading protesters with German foundations that attracted attention and proved critically influential in the formation of public opinion about the Bergama movement. Leading figures were successfully portrayed as those attempting to block 'highly valuable economic investments for the interests of another country', and their followers were depicted as 'deceived by a few leading protesters', and consequently public support for the Bergama movement sharply declined (Özen, 2009). After the withdrawal of the support of many individuals, groups, NGOs and the media, the Bergama movement was considerably weakened in the early 2000s. After the pro-mining bloc's criminalizing efforts, there was a general demobilization, not only of supporters in the wider society, but also of many of the movement's main constituents, such as members of the local agricultural community and others from Bergama.

More importantly, the campaign enabled the political power to reshape mining policy and environmental policy to benefit the interests of mining corporations (Özen and Özen, 2011). In 2002, the authorities began to work on a new mining law in an attempt to block potential 'threats' to future operations. The new mining law (Law no. 5177), which also made amendments to the Law on the Protection of Cultural and Natural Heritage, Environmental

Law, Forests Law and National Parks Law, was enacted in 2004. The new law allows mining developments in formerly protected areas, such as olive groves, coasts, forests, agricultural lands, national parks and historic sites, and eliminates the need for an Environmental Impact Assessment before mining begins. It also exempts gold extraction from Value Added Tax, and prohibits the withdrawal of mining licenses once granted. With the enactment of the new law, the authorities, in fact, attempted not only to increase the attractiveness of Turkey for mining multinationals, but also to block future court decisions against the gold mine operations on the basis of their negative environmental impacts. Although the Bergama protesters raised objections to the new law, these were not successful, in part due to the protesters' reduced credibility in the eyes of the wider public.

In addition to weakening the Bergama movement, one of the immediate effects of the campaign was to encourage the spread of gold mining operations across the country. The number of companies that obtained licenses for gold mining increased to 61, which included operations in areas of natural and historical significance, such as Mount Ida. Another, and perhaps more important effect of the campaign, was the repetition of the same discursive strategies and tactics against those environmental movements that managed to attract popular attention and support. Notable examples are the environmental protest movements opposing gold mining projects in Efemcukuru village in İzmir district, in Esme, a town in the district of Usak, and in Artvin (Akdemir, 2011; Özen and Özen, 2018; Özen and Dogu, 2020), and against resistance to hydroelectric power plants in the Black sea region (Özen, 2014). In all these cases, the projects opposed by the protest movements were presented as of vital importance and, therefore, inevitable for the country's economic development as well as for national interests, while the protesters were accused of conspiring against Turkey in collusion with foreign powers. As such, the discursive strategies and tactics used against the initial environmental gains of the Bergama movement formed the repertoire of anti-environmentalism in Turkey.

CONCLUSION

This study has focused on the anti-environmental campaign launched in response to the popularity and gains of the Bergama movement, which posed the first enduring and substantial challenge to gold mining policies on environmental grounds. It has demonstrated that, in an attempt to overcome the challenges of the Bergama movement and to legitimize the gold mining agenda, this campaign articulated a strongly pro-gold mining discourse. Based on the fabrication of various post-truth claims and on the use of culturally resonant themes, this discourse represented gold mining as vital for the economic progress of the country and for national interests, while painting the protesters as those who hinder economic development and threaten national interests and security in the service of foreign powers. As a strategic maneuver, it avoided positioning itself in a critical relationship to environmentalism of the Bergama movement, and as such, instead of trying to repudiate environmental claims, it remained totally silent on these issues. The success of the anti-environmental campaign against the Bergama movement was proportional to its ability to use this particular blend of silence and voice on gold mining, on the Bergama movement itself, and on the environmental issues it raised. With this blend of silence and voice, it managed, on the one hand, to infuse the image of gold mining with economic development but not with environmental degradation and, on the other, to frame the movement as a foreign conspiracy aimed at curtailing economic development. As such, the campaign also prepared the ground for the repression of the movement while avoiding igniting a public reaction. Specifically, it cast the protesters as agents of repression who deserved to be punished for blocking economic development in the service of foreign powers.

The extant literature on anti-environmentalism shows how counter-movements attack environmental movements and environmentalism by raising doubts about their environmental claims (Boynton, 2015; Dunlap and McCright, 2015; Ferguson, 2009; Jacques et al., 2008; McCright and Dunlap, 2000, 2003), and by prioritizing economic gains over environment (Lomborg, 2001; White et al., 2007; Lewin, 2019). The analysis presented in this study contributes to this literature by showing that anti-environmental counter-movements may not merely focus their efforts on explicitly refuting environmental claims. They may also try to remove environmental issues from the public agenda, or hinder their entrance on to the public agenda. This involves deliberate silence on environmental issues, while at the same time being extremely vocal on other issues such as economic development or national interests. This is potentially an effective strategy for anti-environmental counter-movements in rendering environmental claims invisible and in condemning environmental movements to obscurity.

Another contribution that this study makes to the anti-environmentalism literature is that it demonstrates that anti-environmental groups, in their attempts to curb the influences of environmental movements and to promote pro-corporate practices and legislation, may not be satisfied with a simple appeal to the economic longings and aspirations of the masses. They may additionally attempt to incite popular fears and anxieties, to evoke patriotic and nationalistic sentiments, and to create a sense of insecurity. In short, as Lewin (2019) also confirms in a recent study, they may try to mobilize affect and emotions in favor of ecologically hazardous corporate activities and against environmental movements. In doing this, they may draw on existing narratives and legacies in order to capitalize on meanings and understandings inherent in specific cultural contexts. As we have seen in the Turkish case, the anti-environmental actors emphasized the deployment of culturally and historically specific themes that resonate with wider social segments. More precisely, they drew on nationalism and development discourses as well as conspiracy theories firmly embedded in the national political culture in promoting gold mining, as well as in building up hostility to the Bergama movement. What is more striking in this respect, perhaps, is that in their attempt to demonize the environmental protesters in the eyes of the general public, the anti-environmental actors had no hesitation over attempting to reincarnate historical enmities between different religious groups.

Future research on anti-environmentalism should take into account the strategic silence of anti-environmental counter-movements, as well as the issues that they voice. There should be further exploration of the approaches these movements take to keep environmental issues out of public sight, and the adaptation of these approaches depending on the political context. Comparative studies focusing on authoritarian and democratic polities might be insightful in this regard. There are also interesting research avenues concerning the role of affect and culturally inherent meanings in the constitution and popular appeal of anti-environmentalism. Knowledge can be further advanced by comparing anti-environmental movements' and environmental movements' use of the same or similar cultural themes, and examining how the use of culturally resonant themes obscures pressing environmental problems.

REFERENCES

Adaman, F. and Arsel, M. (2005) Introduction. In: Adaman, F. and Arsel, M. (eds) *Environmentalism in Turkey*. Farnham: Ashgate.

Akdemir, Ö. (2011) *Kuyudaki Taş: Alman Vakıfları ve Bergama Gerçeği*. Istanbul: Evrensel.

Austin, A. (2002) Advancing accumulation and managing its discontents: The U.S. antienvironmental countermovement. *Sociological Spectrum*. **22**(1), pp. 71–105.

Boynton, A. (2015) Formulating an anti-environmental opposition: Neoconservative intellectuals during the environmental decade. *The Sixties*. **8**(1), pp. 1–26.

Buğra, A. (1994) *State and Business in Modern Turkey: A Comparative Study*. New York, NY: SUNY Press.

Buğra, A. and, Savaşkan, O. (2012) Politics and class: The Turkish business environment in the neoliberal age. *New Perspectives on Turkey*. **46**, pp. 27–63.

Cangı, A. (2002) Bergama, Siyanür, Altın, Mahkeme Kararları, Hukuksal Süreç. Available from: http://www.geocites.com/siyanurlealtin/yazi/2002/sureç.html (accessed 18 May 2004).

Cavdar, G. (2012) Heterogeneous transformation of Islamism: The justice and development party and the environment. *The Arab World Geographer*. **15**(1), pp. 1–19.

Dunlap, R.E. and McCright, A.M. (2015) Challenging climate change: The denial countermovement. In: Dunlap, R. and Brulle, R. (eds) *Climate Change and Society: Sociological Perspectives*. New York, NY: Oxford University Press, pp. 300–333.

Ferguson, P. (2009) Anti-environmentalism and the Australian culture war. *Journal of Australian Studies*. **33**(3), pp. 289–304.

Foucault, M. (1978) *The History of Sexuality*. New York, NY: Vintage Books.

Guida, M. (2008) The Sèvres Syndrome and 'Komplo' theories in the Islamist and secular press. *Turkish Studies*. **9**(1), pp. 37–52.

Gürpinar, D. (2013) Historical revisionism vs. conspiracy theories: Transformations of Turkish historical scholarship and conspiracy theories as a constitutive element in transforming Turkish nationalism. *Journal of Balkan and Near Eastern Studies*. **15**(4), pp. 412–33.

Hablemitoğlu, N. (2001) *Alman Vakıfları: Bergama Dosyası*. Istanbul: Otopsi Yayınevi.

Jacques, P.J., Dunlap, R.E. and Freeman, M. (2008) The organization of denial: Conservative think tanks and environmental scepticism. *Environmental Politics*. **17**(3), pp. 349–85.

Kadirbeyoğlu, Z. (2001) *The Transstate Dimension of the Bergama Resistance against Eurogold*. The German–Turkish Summer Institute Working Paper No. 6. Ankara: Orta Doğu Teknik Üniversitesi.

Lester, L. and Hutchins, B. (2012) The power of the unseen: Environmental conflict, the media and invisibility. *Media, Culture & Society*. **34**(7), pp. 847–63.

Lewin, P.G. (2019) Coal is not just a job, it's a way of life: The cultural politics of coal production in central Appalachia. *Social Problems*. **66**(1), pp. 51–68.

Lomborg, B. (2001) *The Skeptical Environmentalist: Measuring the Real State of the World*. Cambridge: Cambridge University Press.

McCright, A.M. and Dunlap, R.E. (2000) Challenging global warming as a social problem: An analysis of the Conservative movement's counter-claims. *Social Problems*. **47**(4), pp. 499–522.

McCright, A.M. and Dunlap, R.E. (2003) Defeating Kyoto: The conservative movement's impact on US climate change policy. *Social Problems*. **50**(3), pp. 348–73.

Öniş, Z. (2004) Turgut Özal and his economic legacy: Turkish neo-liberalism in critical perspective. *Middle Eastern Studies*. **40**(4), pp. 113–34.

Öniş, Z. (2010) Crises and transformations in Turkish political economy. *Turkish Policy Quarterly*. **9**(3), pp. 45–61.

Ovacik Bulletin (2000a) Basın Bildirisi. *Ovacik 2000 Monthly Bulletin*. **2**(4).

Ovacik Bulletin (2000b) Şimdi Sorgulama Zamanı.... *Ovacik 2000 Monthly Bulletin*. **2**(4).

Özen, H. (2009) Located locally, disseminated nationally: The Bergama movement. *Environmental Politics*. **18**(3), pp. 408–23.

Özen, H. (2014) Overcoming environmental challenges by antagonizing environmental protesters: The Turkish government discourse against anti-hydroelectric power plants movements. *Environmental Communication*. **8**(4), pp. 433–51.

Özen, H. and Dogu, B. (2020) Mobilizing in a hybrid political system: The Artvin case in Turkey. *Democratization.* **27**(4), pp. 624–42. Available from DOI: 10.1080/13510347.2019.1711372.

Özen, H. and Özen, Ş. (2011) Interactions in and between strategic action fields: A comparative analysis of two environmental conflicts in gold-mining fields in Turkey. *Organization & Environment.* **24**(4), pp. 343–63.

Özen, H. and Özen, Ş. (2018) What comes after repression? The hegemonic contestation in the gold-mining field in Turkey. *Geoforum.* **88**(1), pp. 1–9.

Özveren, E. and Nas, S.N. (2012) Economic development and environmental policy in Turkey: An institutionalist critique. *Cambridge Journal of Economics.* **36**(5), pp. 1245–66.

Pamuk, S. (2012) Ottoman economic legacy from the nineteenth century. In: Heper, M. and Sayarı, S. (eds) *The Routledge Handbook of Modern Turkey.* London, UK and New York, NY, USA: Routledge, pp. 44–52.

Şenses, F. (2012) Turkey's experience with neoliberal policies since 1980 in retrospect and prospect. *New Perspective on Turkey.* **47**, pp. 11–31.

Somersan, S. (1993) *Olağan Ülkeden Olağanüstü Ülkeye Türkiye de Çevre ve Siyaset.* İstanbul: Metis Yayınları.

Taşkın, S. (1998) *Siyanürcü Ahtapot.* Istanbul: Sel Yayınları.

TMMOB (2003) *Bergama-Ovacık Altın İşletmesi Girişimi Konusunda TUBITAK-YDABCAG Uzmanlar Komisyonu Raporu Elestirisi.* Ankara: TMMOB Jeoloji Muhendisleri Odasi.

Ünalan, D. (2016) Governmentality and environmentalism in Turkey: Power, politics, and environmental movements. In: Özbay, C., Erol, M., Terzioğlu, A. and Türem, U. (eds) *The Making of Neoliberal Turkey.* Burlington: Ashgate, pp. 221–34.

White, D.F., Rudy, A.P. and Wilbert, C. (2007) Anti-environmentalism: Prometheans, contrarians and beyond. In: Pretty, J., Ball, A.S., Benton, T., Guivant, J.S., Lee, D.R., Orr, D., Pfeffer, M.J. et al. (eds) *The SAGE Handbook of Environment and Society.* London: Sage, pp. 124–42.

PART VII

AGRICULTURE AND ANTI-ENVIRONMENTALISM

15. Food sovereignty and anti-regulation from the left
James S. Krueger

1. FOOD SOVEREIGNTY AGAINST AGRICULTURAL REGULATION

Environmentalists and anti-environmentalists are thought to have sharply contrasting perspectives on the role of state law, with environmentalists being 'pro-regulation' and anti-environmentalists 'anti-regulation'. Environmentalists push for stronger collective action to prevent pollution, encourage sustainable land use, and reduce energy consumption, among other things. Anti-environmentalism, to complete the caricature, is a counter-movement that feels that the government has overreached on environmental policy and is hampering otherwise economically beneficial activities and even pro-poor development. Anti-environmentalists might favor using the resources that are available rather than conserving them, and might prefer that more decision-making be left to economic actors, in government or the private sector.

So what happens when self-identifying environmentalists take a position against state regulation? It is of course not unusual for environmentalists to allege that particular industries have captured government agencies, and that the voting public should organize and take back their government so that it works in the public interest. It is something else for a movement to argue that state agencies are not the right loci for regulating economic activities at all and are doing more harm than good when it comes to achieving sustainability. The food sovereignty movement, I will argue, has taken precisely this position. They self-identify as environmentalists, but their anti-regulatory stance presents serious problems for achieving an environmentally conscientious society. Most importantly, they oppose not only state regulation but also non-state forms of control and accountability for farmers.

My argument has several aspects. First, the food sovereignty movement is interesting and relevant to the literature on anti-environmentalism as a counter example that shows the limitations of the environmentalist versus anti-environmentalist binary. Food sovereignty is a movement that self-identifies as environmentalist, but is also anti-regulatory, making it strangely attractive both to environmentally oriented supporters of agroecology and to libertarians, property rights advocates, and farmers whose environmentalism is grounded in what they individually think is best. Second, I provide a constructive critique of food sovereignty's approach to regulation. I highlight their position against some aspects of state regulation but find room for conciliation with nonstate regulation. Third, I argue that the food sovereignty movement, through its anti-regulatory rhetoric, is making it hard to talk about its own quasi-regulatory practices. The movement is not having an open conversation about its own techniques of social control, about the legitimacy of its authority, and about exclusionary practices against outsiders to the movement.

To get from food sovereignty to anti-regulation and anti-environment takes some explaining. Food sovereigntists are the champions of small-scale farmers and food producers – of peasants controlling their own food and destiny – and rightly point to the various ways that state regulation harms smallholders and favors industrial agriculture. Food sovereignty has been defined, in part, as a collective right of peoples 'to define their own food and agriculture system' (Declaration of Nyéléni, 2007). Food sovereignty activists self-identify as pro-environmentalist and pursue agroecology – which is about sustainable and ecologically based farming – as one of their central goals (Martínez-Torres and Rosset, 2014). They also talk about a right of peoples to *regulate* their own agriculture (Rosset, 2003), which would seem to indicate that they are in favor of regulation of some kind. I also am sympathetic to these goals.

Their anti-regulatory stance, at least initially, is also compelling. They argue that state agricultural regulation is designed to facilitate industrial agriculture and that therefore, because industrial agriculture is demonstrably unsustainable, this kind of regulation stands as an obstacle to real sustainable farming. They single out particular types of state law for their ire that are against environmental goals, such as food safety regulations, or incentives for monocropping soybeans or maize, or private ownership of seed varieties through patents. They similarly protest against private food production standards that go together with vertical integration in transnational agricultural supply chains. This is essentially a Polanyian point: large-scale markets and state agricultural regulation actually reinforce one another, rather than oppose one another, such that the debate over market versus government control actually obscures what is going on in industrial farming.

Yet, when it comes to proposing alternative forms of regulation to replace existing pro-industry regulation, their reform agenda falls apart. They go too far with anti-regulatory sentiment. As I will try to show, food sovereignty activists have reservations about both state *and* nonstate forms of regulation, revealing a general distaste for systems of control and accountability over farmers. Their orientation is one of critique: remove the regulatory and policy supports for large industrial agriculture, and local and community-based forms of production will magically self-organize. As a social movement battling powerful actors in industrial agriculture, they tend to imagine long-term success as a continuation of the battle, with comrades bonding over their in-group status, rather than thinking about how to live with others with opposing views in a system of daily regulation and mutually acceptable restraints.

Food sovereignty has an internal contradiction over the role of regulation in people's lives. The movement tends to downplay (or denounce) relations of hierarchy and acts of coercion, but must engage hierarchy and act coercively when it comes to managing the day-to-day relations of food production. In short, food sovereigntists are engaged in regulatory activities – regulating their members for example – but are in denial that they are doing so. By rejecting regulation and hierarchy in rhetoric, food sovereigntists come to be accidental allies of libertarians and anarchists who favor self-organization and freedom from government of any kind.

Yet regulation of some kind is clearly necessary for sustainability. The food sovereignty movement could engage more openly and productively with the question of regulation, particularly in the area of nonstate law. Activists can then raise important questions about who gets to regulate (i.e. questions about the legitimacy of hierarchy and expertise), at what administrative level, following which appropriate procedures. If food sovereignty regulation is to manifest in a particular locality, as a quasi-governmental entity, then it must consider the critical question of how to engage with dissidents who do not agree with its goals.

The problem of the legitimacy of environmental regulators – or indeed the legitimacy of environmental movement actors – has not been addressed sufficiently in the literature on environmentalism or anti-environmentalism, in part because this legitimacy is seen from the perspective of writers and academics who are insiders and sympathizers to the environmental movement. The legitimacy of regulators is too often assumed to be established definitively by some combination of professional expertise, the facts themselves, and personal sincerity and authenticity. Yet clearly one of the main concerns that self-identifying 'anti-environmentalists' bring to the debate about environmental regulation is the legitimacy of regulation – the feeling of being regulated, by untrustworthy others, in the interest of those others. This is a significant but under-addressed issue in the literature on anti-environmentalism, and I take it up here by proxy, by looking at food sovereignty's own questioning of the legitimacy of regulation, and its struggle to introduce new forms of local food governance and new types of legitimacy.

The chapter will look at food sovereignty's problems with regulation – first at problems with state regulation and then at problems with nonstate regulation. It then turns to food sovereignty's internal contradiction – disliking and yet needing to employ regulatory tools like hierarchy and coercion. The contradiction, once expressed, can be resolved into new insights about how to govern social movements and how to use nonstate law. The question of regulation is reframed to ask, what is a social movement's vision of daily governance – of social control – beyond the good feelings generated by participation in the movement?

A side note on my sources and approach is warranted. I am sampling from a very broad and dynamic social movement that is purposefully open to different views and practices of food sovereignty on the ground (Patel, 2009, p. 666). My theoretical engagement with the food sovereignty movement is somewhat disconnected from the peculiarities of food sovereignty activism in particular places and countries. This is partly in keeping with the spirit of food sovereignty itself, which is transnational in scope, but it is more particularly in keeping with my own purpose, which is to explore a theoretical contradiction that exists in the seed of food sovereignty and that can be found anywhere it sprouts.

I rely mainly on the scholarly literature on food sovereignty, which is extensive, and which includes many accounts from farmers and activists who are participating in food sovereignty. I defer at times to statements from La Vía Campesina ('the way of the peasant'), which is a transnational umbrella organization for peasants that has more than any other group articulated and championed food sovereignty.

My goal is to problematize the issue of regulation for food sovereigntists, not pin down any sub-group's definitive views. I aim to be constructively critical, but I should also acknowledge that I am an outsider to the movement. Nonetheless, I benefit from the significant partnership between other academics and food sovereignty activists that makes the academic literature particularly rich in examples and life experience. There are other sources of authority on food sovereignty and differences for example between academics and peasant activists, and between the US and other countries, that I only touch on.

2. FOOD SOVEREIGNTY AND STATE REGULATION

2.1 Overview

US food sovereignty activists have repeatedly and vociferously objected to state regulatory control over farming. Joel Salatin, a radical farmer and local sustainable foods activist, expresses this succinctly in his essay title: 'Everything I want to do is illegal' (2003). The legal system of business licensing, land use planning and zoning, and food safety, according to Salatin, prevents a small farmer from raising an animal, slaughtering it on his farm, and selling it to his neighbor. State regulations can inadvertently put small sustainable farmers out of business (e.g. McMahon, 2014, p. 114). Or, more insidiously, '[Big food industries] are the ones writing the rules ... Food safety rules could more accurately be called Big Food Protection Acts' (Heather Retberg, quoted in Trauger, 2017, p. 75).

Salatin perhaps represents the libertarian strain of food sovereignty, as practiced particularly in the US, but other food sovereignty activists share his sense of unease about state regulators. Outside of the US and the Global North, the state is not effective enough to create many of the impositions that Salatin is talking about, like limitations on on-farm meat processing. Rather, activists in the Global South complain about direct state action in support of large-scale productivist agriculture. The state might recognize private rights over resources that were under customary control and allocate the resources to investors, or might coerce farmers into accepting detailed farming and land use practices in exchange for access to loans or subsidized inputs.

There is a palpable sense of tension, in the US and abroad, between the state policymaking apparatus – which is complex and expert-driven and out-of-reach – and the average smallholder on the ground. Food sovereignty everywhere 'expresses peasant activists' widespread perception that they have no voice in decision-making' (Claeys, 2012, p. 849). Patel and McMichael (2004, p. 249), scholar-allies of the food sovereignty movement, put this bluntly: 'since the state has been captured by capital ... the ability of small farmers to influence state policy ... has been abrogated.'

Despite the general ill-feeling toward state regulation, some food sovereigntists have advocated for alternative state laws that would support food sovereignty. Rosset (2006, pp. 34–5) helpfully lists some specific regulatory interventions, such as direct state action to subsidize and support domestic and small-scale agriculture; maximum limits on farm size; local control over seed, land, water and forest; and an end to patenting seeds. Edelman (2014, p. 970) argues that food sovereignty advocates have not been clear about which institutions will enforce such rules and how those institutions will do it. He considers how the state might enforce limits on farm and firm size and limits on long distance trade and warns about difficulties like lack of political will, ease of circumventing the rules, and cost of enforcement (Edelman, 2014, pp. 970–72).

A more significant underlying problem with food sovereignty's reform suggestions is that the suggestions, while seemingly referring to law, actually are in favor of allocating decision-making powers to local farmer groups or local nonstate councils, away from state regulators. Food sovereigntists at times openly express their desire to break the state's monopoly on lawmaking and allow for other local forms of agricultural regulation (Claeys, 2015, p. 455). Others push for regulation of agriculture on multiple levels of government simultaneously (Schiavoni, 2015, p. 468) but explicitly authorize the local level to act autonomously from higher levels of government.

Several countries have a specific 'food sovereignty' law (Venezuela, Ecuador, Bolivia, Nepal, Mali, Senegal and Egypt) (Anderson, 2018), but no country has a detailed set of national or local regulations for implementing food sovereignty. Such regulations would contradict existing laws (seed patents, subsidies for commodity crops, World Trade Organization, etc.) and other policy goals (agricultural intensification, food safety, etc.) (Bellinger and Fakhri, 2013, p. 48). Considering the difficulty of implementing a real food sovereignty law, activists suspect that existing state food sovereignty laws are for display purposes only. The premier activist group behind food sovereignty, La Vía Campesina, has worried over the dangers of cooption and demobilization when pursuing a legal strategy of institutionalizing food sovereignty at state and international levels (Claeys, 2012, p. 852). There is a real danger of state politicians coopting food sovereignty groups and accommodating peasant demands within the productivist food framework (e.g. Henderson, 2017, p. 36, citing Mexico and Ecuador as two different types of cooption). State laws in favor of food sovereignty are seen by some as an empty victory: 'A few countries make legislative efforts but it looks more like a communication exercise. Is there a real change in agricultural policy?' (La Vía Campesina support staff, in Claeys, 2012, p. 852).

Not surprisingly, most law scholars and practitioners have not taken up food sovereignty's specific suggestions with any great seriousness, and have taken a tepid and cautious approach to reforming food governance in the ways suggested by the food sovereignty movement. The most recent appearances of food sovereignty in the US and Canadian law literature have to do with the illegal sale of raw milk, the illegal sale of meat butchered on-farm, and the rise of local food sovereignty ordinances, particularly in Maine (Almy, 2013; Condra, 2012; Richardson, 2017; Schindler, 2018). Law scholars, as Richardson (2017, p. 211) points out, 'work within existing legal frameworks to identify narrow opportunities to opt out of the status quo rather than to reform agricultural policy from the ground up.' Agricultural law and policies in Canada (as in the US and most of the world) remain 'industrial and productivist' (Richardson, 2017, p. 211). So the revolution in local food democracy has not produced a corresponding revolution in localized law. '[C]ontemporary legal scholars rarely suggest that decentralized publics should be empowered to regulate local economic conditions' (Cohen, 2015, p. 103).

The deeper tensions between food sovereignty and state law and policy are here grouped into three categories: expert versus alternative knowledges; rights versus regulation; and support for smaller-scale over larger-scale markets, political units, and producers. Each of these will be discussed in turn.

2.2 Alternative Knowledges

Part of the food sovereignty program that puts it in tension with state regulation is its support for diverse alternative knowledges. Alternative knowledges include the ways of knowing of small-scale farmers, workers, and Indigenous peoples living in different social and ecological contexts. This diversity of local knowledges is under threat from a somewhat ambiguous enemy, the 'knowledge monoculture' (Martínez-Torres and Rosset, 2014, p. 983) associated with productivist agriculture and the scientists, business people, and lawyers who serve it.

Law's role in creating knowledge monoculture in agriculture varies from theory to theory. One theory is that the state, through intellectual property laws like patents and trademarks (as well as basic laws supporting private property and contracting and advertising), has made farmers dependent on the exclusive knowledge of the elite. In the past, farmers innovated and shared their farming knowledge and seed varieties through farmer-to-farmer networks in communities of local practice. These communities were diverse and were adapted to local ecologies. With the coming of the Green Revolution, however, farmers lost their autonomy. They became dependent on cheap imported food, chemical inputs, patented and specialized seed varieties (that they could not produce themselves on farm), and loans to buy the inputs and seeds. Various laws, like those protecting seed patents, helped police the boundaries of expert knowledge and exclude small-scale farmers. This created knowledge dependency, and it allowed the elite holders of knowledge to impose actual crop monocultures, as well as knowledge monoculture, and extract a larger share of profits from farming (see for example Suppan, 2008, p. 111; Kloppenburg, 2014; Dekeyser et al., 2018, p. 225).

A second version of the critique of knowledge monoculture points directly at law and science experts themselves, unmediated by private business. Over a long period of time, and sometimes through colonialism, science experts in partnership with the state strove to replace the diversity of existing farming knowledges and practices with powerful and simplifying technologies, which helped them to assert their authority across a broad territory (Scott, 1998). This was not always malicious but more often enthusiastic – an outpouring of faith in technological progress shared by capitalist and socialist agronomists alike (Scott, 1998, pp. 196–201). Agricultural officers, trained in centralized education programs with uniform curricula, went out to educate the 'backward' peasantry. Local practices were misunderstood and mistaken as environmentally harmful or unproductive. One thinks of the controlled use of fire by Indigenous peoples in systems of shifting cultivation (e.g. Huffman, 2013), or collective systems of ownership of forest or pasture (e.g. Tang and Gavin, 2015), or innovative intercropping schemes like the three sisters (maize, squash and beans) mound system of the Iroquois that was thought (incorrectly) to be inefficient compared to monocropped maize (Mt. Pleasant, 2006). Although some experts have come around and backed customary knowledge and practices with empirical evidence and the authority of science, this change in position is not universally accepted. Many see it as a dangerous relativism which leaves the science expert – the agronomist – in an awkward position.

A third version of the critique of knowledge monoculture places the blame on managerialism. According to this theory, organizational innovations by managers across law, science and business are driving knowledge monoculture. The manager is trying to deliver on goods and services (like increased agricultural productivity and food safety), and separates himself out from the people being managed for the purposes of manipulating them (Knight, 2017; MacIntyre, 2007). From the perspective of state law enforcers, who have to monitor multiple actors in a big food system, there are clear efficiency advantages of larger facilities and larger farms that follow mandated standard procedures. From the perspective of centralized meat processors and grocery retailers in large national markets, there are clear efficiency advantages of standard food units produced in standard ways.

Of course, the sum of organizational innovations leading to standardization might not be cost-reducing. For example, a larger, more efficient food processing facility might cause a food-borne illness that then prompts heightened food safety measures that are expensive to implement. Certainly the proliferation of micromanaging regulations and standards for agriculture, which farmers complain about, is extremely costly (see for example Schieber, 2013, pp. 256–8) and arguably less efficient than other techniques of management like encouraging trust, discretion, and accountability for bad outcomes. Managers at different governing levels do not necessarily see the systemic rise in costs in regulation. They try to make their own jobs easier by pushing costs out onto others. For example, regulated parties are asked to self-monitor, to achieve cost savings for managers. The cost-savings logic of standardization remains infallible from the perspective of each manager, who does not have a systems view.

A fourth version of the critique of expert knowledge is based on empirical observations from farmers' lived experience. The forces of knowledge monoculture have had a measurable impact on farming landscapes that farmers can see, namely reductions in agrobiodiversity. The diverse knowledges and practices of small-scale farmers have produced the greatest technological innovation in farming that the world knows: diversity of crop landraces and animal breeds. Smallholder participation in the Green Revolution, which selects for and distributes improved (standard) seed varieties across broad regions, has reportedly reduced world agrobiodiversity by a whopping 70 percent (Holt-Giménez and Altieri, 2013, p. 93). Local knowledge of agrobiodiversity, and local reproduction of diverse landraces and breeds, is hanging by a thread, with some people committing acts of food sovereignty resistance on the side in their small plots, unappreciated and unpaid for the work of holding the line against the loss of world agrobiodiversity (Isakson, 2009, p. 755).

For my purposes, all four versions of the problem of expert knowledge suggest that state law is an obstacle to food sovereignty's ideal of transformative change, and more importantly that the problem of expert knowledge is systemic, rather than a set of problems that can be approached piecemeal. Approaching knowledge monoculture as a systemic crisis creates a deep tension with state law.

Most experts, including legal experts, are not ready to throw out expert knowledge-power and prefer instead a piecemeal critique, which avoids taking responsibility for experts' mistakes and for knowledge monoculture and focuses instead on the potential of future partnerships. Jansen (2015, p. 227) argues forcefully that food sovereigntists' 'local-knowledge narrative' is overdrawn and that agroecology would benefit instead from 'joint farmer–science experimentation and debate about what, where and when it works'. Specific problems can be solved piecemeal through cooperation between smallholder farmers and allies in the expert world. The power gradient, and farmer subordination to elite knowledge, can be overcome in specific partnerships and relationships.

There are many piecemeal suggestions for reform of expert knowledge-power, providing a role for experts in partnership with farmers and others on the ground. Some of these suggestions come from allies of the food sovereignty movement. Property can be reformed to protect a commons of open-source seeds (Kloppenburg, 2014), or to protect complex local-level forms of rights and obligations (exemplified by customary land tenure and Indigenous communities) (e.g. Meinzen-Dick and Mwangi, 2008). Law in this way would protect the spaces for local knowledge and local agricultural experimentation and agrobiodiversity. Exceptions to existing laws can be made so that small-scale farmers are not forced to produce to the complex standards of distant experts. Lawmakers are already sensitive to the way that law favors large farmers and, in response, have exempted small farmers from some food safety requirements (see Condra, 2012, pp. 292–4, 311–14 for a US example).

Jasanoff (2015) helpfully has suggested a framework for determining when expert knowledge should inform policy and when localized knowledge should inform policy. She calls this 'epistemic subsidiarity', which is a right to one's own style of reasoning in policy areas lacking expert consensus (Jasanoff, 2015, pp. 1746–8). The 'law work', she explains, is to determine first whether the subsidiarity principle applies and then what form it will take, whether for example two opposing knowledges can coexist in different places. Genetically modified organisms (GMOs) are a 'paradigm case' for peaceful coexistence of knowledges, 'only with an obligation on the part of GM users to prevent contamination of non-GM fields' (Jasanoff, 2015, p. 1747).

Such compromises, however, particularly over GM crops, are not attractive to the mainstream food sovereignty movement. The spirit of compromise cuts against many food sovereignty principles and against their mainline critique of expert knowledge as a kind of political power, imposed on diverse peoples. The power of expert authority creates a hierarchy of knowledge, in which small-scale farmers' own favored social practices and food ways become of secondary importance – a quaint anthropological concern or, at best, a source of novel ideas that science has yet to validate or invalidate.

2.3   Peoples' Rights as Opposed to State Regulation

Food sovereignty is a bottom-up declaration of peoples' *rights* made against existing political configurations (like the state–corporate nexus) that regulate behavior. Different peoples' rights to determine their food system are contrasted with top-down regulation and rule uniformity. Trauger (2017, p. 22) explains: 'Food sovereignty ... envisions not more regulation of agriculture (i.e., food safety laws) but different kinds of rights, many of which provide protection from corporations ... for small-scale farmers.' La Vía Campesina employs a 'rights master frame' at local, state and international levels (Claeys, 2015, p. 453), and uses rights as a unifying theme in the face of the ideological diversity of its member organizations.

Although making a human rights claim is (at least partly) a legal undertaking that can be done before a national or international court, the food sovereignty movement has developed its language of rights outside of the law and at times seems desirous to use the language of rights *against* the law. As Lambek and Claeys (2016, p. 777) explain, 'Unlike the right to food, which has largely been elaborated by academics, lawyers, and non-governmental organizations ..., food sovereignty has been continually defined and redefined from the ground up'.

Again, some food sovereigntists are ambivalent about working 'within the system', in this case at the international level with the United Nations. Some La Vía Campesina activists have expressed a preference for working at the ground level rather than through the UN (Claeys, 2015, p. 457). Nonetheless La Vía Campesina contributed greatly to the UN Declaration on the Rights of Peasants and Other People Working in Rural Areas, adopted in 2018, which it calls 'an important tool' that should be implemented to guarantee 'rural communities the access to and control over land, peasant's seeds, water and other natural resources' (La Vía Campesina, 2018, quoting Elizabeth Mpofu, La Vía Campesina General Coordinator). Unfortunately, UN Declarations, unlike treaties, are not laws that must be implemented. At best they are evidence of customary international law, and customary law requires further evidence of state action to be substantiated and to become binding on states. The law, in other words, falls short, even with regard to this significant accomplishment.

In practice, food sovereigntists advance rights mainly through acts of defiance in opposition to formal law and regulation. The movement is driven, in true Marxist fashion, by the effort to incite radical change in material relations of production on the farm and the relations between sellers and buyers of agricultural produce. Citizenship is not about 'rights and responsibilities guaranteed by the state ... [C]itizenship is claimed and rights are realized through people's own actions' (Pimbert and Farvar, 2006, p. vii). There are many examples of civil disobedience for food sovereignty in the US, particularly against food safety regulations, for example illegal raw milk sales against laws requiring pasteurization, or illegal meat sales against laws requiring meat processing at licensed and inspected facilities, or indeed partly illegal local declarations of independence from state and federal law.

The food sovereignty movement has concentrated on collective rights of peoples rather than individual rights. These collective rights include the right of peoples to self-determination, to land and territory, to seeds, to set prices for farm products, as well as to food sovereignty itself (Claeys, 2015, p. 453; Menser, 2008, p. 32). Collective rights framings are less popular with legal professionals than individual rights. This is in part owing to the liberal legal culture of rights, in which individual liberty is emphasized over responsibility to a local community. (It is not that there is no collectivity in liberal legal culture; it is rather that the only collectivity recognized is the state, leaving the position of 'peoples' and the local community ambiguous; see Freeman, 1995, p. 26.) When US lawyers and courts wade into the GMO debate, they frame it in terms of individual consumers' rights (e.g. to know what they are eating), not in food sovereignty terms of farmers' collective right to autonomous decision-making (Cohen, 2015, p. 119).

Yet there is another reason why legal professionals do not like collective rights. This is because collective rights are a way to privilege the group's internal control of individuals over the state's control of those same individuals. The group's right to regulate itself becomes, in cases of conflict with the state, 'a form of deregulation' or defensive right to non-interference by the state (Schindler, 2018, p. 775). Food sovereigntists in Maine invoke this collective right when they say that local transactions, between a farmer and a local resident, are not the business of the state of Maine or the federal government and so should not be regulated by them (Schindler, 2018, p. 768). Rather, it is the collective right of the local community to regulate its own internal matters.

A defensive right to non-interference by the state is extremely problematic, mainly because it is never clear what is a matter of entirely local concern in the modern world of transnational commerce. US law has taken up this conceptual problem with some seriousness, at least with regard to the respective powers of state and federal governments to regulate farming. In the famous 1942 Wickard v. Filburn case, the US Supreme Court determined that the federal government had the power under the commerce clause to regulate a smallholder farmer who was producing wheat entirely for on-farm consumption. The logic was that, although the farmer's economic activity (planting wheat) might seem to be local, it nonetheless has the potential, together with lots of other farmers' actions, to impact the US economy by its cumulative impact. This case cuts against the logic of US food sovereignty activists who support local ordinances declaring a right to regulate local commerce in farm products (or a right to be free from state regulation of local commerce) (Condra, 2012, p. 284).

In declaring a local right (or collective right) to non-interference, the food sovereignty movement enters confusing and difficult terrain already trodden by other movements, including the right-wing property rights movement that periodically flares up in the Western US (see generally Jacobs, 1998, 2010). The property rights movement makes a claim to an individual right to property, which is meant as a claim to non-interference by the state (which according to property rights activists is over-regulating and unfairly singling out individual property owners, for example, for bearing the burden of supporting the habitat of endangered species). Local food sovereignty ordinances in the US appeal to the same sentiments for local freedom from physically and culturally distant regulators. '[I]t is easy to assume, based on the language of the ordinance, that the goal is de- or no regulation of the food system at the level of producer direct to consumer transactions' (Condra, 2012, p. 308). Condra oddly asserts that this is a misplaced assumption, and that food sovereigntists intend to replace state and federal regulation with local regulation. She nonetheless admits that, 'it does not appear that there have been any replacement regulations for these transactions, only the ordinances that exempt the transactions from state and federal licensing and inspection' (p. 310).

Another option, which has been pursued successfully by some Indigenous groups, is to seek legal recognition for a group and its territory, and with this recognition some right to regulate local matters (and a right to be free from state regulations that interfere with local traditions of resource management). This is a right to collective property that really brings together the goals of the property rights movement and the food sovereignty movement. Interestingly, when it comes to managing internal affairs – that is, coming up with internal rules to replace state law – the very process of seeking legal recognition for the collectivity might change internal relations in potentially negative ways, rendering collective resources as commodities and relationships as contractual arrangements (Fay, 2013).

Unfortunately, asserting non-interference does not help resolve the underlying problem of how to distribute management responsibility (i.e. the positive obligation to regulate) over resources among individual, community and state. This problem of multi-level regulation requires balancing. Sometimes the community's right to regulate trumps the individual's right to manage her own property. Sometimes the state's right to regulate trumps the community's right to regulate a resource like water that flows on to other communities. Declarations of absolute rights at any level put the regulatory system into confusion. After the rights declaration, what level of government will regulate what resource problems? Or indeed, more troublesome yet, what level of government has the right to make the meta-level decision of saying who gets to regulate? In other words, what level of government gets to define what is an externality justifying higher-level government interference (Komesar, 2001)?

All of this rights talk, which is deployed defensively, raises questions about whether and how the food sovereignty movement can regulate its members internally. Importantly, the food sovereignty movement is using the language of rights to position itself, defensively, against regulation of individuals and against the state institutions that regulate. Whereas the rights talk is clear and strong, the corresponding conversation about how to regulate internally, within a community, is muffled at best, and more often entirely absent.

2.4 Small-Scale Markets, Political Units, and Farms

The final area of tension between food sovereignty and state law comes from the localist orientation of food sovereignty, compared to state law's support for larger scales. Food sovereignty is committed to small-scale decision-making – local markets, small-scale political units, and small-scale farms. Localization is a key concept in the Declaration of Nyéléni, one of the few agreed-upon authoritative statements of the food sovereignty movement. The Declaration, adopted at the Forum for Food Sovereignty in 2007, is a paean to local food producers feeding local communities, contrasting their local food ways and local knowledge with the agents of global capitalism who dominate local producers and 'place profits before people, health and the environment' (Declaration of Nyéléni, 2007). At the local level, 'what is produced and how much is produced are determined by social need – not global market price' (Menser, 2008, p. 32).

Food sovereigntists see local markets, unlike transnational 'arm's length' trade, as involving personal relationships; out of these relationships come socially 're-embedded' spaces and obligations to place (Dekeyser et al., 2018, p. 224). Rather than have good agricultural practices determined by expert managers and imposed by legal sanctions, food sovereigntists imagine that good agricultural practices will emerge out of farmers' personal commitments to the people whom they are feeding within a local community. This sentiment is widespread among farmers who want to sell their produce to local residents in face-to-face sales without the intermediation of the state and state regulation (Field and Bell, 2013, p. 43; Richardson, 2017). These local relationships might offer richer opportunities for citizens to express themselves and participate in agricultural policy than state avenues of participation like voting or commenting on public rulemaking. Notably, although food sovereignty prioritizes local markets, it does not reject international trade outright.

Small-scale political units of food producers and consumers are the principal regulators of agriculture in food sovereignty's ideal world (Dekeyser et al., 2018, p. 226; Trauger, 2014, p. 1147). The internal institutional structure of these units is proposed to be radically democratic, with consensus decision-making and diverse other forms of spontaneous self-organization arising out of the solidarity and mutualism that comes from living and working together. Trauger (2017, p. 43) specifically lists the elements of self-rule as: 'consensus decision making, codes of ethics, grievance procedures, a method for choosing rules, and a balance of power between competing interest groups within the community'. Furthermore, these smaller political units might articulate together through 'confederalism': each local unit elects delegates through 'face-to-face democratic assemblies' (Pimbert, 2006, p. xii; 26) who then meet at higher levels (similar to the organizational structure of La Vía Campesina, in which regions elect delegates to meet at the international level).

Finally, in addition to small markets and small political units, food sovereignty activists advocate for farms to be small-scale, against the large farms that are characteristic of modern agribusiness. Agricultural laws and policies have long favored large farms. The US Department of Agriculture for example was famous for telling farmers to 'get big or get out' (see Dyer, 1997, p. 136). Across the developing world, agricultural experts have favored land consolidation policies in order to create large contiguous farms out of scattered smallholder plots (e.g. Dewees, 1995). Much of this work was justified on both productivity and environmental grounds. Larger farms, it was argued, would have enough returns to invest back in the land, allowing them not only to purchase synthetic fertilizers and pesticides and increase productivity, but to have more on-farm trees and soil conservation measures that would reduce soil erosion.

Food sovereigntists hold out the small-scale farmer as the ideal for ecological farming. Agroecology as a science 'is rooted in smallholder systems' (Holt-Giménez and Altieri, 2013, p. 92). The ideal small-scale agroecological farm has low external inputs, is highly diversified, relies on intensive, localized farmer knowledge, and has relatively high productivity potentially on a par with high-input large farms (Holt-Giménez and Altieri, 2013). It is interesting that, in places where smallholders compete with plantations to produce commodity crops like tea, coffee or rubber, the smallholders often prove themselves to be more competitive, despite government subsidies going to plantations (e.g. Dove, 2011, p. 6). Where plantations excel over smallholders is in making themselves visible and governable by rules and standards (Holt-Giménez and Altieri, 2013, p. 22).

What is often lacking in the discussion of smallholder viability and sustainability is the issue of farmer motivation. Smallholders are often doing agroecology out of necessity rather than choice, whereas academics and committed food sovereignty activists are driven to agroecological practices by their beliefs.

Necessity drives smallholders to choose labor-intensive practices and also a risk reduction strategy that mimics natural processes. The classic smallholder farmer, even the one mixing subsistence crops and cash crops, is dominated by a natural fear of total loss. As in natural ecosystems, the strategy of risk aversion is layered, including a number of 'back-up systems' and extensive diversification. The smallholder plants diverse crop species and landraces (intercropping spatially and rotating sequentially), includes subsistence and cash crops when possible, and may even have multiple plots in different locations or at different altitudes with different soil types and weather patterns. The cropping system, including livestock, is also set up to use diverse kinds of labor, including animals, men, women, children, and the elderly. Animals work to provide manure (as well as other sources of protein), children look after animals, elders with extensive ecological knowledge search out wild plants to supplement diets, and so on. Alliances with families in other locations who can donate food in times of localized crisis provide another backstop. This is one material basis for the mutuality championed by the food sovereignty movement – sharing food.

State agricultural laws and policies work to spread risk and insure against farm losses due to weather or market shocks. While this is very important, it has also inadvertently shifted individual farmer risk strategies, so that many choose increased productivity, along with greater exposure to risk of total loss, over the old ecological risk diversification strategies of the classic smallholder farmer.

The distinction between agroecology by necessity and agroecology by choice or belief is important when it comes to self-governance. If smallholders are aligned with agroecology largely out of necessity, rather than choice, then it is not certain that, when given more choices through self-governance, they will choose to continue their agroecological practices. Indeed, when given the opportunity, some smallholder food sovereigntists have shown themselves quite willing to shift over to some of the practices of neoliberal productivist agriculture, for example demanding cheaper chemical pesticides (Henderson, 2017; Jansen, 2015, p. 225; Shilomboleni, 2018).

By emphasizing small-scale markets, political units and farms, food sovereignty activists again widen the gap between their activism and state regulation of agriculture.

3. FOOD SOVEREIGNTY AND NONSTATE REGULATION

Considering the tensions between food sovereignty and state law, it is a bit surprising that the movement has not aligned itself with alternative nonstate ways of regulating people. A few theorists have hinted at the potential for food sovereignty to engage productively with legal pluralism (e.g. Richardson, 2017; Hospes, 2014, 2015), but this spark has not produced much fire. In fact, alternative science, like agroecological techniques or traditional ecological knowledge or some compromise like 'fusion knowledge' (Brown, 2003), has been much more successful than alternative law at finding a place in the imaginary of the food sovereignty movement.

The vast literature on legal pluralism, commons management, and customary land and resource tenure suggests a variety of alternative quasi-legal techniques for regulating productive resources and farming, with rules and social practices around land access and distribution, water use, forest and pasture commons, fire management, fish catch, and erosion control. These systems are often sustainable (or at least sensitive to resource availability for future generations), and research on them has culminated in a new respect for the customs and regulatory practices of smallholder farmers, pastoralists, and Indigenous groups (e.g. Berkes, 2012; Bosselman, 2005; Colding and Folke, 2001; Cox et al., 2014; Krueger, 2016; Meinzen-Dick and Mwangi, 2008; Ørebech and Bosselman, 2005; Ostrom, 1990). Nonstate legal systems provide a number of other benefits aside from sustainability, including increased participation, increased legitimacy, and access to justice (Ellickson, 1991; Galanter, 1981; Pimentel, 2010). There is also a link between diverse local social organization and agrobiodiversity (e.g. Labeyrie et al., 2014).

The main basis for nonstate regulation is group membership (with groups often bound together by economic interdependence). Pospisil (1967, pp. 6–9) traces this idea, which is foundational to legal pluralism, from von Gierke, Ehrlich, Weber, Llewellyn and Hoebel (see also Moore, 2014). Relatedly, Daigle (2019, p. 302) raises the idea of kinship relations in Indigenous communities as a basis for regulations supporting food sovereignty. One of the most severe penalties for not following group rules is being excluded from group activities and ultimately ostracized, perhaps temporarily (Moore, 1973, 2014, p. 9). Moreover, as Ostrom (1990) and others have shown, resource users in various types of group commons will tend to respect rules that they have had a hand in creating, adjusting and enforcing.

The specific contents and methods of nonstate agricultural rules vary greatly from place to place, much as smallholder farming practices vary from place to place. Some rule systems are more processual (requiring particular kinds of deliberation rather than particular outcomes for a given violation). Other rules are more like 'rules of thumb' (Berkes, 2012, p. 194) that approximate good management outcomes with a simple rule, like taboos against eating particular species.

One of the most prominent techniques of nonstate regulation is conditional access to resources. A farmer gets land or water or community labor or access to shared resources like pasture and forest only on condition of good behavior and conformity with local rules of use. The community does not necessarily 'own' these resources. Rather, the community exercises political-legal control over them and reserves a right in extreme cases to confiscate privately held land and resources.

Another aspect of conditional access is the idea of intergenerational obligations (see for example Langton (2010), discussing aboriginal property relations in Australia). A landowner has conditional access to land in the sense that she is an interim manager of the land, which passes from previous generations, to her, and on to future generations. Though she has some individual control over the land, it always reverts to the community, to be given out again to some other individual, in the case of the owner's death or long-term absence. Reversion of land to the community is a common feature of customary land tenure systems.

Although penalties for violating nonstate rules can be harsh, varying from physical and spiritual punishment, to economic punishment, to social ostracization, it is often the case that the penalties have a restorative justice purpose. The penalties might be intended to smooth the way for an individual's continued participation in community life. Restorative justice practices are diverse, but in general the idea is that offenses against the community require an admission of guilt, some kind of token payment (in actual money or in something else), and facing the victim (or the community itself). Through this process the community's norms are affirmed, the victim's harm is ameliorated, and the rule-breaker is restored to some kind of on-going relations with the community. Although restorative justice has been applied mainly in the context of criminal law, it can also be applied productively to administrative violations, to mismanagement of economic assets, and most importantly to harms against the environment (Jenkins, 2018).

The food sovereignty movement has not made a strong connection between its call for local agricultural regulation and the many existing nonstate forms of agricultural regulation. There are a number of reasons why nonstate regulation might be problematic for food sovereigntists. First, customs with path dependency over time are not necessarily democratic, and often represent the authority of elders being imposed on the youth. Second, there is a sense that nonstate rules do not lend themselves well to design – rather they just happen, or not, over time. Third, nonstate rules cannot be disentangled from complex local belief systems and authority structures that might contravene modern science, or cut against Marxist ideology, or upset modernist ideals of gender equality.

Fourth, nonstate social rules and sanctions in rural areas have been rendered invisible, or have been overridden by state law, making it appear as though people are freely associating with one another according to their own culture. This is a misconception that underplays the important role of local political authority and actual institutions that, in the past at least, administered local rules and punishments. After state law usurps and replaces these local institutions, the residual behaviors come to be attributed to 'culture', which seems voluntary and benign. Then dissidents like food sovereignty activists, who are dissatisfied with state rules and punishments, mistakenly turn back to what they perceive is an unregulated or natural or cultural way of life of small-scale agriculture in local communities. The idea that rules and punishments are not just products of modern penal law and capitalism, but in fact exist as an integral part of local food ways, can be jarring to those subscribing to this misconception.

Many of the nonstate options for regulating commons, as Dagan and Heller (2001, p. 552) point out, are 'illiberal', locking group members into communal activities that they might not choose or want. Individuals can only be protected if they are given the option of 'liberal exit' from the community, with compensation from the community for their lost assets (like land) (Dagan and Heller, 2001, p. 568). But this unfortunately upsets one of the main mechanisms for enforcing nonstate rules, which is the threat of being ostracized from the group and losing access to group resources.

Sagy (2011) takes this argument further. She points out that one branch of the legal pluralism literature, referred to as the 'private ordering' literature, is actually about privileging market actors over democratic governments and about subjecting private actors to the whims of the most powerful in their community as they sort out their own problems. Private ordering obviously dovetails with neoliberal ideology about the supremacy of market mechanisms of social coordination (and might therefore be considered by food sovereignty activists as counter-productive). More importantly, Sagy argues that all nonstate orders rely on social hierarchies, and that people being regulated by nonstate legal systems are often forced into the system against their will. As she puts it, 'there is an inherent tension between the social structure that facilitates private ordering and the ability of group members to choose that order or to exit from it' (Sagy, 2011, p. 926).

4. FOOD SOVEREIGNTY'S INTERNAL REGULATIONS

It is common to think of regulation as a form of expert control over otherwise economically beneficial activities. Here I am taking a broader view of regulation and including also community controls and, by extension, the controls that serve to discipline participants in a social movement. Social movement activists, and food sovereigntists, tend not to recognize their own regulatory activities.

Food sovereignty has both general values and specific rules that are non-negotiable. Some food sovereignty values are commitment to local food ways, democratic participation in the food system, sustainability, and diversity of ideas about how to produce food. Its specific rules further define the boundaries of the movement: no use of GMOs, no patenting of seeds, no privatizing local commons, no monopoly power in agriculture, no excluding the poor or other marginalized groups from policymaking, no excluding women, no undercutting the prices of agricultural products, and so on (see for example Rosset, 2003). People who oppose these rules are overtly and covertly silenced, marginalized, or excluded entirely from the movement.

There is a difference between the meta-rules, which are imposed hierarchically, and the regulatory decisions about food and farming made through radical direct democracy and consensus decision-making. Meta-rules are limitations on what can be discussed and decided on through radical democracy. A locally democratic governing body of the food sovereignty movement, like a food policy council, has limits in terms of the food policy it can adopt. Food sovereignty 'is itself constrained by the norms embodied in socially sustainable agriculture' (Menser, 2008, p. 34). Which of the rules are to be imposed on local democratic bodies, and how they are to be imposed, is another matter.

Once food sovereigntists accept that they are imposing regulation, key issues of internal governance become clearer. One of these key issues is about how social movements use exclusion and us-versus-them politics, and mix external advocacy and internal governance. When is it okay to exclude people from a movement? How exclusive can a movement like food sovereignty be when it is engaging in activities very similar to governing territory? How can the harshness of social exclusion be tempered with processes of reconciliation? How can consensus over the standards for good farming be reached across lines of difference?

Food sovereignty is partly governed by a sense of common cause against the enemy, industrial food systems. When it comes to group-level governance, however, it is explicitly pluralist. Paul Nicholson, a leader in La Vía Campesina, explains the shared sense of systemic crisis in agriculture that food sovereignty responds to, contrasted with the diversity of local practice (Wittman, 2009, p. 678): 'It's amazing how we have achieved a sensibility of these diverse cultures, in a common base. This common base is that we understand that the crisis of rural family agriculture is the same all over the world. The causes are the same ... The reality is the same'.

This partly explains some of food sovereignty's standardized meta-rules, which are advocacy against a common crisis and common enemy. There are arguably better ways for local diverse practices to articulate with a broader movement or rule system.

5. WHAT IF FOOD SOVEREIGNTY GOT SERIOUS ABOUT SOCIAL CONTROL AND NONSTATE LAWS?

The preceding sections have emphasized that food sovereigntists are anti-regulatory and have not given enough attention to how they would regulate themselves internally. Yet there is a lot of potential for food sovereignty to engage creatively with the question of regulation, and particularly nonstate regulation, to achieve some of its objectives like agroecology, diversity of farming practice and food ways, and direct farmer participation in, and control over, rural livelihoods. Moreover, there are ways to fit diverse nonstate rules within an overarching system of state law.

Just to show the potential of this kind of engagement, I will mention four techniques of nonstate regulation that bring together state and nonstate authority and that are worthy of deeper study and elaboration. First, there is the idea of community courts or alternative dispute settlement bodies (recognized by state law but staffed by non-professionals). People need a forum for expressing normativity in a more participatory way than is currently allowed by a professionalized judiciary. People also need places where they are ethically exposed before the community and held accountable, in a gentle way, for actions that do not rise to the level of state law crimes. Such non-punitive and potentially restorative forums do not have to apply the same standards as any other community court – that is, they can embrace diverse law knowledges.

Second, there is environmental restorative justice. This can be done in a community court forum. It is aimed at engaging with people who have done things that most people in the community do not like (one thinks of nuisances like pesticide drift). As a deliberative process, restorative justice can arrive at acceptable terms for restoring people to better relations (i.e. to acceptable levels of tension and disagreement) with the community around them.

Third, there is collective responsibility (Krueger, 2015). This idea, though controversial, fits well with collective rights of peoples and helps to reconcile the right to regulate internally and the right to be free from external regulation. In the context of environmental harm, collective responsibility means that an entire group would be liable for its measurable negative externalities (like fertilizer runoff), without having to go through the formal effort of proving individual culpability. Whereas the question of the group's responsibility goes to the state, the question of apportioning blame to individual group members, or not, would be left to the internal decision-making of the group.

Fourth, nonstate law has unique processes for maintaining the legitimacy to regulate. Unlike the case with state experts, who rely on their credentials and scientific expertise, the legitimacy of local nonstate rules must be regularly re-established, drawing from a variety of sources. It has been suggested for example that legitimate political authority in many small-scale communities in the developing world comes from resolving disputes over resources and assigning property rights in resources. The process of successfully authorizing the resource user also authorizes and legitimizes the authority itself (Sikor and Lund, 2009). This would hint at the need for local food sovereignty groups to own collective property (or control territory) and to assign rights to individual members. This provides some leverage for imposing farming rules, and provides the material means to legitimize regulatory power.

6. CONCLUSION

My intention has been to explore an anti-regulatory strain in food sovereignty thinking. This strain starts as a powerful critique of the state regulation that supports industrial agriculture, but leads to an untenable conclusion. Food sovereignty activists struggle to articulate a positive vision for the role of regulation in people's lives and struggle even to engage openly with the ways that they are already regulating people. In some regards, the movement has a hard time differentiating itself from libertarianism and the property rights movement, in which people declare that they want to be free from government so that they can do what they want. Yet there is an opening for food sovereignty activists to think creatively about regulation, and in particular about the many traditions of nonstate regulation, and the different ways that state law might be reformed to accommodate nonstate regulation. To the extent that nonstate regulation also represents diversity of local law ways, to match diversity of local food ways, then this is a nice fit for food sovereignty and its emphasis on diverse local knowledges.

The regulatory challenge for food sovereignty is complicated by the fact that it is a social movement. Many of the 'rules' for food sovereignty are directed against a common enemy, neoliberal industrial agriculture, and draw their energy from the dynamic of us versus them. While this can be motivating and beneficial for the movement, it does not help with building broad-based consensus across ideological differences over what the minimum contents of ethical farming should be in particular places, and how this can be enforced.

It is worth restating that self-identifying environmentalist movements like food sovereignty are not always working for sustainability, and are not necessarily building consensus in any given local area across diverse peoples with diverse farming practices. The movement arguably has greater potential to accomplish these things when less immersed in the battle of environmentalist versus anti-environmentalist, or peasant versus elite businessperson, and when it is made to consider carefully its own internal regulations. A turn inwards, toward self-reflection about internal governance techniques and about the way these techniques articulate with state law, might be particularly fitting for food sovereignty's current stage of development. It has succeeded in challenging industrial agriculture; now it can demonstrate its success in governing people effectively to achieve thriving rural communities and ecological farming.

REFERENCES

Almy, R. (2013) State v. Brown: A test for local food ordinances. *Maine Law Review*. **65**(2), pp. 789–805.

Anderson, F. (2018) Food sovereignty NOW! A guide to food sovereignty. *European Coordination Via Campesina*. Available from: https://viacampesina.org/en/wp-content/uploads/sites/2/2018/02/Food-Sovereignty-A-guide-Low-Res-Vresion.pdf (accessed 10 June 2019).

Bellinger, N. and M. Fakhri (2013) The intersection between food sovereignty and law. *Natural Resources and Environment*. **28**(2), pp. 45–8.

Berkes, F. (2012) *Sacred Ecology: Traditional Ecological Knowledge and Resource Management*. 3rd edn. Philadelphia, PA: Taylor and Francis.

Bosselman, F.P. (2005) Adaptive resource management through customary law. In: Ørebech, P., Bosselman, F., Bjarup, J., Callies, D., Chanock, M. and Petersen, H. (eds) *The Role of Customary Law in Sustainable Development*. Cambridge: Cambridge University Press, pp. 245–81.

Brown, K. (2003) Three challenges for a real people-centred conservation. *Global Ecology and Biogeography*. **12**(2), pp. 89–92.

Claeys, P. (2012) The creation of new rights by the food sovereignty movement: The challenge of institutionalizing subversion. *Sociology.* **46**(5), pp. 844–60.

Claeys, P. (2015) Food sovereignty and the recognition of new rights for peasants at the UN: A critical overview of La Via Campesina's rights claims over the last 20 years. *Globalizations,* **12**(4), pp. 452–65.

Cohen, A. (2015) The law and political economy of contemporary food: Some reflections on the local and the small. *Law and Contemporary Problems.* **78**(1), pp. 101–145.

Colding, J. and Folke, C. (2001) Social taboos: 'Invisible' systems of local resource management and biological conservation. *Ecological Adaptations.* **11**(2), pp. 584–600.

Condra, A. (2012) Food sovereignty in the United States: Supporting local and regional food systems. *Journal of Food Law and Policy.* **8**(2), pp. 281–316.

Cox, M., Villamayor-Tomás, S. and Hartberg, Y. (2014) The role of religion in community-based natural resource management. *World Development.* **54**, pp. 46–55.

Dagan, H. and Heller, M.A. (2001) The liberal commons. *The Yale Law Journal.* **110**, pp. 549–623.

Daigle, M. (2019) Tracing the terrain of indigenous food sovereignties. *The Journal of Peasant Studies.* **46**(2), pp. 297–315.

Declaration of Nyéléni (2007) Declaration of Nyéléni. *Nyeleni.org.* Available from: https://nyeleni.org/spip.php?article290 (accessed 15 June 2019).

Dekeyser, K., Korsten, L. and Fioramonti, L. (2018) Food sovereignty: Shifting debates on democratic food governance. *Food Security.* **10**, pp. 223–33.

Dewees, P.A. (1995) Trees and farm boundaries: Farm forestry, land tenure and reform in Kenya. *Journal of the International African Institute.* **65**(2), pp. 217–35.

Dove, M.R. (2011) *The Banana Tree at the Gate: A History of Marginal Peoples and Global Markets in Borneo.* New Haven, CT: Yale University Press.

Dyer, J. (1997) *Harvest of Rage: Why Oklahoma City Is Only the Beginning.* Boulder, CO: Westview Press.

Edelman, M. (2014) Food sovereignty: Forgotten genealogies and future regulatory challenges. *The Journal of Peasant Studies.* **41**(6), pp. 959–78.

Ellickson, R.C. (1991) *Order Without Law: How Neighbors Settle Disputes.* Cambridge, MA: Harvard University Press.

Fay, D. (2013) Neoliberal conservation and the potential for lawfare: New legal entities and the political ecology of litigation at Dwesa-Cwebe, South Africa. *Geoforum.* **44**, pp. 170–81.

Field, T. and Bell, B. (2013) *Harvesting Justice: Transforming Food, Land, and Agricultural Systems in the Americas.* New York, NY: Other Worlds and U.S. Food Sovereignty Alliance.

Freeman, M. (1995) Are there collective human rights? *Political Studies.* **XLIII**, pp. 25–40.

Galanter, M. (1981) Justice in many rooms: Courts, private ordering, and indigenous law. *The Journal of Legal Pluralism and Unofficial Law.* **13**(19), pp. 1–47.

Henderson, T.P. (2017), State–peasant movement relations and the politics of food sovereignty in Mexico and Ecuador. *The Journal of Peasant Studies.* **44**(1), pp. 33–55.

Holt-Giménez, E. and M.A. Altieri (2013) Agroecology, food sovereignty, and the new green revolution. *Agroecology and Sustainable Food Systems.* **37**(1), pp. 90–102.

Hospes, O. (2014) Food sovereignty: The debate, the deadlock, and a suggested detour. *Agriculture and Human Values.* **31**(1), pp. 119–30.

Hospes, O. (2015) Addressing law and agroecosystems, sovereignty and sustainability from a legal pluralistic perspective. In: Monteduro, M., Buongiorno, P., Di Benedetto, S. and Isoni, A. (eds) *Law and Agroecology: A Transdisciplinary Dialogue.* New York, NY: Springer, pp. 47–56.

Huffman, M.R. (2013) The many elements of traditional fire knowledge: Synthesis, classification, and aids to cross-cultural problem solving in fire-dependent systems around the world. *Ecology and Society.* **18**(4), p. 3.

Isakson, S.R. (2009) *No hay ganancia en la milpa*: The agrarian question, food sovereignty, and the on-farm conservation of agrobiodiversity in the Guatemalan highlands. *The Journal of Peasant Studies.* **36**(4), pp. 725–59.

Jacobs, Harvey M. (1998) The 'wisdom' but uncertain future of the wise use movement. In: Jacobs, H.M. (ed.) *Who Owns America? Social Conflict Over Property Rights.* Madison, WI: University of Wisconsin Press, pp. 29–44.

Jacobs, H.M. (2010) Social conflict over property rights: The end, a new beginning or a continuing conversation? *Housing Policy Debate*. **20**(3), 329–49.

Jansen, K. (2015) The debate on food sovereignty theory: Agrarian capitalism, dispossession and agroecology. *The Journal of Peasant Studies*. **42**(1), pp. 213–32.

Jasanoff, S. (2015) Serviceable truths: Science for action in law and policy. *Texas Law Review*, **93**(7), pp. 1723–49.

Jenkins, B. (2018) Environmental restorative justice: Canterbury cases. Paper presented at the *38th Annual Conference of the International Association for Impact Assessment*, 16–19 May, Durban, South Africa.

Kloppenburg, J. (2014) Re-purposing the master's tools: The open source seed initiative and the struggle for seed sovereignty. *The Journal of Peasant Studies*. **41**(6), pp. 1225–46.

Knight, K. (2017) MacIntyre's critique of management. In: Sison, A.J.G., Beabout, G.R. and Ferrero, I. (eds) *Handbook of Virtue Ethics in Business and Management*. Dordrecht: Springer, pp. 79–87.

Komesar, N.K. (2001) *Law's Limits: The Rule of Law and the Supply and Demand of Rights*. Cambridge: Cambridge University Press.

Krueger, J. (2015) Local corporations: A corporate form to reduce information costs and maintain supportive resources. In: Pistor, K. and de Schutter, O. (eds) *Governing Access to Essential Resources*. New York, NY: Columbia University Press, pp. 336–54.

Krueger, J. (2016) Autonomy and morality: Legal pluralism factors impacting sustainable natural resource management among Miraa farmers in Nyambene Hills, Kenya. *The Journal of Legal Pluralism and Unofficial Law*. **48**(3), 415–40.

La Vía Campesina (2018) Finally, UN General Assembly adopts peasant rights declaration! Now focus is on its implementation. *Vía Campesina website*. Available from: https://viacampesina.org/en/finally-un-general-assembly-adopts-peasant-rights-declaration-now-focus-is-on-its-implementation/ (accessed 15 June 2019).

Labeyrie, V., Rono, B. and Leclerc, C. (2014) How social organization shapes crop diversity: An ecological anthropology approach among Tharaka farmers of Mount Kenya. *Agriculture and Human Values*. **31**, pp. 97–107.

Lambek, N. and Claeys, P. (2016) Institutionalizing a fully realized right to food: Progress, limitations, and lessons learned from emerging alternative policy models. *Vermont Law Review*. **40**, pp. 743–89.

Langton, M. (2010) The estate as duration: 'Being in place' and aboriginal property relations in areas of Cape York peninsula in North Australia. In: Godden, L. and Tehan, M. (eds) *Comparative Perspectives on Communal Lands and Individual Ownership: Sustainable Futures*. New York, NY: Routledge, pp. 75–98.

MacIntyre, A. (2007) *After Virtue: A Study in Moral Theory*. 3rd edn. Notre Dame, IN: University of Notre Dame Press.

Martínez-Torres, M.E. and Rosset, P. (2014) Diálogo de saberes in La Vía Campesina: Food sovereignty and agroecology. *Journal of Peasant Studies*. **41**(6), pp. 979–97.

McMahon, M. (2014) Local food: Food sovereignty or myth of alternative consumer sovereignty. In: Andrée, P., Ayres, J., Bosia, M.J. and Massicotte, M.-J. (eds) *Globalization and Food Sovereignty: Global and Local Change in the New Politics of Food*. Toronto: University of Toronto Press, pp. 111–38.

Meinzen-Dick, R. and Mwangi, E. (2008) Cutting the web of interests: Pitfalls of formalizing property rights. *Land Use Policy*. **26**(1), pp. 36–43.

Menser, M. (2008) Transnational participatory democracy in action: The case of La Via Campesina. *Journal of Social Philosophy*. **39**(1), pp. 20–41.

Moore, S.F. (1973) Law and social change: The semi-autonomous social field as an appropriate subject of study. *Law and Society Review*. **7**(4), pp. 719–46.

Moore, S.F. (2014) Legal pluralism as omnium gatherum. *FIU Law Review*. **10**(5), pp. 5–18.

Mt. Pleasant, J. (2006) The science behind the three sisters mound system: An agronomic assessment of an indigenous agricultural system in the northeast. In: Staller, J., Tykot, R.T. and Benz, R. (eds) *Histories of Maize: Multidisciplinary Approaches to the Prehistory, Linguistics, Biogeography, Domestication, and Evolution of Maize*. Walnut Creek, CA: Left Coast Press, pp. 529–37.

Ørebech, P. and Bosselman, F. (2005) The linkage between sustainable development and customary law. In: Ørebech, P., Bosselman, F., Bjarup, J., Callies, D., Chanock, M. and Petersen, H. (eds) *The Role of Customary Law in Sustainable Development*. Cambridge: Cambridge University Press, pp. 12–42.

Ostrom, E. (1990) *Governing the Commons: The Evolution of Institutions for Collective Action*. Cambridge: Cambridge University Press.

Patel, R. (2009) What does food sovereignty look like. *The Journal of Peasant Studies*. **36**(3), pp. 663–73.

Patel, R. and McMichael, P. (2004) Third worldism and the lineages of global fascism: The regrouping of the Global South in the neoliberal era. *Third World Quarterly*. **25**(1), pp. 231–54.

Pimbert, M. (2006) *Transforming Knowledge and Ways of Knowing for Food Sovereignty*. London: International Institute for Environment and Development.

Pimbert, M. and Farvar, M.T. (2006) Foreword. In: Cohn, A., Cook, J., Fernandez, M., McAfee, K., Reider, R. and Steward, C. (eds) *Agroecology and the Struggle for Food Sovereignty in the Americas*. New Haven, CT: International Institute for Environment and Development, pp. vii–ix.

Pimentel, D. (2010) Can indigenous justice survive? Legal pluralism and the rule of law. *Harvard International Review*. **32**(2), pp. 33–6.

Pospisil, L. (1967) Legal levels and multiplicity of legal systems in human societies. *The Journal of Conflict Resolution*. **11**(1), pp. 2–26.

Richardson, S.B. (2017) Legal pluralism and the regulation of raw milk sales in Canada: Creating space for multiple normative orders at the food policy table. In: Alabrese, M., Brunori, M., Rolandi, S. and Saba, A. (eds) *Agricultural Law: Current Issues from a Global Perspective*. Cham: Springer International Publishing, pp. 211–29.

Rosset, P. (2003) Food sovereignty: Global rallying cry of farmer movements. *Food First Backgrounder*. **9**(4). Available from: https://foodfirst.org/publication/food-sovereignty-global-rallying-cry-of-farmer-movements (accessed 13 June 2019).

Rosset, P.M. (2006) *Food is Different: Why We Must Get the WTO out of Agriculture*. Halifax: Fernwood Publishing.

Sagy, T. (2011) What's so private about private ordering? *Law and Society Review*. **45**(4), pp. 923–54.

Salatin, J. (2003) Everything I want to do is illegal. *Acres USA: A Voice for Eco-Agriculture*. **33**(9). Available from: http://alcoholcanbeagas.com/sites/acbag/files/salatin_illegal.pdf.

Schiavoni, C.M. (2015) Competing sovereignties, contested processes: Insights from the Venezuelan food sovereignty experiment. *Globalizations*. **12**(4), pp. 466–80.

Schieber, G.M. (2013) The Food Safety Modernization Act's Tester Amendment: Useful safe harbor for small farmers and food facilities or weak attempt as scale-appropriate farm and food regulations. *Drake Journal of Agricultural Law*. **18**(1), pp. 239–88.

Schindler, S. (2018) Food federalism: States, local governments, and the fight for food sovereignty. *Ohio State Law Journal*. **79**(4), pp. 761–80.

Scott, J.C. (1998) *Seeing Like a State: How Certain Schemes to Improve the Human Condition Have Failed*. New Haven, CT: Yale University Press.

Shilomboleni, H. (2018) African green revolution, food sovereignty and constrained livelihood choice in Mozambique. *Canadian Journal of African Studies*. **52**(2), pp. 115–37.

Sikor, T. and Lund, C. (2009) Access and property: A question of power and authority. *Development and Change*. **40**(1), pp. 1–22.

Suppan, S. (2008) Challenges for food sovereignty. *The Fletcher Forum of World Affairs*. **32**(1), pp. 111–23.

Tang, R. and Gavin, M.C. (2015) Degradation and re-emergence of the commons: The impacts of government policies on traditional resource management institutions in China. *Environmental Science and Policy*. **52**, pp. 89–98.

Trauger, A. (2014) Toward a political geography of food sovereignty: Transforming territory, exchange and power in the liberal sovereign state. *The Journal of Peasant Studies*. **41**(6), pp. 1131–52.

Trauger, A. (2017) *We Want Land to Live: Making Political Space for Food Sovereignty*. Athens, GA: The University of Georgia Press.

Wittman, H. (2009) Interview: Paul Nicholson, La Vía Campesina. *The Journal of Peasant Studies*. **36**(3), pp. 676–82.

16. Agrarian reform movement in the Betung Kerihun National Park: mobilisation of hunter–gatherer communities against nature protection in Kalimantan

Martin C. Lukas

1. INTRODUCTION

The Betung Kerihun National Park in West Kalimantan protects the largest remaining contiguous expanses of lowland and montane rainforest in Borneo, one of the world's most significant biodiversity hotspots.[1] It harbours more than one thousand tree, bird and fish species, many of which are endemic, numerous amphibian and snake species, crocodiles and turtles. It is also one of the last habitats of threatened iconic mammals, like the Bornean Orangutan (*Pongo pygmaeus*) and other primates. The national park is a key component of the Heart of Borneo conservation agreement, initiated by the World Wide Fund for Nature (WWF) and supported by the governments of Indonesia, Malaysia and Brunei. It covers an area of 800 000 hectares in the upper reaches of the Kapuas River and its tributaries in the remote border region of West Kalimantan with East Kalimantan and Malaysia.

There are two villages inside the national park: Bungan Jaya and Tanjung Lokang (Figure 16.1). Most of their 750 and 500 residents are Indigenous hunter–gatherers of the Punan Hovongan tribe. They gradually adopted a sedentary life in the course of the twentieth century and practise shifting cultivation on a small scale, but still derive much of their income from hunting and gathering.

Figures 1a and 1b show the villages Bungan Jaya (with Nanga Bungan as the main hamlet) and Tanjung Lokang in the remote upper reaches of the Kapuas River in Central Borneo. The villagers' hunting and gathering areas encompass large parts of the upper Kapuas watershed in the southern portion of the Betung Kerihun National Park (elevation data: SRTM).

There is no road or footpath leading into these remote villages. They are accessible only by boat via the Kapuas River. The first section of this trip, from Putussibau, the district capital of Kapuas Hulu, to Matalunai, the last village before the national park, is comparatively easy to navigate. The five-hour trip further up to Nanga Bungan, the main hamlet of Bungan Jaya at the confluence of the Kapuas and Bungan Rivers, can be dangerous at times. It can be done with traditional wooden longboats only and requires experienced boat drivers with a good knowledge of the rapids. The trip from Nanga Bungan further up the Bungan River to Tanjung Lokang through more challenging rapids takes a few hours (Figure 16.2).

I went to these villages twice in the frame of a research project on environmental transformations and changes in natural resource uses and their management along the rivers of West Kalimantan.[2] When I first arrived in Nanga Bungan together with my field research assistant, the national park base camp, a small wooden hut, was nailed up. A national park sign was pulled over. Our introduction to one of the village leaders[3] started with a long conversation

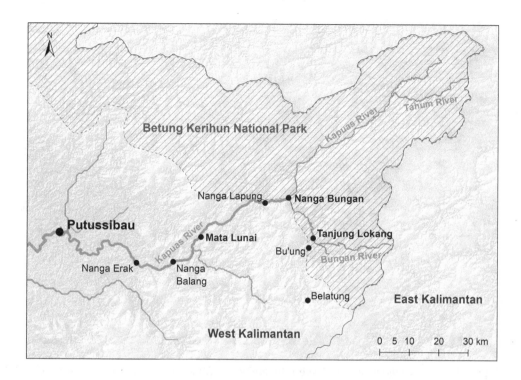

Figure 16.1   1a (top) and 1b (bottom)

between him and our boat driver from Matalunai, in whose house we had stayed the day before. Our boat driver explained our research intentions a few times and emphasised that we were independent researchers without any connection to the national park administration. The tension faded, and we were welcomed to stay.

Our first conversations exposed an atmosphere of friction and rebellion against 'the national park'. Our host explained that they had been free to use all resources from the forest and the rivers until the late 1990s, but since then, various resource uses were supposed to be restricted. He pointed out that the people from the national park monopolised the area and restricted fishing, hunting and gold mining. He noted that youth activists from a non-governmental organisation (NGO) had made the villagers realise that the national park people monopolised their land and their resources, and that they had to fight against this.

These activists from the land reform movement AGRA (*Alliansi Gerakan Reforma Agraria*) had been in Nanga Bungan for a few months. They encouraged villagers to boycott national park programmes, to expand shifting cultivation, and to disobey national park rules. They organised villagers into a 'peasant union' (*Serikat Tani Losing Kovalan*) fighting against the national park and running community activities. Information boards set up throughout the village presented the programme and structure of this 'peasant union'. As a sign of protest against the national park, villagers pulled over national park signs and nailed up the national park authorities' base camps with wooden planks, in both Nanga Bungan and Tanjung Lokang.

306　*Handbook of anti-environmentalism*

Figure 16.2　On the way from Nanga Bungan to Tanjung Lokang, the boat needs to be pulled through river rapids (own photo)

The national park rangers since hesitated to enter the area – because, as villagers assumed, they were afraid and wanted to keep the conflict from boiling over.

As I unexpectedly found myself in the middle of a nature conservation conflict at its highest escalation level, I analysed its causes and emergence, and the trigger, tactics and dynamics of mobilisation.

Conflicts over nature conservation are widespread in Indonesia and other parts of the Global South, where conservation goals often conflict with the interests of local people, who may regard states and conservation agencies as 'illegitimate controllers of local resources' (Peluso, 2015, p. 349), where conservation initiatives run into pre-existing resource conflicts, and particularly where conservation agendas are pursued coercively, under non-responsive authorities, and without genuine participation of local residents. Conservation and natural resource conflicts often exacerbate distrust, produce fear and violence, cause environmental degradation, and undermine conservation goals (Lukas, 2015; Sodhi et al., 2007; Yasmi et al., 2013). It is crucial to understand both the causes and emergence of such conflicts in historical depth (Harrison and Loring, 2020; Lukas, 2015; Sodhi et al., 2007).

The courses of resource and conservation conflicts vary as much as their specific causes. While some conflicts may simmer for years or decades, others escalate and turn violent within short time spans. What drives such conflicts to escalate? Based on a meta-analysis of 118 conflict cases, Yasmi et al. (2006) identified eight escalation stages but found no 'generic' path of escalation that fitted most cases – a finding that they related to the heterogeneity of cases and contexts and that may also reflect limited explicit engagement with escalation courses in many empirical studies.

The conservation conflict in the Betung Kerihun National Park escalated within a very short time span. Historically rooted distrust and deficient communication between authorities and villagers, combined with disappointment and rumours about a lack of programme implementation and corruption constituted conflict-prone pre-conditions. A single critical event – a raid against gold miners – then triggered mobilisation against the national park by the AGRA activists. This pushed the conflict rapidly to high escalation levels, with polarisation, hostility and physical action against national park symbols and infrastructure – the peak on the conflict curve, which Crowley et al. (2017) termed the destructive phase, where chances for constructive dialogue are limited and relationships are being damaged.

Understanding the causes, emergence and escalation of this conservation conflict thus requires analysis not only of the historical context of the hunter–gatherers' transitioning livelihoods at the edge of the state, of their changing natural resource uses, of the establishment, zoning, and management of the national park, and of villager–national park relations. It also requires analysis of the raid against gold miners as a critical event and of the dynamic processes of anti-national park mobilisation it triggered. The role of critical events as triggers of mobilisation has received relatively limited systematic attention in social movement studies.

I thus briefly review scholarship on social movements and mobilisation with regard to the role of critical events in the next section, before I turn to the empirical case of the Betung Kerihun National Park. In the following sections, I provide a brief historical account of the Indigenous hunter–gatherer communities and their changing natural resource uses, and shed light on the establishment, zoning and management of the national park and on villager–national park relations. These sections describe the setting in which mobilisation occurred and provide insight into pre-mobilisation tensions and grievances, as well as cultural and other factors that provided fertile ground for and affected the course of anti-national park mobilisation. I will then elucidate a critical event – a raid against gold miners – that produced anger and public attention and triggered engagement of the AGRA activists, who stirred up tensions between residents and the nature protection agencies and mobilised them against the national park, resulting in polarisation and conflict escalation. I will thereby describe the strategies of mobilisation and direct attention to some contradictions between the perspectives and claims of the movement and realities on the ground.

2. CRITICAL EVENTS IN SOCIAL MOVEMENT STUDIES

Much scholarship on social movements has focused on the social-political environments in which mobilisation occurs. It has analysed social and political structures and contexts that favour or impede mobilisation and influence its prospects, strategies, course and outcomes. Political opportunity (and process) theory emerged as a major conceptual lens of much of this work (Meyer, 2004, p. 126). Eisinger (1973) and Tilly (1978), early contributors to the political opportunity concept, saw the frequency of protest in a curvilinear relationship with political openness – with open political structures tending to pre-empt protest by inviting participation, closed structures discouraging and repressing protest, and a continuum in between that provides more or less fertile ground for social mobilisation (Meyer, 2004).

In the empirical case of the Betung Kerihun National Park discussed in this chapter, a classical political opportunity perspective helps to explain how transformations of the broader social-political environment of Indonesia with diminishing state repression and democratisation since the fall of President Suharto's repressive New Order regime in 1998 have enhanced opportunities for social movements, mobilisation and protest. However, these broader structural changes yield little explanatory insight for the specific causes, timing and course of mobilisation in the national park.

Although it has stimulated fruitful research, political opportunity theory has been critiqued for having little explanatory power across diverse contexts and empirical cases; for the large diversity of understandings of 'political opportunity', which has blurred the concept and obscured distinctions between different aspects; for its deductive bias toward static, structural factors; and for its tendency to neglect non-structural factors, like strategy and agency (the active choices and efforts of actors), as well as cultural factors, which shape, for example, moral visions and emotions prior to and in the process of mobilisation (Goodwin and Jasper, 1999; Jasper, 2011). Hence, Jasper (2010, 2011) called for more inductive empirical research that pays attention to strategic (inter)actions and events.

Surprisingly, relatively few scholars of social movement studies have paid explicit analytical and conceptual attention to critical events as triggers of mobilisation.

In his analysis of anti-nuclear energy mobilisation triggered by a nuclear accident in Pennsylvania, Walsh (1981) emphasised the role of 'suddenly realised' or 'suddenly imposed grievances' in response to a specific event as an important and till then in social movement studies neglected cause of mobilisation. His notion of 'suddenly realised or suddenly imposed grievances' has since sporadically been taken up by others. The extent of grievances, mobilisation, and mobilisation success after critical events depends on a large range of case-specific, situational factors (Koopmans and Duyvendak, 1995).

Staggenborg (1993) described 'redefining critical events' causing shifts in public and elite perceptions, producing public attention, and effecting changes in movements' strategies. Such critical events can be sudden, often unforeseen events, such as a nuclear accident (Walsh, 1981), an oil spill, a police raid (as I describe below), or a food crisis (Shawki, 2012), that trigger mobilisation and social movement formation. Also, political decisions can be such mobilisation-triggering events. Another type of critical events are impactful protests themselves that further promote or change the dynamics of mobilisation. Porta (2008) conceptualised the latter as 'eventful protest' – protest with transformative impacts. A well-known case of mobilisation triggered and promoted by both two types of critical events is the pro-democracy protests in Hong Kong. The intended 'national security' legislation during the SARS epidemic in 2003 triggered abrupt, unpredicted mass-protests on 1 July 2003 – a 'redefining critical event' that kick-started the pro-democracy movement that politicised the formerly 'politically apathetic' city (Lee and Chan, 2011), culminating in a series of critical events in 2019/20: from the planned extradition law amendment bill triggering unprecedented mass-protests, to China's repressive 'national security' law for Hong Kong strategically enacted in the shadow of the SARS-CoV-2 pandemic (Holbig, 2020).

Snow et al. (1998) conceptualised 'quotidian disruptions', that is, disruptions of the taken-for-granted everyday routines, attitudes and expectancies, as trigger of collective action. Ramos (2008) proposed to include critical events as a dimension of the political opportunity concept – through generating contention and awareness, critical events can be opportunities to mobilise. Sewell (1996, 2005) earlier proposed the term of 'eventful temporality' to direct attention to the power of events in history and argued for an 'eventful sociology'. Together with McAdam, he called for more 'event-centred' approaches in the study of social movements with an emphasis on 'transformative events' as key shapers of escalation, de-escalation, and structural change (McAdam and Sewell, 2001). Gillan (2018) sees an 'eventful' approach beginning to make a mark on social movement scholarship.

The mobilisation against the Betung Kerihun National Park that I analyse below would very likely not have occurred without the critical event of a raid against gold miners. The success of mobilisation, however, can be understood only in the historical context of villagers' changing livelihoods and resource uses and their distrustful relations with the national park authorities prior to this critical event. The following sections explore this historical context – a fertile ground for mobilisation.

3. HUNTER–GATHERER SOCIETY IN TRANSFORMATION: A BRIEF HISTORY OF THE 'NATIONAL PARK COMMUNITIES' AT THE EDGE OF THE STATE

The people of the national park villages Bungan Jaya and Tanjung Lokang belong to the Punan Hovongan (or Punan Bungan) tribe, while the people of Matalunai belong to the Bukat, two of the numerous traditional nomadic and semi-nomadic hunter–gatherer groups of Central Borneo, collectively referred to as Punan. The Punan – by their traditional hunter–gatherer way of life – are distinguished from the (traditionally mainly farming) Dayak or seen as a sub-group thereof (MacKinnon et al., 1996; Sellato, 1994). Dayak ('people of the interior') is a collective term referring to numerous tribal groups in the interior of Borneo. They are distinct from the Melayu, another heterogeneous group of people who share a common religion (Islam) and who are concentrated in the coastal areas and in scattered settlements and urban quarters upstream along the rivers.[4]

The Punan Hovongan, like other Punan tribes, lived as nomadic or semi-nomadic hunter–gatherers in the mountainous forest areas of the upper river basins without much contact to the wider world until the early twentieth century. Their subsistence was based on sago, a starch extracted from palm stems, on hunting, gathering and fishing. They also collected forest products, such as resins, honey, camphor, rattan, arrow poison, rhinoceros horn, and hornbill heads and feathers, for barter in exchange for salt, iron, tobacco and other products (Sellato, 1994). Their existence throughout the nineteenth century was marked by fights and headhunting raids[5] between tribes, decimating the population and causing displacements. Their shelters were in hideouts away from the rivers. The Punan's relations to other tribes and people from downstream were marked by distrust and suspiciousness. Strangers were feared and often killed – a fate also met by George Müller, the first European explorer in the Bungan River area in the 1870s/1880s, and a few Dutch people between the 1920s and 1940s.

Interference by pre-colonial Malay rulers from downstream and the colonial administration was very limited until the 1920s (Sellato and Sercombe, 2008). Trade was often done 'silently' without face-to-face meetings via the shifting cultivators downstream, who derived substantial benefits as middlemen and who were regarded as owners of the lands foraged by the Punan (Sellato, 1994). The Dutch tried to abolish headhunting and encouraged the hunter–gatherers to move down to the river, settle, and adopt farming around the 1920s. This accelerated the Punan's transition to a sedentary existence. Yet, only some of them slowly replaced hunting–

gathering by farming (Sellato, 1994). The Punan Hovongan did not adopt rice farming before the 1960s, when Chinese traders in Putussibau generated increasing rice demand. Interventions from outside and villagers' contact with the wider world remained limited until the 1960s and 1970s. The Punan Hovongan of the original settlement of Tanjung Lokang and Nanga Bungan (the village was established in the 1970s) lived virtually outside of state control.

This changed in the 1970s and 1980s, with state authorities initiating programmes to provide access to health care and education, the setting up of a missionary post, and improved transportation. High infant mortality rates and the incidence of deadly diseases, like cholera, started to decline. The introduction of boat engines in the 1980s reduced the travel time from Nanga Bungan to Putussibau from previously one week downstream and two weeks upstream to a few hours. These changes increasingly brought these remote communities into contact with the state, the district town of Putussibau, and urban traders, and enhanced their access to education, information, markets and technology.

This, together with enormously rising prices for certain forest products has enabled them to substantially raise their incomes over the past three decades. Their commercial hunting and gathering of high-priced forest products and species as well as gold mining have put them into a better economic position than many rural and urban poor downstream. At the same time, they have retained a high level of autonomy over the natural resources surrounding them and in many respects of life and community development. They still live at the edge of the state, and this is reflected not only in their location far away from roads and mobile phone networks and the cancellation of most classes in local schools, as teachers prefer to stay in town, but also in villagers' attitudes and ways of life – and this shaped the course of mobilisation against the national park, which I discuss below. In the following, I provide an overview of villagers' control and their changing use, extraction and depletion of high-priced natural resources, which the national park aimed gradually to influence.

4. CHANGING CONTROL, USE AND DEPLETION OF HIGH-PRICED FOREST RESOURCES

In their course of transformation from nomadic or semi-nomadic hunter–gatherers without steady territorial control to a sedentary life, the Punan gained firmer control over large territories rich in high-priced forest resources. As Sellato (2008), who has conducted meticulous research into the hunter–gatherer communities of Central Borneo since the early 1980s, analysed, the Punan gained ground in visibility, land control, and economic advantages over the twentieth century. Through their position at the remote upper ends of river catchments, these small communities have come to control vast areas and have increasingly been acknowledged as rightful users of these resource-rich lands. The villages in the upper Kapuas catchment comprise only about 5 per cent of the population of the district of Putussibau but 60 per cent of its area (Sellato, 2008). Traditionally, the hunter–gatherer tribes had no formal territorial control over these lands. They lived as nomads and were merely regarded as 'guests or visitors' by the farmers downstream, who owned the lands and everything living on it, including the Punan (Sellato, 1994, 2008). The farmers acted as exploitative patrons over the Punan and made them gather forest products, which they sold at high margins (Sellato, 1994, 2005, 2008). The Punan's hunting and gathering grounds were unstable, changing in line with their relations and conflicts with neighbouring groups. Through their gradual settlement in the twentieth century and the state administration's territorial division of sub-villages, villages and districts, they ended up with vast village territories, 'amputated' from the farming groups' territory and comprising the entire upper river catchments (Sellato, 2008). Their rights over these lands and resources have increasingly been recognised (Sellato, 2008), though they had never been the only, exclusive users of these resources. Other tribes, farming groups from downstream, as well as Melayu and Chinese gatherers and traders, have for a long time occasionally exploited forest resources in the area, in the past sometimes leading to conflict and killings (Sellato, 1994, 2005).

Today, most villagers of Nanga Bungan and Tanjung Lokang still derive their major income from hunting and gathering. Shifting cultivation of rice, adopted in the 1960s, remained on a low level and has declined in the past one to two decades. Hunting and gathering is their culture and clearly provides higher returns, as prices for certain forest products have risen enormously. The hunter–gatherers have traditionally been and are still pragmatic, opportunistic, and flexible in choosing subsistence and commercial activities that maximise immediate profits without longer-term labour investment (Sellato, 2005, 2008). In response to new demands and changing market prices and opportunities, and with a focus on maximising immediate returns to labour, they have flexibly switched from one resource to another and, in many cases, hunted or gathered it until depleted.

In addition to the products hunted and gathered for subsistence (e.g. sago, medicinal plants, pigs, deer, birds), villagers have over time switched between numerous resources hunted and gathered for the market – from rhinoceros horns (extinct now), nyatoh resin, tengkawang seeds, damar resin, and geliga (bezoar stones) to rotan, gold, gaharu (eagle wood), swiftlet nests, timber, tor fish (*Tor tambroides*) and hornbills. In the following, I briefly describe the extraction of the latter six resources and species, which have served as the main sources of cash income in Nanga Bungan and Tanjung Lokang from the 1980s onwards. The examples of these six resources and species illustrate the potential conflicts between nature conservation aims and the hunter–gatherers' modes of resource extraction.

Gold Mining

Traditional small-scale gold panning was done in the Kapuas and Bungan rivers throughout the twentieth century. Following a price hike in 1980/1981 and the introduction of compressors in 1988, gold gained importance as a source of income. The compressors allowed diving to collect gold pieces by hand. In the late 1990s, villagers started building boat-like gold mining floats with pipes, engines and sluices (Figure 16.3), a technique adopted from gold miners in the Melawi River, where it had been introduced by miners from Central Kalimantan. With this technique, sediment-water slurry is pumped up from the river and riverbanks through a sluice. The miners first used 3-inch pipes, later 6-inch pipes. This mechanisation raised yields. This, together with rising gold prices turned gold into a major source of income for many households. Villagers of Matulunai leased their river sections to miners from downstream and used 12-inch pipes. This maximised immediate returns to labour but depleted their gold resources. A local gold trader estimated the number of mechanised gold mining units in the upper Kapuas and Bungan Rivers and their tributaries within the national park at 350 to 450. This includes a large number of units operated not by locals, but by Melayu people from Putussibau who started gold mining in the upper-most sections of the Kapuas River and one of its tributaries, the Tahum River, in the late 1990s (Figure 16.4). Mechanised gold mining and mercury use have substantial environmental impacts, from river bank destruction and extreme water turbidity levels, to declining fish stocks, reduced diversity of aquatic life, and health threats. National park initiatives aimed to regulate the practices of local miners. A police raid targeting miners triggered the anti-national park mobilisation that I discuss below.

Figure 16.3 Gold mining unit on the muddy water of the Kapuas River between Matalunai and Nanga Bungan (own photo)

Gaharu

Gaharu, also called agarwood, aloes wood, or eaglewood, has been another major source of income for the villagers in the national park. This fragrant, resinous wood is produced in aquilaria trees through a fungal infection. It is used for incense and perfume, particularly in India and some other Asian and the Arab countries. Gaharu was already collected by hunter–gatherers in Central Borneo in the nineteenth and early twentieth century (Sellato, 2005). Prices rose around 1989/1990, skyrocketed during the Asian Economic Crisis in the late 1990s, and continued to increase thereafter. Villagers receive between IDR 50 000 per kg in the lowest and up to IDR 20 to 400 million per kg in the two highest of five quality levels. They, and collectors from outside, who pay fees to the village, have hence extracted gaharu on a large scale until the resource has been depleted economically. To harvest gaharu, aquilaria trees assumed to be infected with the fungus are felled. As the signs of fungal infection are not visible with certainty beforehand, it does happen that non-infected trees are also felled. Eghenter (2005) observed similar dynamics in East Kalimantan. As the resource is almost

Figure 16.4   A group of Melayu gold miners with fuel and provisions on their way upstream to the gold mining area around the Tahum River (own photo)

depleted on the Indonesian side, some villagers collect gaharu beyond the border on the Malaysian side.

Birds' Nests

Swiftlet nests (edible birds' nests) have also lost their significance as an income source due to resource depletion. They were the major source of income especially in Tanjung Lokang between the 1980s and early 2000s. The nests started to be collected in caves and were sold for IDR 100 000 to 200 000 per kg in 1972. Prices increased to IDR 5 million per kg by the early 2000s. Several hundred kg of swiftlet nests were extracted per year. The person discovering a cave held the rights over it. Due to stealing by locals and outsiders, the caves were guarded. Rights over some caves were sold to outsiders – mostly to finance excessive consumption and pay back corresponding credits; some caves were leased out for up to IDR 5 million per cave per month; and even police and military officers were engaged as guards. Stealing and numerous conflicts among villagers, between villagers and village leaders, and conflicts involving people from other tribes and traders[6] culminated in threats and killings of guards with swords and guns and led to competitive overharvesting of nests. Too early harvesting reduced the quality of the nests and the prices obtained and inhibited reproduction of the birds. Their population hence drastically declined between 2001 and 2005, and swiftlet nests no longer provide incomes to villagers.

Timber

In the late 1990s and early 2000s, during the political vacuum after the fall of President Suharto, the villagers engaged in and substantially benefited from the illegal logging rush. They received chainsaws and fuel on credit from traders. The logs were floated down the river to Putussibau and brought to Pontianak or across the border to Malaysia. Loggers from outside had to pay IDR 50 000 per tree into the village treasury. Villagers achieved very high incomes during this era. 'Logging was even more beneficial than gold here', as one respondent put it. In this case, political regulation rather than resource depletion put an end to this resource boom. Some villagers regret that the logging rush ended with the presidency of S.B. Yudhoyono in 2004, and that the national park since restricts logging.

Tor Fish

Following the depletion of gaharu and swiftlet nests and the logging ban, a fish species of the cyprinidae family, locally called ikan semah putih (*Tor tambroides*), was one of the next high-priced resources, providing substantial cash incomes in Nanga Bungan and Tanjung Lokang. Demand from Malaysia started to raise prices in 2006/2007. Villagers sold it to traders in Putussibau for IDR 600 000 to 800 000 per kg in 2013. A group of three people commonly returns with 10 to 20 tor fishes from a fishing expedition lasting a few days. One fish commonly weighs 3 to 10 kg. As a result of fishing pressure as well as electric and poison fishing,[7] fish stocks declined substantially within two to three years, requiring villagers (and outsiders from Putussibau) to travel to the upper-most river sections to catch this valuable fish.

Helmeted Hornbill

In 2012, villagers began extensively hunting the helmeted hornbill (*Rhinoplax vigil*), locally called *tajak*. The bird's casque (Figure 16.5), a very solid helmet-like structure between its bill and the tip of its head, fetched IDR 2–3 million, large ones IDR 8–11 million. Almost all households of Nanga Bungan started catching the helmeted hornbill. In the beginning, it was not uncommon that one family or hunting group returned with up to 20 to 50 birds from a hunting trip. They attracted the birds with a whistle sound and used shot guns. Both use of shot guns and trade of all hornbill species are prohibited. The abundance of the helmeted hornbill, the mascot of the province of West Kalimantan and sacred for some tribes, thus substantially declined within only one to two years, making it difficult to find. As the species is monogamous, hunting pressure easily threatens reproduction. It is now listed as critically endangered on the IUCN Red List of Threatened Species (BirdLife International, 2019). Apart from the helmeted hornbill, a number of other bird species as well as orangutans (*Pongo pygmaeus*), Bornean gibbons (*Hylobates muelleri*), sun bears (*Helarctos malayanus*) and the Sunda pangolin (*Manis javanica*) are occasionally caught and (parts thereof) fed into illegal wildlife trading chains.

The surprisingly high incomes from the commercial hunting and gathering of these high-priced forest resources and species have made the people of Nanga Bungan and Tanjung Lokang wealthier over the past two to three decades. Some of them own a second house in Putussibau, where they sell their products and buy goods. The high cash incomes have allowed

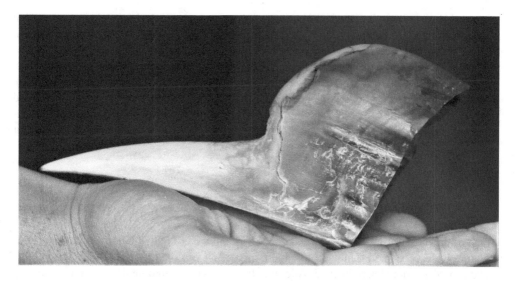

Figure 16.5   Casque of the helmeted hornbill (own photo)

them to buy technical equipment, from engines for boats and gold mining units to chainsaws, and consumer goods.

Yet, immediate spending and squandering and a pronounced reluctance to save and invest repeatedly push many villagers in temporary debt relations with traders and impede a transformation to less resource extractivist livelihoods. As Sellato (2008, p. 87) put it, 'their tenacious "immediate-return" turn of mind has prevented them from investing ... in delayed-return activities. As soon as they bring a load of forest products to the trader, the Punan tend to acquire expensive prestige goods of little practical long-term utility'. In Matalunai, high levels of alcohol consumption limit the potential of incomes from natural resource extraction to enhance living standards – a fate that Nanga Bungan and Tanjung Lokang have stopped through an alcohol ban.

As the examples of the six resources above have shown, villagers '"immediate-return" turn of mind' (Sellato, 2008, p. 87) with a focus on maximising quick returns to labour, and resource competition have kept them in unsustainable modes of resource extraction. This is not a new phenomenon. Resource depletion and extinction of species (e.g. rhinoceros, langur monkey) already occurred earlier when the hunters still relied on traditional tools, like blowpipes and spears (Sellato, 2005). Resource rivalry is also nothing new in the region – hunter–gatherer groups throughout central Borneo staged 'raiding expeditions' to pillage resources in the other tribes' territories in the late nineteenth and early twentieth century, involving open conflicts and headhunting (Eghenter, 2005; Sellato, 2005). Yet, access to markets and technology have considerably raised the levels of resource extraction.

As Sellato and Sercombe (2008, p. 45) in their overview of hunter–gatherer groups of Borneo put it, 'few among them really aim for the long-term, sustainable exploitation of their resources, and many in effect harvest their resources in the same ruthless and unsustainable way as outsiders.' While they tend to manage wild food resources used for subsistence more sustainably, they practise 'severe forms of extractivism' in hunting and collecting forest resources with a trade value but little or no use locally (Sellato, 2005, 2008). The tribal groups of central Borneo 'have had, and still have, no sense that such resources should be managed in a sustainable way for continued use by future generations, since these resources are not needed at the subsistence level' (Sellato, 2005).

This is a challenge for the co-existence of the national park and villagers' resource uses. The national park management plan, drafted by the World Wide Fund for Nature (WWF), and much of the interventions implemented until 2012 took an approach of compromises and gradual transformation. Yet, as I explain below, tensions and distrust soon marked the relations between villagers and the national park authorities, and this provided fertile ground for the AGRA activists to mobilise against the national park.

5. THE NATIONAL PARK: IMPLEMENTATION, PROGRAMMES AND REGULATIONS

Much of the present Betung Kerihun National Park, an area of 600 000 ha, was designated as a Nature Reserve, named Bentuang Karimun, in 1982. It was extended to 800 000 ha in 1992 and declared a national park in 1995. Adopting the names of two mountains, as they are known by local communities (Mt Betung and Mt Kerihun), the name was changed to Betung Kerihun National Park in 1999.

The national park is the largest component of a network of protected areas that represent much of the remaining primary forests of Borneo, one of the world's major biodiversity hotspots, which is severely threatened by logging, extensive land conversions for the rapid expansion of oil palm, rubber, and timber plantations, mining, and unsustainable resource uses. The national park harbours at least 695 tree species, 50 of which are endemic to Borneo, 301 bird species, 24 of which are endemic, 112 fish species, 14 of which are endemic, 51 amphibian species, 21 snake species, crocodiles, and turtles and is one of the last habitats of the Bornean Orangutan (*Pongo pygmaeus*) and six other primates (ITTO et al., 1999; Septiani and Sidabutar, 2015). The park's altitudinal gradient contributes to its conservation significance under climate change (Struebig et al., 2015).

The establishment of the park was supported by the International Tropical Timber Organization (ITTO) and the WWF. The ITTO provided financial support, and the WWF developed concepts and management plans combining nature conservation and support for improving livelihoods in the communities in and around the national park. The management of the park is under the authority of the Ministry of Environment and Forestry, which established a national park office in Putussibau and a number of base camps within the park, two of which are located in Bungan Jaya and Tanjung Lokang.

Villagers and village representatives remember the initiation and establishment phase of the national park in a positive way. Programmes supporting alternative livelihood strategies and various kinds of community support, including the building of health facilities and schools, were promised in kind letters from the government and in friendly meetings. The project documents and management plans from the establishment phase, drafted by the WWF between 1996 and 1999, show a sound knowledge of villagers' natural resource uses and their impacts and put emphasis on linking nature conservation and community development. Developing alternative income sources and enhancing the sustainability of villagers' resource uses were hence defined as some of the central aims of the national park project. The communities living in and around the national park were supposed to benefit.

Aiming to combine nature protection and villagers' resource uses, the national park is divided into six zones, each with different functions and possible uses: *Zona Inti* (core zone), *Zona Rimba* (primary forest zone), *Zona Pemanfaatan* (for limited uses, including tourism), *Zona Tradisional* (for hunting and gathering), *Zona Religion* (spiritual places), and *Zona Khusus* (for settlements, agriculture and other uses). The *Zona Khusus*, a 5 km strip along the rivers, covers an area of 3900 ha and comprises all hamlets within the upper reaches of the Kapuas River and its tributaries. The kinds and methods of villagers' resource uses in the different zones are regulated by national park law – a 'functional territorialisation' (Vandergeest and Peluso, 1995) on paper that has barely been enforced on the ground.

The village communities were encouraged to include regulations banning some of the environmentally most damaging kinds and methods of natural resource extraction in their traditional village law (*adat*).[8] Accordingly, the use of poison and electricity for fishing, which had threatened fish stocks and aquatic life in general, is prohibited according to both national park and *adat* law. Enforcement is difficult, though, in the remote upper river sections, at night, and in the case of outsiders from downstream. In addition, the sizes of machines and pipes used for gold mining were limited and mercury use banned. Only machines up to 5 horsepower and pipes up to 4.5-inch are allowed according to *adat* law. This is a compromise in support of villagers' gold mining methods already used prior to the establishment of the national park. The national park law bans mechanised gold mining and only allows manual panning, but the authorities tolerated mechanised mining that is in line with *adat* law.

To involve the communities, the national park authorities employed two villagers as permanent staff members and ten villagers as local national park guards. They were supposed to support the enforcement of national park and *adat* law, with the latter being the preferred enforcement mechanism and first option used by both the local guards and the guards from the national park authority. Following two warnings, penalties apply. A number of persons accused of poison and electro fishing and miners using machines exceeding the legal limits were warned; a few were punished. Penalties are set and negotiated with the chief of *adat* law (*Ketua Adat*) and take the form of payments of traditional gongs or jars (*tempayan*) or equivalent monetary payments.

In addition to these regulatory measures, the villagers are to be encouraged and supported to gradually adopt alternative livelihood strategies to reduce their dependence on forest resource extraction and further enhance their living conditions. One set of national park initiatives and programmes aims at domesticating high-priced species that villagers have hunted and gathered to date and that are (at risk of being) depleted. Agarwood for gaharu production and tor fish have been covered as the most promising among these species. Following research on the cultivation, fungus infection, and market potential of agarwood, villagers were provided with seedlings, knowledge and equipment and encouraged to cultivate agarwood in and around their villages and on abandoned shifting cultivation plots. The national park authorities also support the development of aquaculture of tor fish. Another set of initiatives aims at tourism development to create new income opportunities for villagers, working as tourist guides, providing accommodation and transportation, and producing handicrafts.

Beyond the national park programmes, the regional government and a village development fund financed a pedestrian's bridge across the river in Nanga Bungan and built micro-hydropower facilities in Nanga Bungan and Tanjung Lokang. The latter are managed by the villagers themselves and replace their individual diesel generators, which produced noise and pollution, and were expensive to operate.

6. VILLAGER–NATIONAL PARK RELATIONS

Despite positive intentions and good ideas on paper, the relations between villagers and the national park authorities were soon compromised by disappointment and distrust. On the one hand, villagers acknowledged that the national park protected their forest from excessive resource extraction by outsiders and from corporate interests – an important consideration, given that large parts of West Kalimantan are being transformed into oil palm plantations, with resource use and control rights shifting in conflictual processes from villagers to companies. On the other hand, villagers were concerned that the national park would regulate their resource uses. In practice, their resource uses were barely affected due to the national park zoning and limited enforcement of regulations. Yet, a lack of flows of information, communication issues across cultural divides, slow implementation of promised programmes, and villagers' perception of corruption, complicated relations and contributed to a climate of distrust.

Villagers noted that funds that the national park administration received from the national government and other sources did not translate into programme implementation on the ground. They noted that funds were diverted, an accusation corroborated by village leaders, insiders from an NGO, and knowledgeable individuals, and that many programmes existed on paper only. An exchange of the head of the national park authority in 2011 reportedly aggravated these issues. Promises regarding schools, health facilities, and fishponds were not met, while a large, representative building was constructed for the national park administration in Putussibau. In fact, only two tor fishponds had been established until 2013 with support by the national park programme. Both of them are owned by relatively wealthy and influential individuals of Bungan Jaya.

The fact that many villagers lacked information about the national park zones, their spatial arrangement, the zone-specific regulations, and the differences between and the supremacy of *adat* vs. national park law in the different zones resulted in confusion. Land and village surveys conducted by representatives of the national park authority without providing sufficient information about the aims of the surveys, and the setting of border stones demarcating the national park boundary without prior notice to the villagers fuelled additional distrust. The involvement of military personnel in the implementation of the agarwood programmes (the distribution of aquilaria seedlings in the villages) caused further irritation.

Furthermore, the historically and culturally rooted tendency of the villagers to meet outsiders and interventions by the state with suspicion, which I discussed above, and the national park authorities' lack of recognition of villagers' customs contribute to the limited effectiveness of programmes and to overall tensions. Governmental representatives, especially if they are from Java, are met by villagers with suspicion and are often not fully understood, as they speak an 'abstract, political language'. Villagers also questioned the quality of the aquilaria seedlings brought from outside and were highly suspicious about the recommended injections, which trigger the fungus infection in the trees leading to the production of gaharu and which they would have to pay for. The national park authorities, in turn, did not take into account villagers' communal tenure with limited private land control and their lacking culture of cultivating, investing, and planning into the future. By determining locations top-down and trying to tell people where to plant the trees, the national park authority simply ignored people's preferences, tenure, and customs, and caused conflict within the villages.

To sum up, a lack of trust and inadequate communication between historically repressive, still not particularly responsive state authorities and the traditional hunter–gatherer communities, who had long lived largely beyond state control and who were wary of losing their autonomy, along with the authorities' inadequate attention to the communities' culture and resource tenure and villagers' disappointment about limited programme implementation and corruption constituted conflict-prone pre-conditions. This latent conflict situation corresponds to the lowest of the eight levels of conflict escalation differentiated by Yasmi et al. (2006), a situation marked by suspicion, rumours and anger, articulated among villagers only. Yet, villagers did not basically oppose the national park until an imprudent police raid targeting gold miners triggered their mobilisation. The issues that I have described in this section as conflict-prone pre-conditions provided fertile ground for and shaped the course of anti-national park mobilisation that I describe in the following.

7. MOBILISATION AGAINST THE NATIONAL PARK TRIGGERED BY A CRITICAL EVENT

A critical event – a raid targeting gold miners – substantially changed the situation in the national park in 2011. This raid, and the way it was conducted, produced grievances locally and public attention, which triggered the AGRA activists' awareness of the national park villages and their engagement in the area.

The raid, which was conducted by police and military personnel, was supposed to primarily target non-local Melayu gold miners who operated with numerous and large machines in the upper-most reaches of the Kapuas River and its tributaries, particularly in the Tahum River, two boat-trip-days upstream from Nanga Bungan. The village representatives received a warning letter two months prior to the raid to allow them to protect the local gold miners. This reflects the cautious approach of the national park authority to avoid conflicts with the national park villagers. Despite this warning, some large gold mining machines owned by local villagers, especially from Nanga Lapung, a hamlet near Nanga Bungan, who also operated upstream, were destroyed, while the raid did not reach the major Melayu gold mining hotspots in the Tahum River area that it was supposed to primarily target. It did not reach this area, as the Melayu boat drivers, whom the organisers of the raid had engaged, reportedly did not take along enough fuel in order to protect the gold miners belonging to their own ethnic group. This injustice caused as much anger among villagers as the destruction of some of their machines.

Their anger provided fertile ground for the activists from the land reform movement AGRA to mobilise them against the national park. The activists, who had not run any programmes in the area before, became aware of the raid and the anger it had caused and decided to engage in this situation. They had started their activities in Tanjung Lokang and Nanga Bungan respectively about 6 and 12 months prior to my first field research. Their engagement substantially stirred up villagers' tensions and distrust, made them boycott any programmes of the national park authority and the WWF, and created a climate of polarisation and confrontation between villagers and the national park. The activists taught villagers about national park regulations and mobilised them to fight against resource use restrictions and the 'monopolisation and appropriation of their land'.

Initiated, facilitated, and in fact led by the AGRA activists, a number of villagers set up an anti-national park action group. This 'peasant union', termed *Serikat Tani Losing Kovalan*, comprised a fairly remarkable organisational structure, including a consultative board and a number of 'departments' covering social themes, like education, members' welfare,

320 *Handbook of anti-environmentalism*

advocacy, youth and women, as well as security and protection (from outsiders who are not conforming to the *adat* law). The activists also planned to set up a local art centre and to build a school – education is a pressing issue that the state has fallen short of addressing for many years. Information boards were set up throughout the village, presenting the programme and structure of the 'peasant union' on formal, professionally designed, colour-printed documents (Figure 16.6). The activists put emphasis on uniting the people of all hamlets, on linking the action group with the traditional institutions and customs of the Punan Hovongan tribe, and on involving the tribal leaders.

Figure 16.6   Information board in Nanga Bungan presenting the 'peasant union', established as anti-national park action group (own photo)

The local *adat* law played a major role in this mobilisation against the national park. The activists aimed at strengthening the *adat* law vis-à-vis the national park law and other legal frameworks of the state and provided support in producing a written version thereof. In the activists' view, any regulation of matters that have been regulated or have been legal according to *adat* law by another law, in this case national park law, is unacceptable. They argued that the national park had weakened the local *adat* law. As *adat* law existed first in this area, according to the argument, outsiders, including the national park authority, cannot come in, set rules, tell people which parts of their land they can use in what way, and enact a law superior to the local *adat* law. A village leader, who was in close exchange with the activists noted that '[t]he national park doesn't use *adat* law. They use their own law. We hope that the national park will then [when we have a written version of the *adat* law] obey to *adat* law.'

The activists regarded the banning of poison and electro fishing and the limitation of the gold mining machines and pipes that the village had included in the *adat* law following recommendations by the national park authority and the WWF, as an unacceptable 'instrumentalisation of the *adat* law' by the national park actors. In another interview, one of the activists argued that gold mining by outsiders had been well regulated by *adat* law, as they had to pay part of their revenues into the village treasury, while the national park, by prohibiting mechanised gold mining, weakened the *adat* law. However, in fact, most gold miners from outside neither obeyed the *adat* law nor did they report and pay their fees to the village as required; the Melayu miners in fact avoided contact with villagers and were feared by some of them to be connected to evil spirits.

The activists' arguments about the supremacy of *adat* law fell on fertile ground among some of the villagers and their leaders. These arguments are well in line with their tradition of autonomy at the edge of the state. The case of a film team that the village leaders denied access to the national park illustrates this. The film team had obtained all necessary permits from the state authorities, including from the national park administration, but did not report to the Ketua *adat* in the village, as required by local *adat* law, and was thus forced to return to Putussibau.

A core phrase that the AGRA activists used in mobilising villagers against the national park labels the establishment of the park as a 'monopolisation of land by the national park authorities.' This phrase reflects AGRA's primary engagement in agrarian conflicts, where farmers struggle to defend their land rights against state-owned or private agro-industrial companies. As one of the activists argued, 'while villagers are allowed to cultivate a few hectares only, the national park authority appropriates thousands of hectares of land'. Some villagers found this perspective not very plausible. Others frequently recited this phrase. A village leader, for example, complained: 'The people from the national park are not helping, but they monopolise the land. They are grabbing land here, peoples' land. They don't care about *adat* law. When they first came, they were very friendly. But look what happens now. They fooled us. They want to monopolise our land.'

The national park authority's lack of communication with villagers and the (resulting) distrust that the latter had developed over time provided fertile ground for these perspectives. The village leader cited above narrated:

> People from the national park came to Nanga Bungan around 2010 and conducted a survey of water quantities used by the people. They might also want to survey the amount of air we breathe. They surveyed the land areas used for *ladang* [shifting cultivation], the yields achieved, and peoples' incomes. But the purpose of the survey was not opened up to us. People were not told what it was done for. The purpose of the survey was perhaps to make a strategy to monopolise our land. The survey was only for the national park people. They fooled us. But now, with the help of the activists, we have become knowledgeable. We resist.

While the national park authorities aim at encouraging villagers to reduce shifting cultivation over the longer term through supporting them in generating alternative incomes, for example through agarwood cultivation and aquaculture, the AGRA activists encouraged them to expand shifting cultivation. According to the activists, the area of 3900 ha (a 5 km strip along the rivers) allocated for shifting cultivation in the national park (*Zona Khusus*) is not large enough. As one of the activists pointed out, '[t]he national park wants villagers to reduce shifting cultivation. But the villagers will expand shifting cultivation'. Their call to expand shifting cultivation is both a symbol of non-compliance with the aims and rules of the national park authority and an expression of AGRA's strong disposition toward subsistence agriculture. However, their ideas contradict the realities on the ground. Satellite images and observations of land use around the villages show that only a portion of the *Zona Khusus* is in fact used for shifting cultivation, and long fallow periods imply that land for shifting cultivation within this zone is not scarce. Furthermore, most families have reduced or even given up shifting cultivation since the 1990s, as they derive substantial cash incomes from commercial hunting and gathering and thus prefer to buy rather than cultivate rice. Thus, the *Zona Khusus*, which had been proposed in its present size by the tribal leaders themselves and which was fully granted when the national park was established, is large enough – as all villagers and village leaders interviewed confirmed. The most distant rice fields are only about 1 km from the river (Figure 16.7).

Figure 16.7   *Shifting cultivation plot above the Kapuas River near Nanga Bungan. The small number of fields and long fallow periods indicate that shifting cultivation land is not scarce (own photo)*

Another contradiction between the AGRA activists' view and realities on the ground concerns the sustainability of some of the villagers' resource uses. The activists consistently framed them as sustainable resource users living in harmony with nature – an imagination that contrasts with, as I described above, villagers' opportunistic shifts from hunting and gathering one species and forest resource after the other until depleted or extinct. This reality was consequently ignored by the activists, and if challenged, they at best attributed it to the capitalistic market. Such contradictions between NGOs' imaginations and realities on the ground are not uncommon. As Sellato (2008) noted, the 'neo-romantic myth' of Borneo's hunter–gatherers as 'children' and 'guardians of the forest' living in harmony with nature constitutes a considerable asset for NGOs. It has been produced, promoted and marketed by anthropologists and NGOs since the 1990s and embraced by donors and the public, often without sufficient inquiry into complex realities on the ground (Eghenter, 2000, 2005; Sellato, 2008). The villagers themselves took up some of this discourse in the process of mobilisation. Adopting the activists' wording, some of them noted that they boycotted the gaharu programmes, which government officials misleadingly termed 'regreening programmes', because their area was already green and managed sustainably, covered by forest as a result of their resource use patterns.

The AGRA activists trained villagers how to react when approached by national park staff and encouraged them to boycott any programmes initiated by the national park and the WWF. Many villagers hence refused to plant aquilaria trees provided in the frame of the national park's gaharu programme. The activists also opposed the performance of traditional music and dances by villagers planned as part of the tourism development programmes as commercialisation of their culture. This perspective was readily taken up by some villagers, who had already looked at the tourism development programmes with scepticism, as they had only limited control over them.

As part of the mobilisation against the national park, eight of the ten village national park guards, employed by the national park administration, resigned. Their chairperson joined the AGRA-initiated anti-national park action group. Some of the former guards turned quiet. They neither wanted to get in conflict with those who mobilised against the national park, nor did they want to join them. The two officially remaining guards did not know how to proceed, and the two villagers employed by the national park administration as permanent staff members paused their already limited activity.

The 6–12 months of AGRA's engagement in Nanga Bungan and Tanjung Lokang resulted in polarisation, with the national park authority framed as an enemy monopolising villagers' lands, and some villagers' arguments in favour of the national park being silenced under the wave of hostility and national park boycott. Some village residents and village leaders, including persons who had not benefited from the national park programmes, stood behind the idea of the national park and did not agree with the viewpoints and activities of the AGRA activists and their followers. They did not see the national park as a land grabbing project but continued to value it as an effort to protect 'their' forest from excessive resource extraction by outsiders and from corporate interests. As one villager put it, 'in areas not protected by the national park, companies enter'. A number of villagers also regarded the banning of electro and poison fishing, which had threatened fish stocks, as a positive result of the establishment of the national park. Yet, to avoid conflict with those who mobilised against the national park, they tended to keep quiet. A few villagers and village leaders openly complained about the activists, for example, they listed everybody who had participated in a first information meeting organised by them as a follower of the anti-national park movement, no matter whether they supported it or not – ironically, a strategy also used by oil palm plantation companies aiming to acquire land from villagers in other areas, outside the national park.

Those who mobilised spread the perspective of the national park as a land monopolisation or land grabbing project and the narrative of a previous harmony that was disturbed by the national park. A village leader noted that '[p]eople here lived in harmony until the national park came and disturbed us'. He looked back to the logging rush in the early 2000s as a good time for the villagers, critiqued the logging ban thereafter, and added: 'and now we face the national park'. As a sign of protest against the national park, villagers pulled over national park signs and nailed up the national park base camps in Nanga Bungan and Tanjung Lokang with wooden planks. Some villages wanted to burn down the base camps but were prevented from doing so by others. This level of polarisation and physical action against national park symbols and infrastructure marked the peak of the conflict, the highest level on the conflict curve, termed the destructive phase by Crowley et al. (2017), where chances for constructive dialogue are limited and relationships are being damaged.

The national park rangers have since hesitated to enter the area. Villagers assumed they were 'not brave enough to enter' and perhaps wanted to keep the conflict from boiling over. After my first field research stay, an NGO representative shared his expectation that the police or military might take action against the AGRA activists, as they were not registered as an NGO in the district of Kapuas Hulu and hence had no licence to run activities in this area.

When I came back nine months later, the AGRA activists were not present any more. A second critical event – the eviction of the AGRA activists – had ended the mobilisation against the national park. A group of representatives from the district administration along with police and military personnel had come to Nanga Bungan, asked the activists about their licence, and evicted them as they did not have one. Letters on information boards now warned the villagers about AGRA, an organisation that has no licence to legally run activities in the area. Polarisation and confrontation had started to fade. Bridging social rifts within the village and between the village leaders requires more time.

8. CONCLUDING REMARKS

The Betung Kerihun National Park protects one of the world's top biodiversity hotspots and one of the largest remaining rainforests in Southeast Asia. It thereby saves the hunting and gathering grounds of the Punan Hovongan and other tribal groups from excessive resource extraction by outsiders as well as from commercial logging, plantation development, and mining, which are wiping out forests and forest-dependent livelihoods throughout Kalimantan at an unprecedented pace. At the same time, it aims at regulating and developing alternatives to some of the unsustainable resource extractions of the hunter–gatherer communities. Extremely high market prices for certain forest products and the adoption of new 'fast and easy' resource extraction techniques, such as electro and poison fishing and mechanised gold mining, combined with a pronounced focus of the traditional hunter–gatherers on maximising short-term returns to labour, their cultural preference of extraction over cultivation and of immediate spending over saving and investing, as well as resource competition have drawn villagers into unsustainable modes of resource extraction.

The management plans for the national park, which aim at combining nature conservation, villagers' resource uses, and community development, and the corresponding zoning concept are, by and large, well thought out and well intended. Yet, lacking implementation, top-down approaches, the suspected diversion of funds, and communication issues complicated relations between the national park authority and villagers, whose tradition of autonomy at the edge of a coercive state a priori tends to limit trust in state authorities. Notwithstanding these issues, villagers did not basically oppose the national park, until a critical event – a raid against gold miners – produced anger and made activists from the land reform movement AGRA mobilise villagers. This led to a climate of polarisation and confrontation between villagers and the national park.

As one of many conflicts over nature conservation, widespread throughout the Global South, the case exemplifies some common challenges of balancing nature conservation goals and local populations' resource uses. Perhaps more importantly, the case illustrates that such conflicts are not necessarily primarily struggles for or against nature protection between those who implement conservation agendas and those who mobilise against them. Rather, conflict and mobilisation may be partly or primarily matters of difficult relations between state authorities and communities, of struggles over control, of distrust and inadequate communication, of a lack of responsiveness and corruption, of a lack of attention to cultural factors, and of numerous other possible issues. Questions of nature and the environment may sometimes be a catalyst for various societal issues. In the process of struggle, they may even be relegated to the background or distorted by rhetoric framings that fit a particular mission.

Some of the ideas, claims and slogans of the AGRA activists exemplify the latter. They reflect their common involvement in struggles against agro-industrial companies. Some of them contradict the context of the national park and realities on the ground. For example, their imagination of the hunter–gatherers as subsistence farmers, eager to expand rice cultivation, contradicts villagers' preference of commercial hunting and gathering over rice cultivation, which they have reduced. The AGRA activists also projected their imagination of Indigenous communities as sustainable resource users living in harmony with nature onto the villagers – an imagination that does not correspond well to reality, which is marked by the depletion and extinction of various forest resources and species, and villagers' opportunistic shift from one depleted resource to another high-priced forest product.

The empirical case directs attention to a number of factors that, as noted in section 2, had been critiqued as being underemphasised in social movement studies. Most importantly, the case highlights the role of critical events as triggers of mobilisation – an aspect that has received relatively limited systematic attention in social movement studies. Notwithstanding pre-existing tensions between villagers and national park authorities, villagers did not basically oppose the national park until a critical event – the raid against gold miners and the way it was conducted – produced anger and triggered the AGRA activists' mobilisation of villagers against the park. This mobilisation would very likely not have occurred without this critical event. The case also directs attention to the relevance of historical trajectories, cultural factors, and pre-mobilisation relations and tensions, shaping the course and outcomes of mobilisation. Another interesting insight is how the activists' strategic mobilisation from within a pre-existing social structure, the traditional tribal structure, and their emphasis on local sovereignty and the local *adat* law contributed to mobilisation success.

The AGRA-initiated insurgency against the national park was coercively stopped but has lasting effects. It has directed attention to the shortcomings of a national park authority that remains focused on its own and its staff members' interests, adheres to top-down approaches, ignores the communities' customs, and falls short on adequately engaging them. Besides polarisation, the insurgency has left behind village communities that engage in controversial debate more actively than before and that demand the national park administration more forcefully to respect their customs, to take into account their interests and concerns, and to actively engage them in the challenging mission of creating a national park that truly integrates and balances nature conservation with sustainable community development and the Punan's culture.

ACKNOWLEDGEMENT

The research was supported by the German Research Foundation (DFG) (Grant-Nos. GZ PY 76/3-1 und FL 392/3-1).

NOTES

1. The island of Borneo is part of the Sunda region, one of the world's five most exceptionally diverse and endemic-rich biodiversity hotspots, which together comprise 20 per cent of the world's plant and 16 per cent of all vertebrate species on a mere 0.4 per cent of the Earth's land surface (Myers et al., 2000). Borneo ranks first in comparative plant biodiversity analyses within the Sunda region and globally (Kier et al., 2005; Roos et al., 2004).
2. In and around the Betung Kerihun National Park, I conducted semi-structured interviews with village heads (*Kepala Desa*), tribal leaders (*Pemangku*), and guardians of the local *adat* law (*Ketua Adat*), with village residents engaged in hunting, gathering, gold mining, shifting cultivation, and other resource uses, traders, local national park guards, representatives of NGOs and the national park administration, and other key informants. I also attended planning discussions of the anti-national park action group.
3. To ensure anonymity, I use the aggregate term 'village leader' in parts of this chapter to refer to different representatives, including tribal leaders (*Pemangku*), the guardians of the traditional local *adat* law (*Ketua Adat*), and the formal village head (*Kepala Desa*).
4. Besides the Dayak and Melayu, ethnic Chinese are another major population group in West Kalimantan. They are descendants of Chinese gold diggers (Heidhues, 2003).
5. Heads were taken during conflicts, as trophies, as proof of strength, and put up next to dwellings to alienate enemies and evil spirits.
6. Ngo (2008) described three of these conflict cases.
7. The traditional use of plant poisons for fishing started to be replaced by herbicides in the 1980s. Electricity fishing was adopted from outsiders who entered the area during the illegal logging rush in the late 1990s and early 2000s. Both poison and electricity fishing are 'quick and easy', but threaten fish stocks and aquatic life. Poison fishing also threatens human health and river water quality.
8. NGOs have supported the tribal groups in and around the national park in building and writing up an *adat* law. This supports their 'traditional' resource rights. As the Punan traditionally abided by the *adat* law of the farming communities downstream, they did not have their own (Sellato, 2008).

REFERENCES

BirdLife International (2019) Rhinoplax vigil (amended version of 2018 assessment). *The IUCN Red List of Threatened Species 2019: e.T22682464A155467793*. Available from DOI: 10.2305/IUCN.UK.2019-3.RLTS.T22682464A155467793.en (accessed 16 May 2020).

Crowley, S.L., Hinchliffe, S. and McDonald, R.A. (2017) Conflict in invasive species management. *Frontiers in Ecology and the Environment.* **15**(3), pp. 133–41. Available from DOI: 10.1002/fee.1471.

Eghenter, C. (2000) What is tana ulen good for? Considerations on indigenous forest management, conservation, and research in the interior of Indonesian Borneo. *Human Ecology.* **28**(3), pp. 331–57. Available from DOI: 10.1023/A:1007068113933.

Eghenter, C. (2005) Histories of conservation or exploitation? Case studies from the interior of Indonesian Borneo. In: Wadley, R.L. (ed.) *Histories of the Borneo Environment: Economic, Political and Social Dimensions of Change and Continuity.* Leiden: KITLV, pp. 87–107.

Eisinger, P.K. (1973) The conditions of protest behavior in American cities. *The American Political Science Review.* **67**(1), pp. 11–28. Available from DOI: 10.2307/1958525.

Gillan, K. (2018) Temporality in social movement theory: Vectors and events in the neoliberal timescape. *Social Movement Studies*. **19**(5–6), pp. 1–21. Available from DOI: 10.1080/14742837.2018.1548965.

Goodwin, J. and Jasper, J.M. (1999) Caught in a winding, snarling vine: The structural bias of political process theory. *Sociological Forum*. **14**(1), 27–54. Available from: www.jstor.org/stable/685013.

Harrison, H.L. and Loring, P.A. (2020) Seeing beneath disputes: A transdisciplinary framework for diagnosing complex conservation conflicts. *Biological Conservation*. **248**, p. 108670. Available from DOI: 10.1016/j.biocon.2020.108670.

Heidhues, M.S. (2003) *Golddiggers, Farmers and Traders in the 'Chinese Districts' of West Kalimantan, Indonesia*. New York, NY: Cornell University Press.

Holbig, H. (2020) Be water, my friend: Hong Kong's 2019 anti-extradition protests. *International Journal of Sociology*. **50**(4), pp. 325–37. Available from DOI: 10.1080/00207659.2020.1802556.

ITTO, WWF Indonesia and Dephut (1999) *Management Plan Betung Kerihun National Park, West Kalimantan, 2000–2024*. International Tropical Timber Organisation (ITTO); World Wide Fund for Nature (WWF); and Directorate General of Nature Conservation and Protection (PKA), Ministry of Forestry.

Jasper, J.M. (2010) Social movement theory today: Toward a theory of action? *Sociology Compass*. **4**(11), pp. 965–76.

Jasper, J.M. (2011) Introduction: From political opportunity structures to strategic interaction. In: Jasper, J.M. and Goodwin, J. (eds) *Contention in Context: Political Opportunities and the Emergence of Protest*. Stanford, CA: Stanford University Press, pp. 1–33.

Kier, G., Mutke, J., Dinerstein, E., Ricketts, T.H., Küper, W., Kreft, H. and Barthlott, W. (2005) Global patterns of plant diversity and floristic knowledge. *Journal of Biogeography*. **32**(7), pp. 1107–116. Available from DOI: 10.1111/j.1365-2699.2005.01272.x.

Koopmans, R. and Duyvendak, J.W. (1995) The political construction of the nuclear energy issue and its impact on the mobilization of anti-nuclear movements in Western Europe. *Social Problems*. **42**(2), 235–51. Available from DOI: 10.2307/3096903.

Lee, F.L.F. and Chan, J.M. (2011) *Media, Social Mobilization, and Mass Protests in Post-colonial Hong Kong: The Power of a Critical Event*. New York, NY: Routledge.

Lukas, M.C. (2015) Reconstructing contested landscapes: Dynamics, drivers and political framings of land use and land cover change, watershed transformations and coastal sedimentation in Java, Indonesia. Ph.D. University of Bremen.

MacKinnon, K., Hatta, G., Halim, H. and Mangalik, A. (1996) *The Ecology of Kalimantan, Indonesian Borneo. The Ecology of Indonesia Series, Volume III*. Periplus Editions (HK) Ltd. Oxford: Oxford University Press.

McAdam, D. and Sewell, W.H. (2001) It's about time: Temporality in the study of social movements and revolutions. In: Tilley, C., McAdam, D., Perry, E.J., Goldstone, J.A., Aminzade, R.R., Tarrow, S. and Sewell, W.H. (eds) *Silence and Voice in the Study of Contentious Politics*. Cambridge: Cambridge University Press, pp. 89–125.

Meyer, D.S. (2004) Protest and political opportunities. *Annual Review of Sociology*. **30**, pp. 125–45. Available from: www.jstor.org/stable/29737688.

Myers, N., Mittermeier, R.A., Mittermeier, C.G., da Fonseca, G.A.B. and Kent, J. (2000) Biodiversity hotspots for conservation priorities. *Nature*. **403**(6772), pp. 853–8. Available from DOI: 10.1038/35002501.

Ngo, M. (2008) Nested disputes: Building mediation procedures for the Punan in West Kalimantan. In: Sercombe, P.G. and Sellato, B. (eds) *Beyond the Green Myth: Borneo's Hunter–Gatherers in the Twenty-First Century*. Copenhagen: Nordic Institute of Asian Studies Press, pp. 160–76.

Peluso, N.L. (2015) Coercing conservation. In: Conca, K. and Dabelko, G.D. (eds) *Green Planet Blues: Critical Perspectives on Global Environmental Politics*. Boulder, CO: Westview Press, pp. 346–57.

Porta, D.D. (2008) Eventful protest, global conflicts. *Distinktion: Journal of Social Theory*. **9**(2), pp. 27–56. Available from DOI: 10.1080/1600910X.2008.9672963.

Ramos, H. (2008) Opportunity for whom?: Political opportunity and critical events in Canadian Aboriginal mobilization, 1951–2000. *Social Forces*. **87**(2), pp. 795–823. Available from DOI: 10.1353/sof.0.0145.

Roos, M.C., Keßler, P.J.A., Gradstein, S.R. and Baas, P. (2004) Species diversity and endemism of five major Malesian islands: Diversity–area relationships. *Journal of Biogeography*. **31**(12), pp. 1893–908. Available from DOI: 10.1111/j.1365-2699.2004.01154.x.

Sellato, B. (1994) *Nomads of the Borneo Rainforest: The Economics, Politics, and Ideology of Settling Down*. Trans. by Stephanie Morgan. Honolulu: University of Hawai'i Press.

Sellato, B. (2005) Forests for food, forests for trade, between sustainability and extractivism: The economic pragmatism of traditional peoples and the trade history of northern East Kalimantan. In: Wadley, R.L. (ed.) *Histories of the Borneo Environment: Economic, Political and Social Dimensions of Change and Continuity*. Leiden: KITLV, pp. 61–86.

Sellato, B. (2008) Resourceful children of the forest: The Kalimantan Punan through the twentieth century. In: Sercombe, P.G. and Sellato, B. (eds) *Beyond the Green Myth: Borneo's Hunter–Gatherers in the Twenty-First Century*. Copenhagen: Nordic Institute of Asian Studies Press, pp. 61–90.

Sellato, B. and Sercombe, P.G. (2008) Introduction, Borneo, hunter–gatherers, and change. In: Sercombe, P.G. and Sellato, B. (eds) *Beyond the Green Myth: Borneo's Hunter–Gatherers in the Twenty-First Century*. Copenhagen: Nordic Institute of Asian Studies Press, pp. 1–49.

Septiani, Y. and Sidabutar, H. (2015) *Biodiversity Survey in the Sub Watershed Embaloh, Betung Kerihun National Park. ITTO PD 617/11 (F) Rev.3. Promoting Biodiversity Conservation in Betung Kerihun National Park (BKNP) as a Transboundary Ecosystem between Indonesia and State of Sarawak, Malaysia (Phase III)*. Jakarta: The International Tropical Timber Organization (ITTO).

Sewell, W.H. (1996) Three temporalities: Toward an eventful sociology. In: McDonald, T.J. (ed.) *The Historic Turn in the Human Sciences*. Ann Arbor, MI: The University of Michigan Press, pp. 245–80.

Sewell, W.H. (2005) *Logics of History: Social Theory and Social Transformation*. Chicago, IL: University of Chicago Press.

Shawki, N. (2012) The 2008 food crisis as a critical event for the food sovereignty and food justice movements. *International Journal of Sociology of Agriculture & Food*. **19**(3), pp. 423–44.

Snow, D.A., Cress, D.M., Downey, L. and Jones, A.W. (1998) Disrupting the 'quotidian': Reconceptualizing the relationship between breakdown and the emergence of collective action. *Mobilization: An International Quarterly*. **3**(1), pp. 1–22.

Sodhi, N., Acciaioli, G., Erb, M. and Khee-Jin Tan, A. (eds) (2007) *Biodiversity and Human Livelihoods in Protected Areas: Case Studies from the Malay Archipelago*. Cambridge: Cambridge University Press.

Staggenborg, S. (1993) Critical events and the mobilization of the pro-choice movement. *Research in Political Sociology*. **6**, pp. 319–45.

Struebig, Matthew J., Wilting, A., Gaveau, D.L.A., Meijaard, E., Smith, Robert J., Abdullah, T., Abram, N. et al. (2015) Targeted conservation to safeguard a biodiversity hotspot from climate and land-cover change. *Current Biology*. **25**(3), pp. 372–8. Available from DOI: 10.1016/j.cub.2014.11.067.

Tilly, C. (1978) *From Mobilization to Revolution*. Reading, MA: Addison-Wesley.

Vandergeest, P. and Peluso, N.L. (1995) Territorialization and state power in Thailand. *Theory and Society*. **24**(3), pp. 385–426. Available from: www.jstor.org/stable/658074.

Walsh, E.J. (1981) Resource mobilization and citizen protest in communities around Three Mile Island. *Social Problems*. **29**(1), pp. 1–21. Available from DOI: 10.2307/800074.

Yasmi, Y., Kelley, L.C. and Enters, T. (2013) Community–outsider conflicts over forests: Perspectives from Southeast Asia. *Forest Policy and Economics*. **33**, pp. 21–7. Available from DOI: 10.1016/j.forpol.2012.05.001.

Yasmi, Y., Schanz, H. and Salim, A. (2006) Manifestation of conflict escalation in natural resource management. *Environmental Science & Policy*. **9**(6), pp. 538–46. Available from DOI: 10.1016/j.envsci.2006.04.003.

17. Wind energy development and anti-environmentalism in Alberta, Canada

Aleksandra Afanasyeva, Debra J. Davidson and John R. Parkins

INTRODUCTION

Indications of anti-environmentalism are pervasive throughout North America. Considering the climate crisis, for example, an article in the *Calgary Herald* stated that over half of Albertans disapprove of the 'Government's climate change strategy' (Wood, 2016), of which wind and solar development is a key component. Furthermore, climate concern is often lacking within many Alberta communities, with one study indicating that 'Alberta residents are the least likely [in Canada] to believe the planet is warming' (Meyer, 2018). In settings like this, with clear opposition to climate policies, resistance to renewable energy is often depicted as an anti-environmentalist sentiment. Scholars link anti-environmentalism to rural-based occupations, property rights advocates, corporate lobby groups, and right-wing political activities (Brick, 1995; Rowell, 1996) – groups that are hostile to environmental protection (Paehlke, 1989) and supportive of ideological positions that reject key environmental concerns such as climate change (Phillips and Dickie, 2015).

Although it is tempting to characterize local opposition to wind power in this way, in this chapter we dig more deeply into local concerns about wind power and examine concerns expressed by people who live in and around these wind energy landscapes. Two questions are at the heart of this analysis. First, is it fair to characterize wind power opposition in Alberta as anti-environmentalist? Second, depending on how we answer this question, what are the implications for making progress on renewable energy?

Attending to this distinction between environmentalism and anti-environmentalism has bearing on energy transitions, because it helps to clarify the nature of oppositional discourses and can assist in developing constructive responses. On one hand, if resistance to wind power represents a straightforward case of anti-environmentalism, then a reasonable response might involve pushing back against this agenda and characterizing this type of resistance as an illegitimate barrier to energy transition. On the other hand, if resistance to wind power represents something other than anti-environmentalism, then a reasonable response might involve a deeper appreciation for local resistance, a desire to learn more about local concerns, and a commitment to ameliorating them. This chapter offers a path towards resolving these questions, starting with detailed definitions of environmentalism and anti-environmentalism.

DEFINING ENVIRONMENTALISM

Environmentalism (McCarthy, 2002; Dunlap and Mertig, 2014; Gottlieb, 2005) from its inception was tied to political and social actions pertaining to the protection of the environment

(Mol, 2000), and since the 1970s, actions on climate change (Jamison, 2010; Antonio and Brulle, 2011). Environmental social movements are broadly defined as 'a collective form of social behavior ... by which human and material resources are mobilized in trying to affect political change' (Jamison, 2010, p. 812). Green energy made its way into environmental discourses surrounding climate change (Klass, 2011; Groth and Vogt, 2014), resulting in substantial global interest in the renewable energy industries (Vasi, 2011; Sine and Lee, 2009).

Arguments for wind energy tend to align with broader environmental and climate change perspectives. Environmental advocates often establish renewable energy as a normative and moral imperative in addressing global climate change. Other pro-wind advocates emphasize that the visual effects of wind energy are justifiable and necessary to avoid drastic and devastating climatic effects (Barry et al., 2008). Refusing the idea of green energy can therefore be categorized as an anti-environmentalist stance and treated akin to so-called Not in My Backyard (NIMBY) campaigns, which have been characterized by some as the selfish pursuits of privileged communities (Van der Horst, 2007). As with local campaigns resisting other forms of development, however, the reality of opposition to wind energy is not so simple.

Against this totalizing view of wind power as green, some authors note the polarizing nature of climate change. Szarka defines this debate as a 'split within green consciousness' where pro-wind advocates claim they are 'saving the planet' whereas anti-wind campaigners argue they are 'saving the environment' (Szarka, 2004, p. 326). Similarly, the split is often referenced in literature as a 'green on green' debate (Warren et al., 2005), whereby both the project proponents and opponents argue for environmental protection. These arguments open up the possibility that wind power may not be entirely synonymous with green energy.

In addition to the 'green on green' debates noted above, notions of environmentalism are also connected to rural and farming landscapes in ways that are distinct from the formal definitions of environmentalism described above. Some authors suggest that farmers have unique social identities guided by unique environmental ethics (Paolisso and Maloney, 2000; Silvasti, 2003). This version of environmentalism entails a more localized relationship with the land, where landowners' 'view of their environmental impacts relies heavily on their immediate, material environments' (Kessler et al., 2016, p. 189). Land stewardship (Ryan et al., 2003) and the concept of the 'good farmer' (Silvasti, 2003) is fundamental to understanding the types of actions that are prioritized by landowners.

One final dimension of environmentalism relates to place and identity. Place identities, community identities, and regional identities (Liebe et al., 2017) can be threatened by large-scale developments that are immobile, permanent and highly visible (Pasqualetti, 2011; Fournis and Fortin, 2017). Emotional content is embodied within physical places and a threat to place identity can result in defensive viewpoints and a framing of wind energy projects as impositions (Jami and Walsh, 2017; Leibenath and Otto, 2014). In turn, those impositions drive actions to protect place, which have been associated with anxiety and sense of loss (Fast et al., 2016). These motivations for place protection are often associated with oppositional views towards wind power, yet they also reflect a type of environmentalism that is consistent with rural farming and stewardship identities.

DEFINING ANTI-ENVIRONMENTALISM

Often called 'green backlash', anti-environmentalism is centered on anti-regulation, anti-government, and anti-environmental policy sentiments (Mol, 2000; Brick, 1995; Rowell, 1996). In its most basic form, anti-environmentalism involves 'actively working *against* someone who is *working for* ecological protection' (Rowell, 1996, n.p.). Some have described it as a 'conservative countermovement that supported neoliberal policies' (Hess and Brown, 2017, p. 64). Others describe anti-environmentalism as having 'traditional strongholds in agriculture, labor, and industry that have consistently resisted the costs imposed by environmental regulations' (Brick, 1995, p. 20). McCarthy argues that the anti-environmentalism counter-movement is:

> composed of members of rural communities, whose livelihoods have long depended on a wide variety of uses of the lands and natural resources surrounding their homes ... the movement's central complaint is that community members are losing access to and control over these lands and resources because of ever more vigorous pursuit of environmental goals by the resource conservation branches of the central governmental trend spurred on largely by the interventions of distant, highly bureaucratic, and professionalized environmental groups. (McCarthy, 2002, p. 1281)

As a key component of this counter-movement, the Wise-Use movement in the United States (initiated by the Center for the Defence of Free Enterprise), is described as: 'a growing coalition of ranchers, miners, loggers, farmers, fishermen, trappers, hunters, off-road vehicle users, property right advocates, industry associations, corporate front groups and right-wing activists who are rising up against the environmental movement across the USA' (Rowell, 1996, n.p.). Overall, one of the core tenets of this counter-movement is a strong critique of environmental over-regulation (Antonio and Brulle, 2011; McCright and Dunlap, 2011). In rural communities across the United States, it entailed the expression of a 'deep-seated frustration with what is perceived to be heavy-handed, arbitrary, and unreasonable federal regulation of public lands' (Babbitt, 1982, p. 853). Given these common characteristics of anti-environmentalism, through our empirical work below we seek to clarify the extent to which rural landowner resistance to wind power in Alberta is linked to these ideas.

RESEARCH SETTING AND METHODS

For this research we implemented a collective case study (Baxter and Jack, 2008) with in-depth interviews of landowners and key informants in the province of Alberta, Canada. The study took place predominantly in Vulcan County around the Blackspring Ridge Wind Project (300 MW capacity), and Paintearth County around Halkirk 1 Wind Project (150 MW capacity). At the time of this study, from June 2017 to August 2018, proponents of the Halkirk 2 Wind Project (about 150 MW capacity) were in discussion with local landowners. Some interviews were conducted outside these counties in Calgary, Edmonton, Pincher Creek, Morin, and Magrath. Two semi-structured interview guides were prepared: one for landowners, and one for key informants. Landowners were asked about their experiences and their views on wind power. Questions focused on understanding landowner experiences of the process, environmental outcomes, and the broader political context surrounding the energy transition. Landowners with a variety of perspectives were interviewed: some were hosting turbines on their property, some were willing hosts, and some were unwilling and had negative views about the development. Key informant interviews included municipal government representatives, industry project proponents, and non-governmental organization (NGO) representatives. Research participants were asked about the broader challenges of implementing wind energy in their communities and in Alberta. Thirty in-depth, face-to-face interview sessions were conducted with 36 individuals. All interviews were audio recorded, transcribed by hand, and analyzed in qualitative data software *NVivo Pro*. Qualitative data in the form of direct transcript quotations were organized in conceptual nodes at both the level of content and the level of discourse. Pseudonyms were assigned to each participant, and quotes are followed by a brief description of the individual's relation to a wind energy project.

DISCOURSES OF ANTI-ENVIRONMENTALISM

Interviewees expressed their positions in relation to environmentalism, climate change, government environmental regulations, and the energy transition mandate in Alberta. The first section of findings identifies discourses that are attributed to anti-environmentalism including anti-regulatory sentiments, climate change skepticism, and deep critique of environmentalism. The second section uncovers discourses of environmentalism and calls for a reconsideration of the landowner perspectives. The second section also reflects on the nuances of local environmental values and why they may be challenged by industrial wind farm development.

Anti-Government, Anti-Regulation, and Politicization of Wind Energy

This section focuses on anti-government and anti-regulatory sentiments surrounding provincial environmental policies. Jared presents his views about the energy transition and policy changes implemented by the NDP (i.e., New Democratic Party – a left-leaning political party in power from 2015 to 2019). Jared is skeptical of whether the benefits of the energy transition will outweigh the costs to the economy of Alberta.

> Having clean energy is never bad. But there is a balance in how far you want to go to trash our economy to do so. And I know that's a political kind of government slogan or whatever, but when I look at it, and this is perhaps more of my view here … is that climate change is happening, but what is actually … like what does that mean? … But do we want to trash our entire way of life for something that could be … when the rest of the world is doing nothing? (Jared, Municipal Government Representative)

A similar sentiment is expressed by Rick, who is critical of the leader of the provincial NDP government:

> She just destroyed our province … I mean there is a ton of people without jobs here, and [it's] directly related to her energy policies and her wind policies. (Rick, Landowner not directly adjacent to the proposed or existing project)

The anti-government sentiment is also expressed in relation to government environmental policies such as the recently implemented province-wide carbon tax. Although the carbon tax is distinct from policies promoting renewable energy, it too is subject to anti-regulatory sentiments. The frustration was evident, and many participants explained how rural communities are negatively impacted by such policies.

> A lot of people just view it as another tax ... It's not gonna help the climate. That's the take on it here. The NDP – their ideology is yes that's their plan to move forward with it and it's quite hurtful for us out here. (Harry, Landowner hosting wind turbines on his property)

Harry and Ruby are landowners who host turbines on their property, and this was their take on why wind energy is received negatively in their community.

> I think it's misinformation. (Harry)

> I think it's got to do with the current government of Alberta, and its resentment because they're bringing in solar and wind power, and it's an underlying resentment against the government. People aren't happy ... I think that we all want to blame somebody, so we'll blame the current government ... It might not be right, but I think that's the mindset. (Ruby)

Dylan is a wind energy developer. From his experience, landowners acknowledge economic benefits rather than discourses surrounding broader environmental goals of wind energy.

> But here in Alberta, yeah, I mean it's really played to what people think about renewables ... as a left-wing kind of ... not conspiracy – it's a left-wing industry, and that's really not the case ... I've always voted for the conservatives. I kind of see conservatism as playing into the renewable energy industry perfectly ... I think for the landowners it's less about the environment and more about the legacy of the farm and being able to diversify their revenue stream for the farm ... So, from the landowner's perspective, I think it is more economic than it is environmental. (Dylan, Wind energy developer)

Similarly, William shares the following when asked about how politics play out in the development of wind energy:

> Some political parties will try to stigmatize the alternative energy industry and try to convince their constituents that all solar and wind and so on is some sort of mistake in policy. But I think it's largely based on misinformation and misdirection, for political ends ... But I'm not seeing that in this region, and this region is very conservative. (William, Municipal Government Representative)

Here the link between conservatism and anti-environmentalism is directly challenged. Both William and Dylan reflect on the dichotomy of ideology that wind energy evokes and suggest that the influence of political ideology is complex. Tom, also a municipal government representative, suggests that politics have been detrimental to the development of renewable energy in the community where he works. Sam highlights how the political environment changed the nature of opposition:

> Um, there has been a little bit of pushback I think based on some of the politics out here in the rural area. I think you can argue that the NDP getting in power was worse for renewable energy ... And it becomes a bit of an, 'us against them' thing as soon as the NDP starts pushing it, then people think well that's associated with killing all the coal plant jobs, right? ... Yah so they're upset about that, and they start associating that with renewable energy, right? (Tom, Municipal Government Representative)

> Well and I think that's you know prior to this, prior to the government involved in renewables, right, you know it was the market that was driving everything. And a lot of these projects went ahead without any major sort of opposition. (Sam, Municipal Government Representative)

Liam is a landowner actively opposing the proposed project who demonstrates his frustration with both the regulation of the industry and the way the government developed the REP program, which he views as pure subsidization:

> They need to have rules in place to encourage the development of clean energy. Not subsidize it – but encourage it ... The direction of our government is they want to become dictators. But they don't understand the rules of what they're dictating ... it would have been supported by all Albertans. But they chose to dictate changes as opposed to engaging changes. (Liam, Landowner unwilling to host turbines)

Mike, a long-time farmer in the area, articulates his reservations despite agreeing to host turbines:

> The Green thing that she's doing – I don't have a real problem with it. I don't. The only problem I have – I just know as a taxpayer, that it's going to cost us a lot of money to put up these windmills. (Mike, Landowner willing to host turbines on property)

Alex in this excerpt presents his frustration and summarizes that in his eyes the trade-off for subsidizing the development of renewable energy is provincial government debt.

> Going billions and billions into debt while saying you're making the world better, by going further into that ... that's a sense of frustration. I'm personally, genuinely disappointed because I have thought okay here is a chance we are going to get a new government ... we can make some changes. You know there's a chance to step in and not be viewed as a left-wing radical [government] – we don't care about the costs or the jobs or anything. (Alex, Landowner adjacent to the proposed project)

The views of these research participants are consistent with published literature noted earlier, linking anti-environmentalism and conservatism, frustration with the use of public money and skepticism about the benefits of government environmental policies and regulations.

Questioning the Premise of Climate Change

Federal and provincial initiatives to phase out coal are premised on the reduction of greenhouse gas emissions to address growing climate concerns. Although the necessity of reducing emissions seems to be widely accepted and understood within the general population, we also observe strongly contrasting perspectives. Many respondents expressed skepticism toward the climate crisis and the role of renewable energy in addressing this challenge. These discourses illustrate why it is tempting to label these wind power opponents as anti-environmentalists.

Shawna, who works for an NGO that deals with energy issues in Alberta, views political polarization as a hindrance to implementing environmental policies.

> That ladder for not taking action on climate ... We start with the science is wrong ... the climate is not changing. Then, the climate is changing ... but it is because of sunspots or other reasons. Then yes, it is changing yes ... because of anthropogenic activities, but we can't do anything about it ... Then, yes, we can do something about it, but Canada shouldn't because it is not our responsibility ... I think

it is tied more to tribalism, and identity politics than it is with a certain economic or political ideology ... How would you define classical conservatism? ... You know there's nothing in there that says you must deny climate science. (Shawna, NGO Representative)

Rick describes his skepticism about climate change and raises an important point about the sources of information people choose to trust. Rick emphasizes his trust for alternative sources of information such as Rebel Media, Friends of Science, and Grassroots Alberta (Centre for the Alberta Taxpayer: Citizens' Initiative). These organizations focus on providing counter-information to mainstream environmentalism. They are deeply critical of government climate policies, including carbon dioxide emission reductions and wind energy development.

Well, I mean it's not fact ... as a person you can't deny the climate changes, but it isn't driven by what they are trying to tell us it is. I mean they aren't scientists ... Friends of Science I mean they have a big organization if you want to find scientific stuff, they have it ... Green energy as so-called is basically close to a religious cult. You know that these people are so sold on green energy they will do anything ... (Rick, Landowner not affected by wind projects)

Both Olivia and Sandra in the following excerpt share their reservations about mainstream climate change information. Despite the fact that they actually accepted wind turbines on their properties, they disagree with the environmental premises:

I think people with their own personal interest are deceiving the public for their own personal gain. It's not that what we are going to do is really going to change where the climate is going. I really don't think it is. But we can use that, to get people to do what we want. (Sandra, Landowner with wind turbines)

Climate change is climate change ... And the only one who made money on the 'climate change' was David Suzuki. (Olivia, Landowner hosting turbines)

Olivia brings to light a deep skepticism about the motives of environmentalists, represented by certain celebrity scientists like David Suzuki. Although it is not essential to support wind energy on the basis of expected environmental benefits, in some cases these environmentalist discourses actually diminished the level of support individuals were willing to express.

On the pro-climate change side ... there is a lot of hypocrisy on their end in their views because they say that these wind projects like this are going to make a world of difference. But, I don't think it is. I really don't think it's going to make a darn bit of difference. (Nick, Landowner with turbines on property)

Nick, a farmer in Vulcan County, rejects the notion that wind energy is a silver bullet solution. Sensitive to these sentiments, Adam, a representative from the wind industry, indicates the reservations of the company to talk about broader climate benefits when securing private land for projects.

Frankly a lot of farmers and ranchers are experiencing climate change at a rapidly advancing rate too ... However, we've always gone in to talk about commercial opportunities. If people want to ask about philosophy, we can talk about it. But for the deal to make sense to someone who is a steward of their land and thinking about the next generation ... And so you basically talk the economics. (Adam, Wind energy industry representative)

In response to the skepticism about environmental benefits from wind power among local landowners, Adam and other wind advocates have opted to highlight locally relevant economic benefits rather than broader environmental benefits.

Refuting Mainstream Environmentalism: 'I'm not an Environmentalist'

> I'm not an environmentalist, but I believe in conservation, and in using your head ... But they better start realizing that it's the consumers, the ultimate taxpayer that – they better consider more than the fantasyland policy, the feel-good notion that we are saving the planet. (Jim, Landowner with wind turbines on property)

In this quote, Jim articulates a resistance to an environmentalist identity, questioning the validity of pro-environmental discourses. Some individuals explicitly distance themselves from what they consider mainstream environmentalism. Rick and Mark are in different positions. Rick is not impacted by wind projects, while Mark hosts part of a large project on his land. Both, however, are critical of the environmental movement and present an anti-environmentalist standpoint.

> Breitbart News ... they most of the time tell you both sides of the issue, but they won't back away from saying that environmentalists are crazy. I mean here you don't want to watch CBC News because they're in the tank. They are the ones that are selling this. (Rick, Landowner not affected by wind projects)

> You know like what the whole environmental movement has done is everybody is pointing at [you] 'you got to change, you got to change' ... But I don't have to change. They're always pointing fingers at somebody, but instead of doing it, and lead[ing] by example. (Mark, Landowner with wind turbines on property)

Marcus, a provincial government employee, explains this polarization as a team-based phenomenon, which defines how information is interpreted.

> If you want to be against things because it's not your team, then you are willing to believe these things that are truthy. Like they sound like they could be right, but they are bogus ... it's your teams, you know. Like that wind turbines are just not the things that I want on my landscape living here. (Marcus, Provincial Government Representative)

Given these findings, there are multiple strands of anti-environmentalism, demonstrating that people contest environmentalism in a variety of ways. Anti-regulatory, anti-government sentiments, climate change skepticism, and a critique of mainstream environmentalists were expressed to differing degrees by many interview participants, but these discourses were not necessarily consistently related to willingness to host turbines. The next section describes the environmental and conservation sentiments of respondents, allowing for a deeper understanding of local reservations and concerns about wind power development in Alberta.

DISCOURSES OF ENVIRONMENTALISM

Although the anti-environmental views summarized above have been noted in a number of other studies of opposition to wind energy, our interviewees also express deeper sentiments that are not often recognized and understood. The same individuals who present anti-environmental discourses also express genuine concern for, and attachment to, their land. Capturing the in-depth reservations of interview participants begs for a reconsideration of the meanings of the term anti-environmentalism. This section sets out to demonstrate the nuances of these motivations and the meaning of environmentalism in rural Alberta.

Anti-Government, but Pro-Regulation

Nearly all interview participants demonstrate a deep concern for the environmental health of their land and community. Many individuals were critical of government policies, and expressed anti-government sentiments, yet also called for stronger regulations for wind energy development, calling into question the extent to which anti-regulatory sentiments describe a generalizable phenomenon. Liam is strongly opposed to wind development in his community and refused it on his land, based on the lack of regulations to limit anticipated impacts to land and wildlife:

> With wind energy, you're seeing more detriments to wildlife because it's affecting the migration zones ... It's affecting the ducks and the geese and the owls and the predator birds that are being disrupted. It's affecting things that people don't talk about yet – the production of livestock ... They weren't regulated on where they could put a tower, or whether they could move dirt from one farm to the next, they weren't regulated on how they had to reclaim when a wind tower was decommissioned. (Liam, Landowner unwilling to host turbines)

In this excerpt Liam questions the assumption that environmental protection is ensured by the wind energy industry. Many interviewees shared the concerns surrounding impacts on wildlife and farming operations, as well as about the standards governing decommissioning and reclamation. Many called for a better assessment of environmental impacts during the construction, operation and reclamation stages.

> Our land use bylaw ... we're updating that to more reflect what our current residents want in terms of wind farm regulations ... we brought it to the province's attention, that there is a lack of provincial policy, on governing of these green energy projects. (Jared, Municipal Government Representative)

Many landowners felt that incoming project proponents do not take these concerns seriously enough. Anthony is a landowner who has refused to host wind turbines and says the following about the regulatory process.

> Yeah, and there are no regulations in the province to protect landowners. That's one of my biggest concerns ... The wind industry has no regulations. They sign up quarters, they figure they have the right to put the towers where they want, they can run their lines in any direction. They don't have to keep their footprint as small as possible. (Anthony, Landowner unwilling to host turbines)

Liam and Anthony are both hesitant to accept wind energy on their land because they perceive it as environmentally deleterious, and insufficiently regulated. One of the most important premises of their opposition is environmental concern for their land. In this case, strong opposition to wind energy is not only portraying a localized protective environmentalism, it is also calling for more government involvement.

Farm-Level Environmentalism: 'My Biggest Concern is That They Don't Wreck our Land'

Localized, farm-level environmentalism is substantially different from versions of environmentalism presented by pro-wind advocates, the wind industry, and the government. The development of wind energy in rural communities brings with it oppositional and conflicting discourses surrounding environmentalism. These discourses challenge the pre-existing notions of environmentalism that farmers subscribe to, often failing to acknowledge genuine concerns, feelings, connections to land, and community. Lola recalls her experience during the construction of a project in the community where she works:

> I had an interesting conversation [with] one of the gentlemen that worked for one of the companies that were here, and he said when he came out from Ontario to be part of this project, he was coming out to teach everybody about green energy, and climate change, and all of this, how to do it ... and he said, and I realized that when I came out, that the farmers and the people in the area are already great stewards of the land. Like they have to be because their livelihood depends on it. (Lola, Municipal Representative)

Lola emphasizes how stewardship is a priority for landowners. Farmers in her community have dedicated a significant amount of time and effort to better the environment. She says there is a lack of acknowledgment of these efforts in the broader discourses surrounding environmentalism and wind energy:

> You can't tell people how they have to be good stewards of the land. You can't tell people how they have to embrace climate change. You can't tell people how they have to switch their energy sources because it would not matter if they supported you, the majority of the people when you tell them they have to – they're going to fight you on it. (Lola, Municipal Representative)

Alex is critical of a proposed development adjacent to his property and does not accept the discourses surrounding its environmental benefits. He reflects on the motivations, and sense of responsibility that guide his own environmental position as a landowner.

> My stance on the environment is, especially being close to the environment, as I am, I'm one of the ones ... before all of the programs were coming in to preserve riparian areas and to preserve native grasslands and all this ... We were ahead of that ... If you're concerned at all about the environment and you're moving somewhere to be ... you know, to probably put yourself in a little better position to help out, personally. You do take the environment personally. (Alex, Landowner near proposed project)

A similar idea was presented by Mavis, who is a willing host to turbines as part of the proposed project. She emphasizes the challenges she is facing in her community, and the divisions she is witnessing. Living in rural Alberta, she believes, entails a different kind of environmentalism. It is disconnected from broader climate change and energy transition discourses and is about the realities of rural farm life:

> I think climate change would be more accepted if they included the stewards of the land ... So, the people that are making the decisions for climate change don't live in rural Alberta, don't own land, don't own animals, generally. They may have an understanding of it, but they don't live it ... Again, farmers worry about their farm and their family. And not that people in the city and in town don't. It's

just that what we have to do for our farm to survive, may or may not be in line with climate change, but it doesn't mean we don't care about the environment. (Mavis, Landowner willing to host turbines)

Mavis challenges the assumptions about rurality and farmer attitudes towards environmentalism. Similarly, Mike is candid about his concerns regarding wind turbines. His property gives him a sense of place, and he does not take environmental risks lightly. Mike is hopeful the company will treat his land with respect.

If they're coming, we understand, we've already signed up, we agreed that they are coming. My biggest concern is that they don't wreck our land. And that's my wife's biggest concern ... guys just come and say well it's just a piece of dirt. That piece of dirt means a lot to us ... I said can I come to your front lawn in the city and rip it up and then you look at it? It's the same as us out there. That piece of dirt means as much to us as our front lawn, you know? And we just don't want our land wrecked. That's our biggest concern. (Mike, Landowner willing to host turbines)

Stewardship and localized environmentalism were in many cases at the heart of local concerns about wind power. In the following excerpt, Alex calls for a change to the way wind energy companies approach the question of environmental responsibility.

If they go broke, or if their wind towers fall on their head, they're not responsible financially. And that is just, that is just simply business ... If you're a stockholder or shareholder it's a great business ... if you're environmentally responsible, I view that you should be responsible for your projects, as someone who cares about the land and the landscape. (Alex, Landowner near proposed project)

Alex suggests landowners need to feel that their concerns about environmental responsibility and outcomes for the health of their land are respected. Anti-government sentiments, climate change skepticism, and critique of mainstream environmentalism alone do not encompass the source of resistance heard in this study. The core tenets of anti-environmentalism do not stand alone but are accompanied by paradoxical discourses of localized environmentalism centered on land care and a desire for greater regulatory attention to the impacts of project development.

CHARACTERIZING WIND POWER OPPOSITION

Is it fair to characterize wind power opposition in Alberta as anti-environmentalist? Our answer to this question is a qualified 'no'. The dichotomy of environmentalism and anti-environmentalism provides a lens through which opposition to green energy initiatives can be assessed but it may be too simplistic to characterize local opposition as anti-environmentalist. This analysis offers insights into the broader contemporary context of deep polarization toward environmental policies (Antonio and Brulle, 2011). As Alberta moves through the energy transition, it is important to understand the polarizing discourses surrounding green energy mandates and environmental policies more broadly. Through this analysis we can begin to anticipate and unpack the social implications of the energy transition. When it comes to wind energy development in Alberta, discourses of environmentalism play an important role in influencing the views that individuals hold about wind energy projects and whether they actively or passively, support or oppose, projects in their communities. Findings suggest that there are no fixed patterns between the perspectives that interviewees articulate and the positions they take about wind energy development in their communities. Individuals who criticize the government and environmental policies, deny climate change, and refute environmentalism are simultaneously demonstrating a deep concern for their land and community. These same individuals also host wind turbines despite a deep-set criticism of the widely accepted premises behind wind energy development. In short, patterns of anti-environmentalism are not synonymous with opposition to wind power.

RECONSIDERING ANTI-ENVIRONMENTALISM

What are the implications for making progress on renewable energy? Based on our findings, a partial answer to this question involves closer attention to how we talk about wind energy development in the context of deeply held skepticism around the science and the urgency of climate action. Many arguments for wind energy as presented by both the energy transition policies of the government and pro-wind energy advocates do not carry the same meaning for rural landowners. In recent decades, wind energy has become a hallmark for addressing climate change and broader environmental issues (Vasi, 2011; Groth and Vogt, 2014; Jamison, 2010). Yet, these claims about wind power as a solution to climate change caused some interview participants to be more skeptical about wind energy. This finding is consistent with the recent waves of anti-environmentalism that conflict sharply with climate science and associated public policies (McCright and Dunlap, 2011). Given the persistence of climate skepticism in many parts of North America, arguments in support of wind power development are likely to take on more salience if they are situated outside of the climate change context.

A second response to the question above involves attention to scales of environmental concern. The land stewardship of farmers is well documented (Ryan et al., 2003; Silvasti, 2003), but these expressions of local environmentalism are almost entirely delinked from mainstream environmental discourses that are trained on issues of climate change and other measures of environmental pollution from agriculture. In this sense, the idea of environmentalism has a scalar dimension whereby local landowners are tuned into local environmental impacts whereas mainstream environmentalists are often focused on the global scale. The 'green on green' characterization of wind energy conflicts offers one way of representing the different scales (Szarka, 2004). But as this study shows, instead of environmentalists in conflict with each other (Warren et al., 2005), as is the conventional formulation of green-on-green, in this case we observe scales of environmentalism that are in tension with each other, and these scales bring together a set of actors that extend beyond the mainstream environmentalist community.

The notion of scale, however, is only one way of understanding these conflicting versions. Interviewees expressed concern for the local landscape and highlighted a kind of skepticism about the extent of benefits of the energy transition, and Alberta's role in addressing global climate change. Several authors have approached skepticism about renewable energy and demonstrated a misalignment with conventional environmental talking points (Barry et al., 2008; Warren et al., 2005). For example, in Texas, researchers identified a 'reflexive environmental skepticism' and general support for wind energy (Jepson et al., 2012). In this study, findings suggest that mainstream environmentalism is misaligned with farm-level environmentalism. Therefore, to make progress on renewable energy, attention to the local scale of environmentalism will be required. This involves an understanding of these local sentiments and meaningfully working to remedy local environmental concerns in the design and implementation of wind energy.

In summary, the term 'anti-environmentalist' does not adequately describe the position of local residents expressing concern about wind energy projects. There are nuances and paradoxes in discourses that we need to consider. An analysis of this nature helps to understand why we need to be careful about the polarizing nature of terms, and rather than dismissing perspectives, we need to attempt to uncover the motivations behind what is being said, rather than take it at face value. The implications of (mis)diagnosing local opposition to wind power as anti-environmentalist could have lasting effects and slow the potential for renewable energy transition.

CONCLUSION

This study explores diverse perspectives on wind energy in rural Alberta. Based on in-depth interviews, we provide a way of understanding the polarizing nature of debates about wind energy and the broader energy transition mandated by provincial and federal governments. Results from interviews with municipal, government, industry representatives, and landowners demonstrate clear differences in how people express their environmental values. We argue that political conservatism, anti-government sentiments, climate skepticism as well as a rejection of mainstream environmentalism can, at face value, reflect an anti-environmentalist stance. However, dismissing landowners' concerns as simply anti-environmentalist is detrimental to the fundamental understanding of local notions of environmentalism that are unique to rural farming areas. Dismissal serves to take away from the understanding of legitimate environmental concerns and protective actions of landowners. Given the polarization in contemporary politics and the tendency to construct enemies of energy transition, this chapter offers a caution against such easy characterizations. Our goal is to make visible a more nuanced set of concerns about wind energy development, with a view to appreciating these concerns, and working towards more acceptable forms of renewable energy development.

REFERENCES

Antonio, R.J. and Brulle, R.J. (2011) The unbearable lightness of politics: Climate change denial and political polarization. *The Sociological Quarterly*. **52**(2), pp. 195–202.

Babbitt, B. (1982) Federalism and the environment: An intergovernmental perspective of the Sagebrush Rebellion. *Environmental Law*. **12**(4), pp. 847–61.

Barry, J., Ellis, G. and Robinson, C. (2008) Cool rationalities and hot air: A rhetorical approach to understanding debates on renewable energy. *Global Environmental Politics*. **8**(2), pp. 67–98.

Baxter, P. and Jack, S. (2008) Qualitative case study methodology: Study design and implementation for novice researchers. *The Qualitative Report*. **13**(4), pp. 544–59.

Brick, P. (1995) Determined opposition: The wise use movement challenges environmentalism. *Environment: Science and Policy for Sustainable Development*. **37**(8), pp. 17–42.

Dunlap, R.E. and Mertig, A.G. (2014) The evolution of the US environmental movement from 1970 to 1990: An overview. *Society & Natural Resources*. **4**(3), pp. 13–22.

Fast, S., Mabee, W., Baxter, J., Christidis, T., Driver, L., Hill, S., McMurtry, J. and Tomkow, M. (2016) Lessons learned from Ontario wind energy disputes. *Nature Energy*. **1**(2), pp. 1–7.

Fournis, Y. and Fortin, M.J. (2017) From social 'acceptance' to social 'acceptability' of wind energy projects: Towards a territorial perspective. *Journal of Environmental Planning and Management.* **60**(1), pp. 1–21.

Gottlieb, R. (2005) *Forcing the Spring: The Transformation of the American Environmental Movement.* Washington, DC: Island Press.

Groth, T.M. and Vogt, C.A. (2014) Rural wind farm development: Social, environmental and economic features important to local residents. *Renewable Energy.* **63**, pp. 1–8.

Hess, D.J. and Brown, K.P. (2017) Green tea: Clean-energy conservatism as a countermovement. *Environmental Sociology.* **3**(1), pp. 64–75.

Jami, A.A. and Walsh, P.R. (2017) From consultation to collaboration: A participatory framework for positive community engagement with wind energy projects in Ontario, Canada. *Energy Research and Social Science.* **27**, pp. 14–24.

Jamison, A. (2010) Climate change knowledge and social movement theory. *Wiley Interdisciplinary Reviews: Climate Change.* **1**(6), pp. 811–23.

Jepson, W., Brannstrom, C. and Persons, N. (2012) 'We don't take the pledge': Environmentality and environmental skepticism at the epicenter of US wind energy development. *Geoforum.* **43**(4), pp. 851–63.

Kessler, A., Parkins, J.R. and Huddart Kennedy, E. (2016) Environmental harm and 'the good farmer': Conceptualizing discourses of environmental sustainability in the beef industry. *Rural Sociology.* **81**(2), pp. 172–93.

Klass, A.B. (2011) Property rights on the new frontier: Climate change, natural resource development, and renewable energy. *Ecology Law Quarterly.* **38**, pp. 63–119.

Leibenath, M., and Otto, A. (2014) Competing wind energy discourses, contested landscapes. *Landscape Online.* **38**, p. 1–18.

Liebe, U., Bartczak, A. and Meyerhoff, J. (2017) A turbine is not only a turbine: The role of social context and fairness characteristics for the local acceptance of wind power. *Energy Policy.* **107**, pp. 300–308.

McCarthy, J. (2002) First World political ecology: Lessons from the Wise Use movement. *Environment and Planning A.* **34**(7), pp. 1281–302.

McCright, A.M. and Dunlap, R.E. (2011) The politicization of climate change and polarization in the American public's views of global warming, 2001–2010. *The Sociological Quarterly.* **52**(2), pp. 155–94.

Meyer, C. (2018) 'Vicious' right-wing politics fueling climate denial in Alberta, says environment minister Phillips. *National Observer.* Available from: https://www.nationalobserver.com/2018/05/22/news/vicious-right-wing-politics-fueling-climate-denial-alberta-says-environment-minister.

Mol, A.P. (2000) The environmental movement in an era of ecological modernization. *Geoforum.* **31**(1), pp. 45–56.

Paehlke, R.C. (1989) *Environmentalism and the Future of Progressive Politics.* New Haven, CT: Yale University Press.

Paolisso, M. and Maloney, R.S. (2000) Recognizing farmer environmentalism: Nutrient runoff and toxic dinoflagellate blooms in the Chesapeake Bay region. *Human Organization.* **59**(2), pp. 209–21.

Pasqualetti, M.J. (2011) Opposing wind energy landscapes: A search for common cause. *Annals of the Association of American Geographers.* **101**(4), pp. 907–17. Available from DOI: 0.1080/00045608.2011.568879.

Phillips, M. and Dickie, J. (2015) Climate change, carbon dependency and narratives of transition and stasis in four English rural communities. *Geoforum.* **67**, pp. 93–109.

Rowell, A. (1996) *Green Backlash: Global Subversion of the Environmental Movement.* London: Routledge.

Ryan, R.L., Erickson, D.L. and De Young, R. (2003) Farmers' motivations for adopting conservation practices along riparian zones in a mid-western agricultural watershed. *Journal of Environmental Planning and Management.* **46**(1), pp. 19–37.

Silvasti, T. (2003) The cultural model of 'the good farmer' and the environmental question in Finland. *Agriculture and Human Values.* **20**(2), pp. 143–50.

Sine, W.D. and Lee, B.H. (2009) Tilting at windmills? The environmental movement and the emergence of the US wind energy sector. *Administrative Science Quarterly.* **54**(1), pp. 123–55.

Szarka, J. (2004) Wind power, discourse coalitions and climate change: Breaking the stalemate? *European Environment.* **14**(4), pp. 317–30.

Van der Horst, D. (2007) NIMBY or not? Exploring the relevance of location and the politics of voiced opinions in renewable energy siting controversies. *Energy Policy.* **35**(5), pp. 2705–14.

Vasi, I.B. (2011) *Winds of Change: The Environmental Movement and the Global Development of the Wind Energy Industry.* New York, NY: Oxford University Press.

Warren, C.R., Lumsden, C., O'Dowd, S. and Birnie, R.V. (2005) 'Green on green': Public perceptions of wind power in Scotland and Ireland. *Journal of Environmental Planning and Management.* **48**(6), pp. 853–75.

Wood, J. (2016) New poll shows strong opposition to Alberta carbon tax. *Calgary Herald* (online). Available from: http://calgaryherald.com/news/politics/new-poll-shows-strong-opposition-to-alberta-carbon-tax (accessed 6 June 2018).

PART VIII

ETHNICITY AND RACE

18. The end of population-environmentalism: dissonance over human rights and societal goals
Pamela McMullin-Messier

> The environmental movement has been taken over by the radical left, where they have anti-environmental goals. 'Global goals' has changed the nature of discussion. We cannot help the world if we add population to the U.S. They consume at our levels, and continue raising negative problems, such as contributing to greenhouse gases. To be a true environmentalist, you have to stop growth. (Virginia Abernethy, personal conversation, 2000)

Population-environmentalism, as an ideology, perceives relative imbalance between people and resources, where greater numbers of people use more resources, and produce more waste, which leads to dire predictions in shortages of clean water and food. Population numbers are used to support this perspective and demonstrate impact in terms of the growth in population size over time. For example, the population of the United States has more than tripled over the past century, with net migration projections increasing and expected to double in size over the next century. Messaging in the media emphasizes stark depictions warning of impending chaos and doom upon humanity, including images of war-ravaged landscapes, children dying in their mothers' arms, and starvation resulting from competition for scarce resources, with the end message being: we must stop population growth before it is too late (Hardin, 1993).

This oft-stated need for population control has long been part of the environmental movement's rhetoric and a popular topic in speeches given on the first Earth Day in 1970. Interest in population-environmentalism was ignited by *The Population Bomb* (Ehrlich, 1968), *The Limits to Growth* (Meadows et al., 1972), and 'The Tragedy of the Commons' in *Science* (Hardin, 1968). Mobilization began with a population advocacy organization, Zero Population Growth (ZPG), in linking population growth to environmental degradation, and they worked with the Sierra Club, a mainstream environmental group, on constructing momentum for population-environmental policy. The Sierra Club was one of the first to call for stabilizing population: 'a rapid end to population growth in this country and around the world is an essential part of any effort to protect the environment, sustain the ability of the earth to support life, and enhance the quality of life for all human beings.'

When it was reported that the US had reached replacement level fertility in the 1970s, population-environmentalism shifted towards international issues and global population growth. In the 1980s, the mainstream focus shifted towards economic and social development for sustainable population growth and the environmental movement focused on conservation, preservation, and resource management (Dunlap and Mertig, 1992). While the 1990s witnessed a resurgence of interest in population, this interest was concerned with sustainability through the lens of environmental and reproductive justice (Cohen, 1993). Conversely, in the twenty-first century, population disappeared from the lexicon of environmental groups with controversy surrounding immigration and the 'greening of hate', although connections

Table 18.1 Ideology groupings

Grouping	Concern
Human Rights	Anti-environmental organizations that challenge mainstream, advocacy, and numbers impact groups; focus on human rights and social inequality
Mainstream Environment	Environmental organizations representing mainstream attitudes about population growth and environmental connections
Numbers Impact	Anti-environmental organizations that challenge mainstream, advocacy, and human rights groups; focus on population numbers and carrying capacity
Population Advocacy	Stakeholder organizations that work with mainstream groups; focus on sustainable population growth and environmental connections

between population and the environment had not been resolved (Lutz and Shah, 2002; Mazur, 2009).

This chapter explores the influence of anti-environmental ideologies connected to immigration and how it polarized population-environmentalism (McMullin-Messier, 2006). This study analyzed 30 interviews with population, environmental, immigration and human rights advocates, 17 organizational websites, and print media. Interview questions focused on affiliations with other organizations, stances on population policies, perceptions about the Sierra Club and ZPG's positions, and how they felt about the term 'greening of hate'. The objective was to evaluate perceptions about changes in discourse over population-environmentalism. Interviews were conducted with activists/advocates who represented a variety of viewpoints concerning immigration, population, and environmental issues. Representatives were identified by: (1) exposure in print media and organizational e-mailing lists (listservs); (2) activist experiences within environmental and population advocacy organizations; and (3) word of mouth from other activists or advocates, which developed into a snowball sample representing voices from across the spectrum.

The groupings are identified by ideology (Table 18.1): (1) *human rights* (environmental justice, feminists, and immigrant rights); (2) *mainstream environment* (mainstream population and environmental groups); (3) *numbers impact* (groups pushing for controls and/or restrictions on population growth); (4) *population advocacy* (population advocates who understand where other groups are coming from and work towards building bridges). There is overlap between groups, as people may have divergent points of view based on membership with other organizations; therefore, interviews were evaluated based upon ideologies expressed:

Five frames emerged to compare and contrast interviews from the groupings: environment, population, immigration, greening of hate, and future. Frame analysis offers another view on comparing population-environmentalisms (Hunt et al., 1994; Wilmoth and Ball, 1995): (1) limits to growth; (2) population pressure; (3) quality of life; (4) greening of hate; (5) human rights; and (6) globalization. Negotiation analysis compares competing points of view and uncovers common ground to develop a 'zone' of possible agreement (Sebenius, 1991) and identify main interests, clarify ideologies, and examine actions utilized by the groups (Habermas, 1984). Campbell's 'competing schools of thought' (1998) perspective was used to compare the negotiation process between these groups and distinguish areas of symmetry and commonality for how the discourse had a splintering impact and created an anti-environmentalist shift (Taylor, 2000).

SPLINTERING OVER IMMIGRATION

The controversy surrounding immigration within population-environmentalism was not new; the Federation for American Immigration Reform (FAIR) was created in 1979 to focus on immigration issues, which splintered from Zero Population Growth (Lutton and Tanton, 1994). Environmentalists revisited immigration as a subject of concern particularly in conversations surrounding sustainable growth in the 1990s, as analysis of US Census data indicated that projected growth was due to recent immigration and childbearing among immigrants since the 1970s (Camarota, 2005; Cohn, 2005). This began a new discourse to address immigration by focusing on stabilizing population growth in the US and around the world (Beck and Kolankiewicz, 2000; Bouvier and Grant, 1994).

This contention over immigration continued to grow within ZPG. ZPG's focus had been to encourage grassroots organizing at the local level and the most significant conflict occurred when California ZPG split off and formed Californians for Population Stabilization, as other sections (e.g. Florida and Colorado, among many others) followed suit. Although ZPG has a statement in their policy about the role of immigration and population growth, their larger focus has been family planning and consumption. ZPG's Board of Directors revised their policy regarding immigration in 1994 and re-affirmed in 1997 to focus instead on 'addressing factors which compel people to leave their homes and family and immigrate to the United States'. They felt that 'no forcible exclusion policy [would] successfully prevent people from seeking to relocate into the United States'. However, ZPG did believe that 'the United States should adopt an overall goal for immigration as a part of its national population policy ... to plan for demographic changes and to slow population growth.'

While ZPG focused on the importance of a national population policy, it refused to go out on a limb for how this should take place. In addition, after discussing future goals of the organization and the original purpose behind the name of their organization, in 2002 they decided to change their name to Population Connection.

The Sierra Club had similar issues regarding taking positions on national population policy. In 1992, the Board of Directors revised its population policy, as 'a rapid end to population growth in this country and around the world is an essential part of any effort to protect the environment, sustain the ability of the earth to support life, and enhance the quality of life for all human beings.' However, in 1996 the Board of Directors revised the policy to exclude migration in official Club policy efforts to limit US population growth and refused efforts from the grassroots level. In 1998, a ballot initiative was introduced to consider migration in the official policy. The Sierra Club differs from ZPG as a democratic organization that relies on its membership to vote on the Board of Directors and official club policy. A group that had splintered from the Sierra Club, Sierrans for US Population Stabilization (SUSPS), began lobbying for an immigration policy initiative on the ballot. After much consternation, the Sierra Club decided that the ballot initiative would ask members to choose between two alternatives (Table 18.2).

In effect, the Sierra Club was asking its members to consider the problem about the relationship between population and resources as either a national issue or a global issue. Option A (SUSPS' position) asked for consideration about the role immigration plays in population growth in the United States and advocated a larger conversation about how to address it. Option B (SC Board of Directors) asserted that the problem was not about immigration but

Table 18.2 Sierra Club ballot alternatives

Alternative A (SUSPS's Position)	Alternative B (Sierra Club's Position)
Shall the Sierra Club reverse its decision adopted 2/24/96 to 'take no position on immigration levels or on policies governing immigration into the United States'; and adopt a comprehensive population policy for the United States that continues to advocate an end to U.S. population growth at the earliest time possible through reduction in natural increase (births minus deaths) but now also through reduction in net immigration (immigration minus emigration)?	Sierra Club affirms the decision of the Board of Directors to take NO position on U.S. immigration levels and policies. Sierra Club can more effectively address the root causes of global population problems through its existing comprehensive approach: Sierra Club will build on its effective efforts to champion the right of all families to maternal and reproductive health care, and the empowerment and equity of women; Sierra Club will continue to address the root causes of migration by encouraging sustainability, economic security, health and nutrition, human rights and environmentally responsible consumption.

instead about global population growth, and the environmental movement should only advocate for family planning and sustainable development goals.

This debacle received widespread national attention in the media about whether the environmental movement had any business talking about immigration. Mainstream environmental groups were accused of being racist, elitist, xenophobic, and nativist; this was in part because the Sierra Club vote was within four years of a controversial vote on Proposition 187 in California, which called for restriction on immigrant assistance. The rhetoric that dominated the news cycle was to call any position taken on by mainstream environmental organizations about immigration as representing the 'greening of hate', which was a catch phrase used in the media as part of a strategic media campaign started by the Political Ecology Group, an environmental justice organization (Silliman and King, 1999). This term was intended to challenge anti-immigrant groups that used arguments about controlling US population growth and urged environmentalists to support a moratorium on immigration. The belief was that this scapegoated immigrants and diverted attention from what was considered to be real causes of environmental degradation and intended to divide groups over environmental and human rights. 'Greening of hate' represented a taint of racism for population-environmentalism whenever the topic of immigration came up in connection to population and environment issues and it damaged organizational reputations.

While Alternative A was voted down, many Sierrans expressed publicly in print media and privately in discussions via Sierra Club listservs their concern about the way the issue damaged Sierra Club's credibility; 40 percent of Sierra Club members voted for measure A. The issue came up again on the ballot in 1998 with the Sierra Club Board of Directors election where 22 candidates were vying for five positions. Petition candidates (not endorsed) who made their position known to be in favor of the Alternative A initiative lost the election; however, 12 candidates mentioned 'population' in their statements, which indicated the importance of this issue to the Club's priorities and campaigns. These two campaigns highlighted dramatic differences among environmentalists about perceptions on the balance between people and resources and the third rail of immigration.

While mainstream groups now avoid addressing immigration, other groups have taken it on and made connections to population-environmentalism, such as linking sprawl to advocacy for immigration restrictions. This issue continues to haunt the Sierra Club with struggles over population policy and elections for the Board of Directors; splinter groups targeted the Sierra Club leadership when they could not address policy at the grassroots level. The imbalance between people and resources is critical and complex, but cannot be addressed by mainstream groups because of substantial differences in positions.

Anti-Environmental Influences

In the 1990s, there had been an important paradigm shift in population policy to change the focus from economic development and individual agency to improving the role of women and reducing income inequality for sustainable population growth (Dixon-Mueller, 1993; Ashford, 2001). This shift in ideology opened the door for population-environmentalists who were upset by this change in value orientation to challenge it (Greene, 1999). Connecting this to Abernethy's concern (1993) about anti-environmentalist forces and their impact on the population-environmentalism connection, we can begin to understand how competing interest groups exerted influence on the larger discourse (Benford and Hunt, 1992; Brulle, 2000). There is a need to recognize this historical context to identify how organizations from both the left and right influenced the discourse, as some groups redirected and diminished concerns about population while attacking environmentalists. The deliberate splintering of mainstream organizations over immigration by these outside groups' influence is anti-environmental at its core, as the controversy over 'greening of hate' made population a taboo subject. There has always been a strong connection between population and the environment, beginning on the first Earth Day, with population embraced as a core concern by many environmental organizations. Allies often cite that what happened to the Sierra Club and ZPG was where mainstream conversation surrounding population stopped, which is essential to examining the influence of population and environmental groups and anti-environmental stakeholders.

Immigration became the third rail for mainstream environmental groups because existing data do not demonstrate whether immigrants have a negative impact on the environment. Most mainstream groups believe the focus of population efforts should be on sustainable consumption; the US constitutes approximately 5 percent of the world's population yet consumes 25 percent of the world's resources. First-wave environmentalists of the 1970s viewed over-population primarily as a problem of numbers, while the newer generation of environmentalists believes that intersectionality needs to be included in any discussion about population. The key to bridging the gap between the generations lies in finding a new way to frame the conversation (King, 2007).

POPULATION–ENVIRONMENT CONNECTION

The partnership between mainstream environmental and population advocacy groups began in 1965 with the Sierra Club's creation of population-environmentalist policy. As best expressed by David Brower in 1966, executive director of the Sierra Club, 'you don't have a conservation policy unless you have a population policy'.

Population-environmentalism took off in the 1970s with a neo-Malthusian manifesto, which made a statement about the alarming problem of human population growth and how the impacts of this growth indicated the imminent destruction of the planet earth, unless things turned around soon. A term often used at that time was zero population growth, coined by Kingsley Davis, described limiting population increase to the number of live births needed to replace the existing population. Paul Ehrlich, Charles Remington, and Richard Bower used this term to incorporate a new organization 'Zero Population Growth' in 1968. This organization got off the ground after the first Earth Day, where environmental degradation linked with population growth to create the foundation of population-environmentalism.

The focus on population as a crisis needed to change when the total fertility rate in the United States fell below 2.1 births per woman in 1972, dropped to 1.7 in 1976 and remained steady until the 1990s. Population-environmentalism zeroed in on support of international family planning programs while still advocating for 'stop at two' in educational and advocacy programs for the United States. In the 1990s, the metaphor of the population 'bomb' was transformed into an 'explosion', to represent the amount of growth globally that had transpired over 20 years. Usage of the 'I = PAT' equation (Impact = Population * Affluence * Technology) (Ehrlich and Holdren, 1971) became a mainstay in discussions surrounding sustainability, carrying capacity, and overpopulation arguments and thus began a renewed interest in population-environmentalism.

While the mainstream environmental movement had been rooted in conservation and preservation, new concerns were beginning to take root with a shift in focus to the human environment and health issues regarding clean air and water. There was also the start of discussions on the unfair distribution of resources and profitable technologies, in how economic systems impact the environment (Hunter, 2000). However, conservationists and preservationists were still concerned about population growth, especially in watching wilderness and habitats disappear. They made the connection to the growth of the Baby Boom generation and were able to retain this tenet in population-environmentalism until the late 1990s, with a change of focus to environmental justice and human rights.

The United Nations conferences of the 1990s also had an incredible influence on the changing context of discussions in the mainstream environmental movement and the population advocacy organizations, particularly with involvement of non-governmental organizations (NGOs) actively participating in the proceedings. Three conferences – Rio, Cairo, and Beijing – had the largest effects in changing the discourse surrounding population-environmentalism and resulted from the diversity of voices represented. Rio linked environmental degradation to population growth, Cairo linked development with improving women's rights, and Beijing focused on women's rights as human rights; therefore, the impact of NGOs is critical to connect shifting paradigms of thought in population-environmentalism (Hodgson and Watkins, 1997).

Mainstream Environment

The Sierra Club was one of the first environmental organizations to define population-environmentalism in stating that population growth was the root of environmental degradation. Another distinction of the Sierra Club from the other mainstream environmental groups is that democratic membership is the core mission of the organization where every member is a voting member on Club policy and elects their own Board of Directors. Population-environmentalism campaigns of the Sierra Club adapted over time, but they have always been pro-choice. There were other mainstream environmental organizations that had active population programs and/or policies, including the Audubon Society, Izaak Walton League, National Wildlife Association, and Wilderness Society. Since the early 2000s, though, most environmental organizations have had a change in leadership within their infrastructure and population programs.

Table 18.3   Mainstream environment representations

Frame	Clusters
Environment	Justice; Management; Habitat/Resource
Population	Family Planning Programs: Family Size and Health; Optimal Levels; Global Issues; Carrying Capacity/Sustainability; Consumption/Domestic Issues; Future Generations
Immigration	Controversy/Polarization; Dilemma; Population Connections; Priorities
Greening of Hate	Exaggeration; Polemical; Intentional
Future Goals	Dialogue; Representations – 'At the Table'; Vision: Values and Beliefs; Coalition

A former environmental group administrator who had been with one of the mainstream environmental organizations, leading the population program since the 1980s and having a long history with population-environmentalism, represented the views of mainstream environmental groups (Table 18.3). This interviewee shared experiences of coalition building and institutional memories that pre-dated the Sierra Club vote in 1998.

Discussion on population focused on support of international family planning programs, particularly examining the importance of the role of health and education in the lives of women and families on a global level. There was much discussion surrounding 'carrying capacity', 'sustainability', as most of the impacts of population growth are viewed as environmental with resource impacts, and consideration into what effect current programs will have on future generations, particularly in the developing world. However, in domestic issues, consumption rates and future impact are the main issues concerning the United States in comparison to other countries. Growth in the United States results from migration, but population growth will stabilize through endorsement of voluntary family planning programs.

Most of the conversation about immigration focused on the dilemma/controversy surrounding immigration and whether environmental groups should have policy statements on setting limits or focus on where the growth is coming from (e.g. fertility levels by racial/ethnic groups). There was discussion of the polarization that occurred within the Sierra Club and how other groups wanted to avoid the controversy; their priorities were examining connections to population growth in the United States and considering how much growth is good for the future of the nation.

Discussion on the environment focused on how to manage growth, particularly for the impact upon habitat and resources for present and future generations. Environmental justice and power are issues that need to be considered, as the environmental movement is known to be more represented by mostly middle-class white people and needs to see things from a bigger perspective of how communities, at both racial and class levels, are affected differently. Quality of life for all, as a comprehensive point of view, considered an important conservation strategy for survival of the planet.

Assessment on the greening of hate determined that the term was an exaggeration, but splinter groups made it polemical as using that term was name calling and not well intentioned. While there was some truth in environmental groups mostly consisting of white people, there needs to be more sensitivity about how issues are discussed and who is included in those discussions. It is a complex issue in talking about policy and population, but a greater dialogue needs to take place, rather than just accusations, which are too one-sided.

Future goals involved dialogue about the development of coalitions. Different groups need to be represented and have 'places at the table', to encourage a more open and broader discussion. A new vision needs to focus on quality of life on a global level – both domestically and globally, where values and beliefs need to find the commonality and build from there. Isolationism is not the answer, but consensus and coalition are.

Population Advocacy

Advocacy for population-environmentalism came from linking population growth with environmental degradation in the creation of Zero Population Growth. However, examining the roots of population concerns beyond Malthus, there is connection with the eugenics movement and Social Darwinism, particularly in discussions of whose fertility needed to be controlled (Finkle and McIntosh, 1994; Greene, 1999). However, in terms of its affirmative aspects, population concerns are also rooted in the feminist movement, as seen in Margaret Sanger's advocacy for family planning and in the creation of Planned Parenthood. Organizations that advocated for population issues and mentioned concern about environmental issues as part of their mission statements were included.

The first population advocacy organization was Zero Population Growth, founded in 1968, and policy recommendations focused on reducing US population growth:

> Zero Population Growth Inc. is an organization which has been formed to bring the crucial issue of over-population to the attention of the general public, and more specifically, to the attention of our legislators (state and federal): the ultimate goal of ZPG to form a lobby group to press for legislation to implement birth control programs, repeal archaic legislation that runs counter to these objectives, press for allocation of funds for more research into population problems and research for better methods of contraception, and press for tax laws that, instead of offering incentives for having more children, will emphasize the need for population control.

ZPG changed their name to Population Connection on 1 May 2002, as board members felt that ZPG had passed into common usage as a concept that prompted discussion for name change. This was not the first time that ZPG had questioned whether they had outgrown their initial goals; in 1978, a splinter movement formed the Federation for American Immigration Reform when leaders of ZPG decided that it would be better to avoid immigration and concentrate on impediments to family planning programs. Population Connection continues to work on issues concerning population and reproductive rights and their focus remains on educational efforts: 'Overpopulation threatens the quality of life for people everywhere. Population Connection is the national grassroots population organization that educates young people and advocates progressive action to stabilize world population at a level that can be sustained by Earth's resources.'

Population Action International (PAI), which began as Population Crisis Committee in 1965, is a policy advocacy organization that is 'committed to advancing universal access to family planning and related health services and to educational and economic opportunities, especially for girls and women. These strategies promise to improve the lives of individual women and their families, while helping to slow the world's population growth and preserve the environment.' Other population advocacy organizations examined include Population Communications International, Population Coalition, Population Media Center, and three splinter organizations created by activists dissatisfied with ZPG's lack of focus on immigration issues and that are anti-environmental at their core despite their names: Population Environment Balance, Negative Population Growth, and Carrying Capacity Network.

Table 18.4 Population advocacy representations

Frame	Clusters
Environment	Impacts of Growth; Consumption of Resources; Stewardship – Planet
Population	Stabilization; Reproductive Health and Accessibility; International; Generations; Sustainability; Connections
Immigration	Political/Debate; Migration; Trends/Levels; Economics
Greening of Hate	Blame; Diversity
Future Goals	Coalitions; Dialogue

A member actively involved with population advocacy work since the 1990s and as an environmental journalist represented views of population advocacy groups (Table 18.4) with their active involvement with various government and non-profit organizations and rational approach to the issues. Part of the frustration with the interviews, similar to the environmental organizations, was the reluctance to discuss anything about 'the greening of hate' without anger about what the term did to the credibility of the movement and organizations and activists involved in the issues.

Population advocacy focused on demographics in a comparative sense and on international concerns supporting family planning programs for sustainable growth, particularly reproductive health and accessibility to care for women and families. To balance the discussion, there is mention of worldwide population slowing down, but in the US, population growth is speeding up. It becomes difficult to describe what is causing the growth, as it has to do with how we define who is an immigrant versus who is a native related to issues of time. There is discussion on stabilizing growth, sustainability, and connecting to other larger issues, such as the environment and consumption of finite resources. The impact on future generations was also important, in terms of reductions in growth.

Discussion about the environment focused on linkages made between population growth and impact on clean water, air, and resources, mostly in setting consumption and sustainability goals. Also, there was discussion of stewardship as a goal within the confines of sustainability (e.g. Pew Global Stewardship Initiative), where there is a need to advocate for developing individual responsibility for the needs of the many and future generations as long-term goals, instead of policies that focus on short-term or short-sighted goals for the future. Long-term goals focus on consumption of resources and sustainability.

Discussion about immigration focused on racial overtones used in the media. Much of the discussion of population growth within the United States resulted from migration flows and fertility levels of recent immigrants. However, there is a difference in determining new immigrants versus established residents in terms of speculation of where the growth is coming from: 'We are all progeny of immigrants, including Native Americans. At what point do you stop calling people immigrants and say "Okay, they're natives now"? That's the frustrating thing about this discussion ... the groups ... have over-simplified it.' Also numbers are played up in the media, as focus relates to what people fear (change) instead of how immigration relates to growth overall and the impact on resource consumption. The problem came down to the fact that they could not find a way to make the case that migration is important as a process and in how it impacts the environment, rather than focusing on the migrants themselves.

Future goals focused on coalition and group-based work, not just between population and environmental groups, but including sustainable development and poverty alleviation. There is a need for different ideological lenses or points of view, for purposes of inclusion in order to make the larger connections between population and environment, particularly from a global point of view. There is a need to connect the United States to the rest of the world. It is critical to have a global perspective, but discussion needs to be brought back to the national level. What would help the dialogue would be to make the connection between demographic processes and environmental impacts: 'The other key things to be thinking about are ... long-time scales ... the long-term trends that are happening in this country ... looking at how many people will we ultimately have and what will be the environment?'

The problem remains political sensitivity and finding common ground, leading to discussion about the greening of hate and connecting to the lack of racial and ethnic diversity in the leadership and representation within organizations. The framing of the greening of hate came down to the blame game and a need to change the causality in arguments made with a tendency to blame:

> This is all based on this kind of reduction in view of human affairs ... if people would ... shift their language to looking at processes themselves ... rather than demonizing people or individuals and then demonizing your opponent and accusing them of demonizing ... well, it's very hard to keep the debate civil. Once they lose this ability, everybody's kind of accusing everyone else of being whatever.

In any case, the 'greening of hate' was a reflection of poverty of being unable to articulate a difference in point of view and the inability to have an open conversation.

Mainstream environment and population advocacy
In comparing and contrasting these groupings, they do not represent opposite sides. While there are people active in both mainstream environment and population advocacy organizations that are similar in how they see population-environmentalism, they are different in their approaches. They differ in their goals, where the mainstream environment's goal is to protect and conserve the environment, and population advocacy's goal is to educate the public on population and its connections to environmental impact. However, there is symmetry between these two groupings in four specific areas: (1) core beliefs on population; (2) policy actions; (3) ethical standpoints; and (4) working goals for the future. They believe in limits to growth (carrying capacity, consumption), quality of life (sprawl, threats to freedom), individual rights, and globalization (global impact/concerns). They both believe in goals pertaining to future generations, community rights, quality of life, and global concerns, and identified dialogue and coalitions as future working goals for their respective social movement organizations.

HUMAN RIGHTS VS. SOCIETAL GOALS

The splintering within population-environmentalism represents a conflict between Numbers Impact and Human Rights; these divergent paradigms emerged as points of conflict about unmet needs and a vocal minority feeling unheard. Both groupings represent anti-environmentalist goals, but there is also a larger context with changes in immigration policy to connect with disagreements over population-environmentalism.

The US population is projected to rise to 420 million in 2050, a 49 percent increase from 2000. After 2030, the rate of increase will decrease as the Baby Boom generation continues to age and die (Alonso-Zaldivar, 2004). However, the racial make-up of the population of the United States will become more diverse as the numbers of Latinos and Asians will triple over the next half century, as the white population will continue to decline. There will be two Americas: 'One America will be white, middle class and graying and then you'll have this new kind of globalized America coming to the fore, essentially a racial generation gap will occur.' (Frey, 1995).

Immigration has had a varying effect on population growth throughout US history. From a global perspective, about 175 million people, approximately 3 percent of the world population, are international migrants (IOM, 2003). A large majority of migrants to the US are from less developed countries. People move to take advantage of better economic opportunities, and some are refugees seeking asylum after leaving countries because of political violence or threat of persecution. Immigration has always been a point of contention in our nation with a long history of racism and nativism (Feagin, 2000). As Gunnar Myrdal (1944) demonstrates:

> There was a growing feeling in America against the 'new' immigrants pouring into the country whose last frontier was now occupied and congregating in the big cities where they competed with American labor. In addition to the social friction they created, the idea that these newcomers represented an inferior stock provided much of the popular theory for the restrictive legislation. Immigration legislation has also changed from a strict quota system to focus on family reunification, labor needs, and asylum/refugees.

A further example of the schism over immigration is demonstrated in 1977 at a Conference on the Ethics of Exclusion: The Crisis of US Immigration Policy held at the Center for the Study of Democratic Institutions at the University of California (UC) Santa Barbara, between Jorge Bustamante and Garrett Hardin. Hardin, a human ecologist from UC Santa Barbara, is known for carrying capacity and lifeboat analogy in terms of the impact of growth in a finite world of resources. Bustamante founded and served for many years as President of El Colegio de la Frontera Norte, a Mexican research center for the study of social issues affecting the border region between the United States and Mexico; he is an outspoken advocate of human and labor rights for immigrants worldwide and particularly Mexico. Hardin and Bustamante set the stage for how dialogue comes down to politics of undocumented immigrant rights pitted against strictly limiting immigration numbers. Bustamante was addressing the problem as an international issue (relationship between nations) whereas Hardin was addressing the problem solely as a domestic issue (impact on US growth and change). These are distinct and separate approaches in how problems and actions are defined, yet they both address *illegal* immigration, which should be separate from legal migration, but are sandwiched together. Mexican migration tends to take center stage in discussions surrounding migration as 60 percent of undocumented migrants/laborers come from Mexico. The same issues are relevant in current discussions on border enforcement, employer sanctions, adjustment of status, and temporary residential alien status.

Both Human Rights and Numbers Impact perspectives are anti-environmental in how they clash and lead to splintering of mainstream discussions in their attempts to influence population-environmentalism over human rights versus societal goals.

Human Rights

Human rights is defined as basic rights and freedoms to which all humans are entitled, including the right to life and liberty, freedom of thought and expression, and equality before the law.

The human rights grouping invokes an environmental justice paradigm that views race, class, and gender as interconnected components. The environmental justice movement sprang from concerns about pollution and chemicals affecting the human environment and differed from not in my backyard (NIMBY) groups in that communities of color started banding together to fight environmental racism. A portion of this movement confronted mainstream environmental groups and accused them of racism, to the degree that they did not represent people of color (mainstream groups are mostly white middle-class members), and challenged them to change and become more diverse in membership and approaches to policy and representation (Melosi, 2000).

The UN conferences in Rio, Cairo, and Beijing also had a significant change with the inclusion of non-governmental organizations and a wider range of voices in the discussion of linking population and environment (McIntosh and Finkle, 1995). The divergence of discussion was also along racial, class, and gender lines, as environmental justice, immigrant rights, and feminist groups are represented in this grouping. The groups responsible for having an influence on changes in Sierra Club population policy and on the framing of the 1998 elections were: Committee for Women, Population and the Environment; Political Ecology Group; and National Network for Immigrant and Refugee Rights.

The Committee for Women, Population and the Environment is 'a multi-racial alliance of feminist activists, health practitioners and scholars. [It is] committed to promoting the social and economic empowerment of women in a context of global peace and justice; and to eliminating poverty, inequality, racism, and environmental degradation.' What they have contributed to the dialogue is that they challenge the belief that population growth is the primary cause of environmental degradation, conflict, and growing poverty as well as 'educating population and environmental organizations on the problems of using demographic alarmism and rationales in explaining the causes of global problems.' They were also credited with creating the term 'greening of hate' (Silliman and King, 1999).

The Political Ecology Group (PEG) was founded in 1990 and its initial goals were to combine social justice and environmental concerns. Its work has focused on exposing the 'greening of hate' in the environmental movement and also had an environmental justice campaign focus on Methyl Bromide in communities of color. PEG is a grassroots, multi-racial and multi-issue organization working for environmental justice locally, nationally, and internationally. It works toward a future in which our environment, healthy communities, and human rights come first. PEG's campaigns build alliances to confront racism, corporate power, and environmental destruction. PEG brings people together for participatory education and leadership development to reframe public debate and to take collective action.

What these organizations did for the Sierra Club 1998 elections was an aggressive media campaign to capitalize on exposing the 'greening of hate' among the groups who had heavily campaigned to members of the Sierra Club in favor of their own agendas for immigration control. Other groups involved in the analysis included the National Network for Immigrant Rights, Center for Development and Population Activities, Center for Health and Gender Equity, and Alliance of Ethnic and Environmental Organizations.

Advocates who served as the bridge for all three organizations in attempting to work with the Sierra Club represented this perspective (Table 18.5).

Discussion on the environment does not center on the natural environment or resources, but includes people. These groups look at it as a natural system, an ecology of well-being overall and focus on the damage to ecosystems. Discussion on health included quality of life issues

Table 18.5   *Human rights representations*

Frame	Clusters
Environment	Health, Clean Air/Water; Community; Global Economy; Women; Consumption
Population	Malthus; Control; Family Planning; Poverty
Immigration	Human Rights; Scapegoats; Racism/White Privilege; Border; Overpopulation
Future Goals	Social Justice; Environmental Protection; Health

and access to care. Discussion on clean air and water focused on the need to protect from pollution and sanitation issues. The main concern was about accessibility to these resources for all people. In considering the larger community, they have a holistic perspective and look at who is responsible. The safety of the environment is a challenge for the global economy with market forces. There is concern about workers' and laborers' rights and protection. People are a part of the social environment, in terms of securing reproductive health and rights with literacy and educational issues. The last issue discussed within the environment is that of consumption and Western culture. The problem was perceived as an impact on the environment with waste and use of fossil fuels. Industrial waste and contamination are the real issues, with the role of corporations and technology at the less powerful people's expense. Privilege and lifestyles of the First World are considered to be more of a problem then Third World fertility, with the long-term effects and reach of Western ideology and consumer culture on our global world.

Population was discussed as a critique of the population control mindset that has dominated policy discussions; the lens of 'overpopulation' permeated discussions surrounding finite amounts of natural resources. It is a complex issue of interactions between people and the environment. The frame of Malthusianism suggests impending doom with population increase, utilizes threatening images, and is perceived to be eugenicist or survival of the fittest (fit vs. unfit stock). There is reference to a war-like older generation, called 'population hawks' who are perceived to be protecting their own. They discussed Ehrlich and 'I = PAT' as being too simplistic or narrow-minded in its approach. Herein is a critique of control and coercion of population, where it is seen as manipulation and ultimately Third World versus First World, which is perceived to be damaging and offensive. What they find as sincere aspects of population programs are those of family planning, if combined with reproductive rights and maternal and children's health issues. There is general agreement that smaller families with fewer children are a positive benefit of family survival and reduce infant mortality. However, there is concern mostly about how the real problem is redistribution of wealth and resources; a need for a revolution of thought for human needs, entitlement for all instead of a select few.

The perspective of immigration as a social problem does not consider how groups focus on the immigrants themselves, stigmatizing them and blaming them for society's ills. Discussion centered on hazards that immigrants are exposed to being ignored and not considered as rights of immigrants. Immigrants are often scapegoated and treated as second-class citizens and blamed for problems in society, like rising crime or sprawl. There was also discussion on racism and white privilege, with cultural change in society blamed on immigrants. Greening of hate is a reference to the link with white supremacy issues. They perceive the problem with an agenda to protect the borders, as the focus is on illegal immigration, and misses the complexity of the economy and market forces that drive migration. The overpopulation lens refers to population control versus human rights – whose numbers are to be controlled?

Discussion about future goals centered on welfare of all people, regardless of citizenship, as a priority. Environmental justice at community levels needs to be considered and the focus should be on environmental protection, fragility of ecosystems, and protection of species. Quality of life should be for everyone, particularly those taken advantage of because of their powerlessness.

Numbers Impact

To paraphrase the numbers impact organizational perspective in one phrase would be 'all growth is bad'. While organizational goals are about reformulating immigration policy, they would be characterized as tackling the problem of numbers and their social impact, following the 'I = PAT' ideology. Their motto was, 'If we can't change how much we consume, at least we can control our numbers.' A political cartoon that Sierrans for US Population Stabilization used in their campaign in 1998 had a janitor looking at an overflowing sink, where he pondered whether he should first fix the spigot or mop up the water. The spigot represented migration and the overflowing water represented fertility; the logical approach would be to turn the spigot off.

Many people from these groups considered themselves to be environmentalists, but experienced a turning point in viewing how their world had changed and concluded that it was not necessarily for the better. They grew up at a time where progress was measured by growth and prosperity (e.g. 'growth is good'), which involved urbanization, sprawl, and migration. An oft-used refrain was 'I remember when none of this used to be here', when describing the loss of open space, untouched forest and smaller towns that had since blossomed intro metropolises. For example, one could look at the traffic congestion in areas such as Los Angeles and blame the change on too many people – never mind too many cars, poor urban planning, or the lack of an accessible public transportation system.

What happened within the structures of the Sierra Club and ZPG happens to social movements; fragmentation is an inexorable consequence of expansion, particularly when there is diversity of opinion on where the movement should be headed (Dunlap and Mertig, 1992). This fragmentation over ideology leads to splinters from the mainstream movement in the creation of alternative groups.

Sierrans (now 'Support') for US Population Stabilization broke away from the Sierra Club when the Board of Directors changed the population policy in 1996 to be 'neutral' on immigration. They are responsible for placing the ballot initiative in 1998 on asking the membership of the Sierra Club to reconsider the official policy of SC. SUSPS is a network of thousands of individuals who are Sierra Club members and activists, many with decades of Sierra Club experience; it is not an official body of the Sierra Club, but a network:

> We support Sierra Club policies and principles with the exception of current Sierra Club U.S. population policy, which we believe is inadequate in addressing U.S. overpopulation. We support U.S. population stabilization purely for ecological reasons. This requires we reduce both birth rates and migration to the U.S. to sustainable levels. Unending population growth and increasing levels of consumption together are the root causes of the vast majority of our environmental problems, as is the case in many other countries.

Federation for American Immigration Reform (FAIR) was an offshoot of ZPG, as there was much division within the organization concerning how to approach immigration. It was

Table 18.6   Numbers impact representations

Frame	Clusters
Environment	Clean Air/Water; Sprawl; Protection; Future; Choices
Population	Family Size; Linkages; Growth/Sprawl; Quality of Life
Immigration	Levels; Reforms; Legal/Illegal; Racism/Eugenics; Human Rights
Future Goals	Coalitions; Individual vs. Environment; Stakeholders; Ethics; Stabilization

determined that FAIR would be able to do a better job of focusing on one issue, rather than stretching ZPG beyond its original confines: 'FAIR seeks to improve border security, to stop illegal immigration, and to promote immigration levels consistent with the national interest—more traditional rates of about 300,000 a year.'

Other organizations represented in this grouping include Numbers USA, Population Environment Balance, and Californians for Population Stabilization. Representing this perspective were advocates who had been actively involved with these organizations (Table 18.6), where they discussed how they had become overwhelmed by the role and impact of migration on population growth and environmental degradation: 'The success of the environmental movement is in danger. Immigration has had a profound effect on growth. Perpetual growth will undermine our efforts.'

The environment is viewed as a resource; it is seen as both man-made and natural, in terms of the loss of nature. Within this framework, the desire to protect air and water quality for society, and restoration, quality of life, and standards are keywords. They focus on sprawl, where the perception is that population growth leads to environmental degradation, particularly in the decrease in farmland and paving over habitat. Environment is something to be sustained, stabilized and protected. For that reason, they consider themselves to be stakeholders, and have a sense of responsibility for future generations, for the nation to come. They see their purpose to help to see the truth, validity, justification of numbers for population stabilization, as there are perceived priorities to set long-range goals for the nation, and make community decisions as a democracy. There is a sense of self-determination, in feeling obligations but not coercion.

Population is viewed as seeing people as a whole and focusing on issues at the societal level as an investment in the future. Family size was one issue, where stabilization was encouraged at two children, but that it was a choice and related to women's issues. Discussion centered on the role of ethics, in terms of goals and responsibilities, in comparing society versus individual needs. While focus was on government involvement, they recognized the level of conflict with individual freedom. There were frequent remarks about the link to the environment, in terms of stability in the face of demographic change and growth leading to sprawl. This discussion was on the change and transformation of the landscape, and *damage* was one word that came up frequently. Finally, there was discussion in terms of quality of life issues: life, liberty, and the pursuit of happiness, but pitting the personal against the collective.

Immigration centered on numbers, where levels are above average and expected to increase. The only solution is reform, with reductions and changes in policy and needed government intervention. A problem that arose was how legal and illegal immigration are grouped or lumped together, not seen separately. Responding to the 'greening of hate', the calls of racism and hate were strong and powerful, but were quite effective tools, as they linked to McCarthyism and fear. However, guilt by association and connections to the past were seen as invalid for present concerns. Finally, human rights is an issue pitting society versus individual needs; economic fairness with labor and worker concerns.

Table 18.7 Areas of symmetry and commonality

Points of Difference	Points of Similarity
Individual Rights vs. Societal Goals	*Protection*
Differences come down to focus on human and civil rights protections for the present or goals for future generations to come. There is no common ground, except balancing needs with sacrifices for deserving versus undeserving groups.	Both agree that clean air and water are critical and natural resources need protection for both current and future needs.
Inequality vs. Rationality	*Critical of Consumption*
Differences come down to focusing on societal and economic inequality and problems with regulating corporations versus focus on growth and its overall impact on present and future needs of society; it is difficult to see inequality if it does not directly affect one's way of life.	Both recognize that consumption is a bigger part of the battle in reducing environmental impact; both also recognize government intervention is necessary, as well as individual responsibility to reduce the human footprint.
Justice vs. Health	*Quality of Life*
Difference come down to focus on inequality in communities of color and social class versus focus on the environment from a societal point of view; this is the same issue human rights groups have with mainstream groups.	Both agree about concern for quality of life, but differ on whose (society versus individual), which goes back to views on environmental justice, health, and systemic inequality.

As for future goals, they felt environmental groups dropped population and stopped making it an issue, an educational void – and needed to reorganize their principles. Discussion centered on how environmentalists needed to include immigration reform organizations and labor/worker groups in building coalitions. In pitting the individual against the environment, there was a perception that women's issues were at odds with the environment. Responsibility was a keyword, as in 'the survival of future generations are at stake'. There was also discussion about short-term versus long-term goals, with societal and individual needs on the level of quality of life for all instead of the few. Finally, stabilization was discussed: continued and perpetual population growth keeps us (society) from reaching our goals and undermines success for the future.

Human rights versus numbers impact
In comparing and contrasting the frames and clusters of these groupings, several areas of symmetry and commonality emerged (Table 18.7). In terms of similarities, both groups value environmental protection and are critical of the impact of consumption: however, while they both value the quality of human life, they disagree on whose life is more valuable. The points of difference form the basis of contention between the groups' values and positions which cannot be negotiated. In summary, it appears to pit individual rights, social inequality, and environmental justice against nationalist goals for the future of society.

NEGOTIATING POPULATION-ENVIRONMENTALISM

Negotiation analysis looks for areas of commonality or symmetry across the groupings and defines common ground based on similarities that emerge. In Table 18.8, there are five different aspects examined from summation of information and collective action from the organizations: primary organizational interests (mission and organizational goals), issues

Table 18.8   Negotiation analysis

	Mainstream Environment	Population Advocacy	Human Rights	Numbers Impact
Primary organizational interests	Protect and conserve the environment	Education on population and its connections	Protect rights for minority groups	Reduce growth, focused on future impact
Issues and beliefs on population and immigration*	• Limits to growth • Quality of life • Rights • Globalization	• Limits to growth • Quality of life • Rights • Globalization	• Quality of life • Race • Rights • Globalization	• Limits to growth • Quality of life • Population pressure • Race
Chosen policy actions on population and immigration	Neutrality. Policy positions stated, but no action taken**	Neutrality. Policy positions stated, but no action taken**	Policy and advocacy for protection of human rights	Policy and advocacy for reduction in numbers
Ethical standpoints ***	1) Future 2) Community 3) Total 4) Accessible 5) Global	1) Future 2) Community 3) Total 4) Accessible 5) Global	1) Present 2) Community Individual 3) Total 4) Equality 5) Global	1) Future 2) Community Society 3) Average 4) Protection 5) Local
Working goals for the future	Dialogue Coalition Stewardship	Dialogue Coalition	Coalition Social Justice Protection	Coalition Stabilization Stewardship

Notes: *Adapted Wilmoth and Ball's (1995) categorical frames for population issues discourse: The 'growth is good' frame was irrelevant and the 'race' frame was adapted with discourse on nativism. Two new frames were added: (1) rights and (2) globalization. **Organizations with policy statements about population and immigration, and advocated for reducing future growth, but did not set limits on migration. Actions included lobbying for family planning and advocacy for protection of rights. ***Adapted Campbell's (1998) discussion on ethical questions surrounding population policy: (1) responsibility to present versus future generations; (2) individual versus community rights and benefits; (3) average versus total quality of life; and (4) distribution of resources and opportunity. We added an additional question: (5) local versus global focus.

and beliefs on population and migration, chosen policy actions on population and migration, ethical standpoints on population, and working goals for the future.

Among three of the groupings (mainstream, advocacy, and numbers impact), there is agreement on several fronts: there are perceived needs to limit population growth, consider the role of human rights in population policy, and consider the global impact of these concerns beyond our borders. Among all four of the groupings, there is agreement on the need to consider quality of life, with how population growth and changes in environment have effects on human beings. However, there is disagreement on whose quality of life, society overall or individuals, who may be affected differently. In examining the ethical standpoints of the various groupings, there is overlap among three (mainstream, advocacy, and numbers impact) on a focus on future generations and a global focus on community needs, but it differs over individual impacts or society levels. All four groupings agree that coalition building should be the ultimate goal for the future of the movement.

However, that is where it ends on the level of agreement, or symmetry, between the groups. The largest levels of dissymmetry exist between human rights against the numbers impact grouping over issues related to perceptions of population control versus population pressure in the basic core of their belief systems, as this is inextricably linked to their views on race, class, and gender. These groups also differ in their ethical standpoints between equality of access to resources and opportunities versus protection for the good of society. This is where the biggest difference lies, in nativist versus global concerns.

There were attempts to bridge between the groups, such as the Alliance of Ethnic and Environmental Organizations (Gelobter et al., 2005). There were also funders of environmental organizations, such as Turner Foundation, Pew Global Initiative, and Hewlett Packard, where there was investment of money, time, and resources into the environmental movement to assist in coming up with a way to tie population with the environment. However, conflicts over family planning and immigration prevented them from being able to accomplish these goals. This occurred particularly out of the public discussions that emanated from the UN conferences in Rio and Cairo, in making the connections between population and the environment. However, what the funding organizations like Pew and Hewlett-Packard found was that all of these groups have very different visions for how they see the world and how they see or define the problem. Without a common goal or definition, there are no ready-made solutions.

Anti-Population-Environmentalism

The catch phrase 'greening of hate' hit a raw nerve within the population-environment community, as it provoked an image of exclusiveness and protection. It is a polarizing and politicizing term, in that it pushed people into neutral territory for fear of being perceived as racist, and was seen as a catch-22 situation, which was a no-win for anyone. However, it also shone a light on a glaring crack in the structure of the environmental movement, where the movement did not necessarily represent the needs or issues of environmental protection for all (Pellow, 1999). Concerning the usage of 'greening of hate', it continues to be linked with any environmental discussion surrounding limits to immigration (Aufrecht, 2012). However, it is not just about migration as much as it is about the struggle over human rights versus societal goals (Taylor, 2000). It is not about who is a racist, but more about nativism versus globalism (Bonilla-Silva, 2003). It is about limited thinking within the constraints of a dominant paradigm of thought, as it pits the needs of individuals versus those of society overall (Loh and Gore, 1995; Sinding, 1993). The constraints of discourse came down to saving either the United States or the world, with images of 'us versus them' or 'must it be the rest against the west', with very little room for compromise (Dowie, 1995; Gottlieb, 1993).

This myopia continues to resonate in the mainstream environmental movement, as leaders are predominantly white people who represent middle-class American values. Shellenberger and Nordhaus (2004) argued that American environmentalism was ill-equipped to face massive global challenges, which require more long-term solutions than defense against the 'plunder-the-earth' and cornucopian corporate world philosophies and excess. However, the environmental movement has adjusted its vision and approach to a brave new globalized world, to focus on human rights and social justice for social change. Their call for a renewed political strategy encompasses a broader and more inclusive social movement and works to bridge environmental justice to merge with the civil rights orientation that initially drew crowds on that first Earth Day in 1970, and to build new partnerships for change. Any future dialogue connected to population-environmentalism, however, will continue to remain off the table because of the resultant stigmatization from anti-environmental influences. Nonetheless, it is obvious to anyone paying attention to the impacts of climate change how important population is.

REFERENCES

Abernethy, V. (1993) *Population Politics: The Choices That Shape Our Future*. New York, NY: Insight Books.

Alonso-Zaldivar, R. (2004) Census projects an America of greater racial diversity by 2050. *Los Angeles Times*. Available from: https://www.latimes.com/archives/la-xpm-2004-mar-18-na-census18-story.html.

Ashford, L.S. (2001) New population policies: Advancing women's health and rights. *Population Bulletin*. **56**(1). Available from: https://www.prb.org/wp-content/uploads/2001/03/56.1NewPopPoliciesWomen_Eng.pdf.

Aufrecht, M. (2012) Re-thinking 'Greening of Hate'. *Ethics and the Environment*. **17**(2), pp. 51–74.

Beck, R. and Kolankiewicz, L. (2000) The environmental movement's retreat from advocating U.S. population stabilization (1970–1998): A first draft of history. *Journal of Policy History*. **12**(1), pp. 123–56.

Benford, R.D. and Hunt, S.A. (1992) Dramaturgy and social movements: The social construction and communication of power. *Sociological Inquiry*. **62**(1), pp. 36–55.

Bonilla-Silva, E. (2003) *Racism Without Racists: Racism and the Persistence of Racial Inequality in the United States*. Lanham, MD: Rowman and Littlefield.

Bouvier, L.F. and Grant, L. (1994) *How Many Americans? Population, Immigration and the Environment*. San Francisco, CA: Sierra Club Books.

Brulle, R.J. (2000) *Agency, Democracy, and Nature: The U.S. Environmental Movement from a Critical Theory Perspective*. Cambridge, MA: MIT Press.

Camarota, S. (2005) Births to immigrants in America: 1970–2002. *Center for Immigration Studies*. Available from: https://cis.org/Report/Births-Immigrants-America-1970-2002.

Campbell, M.M. (1998) Schools of thought: An analysis of interest group influence in international population policy. *Population and Environment*. **19**(6), pp. 487–512.

Cohen, S.A. (1993) The road from Rio to Cairo: Toward a common agenda. *International Family Planning Perspectives*. **19**(2), pp. 61–71.

Cohn, D. (2005) Hispanic growth surge fueled by births in U.S. *Washington Post*. Available from: https://www.washingtonpost.com/archive/politics/2005/06/09/hispanic-growth-surge-fueled-by-births-in-us/3390d048-9c67-4638-95e6-ae485017f58b/.

Dixon-Mueller, R. (1993) *Population Policy and Women's Rights: Transforming Reproductive Choice*. Westport, CT: Praeger.

Dowie, M. (1995) *Losing Ground: American Environmentalism at the Close of the Twentieth Century*. Cambridge, MA: MIT Press.

Dunlap, R.E. and Mertig, A. (eds) (1992) *American Environmentalism: The U.S. Environmental Movement, 1970–1990*. Philadelphia, PA: Taylor and Francis.

Ehrlich, P. (1968) *The Population Bomb*. New York, NY: Sierra Club/Ballantine Books.

Ehrlich, P.R. and Holdren, J.P. (1971) Impact of population growth. *Science*. **171**(3977), pp. 1212–17.

Feagin, J.R. (2000) *Racist America: Roots, Current Realities, and Future Reparations*. New York, NY: Routledge Press.

Finkle, J. and McIntosh, C.A. (eds) (1994) *The New Politics of Population: Conflict and Consensus in Family Planning*. New York, NY: Population Council.

Frey, W.H. (1995) Immigration and internal migration 'flight': A California case study. *Population and Environment*. **16**(4). Available from: http://www.frey-demographer.org/reports/R-1995-4_ImmigrationInternal.pdf.

Gelobter, M., Dorsey, M., Fields, L., Goldtooth, T., Mendiratta, A., Moore, R., Morello-Frosch, R. et al. (2005) The soul of environmentalism: Rediscovering transformational politics in the 21st century. Oakland, CA: Redefining Progress. Available from: https://community-wealth.org/sites/clone.community-wealth.org/files/downloads/paper-gelobter-et-al.pdf.

Gottlieb, R. (1993) *Forcing the Spring: The Transformation of the American Environmental Movement*. Washington, DC: Island Press.

Greene, R. (1999) *Malthusian Worlds: US Leadership and the Governing of the Population Crisis*. Boulder, CO: Westview Press.

Habermas, J. (1984) *The Theory of Communicative Action, Volume One, Reason and the Rationalization of Society*. Boston, MA: Beacon Press.
Hardin, G. (1968) The tragedy of the commons. *Science*. **162**, pp. 1243–8.
Hardin, G. (1993) *Living Within Limits*. New York, NY: Oxford University Press.
Hodgson, D. and Watkins, S.C. (1997) Feminists and neo-Malthusians: Past and present alliances. *Population and Development Review*. **23**(3), pp. 469–523.
Hunt, S.A., Benford, R.D. and Snow, D.A. (1994) Identity fields: Framing processes and the social construction of movement identities. In: Larana, E., Johnston, H. and Gusfield, J.R. (eds) *New Social Movements: From Ideology to Identity*. Philadelphia, PA: Temple University Press, pp. 185–208.
Hunter, L.M. (2000) *The Environmental Implications of Population Dynamics*. Santa Monica, CA: RAND Corporation.
IOM (2003) World Migration Report. *International Organization for Migration*. Available from: https://www.iom.int/world-migration-report-2003
King, L. (2007) Charting a discursive field: Environmentalists for U.S. population stabilization. *Sociological Inquiry*. **77**(3), pp. 301–325.
Loh, P. and Gore, J. (1995) *Beyond Fear: Addressing Population and Sustainability Concerns in California*. EDGE Position Paper, Post-Conference Synthesis. Los Angeles, CA.
Lutton, W. and Tanton, J. (1994) *The Immigration Invasion*. Petoskey, MI: The Social Contract Press.
Lutz, W. and Shah, M. (2002) Population should be on the Johannesburg (UN Sustainable Development) agenda. *Nature*. **418**(17).
Mazur, L.M. (ed.) (2009) *A Pivotal Moment: Population, Justice and the Environmental Challenge*. Washington, DC: Island Press.
McIntosh, C.A. and Finkle, J. (1995) The Cairo conference on population and development: A new paradigm? *Population and Development Review*. **21**(2), pp. 223–60.
McMullin-Messier, P. (2006) Dissonance in the population-environment movement over the politics of immigration: Shifting paradigms of discourse vis-à-vis individual rights and societal goals. Unpublished Dissertation (Ph.D.), University of Southern California.
Meadows, D.L., Randers, J. and Behrens, W.W. (1972) *The Limits to Growth*. New York, NY: Universe.
Melosi, M.V. (2000) Environmental justice, political agenda setting, and the myths of history. *Journal of Policy History*. **12**(1), pp. 43–71.
Myrdal, G. (1944) *An American Dilemma: The Negro Problem and Modern Democracy*. New York, NY: Harper and Brothers Publishers.
Pellow, D.N. (1999) Framing emerging environmental movement tactics: Mobilizing consensus, demobilizing conflict. *Sociological Forum*. **14**(4), pp. 659–83.
Sebenius, J. (1991) *Negotiation Analysis, International Negotiation: Analysis, Approaches, Issues*. San Francisco, CA: Jossey-Bass Publishers.
Shellenberger, M. and Nordhaus, T. (2004) *The Death of Environmentalism: Global Warming Politics in a Post-Environmental World*. Presented at Environmental Grantmakers Association Meeting.
Silliman, J. and King, Y. (eds) (1999) *Dangerous Intersections: Feminist Perspectives on Population, Environment and Development*. Cambridge, MA: South End Press.
Sinding, S. (1993) Getting to replacement: Bridging the gap between individual rights and demographic goals. In: Senanayake, P. and Kleinman, R.L. (eds) *Family Planning: Policy Challenges, Priority Choices*. Lancaster: The Parthenon Publishing Group, pp. 23–34.
Taylor, D.E. (2000) The rise of the environmental justice paradigm: Injustice framing and the social construction of environmental discourses. *American Behavioral Scientist*. **43**(4), pp. 508–80.
Wilmoth, J.R. and Ball, P. (1995) Arguments and action in the life of a social problem: A case study of 'overpopulation', 1946–1990. *Social Problems*. **42**(3), pp. 318–43.

19. The environmental state and the racial state in tension: does racism impede environmentalism?
Ian R. Carrillo

INTRODUCTION

For scholars studying environment and sustainability, *the environmental state* has been the central framework for understanding the political economy of environmental change. The debate on the environmental state focuses on how the state mediates relations between business, society and the environment. Two competing views of the environmental state exist. Ecological modernization theory contends that the state can prod and goad market actors toward adopting sustainable practices, a goal achieved through green consumerism, business-friendly regulations, and technology. The treadmill of production (ToP) posits that the state is largely allied with pro-growth business groups who favor increasing pollution and oppose measures that sacrifice short-term profits to improve environmental outcomes.

While these two environmental state theories have been useful for investigating problems, politics and policy, they tend to obscure how race and racism shape the political economy of environmental change. This chapter argues that, rather than being a peripheral feature of environmental governance, race and racism are central for how the state and market determine the people and places that bear toxic burdens. In this sense, a discussion of political economy absent of race fails to understand the logic and mechanisms that produce anti-environmentalism.

By centering environmental politics and policy on the issues of race, with a focus on the US experience, this chapter engages long-standing debates on the role of the state in driving environmental change. I ask two interconnected questions: (1) How are race and racism building blocks for anti-environmentalism? (2) How does the state use race to impede environmentalist efforts? In answering these questions, I do not claim that race and racism are the sole explanatory forces for US anti-environmentalism. However, this chapter does claim that it is difficult to explain anti-environmentalism *without* accounting for race and racism. For instance, according to Coates (2017), an animating ideal for Trump, as the first of 43 white presidents to follow a black president, is to restore and redeem whiteness while rejecting his predecessor's pluralistic tendencies. While Trump stoked racial tensions to win votes to enact an anti-environmentalist agenda, centuries of racism laid the groundwork for such a strategy to be electorally viable.

In contrast to the environmental state, *the racial state* framework contends that a major objective for the US government has been to distribute resources, opportunities and privileges in a way that advantages whites and disadvantages black and brown communities (Omi and Winant, 1987). In this approach, race is an organizing principle of the political economy, with the state buttressing the racialized provision of power, wealth and resources. For the racial state, inequalities are neither an anomaly nor an aberration, but are rather the intended outcome of systemic design. The racial state framework thus challenges and contributes to the environmental state by delineating the mechanisms and processes that reproduce inequalities.

This chapter defines environmentalism in line with environmental justice, which is the 'principle that all people and communities are entitled to equal protection of environmental and public health laws and regulations' (Bullard, 1996, p. 493). In contrast, anti-environmentalism refers to an array of polluting practices that are the result of current activities or the accumulation of historical patterns. Examples of anti-environmentalism include, but are not limited to: toxins and other waste from chemical, extractive and industrial activities that contaminate homes, buildings, land, air and water; the discriminatory siting of hazardous facilities; CO_2 that contributes to planetary climate change; and discrimination, such as systemic racism and exclusion from democratic participation, that impedes an individual's or community's ability to mitigate an environmental risk.

The chapter comprises five sections. Following the introduction, the second section details how the racial state is an important lens for understanding how race influences the political economy of the environmental change. The third section illustrates how the provision of public goods and distribution of negative externalities follows racialized patterns. In the fourth section, I describe the relationship between racial identity politics, elections and anti-environmentalism. The fifth section concludes the chapter.

THE RACIAL STATE AND ENVIRONMENTAL STATE IN TENSION

Race scholars have long viewed the state as key to maintaining the racial hierarchy. In what they call *the racial state*, Omi and Winant (1987) argue that the state, as the principal interlocutor between businesses and society, creates, enshrines and enforces rules for the racial order. The state does so to reproduce the racial divisions that served as the basis of the nation's founding and subsequent development.

The racial state is important for racial formation, which refers to 'the sociohistorical process by which racial categories are created, inhabited, transformed, and destroyed' (Omi and Winant, 1987, p. 55). In this sense, race and racism are crucial to the formation of institutions, economic growth and social organization. Racial projects, the 'building block' of racial formation, function as 'an interpretation, representation, or explanation of racial dynamics, and a simultaneous effort to reorganize and redistribute resources along particular racial lines' (Omi and Winant, 1987, p. 56). Racial projects, such as slavery and the suppression of non-white voters, put into practice ideologies and beliefs. A principal objective of the state is to use laws, institutions and democratic mechanisms to help realize racial formation and racial projects, which are fundamental for the uneven distribution of resources.

This chapter argues that the racial state is also critical for the management of natural and environmental resources. Research shows that black and brown communities disproportionately bear environmental harms, while white communities tend to hoard environmental goods. The racial state plays an important role in this allocation of goods and risks, as it controls legislative mechanisms and resources and budgeting for regulatory activities. Thus, when the state considers environmental policy, similar to policies for housing, policing and immigration, race and racism deeply shape the political and regulatory process.

In the landmark book *The Environmental State Under Pressure* (Mol and Buttel, 2002), social scientists debated the state's role in the political economy of environmental change. Ecological modernization theory (EMT) takes an optimistic view of the state's ability to steer economic growth toward sustainability. In the chapter 'Ecological modernization and the environmental state', Mol and Spaargaren (2002) argue that one of the main reasons that traditional economic growth has produced environmental degradation is that societies and markets have failed to adequately value and price ecosystem resources. The state uses 'soft' means, such as promoting green consumerism, market-friendly regulations, and green technology, to reduce environmental harms while not threatening economic growth. For this reason, EMT sees voluntary transactions in the market, more so than state coercion, as the main pathway for resolving environmental problems. However, by taking a non-racial view of the political economy, EMT overlooks the role of race and racism in creating many negative externalities. This is problematic because EMT assumes that heightened morality will lead government, businesses and consumers to resolve environmental problems. For this prediction to materialize, there would need to be awareness and visibility of injustice coupled with a willingness of the major political economic actors to reverse the effects of racism. Thus, adopting an anti-racist consciousness is a requisite for EMT to fulfill its predictions, a stance the framework currently lacks.

In the chapter 'The treadmill of production and the environmental state', Schnaiberg et al. (2002) argue that the state's relationship with large businesses is based on a pro-growth outlook that facilitates exponential resource withdrawal from and waste expulsion into ecosystems. Within the treadmill, not only do big businesses capture governmental and democratic mechanisms to serve polluting interests, but workers also support treadmill acceleration by voting for candidates who remain committed to economic growth and employment stability. In studying the relationship between space and waste, ToP insightfully studies class, politics and technology, yet overlooks the influence of race and racism. This absence raises two issues. First, the long-held association between race and space in US society (Massey and Denton, 1993) means that many environmental problems are also racial problems. Second, we fail to understand how race shapes the 'spatial fix' (Harvey, 1982), which refers to the process of relocating polluting activities to a new geographic area with better conditions for investment. ToP scholars argue that, when polluters confront a barrier to profitability, such as a regulatory problem or technological bottleneck, they will often seek a spatial fix that allows the treadmill to continue accelerating. Yet, when seeking a spatial fix, government and businesses often see racial minority communities as ideal sites, as they are structurally vulnerable and lack the resources to resist siting and to demand removal and clean-up.

While racial inequalities are a main focus of the environmental justice literature, the forces of anti-environmentalism, particularly within the environmental state, have been under-examined. Some scholars use a racial framework to understand environmental politics and the state's relationship with polluters, but do not consider processes of treadmill deceleration or acceleration (Sbicca and Myers, 2017; Richter, 2017; Kurtz, 2009). Others investigate environmental justice conflicts, such as 'site fights' (Aldrich, 2008), within the ToP framework, but often take a citizenship approach that considers race and class on similar footing. For example, Weinberg et al. (2000) study working class resistance to waste siting in urban areas, while others analyze grassroots effort to politically challenge treadmill elites through a lens based on class and citizenship (Gould et al., 1996; Pellow, 2002; Sbicca, 2012).

Overall, the environmental state overlooks two important ways in which race and racism shape the political economy of environmental change. First, EMT fails to consider how race and racism often undergird the devaluation of environmental inputs and shape the distribution of negative externalities. Second, by taking a non-racial approach to the spatial fix, ToP undertheorizes how race influences polluting and dumping practices. Given that businesses and government consider vulnerable communities ideal for hazardous siting, it is important to consider how race and racism create the vulnerability necessary for economic growth. By not interrogating the role that race plays in creating and reproducing environmental problems, scholars and policymakers are likely to misdiagnose the origins of and solutions for environmental disparities. In contrast, the racial state offers a useful framework for understanding the institutional and structural mechanisms necessary to address environmental racism.

THE RACIALIZATION OF PUBLIC GOODS AND EXTERNALITIES

This section examines public goods and negative externalities to delineate the tension between the racial state and the environmental state. The state is primarily responsible for provisioning public goods and regulating externalities. A public good is a non-exclusive, non-rivalrous good that can be made available cheaply but is difficult to prevent others from consuming once available. Negative externalities are spillover costs, such as pollution, borne by third parties who were not involved in the initial transaction or production process. The state's regulation of externalities determines the distribution of environmental harms and the costs third parties bear. For instance, the state has the power to criminalize or neglect pollution, which makes environmental regulation an important public good in and of itself. This section details how: (1) the provision of public goods has been oriented to benefit whites; (2) whites are likely to withdraw support for public goods when non-whites benefit from their provision; and (3) negative externalities are disproportionately imposed on non-white populations.

In the US, an explicit aim of the state has been to provision public goods to advantage white populations. For instance, the federal government used the military, a classic public good, to seize ancestral land from Native Americans and Mexicans. Homesteading policies transferred millions of acres to European settlers throughout the nineteenth century. Federally enforced slave codes provided vast labor subsidies for agriculture and industry. After abolition, segregationist laws created racialized access to many public goods, such as housing, education, and labor protections (Feagin, 2006).

In the twentieth century, race was a guiding principle for the formation of the welfare state. Following the Great Depression, the US government instituted the New Deal, a Keynesian package of federal policies meant to stimulate the US economy through anti-poverty, housing, education, and employment subsidies targeting the working class. However, due to a racial bargain that Congress and the presidency struck during the legislative process, whites were able to systematically hoard the New Deal's middle-class opportunities (Quadagno, 1994). As Katznelson details in *When Affirmative Action Was White* (2005), in exchange for congressional votes, racially conservative Democrats from the south demanded that New Deal legislation make employment fields where African–Americans were overrepresented – domestic and agricultural work – ineligible for social security and minimum wage benefits. While white veterans accessed higher education through the G.I. Bill – a government program that provided former soldiers with college financing – black veterans were excluded because they were generally barred from enlisting in the military and, for those that did enlist, local military offices refused to disburse benefits. The Federal Housing Administration (FHA) – the federal program charged with executing government housing programs – underwrote mortgages for white homeowners, but denied financing for black and brown citizens and created the widespread segregation that exists today.

In the post-Civil Rights era, there is little evidence to suggest that the racialized provision of public goods has ceased. Reskin (2012) shows that race continues to be the primary factor that determines the quality of public goods that citizens can access. We also see that the state provides stronger environmental protection for white communities in comparison to minority communities, a tendency that is an extension of the historical patterns of discrimination that have long been part of the blueprint for economic growth and social organization in the US.

Race also contributes to the dismantling of public goods. Recent research demonstrates the linkages between racial backlash and public goods disinvestment. For instance, when whites perceive that their relative position in the racial status hierarchy is threatened, their resentment towards non-whites increases and they will reduce support for social safety net programs that are viewed as disproportionately benefiting minorities (Wetts and Willer, 2018). Moreover, when non-whites begin using public goods that whites have traditionally used, whites are likely to erect new barriers that impede non-white access (Enos, 2017).

In seeking to understand this racial backlash, scholars have studied how politicians use 'dog-whistle politics', speech that is racially coded but not explicitly racist, as a way to corrode white support for government programs. These discursive techniques became prominent following Civil Rights victories, when it became socially unacceptable to use explicitly racist speech and illegal to exclude non-whites from access to public goods (Mendelberg, 2001; Haney-Lopez, 2014). Since the 1970s, dog-whistle politics have been central to the electoral strategy of racial conservatives, who initially used the tactic in the Southern Strategy to prise whites aggrieved by Civil Rights victories away from the Democratic Party but eventually expanded the approach to the national level (Haney-Lopez, 2014).

These tactics followed the playbook of Lee Atwater, a pioneer of dog-whistle politics and the Southern Strategy, who was a former aide to Ronald Reagan and chief campaign strategist to George H.W. Bush. In an interview (Perlstein, 2012), Atwater described the logic behind using racially coded language as a way to turn white voters against government programs:

> You start out in 1954 by saying, 'n*****, n*****, n*****.' By 1968 you can't say 'n*****' – that hurts you, backfires. So you say stuff like forced busing, states' rights, and all that stuff, and you're getting so abstract. Now, you're talking about cutting taxes, and all these things you're talking about are totally economic things and a byproduct of them is, blacks get hurt worse than whites ... 'We want to cut this' is much more abstract than even the busing thing, and a hell of a lot more abstract than 'n*****, n*****'.

Atwater hypothesized that once you code a government program as a 'minority' program, it is much easier to convince white voters to support its elimination, even if whites benefit from it. Not only did Atwater's strategy provide a racial subtext for rolling back welfare programs, it also sought to discredit government intervention in general.

By creating the impression that state programs unfairly distribute resources and opportunities away from white populations, politicians created a permission structure in which they could disassemble public goods. This had important consequences for efforts to regulate environmental pollution. For instance, conservative politicians used coded racism not just to attack government programs, but also the principle of environmental regulation itself, thus creating white support for defunding the environmental protection agency (EPA), weakening air and water standards, and reneging on planetary climate agreements. In doing so, they undermined Nixon and Reagan's environmental achievements, such as founding the EPA, implementing federal acts for clean air and water, and signing the Montreal Protocol. In an ironic turn, Nixon and Reagan's early use of coded racism to delegitimize government contributed to the eventual undoing of their own environmental legacies. Importantly, these moments reveal how not only race shapes the formation of social policy, but also environmental policy.

Within this socio-historical context, it is unsurprising that we see the racialized distribution of negative externalities. The weight of evidence in environmental justice research shows that black and brown communities are more likely than white communities to be exposed to environmental hazards. Some studies provide snapshot, city-level documentation of toxic burdens. For example, research shows that black children in Chicago have higher rates of lead poisoning, and black neighborhoods in Detroit have greater exposure to industrial pollutants (Sampson and Winter, 2016; Downey, 2006). Other studies take a regional and national approach, finding that non-white populations are more likely to live near hazardous facilities, be exposed to airborne pollutants, and face environmental risks (Been, 1995; Ringquist, 2005; Daniels and Friedman, 1999; Ash and Fetter, 2004; Morello-Frosch and Jesdale, 2006; Downey and Hawkins, 2008; Downey et al., 2008; Bell and Ebisu, 2012; Zwickl et al., 2014).

Other longitudinal studies document changes in toxic exposure over time, the interaction between race, income and residential mobility, and the contexts in which siting decisions were made. Research at the city and state level uncovered relational dynamics whereby unwanted hazardous facilities were diverted from white neighborhoods to non-white neighborhoods, thus suggesting that the logic of racism and racial privilege shaped siting decisions (Hamilton, 1995; Pastor et al., 2001; Pulido, 2000; Saha and Mohai, 2005). National-level research shows that race remains consequential to environmental risks and toxic exposure over the life-course, even taking into account class and residential mobility (Crowder and Downey, 2010; Pais et al., 2014; Ard, 2015; Downey et al., 2017). Moreover, a national analysis over a 30-year period shows that polluting companies tend to target racial minority communities when making their siting decisions (Mohai and Saha, 2015).

Environmental justice research illustrates that there is a strong relationship between race, space and waste. These dynamics are outcomes of processes that were neither organic nor freely made, but rather materialized through explicit policies to achieve geographic and racial sorting. For example, in the twentieth century, New Deal policies institutionalized segregation in employment, housing and higher education policies, whereas 'sundown town' practices impeded the settlement of black Americans in rural areas outside of the south, further amplifying racial segregation in urban areas (Katznelson, 2005; Loewen, 2006; Miraftab, 2016).

These socio-historical processes force us to re-think the environmental state debates. Although ToP research emphasizes the spatial fix, the framework does not theorize how race is often the lynchpin that binds together the relationship between waste and space. I argue that the spatial fix is often a 'racial fix', as minority communities are often either targeted for polluting activities or have demands for clean-up neglected. This history shows that the racial state plays an important role in creating the residential segregation that makes environmental racism not only possible, but also efficient for government and business officials. That is, the suite of segregationist policies brings an efficiency to Not-In-My-Backyard-ism (NIMBY-ism) that may not otherwise exist. While EMT predicts that heightened morality in voluntary market transactions will foment sustainability, the historical and environmental evidence illustrates the scope and difficulty of such a path. Doing so requires widespread recognition of the relationship between racial segregation and environmental harms, as well as the consciousness and political will to undertake anti-racist actions that improve environmental outcomes.

There are three interrelated points to glean from the evidence on the racialized distribution of environmental harms. First, the relationship between race, space and waste has always been highly regulated. By segregating neighborhoods and racializing hazardous siting, government and business succeeded in ensuring that many environmental problems, such as lead poisoning in Flint, are coded as *minority* problems. Second, the geographic and racial removal of environmental problems enables white populations to deny and neglect the existence of such problems. Third, the weak political representation and economic strength of racial minority neighborhoods makes it likely that government and business elites can ignore environmental racism without suffering electoral or economic retribution. Above all, spatial and racial segregation makes possible an 'out of sight, out of mind' mentality that not only allows injustices to persist, but also makes such problems, once identified, difficult to resolve given pre-existing racial divisions. The next section elaborates on this point.

RACIAL IDENTITY POLITICS, ELECTIONS AND ANTI-ENVIRONMENTALISM

In November 2016, Donald Trump won the presidential election in spite of losing the popular vote to Hillary Clinton by 2.8 million votes. By winning about 80 000 votes across Michigan, Pennsylvania and Wisconsin, Trump eked out a victory in the Electoral College, the system of state-level delegations that actually determine presidential elections. Once inaugurated, the Trump administration enacted a broad anti-environmentalist agenda, including backing out of the Paris Climate Accord, weakening the rights of states to set their own air quality standards, and giving certain industries, such as fossil fuels, chemicals and auto, more freedom to pollute. In this section, I ask: how do race and racism influence the electability of anti-environmentalist politicians? To answer this question, I review (1) how the politics of whiteness shapes anti-environmentalism and (2) how the persistence of white majorities has been an explicit racial project.

Similar to Quadagno's (1994) claim that race was a guiding principle for the formation of welfare policy, I argue that white identity politics influences environmental policy. Recent research bolsters this assertion. For instance, whites are more likely than non-whites to have polarizing views on climate change (Schuldt and Pearson, 2016). These findings have implications for understanding the environmental politics of white liberals and conservatives. The former group has tended to dominate the environmental movement since the 1960s. Although these movements have won environmental victories, their organizational efforts tended to focus on white communities (Taylor, 2016). As Mohai et al. (2009) note, NIMBY-ism in white communities at times displaced hazardous facilities into minority communities. Moreover, the widespread belief among white liberals that the ideal approach to race relations is colorblindness, rather than anti-racism (Bonilla-Silva, 2003), has probably hindered addressing problems of environmental racism.

For conservatives, white identity politics is a key driver of anti-environmentalism. For example, racial prejudice is highly correlated with views on climate change and climate science, even when controlling for partisanship, ideology and education (Benegal, 2018). Hochschild (2016) finds that white Tea Party members – a far-right group who arose in opposition to the Obama presidency – in Louisiana harbor suspicion of government out of the belief that the federal government unfairly supports racial minorities and immigrants. Although these individuals live in highly polluted areas, their perception that government provides unfair advantages to non-whites contributes to their opposition to environmental regulation. Further, Willer et al. (2016) find that anxiety over a 'decline in whiteness' is the primary motivating factor for identifying as a Tea Party member. In this group, a major support base for Trump, 71 percent of members deny claims of anthropogenic climate change (Yale Project on Climate Change Communication, 2011).

Two additional social forces – evangelicalism and nativism – link whiteness and anti-environmentalism. During the Obama presidency, these forces helped push conservatives away from supporting modest environmental regulations, such as carbon taxes, and toward extreme opposition to any regulation. In the process, the Republican Party became the most anti-environmentalist conservative party among Western democracies (Batstrand, 2012).

Evangelicals comprise 35 percent of Trump's base of support, arguably making them the Republican Party's dominant constituency (Cox and Jones, 2017). A white Christian worldview has long permeated evangelicalism, with adherents seeing racial inequalities and white supremacy as ordained by God. Not only did many evangelicals display ardent support for Native American dispossession, slavery and Jim Crow, but they also backed the dog-whistle politics that helped to delegitimize and dismantle government social programs (Dochuk, 2010; Harvey, 2005; Noll, 2010). Furthermore, the perception among evangelicals that the white Christian worldview was under assault from the Obama administration spurred a backlash in which 81 percent of evangelicals voted for Trump, a bigger share than the past four elections (Smith and Martinez, 2016; Wong, 2018).

This worldview also shapes environmental politics. Among evangelicals, 72 percent do not support the claim of anthropogenic climate change, the highest of any religious group (Funk and Alper, 2015). Such skepticism is grounded in the belief that God has given humans dominion over nature, which puts the anthropogenic thesis fundamentally at odds with God's desires for humanity. Trump's first EPA director, Scott Pruitt, a devout evangelical, used this logic to deregulate polluting activities, arguing that government intervention to mediate environmental problems is an attack on heavenly endowed personal liberty. In criticizing the notion that human activity harms the climate, Pruitt stated: 'The biblical worldview with respect to these issues is that we have a responsibility to manage and cultivate, harvest the natural resources that we've been blessed with to truly bless our fellow mankind' (Brody, 2018).

Nativism – the idea that descendants of Europeans are the rightful benefactors of the US project – is an animating principle for the white conservative base. Racial resentment, rather than economic anxiety, was the main predictor for casting a vote for Trump (McElwee and McDaniel, 2017; Fowler et al., 2017), who stoked the racial anxiety of white voters, particularly by conflating the growing non-white population with American decline. Other empirical research bolsters the association between demographic change and increasingly conservative racial attitudes among whites (Richeson and Sommers, 2016; Craig, Rucker, and Richeson, 2018; Sides et al., 2018a, 2018b). Key statements and policies – the border wall, the separation of immigrant families, the disparagement of Black Lives Matter activists, the Muslim ban, and defending white supremacists – place nativist issues at the forefront of Trump's agenda for campaigning and governing. Through these strategies, Trump has not only enacted an anti-environmentalist agenda, but also has appointed conservative judges who will use the courts to impede environmentalist legislation for decades.

Evangelicalism and nativism are therefore twin forces for electing anti-environmentalist politicians. For the former, government policies that seek to redress racial discrimination and environmental problems are viewed as an affront to God's will. For the latter, a perceived loss in racial status and diminishing racial advantages triggers a panic among aggrieved whites. Nativism and evangelicalism in this context operate as counter-revolutionary forces that seek to restore the status quo (Robin, 2017), in which anti-environmentalism is both a cause and consequence.

To understand how the anti-environmentalist tendencies of white identity politics translate into real-world policies, it is important to examine the racial projects that produce white majorities. Three racial projects are notable. First, immigration policies consistently impeded the entry of non-whites into the US. For example, the 1924 Immigration Act codified eugenics logic in population policies. The Act gave preferential treatment to Western Europeans, who were perceived to be ideal, and denied entry to Africans, Latin Americans, Asians and European Jews, who were considered genetically inferior and thus not suited to be part of the US project. This immigration policy was critical for replenishing the white population and slowing non-white population growth, thus reproducing white majoritarian status throughout the twentieth century.

Second, the electoral mechanisms of US democracy have been oriented to favor whites over non-whites. As Feagin (2012) shows, this tendency has centuries-long roots. Slaveholding states, whose large non-citizen population disadvantaged them in national elections, lobbied to institute the Electoral College, thus blocking the emergence of a one-person-one-vote system for presidential elections. Even after black citizens won the right to vote, whites erected barriers to suppress black voter turnout, including poll taxes, literacy tests and lynching.

The third racial project involves suppressing non-white voting power in an era of declining white majoritarian status. After the 1965 Voting Rights Act, racially conservative politicians devised new strategies to hinder minority voters, such as barring felons from voting and implementing new identification requirements for voting (The Sentencing Project, 2014; Brennan Center, 2017). Proponents of such programs claim they are necessary to combat widespread voter fraud carried out by non-white citizens and immigrants, accusations that research reveals to be non-existent (Ansolabehere et al., 2014; Huseman, 2018). Racial conservatives have also intensified gerrymandering, a strategy in which political parties redraw electoral maps to win more seats with fewer votes. Analyses show that Republicans benefit more from gerrymandering than Democrats, with black and brown voting power especially diluted (Lieb, 2017). As demographic shifts threaten white majoritarian status, the Trump administration had manipulated the US census to re-allocate electoral power from growing non-white populations to shrinking white populations. Many racially conservative politicians see these voter suppression strategies as the only pathway to power, as Republicans have won the popular vote for president just once since 1992 (Alston, 2017; Scherer, 2018; Gelman and Kremp, 2016). Overall, these three racial projects consistently preserved white voting power through both majoritarian and counter-majoritarian strategies, thus helping translate the anti-environmentalism of white identity politics into public policy.

As Ashwood and MacTavish (2016) argue, majoritarian status confers a utilitarianism whereby it is simply logical for democracy and capitalism to fulfill the majority's will. If minorities speak out to have their grievances addressed, majority defenders will argue that doing so runs counter to the logic and reason of utilitarianism. The problems of minority communities will appear foreign and non-mainstream, making it less likely that politicians will seek solutions. This is especially true in cases of environmental injustice, when the business community, elected officials, and courts side with the majority's view that it is politically and economically expedient to dump costs on minority communities (Taylor, 2014). However, as white majoritarian status declines at the national level, racial conservatives increasingly seek to discredit majoritarianism, as it no longer confers the advantages it once did (Robin, 2020).

While the racial state framework sees the previous examples of racial projects as explicit goals of the government, the environmental state struggles to theorize how capitalism and democracy reproduce environmental racism. On the one hand, ToP considers vulnerable communities and spaces as ideal sites for siting the environmental harms that underpin economic growth. However, as this section shows, the racialized way in which the US historically constructed white majoritarian status means that politicians and business leaders often steer unwanted polluting and dumping into minority communities. Moreover, the persistence of white majoritarian status often means that racial minority communities lack the resources to achieve environmental justice. On the other hand, EMT assumes that a majority of consumers and voters are likely to pressure business and government to bring negative externalities internal to the market. Yet, the US's socio-historical experience indicates that business and government are likely to neglect the environmental problems of racial minority communities, as minorities lack the democratic and economic power to influence electoral politics and white voters who comprise the majority will likely not prioritize the environmental problems that afflict minority communities.

For Pulido et al. (2019), Trump used 'spectacular racism' and white supremacy to elevate his anti-environmentalist agenda. While Trump was the most visible manifestation of white supremacist tendencies, whiteness operates in complex ways to shape the electoral politics that underpin environmental policymaking. As Coates (2017) notes, despite the fact that Trump voters had above average income, the 2016 election saw the fetishization of the white working class across the political spectrum. For instance, *The New York Times*' liberal columnist Nicholas Kristof denied that Trump's racist appeals may be tapping into authentic racist attitudes in the white working class, whereas Bernie Sanders chastised Latinx identity politics while celebrating the identity politics of the white working class. Coates elaborates on the double-standard between sympathy for working-class whites and punishment for working-class blacks:

> Black workers suffer because it was and is our lot. But when white workers suffer, something in nature has gone awry. And so an opioid epidemic among mostly white people is greeted with calls for compassion and treatment, as all epidemics should be, while a crack epidemic among mostly black people is greeted with scorn and mandatory minimums. Sympathetic op-ed columns and articles are devoted to the plight of working-class whites when their life expectancy plummets to levels that, for blacks, society has simply accepted as normal ... This dynamic serves a very real purpose: the consistent awarding of grievance and moral high ground to that class of workers which, by the bonds of whiteness, stands closest to America's aristocratic class.

Given this double-standard and the fact that the racial conservatism is considered a centrist position in the US, there is a higher price to be paid for anti-racism than racism in electoral politics.

CONCLUSION

This chapter asks two questions: (1) How are race and racism building blocks for anti-environmentalism? (2) How does the state use race to impede environmentalist efforts? I answer these questions by drawing from racial formation theory, which conceptualizes the state as an entity that organizes the distribution of power and resources along racial lines. With race as an organizing principle of the political economy, the state is an important mediator between business and society. The state has been critical in ensuring not only that the provision of public goods and the distribution of negative externalities follow racialized patterns, but also that the balance of power remain in favor of anti-environmentalist voters, politicians and businesses.

This chapter delineates the tension between the racial state and the environmental state. For ToP, systemic and structural racism not only devalue non-white communities to make them ideal locations for hazardous siting, but weakened power in democracy and capitalism also means that such communities have fewer resources to resist. In this sense, race and racism are fundamentally important for the political economy, as they create the conditions that make the spatial fix possible, thus allowing the treadmill to continue accelerating. While the EMT model assumes that heightened morality among businesses, consumers and government will reduce negative externalities, its non-racial approach views the environmental problems that afflict white and non-white communities as having the same origins and solutions. The US's socio-historical development illustrates that realizing EMT predictions requires adopting an anti-racist approach to environmental policymaking.

It is also important to consider how white supremacist ideology shapes environmental policy formation within the context of settler colonialism, as found in, among other places, Australia, New Zealand, Canada and the US. For Whyte (2016), there are three main pillars that bind together settler colonialism and environmental injustice. The first are moral terrains, which constitute 'the web of value layered over places through discourse that establish normative practices and socio-environmental belonging' (Figueroa and Waitt, 2008, p. 328). For instance, the touristic climbing of the Uluru rock in Australia's Uluru-Kata Tjuta National Park violates the Anangu people's Tjukurpa law, which considers moral and biophysical processes to co-exist in the sacred Uluru. The second pillar – systems of responsibility – refers to the idea that a complex ecosystem exists in which material and nonmaterial entities operate interdependently to support Indigenous peoples. With each entity, such as water, plants, animals and humans, each seeking to fulfill their specific responsibilities, they can jointly continue living. However, acts of environmental injustice, such as water pollution, can impede one or more entities from fulfilling their responsibilities, thus upending the entire system. Third, collective continuance refers to the notion that systems of responsibilities can adapt to outside change, such as ecological shifts or man-made change, while keeping their primary internal features intact. For Whyte (2016, p. 166): 'Collective continuance is relevant to EJ because if one society interferes with or erases another society's capacity to adapt to external forces, then the former society – in promotion of its own self-interest – can impose preventable harm on the latter society's members.' These three pillars illustrate how environmental injustice is a key instrument in settler colonial projects for undermining Indigenous societies and imposing racial domination. However, following Roediger and Esch (2014), this settler colonial perspective should be viewed as complementary to, rather than competing with, an anti-blackness framework. In the US, the ideological justification for native genocide and land dispossession was critically aided by the slave plantation experience, where white supremacist ideas around race, labor and business management were honed and extended into settler colonialist projects.

Finally, what is the path forward? By offering a critical perspective on how race and racism influence anti-environmentalism, this chapter lays out the scope of the challenges ahead. Above all, a commitment to anti-racism is imperative for resolving environmental problems and promoting sustainability. While a colorblind approach is ineffective against the historical and institutional inertia of racism, the *existing* forces of racism that energize environmental injustice can only be combated with anti-racist tactics. Several strategies include, but are not limited to: (1) Empower local communities to use democratic and legal means to resist hazardous siting; (2) Reduce segregation and promote integrated communities; (3) Eliminate gerrymandering and encourage competitive elections; (4) Increase democratic access for all citizens; and (5) Strengthen environmental regulations, including the capacity to enforce laws, cite offenders, and collect fines. Such strategies can provide countervailing forces to the logic and mechanisms that currently guide democracy, capitalism and social organization in the US.

REFERENCES

Aldrich, D. (2008) *Site Fights*. Ithaca, NY: Cornell University Press.
Alston, J. (2017) The rust belt elevated Trump, but its electoral power is dwindling. *FiveThirtyEight* (online). Available from: https://fivethirtyeight.com/features/the-rust-belt-elevated-trump-but-its-electoral-power-is-dwindling/ (accessed 1 March 2017).
Ansolabehere, S., Luks, S. and Schaffner, B. (2014) The perils of cherry picking low frequency events in large sample surveys. *Electoral Studies*. **40**, pp. 409–410.
Ard, K. (2015) Trends in exposure to industrial toxins for different racial and socioeconomic groups: A spatial and temporal examination of environmental inequality in the U.S. from 1995 to 2004. *Social Science Research*. **53**, pp. 375–90.
Ash, M. and Fetter, T.R. (2004) Who lives on the wrong side of the environmental tracks? Evidence from the EPA's risk-screening environmental indicators model. *Social Science Quarterly*. **85**(2), pp. 441–62.
Ashwood, L. and MacTavish, K. (2016) Tyranny of the majority and rural environmental injustice. *Journal of Rural Studies*. **47**, pp. 271–7.
Batstrand, S. (2012) More than markets: A comparative study of nine conservative parties on climate change. *Politics & Policy*. **43**(4), pp. 538–61.
Been, V. (1995) Analyzing evidence of environmental justice. *Journal of Land Use and Environmental Law*. **11**(1), pp. 1–36.
Bell, M. and Ebisu, K. (2012) Environmental inequality in exposures to airborne particulate matter components in the United States. *Environmental Health Perspectives*. **120**(12), pp. 1699–705.
Benegal, S. (2018) The spillover of race and racial attitudes into public opinion about climate change. *Environmental Politics*. **4**, pp. 733–56.
Bonilla-Silva, E. (2003) *Racism without Racists: Color-Blind Racism and the Persistence of Racial Inequality in the United States*. Lanham, MD: Rowman & Littlefield.
Brennan Center (2017) Debunking the voter fraud myth. *Brennan Center for Justice* (online). Available from: https://www.brennancenter.org/analysis/debunking-voter-fraud-myth (accessed 30 March 2018).
Brody, D. (2018) Unraveling the 'weaponization' of the EPA is top priority for Scott Pruitt. *CBNNews* (online). Available from: http://www1.cbn.com/cbnnews/us/2018/february/unraveling-the-weaponization-of-the-epa-is-top-priority-for-scott-pruitt (accessed 1 June 2018).
Bullard, R. (1996) Environmental justice: More than waste facility siting. *Social Science Quarterly*. **77**, pp. 493–9.

Coates, T. (2017) The first white president. *The Atlantic* (online). Available from: https://www.theatlantic.com/magazine/archive/2017/10/the-first-white-president-ta-nehisi-coates/537909/ (accessed 1 June 2018).

Cox, D. and Jones, R. (2017) America's changing religious identity. *Public Religion Research Institute* (online). Available from: https://www.prri.org/research/american-religious-landscape-christian-religiously-unaffiliated/ (accessed 15 January 2018).

Craig, M., Rucker, J. and Richeson, J. (2018) Racial and political dynamics of an approaching 'majority-minority' United States. *Annals of the American Academy of Political and Social Science.* **677**(1), pp. 204–14.

Crowder, K. and Downey, L. (2010) Inter-neighborhood migration, race, and environmental hazards: Modeling microlevel processes of environmental inequality. *American Journal of Sociology.* **115**(4), pp. 1110–49.

Daniels, G. and Friedman, S. (1999) Spatial inequality and the distribution of industrial toxic releases: Evidence from the 1990 TRI. *Social Science Quarterly.* **80**(2), pp. 244–62.

Dochuk, D. (2010) *From Bible Belt to Sunbelt*. New York, NY: W.W. Norton.

Downey, L. (2006) Environmental racial inequality in Detroit. *Social Forces.* **85**(2), pp. 771–96.

Downey, L. and Hawkins, B. (2008) Race, income, and environmental inequality in the United States. *Sociological Perspectives.* **51**(4), pp. 759–81.

Downey, L., Crowder, K. and Kemp, R.J. (2017) Family structure, residential mobility, and environmental inequality. *Journal of Marriage and Family.* **79**(2), pp. 535–55. Available from DOI:10.1111/jomf.12355.

Downey, L., Dubois, S., Hawkins, B. and Walker, M. (2008) Environmental inequality in metropolitan America. *Organization & Environment.* **21**(3), pp. 270–94.

Enos, R. (2017) *The Space between Us*. Cambridge: Cambridge University Press.

Feagin, J. (2006) *Systemic Racism: A Theory of Oppression*. New York, NY: Routledge.

Feagin, J. (2012) *White Party, White Government: Race, Class, and U.S. Politics*. New York, NY: Routledge.

Figueroa, R. and Waitt, G. (2008) Cracks in the mirror: (Un)covering the moral terrains of environmental justice at Uluru-Kata Tjuta National Park. *Ethics, Place, & Environment.* **11**(3), pp. 327–49.

Fowler, M., Medenica, V. and Cohen, C. (2017) Why 41 percent of white millennials voted for Trump. *Washington Post* (online). Available from: https://www.washingtonpost.com/news/monkey-cage/wp/2017/12/15/racial-resentment-is-why-41-percent-of-white-millennials-voted-for-trump-in-2016/?utm_term=.abc17a5e4296 (accessed 30 January 2018).

Funk, C. and Alper, B. (2015) Religion and views on climate and energy issues. *Pew Research Center* (online). Available from: http://www.pewinternet.org/2015/10/22/religion-and-views-on-climate-and-energy-issues/ (accessed 15 January 2018).

Gelman, A. and Kremp, P.A. (2016) The electoral college magnifies the power of white voters. *Vox* (online). Available from: https://www.vox.com/the-big-idea/2016/11/22/13713148/electoral-college-democracy-race-white-voters (accessed 1 March 2017).

Gould, K., Weinberg, A. and Schnaiberg, A. (1996) *Local Environmental Struggles*. Cambridge: Cambridge University Press.

Hamilton, J. (1995) Politics and social costs: Estimating the impact of collective action on hazardous waste facilities. *RAND Journal of Economics.* **24**(1), pp. 101–25.

Haney-Lopez, I. (2014) *Dog Whistle Politics*. New York, NY: Oxford University Press.

Harvey, D. (1982) *Limits to Capital*. London: Verso Books.

Harvey, P. (2005) *Freedom's Coming*. Chapel Hill, NC: University of North Carolina Press.

Hochschild, A. (2016) *Strangers in their Own Land*. New York, NY: The New Press.

Huseman, J. (2018) How the case for voter fraud was tested – and utterly failed. *ProPublica* (online). Available from: https://www.propublica.org/article/kris-kobach-voter-fraud-kansas-trial (accessed 1 July 2018).

Katznelson, I. (2005) *When Affirmative Action Was White*. New York, NY: W.W. Norton and Company.

Kurtz, H. (2009) Acknowledging the racial state: An agenda for environmental justice research. *Antipode.* **41**(4), pp. 684–704.

Lieb, D. (2017) Analysis indicates partisan gerrymandering has benefited GOP. *Associated Press.* Available from: https://apnews.com/fa6478e10cda4e9cbd75380e705bd380/AP-analysis-shows-how

-gerrymandering-benefited-GOP-in-2016?utm_campaign=SocialFlow&utm_source=Twitter&utm_medium=AP (accessed 1 February 2018).

Loewen, J. (2006) *Sundown Towns: A Hidden Dimension of American Racism*. New York, NY: Touchstone.

Massey, D. and Denton, N. (1993) *American Apartheid*. Cambridge, MA: Harvard University Press.

McElwee, S. and McDaniel, J. (2017) Economic anxiety didn't make people vote Trump, racism did. *The Nation* (online). https://www.thenation.com/article/economic-anxiety-didnt-make-people-vote-trump-racism-did/ (accessed 1 November 2017).

Mendelberg, T. (2001) *The Race Card*. Princeton, NJ: Princeton University Press.

Miraftab, F. (2016) *Global Heartland*. Bloomington, IN: Indiana University Press.

Mohai, P. and Saha, R. (2015) Which came first, people or pollution? Assessing the disparate siting and post-siting demographic change hypotheses of environmental injustice. *Environmental Research Letters*. **10**(12), pp. 1–18.

Mohai, P., Pellow D. and Roberts, J.T. (2009) Environmental justice. *Annual Review of Environment and Resources*. **34**, pp. 405–30.

Mol, A. and Buttel, F. (eds) (2002) *The Environmental State Under Pressure*. Bingley: Emerald Insight.

Mol, A. and Spaargaren, G. (2002) Ecological modernization and the environmental state. In: Mol, A. and Buttel, F. (eds) *The Environmental State Under Pressure*. Bingley: Emerald Insight, pp. 33–52.

Morello-Frosch, R. and Jesdale, B. (2006) Separate and unequal: Residential segregation and estimated cancer risks associated with ambient air toxics in U.S. metropolitan areas. *Environmental Health Perspectives*. **114**(3), pp. 386–94.

Noll, M. (2010) *God and Race in American Politics*. Princeton, NJ: Princeton University Press.

Omi, M. and Winant, H. (1987) *Racial Formation in the United States*. New York, NY: Routledge.

Pais, J., Crowder, K. and Downey, L. (2014) Unequal trajectories: Racial and class differences in residential exposure to industrial hazard. *Social Forces*. **92**(3), pp. 1189–215.

Pastor, M., Sadd, J. and Hipp, J. (2001) Which came first? Toxic facilities, minority move-in, and environmental justice. *Journal of Urban Affairs*. **23**(1), pp. 1–21.

Pellow, D. (2002) *Garbage Wars*. Cambridge, MA: MIT Press.

Perlstein, R. (2012) Exclusive: Lee Atwater's infamous 1981 interview on the southern strategy. *The Nation* (online). Available from: https://www.thenation.com/article/exclusive-lee-atwaters-infamous-1981-interview-southern-strategy/ (accessed 30 January 2018).

Pulido, L. (2000) Rethinking environmental racism: White privilege and urban development in southern California. *Annals of the Association of American Geographers*. **90**(1), pp. 12–40.

Pulido, L., Bruno, T., Faiver-Serna, C. and Galentine, C. (2019) Environmental deregulation, spectacular racism, and white nationalism in the Trump era. *Annals of the American Association of Geographers*. **109**(2), pp. 520–32.

Quadagno, J. (1994) *The Color of Welfare*. New York, NY: Oxford University Press.

Reskin, B. (2012) The race discrimination system. *Annual Review of Sociology*. **38**, pp. 17–35.

Richeson, J. and Sommers, S. (2016) Toward a social psychology of race and race relations for the twenty-first century. *Annual Review of Psychology*. **67**, pp. 439–63.

Richter, L. (2017) Constructing insignificance: Critical race perspectives on institutional failure in environmental justice communities. *Environmental Sociology*. **4**(1), pp. 107–21.

Ringquist, E. (2005) Assessing evidence of environmental inequities: A meta-analysis. *Journal of Policy Analysis and Management*. **24**(2), pp. 223–47.

Robin, C. (2017) *The Reactionary Mind*. New York, NY: Oxford University Press.

Robin, C. (2020) The tyranny of the minority, from Iowa caucus to Electoral College. *The New York Review of Books*. Available from: https://www.nybooks.com/daily/2020/02/21/the-tyranny-of-the-minority-from-iowa-caucus-to-electoral-college/ (accessed 24 February 2020).

Roediger, D. and Esch, E. (2014) *The Production of Difference: Race and the Management of Labor in U.S. History*. New York, NY: Oxford University Press.

Saha, R. and Mohai, P. (2005). Historical context and hazardous waste facility siting: Understanding temporal patterns in Michigan. *Social Problems*. **52**(4), pp. 618–48.

Sampson, R. and Winter, A. (2016) The racial ecology of lead poisoning: Toxic inequality in Chicago neighborhoods, 1995–2013. *Du Bois Review*. **2**, pp. 261–83.

Sbicca, J. (2012) Elite and marginalised actors in toxic treadmills: Challenging the power of the state, military, and economy. *Environmental Politics*. **21**(3), pp. 467–85.

Sbicca, J. and Myers, J. (2017) Food justice racial projects: Fighting racial neoliberalism from the Bay to the Big Apple. *Environmental Sociology*. **3**(1), pp. 30–41.

Scherer, M. (2018) Potential citizenship question in 2020 census could shift power to rural America. *Washington Post* (online). Available from: https://www.washingtonpost.com/politics/potential-citizenship-question-in-2020-census-could-shift-power-to-rural-america/2018/01/23/c4e6d2c6-f57c-11e7-beb6-c8d48830c54d_story.html (accessed 30 March 2018).

Schnaiberg, A., Pellow, D. and Weinberg, A. (2002) The treadmill of production and the environmental state. In: Mol, A. and Buttel, F. (eds) *The Environmental State Under Pressure*. Bingley: Emerald Insight, pp. 15–32.

Schuldt, J.P. and Pearson, A.R. (2016). The role of race and ethnicity in climate change polarization: Evidence from a U.S. national survey experiment. *Climatic Change*. **136**(3), pp. 495–505. Available from DOI: 10.1007/s10584-016-1631-3.

The Sentencing Project (2014) Felony disenfranchisement laws in the United States. *The Sentencing Project*. Available from: https://www.sentencingproject.org/publications/felony-disenfranchisement-laws-in-the-united-states/ (accessed 1 April 2018).

Sides, J., Tesler, M. and Vavreck, L. (2018a) Hunting where the ducks are: Activating support for Donald Trump in the 2016 Republican primary. *Journal of Elections, Public Opinion and Parties*. **28**(2), pp. 135–56.

Sides, J., Tesler, M. and Vavreck, L. (2018b) *Identity Crisis*. Princeton, NJ: Princeton University Press.

Smith, G. and Martinez, J. (2016) How the faithful voted: A preliminary 2016 analysis. *Pew Research Center*. Available from: http://www.pewresearch.org/fact-tank/2016/11/09/how-the-faithful-voted-a-preliminary-2016-analysis/ (accessed 15 January 2018).

Taylor, D. (2014) *Toxic Communities: Environmental Racism, Industrial Pollution, and Residential Mobility*. New York, NY: New York University Press.

Taylor, D. (2016) *The Rise of the American Conservation Movement: Power, Privilege, and Environmental Protection*. Durham, NC: Duke University Press.

Weinberg, A, Pellow, D. and Schnaiberg, A. (2000) *Urban Recycling and the Search for Sustainable Community Development*. Princeton, NJ: Princeton University Press.

Wetts, R. and Willer, R. (2018) Privilege on the precipice: Perceived racial status threats lead white Americans to oppose welfare programs. *Social Forces*. **97**(2), pp. 793–822.

Whyte, K. (2016) Indigenous experience, environmental justice and settler colonialism. In: Bannon, B. (eds) *Nature and Experience: Phenomenology and the Environment*. London: Rowman & Littlefield Publishers, pp. 157–74.

Willer, R., Feinberg, M. and Wetts, R. (2016) Threats to racial status promote tea party support among white Americans. *SSRN Working Paper*. Available from: https://ssrn.com/abstract=2770186.

Wong, J. (2018) *Immigrants, Evangelicals, and Politics in an Era of Demographic Change*. New York, NY: Russell Sage Foundation.

Yale Project on Climate Change Communication (2011) Politics & global warming. *Yale Project on Climate Change Communication*. Available from: http://climatecommunication.yale.edu/wp-content/uploads/2016/02/2011_09_Politics-and-Global-Warming.pdf (accessed 15 January 2018).

Zwickl, K., Ash, M. and Boyce, J. (2014) Regional variation in environmental inequality: Industrial air toxics exposure in U.S. cities. *Ecological Economics*. **107**, pp. 494–509.

PART IX

OTHER SPHERES OF ANTI-ENVIRONMENTALISM

20. Skin in the game: the struggle over climate protection within the US labor movement
Todd E. Vachon

> Climate change, to those of us who don't believe in voodoo but believe in science, is a real serious concern ... There is a group of people who are committed to gaining employment any way you can have it ... That's unfortunate. We have to be more thoughtful about the impact.
> Larry Hanley, Amalgamated Transit Workers Union[1]

> Some of our so-called brothers and sisters in the trade union movement have abandoned solidarity with the working class and are instead throwing in with environmentalists ... it will not put a single one of their members to work yet they choose to take food off of our members' tables.
> Terry O'Sullivan, Laborer's International Union of North America[2]

Jobs vs. the environment. That has been the mantra of the mainstream media when it comes to unionized workers and environmental issues in the United States (US). High-profile cases like the struggle between unionized construction workers and environmentalists over the Keystone XL Pipeline have served as great news stories for media outlets that have portrayed labor unions as anti-environmental organizations. Like other entities engaged in anti-environmentalism, these unions have attempted, and in many cases succeeded, in countering the demands made by environmentalists, by diminishing public concern about the environment, attacking environmental activists, and persuading elected officials to oppose increased environmental regulation (Beder, 1997; Helvarg, 1994; Rowell, 1996). However, it is equally important to note the countless instances of labor advocacy for the environment, such as joint support for environmental legislation like the Clean Air and Clean Water Acts (Obach, 2004; Dewey, 1998), support for renewable energy projects in the northeast (Cha and Skinner, 2017), and recent research that has found union members to hold more pro-environmental attitudes than the general public (Vachon and Brecher, 2016). To be sure, there are specific instances in which some unions clash with environmental interests and others when they cooperate, but the outstanding question remains: what factors lead some unions to engage in anti-environmental activity?

This chapter will partially answer that question by surveying some of the major political-economic, institutional, and cultural explanations for anti-environmental behavior by unions. In particular, the chapter will focus on the case of climate change and efforts by some unions to undermine efforts to reduce greenhouse gas (GHG) emissions in the US. Based in part on data from participant observation with three labor–climate movement organizations and 34 in-depth interviews with union leaders, this chapter will proceed in four sections. First, a brief history of labor–environmental relations in the US to provide context for readers unfamiliar with the labor movement. Second, an examination of the major political-economic, institutional, and cultural explanations for opposition to climate protection measures by some unions.[3] Third, an introduction to the nascent labor–climate movement working within the US labor movement to overcome these many structural barriers and move labor as a whole to a more progressive stance on this crucial issue. Finally, a step back away from the US case to consider broader implications for understanding the relationship between organized labor and anti-environmentalism.

Although severely weakened in recent decades, unions still hold a considerable amount of political influence in the US, particularly at the state and local level (Vachon and Wallace, 2013). Understanding the causes for resistance to climate protection by some unions provides valuable insight into the types of policies and actions that are needed to build the broad-based consensus required to adequately address the climate crisis (Brecher, 2017). Unlike previous environmental protections that have spurred jobs vs. the environment clashes, climate change poses an 'existential threat' to the very existence of humanity, making the questions posed in this chapter even more urgent (Xu and Ramanathan, 2017).

A HISTORY OF CONFLICT AND COOPERATION

The history of labor–environmental relations in the US is a story both of conflict and of cooperation, of campaigns for healthy workplaces and communities and of jobs vs. the environment clashes.[4] Dating back to at least the 1940s, labor's initial involvement with environmental issues has frequently been an extension of its concern with health and safety issues inside the workplace to the effect of industrial processes outside the workplace. From anti-pollution campaigns to wilderness preservation, the labor movement in the decades immediately following World War II in many ways helped lay the foundation for what would become the modern environmental movement decades later (Dewey, 1998).

Early Labor-Environmentalism

A seminal event for labor-environmentalism occurred on Halloween night, 1948 in Donora, Pennsylvania, when fluoride released by plants of the US Steel Corporation caused a toxic cloud that killed 20 people and left hundreds of others sick. The 'Donora death fog', as it was called, led the then recently formed United Steelworkers (USW) union to recognize the close connection between environmental issues in the plant and those in surrounding communities (Obach, 2004). As a result, the union became a strong supporter of environmental protection (Mayer, 2009). By 1958, national labor representatives regularly testified in favor of federal proposals to control pollution, and American Federation of Labor-Council of Industrial Organizations (AFL-CIO) officials served on the steering committees for the first two National Conferences on Air Pollution in 1958 and 1962. In 1963 USW supported the very first Clean Air Act (Vachon and Brecher, 2016).

In addition to these early anti-pollution efforts, the AFL-CIO also recognized the need to conserve land for recreation use by workers who lived and toiled in industrial cities which lacked wild spaces. In testimony in support of the bill to create the National Wilderness Preservation System in 1958, AFL-CIO legislative representative George D. Riley stated: 'We [also] favor the preservation of wilderness areas for reasons other than recreation. Wilderness has practical values. Even though they cannot be measured in dollars,' he continued, 'the scientific value of wilderness should be stressed' (Senate Committee on Interior and Insular Affairs, 1958).

As labor historian Scott Dewey (1998) notes in his history of early labor-environmentalism, the labor movement was one of the first organizations to combine the concern for wilderness protection and pollution reduction into one organizational structure. Through the mid-1960s, most Americans viewed conservationism and anti-pollutionism as separate and unrelated issues. Unions were in the unusual position of showing interest in reducing pollution before most conservation organizations and simultaneously expressing concern for nature conservation before most public health advocates. These different concerns gradually fused together into the modern environmental movement in the late 1960s and early 1970s (Dewey, 1998).

Labor-Environmental Cooperation

Following the rise of the environmental movement, unions and environmentalists often worked together to fight corporate enemies of both labor and the environment by demanding that people and planet be put before profit. For example, in 1973 the Oil, Chemical, and Atomic Workers (OCAW) union struck at five Shell Oil refineries, demanding a national health and safety agreement that would have significantly reduced the dangers of environmental contamination. The Sierra Club and nearly a dozen other environmental organizations supported OCAW's strike, recognizing that working people were among the hardest hit by the hazards of pollution. Other unions like the United Auto Workers (UAW) and the American Federation of State, County, and Municipal Workers helped initiate Earth Day (UAW, 1970). As the coordinator of the first Earth Day, Denis Hayes, recalls:

> The UAW was by far the largest contributor to the first Earth Day, and its support went beyond the merely financial. It printed and mailed all our materials at its expense – even those critical of pollution-belching cars. And, of course, Walter [Reuther, President of the UAW] then endorsed the Clean Air Act that the Big Four [auto companies] were doing their damnedest to kill or gut. (Uehlein, 2010)

In 1979, unions and environmental groups like the Sierra Club and Friends of the Earth formed the OSHA Environmental Network with active coalitions in 22 states. The Network, initiated by and housed in the Industrial Union Department of the AFL-CIO, helped pass legislation that gave both workers and communities the right to know about toxic substances being used in workplaces (Obach, 2004; Mayer, 2009). In 1999, the labor movement and many environmental organizations jointly demanded protection of workers and the environment in international trade agreements and joined together to protest the founding meeting of the World Trade Organization (WTO) in Seattle. When young environmentalists, some wearing turtle costumes to represent threatened species, arrived at rallies and demonstrations with union workers, the slogan rapidly spread, 'Turtles and Teamsters, together at last!' The ensuing 'Battle of Seattle' shut down the global summit called to establish the WTO (Brecher et al., 2000). In the aftermath of the Battle of Seattle, several labor–environmental alliances sprang up, including the Apollo Alliance in 2003, which brought together labor, environmental, and business groups to promote clean energy, and the Blue–Green Alliance in 2006 to fight for green jobs.

Jobs vs. the Environment Conflicts

Despite these and countless other examples of labor–environmental cooperation, there are also many instances when the environmental movement faced opposition from labor, particularly when pro-environmental demands involved the loss of jobs for union members. In the late

1970s and early 1980s, nuclear power plant construction sites from Seabrook, New Hampshire to Diablo Canyon in California were ground zero for these types of jobs vs. the environment struggles. When anti-nuclear activists opposed the building of the Three Mile Island nuclear plant in Middletown, Pennsylvania, a local union distributed a bumper sticker reading 'Hungry and Out of Work? Eat an Environmentalist!' The construction project employed over 3000 unionized workers between 1968 and 1974. Five years after going online, in 1979, it was the site of the most serious commercial nuclear power disaster in US history (US Nuclear Regulatory Commission, 2019). After the incident was contained, the plant continued to operate, employing 300–400 full-time, full-year workers until its closure in 2019. Such labor–environmental conflict has arisen around not only nuclear energy, but also coal mining, 'smart growth' restrictions on development, climate change mitigation, and many other issues locally, regionally, and nationally.

This division between labor and environmentalists often occurs around the question of economic growth. Historically, unions have supported economic growth as a means to achieve full employment—a way to provide a better life for all—and as an aspect of human progress. Unfortunately for most workers, beginning in the 1970s the pro-growth agenda became synonymous with the neoliberal agenda and focused on deregulation, deunionization, and the decoupling of productivity gains from wage gains. For environmentalists, the negative consequences of economic growth such as the pollution of air, water, and land; the harm to human health; and the threat to the Earth's climate remained front and center in their thinking and activism (York, 2004; Schnaiberg, 1980). This difference of view has been at the center of recent battles over fossil fuel construction projects such as the Keystone XL (KXL) Pipeline and the Dakota Access Pipeline (DAPL).

In the case of both pipelines, as with many other fossil fuel infrastructure projects, the leaders of the nation's building trade unions saw the projects as great job opportunities for their unemployed members—especially in the wake of the Great Recession. And indeed, both projects were good opportunities as the companies responsible for construction of the pipelines signed employment contracts, known as project labor agreements, promising that all of the jobs building the pipelines would pay union wages and benefits if they were to get regulatory approval. For environmentalists, these fossil fuel pipelines represented a direct threat to local water supplies because of their tendency to leak, but they also posed a further threat to the Earth's climate by bringing more greenhouse gas (GHG)-producing fossil fuels to the market during a period when the science says we should be reducing our reliance on carbon-based fuel sources. In the case of DAPL, the pipeline posed an additional threat to sacred lands of the Standing Rock Sioux Tribal Nation.

Contested Terrain

It is important to note that both labor and environmental groups are often divided internally on these and other issues. For example, many environmental groups joined with labor in opposing the North American Free Trade Agreement in 1993–1994, but others supported it. The United Steelworkers supported the Kyoto Protocol on global warming in 1997 while the United Mineworkers of America and others opposed it and eventually persuaded the AFL-CIO to do so as well. While the AFL-CIO has come to recognize the reality of climate change and to support policies to expand green jobs, it has also lobbied against incorporating the targets and timelines recommended by climate scientists in international agreements (Sweeney, 2015;

Brecher, 2013). For example, during the negotiations that led to the historic United Nations Paris Climate Accord in 2015, the AFL-CIO opposed the inclusion of legally binding emissions reduction targets and instead supported the nationally determined, voluntary commitments that the Obama Administration ultimately signed on to (and the Trump Administration had vowed to step away from). While not all US unions are affiliated with the AFL-CIO, its stance on climate issues still sets limits on the actions of the movement as a whole.

Regarding KXL and DAPL, a handful of national unions, including the Amalgamated Transit Union, National Nurses United (NNU), American Postal Workers Union, the Service Employees International Union (SEIU), and the Communication Workers of America (CWA) were vocal in their opposition to the projects. A statement by the CWA read in part: 'CWA will continue to fight against the interests of the 1% and corporate greed and firmly stand in solidarity with our brothers and sisters of the Standing Rock Sioux tribe against the environmental and cultural degradation of their community' (CWA, 2016). In response, Terry O'Sullivan, president of the Laborer's International Union (LIUNA), said:

> [these] self-righteous unions ... know little about the project and have no job equity in it ... A central tenet of the labor movement has always been that when it comes to a project in which you have no equity at stake, you either support it or remain silent. We look forward to reciprocating the 'solidarity' shown to LIUNA members by these unions'. (LIUNA, 2016)

EXPLAINING LABOR RESISTANCE TO CLIMATE PROTECTION IN THE US

The major takeaway from the previous, very brief review of the history of labor–environmental relations in the US is that it is a complicated matter. There is not one singularly defined relationship between unions and environmental protection measures. However, that does not mean there is a lack of patterns or trends that can be identified to help us understand labor–environmental relations. In this section, I will draw from my personal experiences in the labor movement as a union construction worker from 2004 to 2010, a union organizer and local union president from 2013 to 2018, and a participant in several labor-environmental organizations since 2013, to identify some of the major explanations for opposition to climate protection measures by some US unions. The analysis also draws from 34 in-depth interviews with union leaders regarding labor and climate change between 2014 and 2018.

In sum, I identify twelve major structural and cultural explanations for labor opposition to climate change mitigation. While distinct, these explanations are deeply intertwined, overlapping and reinforcing. All are underpinned by the powerful free market ideology that dominates American political-economic discourse: neoliberalism. This belief system, rooted in what Adam Smith referred to as 'the unseen hand of the market', dictates what can and cannot be on the table for political discussion (Harvey, 2005). In general, government intervention in the market in order to solve social problems—including climate change, lack of health care, student debt, job loss—is akin to heresy from this perspective. For workers, this constraint on democracy often leads to a false choice between having good jobs or having a healthy environment in which to live and work. Workers in the fossil fuel industry become acutely aware of this dichotomy when federal, state, and local governments discuss solutions to the crisis of climate change that involve decarbonizing the economy. The hardships associated with job loss that result from the lack of a strong social safety net and the lack of good job alternatives for displaced workers are two examples of the ways in which the hegemonic neoliberal ideology can fuel anti-environmental activity on the part of unions. Each of these and other explanations will be outlined below.

Job Blackmail

Since the establishment of environmental and workplace protections in the early 1970s, private employers have resisted further curbs on corporate conduct by threatening job destruction (Kazis and Grossman, 1982). The refrain has been that environmental standards wipe out existing jobs and make new ones impossible. Kazis and Grossman (1982) showed in detail the use of this job blackmail to peel off trade unionists from environmentalists, making unnatural enemies of those who should be allies. The interest of workers in protecting their jobs is used by employers to achieve their own policy objectives and thus workers are often presented as the public face of opposition to environmental protection. This tactic works to the advantage of employers who are opposed to both workers and environmental protection, allowing them to maximally exploit labor and nature for profit (Brecher, 2013).

Workers are susceptible to this sort of blackmail for a variety of reasons, including the lack of viable alternatives and the lack of a social safety net, but also because of the importance of work in people's lives. Literature from the sociology of work tells us that a job is much more than just a source of income for working people. It provides a sense of purpose, an identity, and a feeling of dignity (Hodson, 2001). Conversely, unemployment is highly stigmatized in American culture—especially among men. For these reasons, the prospect of job loss is frightening for most workers, particularly those without a college education who are fortunate enough to hold a well-paying job.

Actual Job Loss

Addressing the causes of climate change will not only radically alter the way we generate electricity, travel, heat our homes, and consume goods and services, but it will also disrupt labor markets, employment, and work in whole industries. Replacing fossil fuels with renewable energy sources will reduce the number of jobs in the fossil fuel industry while simultaneously increasing the number of jobs in renewable power generation. Electric cars do not require oil changes but do require battery replacements. Energy efficient buildings will require fewer oil and gas deliveries, but more smart grid technicians to maximize the efficiency of operations. Offshore wind farms do not require plant operators but do require wind turbine technicians. Unlike the *threat* of job loss by employers described above, decarbonizing the economy is guaranteed to eliminate a certain number of jobs in the fossil fuel industry.

Most studies on the relationship between environmental protections and employment conclude that on average, legislative efforts to protect the environment have typically created more jobs than they have destroyed (Goodstein, 1999). However, this fact is of little comfort to the individual worker who loses *their* job as a result of government policy. It does not consider whether the new jobs are located in the same geographic region or if they require the same set of skills. It also does not take into consideration the quality of the new jobs compared to the jobs that are lost. The only real certainty is that many of the existing jobs in the fossil fuel industry will go away as a result of decarbonizing the economy. For unions, one existing job today is worth more than a million potential jobs promised by a politician and is thus worth fighting for.

Loss of Bargaining Power

Fossil fuel jobs in the energy sector, ranging from extraction to transportation to power plant operations, are very high paying jobs that do not require a college degree. These jobs were not always good jobs but became increasingly better over the course of the twentieth century due to the collective efforts of workers, predominantly through unions, to protest and bargain for increases in wages, benefits, and workplace safety. Many of the new green energy jobs, particularly in the residential solar industry—the largest employer in the renewable energy sector—do not offer wages or benefits comparable to jobs in the fossil fuel industry. For example, in 2018 the mean annual salary for a fossil fuel power plant operator was $78,030 while the mean annual salary for rooftop solar installer was $46,010 (Bureau of Labor Statistics, 2018).

This difference in pay is due in large part to the disparity in worker power between these two industries. In the fossil fuel sector, workers have a long history of unionization and bargaining over wages, hours, and working conditions. The solar sector is characterized by at-will employment and anti-union employers that invest heavily in union avoidance campaigns to prevent workers from bargaining collectively for higher wages (Eidelson, 2018). Through concerted action by workers, residential solar jobs could become as high paying as fossil fuel jobs over time; however, the initial experience for a worker shifting from one occupation to the other is an immediate reduction in salary and benefits. For unions, organizing new workers in the private sector has become increasingly difficult. The steady weakening of labor protections over the past 50 years coupled with extreme anti-union sentiment among employers makes new union organizing considerably more challenging than in the years immediately following the National Labor Relations Act of 1935 when many of the fossil fuel unions were formed.

Dearth of Alternatives for Blue Collar Workers

Related to the disparities in bargaining power between the fossil fuel and renewable energy industries is the general lack of good union job alternatives for blue collar workers. The ongoing history of globalization and deindustrialization—the shipping of jobs overseas in order to pay lower wages and pollute more in order to maximize profits in a competitive global market—has hollowed out the middle-class labor market (Bluestone and Harrison, 1982). The decline in well-paying, blue-collar manufacturing jobs has left few good alternatives for displaced workers without a college degree. Those that still hold one of the few union jobs left in the private sector, just 6 percent of workers in 2018, understand very well just how privileged they are in the contemporary American economy and are not prepared to give up those jobs for themselves or their children. They also know that the majority of alternatives readily available are low-paying, service sector jobs without union representation or fringe benefits.

Weak Social Safety Net

Unlike most other rich capitalist democracies, the US has a very weak social safety net. When workers lose their jobs, they not only lose their income, but they also lose health insurance for their families. Training and education is an expensive endeavor that places nearly all of the risk, usually in the form of debt, on the individual worker, with no guarantee that the investment will lead to a job in the end. The transition for workers from one occupation to another is made easier when education is free or highly subsidized and when health insurance and other benefits exist during the interim period of unemployment. This has been cited as one of the major reasons for the difference in support for climate protection measures between unions in the European context and the American context (Hyde and Vachon, 2019).

The stinginess of the US social safety net is even more pronounced in its programs designed to help workers who are displaced from jobs as a result of government policy. One example is the Trade Adjustment Assistance program, which was designed to assist workers harmed by international trade agreements such as the North American Free Trade Agreement. The program is generally seen as inadequate for a number of reasons, including the limited number of workers that actually qualify for assistance, the level of assistance, and the inability of the job retraining program to guarantee a job at the end. In fact, most workers who received training with the program did not end up with jobs in the fields they had trained for (Barret, 2001). In effect, most workers who lost well-paying blue-collar jobs went through an inadequate job placement program and ended up with low-paying service sector work in the end, which they could have found without the program. This has led many unions to be highly skeptical of government transition programs. AFL-CIO president, Richard Trumka, even went so far as to refer to just transition as a 'fancy funeral'. The inadequacy of the social safety net and existing transition programs is largely a result of the neoliberal governing ideology, which loathes taxation and social spending and opposes most forms of state intervention into markets.

Geographic Economic Factors

The energy infrastructure of the nineteenth and twentieth century was built around supplies of fossil fuels. Coal mining requires an underground supply of bituminous coal and oil drilling requires an underground supply of crude oil. The transition to renewable energy sources that is required to reduce GHG emissions will be built around a different set of resources. Wind power requires a steady flow of air, offshore wind requires a shoreline, and solar power requires prolonged sun exposure. These renewable resources may or may not be available in the same locations as fossil fuel resources, which means the transition away from fossil fuels to renewables could harm the economy in some localities while benefiting it in others.

These geographic factors can contribute to resistance to climate protection measures by unions, particularly in rural or isolated areas with less diversified economies. There are countless cities and towns scattered across the map that are reliant on just one fossil fuel employer for the majority of wages and local tax revenue. For these communities, the economic impact of decarbonization can result in deep and widespread economic hardships. For workers and unions in these regions, such as Appalachia, the consequences of job loss are amplified considerably. Alternatively, unions in areas where new green infrastructure projects are likely to be built see an increase in job opportunities.

'All of the Above' Construction Policy

Commercial construction workers are responsible for building fossil fuel power plants and pipelines as well as wind farms and commercial solar plants. Like fossil fuel jobs in the energy sector, unionized commercial construction jobs are highly paid blue-collar occupations that do not require a college degree. However, unlike most fossil fuel industry jobs, employment in construction is sporadic and comes in fits and starts depending on the state of the economy and level of investment in construction projects. An average construction worker may work for two or three different employers in a given year and dozens more over the course of their career. They may also spend several months each year unemployed, waiting for a construction project to begin.

Unlike other sectors of the labor movement, construction unions (known as the building trades) serve as an employment service, connecting workers looking for jobs to construction companies looking to hire large numbers of skilled workers on short notice for temporary jobs. The workers in return are guaranteed the same negotiated pay rate and benefits regardless of the employer and carry their benefits with them seamlessly throughout their career from one employer to another, even across durations of unemployment. Unlike a typical factory worker who becomes a union member by way of employment at a particular workplace and only maintains membership so long as they are employed by that company, construction workers are union members first and employees of a particular company second. In other words, they are connected to the labor market via the union hiring hall.

The sporadic nature of construction work combined with the hiring hall structure creates an incentive for building trades unions to offer political support for any and all construction projects in order to secure adequate employment opportunities for their members. This 'all of the above' approach often leads building trades unions to support projects that might otherwise be harmful to their members' communities, such as waste incinerators, casinos, and coal-fired power plants. It can also lead unions to become 'junior partners' to capital as they drum up political support for construction projects that large corporations are pursuing.[5]

Importantly, the 'all of the above' approach has also led some building trades unions to support renewable energy projects. An example of this was the construction of the Block Island Offshore Wind Farm—America's first offshore wind farm. In this case the Rhode Island building trades unions worked closely with environmentalists and renewable energy activists to win approval for the wind farm. The project created hundreds of local union construction jobs and replaced Block Island's dirty diesel generator with clean, renewable wind power. This example is largely a result of geographic factors that shaped the realm of possible construction projects to be supported by local unions wishing to stimulate job opportunities for their unemployed members.

Job Bribery

Where fossil fuel workers are often coerced into opposing environmental protections as a result of job blackmail by employers, construction workers face a different form of employer influence—a legal bribe in the form of a project labor agreement (PLA). For building trades unions, the PLA is the gold standard for proposed construction projects. A PLA, also referred to as a community workforce agreement, is a pre-hire collective bargaining agreement between construction companies and labor organizations that establishes the terms and conditions of employment for a specific construction project before it begins. For construction companies it creates a broad base of support for their projects; for unions it offers some assurance that their members will get jobs.

Building trades unions typically offer their political support for construction projects in exchange for a guarantee that the jobs will pay union wages once the work begins (they also oppose non-union construction projects). The PLA essentially creates an incentive for employers and unions to work together to expand the pro-growth agenda of the construction industry and ensure that a percentage of that growth is shared fairly with the workers that perform the required jobs. As the threat of climate mitigation began to loom over the fossil fuel industry, corporations became increasingly supportive of signing PLAs with building trades unions to garner their powerful political support for projects that would face another form of organized political opposition—the environmental movement. While PLAs themselves are not inherently a bad thing—they certainly help to ensure that labor gets a fair share of the pie—the increased weaponization of them by employers to effectively hire unions as an anti-environmental political army has led to several jobs vs. the environment clashes, such as those associated with the KXL and DAPL pipeline projects. If renewable energy companies were not so anti-union, they too could sign PLAs with building trades unions, which could build a powerful pro-green political alliance and turn the tide of labor support away from fossil fuel projects.

The Structure of the AFL-CIO

Union confederations are umbrella organizations with which unions in a geographically defined area may choose to affiliate in order to build cross-sector solidarity and increase workers' power for collective actions and legislative efforts. Examples of union confederations include: central labor councils, which operate at the county or metropolitan level and typically comprise union locals; state federations, which operate at the state level and typically comprise local- and state-level unions; and the AFL-CIO, which is a national confederation of unions comprising 55 national unions, representing some 12.5 million workers in almost all industries. Most major unions are affiliated with the AFL-CIO, with a handful of notable exceptions, such as the SEIU, the Teamsters, the United Brotherhood of Carpenters, and the International Longshore and Warehouse Union (ILWU). The building trades unions have their own national-level confederation in the US called North America's Building Trades Unions, which, as a block, has significant influence within the AFL-CIO.

Union confederations often take stances on political and economic issues based on the interests of their member unions. However, since confederations rely on voluntary membership dues in order to operate, they are often at the mercy of any one union or group of unions that can effectively veto an issue by threatening to disaffiliate from the confederation. This structural feature of union confederations is critically important in shaping labor's position on climate change mitigation policies. In fact, the AFL-CIO has a long history of supporting coal and other fossil fuels because of the influence of member unions with individual members who work for mining, drilling, transportation, and power generation companies. As a result, the confederation has generally taken a very cautious, conservative approach to climate policy. Unlike the International Trade Union Confederation, and national confederations in other countries, the AFL-CIO has never supported either the Kyoto Protocol or other science-based emissions reduction targets. Historically, the AFL-CIO's climate and energy policy has been shaped predominantly by a small number of unions in extraction and construction who form the very powerful Energy Committee, and the rest of the confederation—unions representing the vast majority of union members—have mostly steered clear of what is, or could be, a divisive issue.

Business Unionism and the Politics of Solidarity

A common refrain uttered by leaders of fossil fuel and building trades unions when responding to environmentalists or other unions that support climate protection measures is that they do not have 'skin in the game' or that they lack 'equity' on the issue. The point is that it is easy for organizations whose members will not lose jobs from climate protection to support climate protection. However, as other unions that support climate protection have noted, climate change impacts *all* workers and thus all unions have a stake in it. In the end, this difference in perception comes down to two distinct understandings of what is meant by union solidarity.

For building trades unions, solidarity generally means supporting, or at least not opposing, the interests of unions who have jobs on the line. For unions that are taking a more progressive stance on climate protection, solidarity means coming together to demand solutions that protect the entire working class, including the fossil fuel workers who face job displacement, but also the workers from frontline communities that are already being devastated by the ill effects of climate change. As Joe Uehlein, President of the Labor Network for Sustainability, stated: 'Solidarity has to be thought of in the context of broader human solidarity.' In between these two poles lies the majority of the labor movement, which, for fear of dividing the movement or drawing the ire of the building trades and extraction unions, chooses to remain silent on the issue all together, effectively providing support for the status quo, which is the anti-climate protection stance.

In academic terms, the first approach is akin to what labor studies scholars and sociologists have referred to as 'pure and simple business unionism' (Buhle, 1999; Perlman, 1949; Commons, 1918). The second approach is often referred to as 'social movement unionism' (Clawson, 2003; Robinson, 2000; Moody, 1997; Waterman, 1991). From the business union perspective, unions are not inherently antagonistic toward the capitalist order, but rather just one of the countless interest groups acting within a pluralistic society. There is no class consciousness or class-based political goal, merely aggregates of working people that when confronted with incidents of scarcity develop 'job consciousness' and band together for the purpose of protecting their jobs and apportioning available opportunities on an equal basis (Perlman, 1949). The business union theory was developed in the US as a means of explaining the very different form of unionization that took hold there compared to mainland Europe.

The social movement union perspective envisions the labor movement as a working-class social movement rather than an instrumentalist organization. While there is not one authoritative definition of social movement unionism, a review of the literature reveals a number of common characteristics (Scipes, 2014; Schiavone, 2007; Robinson, 2000; Moody, 1997; Waterman, 1991). First, social movement unions are highly democratic organizations with a high degree of rank-and-file participation. Second, they struggle for more than just wage increases for more than just their members. Third, they work regularly in conjunction with other community-based groups and social movements on equal footing (e.g., environmentalists, women's rights groups, faith groups, peace groups, etc.). Fourth, they are highly committed to organizing new members, regardless of race, ethnicity, gender, sexual orientation, or country of origin. And finally, they utilize innovative strategies and non-institutional tactics to achieve their organizing goals.

The culture of business unionism and its correspondingly narrow understanding of solidarity is one of the major organizational-cultural explanations for anti-environmentalism by some unions. From a business union perspective, fighting to protect fossil fuel jobs rather than fighting to address climate change for all working people is perfectly logical. The primary focus is always on the immediate material interests of the dues-paying members. This job consciousness perspective is very different from a class consciousness perspective and, as we have seen, can lead to a very different understanding of what it means to show solidarity. The following quote from a statement by NNU regarding climate change neatly summarizes the alternative: 'The future for labor should not be scrambling for elusive crumbs thrown down by corporate partners, but advocating for the larger public interest, the reputation labor deservedly earned in the 1930s and 1940s, the period of labor's greatest growth and the resulting emergence of a more egalitarian society' (NNU, 2013).

Bad Experiences with Environmentalists

Another factor contributing to anti-environmentalism by some unions is a history of negative encounters with environmentalists. Obach (2004) provides several examples of instances when environmentalists showed up outside of plants to protest, berating workers as they entered or left work as if they were responsible for the plant's pollution. Tree spiking, monkeywrenching, and other forms of eco-sabotage have put unwitting workers in harm's way. A union whose members have been the victim of such acts or even attempted acts is likely to mistrust environmentalists and develop a negative attitude toward their activities. The open hostility of many environmentalists to the timber workers in the Pacific Northwest during the battle over spotted owls in old growth forests continues to resonate in that region today.

Additionally, starting in the 1980s, many environmental organizations turned their energy away from alliance-building and toward legal battles to win environmental protections. This change in strategy led to a decline in interaction with unions as well as an almost singular focus on fundraising. Becoming more reliant on big donors, many environmental organizations became indifferent to the lived experience of workers, appearing to be 'out-of-touch with reality' and elitist from the perspective of many unions.

Union Democracy and Leadership

This final explanation deals with the beliefs and values of individual workers, nested within local cultures, that are transmitted upward through democratic channels to shape the political stance of their unions. For example, the depth and breadth of support for coal in places like West Virginia, Kentucky and Western Pennsylvania goes beyond the fear of further job losses and the erosion of the local tax base. Coal has been woven into the fabric of Appalachian life for more than a century. Mining is not just a job; it is a cultural identity. It has a rich oral, musical, and cultural legacy. Songs like 'Dark as a Dungeon', written by Merle Travis in 1946, have alternately been used during struggles by miners decrying deadly working conditions in the mines, but also in celebration of the dignity involved in doing an honest, albeit deadly, day's work to support one's family and power the US economy. For many in Appalachia, the emotional response to what has been dubbed by the industry as a 'war on coal' is part anger at job loss, but also part sorrow for what is slipping away, a culture that is deeply rooted in a place, and part fear at what the future may bring for that place.

These individual and community concerns are projected into union politics. Just as an aggregate of individuals can promote their political ideology into government policy through elections and lobbying, the same is true within labor organizations. While the extent of union democracy varies greatly across unions, it is true that even in the most oligarchic unions the leadership is still accountable to the expressed interests of the membership. If the members are opposed to environmental regulations because they don't believe in the science of climate change, or they don't want to change their fossil fuel-based lifestyle, or they fear that it will eliminate their job and undermine their way of life, then the leadership is likely to respond to these cues and act accordingly 'in the interests' of their members.

It takes courageous leadership to stand before the members of a union and tell them that their jobs will need to be eliminated for the common good and that the union will not fight to save those jobs, but will instead fight to ensure that the members are taken care of economically when their jobs are eliminated. One such leader was Tony Mazzocchi from OCAW. His union represented a variety of workers, including those who designed and built nuclear weapons for the US military. He was also keenly aware that the product they were making was devastating to the environment, the workers, and ultimately all life on Earth. He took a very bold stand by opposing nuclear weapons and calling for the creation of a 'superfund for workers' to ensure that his members who could lose their jobs as a result of halting nuclear arms manufacturing were taken care of economically (Leopold, 2007). For this he is generally credited with pioneering the concept of a 'just transition'.

Barring the occasional emergence of brave and charismatic leaders that have a clear vision of the common good, the democratic nature of unions means that leaders will typically espouse and act on the beliefs and values expressed by their members. For some unions, such as the nurses, this means taking a very progressive stance on climate change because of the ill health effects the members see in their work every day. For other unions, it means opposing climate protection measures because the members attribute declining employment in their sector and economic devastation in their communities to the work of environmental activists. However, the democratic nature of unions also creates opportunities for member activists to organize within their unions to shift the organization's position on issues like climate change—which many have been doing.

TOWARD A GREEN NEW DEAL?

Despite many instances of anti-climate protection by some unions, other unions have been leading the fight for climate protection. Unions in healthcare, education, the public sector, services, and transportation are among the most progressive when it comes to addressing climate change. Much of this is as a result of concerted efforts by activist members and local-level leaders constituting what I call the 'labor–climate movement' within US labor that is pushing unions from within to take action. By demanding both good jobs and a livable climate, they are challenging the dominant free market ideology of American governance. They are also employing the social movement approach to unionism by making demands that benefit the whole of the working class, not just the material interests of their dues-paying members.

One such union, NNU has supported legislation to ban fracking, citing the inherent risks to public health, especially the health of children, who are most vulnerable. They have also promoted a Robin Hood Tax as a means to generate government funding for a transition to a green economy:

The Robin Hood Tax can fund the transition to a non-fossil-fuel based economy. Wall Street reaps billions from oil companies, it's time for them to pay us back—to address the effects of climate change and support a sustainable economy. Green manufacturing, clean energy and mass transit, funded by a tax on Wall Street transactions. (NNU, 2015)

SEIU 32BJ has pioneered programs in green building management to 'ensure the gains made through retrofits are fully realized by a well-trained property services workforce' (SEIU, 2016). California Local 1000 proposed the creation of a 'Joint Labor–Management Committee on Greenhouse Gas Emissions Reduction' during bargaining in 2008. CWA and the Teamsters played a central role in organizing and coordinating labor's participation in the historic People's Climate March in New York in 2014. The union 32BJ was also one of the first to come out in support of the Green New Deal (GND) resolution introduced to congress by Representative Ocasio-Cortez and Senator Markey in 2019.

The GND resolution provides a bold vision for a more sustainable and equitable future by sketching a roadmap 'to achieve net-zero greenhouse gas emissions through a fair and just transition for all communities and workers' (US House Resolution 109, 2019). It confronts many of the issues addressed in this chapter, including the need for green jobs to be good jobs with union rights and livable wages, the need for PLAs for renewable energy projects, the need for a robust social safety net to protect displaced workers, including single-payer healthcare and tuition-free college education, and the federal guarantee of a living-wage job for anyone seeking employment who is unable to find work in the private sector. The proposal is nothing short of transformational in its challenge to the market logic that has guided most climate and employment legislation in the US up to this point. Most importantly, the resolution seeks the active participation by labor unions and other stakeholders in helping to shape the legislation that will make that vision a reality. As stated in the resolution: 'a Green New Deal must be developed through transparent and inclusive consultation, collaboration, and partnership with frontline and vulnerable communities, labor unions, worker cooperatives, civil society groups, academia, and businesses' (US House Resolution 109, 2019).

For labor–climate activists, the GND is the ideal solution to the dual crisis of climate and inequality. Labor just needs to come to the table and help shape the legislation to ensure that the interests of workers are reflected in the plan. For the energy unions and the AFL-CIO, it is still pie in the sky. The promise of future jobs does not outweigh the protection of existing jobs. They also remain highly skeptical about the government's ability to ensure a truly just transition for displaced workers. As Cecil Roberts of the United Mine Workers of America said about just transition: 'I've never seen one.' In a letter to the authors of the GND resolution, members of the AFL-CIO's Energy Committee stated: 'We will not stand by and allow threats to our members' jobs and their families' standard of living go unanswered.' They did go on to state their belief in climate science and support for efforts to address it, including investing in energy efficiencies for buildings and constructing green infrastructure, but they also called for the development and use of carbon capture technologies and rehashed the largely disproven 'bridge fuel' argument in support of new natural gas power plants.

This fissure between the pro- and anti-climate protection unions underscores a theme that is present throughout labor's storied history with environmental issues. Namely, the goal of protecting *jobs* can sometimes come into conflict with the goal of protecting *workers* in general—a reflection of the recurring distinction between what Perlman (1949) called 'job consciousness' and what Marx called 'class consciousness'—that is at the heart of the climate debate within labor. Despite this rift, many labor activists still have hope that the GND can serve as a unifying vehicle to create the kind of change that is needed. They have been speaking with fellow union members, organizing town hall meetings, and drafting union resolutions in support of the GND. Groups such as the Labor Network for Sustainability and Trade Unions for Energy Democracy have been growing steadily and offering a counter-narrative to the 'jobs vs. the environment' frame put forth by anti-climate protection unions in the mainstream media.

As these labor–climate activists know well and articulate to varying degrees, overcoming the many obstacles blocking the pathway to a more just, equitable, and sustainable world requires challenging the dominant neoliberal ideology that at every corner blocks efforts to regulate the economy in order to combat climate change, attacks efforts by workers to unionize in the renewable sector, eschews plans to create a social safety net and provide a just transition for displaced workers, opposes a public jobs guarantee, and forces many workers to make a false choice between having a good job or a livable planet. To truly address climate change, the fossil fuel jobs will have to go away. The question in the end is not *whether* the transition will happen, but *when* it will happen and whether it will happen *to* workers or *with* workers. The only way to ensure that the transition is fair and just for workers is for unions to come to the table and fight for it as hard as they are fighting now to protect fossil fuel jobs that are destined to decline. Building trades unions, service sector unions, transportation unions, extraction unions, healthcare unions, education unions, manufacturing unions, public sector unions, all unions. When it comes to addressing climate change, everyone has skin in the game.

DISCUSSION AND CONCLUSION

The case study of American unions examined in this chapter offers important insight into our theoretical understanding of anti-environmentalism. Overall, the case suggests that political economic institutions can play an important role in fostering anti-environmental activity in capitalist societies. At the economy level, the combination of a weak social safety net and a dearth of good job alternatives in the US have worked together to significantly increase the likelihood of unions engaging in anti-environmental behavior to preserve unionized jobs. The neoliberal nature of the American economy leaves workers with little social support in the event of job loss, and the greater the loss is perceived to be, the more that workers and their unions can be expected to fight to avoid that loss.

At the government level, the relative inability of stakeholders, including workers and environmentalists, to cooperatively shape policy may also contribute to anti-environmental behavior. Governance systems can be said to fall along a continuum between pluralism and corporatism based upon the extent of interest aggregation and policy 'concertation'. Pluralist systems like the US are characterized by limited policy concertation and more decentralized and competitive interest groups. The government receives input from numerous small interest groups and then makes policies in an attempt to 'please' all groups, or at least minimize the damage to all groups. The result is that policy tends to be heavily contested from the time it appears on the agenda all the way through implementation. This fragmentation of interests can make it very difficult to overcome collective action problems because any gain for one group can be seen as a loss for another in a classic zero-sum fashion.

In contrast, corporatist governments, as have existed in parts of Western Europe and in particular the Nordic countries, have a relatively high level of interest aggregation and policy concertation. Government policymakers consult extensively with a small number of peak associations representing distinct interest associations—the two dominant associations being employers and unions. The role of labor and business groups in representing their group interests, and then regulating their members in compliance with agreements they negotiate, provides great opportunities to overcome the perennial collective action problems associated with the provision of public goods—such as a healthy environment.

At the employer level, the power that corporations wield over their workers can shape their attitudes and behaviors toward the environment as well. When employers are opposed to environmental protections for fear of being less competitive in the global market, they are able to activate their employees to oppose such protections by threatening the destruction of their jobs. This imbalance in power between workers and employers makes unions susceptible to becoming the public relations wing of corporate anti-environmental campaigns in the name of saving their members' jobs. At the organizational level, unions are democratic organizations that are accountable to the demands of their members. This can often be the deciding factor when an organization decides to either side with or oppose efforts to protect the environment. A union with anti-environmentalist members is likely to engage in anti-environmentalist activity, just like a union with environmentalist members is more likely to engage in pro-environmental activity.

The insights from this case motivate several additional research questions and lines of inquiry for understanding the social dynamics of anti-environmentalism. For example, to what extent do the political-economic explanations identified in this chapter influence the stance of workers and unions toward environmental protections in other countries? Are workers in countries with stronger social provisions, including universal healthcare, free or reduced-cost college education, and extended unemployment benefits less likely to engage in anti-environmental activism to protect jobs? Do more inclusive governing structures such as corporatism and tripartite governance help to overcome stalemates between entrenched interests such as those seeking to protect jobs and those protecting the environment? Are workers in particular occupations or industries more or less likely to engage in anti-environmentalism compared to others? Are unionized workers more or less likely to engage in anti-environmentalism compared to non-union workers? Future research into these and other questions about the relationship between workers, their organizations, and environmental protections can help strengthen our understanding of the causes and possible solutions to anti-environmentalism in the twenty-first century.

NOTES

1. Speaking about the Keystone Access Pipeline project (Brown, 2011).
2. Speaking about unions opposing the Dakota Access Pipeline (LIUNA, 2016).
3. This chapter is focused on the positions and actions of unions as organizations and thus does not deal at length with the reasons that individual workers may oppose climate protection.
4. For a more thorough history, see Dewey (1998), Mayer (2009), Obach (2004), and Silverman (2006).
5. It is important to note that despite this one perverse outcome of the hiring hall structure, it successfully addresses a very serious structural problem in the construction industry: sporadic unemployment. Without this structure or a very strong social safety net, construction workers would be in perpetual poverty or very few people would pursue a career in the trades long enough to develop the skills required to safely build large-scale infrastructure projects.

REFERENCES

Barret, J. (2001) *Worker Transition and Global Climate Change.* Pew Center on Global Climate Change.
Beder, S. (1997) *Global Spin: The Corporate Assault on Environmentalism.* Totnes: Green Books.
Bluestone, B. and Harrison, B. (1982) *The Deindustrialization of America: Plant Closings, Community Abandonment, and the Dismantling of Basic Industry.* New York, NY: Basic Books.
Brecher, J. (2013) Stormy weather: Climate change and a divided labor movement. *New Labor Forum.* **22**(1), pp.75–81.
Brecher, J. (2017) *Against Doom: A Climate Insurgency Manual.* Oakland, CA: PM Press.
Brecher, J., Costello, T. and Smith, B. (2000) *Globalization from Below: The Power of Solidarity.* Cambridge, MA: South End Press.
Brown, J. (2011) Oil Pipeline Fight Roils Unions. *Labor Notes* (online). Available from: https://www.labornotes.org/2011/11/oil-pipeline-fight-roils-unions (accessed 22 May 2019).
Buhle, P. (1999) *Taking Care of Business: Samuel Gompers, George Meany, Lane Kirkland, and the Tragedy of American Labor.* New York, NY: Monthly Review Press.
Bureau of Labor Statistics (2018) *Occupational Employment Statistics.* Bureau of Labor Statistics (online). Available from: https://www.bls.gov/oes/current/oes_stru.htm#00-0000 (accessed 22 May 2019).
Cha, J.M. and Skinner, L. (2017) *Reversing Inequality, Combatting Climate Change: A Climate Jobs Program for New York State.* ILR Worker Institute (online). Available from: https://archive.ilr.cornell.edu/sites/default/files/InequalityClimateChangeReport.pdf (accessed 12 February 2020).
Clawson, D. (2003) *The Next Upsurge: Labor and the New Social Movements.* Ithaca, NY: Cornell University Press.
Commons, J.R. (1918) *History of Labour in the United States.* New York, NY: Beard Books.
CWA. (2016) Statement by the CWA Committee on Human Rights in Support of the Standing Rock Sioux Tribe. *Communications Workers of America* (online). Available from: https://cwaunion.org/news/releases/statement-cwacommittee-on-human-rights-in-support-ofstandingrock-sioux-tribe (accessed 22 May 2019).
Dewey, S. (1998) Working for the environment: Organized labor and the origins of environmentalism in the United States, 1848–1970. *Environmental History.* **3**(1), pp. 45–63.
Eidelson, J. (2018) Tesla workers start a drive to unionize solar-panel factory. *Bloomberg Law.* Available from: https://news.bloomberglaw.com/daily-labor-report/tesla-workers-start-a-drive-to-unionize-solar-panel-factory-1.
Goodstein, E. (1999) *The Trade-Off Myth: Fact and Fiction about Jobs and the Environment.* Washington, DC: Island Press.
Harvey, D. (2005) *A Brief History of Neoliberalism.* Oxford: Oxford University Press.
Helvarg, D. (1994) *The War Against the Greens: The 'Wise-Use' Movement, the New Right, and Anti-Environmental Violence.* San Francisco, CA: Sierra Club Books.
Hodson, R. (2001) *Dignity at Work.* Cambridge, MA: Cambridge University Press.
Hyde, A. and Vachon, T.E. (2019) Running with or against the treadmill? Unions, institutional contexts, and greenhouse gas emissions in a comparative perspective. *Environmental Sociology.* **5**(3), pp. 269–82. Available from DOI: 10.1080/23251042.2018.1544107.
Kazis, R. and Grossman, R.L. (1982) *Fear at Work: Job Blackmail, Labor and the Environment.* New York, NY: Pilgrim Press.
Leopold, L. (2007) *The Man Who Hated Work and Loved Labor: The Life and Times of Tony Mazzocchi.* White River Junction, VT: Chelsea Green.
LIUNA. (2016) LIUNA re-elects leadership and charts determined, optimistic agenda at its international convention. *LIUNA* (online). Available from: http://www.liuna.org/news/story/liuna-re-elects-leadership-and-charts-determined-optimistic-agenda-at-its-international-convention (accessed 22 May 2019).
Mayer, B. (2009) *Blue-Green Coalitions: Fighting for Safe Workplaces and Healthy Communities.* Ithaca, NY: Cornell University Press/ILR Press.
Moody, K. (1997) *Workers in a Lean World: Unions in the International Economy.* New York, NY: Verso.

NNU (2013) Nurses Oppose the KXL Pipeline – and all of labor should too. *National Nurses United* (online). Available from: http://www.nationalnursesunited.org/blog/nurses-oppose-kxl-pipeline-and-alllabor-should-too (accessed 22 May 2019).

NNU (2015) Populist proposals remind why nurses trust Bernie Sanders to heal America. *National Nurses United* (online). Available from: https://www.nationalnursesunited.org/blog/populist-poposalsremind-why-nurses-trust-bernie-sanders-heal-america (accessed 22 May 2019).

Obach, B.K. (2004) *Labor and the Environmental Movement: The Quest for Common Ground.* Cambridge, MA: MIT Press.

Perlman, S. (1949) *A Theory of the Labor Movement.* New York, NY: AM Kelley.

Robinson, I. (2000) Neoliberal restructuring and U.S. unions: Toward social movement unionism? *Critical Sociology.* **26**, pp. 109–38.

Rowell, A. (1996) *Green Backlash: Global Subversion of the Environment Movement.* London, UK and New York, NY, USA: Routledge.

Schiavone, M. (2007) Moody's account of social movement unionism: An analysis. *Critical Sociology.* **33**(1–2), pp. 279–309.

Schnaiberg, A. (1980) *The Environment: From Surplus to Scarcity.* Oxford: Oxford University Press.

Scipes, K. (2014) Social movement unionism or social justice unionism? Disentangling theoretical confusion within the global labor movement. *Class, Race and Corporate Power.* **2**(3), pp. 1–43.

SEIU (2016) About the green supers program. *32BJ Training Fund* (online). Available from: http://training.32bjfunds.org/en-us/green.aspx (accessed 22 May 2019).

Senate Committee on Interior and Insular Affairs (1958) *National Wilderness Preservation Act: Hearings before the Committee on Interior and Insular Affairs.* 85th Congress, 2nd session, pp. 203–204.

Silverman, V. (2006) Green unions in a grey world. *Organization and Environment.* **19**(2), pp. 191–213.

Sweeney, S. (2015) Standing rock solid with the frackers: Are the trades putting labor's head in the gas oven? *New Labor Forum.* **26**(1), pp. 94–9.

UAW. (1970) Gaylord Nelson and Earth Day: The UAW steps up for Earth Day. Gaylord Nelson and Earth Day (online). Available from: http://nelsonearthday.net/collection/coalition-uawflyer.htm (accessed 22 May 2019).

Uehlein, J. (2010) Earth day, labor, and me. *Common Dreams* (online). Available from: http://www.commondreams.org/views/2010/04/19/earth-day-labor-and-me (accessed 22 May 2019).

US House Resolution 109 (2019) Recognizing the duty of the Federal Government to create a Green New Deal. *US Congress* (online). Available from: https://www.congress.gov/bill/116th-congress/house-resolution/109/text (accessed 22 May 2019).

US Nuclear Regulatory Commission (2019) Backgrounder on the Three Mile Island accident. *Nuclear Regulatory Commission* (online). Available from: https://www.nrc.gov/reading-rm/doc-collections/fact-sheets/3mile-isle.html (accessed 22 May 2019).

Vachon, T.E. and Brecher, J. (2016) Are union members more or less likely to be environmentalists? Some evidence from surveys. *Labor Studies Journal.* **41**(2), pp. 185–203.

Vachon, T.E. and Wallace, M. (2013) Globalization, labor market transformation, and union decline in U.S. metropolitan areas. *Labor Studies Journal.* **38**(3), pp. 229–55.

Waterman, P. (1991) Social movement unionism: A new model for a new world. Working Paper No. 110. Amsterdam: International Institute for Research and Education.

Xu, Y. and Ramanathan, V. (2017) Well below 2°C: Mitigation strategies for avoiding dangerous to catastrophic climate changes. *Proceedings of the National Academy of Sciences.* **114**(39), pp. 10315–23.

York, R. (2004) The treadmill of (diversifying) production. *Organization & Environment.* **17**(3), pp. 355–62.

21. Reflexive religious anti-environmentalism on Indigenous lands: decolonization and religious environmental organizations (REOs) in the Trans Mountain resistance
Victor W.Y. Lam

INTRODUCTION: SITUATING RELIGION IN ENVIRONMENTALISM AND ANTI-ENVIRONMENTALISM

Pope Francis' encyclical *Laudato Si* (subtitled 'On care for our common home'), often hailed as a milestone in moving the dial on religious responses to climate change (Landrum and Vasquez, 2020; Pou-Amérigo, 2018), represents one of many monumental shifts renewing interest in the ways religions are responding to environmentalism. Contrary to this popularization, however, is also identification of the ways religion can fuel classic forms of anti-environmentalism. In the US, conservative politicians and religious leaders draw upon apocalyptic visions of 'end times' in anticipation of divine judgment and destruction of the earth, resulting in persistent efforts to promote climate change denial (Zaleha and Szasz, 2015). Such polarizing examples raise critical questions for the place of religion in shaping anti-environmental attitudes, structures and actors.

Recognizing the various configurations of religion in environmental politics highlights how religious discourse may fuel pro- and anti-environmental rhetoric and endeavors (Hoffman, 2011; Wardekker et al., 2009). Features of religion in environmentalism and anti-environmentalism have been extensively documented on Christianity in the US (Caniglia et al., 2015; Taylor et al., 2016; Veldman et al., 2014). Evangelical Environmental Network, an organization that promotes reformed interpretations of stewarding the earth and framing environmental issues as spiritual issues, highlights evangelical discourses to care for the earth and tackle climate change as a means to show neighborly love for the poor (Wardekker et al., 2009; Wilkinson, 2012). In contrast, the Cornwall Alliance, a coalition of theologians, scholars and church leaders who alternatively frame stewardship as commanding the wise use of resources for human benefit while dismissing anthropogenic climate change (Zaleha and Szasz, 2015) exemplifies discourses of developmental stewardship that emphasize the 'god-given' right to use resources and belief that God is in control of the climate (Caniglia et al., 2015; Roser-Renouf et al., 2016; Zahela and Szasz, 2015). These diametric opposites epitomize recent debates on religious environmentalism and anti-environmentalism. Yet, claims on religious environmentalism of either form have to be carefully weighed alongside socio-demographic factors such as denominational differences, political leanings, race and ethnicity (Pew Research Center, 2015).

Importantly, religious environmentalisms have emerged worldwide (Veldman et al., 2014), illustrating the need for context-specific and integrated accounts. Variations of religious environmentalisms have been noted in Africa, where Orthodox Christian churches become co-habitants of sacred spaces and Indigenous plant species (Bongers et al., 2006; Kent and Orlowska, 2018; Ruelle et al., 2018). Religious environmentalism can emerge in the revitalization of religions. Prior to colonization, Indigenous religions in the Asante Sekeyere community in Ghana held critical access to knowledge systems that preserved the fundamental connection between spirituality and the environment (Botchway and Agyemang, 2012). In Indonesia, Islamic environmental organizations have developed eco-theology that combines canonical texts and local networks to inform adherents of environmental degradation, combat deforestation, and foster alternative livelihoods (Amri, 2014). Language of protecting the environment in Western religions, which presupposes a rigid division between humans and nature, contrasts with Tomalin's (2009) findings of Hindu 'bio-divinity' in India, which imbue sacredness of the natural world. Examining the emergence of religious environmentalism outside Western contexts expands the range of ways religions mediate knowledge and relationships between humans and their natural environments (Sachdeva, 2016; Taylor, 2016). As religions become increasingly aware of the need to adapt thoughts and practices to confront environmental crises (Grim and Tucker, 2014; Taylor, 2016), not only is it necessary to examine the evolving practices in religious environmentalism, but it is equally important to account for emerging religious frameworks that prescribe, diagnose and explain shifting society–nature relationships. Offering integrated accounts of religious environmentalisms that attend to the scales, politics and cultures that shape religions may enhance understanding of the diversity, alignments and tensions that underlie the partial and incomplete picture of religious environmentalism in the face of anti-environmentalism. Taking religious environmentalism and religious anti-environmentalism under this frame may offer opportunities to examine the reflexive capacities from within.

Drawing upon activist accounts and documents from religious environmental organizations (REOs) in the Trans Mountain pipeline expansion resistance in Canada, this chapter proposes the possibility of decolonization of religious actors in reflexive anti-environmentalism. Decolonizing religious actors signifies two potential leverage points in reflexive anti-environmentalism. Notably, they are the socio-historical dynamics embedded in the complicit roles of religious institutions in settler colonialism, which foregrounded REO commitments to front line actions and destabilization of religious and settler identities of individual activists over the course of the resistance. Although the case draws from Western religious traditions, this chapter initiates a timely and constructive discussion on the inner workings of religion, its colonial assumptions, and its impact on the environment.

The remaining subsections characterize the study of religious environmental movements and offer two potential lines of reflexivity in religious forms of anti-environmentalism. The next section then offers an account of reflexive anti-environmentalism in the decolonization of REOs in the Trans Mountain resistance. The chapter concludes by offering several potential research themes and questions for the broader religious anti-environmentalism literature.

Characterizing Religious Environmental Movement(s) as Response to Anti-Environmentalism

The religious environmental movement[1] is an upsurge of religious interest that repositions environmental issues in religious and moral terms (Ellingson, 2016; Grim and Tucker, 2014; Nita, 2016; Smith and Pulver, 2009; Tomalin, 2009). Religious environmentalism has emerged in light of the greening of religion debate stemming from the Lynn White thesis (Bauman et al., 2011; Taylor, 2016; White, 1967). Central to White's thesis, which asserted that Christianity is the root of the ecological crisis, is the diagnosis of the anthropocentric undertones of religion that shape anti-environmental attitudes (LaVasseur and Peterson, 2017). As some scholars have argued, the problem is not restricted to Christianity per se, but certainly his assertions have been most hard-hit among Christian apologetics (Berry, 2013; LaVasseur and Peterson, 2017). Despite subsequent debates that have intensely criticized White's assertions (LaVasseur and Peterson, 2017), White's essay spurred development of new fields such as religion and ecology, which has claimed that the world's predominant religions are greening (Bauman et al., 2011; Berry, 2013; Grim and Tucker, 2014). Recent reviews of the literature to test this claim however have yielded mixed results (Taylor, 2016; Taylor et al., 2016).[2]

At their core, Lynn White's argument and its subsequent debates fundamentally recognized that the emergence of religious environmentalism was a response to the ways religion had been used to further anti-environmentalism. This insight was reflected in White's reading of the historical relationship between Christianity and Western science and technology (Stoll, 2017). From the seventeenth century onwards, the emerging Protestantism, alongside growing capitalism, beliefs in progress and science, and industrialization and resource exploitation through colonization, paved the way for massive environmental transformation (LeVasseur and Peterson, 2017; Northcott, 2017; Worthy et al., 2018). Religion, notably Christianity, cemented the foundation of the Western mind and its alienation of nature. These consequences could be seen reverberating throughout settler colonial states.[3] In effect, Lynn White's broader recognition of anti and indifferent attitudes embedded in religion galvanized an introspective inquiry into religious greening. Reckoning with this backstory of religious environmentalism underscores the multiple ways religion mediates visions of harmony or incitement of conflicts in society–nature relationships. Characterizing religious environmental movements therefore requires not only careful description of evolving practices in reconciling with its ambivalent or anti-environmental remnants, but also demonstrating how religious frameworks may steer its adherents towards greater connectivity with or separation from ecology.

Unpacking this backstory explains the motivations behind empirical research on religious environmental movements. Recent empirical assessments have highlighted the diversity of religious traditions and scale of religious actors (Ellingson, 2016; Johnston, 2013; Smith and Pulver, 2009; Nita, 2016; Veldman et al., 2014). Examining religious environmental movements thus underscores the importance of observing, identifying and assessing the multitude of actors, discourses and dynamics across multiple scales that point towards the relational nature of religious actors in response to its socio-ecological context. In particular, cosmologies that make epistemic and ontological claims about the nature of reality and sources of knowledge that are not verifiable solely by science warrant studying religious systems on their own terms (Veldman et al., 2014, p. 4). As such, religious vernaculars to examine how religious phenomena define environmentalism and anti-environmentalism on their respective terms allow for some degree of cross-scalar comparability and generalizability.

Religious environmental movements can be further classified across responses, actors and socio-demographic factors. The primarily US-centered religious environmentalism literature has found diverse responses from a multitude of actors, which have been popularized by institutional positions (e.g. Earth Charter, Laudato Si, Islamic Declaration on Climate Change) (Grim and Tucker, 2014; Taylor et al., 2016; UNEP, 2016). The composition of responses has come from ecumenical and interfaith coalitions, figures of authority (Bauman et al., 2011; Veldman et al., 2014), as well as communities, congregations (Veldman, 2016) and religious environmental organizations (Baugh, 2017; Ellingson, 2016; Johnston, 2013; Nita, 2016; Smith and Pulver, 2009). Race, ethnicity, gender and class in religious environmental movements have been examined to a limited extent (Baugh, 2017; Tomalin, 2009). Still, religious environmental movements have also emerged beyond the US (Amri, 2014; Botchway and Agyemang, 2012; Fair, 2018; Lysack, 2014; Tomalin, 2009; Veldman et al., 2014), highlighting contextualized expressions and trans-local linkages.

In summary, a majority of the religious environmentalism literature presents emergences of 'greening' at institutional and to some extent meso- and micro-levels. Accounting for religious environmentalism in multifaceted forms offers an array of approaches that capture the revolving relationships between religious environmentalism as response to religious anti-environmentalism. Nevertheless, to what extent such macro-scale efforts trickle into networks, materials and human resources needed in sustaining environmental campaigns and practices at the local levels (Ferber and Haluza-DeLay, 2015; Taylor et al., 2016, pp. 348–9) are areas in need of further examination. A critical task ahead then is to connect the normative dimensions of religious environmentalism (i.e. what religions interpret, teach or foster in greening their tradition) with the empirical evidence of emerging practices among religious actors.

How Can Religious Anti-Environmentalism Be Reflexive?

A less understood area of religious anti-environmentalism is its reflexive capacity. Reflexivity in religious anti-environmentalism is not entirely new. One can certainly make the case that academic reflexivity underlies the greening of religion debate and pioneering field of religion and ecology (Bauman et al., 2011; Grim and Tucker, 2014; Jenkins et al., 2018; Taylor, 2016). As Bauman and colleagues (2011, p. 5) note, the reflexive process among scholars and activists of religion and ecology through the combination of intellectual traditions of religions and everyday practices and actions of religion on the ground have been methodologically central to expanding the field. The activist-scholar field of religion and ecology thus forms a vital component of the reflexive intellectual state of religious environmentalism. More recently, Jenkins and colleagues (2018) noted their own reflexivity in academic arenas as they reviewed the literature on the relationship of religious systems and meanings of climate change. In their documentation of historians of religion who traced the links between the relationship of climate change and major periods of religious change, they found that formal religious bodies engaged in reflexivity by accelerating religious processes of interpretation and ritualization in response to massive climate and ecological changes. However, major disruptions to categories in religion also shape the relationship between religion and climate. As Jenkins and colleagues subsequently acknowledged, the categories of religion and climate change must be destabilized in the face of Indigenous[4] ways of perceiving climate. The socio-historical dynamics embedded in the category of religion, notably in its use during European colonization to legitimize colonialism, is problematic in how religion gets interpreted. Academic self-reflexivity on the relationship between religion and Indigenous knowledge systems has further prompted scholars of critical religious studies to initiate projects aiming to disentangle the complicity of religion and the discipline of religious studies in colonialism (Graber and Klassen, 2020; Nye, 2019). These illustrations of reflexivity reposition and chart out future lines pertaining to the academic study of religion and environmentalism.

This chapter positions reflexivity in the way religious actors come to practice religious anti-environmentalism. In practicing reflexive anti-environmentalism, religious actors may identify the potential tensions or conflicts that lie within existing structures of power, they may be able to self-correct, and offer alternative understandings that complement existing approaches. Adopting this general framing, two lines of reflexivity could be identified.

The first line of reflexivity may take aim at institutional bodies to foster the middle ground between religious institutions who are pushing greening efforts and the need to meet grassroots objectives and direct-action efforts of localized actors at mobilization sites. Endowed with resources and influence, religious institutions indeed are well positioned to lead greening efforts. Institutional resources and effort enabled, for instance, the United Church of Christ's Commission for Racial Justice to pull together the landmark report *Toxic Wastes and Race in the United States*, which brought nationwide attention to grassroots environmental justice movements and environmental racism in the US (Bullard et al., 2008). While such leadership moments to further greening efforts are encouraging, the institutional approach may neglect the emergence and agency of micro- and meso-level religious actors who simultaneously engage in greening efforts with greater relational proximity to affected communities in environmental conflicts. Actors operating at these levels may fine tune frameworks that conceive the relationship between practiced religion and connections to the natural world. Reflexive religious actors may find themselves negotiating their own positions in relation to the institutional hierarchies that may inhibit them from taking stronger actions (Lysack, 2014; Nita, 2016). This agential–structural tension suggests greater attention towards understanding the political spectrum and alignment of religious actors relative to their affiliated institutional counterparts. Meso- or micro-level religious actors that operationalize reflexivity could offer more grounded and fresh perspectives, build trust with impacted communities, commit to grassroots coalitions and resources, engage in advocacy, and participate in activism. These actors present among affected communities from environmental injustice may be more likely to act autonomously and position themselves in campaigns apart from their institutional counterparts. For instance, some religious groups and individuals who have connections with Indigenous communities who have reckoned with and are speaking up about the colonial past of their affiliated institutions are more inclined to support the Idle No More movement and participate in the Truth and Reconciliation Commission hearings in Canada (Denis and Bailey, 2016; Gilio-Whitaker, 2015). Exposing Indigenous–settler relations in the dynamics of religious environmentalism expands the range of possibilities, challenges and limitations for grassroots mobilizations. Underscoring the multiple logics of bottom-up reflexive religious anti-environmentalisms may unlock a broader set of messages and actions that may complement top-down approaches.

The second line of reflexivity taps into the multiple existing identities of activists in religious environmental movements. Socio-demographic factors, notably racial, gender and class identities, are becoming increasingly critical in understanding the diverse processes behind religious greening (Baugh, 2017; Bauman et al., 2011; Tomalin, 2009). These characteristics are shared across religious and mainstream environmental movements, even when the common treatment in the literature has been to distinguish activists and groups in religious environmentalism as distinct from mainstream environmentalism movements solely on the basis of religious affiliation (Smith and Pulver, 2009; Johnston, 2013; Ellingson, 2016). However, more recent evidence points to blurred lines between religious environmentalism and mainstream environmentalism. Nita's (2016) ethnographic study of Christians and Muslim activists in the Transitions Town movement in the UK and Lysack's (2014) observation of the splintering activists from the national conversation on religious unity on climate change across different religious traditions in Canada add to growing evidence of potential intermingling and identity switching present among activists who straddle both the religious and environmental movements. Furthermore, carving out religious identities in relation to their self-location to the political state as settlers or Indigenous peoples may add another layer to activist identities. In particular, the literature's reliance on pre-set jurisdictional boundaries as the setting of analysis has resulted in a vernacular of religious environmentalism that fixates on the substance of greening. However, it has neglected the broader historical-political dynamics of religious encounters with already existing Indigenous knowledge systems in settler colonial states. Deconstructing the geographical boundaries, histories, and settler identities in these states may complicate conventional understandings of religion and the environment (Jenkins et al., 2018) (see note 2). In this manner, reflexive religious actors can confront potential tensions and power structures underlying religious environmentalism such as unsettling religious history and its embeddedness in colonial formation. Extricating the multiple identities of religious actors thus exposits the relationship of religion in relation to place and history.

These two lines of reflexivity in religious anti-environmentalism offer starting points to situate the reflexivity of religious actors by evaluating the conditions underlying the progressions, successes and failures of emerging religious environmental movements. REOs' involvement in Indigenous-led pipeline resistance in Canada offers a concrete case that demonstrates how decolonization acts as a form of reflexivity in religious anti-environmentalism.

SITUATING REFLEXIVE RELIGIOUS ANTI-ENVIRONMENTALISM IN CANADA: INTERROGATING POLITICAL RESPONSIBILITIES AND IDENTITIES IN THE ERA OF 'RECONCILIATION'

This chapter argues that the decolonization of religious environmentalism in Indigenous-led resistance represents an emerging form of reflexive religious anti-environmentalism. This section begins by situating the Trans Mountain pipeline expansion project (TMX) resistance and the theoretical background concerning religious settler identities and claims to reconciliation. Reflexive religious environmentalism through decolonization can be demonstrated in two ways. First, members of REOs assumed political responsibility to honor commitments to reconciliation by engaging on the front lines. And second, members of REOs destabilized their own religious and settler identities.

Findings were based on a stratified, purposeful criterion sample (Marshall and Rossman, 2011) of seven REOs from Christian, Quaker, Unitarian and multi-faith traditions. REOs were found based on iterative searches and on ground observations by the research team in the field. REOs consisted of a spectrum of autonomous, semi-autonomous and institutionally affiliated organizations. They were fairly small in size, generally consisting of a few to tens of core members depending on respective characterizations. As REOs reflected a small subset of critical voices, their views and actions on Indigenous–settler dynamics did not necessarily reflect that of affiliated institutions (cf. Lysack, 2014 and Moyer, 2018).

Fifteen in-depth, semi-structured interviews with key informants were conducted from October to December 2018. Interviews were audio-recorded, transcribed verbatim, and member checked by interviewees. Interviews were triangulated with 107 movement texts of REOs (e.g. website posts, organizational statements, event pages), media sources, and documents from major resistance actors such as First Nations, environmental, and grassroots groups. Content and discourse analyses generated iterative themes and codes that centered on justice-based messages and Indigenous–settler dynamics.

The Trans Mountain Pipeline Expansion Project Conflict

The existing Trans Mountain pipeline carries approximately 300 000 barrels of refined petroleum and synthetic, light, and heavy crude per day from Alberta to the Westridge Marine Terminal in Burnaby, British Columbia, with connections to refineries in Washington State (NEB, 2016). The proposed Trans Mountain pipeline expansion project (TMX) would twin the existing pipeline, triple system capacity, allow for dual line operations, and serve up to 37 tankers per month (NEB, 2016). TMX faced numerous legal challenges and underwent two rounds of consultations and approvals, in 2016 and 2019 respectively. The National Energy Board's initial approval in 2016 stated that Kinder Morgan, the project owner at the time, must satisfy 157 conditions throughout the project lifecycle (NEB, 2016). However, in August 2018, the Federal Court of Appeal ruled that the federal government failed to fulfill its constitutional duty to engage in meaningful dialogue with affected First Nations. The Court subsequently tasked the National Energy Board to conduct another review that expanded consultation with Indigenous communities and focused on tanker traffic impact to marine ecosystems (Harris, 2018). The federal government's purchase of the Trans Mountain system in May 2019 and re-approval shortly after secured the fate of TMX.

The main controversy behind TMX stemmed from contrasting interpretations by different parties on the status of Indigenous consent (Hoberg, 2018b). Although TMX proponents upheld the importance of the process of consultation, they nevertheless claim that the lack of consent does not translate into a direct veto to the project (Hoberg, 2018b, p. 79), whereas First Nations groups, environmental, and grassroots groups as well as religious environmental organizations have primarily framed project opposition over the lack of Indigenous consent.[5] Opponents upheld the importance of consent and procedural rule within the respective legal framework of the United Nations Declaration for the Rights of Indigenous Peoples (UNDRIP) and laws within respective Indigenous community territories (Hoberg, 2018b, pp. 84–5). These divisions marked the differences in interpreting consultation and accommodation as a procedural step rather than respecting the right of Indigenous communities to consent to projects affecting their lands and titles (Hoberg, 2018b, p. 88). In the TMX resistance, opponents deployed numerous campaign tactics such as speaking out at National Energy Board hearings, organizing multiple petitions, rallies, demonstrations, and coordinating efforts to engage in civil disobedience.

Decolonization as Destabilizing Religious Settler Identities and Conferring Political Responsibility in 'Reconciliation'

Settlers may refer to anyone with the intention to make a new home and derive source of capital on appropriated Indigenous lands and '[insist] on settler sovereignty over all things in their new domain' (Tuck and Yang, 2012, p. 5). A synonymous but distinct term is 'settler colonialism', which is 'shaped by and shaping interactive relations of coloniality, racism, gender, sexuality and desire, capitalism and ableism' (Snelgrove et al., 2014, p. 2). Settler colonialism is specified through its approach to place, culture and relations of power and reflected in the ways settler states govern their subjects (Snelgrove et al., 2014). The set of power relations between Indigenous peoples and settlers is made and reproduced for sustained understandings of temporal and spatial forms of settler colonialism (Snelgrove et al., 2014, p. 5). Re-ordering human–land relations, settler colonialism disrupts and destroys Indigenous ontological, epistemological and cosmological relationships to land (Tuck and Yang, 2012, p. 5). This prerogative in settler colonial states recognizes that climate change, as much as it objectifies anthropogenic climate change, is constructed upon settler colonial relations with Indigenous peoples and its transformations of political relations with the land (Whyte, 2016a, p. 3). The responsibility of settler colonialism as the base of climate change threatens Indigenous cultures and self-determinations, limiting the ability of Indigenous peoples to adapt to climate change (Whyte, 2016a, p. 7).

Conceptualizing 'religious settler'[6] offers an additional analytical layer to the identity of religious environmentalists as they wrestle with the expectations of and shortcomings in decolonization. Illuminating the religious dimensions of settlers emphasizes the concurrent cosmologies, relationships and ethics that could intersect or conflict with Indigenous knowledge systems. At the same time, religious identities connote historical realities that may become evident in the settler's self-location in light of settler colonial structures that emerge from Indigenous struggles. Deconstructing one's knowledge of the settler history and to step into Indigenous stories of the land that one stands on represents a posture to re-orienting political–ecological–cosmological relations in settler colonial contexts. Calls to decolonization therefore initiate a lifelong destabilization of the meanings and responsibilities of being religious and settler on Indigenous lands.

Religious settler consciousness and transformation under decolonization may offer a pathway to reflexive religious anti-environmentalism (Davis et al., 2017; Denis and Bailey, 2016; Heinrichs, 2018). However, well-intentioned attempts of settlers, settler states and settler institutions may risk using reconciliation as an abolition of guilt (Jung, 2018; Tuck and Yang, 2012). Such efforts towards decolonization may continue to perpetuate reconciliation as a project of affirmation or move towards innocence in hopes of finding closure or achieving redemption through the act of listening (Davis et al., 2017; Jung, 2018; Tuck and Yang, 2012). In the Canadian and US settler colonial contexts, Christianity is often implied to be the culprit regarding the colonial legacies that continue to govern discriminatory policies against Indigenous peoples (Heinrichs, 2016, 2018; Yellowhead Institute, 2019). Christian settlers and institutions, for instance through sacraments, may offer apologies in exchange for forgiveness but could instill settler normalcy and absolution of any future accountability of past wrongs (Jung, 2018). Such moves to innocence have been criticized for relieving persons or communities of guilt and responsibility without fundamentally changing the initial conditions or wrongs (Jung, 2018; Tuck and Yang, 2012). Religious settlers may find that well-intentioned efforts towards reconciliation with Indigenous peoples (e.g. participating in Truth and Reconciliation Commission hearings) aside from statements require calls to the broader struggle for Indigenous rights and sovereignty (Denis and Bailey, 2016; Heinrichs, 2016). Response of religious settlers to Indigenous–settler reconciliation in an ambivalent or negative light is also plausible. Religious settlers may be assured that there is no compelling reason to recognize the inherent rights and self-determination of Indigenous peoples, or even go so far as to deny any wrongdoing to Indigenous peoples and perpetuate inscriptions of empire in political, economic and social structures.

Claims to reconciliation thus demand interrogating how religious settlers begin decolonizing by taking political responsibility to Indigenous peoples on the legacy of settler colonialism (Maddison and Statsny, 2016, p. 232). Some religious settlers and Indigenous leaders have pointed to the importance of unlearning one's tradition and reliance on colonial assumptions (Heinrichs, 2016; 2018). Unlearning is integral to unsettling one's identity or else reconciliation initiatives may offer false optimism when it fails to promote substantive change (Davis et al., 2017, p. 408). Indeed, any attempts at reconciliation necessarily encompass settlers who commit towards helping in the restoration of Indigenous rights, sovereignty, and land repatriations under Indigenous resurgence (Asch et al., 2018; Tuck and Yang, 2012; Whyte, 2018a; Yellowhead Institute, 2019). In the context of resources development, heeding Indigenous sovereignty and governance fundamentally means that Indigenous peoples have the final say to decide on activities on their lands (Yellowhead Institute, 2019). In striving towards eco-justice or environmental justice, religious settlers have an obligation to face the history of religious complicity in settler colonialism to make amends on reconciliation.

While the above discussion stems from the perspective of Indigenous–religious settler relations in Canada and the US, its potential lies in destabilizing the assumptions underlying the US-centered forms of religious environmentalisms which have thus far neglected to account for the history of the land religious environmentalism states it is practicing upon. Ultimately, decolonizing religious environmentalism could materialize into a reflexive posture that unsettles one's own religious traditions and complicity to settler colonial thoughts and structures while concurrently attending to broader calls to participate in Indigenous-led struggles.

Justice-Based Messaging on Reconciliation

The history and relationship between religious institutions and Indigenous peoples in Canada foregrounded the justice messaging of REOs in the TMX resistance. Centering on justice presents deep introspection into the religious history of Canada, thanks largely to the legacy of Christianity and its permanence in colonial discourse of the 'founding' of Canada as a 'young' nation (Regan, 2010). The course of 'reconciliation' responses within specific religious denominational bodies in Canada had been framed in response to the legacy and impacts of *terra nullius* (or vacant land) and the Doctrine of Discovery (Anglican Church of Canada et al., 2016; Canadian Conference of Catholic Bishops, 2016; TRCC, 2015b). Originating from fifteenth-century Papal Bulls, *terra nullius* and the Doctrine of Discovery effectively asserted that Indigenous peoples had no sovereign rights in relation to their own land, thus legitimizing European seizure of Indigenous lands (Newcomb, 2008; Reid, 2010). The monumental impact of the Doctrine of Discovery in Canada continues to linger in contemporary legal disputes underlying Indigenous land claims and resource development (Reid, 2010; Yellowhead Institute, 2019).

Recent national conversations over reconciliation stemming from the Truth and Reconciliation Commission of Canada (TRCC) further compounded the case to honor historical treaties and respect Indigenous rights and sovereignty. Launched in 2010, the TRCC held hearings across Canada, placing in the public spotlight the testimonies of Indian Residential School survivors from their experiences of the committed atrocities in the Indian Residential School system. Establishment of the school system, in the words of the TRCC, 'was based on an assumption that European civilization and Christian religions were superior to Aboriginal culture, which was seen as being savage and brutal' (TRCC, 2015a, p. 4). A central piece of the

Canadian government's policy to assimilate Indigenous peoples into settler society, the Indian Residential School system enrolled over 150 000 First Nations, Métis and Inuit children in over 100 years of operations, with the last school closing in the 1990s (TRCC, 2015a, p. 33). Schools were poorly maintained, heated and staffed; Indigenous languages and cultures were denied and suppressed; and students were regarded as intellectually inferior, obliged to complete chores to sustain school operations, and physically and sexually abused by staff (TRCC, 2015a, pp. 3–4). Centrally, the TRCC brought to national awareness the genocide and lasting trauma inflicted upon Indigenous peoples. In 2015, the TRCC published the six-volume report and recommended 94 Calls to Action for all sectors of Canadian society, from governments, institutions, to businesses, schools and church organizations in hopes of educating Canadians about their colonial history and urging them to assume responsibility towards a reconciled relationship with Indigenous peoples (TRCC, 2015a, 2015b). Despite the national discourse over reconciliation, Indigenous scholars such as Glen Coulthard (2014) remain skeptical over the politics of recognition infused in reconciliation rhetoric. Such views have been compounded by ongoing disparities in Indigenous communities on public health, treaty rights and land claims, and natural resource development (Roache, 2015; Yellowhead Institute, 2019). Recent flashpoints such as the Wet'suwet'en land defences against a proposed natural gas pipeline project in northern BC have led some Indigenous writers and land defenders to conclude that 'reconciliation is dead' (Ballingall, 2020; Talaga, 2020).

Religious responses to the TRCC's Call to Actions have coalesced religious actors in an attempt to take responsibility for the legacy of the Doctrine of Discovery and educate religious communities on the history of colonialism in Canada. While religious institutions that ran Indian Residential Schools have respectively issued statements apologizing for their complicities in the school system and towards Indigenous peoples, the Roman Catholic Church has yet to apologize officially (Anglican Church of Canada, 2015; Dube, 2016). Other informal and grassroots religious efforts such as KAIROS and Citizens for Public Justice have similarly responded by leading efforts on decolonization, reconciliation education, and policy discussions to respond to TRCC's Calls to Action (KAIROS Canada, 2010; Munn-Venn, 2018). Other attempts to engage in reconciliation have come in the form of deconstructing the linkage of Christianity and settler colonialism. A cluster of First Nations and Christian thinkers have called for more grassroots attempts to advocate for the implementation of UNDRIP and advocate alongside Indigenous peoples on the front lines of Indigenous-led movements (Heinrichs, 2016).

The broader context of Indigenous–religious reconciliation broadly informed religious actors at all levels in framing opposition to resource development projects as contradictory to the aims of reconciliation. In particular, national religious bodies such as the Anglican Church, Canadian Friends Service Committee, KAIROS, Mennonite Church, and the United Church have issued public statements in support of Indigenous opposition to TMX (Canadian Friends Service Committee, 2014; Dueckman and Muir, 2018; KAIROS Canada, 2018; Kidd, 2018; and United Church of Canada, 2016). Statements expressed regret and opposition because of TMX's resulting climate change impacts and breaching of free, prior and informed consent principles under UNDRIP.

REOs echoed calls to justice similar to their institutional counterparts. At the meso- and micro-levels, REOs articulated motivations and goals of religious responses to Indigenous reconciliation, stressing the importance of free, prior and informed consent among Indigenous communities opposing TMX. Their emphasis on respecting the consent of First Nations to the project can be read most directly in view of the direct opposition from the Tsleil-Waututh Nation, the local First Nation whose traditional territory encompasses the terminus of TMX.

Yet, REOs differed from institutional counterparts in their extensive engagements on the ground to commit to solidarity actions in the TMX resistance. REOs had been involved in the resistance since 2012 during the initial project proposal. REO members were immersed in various activist circles that informed their positions and strategies in advancing resistance efforts. The Unitarian Church of Vancouver initiated one of the first responses, where they issued a rare public statement expressing the congregation's opposition to the project. Other REOs such as Earthkeepers and Vancouver Quakers spoke out in opposition at National Energy Board hearings. The first wave of organized protests in 2014 catalyzed subsequent REO mobilizations and network building between 2015 and 2017. During this period, individual activists coalesced to form new REOs (e.g. Earthkeepers and Salal + Cedar), collaborated on events (e.g. Ecological Stations of the Cross), and broadly participated in wider campaign events. The first few months of 2018 highlighted the convergence of religious environmental efforts with the broader resistance. Events in February and March 2018 became turning points in gathering movement momentum for First Nations and environmental groups such as Protect the Inlet, Greenpeace, and 350.org in rallying broader resistance. Semi-organized actions by members of Salal + Cedar, Justin Trudeau Brigade, and other local activists from Burnaby Residents Opposing Kinder Morgan offered additional support and resources to the front lines where they disrupted ongoing geotechnical assessments. This wave of action was followed by a march of thousands of people on Burnaby Mountain on 10 March prior to an indefinite injunction order surrounding the Trans Mountain facility in mid-March (Protect the Inlet, n.d.). With injunction restrictions on public gatherings around the facility, Protect the Inlet, one of the forefront First Nations groups, announced a new wave of protests, including a wide call for mass civil disobedience outside the gates of the facility. The call for civil disobedience resulted in arrests of more than 170 activists on the week of 17–24 March (Protect the Inlet, 2018c). Between arrests of high-profile activists, politicians, artists, retired professionals, and other citizens from March to May 2018 (Protect the Inlet, n.d.), media coverage from mainstream outlets and Indigenous campaigns additionally featured the arrests of members from REOs and other faith communities on 20 April, 28 April and 28 May (Coast Protectors, 2018; Pawson, 2018; Protect the Inlet, 2018a, 2018b).

The Faith Day of Action on 28 April 2018 emerged as a key event that coalesced religious responses to Indigenous calls for solidarity. The event materialized as a result of collaborative discussions behind the scenes between one key REO, Salal + Cedar, as well as leaders from First Nations and environmental groups. This collaboration subsequently materialized into a statement by Will George of the Tsleil-Waututh Nation. In the statement, George not only emphasized the urgency in stopping Kinder Morgan and its threats to Coast Salish lands, waters, culture and spirit, but urged people of faith to take bold action against Kinder Morgan on 28 April by standing with Coast Salish peoples as they asserted their traditions and practices on their territory, for the sake of 'reconciliation and decolonization'. That day, over one hundred members from REOs as well as individuals from faith communities comprising Christians, Muslims, Jews and Buddhists gathered outside the Kinder Morgan facility, with some activists engaging in civil disobedience by trespassing on the injunction line (Pawson, 2018). Responding to the direct call from the local First Nation signified a notable instance of a direct call of First Nations leadership for solidarity from religious communities. In spite of national calls for reconciliation, ongoing faith-based actions throughout the resistance and particularly on the Faith Day of Action underscored the timeliness of REOs in embodying the call to action.

In summary, REOs engaged in various courses of direct action, underscoring their autonomy to nimbly respond to local and immediate calls to action. Partnering with other REOs to organize events, engaging in advocacy, providing front-line support, and participating in acts of civil disobedience highlighted the inter-organizational efforts of REOs in forming a nascent religious environmental movement. Even so, formation of this movement has to be understood within the broader coalitional efforts of First Nations, environmental and grassroots groups.

The reflexive nature of REOs in activism further points to the internal dynamics between religious institutions and meso- and micro-level actors such as REOs. REOs pressed forward with commitments to step up on the front lines in response to calls of Indigenous communities which went further than the institutional statements on reconciliation at the level of national religious bodies. Foregrounding Indigenous–settler dynamics and identities paved way for justice-based messaging of religious actors. REOs leveraged their relatively autonomous nature to adopt a stronger stance in opposing TMX. REOs thus adopted a grounded approach and fostered relationships with other resistance actors, which hinted at how religious actors can begin reflexivity on the grounds of resistance.

Destabilizing Religious and Settler Identities

A second way that religious actors demonstrated reflexivity under decolonization was in the destabilization of religious and settler identities. As REO members revealed, decolonization entailed a lifelong process of deconstructing colonial patterns that shaped religious thoughts, attitudes, structures and practices. Their accounts offered two ways in which decolonization can take place. First, REO members awakened to climate injustice through the lived experiences of Indigenous peoples. And second, REO members interrogated their religious and settler identities. Reckoning with the complicity of their religion in settler colonialism, the reflexivity of religious settlers forged new and sometimes unexpected pathways of practicing religion and learning the responsibilities of being a settler on Indigenous lands.

Reconciliation and climate change: seeing climate injustice through Indigenous experiences

REOs recognized the imperative of reconciliation to ground and articulate the realities of climate change. Messaging of REOs on reconciliation is explicitly recognized as a present-day issue between relations of settlers and Indigenous peoples linking the historical continuity of the sources and causes of climate change to Indigenous land dispossession. Particularly, the experiences of Indigenous peoples and other marginalized voices were perceived to exemplify the human toll of climate change. For Streams of Justice, a REO that articulated liberation theology in connecting global struggles to personal action, their members had actively worked on the intersections of Indigenous rights, migrant labor, poverty, and climate justice. When asked how climate change is framed in the REO, one member contrasted the global framing of climate change as a problem and its personal relevance:

> climate change is this kind of universalizing ... it's going to affect everyone, and now we should care about it because suddenly my interests are threatened, but I think that just sort of exposes the inequalities in terms of environmental risks that people have based on social inequalities ... the way

I have understood the framing [of climate change is] more about these historical and ongoing and much more immediate kinds of threats.

Personalizing climate change through the lens of Indigenous peoples in terms of inequality of risks and harms suggests that the significance of validating subjective experiences on climate change is just as valuable as the universalizing impact of climate change. In the context of resource development of Canada, historicizing climate change in its immediacy and perceptiveness of threats from the direct experiences of particular people groups points towards the power of human experiences as proxies of climate change (Tschakert et al., 2017; Yellowhead Institute, 2019). Understanding the values and struggles of Indigenous peoples on addressing climate change, some members of Streams of Justice worked closely with various front-line Indigenous activists and groups resisting TMX and other natural resources development projects in Canada. Similarly, a member from the independent Catholic REO, Our Lady of Guadalupe Tonanzin Community Society, acknowledged the link of climate change with Indigenous reconciliation, 'we've done all these studies [on climate change], that's where the umbrella framework comes from. But where the actual action is has been in reconciliation and Indigenous issues.'

Framing climate change on the grounds for consent of First Nations implied not only that the stakes of climate change rested on the historical contributions of greenhouse gas emissions but that non-Indigenous decision-makers wielded enormous power and influence over changing land use. Issues of land recognition, rights and sovereignty had been inextricably tied to the marginalization of Indigenous communities to decision-making and consent in the history and current development of natural resources projects. As such, messaging of REOs on reconciliation highlighted Canada's simultaneous failures regarding economic, legal and political reconciliation with Indigenous peoples as well as failures to limit carbon emissions.

Reconciliation was also expressed as a process of finding common ground and heeding Indigenous voices. Earthkeepers, a Christian ecumenical REO, echoed this posture. Their web blog pointed to the significance of speaking up to honor the commitments to Indigenous reconciliation, while also challenging the inaction among the wider Christian community in response to TMX, 'If we as Christians want to be serious about reconciliation, then we have to ask: where is harm continuing to happen? ... And since silence is complicity, what will we as the church actually do about that harm?'

Messaging on reconciliation operationalized as a frame for REO members to see the direct connections between climate change and purpose behind Indigenous-led resistance. In illuminating the inactions of religious institutions, reflections of REO members underscored what they viewed as ways to offer tangible support and link the impending need to address climate change and urgency towards decolonization. This insight has been observed by Indigenous and non-Indigenous scholars who argue the inextricable links between settler colonialism, terraforming processes, and the underlying logic of severing relations (Asch et al., 2018; Davis and Todd, 2017; Whyte, 2016b). As Heaton Davis and Zoe Todd (2017, p. 774) further note, the processes of decolonization and addressing climate change and other environmental catastrophes involve not only Indigenous self-governance, return of stolen lands, and reparations, but also questioning the legitimacy of the nation-state structure. For religious settlers, the history of religion in Canada and its embeddedness with settler colonialism and formation of the Canadian settler state has to be first acknowledged before one can awaken to the ways climate change connects with ongoing injustices upon Indigenous peoples.

However, as the next subsection shows, how decolonization is approached individually could bring to light the representation and power dynamics that foregrounded the politics of solidarity with Indigenous peoples.

Interrogating religious and settler identities
Unpacking the motives for reconciliation opened up new and unexpected pathways for REO members to unsettle religious and settler identities in connection with the role of religion in settler colonialism. As Australian settler scholar Clare Land (2015, pp. 162–3) describes in her study of primarily non-Indigenous, White Australians engaging in solidarity with Indigenous peoples, this process of getting to know oneself or themselves in a historical and political context involves decolonizing one's thinking and minds and gaining a clearer view of the workings of race, privilege and complicity to colonialism at personal and structural levels.

REO members acknowledged one's privilege and position on the land they stood on. Although some respondents were more explicit than others, the general acknowledgement of one's identity hinted at the power dynamics that were often unconsciously exercised in posturing engagement with Indigenous peoples on their lands. One member from Earthkeepers candidly illustrated the framed conflict of TMX between settler and Indigenous rights to resources and sovereignties over unceded Indigenous lands:

> We as Settlers, as people who historically were not Indigenous, we were part of this because we wanted all this and this land. We didn't want to share it with people who were originally here. And yet, why are we the ones who are saying, we need to build the pipeline?

Her rhetorical question juxtaposed the paradox in pipeline support and opposition in the broader process of settler colonialism. Settlers have had the power to determine the use of resources, while the voices and rights of Indigenous peoples had been and continue to be marginalized. Nevertheless, as this member and others at Earthkeepers have demonstrated, awakened settlers have the power and privilege to shift the terms of debate by channeling their stories of settler awakening in the messages and actions of REOs in support of Indigenous rights. Yet, the privileges afforded by settlers simply for being non-Indigenous may stand in the way of allying in Indigenous struggles. Another member of Earthkeepers acknowledged his privilege in recalling his experiences confronting the police in the early demonstrations and acts of civil disobedience against TMX in 2014:

> It wasn't going to change things in and of itself and with the recognition that as a White, middle-class, cis-gender … settler, I have a whole bunch of privilege and I am not treated the same way as people of color or are Indigenous when they confront the police.

This member's reflection underscored the workings of race, class and gender that intersected one's position and access to the afforded spaces of religious environmental activism. Race, class and gender also resonated in a different light during the court testimony of a member from Streams of Justice who engaged in civil disobedience on the Faith Day of Action in 2018:

> I am here today as I was on the day I was arrested for participating, like others, in nonviolent civil disobedience – standing in solidarity with Indigenous people, here on these territories, and across Turtle Island. I mean no disrespect to the court in my actions. I simply wish to live in a way that honours those whose voices, stories, and wisdom predate the court system on these lands, and whose rights remain unrecognized. Myself, I come from a migratory people, a family tree with a history

of displacement like many living in diaspora. It is here on these territories that Indigenous Elders, siblings, and friends have generously taught me the beauty and resonance in being rooted to a place, in speaking to ancestral knowledge, power, and pride, in protecting the land and water as sacred.

As a self-identified Chinese woman, her testimony pointed to the potential for religious, Colored settlers to reflect on their own stories and encounters with Indigenous peoples on these lands. Deciding where one stood on the Trans Mountain decision was an initiation to either reject, remain indifferent to, or heed the calls of Indigenous peoples. Actions out of reconciliation thus crystallized the praxis of self-reflexivity among religious settlers, pulling them towards a common purpose of defending lands alongside local Indigenous nations.

Beyond activism, unlearning one's identity as a religious settler also represented a longer process of educating on decolonization. The logic behind unlearning implied a process of abandoning thought and practices that perpetuated the colonial mindset in the first place. Religious settlers can be open to experimenting with alternative expressions in their traditions as they learn about Indigenous issues and promote renewed, sustained engagement (Nadeau, 2016). As part of the wider network of KAIROS Canada, the Vancouver Quakers regularly organized the Blanket Exercise.[7] The exercise would immerse participants in the experiences of Indigenous peoples on the land as they endured the legacy of and in resisting ongoing settler colonialism.

An extension of this education process entailed trenchant critique of colonial patterns, structures and interpretations including that of their affiliated religious institutions. Unlearning one's own knowledge about the political and religious institutions in relation to colonial processes opened up alternative lines of interpretations and teachings. For some members of Earthkeepers, reconciliation demanded rejection of existing interpretations in favor of post-colonial interpretations that justified actions on the lines of Indigenous resistance. Two founding members of Earthkeepers argued for readings of liberation of peoples to override readings of 'consumerist and capitalist influence'. One member attributed this latter 'therapeutic' reading of the gospel as a narrow interpretation rooted in Western evangelical Christianity that strictly focused on the inner peace of the individual and family. Such expressions remained mute on matters beyond personal circumstances. Instead, this member pushed forward an interpretation of the Christian gospel that was rooted in the liberation narrative of peoples and their relationship with the land. Similarly, another member of Earthkeepers stressed that religious settlers be respectful in residing on unceded Indigenous lands and commit to long-term engagement and solidarity with local Indigenous communities who were on the front lines of resistance against resource extraction. For these members of Earthkeepers, their pursuit for alternative lines of interpretations represented liberation from colonial interpretations and ushered new ways of circumscribing relationships with neighbors and the earth. Individual experiences with their institutional bodies validated their diagnosis of the historical problems and patterns that continued to fashion church structure and practices.

Linked to this structural critique in decolonial reflexivity was the corporate unlearning of colonial thought and language couched in Whiteness that remained present in Christian institutions. A member of Streams of Justice bluntly pointed to the 'White man's education curriculum' and ties of Christianity to empire as responsible for dispossessing and eliminating Indigenous peoples from their lands. Their own efforts towards solidarity with Indigenous struggles and their own paths of decolonization were therefore inseparable with decentering Christianity from Whiteness and its severance of relationships with the land. Another member of Streams of Justice further noted the importance of de-constructing these ideologies and rhythms which have shaped the historical and present-day Christian church. Unlearning these patterns therefore would magnify the platforms of affected Indigenous peoples. Institutional critiques served to deconstruct the role of religious institutions in continuing to perpetuate and guide such ideologies that bore the racism and genocide committed upon Indigenous peoples. In this process, religious settlers may face contradictions of living within the system, while also becoming agents seeking reforms (Denis and Bailey, 2016; Land, 2015). Engagements in unlearning and relearning became opportunities for critical reflection, transforming White and Colored religious settlers in the process of unlearning their own past and committing to Indigenous solidarity.

The political implications of religious settler reflexivity in Indigenous-led resistance challenge static and rigid binaries in religious and settler identities. Unsettling accounts of REO members complicated the fixation of 'greening' of religious traditions as these accounts exposed the colonial assumptions embedded in their very intellectual traditions and everyday practices of religion. Destabilizing society–nature relationships and assumed political relations of ownership and sovereignty in religious environmentalisms revealed the historical linkages and complicity of namely White, cis-gender, Euro-American Christianity that has fashioned anthropocentric human–land relationships on Turtle Island. If the purpose of religious environmentalism intends to re-establish cosmological, planetary and ecosystem relationships in religious traditions, then it would be imperative to unmask the complicity of religious environmentalism in settler colonial history, posture openness towards reconciliation, and re-imagine socio-political factions.

A corollary discussion in interrogating religious and settler identities is the lens of race, class and gender in connection to decolonization. Placing religious actors as the subjects of destabilizing religion, colonialism and race unsettled their own affiliated religions or the state-inscribed religion, along with their own burdens of settler privilege and race. The simultaneous involvement of some REO members in struggles for migrant and sexual minority rights added further weight to exposing the uncomfortable questions that may be unwelcome in institutional settings. Yet, their own undertakings and actions did not fully reject their affiliated institutions. Instead, their criticism was directed towards recognition that institutions that had been complicit in systematic injustices may also serve as a voice for the oppressed (Heinrichs, 2016, 2018). In this manner, interrogation of religious and settler identities along racial, class and gendered lines represented a fundamental acknowledgement of the many imperfections of institutions while seeking to address power dynamics and rectify injustices. Exposing the complex structural politics of religion, however, has not discouraged individual religious settlers across different backgrounds from forging new pathways towards repairing relationships with Indigenous communities and the land.

Interrogating religious and settler identities further raised questions on how religious actors conceive their relationship with climate. Indigenous writers and scholars have written extensively on the irreconcilable link between the impacts of climate change from centuries of settler colonial transformation of the land (Davis and Todd, 2017; Whyte, 2018b). Potawatomi scholar Kyle Powys-Whyte notes that for many Indigenous peoples, ecological change represents not only a déjà vu (Whyte, 2018a) but relational tipping points (Whyte, 2019). Indigenous-led resistances have ignited possibilities and pushed the boundaries of conventional wisdom in reflexive religious anti-environmentalism, challenging the ways religious language can be couched in human–nature binaries and its assumptions under settler colonialism. The decolonizing accounts of REO members not only captured glimpses of small but important starting points that inform the iterative process of awakening to settler responsibilities to Indigenous peoples and the land. They also add weight to the transformations that are needed at meso- and micro-levels for scalar and context-based reflexive religious anti-environmentalism. The richness of this bottom-up strand of reflexive anti-environmentalism not only surfaces the multiple ways of knowing among religious actors in relation to place but points out the limits of clear-cut categorizations and top-down approaches embedded in academically driven and institutionally-led efforts in religious environmentalisms.

CONCLUSION: CONTENDING A DECOLONIAL REALITY IN REFLEXIVE RELIGIOUS ANTI-ENVIRONMENTALISM(S)

This chapter has argued that decolonization represents a form of reflexive anti-environmentalism. Examining responses of REOs to responsibly honor commitments to reconciliation and personal destabilization of religious and settler identities in the TMX resistance has revealed starting points in articulating reflexivity of religious anti-environmentalism under decolonization. The findings further highlighted the reflexivity of micro- and meso-level actors who were committed to working to address environmental imperatives, concretize institutional messages on the front lines, but also confronted with shortcomings of top-down approaches. Religious undertones in legitimizing colonization and equipping state-led violence upon Indigenous peoples underscored the obligations of actors to develop self-correcting critiques of their traditions while also engaging with affected communities. Such spaces for criticism, introspection and action establish the parameters of reflexivity for religious actors in anti-environmentalism. If decolonization of broader religious environmentalism and indeed of entire religious traditions is to be taken seriously, religious actors of all stripes including gatekeepers have a critical role to play in reconciling their own relationship and responsibility in relation with affected Indigenous communities. Acknowledgement of the harms done in the name of religion and taking the reins to rectify the harms represents only the beginning of restitution from centuries of colonialism.

Focusing on the potential of reflexive religious anti-environmentalism in the Canadian context raises a number of research themes for religious anti-environmentalism scholarship. The two lines of reflexivity proposed in this chapter are by no means exhaustive. Similar examinations to compare global and far-reaching impacts of religious anti-environmentalisms across segments of society could provide a macro snapshot and explanation of varying emergences. In particular, identifying contextual logics of religious anti-environmentalism in their interactions with the socio-political terrain can mature conceptualization and spectrum of approaches. With the participation of religious actors in environmental and climate movements (Stoddart et al., Chapter 1 in this volume), potential collaborations or fractures may emerge. As such, religious anti-environmentalism may have to negotiate its own place in relation to the global climate movement and other simultaneous movements operating at corresponding levels. Furthermore, repeated calls for sustained activism and acts of civil disobedience in the climate movement (Dietz and Garrelts, 2014) also raise questions on demarcating the blurry identities of religious actors (Nita, 2016). A decolonial form of religious anti-environmentalism could translate to upholding Indigenous rights and supporting and defending land defenders or water protectors as in the case of #NoDAPL (Sullivan-Clarke, 2020). Examining lines of solidarity and fracture in environmental resistance movements across Canada, the US as well as other Anglo-American settler colonial countries, such as Australia and New Zealand, could offer meaningful comparisons of reflexive processes and challenges to religious settler identities. These questions could be further extended to Global South contexts where the majority of religiously affiliated people now live (Pew Research Center, 2018). The lived realities for many marginalized communities, especially Indigenous peoples who are rarely consulted or placed foremost in considerations for extractive projects in 'post-colonial' states in the Global South, suggest that religious actors have an increasingly important role to play in rethinking how their traditions have established a precedent for these ecologically destructive forms of development. Vertical and horizontal examinations are further needed to better assess how religious actors adapt and respond to structural and historical critiques, and whether such efforts can be sustained and entrenched in the long term across all levels. Across these endeavors, focused conceptualizations and comparisons of the characterization of religious settlers as proposed earlier in this chapter could refine its operationalizations of individual as well as corporate responsibilities across religious traditions in Indigenous–settler relations.

Finally, future research on the role of religion in anti-environmentalism should consider the dialectical relationship of religion as a framework in understanding religious environmentalism and anti-environmentalism. Religion as a dynamic force cuts across economic, political, social (e.g. race, gender and class) and environmental dimensions. Viewing religion under these lenses redirects the attention from simply demonstrating simplistic assertions of religion as either pro- or anti-environment to comprehensively examining the interactive ways religion can take on classic or reflexive anti-environmental modes (Stoddart et al., Chapter 1 in this volume). Indeed, revisiting the force of religion in the classic anti-environmentalism literature therefore is not only warranted and timely but deeply relevant to identify pathways to disentangle religious problems. Socio-cultural relationships underlying the motivations of and impacts to religious actors with sites or materials that sustain environmental impacts and injustices (for example, see Dochuk, 2019) could offer critical discussion of the social, cultural and religious assemblages that may impede or facilitate transitions to new climate and energy realities for the twenty-first century. As scholarship in religious anti-environmentalism matures, employing this dialectical approach to understanding religious environmentalism and anti-environmentalism may prove pivotal to explaining how religion as a major force continues to shape responses to our ecological predicament.

ACKNOWLEDGEMENTS

The author would like to thank the editors for their critical comments and suggestions on earlier versions of this chapter. Materials presented in this chapter originated from the author's Master's thesis project. As such, the author would like to additionally thank George Hoberg, Leila Harris and Candis Callison for their supervision and guidance on the project.

NOTES

1. A core assumption in the literature on religious environmentalism is its treatment of Indigenous spirituality on a par with other 'world religions' in religious studies scholarship (Grim and Tucker, 2014). However, such equivalency of Indigenous spirituality is a simplification of Indigenous

spirituality, knowledges, culture and practices (Jenkins et al., 2018). As Jenkins and colleagues (2018, p. 15) state, '"religion" may be a distortive category to describe the biocultural ways of Indigenous peoples' as religion not only discriminates against Indigenous ways of life by separating 'supernatural' and 'scientific' ideas, but also religion 'was used as a category in the colonial period to delineate "primitive" from advanced cultures, and thereby legitimate colonialism.' It is important therefore to take a historically contextualized account of the complex discussions and associations between religious traditions and Indigenous spiritualities and Indigenous peoples.

2. Discussion of the intricacies of religion and the environment are beyond the scope of the chapter. Readers who wish to pursue further research on the greening of religion debate may be interested in Bron Taylor's extensive two-part review where he provides a recent and comprehensive assessment on the literature.

3. North American Christianity and its role in the myths of US nationalism and exceptionalism can be taken as a key example of religion serving as a force for anti-environmentalism. Some scholars have offered more nuanced interpretations, arguing that Christianity and religiosity helped forge modern American environmental thought, such as espousing intrinsic values of nature and promoting conservation policies (Berry, 2015; Stoll, 2015). Yet, such claims to early remnants of religious environmentalism privilege a one-sided Euro-Western, White, male-centered interpretation of environmental history. What can be presented as supposedly 'ecological' visions and policies may actually mask settler colonial violence and reinforce erasure of already existing socio-ecological relations of Indigenous peoples over the land prior to colonization (Hixson, 2013; Newcomb, 2016).

4. This reference to 'Indigenous' is generally used as an umbrella term referring to Indigenous peoples worldwide both as part of a larger collective identity shaped by common ancestral traditions on land and troubled relations with European settlement. Subsequent references in the chapter to 'Indigenous peoples' in the context of Canada refer specifically to First Nations, Inuit and Métis identities. Indigenous Foundations at the University of British Columbia offers a more comprehensive description and explanation: https://indigenousfoundations.arts.ubc.ca/aboriginal_identity _terminology/.

5. Climate change also foregrounds the pipeline conflicts across Canada (Hoberg, 2018a, 2018b). Critics have warned that TMX may become a catalyst for oil sands expansion, which could jeopardize Canada's goals to meet its emissions targets under the Paris Agreement (Sherlock, 2019).

6. Authors in the edited volume by Heinrichs (2016) respectively coin religious settlers and organized bodies of religious settlers on Indigenous lands as 'Settler Christians' and 'Settler Church'. Such conceptualizations could conceivably be extended to settlers of other religious identities, such as Settler Muslims, Hindus or Buddhists, but require further specification without risking over-generalization.

7. The KAIROS Blanket Exercise, created in 1997 in response to the Report of the Royal Commission on Aboriginal Peoples, invites participants to step into the role of Indigenous peoples walking on blankets that represented the land. The facilitator reads scrolls and carrying cards that ultimately determine the outcome of participants as they experience pre-contact, treaty-making, colonization, and resistance with European explorers and settlers. Participants conclude by debriefing their experiences.

REFERENCES

Amri, U. (2014) From theology to a praxis of 'eco-jihad': The role of religious civil society organizations in combating climate change in Indonesia. In: Veldman, R.G., Szasz, A. and Haluza-DeLay, R. (eds) *How the World's Religions are Responding to Climate Change: Social Scientific Investigations*. London: Routledge, pp. 75–93.

Anglican Church of Canada (2015) Response of the churches to the Truth and Reconciliation Commission of Canada. *The General Synod of the Anglican Church of Canada*. Available from: https://www.anglican.ca/tr/response-of-the-churches-to-the-truth-and-reconciliation-commission-of -canada/ (accessed 29 June 2019).

Anglican Church of Canada, Evangelical Lutheran Church in Canada, The Presbyterian Church in Canada, Religious Society of Friends (Quakers), The Salvation Army, and The United Church of Canada (2016) An ecumenical statement on the United Nations Declaration on the Rights of Indigenous Peoples: Responding to the Truth and Reconciliation Commission's call to action 48. *The Presbyterian Church in Canada.* Available from: http://presbyterian.ca/downloads/27656/.

Asch, M., Borrows, J. and Tully, J. (2018) *Resurgence and Reconciliation: Indigenous–Settler Relations and Earth Teachings.* Toronto: University of Toronto Press.

Ballingall, A. (2020). 'Reconciliation is dead and we will shut down Canada', Wet'suwet'en supporters say. *The Toronto Star.* Available from: https://www.thestar.com/politics/federal/2020/02/11/reconciliation-is-dead-and-we-will-shut-down-canada-wetsuweten-supporters-say.html.

Baugh, A.J. (2017) *God and the Green Divide: Religious Environmentalism in Black and White.* Oakland, CA: University of California Press.

Bauman, W., Bohannon, R. and O'Brien, K.J. (2011) *Inherited Land: The Changing Grounds of Religion and Ecology.* Eugene, OR: Pickwick Publications.

Berry, E. (2013) Religious environmentalism and environmental religion in America. *Religion Compass.* 7(10), pp. 454–66. Available from DOI: 10.1111/rec3.12065.

Berry, E. (2015) *Devoted to Nature: The Religious Roots of American Environmentalism.* Oakland, CA: University of California Press.

Bongers, F., Wassie, A., Sterck, F.J., Bekele, T. and Teketay, D. (2006) Ecological restoration and church forests in northern Ethiopia. *Journal of the Drylands.* **1**(1), pp. 35–44.

Botchway, D.-V. and Agyemang, Y.S. (2012) Indigenous religious environmentalism in Africa. *Religions: A Scholarly Journal.* **2012**(1). Available from DOI: 10.5339/rels.2012.environment.6.

Bullard, R.D., Mohai, P., Saha, R. and Wright, B. (2008) Toxic wastes and race at twenty: Why race still matters after all of these years. *Environmental Law.* **38**(2), pp. 371–411. Available from: http://www.jstor.org/stable/43267204.

Canadian Conference of Catholic Bishops (2016) The 'doctrine of discovery' and terra nullius: A Catholic response. *Canadian Conference of Catholic Bishops.* Available from: https://www.cccb.ca/site/images/stories/pdf/catholic%20response%20to%20doctrine%20of%20discovery%20and%20tn.pdf.

Canadian Friends Service Committee (2014) CFSC supports nonviolent work on Burnaby Mountain. *Canadian Friends Services Committee.* Available from: https://quakerservice.ca/news/cfsc-supports-nonviolent-work-burnaby-mountain/ (accessed 14 June 2019).

Caniglia, B.S., Brulle, R.J. and Szasz, A. (2015) Civil society, social movements, and climate change. In: Dunlap, R.E. and Brulle, R.J. (eds) *Climate Change and Society: Sociological Perspectives.* New York, NY: Oxford University Press, pp. 235–68.

Coast Protectors. (2018) Faith leaders arrested at Kinder Morgan gates. Available from: https://www.coastprotectors.ca/faith_leaders_arrested_at_kinder_morgan_gates.

Coulthard, G.S. (2014) *Red Skin, White Masks: Rejecting the Colonial Politics of Recognition.* Minneapolis, MN: University of Minnesota Press.

Davis, H. and Todd, Z. (2017) On the importance of a date, or decolonizing the Anthropocene. *ACME: An International Journal for Critical Geographies.* **16**(4), pp. 761–80. Available from: www.acme-journal.org/index.php/acme/article/view/1539.

Davis, L., Hiller, C., James, C., Lloyd, K., Nasca, T. and Taylor, S. (2017) Complicated pathways: Settler Canadians learning to re/frame themselves and their relationships with Indigenous peoples. *Settler Colonial Studies.* **7**(4), pp. 398–414. Available from DOI: 10.1080/2201473X.2016.1243086.

Denis, J.S. and Bailey, K.A. (2016) 'You can't have reconciliation without justice': How non-indigenous participants in Canada's Truth and Reconciliation Process understand their roles and goals. In: Maddison, S., Clark, T. and de Costa, R. (eds) *The Limits of Settler Colonial Reconciliation: Non-Indigenous People and the Responsibility to Engage.* Singapore: Springer, pp. 137–58.

Dietz, M. and Garrelts, H. (2014) *Routledge Handbook of the Climate Change Movement.* Abingdon: Routledge.

Dochuk, D. (2019) *Anointed with Oil: How Christianity and Crude Made Modern America.* New York, NY: Basic Books.

Dube, S. (2016) Aporia, atrocity, and religion in the Truth and Reconciliation Commission of Canada. In: Bradford, J.T. and Horton, C. (eds) *Mixed Blessings: Indigenous Encounters with Christianity in Canada*. Vancouver: UBC Press, pp. 145–63.

Dueckman, A. and Muir, R.W. (2018) Mennonites join in Kinder Morgan pipeline protest: Indigenous rights, climate change prompt action. *Canadian Mennonite*. Available from: https://canadianmennonite.org/stories/mennonites-join-kinder-morgan-pipeline-protest.

Ellingson, S. (2016) *To Care for Creation: The Emergence of the Religious Environmental Movement*. Chicago, IL: The University of Chicago Press.

Fair, H. (2018) Three stories of Noah: Navigating religious climate change narratives in the Pacific Island region. *Geo: Geography and Environment*. **5**(2), e00068. Available from DOI: 10.1002/geo2.68.

Ferber, M.P. and Haluza-DeLay, R. (2015) Scale-jumping and climate change in the geography of religion. In: Brunn, S. (ed.) *The Changing World Religion Map*. Dordrecht: Springer, pp. 203–15.

Gilio-Whitaker, D. (2015) Idle No More and fourth world social movements in the new millennium. *South Atlantic Quarterly*. **114**(4), pp. 866–77. Available from DOI: 10.1215/00382876-3157391.

Graber, J. and Klassen, P.E. (2020) North America, Turtle Island, and the study of religion. *Numen*. **67**(2–3), pp. 313–25. Available from DOI: 10.1163/15685276-12341581.

Grim, J. and Tucker, M.E. (2014) *Ecology and Religion*. Washington, DC: Island Press.

Harris, K. (2018) Ottawa gives pipeline regulator 22 weeks to review Trans Mountain expansion project. *CBC News*. Available from: www.cbc.ca/news/politics/natural-resources-trans-mountain-1.4832759.

Heinrichs, S. (2016) *Wrongs to Rights: How Churches Can Engage the United Nations Declaration on the Rights of Indigenous Peoples*. Intotemak.

Heinrichs, S. (ed.) (2018) *Unsettling the Word: Biblical Experiments in Decolonization*. Mennonite Church Canada.

Hixson, W.L. (2013) *American Settler Colonialism: A History*. 1st edn. New York, NY: Palgrave Macmillan.

Hoberg, G. (2018a) A line in the sand: How oil sands pipeline conflicts transformed climate politics in North America. Paper presented at the Annual Meeting of the International Studies Association, 4–7 April, San Francisco.

Hoberg, G. (2018b) Pipelines and the politics of structure: Constitutional conflicts in the Canadian oil sector. *Review of Constitutional Studies*. **23**(1), pp. 53–89.

Hoffman, A.J. (2011) Talking past each other? Cultural framing of skeptical and convinced logics in the climate change debate. *Organization & Environment*. **24**(1), pp. 3–33. Available from DOI: 0.1177/1086026611404336.

Jenkins, W., Berry, E. and Kreider, L.B. (2018) Religion and climate change. *Annual Review of Environment and Resources*. **43**(1), pp. 85–108. Available from DOI: 10.1146/annurev-environ-102017-025855.

Johnston, L.F. (2013) *Religion and Sustainability: Social Movements and the Politics of the Environment*. Sheffield: Equinox.

Jung, C. (2018) Reconciliation: Six reasons to worry. *Journal of Global Ethics*. **14**(2), pp. 252–65. Available from DOI: 10.1080/17449626.2018.1507000.

KAIROS Canada (2010) Indigenous rights: A KAIROS strategy. *KAIROS Canada*. Available from: https://www.kairoscanada.org/wp-content/uploads/2015/09/Indigenous-Rights-A-KAIROS-Strategy.pdf.

KAIROS Canada (2018) KAIROS Statement: Kinder Morgan Trans Mountain pipeline expansion project. *KAIROS Canada*. Available from: https://www.kairoscanada.org/kairos-statement-kinder-morgan-trans-mountain-pipeline-expansion-project.

Kent, E.F. and Orlowska, I. (2018) Accidental environmentalists: The religiosity of church forests in highlands Ethiopia. *Worldviews: Global Religions, Culture, and Ecology*. **22**(2), pp. 113–42. Available from DOI: 10.1163/15685357-02201101.

Kidd, J. (2018) National Indigenous Anglican Bishop 'grieved' over pipeline purchase. Available from: https://www.anglicanjournal.com/national-indigenous-anglican-bishop-grieved-over-pipeline-purchase/ (accessed 30 September 2019).

Land, C. (2015) *Decolonizing Solidarity: Dilemmas and Directions for Supporters of Indigenous Struggles*. London: Zed Books.

Landrum, A.R., and Vasquez, R. (2020) Polarized U.S. publics, Pope Francis, and climate change: Reviewing the studies and data collected around the 2015 Papal Encyclical. *WIREs Climate Change*, e674. Available from DOI: 10.1002/wcc.674.

LeVasseur, T. and Peterson, A. (2017) Introduction. In: LeVasseur, T. and A. Peterson, A. (eds) *Religion and Ecological Crisis: The 'Lynn White Thesis' at Fifty*. New York, NY, USA and Abingdon, UK: Routledge, pp. 1–18.

Lysack, M. (2014) Stepping up to the plate: Climate change, faith communities, and effective environmental advocacy in Canada. In: Veldman, R.G., Szasz, A. and Haluza-DeLay, R. (eds) *How the World's Religions are Responding to Climate Change: Social Scientific Investigations*. Abingdon: Routledge, pp. 157–73.

Maddison, S. and Statsny, A. (2016) Silence or deafness? Education and the non-indigenous responsibility to engage. In: Maddison, S., Clark, T. and de Costa, R. (eds) *The Limits of Settler Colonial Reconciliation: Non-Indigenous People and the Responsibility to Engage*. Berlin and Heidelberg: Springer, pp. 231–48.

Marshall, C. and Rossman, G.B. (2011) *Designing Qualitative Research*. 5th edn. London: Sage.

Moyer, J. (2018) Faith-based environmental work in Canada: A profile. *Western Geography*. **23**, pp. 60–85.

Munn-Venn, K. (2018) *Towards Reconciliation*. Available from: https://cpj.ca/towards-reconciliation.

Nadeau, D. (2016) Decolonizing religious encounter? Teaching 'indigenous traditions, women, and colonialism'. In: Bradford, J.T. and Horton, C. (eds) *Mixed Blessings: Indigenous Encounters with Christianity in Canada*. UBC Press, pp. 164–82.

NEB (2016) National Energy Board Report: Trans Mountain Expansion Project. *National Energy Board*. Available from: https://docs2.neb-one.gc.ca/ll-eng/llisapi.dll?func=ll&objId=2969681&objaction=download&viewType=1.

Newcomb, S.T. (2008) *Pagans in the Promised Land: Decoding the Doctrine of Christian Discovery*. Golden, CO: Fulcrum Publishing.

Newcomb, S.T. (2016) Original nations of 'Great Turtle Island' and the genesis of the United States. In: McGraw, B.A. (ed.) *The Wiley Blackwell Companion to Religion and Politics in the U.S.* Chichester: John Wiley & Sons, pp. 5–17.

Nita, M. (2016) *Praying and Campaigning with Environmental Christians*. 1st edn. Nature America Inc.

Northcott, M.S. (2017) Lynn White Jr. right and wrong: The anti-ecological character of Latin Christianity and the pro-ecological turn of Protestantism. In: LeVasseur, T. and Peterson, A. (eds) *Religion and Ecological Crisis: The 'Lynn White Thesis' at Fifty*. New York, NY, USA and Abingdon, UK: Routledge, pp. 61–74.

Nye, M. (2019) Decolonizing the study of religion. *Open Library of Humanities*. **5**(1), p. 43. Available from DOI: 10.16995/olh.421.

Pawson, C. (2018) 7 arrested as faith leaders protest Trans Mountain pipeline expansion in Burnaby. *CBC News*. Available from: http://www.cbc.ca/news/canada/british-columbia/faith-leaders-trans-mountain-protest-burnaby-1.4640502.

Pew Research Center (2015) Religion and views on climate and energy issues. *Pew Research Center*. Available from: https://www.pewresearch.org/science/2015/10/22/religion-and-views-on-climate-and-energy-issues/ (accessed 1 September 2020).

Pew Research Center (2018) *The Age Gap in Religion Around the World*. Pew Research Center. Available from: https://www.pewforum.org/wp-content/uploads/sites/7/2018/06/ReligiousCommitment-FULL-WEB.pdf.

Pou-Amérigo, M.-J. (2018) Framing 'Green Pope' Francis: Newspaper coverage of Encyclical Laudato Si' in the United States and the United Kingdom. *Church, Communication and Culture*. **3**(2), pp. 136–51. Available from: 10.1080/23753234.2018.1478229.

Protect the Inlet (n.d.) *Media*. Protect the Inlet. Available from: https://protecttheinlet.ca/media/.

Protect the Inlet (2018a) Faith leaders arrested at Kinder Morgan tank farm. *Protect the Inlet*. Available from: https://protecttheinlet.ca/faith-leaders-arrested-at-kinder-morgan-gates/.

Protect the Inlet (2018b) Faith leaders arrested blocking gates at Kinder Morgan marine terminal. *Protect the Inlet*. Available from: https://protecttheinlet.ca/faith-leaders-arrested-while-blocking-gates-at-kinder-morgan-westridge-marine-terminal/.

Protect the Inlet (2018c) Over 170 people arrested. *Protect the Inlet*. Available from: https://protecttheinlet.ca/988-2/.

Regan, P. (2010) *Unsettling the Settler Within: Indian Residential Schools, Truth Telling, and Reconciliation in Canada*. Vancouver: UBC Press.

Reid, J. (2010) The doctrine of discovery and Canadian law. *The Canadian Journal of Native Studies*. **30**(2), pp. 335–59. Available from: http://www3.brandonu.ca/cjns/30.2/06reid.pdf.

Roache, T. (2015) Top 5 Indigenous issues all Canadians should care about. *APTN National News*. Available from: https://www.aptnnews.ca/national-news/top-5-indigenous-issues-all-canadians-should-care-about/.

Roser-Renouf, C., Maibach, E., Leiserowitz, A. and Rosenthal, S. (2016) *Global Warming, God, and the 'End Times'*. Yale Program on Climate Change Communication. Available from: http://climatecommunication.yale.edu/wp-content/uploads/2016/07/Global-Warming-God-and-the-End-Times.pdf.

Ruelle, M.L., Kassam, K.-A. and Asfaw, Z. (2018) Human ecology of sacred space: Church forests in the highlands of northwestern Ethiopia. *Environmental Conservation*. **45**(3), pp. 291–300. Available from DOI: 10.1017/S0376892917000534.

Sachdeva, S. (2016) *Religious Identity, Beliefs, and Views about Climate Change*. Oxford Research Encyclopedia. Available from: http://oxfordre.com/climatescience/view/10.1093/acrefore/9780190228620.001.0001/acrefore-9780190228620-e-335.

Sherlock, T. (2019) IPCC authors urge NEB to consider climate impacts of Trans Mountain pipeline expansion. *National Observer*. Available from: https://www.nationalobserver.com/2019/01/21/news/ipcc-authors-urge-neb-consider-climate-impacts-trans-mountain-pipeline-expansion.

Smith, A. and Pulver, S. (2009) Ethics-based environmentalism in practice: Religious-environmental organizations in the United States. *Worldviews: Global Religions, Culture, and Ecology*. **13**(2), pp. 145–79. Available from DOI: 10.1163/156853509X438580.

Snelgrove, C., Dhammon, R. and Corntassel, J. (2014) Unsettling settler colonialism: The discourse and politics of settlers, and solidarity with Indigenous nations. *Decolonization: Indigeneity, Education & Society*. **3**(2), pp. 1–32. Available from: https://jps.library.utoronto.ca/index.php/des/article/view/21166/17970.

Stoll, M. (2015) *Inherit the Holy Mountain: Religion and the Rise of American Environmentalism*. New York, NY: Oxford University Press.

Stoll, M. (2017) Sinners in the hands of an ecologic crisis: Lynn White's environmental jeremiad. In: LeVasseur, T. and Peterson, A. (eds) *Religion and Ecological Crisis: The 'Lynn White Thesis' at Fifty*. New York, NY, USA and Abingdon, UK: Routledge, pp. 47–60.

Sullivan-Clarke, A. (2020) Decolonizing 'allyship' for Indian country: Lessons from #NODAPL. *Hypatia*. **35**(1) pp. 178–89. Available from DOI: 10.1017/hyp.2019.3.

Talaga, T. (2020) Reconciliation isn't dead. It never truly existed. *The Globe and Mail*. Available from: https://www.theglobeandmail.com/opinion/article-reconciliation-isnt-dead-it-never-truly-existed/.

Taylor, B. (2016) The greening of religion hypothesis (Part One): From Lynn White, Jr and claims that religions can promote environmentally destructive attitudes and behaviors to assertions they are becoming environmentally friendly. *Journal for the Study of Religion, Nature and Culture*. **10**(3), pp. 268–304. Available from DOI: 10.1558/jsrnc.v10i3.29010.

Taylor, B., Van Wieren, G. and Zaleha, B. (2016) The greening of religion hypothesis (Part Two): Assessing the data from Lynn White, Jr, to Pope Francis. *Journal for the Study of Religion, Nature and Culture*. **10**(3), pp. 306–378. Available from: 10.1558/jsrnc.v10i3.29011.

Tomalin, E. (2009) *Biodivinity and Biodiversity: The Limits to Religious Environmentalism*. Farnham: Ashgate.

TRCC (2015a) *Honouring the Truth, Reconciling for the Future: Summary of the Final Report of the Truth and Reconciliation Commission of Canada*. Truth and Reconciliation Commission of Canada.

TRCC (2015b) *Truth and Reconciliation Commission of Canada: Calls to Action*. Truth and Reconciliation Commission of Canada.

Tschakert, P., Barnett, J., Ellis, N., Lawrence, C., Tuana, N., New, M., Elrick-Barr, C. et al. (2017) Climate change and loss, as if people mattered: values, places, and experiences. *WIREs Climate Change*. **8**(5), p. e476. Available from DOI: 10.1002/wcc.476.

Tuck, E. and Yang, W.K. (2012) Decolonization is not a metaphor. *Decolonization: Indigeneity, Education & Society.* **1**(1), pp. 1–40.

UNEP (2016) *Environment, Religion and Culture in the Context of the 2030 Agenda for Sustainable Development.* United Nations Environment Programme.

United Church of Canada (2016) Letter on the Trans Mountain Pipeline. *United Church of Canada.* Available from: https://www.united-church.ca/news/trans-mountain-pipeline-decision-united-church-response.

Veldman, R.G. (2016) What is the meaning of greening? Cultural analysis of a Southern Baptist environmental text. *Journal of Contemporary Religion.* **31**(2), pp. 199–222. Available from DOI: 10.1080/13537903.2016.1152676.

Veldman, R.G., Szasz, A. and Haluza-DeLay, R. (2014) *How the World's Religions are Responding to Climate Change: Social Scientific Investigations.* 1st edn. Abingdon: Routledge.

Wardekker, J.A., Petersen, A.C. and van der Sluijs, J.P. (2009) Ethics and public perception of climate change: Exploring the Christian voices in the US public debate. *Global Environmental Change.* **19**(4), pp. 512–21. Available from DOI: 10.1016/j.gloenvcha.2009.07.008.

White, L. (1967) The historical roots of our ecologic crisis. *Science.* **155**(3767), pp. 1203–207. Available from: http://www.jstor.org/stable/1720120.

Whyte, K. (2016a) Indigenous peoples, climate change loss and damage, and the responsibility of settler states. *SSRN Electronic Journal.* Available from DOI: 10.2139/ssrn.2770085.

Whyte, K. (2016b) Is it colonial déjà vu? Indigenous peoples and climate injustice. In Adamson, J. and Davis, M. (eds) *Humanities for the Environment: Integrating Knowledge, Forging New Constellations of Practice.* Routledge, pp. 88–105.

Whyte, K. (2018a) On resilient parasitisms, or why I'm skeptical of Indigenous/settler reconciliation. *Journal of Global Ethics.* **14**(2), pp. 277–89. Available from DOI: 10.1080/17449626.2018.1516693.

Whyte, K. (2018b) Settler colonialism, ecology, and environmental injustice. *Environment and Society: Advances in Research.* **9**(1), p. 125. Available from DOI:10.3167/ares.2018.090109.

Whyte, K. (2019) Too late for indigenous climate justice: Ecological and relational tipping points. *Wiley Interdisciplinary Reviews: Climate Change*, p. e603. Available from DOI: 10.1002/wcc.603.

Wilkinson, K.K. (2012) *Between God and Green: How Evangelicals are Cultivating a Middle Ground on Climate Change.* New York, NY: Oxford University Press.

Worthy, K., Allison, E. and Bauman, W.A. (2018) Introduction. In: Worthy, K., Allison, E. and Bauman, W.A. (eds) *After the Death of Nature: Carolyn Merchant and the Future of Human-Nature Relations.* New York, NY: Routledge, pp. 1–16.

Yellowhead Institute (2019) Land back: A Yellowhead Institute red paper. *Yellowhead Institute.* Available from: https://redpaper.yellowheadinstitute.org/wp-content/uploads/2019/10/red-paper-report-final.pdf.

Zaleha, B.D. and Szasz, A. (2015) Why conservative Christians don't believe in climate change. *Bulletin of the Atomic Scientists.* **71**(5), pp. 19–30. Available from DOI: 10.1177/0096340215599789.

22. Anti-environmentalism in critical social science and new conservation
Helen Kopnina, Haydn Washington and Joe Gray

INTRODUCTION: DIFFERENT ASPECTS OF ENVIRONMENTALISM

Environmentalism and environmental activism have many different faces. This varies depending on the specific national or international context in which the group or individuals are defined, and also by whether it is individuals within, or inspired by, the movement doing the defining, or if it is those outside it. Sometimes environmental non-governmental organizations (ENGOs), 'environmental organizations', 'activists', 'conservationists' and grass-roots protest movements are lumped together with environmental government agencies or ministries concerned with regulating, managing or profiting from natural resources. Indeed, under the label of 'environmentalists', we can speak of many different organizations, movements, institutions, groups and individuals inspired – for one reason or other – to protect the environment and the nature of their region. One of the unifying features of these motivationally, ethically and operationally diverse groups is a concern to retain nonhuman life, be it on farmland or in forests, rivers, seascapes or other natural areas.

In the way that a generalized 'environmentalism' exists, we can also consider the opposite – a generalized 'anti-environmentalism'. This chapter will outline a number of areas in which anti-environmentalism represents an important challenge for environmental protection. 'Environmental protection' can refer to a simple act of a person recycling paper, but it can also refer to the much larger efforts to mitigate climate change, and even to the direct goals of biological conservation – addressing biodiversity loss by conserving natural areas and protecting threatened species. Conversely, anti-environmentalism is a very broad spectrum that runs from a municipal failure to facilitate paper recycling, say, to the murder of environmental activists protesting against damaging activities such as logging or poaching.

Social psychologist Paul Stern (2000) has made a distinction between behaviours that directly cause environmental change, such as the clear-cutting of forests, and behaviours that have an indirect impact on the environment. An example of the latter is the investment of pension funds in fossil fuels; this and other indirect behaviours shape the context in which choices are made that directly cause environmental change (Stern, 2000, p. 408). Following Stern's classification of direct and indirect environmental impact, we can also apply such a distinction to anti-environmentalism, of which there are passive or indirect effects on environmentalism, as well as direct ones, such as violent action. We will focus mostly on the indirect anti-environmentalism that subtly manipulates ethical discourse to position anthropocentrism as normative while ignoring ecocentric positions. This, we shall argue, has potentially devastating consequences in contexts where environmental action is needed the most. Here, we shall consider in detail the case of biological conservation at a time of major extinction crisis (e.g. IPBES, 2019). We will also investigate the causes of anti-environmentalism. First, we consider a number of examples of direct violent anti-environmentalism.

DIRECT ANTI-ENVIRONMENTALISM

Between the 1990s and the present, many hundreds of environmental activists have been murdered in South and Central America (Spanne, 2016; Watts and Vidal, 2017; Watts, 2018), Asia (Global Witness, 2013; Blet, 2018), Africa (Nixon, 1996; Burke, 2018) and elsewhere (Holmes, 2016). In Africa, for example, many environmental activists have been killed for protesting against the oil industry (Nixon, 1996) or defending wildlife against poachers in national parks (Burke, 2018).

In 2018, 20 environmental and land rights activists were killed in Guatemala alone (Vidal, 2018), part of a global total of at least 83 environmental defenders killed in the first 10 months of the year (The Guardian, 2018). As environmental protests have erupted around the globe, the killing continues. There is evidence that such murders are increasing in frequency: the rate of murders may be as high as four activists each week (The Guardian, 2018). Behind each murder is a tragic personal story. For instance, Jairo Mora Sandoval, a Costa Rican conservationist, was murdered on the same beach where he tried to protect turtles, his hands tied behind his back while he sustained grave injuries to his head (Fendt, 2015). Elsewhere in Central America, Berta Cáceres Flores and other environmentalists were killed in Honduras in 2016 (Spanne, 2016), while Isidro Baldenegro López, an Indigenous opponent of illegal logging, and other protestors were killed in Mexico in 2017 (Watts and Vidal, 2017).

In Western Europe, many climate change and biodiversity-related strikes have taken place in the last few years. In Europe, 'governing with the greens was never easy', as one article in *The Economist* (2014, p. 27) laments, reflecting on the death of French environmental activist Remi Fraisse, who was killed while protesting against the building of a dam that threatened biodiversity. Since October 2018, a group called Extinction Rebellion has blocked the streets of London and taken action in other areas to draw attention to the contribution to climate change and extinction of governments, through their consistent inability to act, and citizens, through private actions such as driving cars. The group members blocking the roads received threats by car owners and some were arrested (Laville, 2018; BBC, 2019). The protests in London received significant press coverage, but elsewhere in Europe, especially in the east, activism is often less well reported on. Even so, some news does appear; for example, in 2018, it emerged that Andrei Rudomakha, a Russian environmentalist and coordinator of the Environmental Watch on North Caucasus, had been severely beaten (The Moscow Times, 2018). Another recent example of violence comes from when peaceful protests to protect trees in a park in Istanbul, Turkey, escalated to police violence. This was reported to be another example of an old problem: 'the violence against environmental protesters began decades ago' (Aksogan, 2013). Also in Turkey, in 2017, Aysin and Ali Büyüknohutçu, who were beekeepers and environmental defenders, were murdered, and at the time of writing, no convictions have been made from what have been described as 'sham' trials (Watts, 2018).

In Asia, environmental activism – ranging from the opposition of logging and mining, through protests calling political attention to climate change, to actions to protect threatened species – has recently intensified. In Hanoi, Vietnam, protestors challenged the cutting down of centuries-old trees (The Economist, 2015). In 2017, a Vietnamese environmental activist

Nguyen Ngoc Nhu Quynh was sentenced to 10 years in prison for 'distributing propaganda against the state' (Nguen and Datzberger, 2018). In China, Lei Yang, who worked for the Chinese Association for Circular Economy, died following an arrest (Tatlow, 2016). Despite the popularity of the Chinese documentaries *Beijing Besieged by Waste* and *Under the Dome*, which exposed pollution, not much has changed as far as persecution of environmental protestors is concerned (Babones, 2017; Standaert, 2017).

In Cambodia, the anti-logging activist Chut Wutty was murdered following his protests (Vrieze and Naren, 2012; Global Witness, 2013). In 2016, three employees of ENGOs were convicted without evidence or proper trial in Cambodia (The Economist, 2016).

In the Middle East, there are similar cases. Reports have emerged, for instance, of environmental activists being imprisoned and tortured (Human Rights Watch, 2019; Margit, 2019).

Since the turn of the century in the United States, radical environmentalists have been labelled a number one terrorist threat (Liddick, 2006). In *The War Against the Greens*, David Helvarg (1989) describes Texan ranchers and loggers uniting against the environmentalists (p. 359). In the era of President Donald Trump, more indirect forms of anti-environmentalism have been reported (Greshko et al., 2019). Media articles have revealed a range of examples of institutional anti-environmentalism, including manipulation of bodies dealing with environmental protection and the cutting of funding for research into effects of climate change (e.g. Davenport and Landler, 2019) and biodiversity loss (Milman, 2019).

ANTI-ENVIRONMENTALISM IN ACADEMIA

Indirect or passive anti-environmentalism can be equally devastating, and perhaps even more so because its consequences are more covert. One type of academic anti-environmentalism can be summed up as 'denial', or in some cases, 'denial of denial'. Bjørn Lomborg (2001), for example, argues that claims of overpopulation, declining energy resources, deforestation, the loss of biodiversity, and climate change are not supported by scientific data. In his later work, Lomborg (2010) seems to accept the reality of climate change (thus denies denial), but remains very optimistic about easy techno-fix solutions. Especially in the United States, the industry-supported think tanks such as the Breakthrough Institute (n.d.), promote scepticism about the scientific evidence of climate change or biodiversity loss as a key tactic of the anti-environmental counter-movement (Jacques, 2012) and stimulate techno-optimism (Kopnina et al., 2020) that frames environmentalists as overtly alarmist and pessimist. The politically and media-orchestrated 'shallow' forms of anti-environmentalism pervade other arenas that shape broader cultural views and values (Norgaard, 2006).

A more tacit anti-environmentalism is the promotion of economic growth policies by governments that result in an increase in production and consumption and thus put escalating pressure on wild places, framed as 'natural resources' (Crist, 2012). This support of one type of economy-centred discourse simultaneously distances other discourses, creating what Norgaard (2006) describes as *collective avoiding*. Emotions play a pivotal role in this social organization of denial, with various psychological and socio-cultural factors responsible for reasons why people prefer to avoid or contradict scientific evidence. Emotion management, and social narratives, according to Norgaard, are central to denial, 'perspectival selectivity' and 'selective interpretation'.

Recently, though, indirect anti-environmentalism has appeared from an unexpected source, from academic disciplines that have 'environment', 'ecology' or 'conservation' in their titles, namely environmental anthropology, political ecology and conservation science. The emergence of so-called 'critical social science' and the 'new conservationists' (Kopnina et al., 2018), exposed by the 'Future of Conservation' debate, provided a venue for moral attacks against both the underlying ethic and practice of conservation, as well as against a generalized group of 'environmentalists' (Kopnina et al., 2018).

In the view of these various critical scientists, 'environmentalists' endanger poor people's livelihoods and violate human rights by punishing impoverished poachers and by imposing their own Western and elitist view of nature on poor communities (Kopnina et al., 2018). Some critical social scientists have focused their research and considerations on the social and economic rights of disadvantaged communities, on the unfair distribution of the benefits of conservation, or on the grievances caused by the establishment of protected areas (Brockington, 2002; Holmes, 2013; Büscher, 2014; Duffy et al., 2016). As described in more detail below, environmentalists are portrayed as a generalized group of neoliberal profit-seekers that displace local communities to welcome wealthy tourists (Chapin, 2004; West and Brockington, 2012; Minter et al., 2014). Critical social scientists and new conservationists have argued that environmentalists entrench economic inequality, as they marginalize local communities in order to generate conservation revenue (e.g. West and Brockington, 2012; Baviskar, 2013). While critical social scientists are usually opposed to neoliberalism and the growth economy, the new conservationists actually embrace the capitalist economy (Miller et al., 2014) and see technology as a solution to environmental crises.

Open acknowledgment of anti-environmentalism in academia is rare. A few academics have openly stated their position, such as Kalland (2009), who has acknowledged that his sympathy lies with the whalers and not with whales. In anthropocentrically motivated attacks on conservationists and 'environmentalists', the entitlements to the benefits derived from the exploitation of wildlife are often ethically unquestioned – as long as local, vulnerable or poor communities profit from it. Some environmental anthropologists, ecological economists, social geographers and political ecologists such as Rosaleen Duffy, Bram Büscher, Paige West, Dan Brockington, George Holmes and Robert Fletcher, and organizations such as Cultural Survival, have attacked a generalized group of 'neoliberal conservationists' that they often broadly label 'environmentalists' (Colchester, 2004). Their accusation is that conservation organisations profit from conservation at the expense of poor communities (e.g. Corry, 2011; Nonini, 2013; Fletcher et al., 2015). According to these critics, environmentalists create 'dominant discourses about wildlife, poaching, and the extinction crisis' (Holmes, 2013, p. 74) and perpetuate the 'politics of hysteria in conservation' (Büscher, 2015). West and Brockington (2012, p. 2) state that environmentalism went south and 'got snugly in bed with its old enemy, corporate capitalism'. Brockington (2008) also speaks of 'celebrity environmentalism', opening his article with the discussion of Edward Abbey's (1975) *The Monkey Wrench Gang*, a fictional work written in the 1970s describing a group of environmentalists that sabotaged capitalist industrial development in the USA. While Brockington acknowledges the fact that environmentalists are very diverse, he swiftly moves from fictional American characters in Abbey's book to eco-tourism in poor countries, blaming 'environmentalists' in displacing local communities for the sake of profit. We question the logic of such a comparison.

Supposedly, environmentalists are 'wistful[ly] harkening after a "Green Adolph"' (Schantz, 2003) and 'waging war' on poor people to save biodiversity. According to Duffy and St John

(2013, p. ii), poaching in Sub-Saharan Africa is the result of the historical legacy of colonialism. Likewise, Holmes (2013, p. 75) states that in Amboseli National Park, the resistance of local people to conservation policies in the form of killing of wildlife is akin to the 'weapons of the weak'. Such local resistance, Holmes continues, 'can have some impact in limiting or delaying certain protected area policies', but is 'generally unable to seriously challenge the existence of protected areas or their ability to protect biodiversity.'

This 'resistance' is excused (or in fact tacitly supported) as long as local people profit from it. For example, according to Von Hellermann (2007), illegal deforestation in Lagos provides a vital source of livelihood for the many farmers and traders, implying that this 'illegality' needs to be questioned or made legal. In a similar way, it is argued that since a lot of poaching occurs among the poor local communities, its criminalization needs to be questioned (Duffy and St John, 2013; Duffy, 2014; Büscher and Ramutsindela, 2016). These authors pose a loaded question: should the international community deprive developing countries of the 'right' to use their natural resources for the economic benefit of their populations (Duffy and St John, 2013; Duffy, 2014)?

It needs to be noted that certainly not all anthropologists or social geographers are anthropocentric in their orientation. In her chapter 'Requiem for roadkill', anthropologist Jane Desmond (2013) calls for an ethical recognition of animal victimhood. Another anthropologist, Barbara Noske (1989), has called her colleagues to heed the deep green side of environmental ethics and engage with animal rights and welfare literature. In environmental ethics, the definition of Land Ethics comes to mind: '[a] thing is right when it tends to preserve the integrity, stability, and beauty of the biotic community. It is wrong when it tends otherwise' (Leopold, 1949, pp. 224–5). A few decades later, the deep ecology movement has emerged endorsing 'biospheric egalitarianism' (Naess, 1973), the view that all living things are alike in having value in their own right, independent of their usefulness to humans.

However, these ethical/philosophical developments have not necessarily affected disciplines most concerned with preservation of nature. Within the field of biological conservation, there is also a group called 'new conservation', such as Kareiva and Marvier (e.g. Kareiva et al., 2011) or the work of the Breakthrough institute (e.g. Shellenberger and Nordhaus, 2004), a conservative think-tank, that comes from a neoliberal stance and yet shares an anthropocentric approach with these critical social scientists (for a discussion of this group see Miller et al., 2014; Doak et al., 2014; Kopnina et al., 2018). Much like the neo-Marxist group of critical social scientists concerned with local communities, the new conservationists and Eco modernists accuse 'environmentalists' in being naive in trying to preserve pristine wilderness.

Let us examine and address the accusations and false claims one by one.

False Claim: 'Environmentalists Evict Local Communities from Their Land'

When environmentalism is inspired by ecocentrism or deep ecology, the guiding principle is respect for *all* communities – where the term 'community' is used for both humans and non-humans (Crist, 2012, 2015; Kopnina, 2012a, 2012b, Crist and Kopnina, 2014; Sinclair, 2015; Piccolo et al., 2018; Washington et al., 2018). This follows on from Leopold's (1949) idea of the 'Land Ethic', in which humanity is just a plain member of the living community. Many conservation and environmental protection efforts historically in the West were 'at home', as in Abbey's fiction book quoted by Brockington (2008), whereas most evictions historically in the West have been done in the name of 'progress' – industrial or municipal development. In some cases that affect communities in more 'traditional' settings, it is important to consider the argument that the idea of 'Indigenous' or 'local' can apply to humans *and* nonhumans alike. When the local human populations push for expansion of agricultural activity, they threaten Indigenous *nonhuman* species. There is thus a need for a careful ethical consideration that balances different interests, rather than an a priori privileging of one species (i.e. humans).

To return to the question posed by Duffy (2000): should the international community deprive developing countries of the right to use their natural resources for the economic benefit of their populations? The obvious thing to note here is that the 'populations' referred to are purely those of humanity, not the nonhuman world. Another thing to consider is that the only 'right' considered is a right for humans, with no consideration of the rights of nature. In addition, the answer depends on what is found normative. In this question, the right of exploitation and the right to benefit economically is seen as a moral priority, and thus critical social scientists see their stance as a 'balanced approach to sustainable utilization' (Duffy, 2000) in order to enable 'sustainable' economic benefit.

Yet, this assumption has little pragmatic or ethical grounding because, practically speaking, it is highly questionable whether there will be any 'natural resources' to go around. There is a significant difference between prohibiting some activities, such as hunting in certain areas, and thus endangering one part of cultural tradition – and physically endangering individual animals, groups or even entire species with extinction. Research shows that unrestricted access to land or even traditional agricultural activity can lead to over-exploitation when done with a greater number of people and in a greater number of localities, by using, for example, slash-and-burn techniques (Henley, 2011). Hunting endangered species as 'bushmeat' to the point of extinction has become common (Benítez-López et al., 2019), especially in situations where local communities have expanded both demographically and in terms of consumptive and economic practices (Ripple et al., 2016). Ethically, it is simply not explained what gives one single species the right to use all other species as resources for its own benefit (Crist, 2012).

Despite the dangers that expansion of local communities' activity poses to wildlife, it is not the 'environmentalists' that cause evictions but mostly local authorities, mining or logging companies, agricultural plantation owners, development agencies, and other stakeholders that seek to make even more profit off the land (Borras et al., 2012). While Indigenous species of nonhumans are wiped out, and Indigenous people are driven from their land by 'developers', 'conservation' as the generalized practice is blamed and used as a 'scapegoat'. As Crist (2015, p. 93) has stated:

> The literature challenging traditional conservation strategies as locking people out, and as locking away sources of human livelihood, rarely tackles either the broader distribution of poverty or its root social causes; rather, strictly protected areas are scapegoated, and wild nature, once again, is targeted to take the fall for the purported betterment of people, while domination and exploitation of nature remain unchallenged. The prevailing mindset of humanity's entitlement to avail itself of the natural world without limitation is easily, if tacitly, invoked by arguments that demand that wilderness ... offer up its 'natural resources' – in the name of justice.

It is actually often environmentalists from local communities that take a stance against displacement, land grabbing and rapacious industrial or agricultural development, as described in the cases of environmentalists who stood up for nature above. What are responsible for evictions of people from their land are industrial or agricultural corporate players, local authorities and all those trying to make a profit, not 'environmentalists'.

False Claim: 'Environmentalists Violate Human Rights by Punishing Impoverished Poachers'

As Goodall (2015) has stated, poachers are overwhelmingly not impoverished people from local communities but highly organized criminal networks. When talking about 'celebrity conservationists', Brockington does not explain that the 'late' George and Joy Adamson and Dian Fossey were brutally murdered when trying to defend animals. Nor does Brockington mention the fact that the fighters against the illegal ivory trade, such as Esmond Bradley Martin (Van der Zee, 2018) or Wayne Lotter, a South African wildlife conservationist were murdered (IUCN, 2017). Is this the fame that the supposed 'celebrity conservationists enjoy' (Brockington, 2008, p. 563), along with hundreds of local park guards killed defending wildlife, such as Venant Mumbere Muvesevese and Fidèle Mulonga Mulegalega, who were murdered in Virunga National Park in the Democratic Republic of the Congo (Vidal, 2016)?

False Claim: 'Environmentalists Are Western Neo-Colonial Elitists'

The sad legacy of murdered, tortured and ostracized environmentalists across the globe serves as evidence that environmentalism is widespread among non-Western nations, and that the environmental movement is *not* at all a Western (elitist, rich, Euro-American etc.) enterprise, as critics claim, but in fact a truly global phenomenon. Grassroots environmentalism indeed knows many variations, and it transcends national and racial boundaries (e.g. Dunlap and York, 2008). While there is mounting evidence that environmentalism is a cross-cultural phenomenon (e.g. Shoreman-Ouimet and Kopnina, 2015b; Milfont and Schultz, 2016), critical social scientists insist that environmentalists are Western elitists. It is certainly ironic that most people who make these accusations have comfortable academic appointments and steady jobs in Western universities. It is strange to see the word 'elite' being used in such a way, supposedly outside of the cynical politics of grievance studies (Lindsay et al., 2018).

While the list of Western conservationists and environmentalists continues to lengthen, there is an even longer list of Indigenous environmental activists (Kopnina, 2015; Shoreman-Ouimet and Kopnina, 2015b). Besides the internationally recognized activists, such as the founder of the Green Belt Movement, Wangari Muta Maathai, there are many less-known non-Western activists, many of whom have been murdered for defending nature, including Jairo Mora Sandoval, Berta Cáceres Flores and Isidro Baldenegro López, all of whom are described earlier in the chapter.

When Brockington (2008) talks of 'celebrity environmentalism', he mentions 'African celebrity conservationists' who supposedly have a 'dual claim to authenticity' to promote their extravagant and profit-driven cause:

> First, they represent 'the real Africa', the people-less Eden that is popularly believed to have existed before it was spoilt by discovery, exploration, and development ... Second, their common motif is closeness to and communion with nature. Consider Jane Goodall, the late George and Joy Adamson, Iain Douglas-Hamilton, Cynthia Moss and the late Dian Fossey. All are famous for their special closeness to large charismatic wildlife ... Many people yearn for the sort of intimacy with wildlife and nature which celebrity conservationists enjoy. (Brockington, 2008, p. 563)

There is a special disjuncture between the anthropocentrism of environmental justice (just for people) proponents and their lofty ideas of equity and equality, and sometimes a distinct ferocity in the way it is expressed. This is amplified by the supporters' humanistic rhetoric and moral outspokenness. While the 'critical social scientists' have a point about criticizing neoliberal *conservation* (such as the new conservationists) that only aims to profit from biodiversity, they also create a kind of normative ethical climate in which only the rich Western 'exploiters' and the poor Indigenous/local (human) 'sufferers' matter. The interests of *Indigenous* nonhuman species (who, evolutionarily, have been Indigenous to the place longer than human groups) are simply left out of any moral consideration.

The accusation is that the generalized group of 'environmentalists' create 'dominant discourses' (Holmes, 2013, p. 74) and are said to perpetuate the 'politics of hysteria in conservation' (Büscher, 2015). This seems to actually perpetuate another rhetoric – that of human supremacy and domination over every other living being on this planet (Crist, 2012). At the same time, the polemic against environmentalists seems to excuse blatant human rights abuses and even murder of those that stand up for nature. This testifies to the worst kind of endorsement of planet-wide colonization of ethics and action by one single species under the guise of caring about power inequalities.

False Claim: 'Environmentalism Got Snugly in Bed with Its Old Enemy, Corporate Capitalism'

While some critical social scientists have made good points warning about 'conservation for profit' or 'neoliberal conservation' and the dangers of commodification for capitalist accumulation, it is certainly not true that the generalized group of 'conservationists' and 'environmentalists', especially of the kind discussed in examples at the beginning of this chapter, are complacent in 'getting into bed with the enemy' (West and Brockington, 2012). There is an irony here, in that the only group that could truly be said to be 'neoliberal' in conservation are the 'new conservation' movement, who are just as anthropocentric as the critical social scientists (Miller et al., 2014; Kopnina et al., 2018). The issue here is that both new conservation and critical social science groups appear not to recognize the type of environmentalism that is urgently needed for addressing the most severe conservation problems such as biodiversity loss and extinction. Critical social scientists imply that only when social inequalities are resolved, will the problems cease, while new conservation proponents suggest that economic development and technology will solve the problems. The critical social scientists do not provide data to support the claim that societies in which social inequality has been properly addressed are a solution to the biodiversity crisis (nor do they supply an example of such societies), while new conservation proponents fail to show how economic growth and technology can solve this crisis.

In fact, as witnessed by all objective biodiversity measures (IUCN, 2017; IPBES, 2019), the problems are far from solved. Environmental problems still occur in Communist or socialist countries such as China or Vietnam and relatively egalitarian, technologically advanced and high-GDP Scandinavian countries. While the Communist and socialist countries might actually have a worse track record concerning human rights in relation to persecution of environmentalists (as indicated in some examples above, e.g. The Economist, 2015; Tatlow, 2016; Standaert, 2017; Nguen and Datzberger, 2018), the high-GDP capitalist countries, despite the 'superior' technology and economic base to supposedly enter the era of 'eco-modernism' (BI), tend to have the highest levels of consumption (e.g. Eurostat, 2017; Grunwald, 2018).

As opposed to more 'left' (socialist, neo-Marxist) critical social scientists, however, these eco-optimists see neoliberal capitalism and technological and industrial progress as a solution for environmental problems. The founding fathers of Breakthrough Institute, Shellenberger and Nordhaus (2004) do not deny the severity of biodiversity loss, but promote a 'post-environmental approach' warning environmentalists to 'stop trying to scare the pants off of the American public'; to recognize that 'the solution to the ecological crises wrought by modernity, technology, and progress will be more modernity, technology, and progress'. Thus, it seems that it is not environmentalists that got snugly into bed with capitalism, but new conservation, Eco modernist and other proponents of industrial growth.

The Underlying Ethics of Anti-Environmentalism in Academia

Either way, 'environmentalists' are portrayed as either neo-colonial, naive, or misanthropic. Anthropocentric orientation, simply put, is one overarching theme that links the critique of both critical social scientists and new conservationists (Kopnina et al., 2018). The critical social science camp can be positioned to the far left of the political spectrum, and many political ecologists can be classified as neo-Marxist. Neo-Marxist ideology is embodied in Shantz's (2003) critique of environmentalism as an anti-worker movement, stating that the 'fundamentalist versions of ecology', exemplified according to the author by the theory of deep ecology and the social movement Earth First!, have mistakenly proposed social scarcity as a means to overcome natural scarcity. According to Shantz, because deep ecologists do not engage with capitalist forces of power, they have moved away from an analysis of the power relations that underlie social inequality and the destruction of nature. Shantz uses the terms 'neo-Malthusian' and 'anti-worker perspectives', blaming environmentalists in shifting responsibility for ecological crises away from capitalist structures of inequality and towards personal consumption practices. More generally, neo-Marxist political ecologists and environmental anthropologists tend to discount population growth, demographic pressures on the environment and individual responsibility for ecological degradation. In fact, instead of the 'green Hitlers' imagined by neo-Marxist critiques (e.g. Shantz, 2003), the war is waged in the name of the same power that critical social scientists try to expose, that of rapacious capitalist development. We need to add here that the lived experience of socialism in regard to nature conservation, if this is seen as an alternative to capitalism, is not much more harmonious, judging from atrocities against human rights and nature committed by nominally Communist (and in practice socialist) regimes (see discussion in Kopnina, 2016c). The real culprit of environmental destruction is industrial and agribusiness development and the cult of economic growth (present in both socialist and capitalist countries) as well as population growth (Washington et al., 2018).

Some are more positioned to the 'right', such as new conservationists (Miller et al., 2014; Doak et al., 2014; Kopnina et al., 2018). The Breakthrough Institute (BI) also clearly falls into this category in its support of 'eco-modernism' (https://ecomodernistmanifesto.squarespace.com/). As discussed in the section above, however, what unites both the leftist critical social scientists and the conservative new conservationists is their strong anthropocentric stance (Kopnina et al., 2018). Thus, while there are differences between new conservation (more market-oriented, neoliberal, growth-oriented, belief in technology as a solution) and critical social scientists (neo-Marxist, anti-capitalist, anti-growth, belief in social equality as a solu-

AN ALTERNATIVE VISION FOR SURVIVAL: ECOCENTRISM, ECOJUSTICE AND ECODEMOCRACY

Washington et al. (2017, p. 35) note:

> Ecocentrism is the broadest term for worldviews that recognize intrinsic value in all lifeforms and ecosystems themselves, including their abiotic components. Anthropocentrism, in contrast, values other lifeforms and ecosystems insofar as they are valuable for human wellbeing, preferences, and interests.

Ecocentrism rejects the dualistic worldview common in Western society where humans are seen as separate from nature, in favour of a more holistic worldview of humans being part of nature. Ecocentrism has been conceptualized from the early twentieth century but has been recently revisited in the writings of, among others, Corry (2011); Rolston (2012); Gray (2013); Crist (2015); Kopnina (2016a, 2016b); Strang (2017); Washington et al. (2017); Piccolo et al. (2018); and Washington (2019).

Inspired by ecocentric thought, Vilkka (1997) makes the case for 'ethical extensionalism', where intrinsic value has extended from (1) just humanity; (2) to sentient beings; (3) to all of life; (4) to ecosystems; (5) to geodiversity; (6) to the whole planet (Washington, 2019). Curry (2011) also supports the idea that existing human ethics can be 'extended' to address the current ecological crisis, showing that a truly ecological ethic is both possible and urgently needed. A major implication of ecocentrism is the idea of ecological justice, in which non-human nature, like the human species, is considered to also deserve justice (Baxter, 2005; Washington et al., 2018). Another implication of ecocentrism is the need to make governance more Earth-centred. Gray and Curry (2016) proposed the following definition of an ecocentrically motivated democracy or 'ecodemocracy':

> Groups and communities using decision-making systems that respect the principles of human democracy while explicitly extending valuation to include the intrinsic value of non-human nature, with the ultimate goal of evaluating human wants equally to those of other species and the living systems that make up the ecosphere. (p. 21)

In ecodemocracy, the intrinsic value should be assigned both to biotic and abiotic components of the ecosphere (Gray, 2013), such as the geodiversity of landforms, rivers and soil. All aspects of ecocentrism (including ecojustice and ecodemocracy) recognize the fact that species extinction is moral evil (Cafaro and Primack, 2014). In this framing, an alternative for the survival of nonhuman species – *and* human cultural survival – is to embrace biospheric egalitarianism and ecojustice (Kopnina, 2014, 2015, 2016a, 2016b; Shoreman-Ouimet and Kopnina, 2015a, 2015b; Strang, 2017; Washington et al., 2018). In this context, the objective of keeping the wild for the sake of the wild (Wuerthner et al., 2014; Wakild, 2015; Washington et al., 2018; Johns, 2020) offers a moral and legal basis to counteract anti-environmentalism. A deeper problem with anti-environmentalism in academia is the lack of legal, political and ethical consideration of nonhumans as perhaps the most important stakeholders in their own destiny. Their voice gets ignored (Gray and Curry, 2019), just because we do not speak their language. The need to consider the more humble human place in nature and nature's legal rights has been expressed in two significant articles in *Science* (Crist, 2018; Chapron et al., 2019).

CONCLUSION

There are numerous instances of Indigenous people and local individuals that have defended nature across the globe, when local governments, or indeed international conservation organizations, have failed. Concern about the environmental crisis is present *everywhere* in the world. This chapter has considered the worrying extent of direct and violent anti-environmentalism, with hundreds of environmental activists being killed each year around the world (a number that seems to be growing). Most of these are people in developing nations seeking to conserve their land and nature.

The chapter then analyzed anti-environmentalism within academia, considering the various accusations made about conservation and environmentalism. The chapter then considered the underlying ethics within academia that are responsible for anti-environmentalism, showing that the key cause was a deep (if never openly declared) anthropocentrism that amounts to human supremacy. This has led to a situation where some espousing 'nature conservation' now argue that it should be undertaken not for the benefit of nature, or because society upholds a commitment to ecojustice, but purely for the benefit of humans, predicated only on social justice concerns. The chapter then concluded by considering an alternative ethic for survival – ecocentrism, ecojustice and ecodemocracy. If academia were to embrace such an ethic, then anti-environmentalism would wither away, and we could all move forward constructively to ethics and justice that embrace both humanity *and* the rest of nature. Given that society is fully dependent on nature to survive, we believe such an ethic makes excellent practical – as well as ethical – sense.

REFERENCES

Abbey, E. (1975) *The Monkey Wrench Gang.* New York, NY: Avon Books, HarperCollins.
Aksogan, P. (2013) The fight to protect Turkey's green spaces began decades ago. *The Guardian blog.* Available from: https://www.theguardian.com/environment/blog/2013/jun/04/turkey-protests-protect-green-spaces.
Babones, S. (2017) Red alert for China's pollution protesters. *Al Jazeera.* Available from: https://www.aljazeera.com/indepth/opinion/2017/02/red-alert-china-pollution-protesters-170217111717375.html.
Baviskar, A. (2013) Hallsworth plenary debate: Justice for people should come before justice for environment. Paper presented for the World Anthropology Congress. ASA-IUAES conference, 5–10 August, Manchester. Available from: http://www.youtube.com/watch?v=oldnYTYMx-k.
Baxter, B. (2005) *A Theory of Ecological Justice.* New York, NY: Routledge.
BBC (2019) Extinction Rebellion London protest: 290 arrested. *BBC News.* Available from https://www.bbc.com/news/entertainment-arts-47945397.
Benítez-López, A., Santini, L., Schipper, A.M., Busana, M. and Huijbregts, M.A. (2019) Intact but empty forests? Patterns of hunting-induced mammal defaunation in the tropics. *PLoS Biology.* **17**(5), p.e3000247.

Blet, R. (2018) Five Asian environmental activists killed for defending land and natural resources against exploitation. *South China Morning Post*. Available from: https://www.scmp.com/lifestyle/article/2156958/five-egregious-deaths-asian-environmental-activists-killed-defending-land.

Borras Jr, S.M., Kay, C., Gómez, S. and Wilkinson, J. (2012) Land grabbing and global capitalist accumulation: Key features in Latin America. *Canadian Journal of Development Studies/Revue Canadienne d'Etudes du Développement*. **33**(4), pp. 402–16.

Breakthrough Institute (n.d.) Home Page. *The Breakthrough Institute*. Available from: https://thebreakthrough.org/.

Brockington, D. (2002) *Fortress Conservation: The Preservation of the Mkomazi Game Reserve, Tanzania*. Indianapolis, IN: Indiana University Press.

Brockington, D. (2008) Powerful environmentalisms: Conservation, celebrity, and capitalism. *Media, Culture & Society*. **30**(4), pp. 551–68.

Burke, J. (2018) Six Virunga Park rangers killed in DRC wildlife sanctuary. *The Guardian*. Available from: https://www.theguardian.com/weather/2018/apr/09/six-virunga-park-rangers-killed-in-drc-wildlife-sanctuary.

Büscher, B. (2014) Nature on the move: The value and circulation of liquid nature and the emergence of fictitious conservation. In: Büscher, B., Dressler, W. and Fletcher, R. (eds) *Nature™ Inc: New Frontiers of Environmental Conservation in the Neoliberal Age*. Tuscon, AZ: University of Arizona Press, pp. 183–204.

Büscher, B. (2015) 'Rhino poaching is out of control!' Violence, heroes and the politics of hysteria in online conservation. Paper presented at the British International Studies Association, 16–19 June, London.

Büscher, B. and Ramutsindela, M. (2016) Green violence: Rhino poaching and the war to save Southern Africa's Peace Parks. *African Affairs*. **115**(458), pp. 1–22.

Cafaro, P. and Primack, R. (2014) Species extinction is a great moral wrong: Sharing the Earth with other species is an important human responsibility. *Biological Conservation*. **170**, pp. 1–2.

Chapin, M. (2004) *A Challenge to Conservationists*. World Watch Institute.

Chapron, G., Epstein, Y. and López-Bao, J.V. (2019) A rights revolution for nature. *Science*. **363**(6434), pp. 1392–1393.

Colchester, M. (2004) Conservation policy and Indigenous peoples. *Cultural Survival*. Available from: http://www.culturalsurvival.org/publications/cultural-survival-quarterly/none/conservation-policy-and-indigenous-peoples.

Corry, S. (2011) *Tribal Peoples for Tomorrow's World*. London: Survival International.

Crist, E. (2012) Abundant Earth and population. In: Cafaro, P. and Crist, E. (eds) *Life on the Brink: Environmentalists Confront Overpopulation*. Athens, GA: University of Georgia Press, pp. 141–53.

Crist, E. (2015) I walk in the world to love it. In: Wuerthner, G., Crist, E. and Butler, T. (eds) *Protecting the Wild: Parks and Wilderness, The Foundation for Conservation*. Washington, DC, USA and London, UK: The Island Press, pp. 82–95.

Crist, E. (2018) Reimagining the human. *Science*. **362**(6420), pp. 1242–4.

Crist, E. and Kopnina, H. (2014) Unsettling anthropocentrism. *Dialectical Anthropology*. **38**, pp. 387–96.

Curry, P. (2011) *Ecological Ethics: An Introduction*. 2nd edn. Cambridge: Polity Press.

Davenport, C. and Landler, M. (2019) Trump administration hardens its attack on climate science. *New York Times*. Available from: https://www.nytimes.com/2019/05/27/us/politics/trump-climate-science.html.

Desmond, J. (2013) Requiem for roadkill. In: Kopnina, H. and Shoreman-Ouimet, E. (eds) *Environmental Anthropology: Future Trends*. London: Routledge.

Doak, D.F., Bakker, V.J., Goldstein, B.E. and Hale, B. (2014) What is the future of conservation? *Trends Ecological Evolution*. **29**, pp. 77–81.

Duffy, R. (2000) *Killing for Conservation: Wildlife Policy in Zimbabwe*. Oxford: James Currey.

Duffy, R. (2014) Waging a war to save biodiversity: The rise of militarised conservation. *International Affairs*. **90**(4), pp. 819–34.

Duffy, R. and St John, F.A.V. (2013) Poverty, poaching, and trafficking: What are the links? *Evidence on Demand*. Available from DOI: 10.12774/eod_hd059.jun2013.duffy.

Duffy, R., St. John, F.A.V., Büscher, B. and Brockington, D. (2016) Towards a new understanding of the links between poverty and illegal wildlife hunting. *Conservation Biology*. **30**(1), pp. 14–22.

Dunlap, R.E. and York, R. (2008) The globalization of environmental concern and the limits of the post-materialist values explanation: Evidence from four multinational surveys. *The Sociological Quarterly.* **49**, pp. 529–63.

Eurostat (2017) GDP per capita, consumption per capita and price level indices. *Eurostat.* Available from: https://ec.europa.eu/eurostat/statistics-explained/index.php/GDP_per_capita,_consumption_per_capita_and_price_level_indices.

Fendt, L. (2015) Who killed Costa Rica's turtle advocate? *Outside.* Available from: http://www.outsideonline.com/1928971/who-killed-costa-rica%E2%80%99s-turtle-advocate.

Fletcher, R., Dressler, W. and Büscher, B. (2015) Nature™ Inc: Nature as capitalist imaginary. In: Bryant, R. (ed.) *Handbook of Political Ecology.* Cheltenham, UK and Northampton, MA, USA: Edward Elgar Publishing, pp. 359–72.

Global Witness (2013) Cambodia marks 1 year anniversary of Chut Wutty's murder. *Global Witness.* Available from: http://www.globalwitness.org/library/cambodia-marks-1-year-anniversary-chut-wutty%E2%80%99s-murder.

Goodall, J. (2015) Caring for people and valuing forests in Africa. In: Wuerthner, G., Crist, E. and Butler, T. (eds) *Protecting the Wild: Parks and Wilderness, The Foundation for Conservation.* Washington, DC, USA and London, UK: The Island Press, pp. 21–6.

Gray, J. and Curry P. (2016) Ecodemocracy: Helping wildlife's right to survive. ECOS. **37**(1), pp. 18–27.

Gray, J. and Curry P. (2019) Ecodemocracy and political representation for non-human nature. In: Kopnina, H. and Washington, H. (eds) *Conservation: Integrating Social and Ecological Justice.* Cham: Springer, pp. 155–66.

Gray, M. (2013) *Geodiversity: Valuing and Conserving Abiotic Nature.* 2nd edn. Hoboken, NJ: John Wiley and Sons.

Greshko, M., Parker, L., Howard, B.C., Stone, D., Borunda, A. and Gibbens, S. (2019) A running list of how President Trump is changing environmental policy. *National Geographic.* Available from: https://news.nationalgeographic.com/2017/03/how-trump-is-changing-science-environment/.

Grunwald, A. (2018) Diverging pathways to overcoming the environmental crisis: A critique of eco-modernism from a technology assessment perspective. *Journal of Cleaner Production.* **197**, pp. 1854–62.

Helvarg, D. (1989) *The War Against the Greens.* San Francisco, CA: Sierra Club Books.

Henley, D. (2011) Swidden farming as an agent of environmental change: Ecological myth and historical reality in Indonesia. *Environment and History.* **17**, pp. 525–54.

Holmes, G. (2013) Exploring the relationship between local support and the success of protected areas. *Conservation and Society.* **11**(1), pp. 72–82.

Holmes, O. (2016) Environmental activist murders set a record as 2015 became the deadliest year. *The Guardian.* Available from: https://www.theguardian.com/environment/2016/jun/20/environmental-activist-murders-global-witness-report.

Human Rights Watch (2019) Iran: Environmentalists' flawed trials: Detainees allege torture in detention. *Human Rights Watch.* Available from: https://www.hrw.org/news/2019/02/05/iran-environmentalists-flawed-trial.

IPBES (2019) Media release: Nature's dangerous decline 'unprecedented' species extinction rates 'accelerating'. *Intergovernmental Science-Policy Platform on Biodiversity and Ecosystem Services (IPBES).* Available from: https://www.ipbes.net/news/Media-Release-Global-Assessment.

IUCN (2017) IUCN and the World Commission on Protected Areas mourn the loss of wildlife defender Wayne Lotter. *International Union for Conservation of Nature.* Available from: https://www.iucn.org/news/secretaria/201708/iucn-and-world-commission-protected-areas-mourn-loss-wildlife-defender-wayne-lotter.

Jacques, P.J. (2012) A general theory of climate denial. *Global Environmental Politics.* **12**(2), pp. 9–17.

Johns, D. (2020) With friends like these wilderness and biodiversity do not need enemies. In: Kopnina, H. and Washington, H. (eds) *Conservation: Integrating Social and Ecological Justice.* Dordrecht: Springer, pp. 59–72.

Kalland, A. (2009) *Unveiling the Whale: Discourses on Whales and Whaling.* New York, NY: Berghahn Books.

Kareiva, P., Lalasz, R. and Marvier, M. (2011) Conservation in the Anthropocene: Beyond solitude and fragility. In: Shellenberger, M. and Nordhaus, T. (eds) *Love Your Monsters: Postenvironmentalism and the Anthropocene*. Oakland, CA: Breakthrough Institute.

Kopnina, H. (2012a) Towards conservational anthropology: Addressing anthropocentric bias in anthropology. *Dialectical Anthropology*. **36**(1), pp. 127–46.

Kopnina, H. (2012b) Re-examining culture/conservation conflict: The view of anthropology of conservation through the lens of environmental ethics. *Journal of Integrative Environmental Sciences*. **9**(1), pp. 9–25.

Kopnina, H. (2014) Environmental justice and biospheric egalitarianism: Reflecting on a normative-philosophical view of human–nature relationship. *Earth Perspectives*. **1**(8). Available from: https://earth-perspectives.springeropen.com/articles/10.1186/2194-6434-1-8.

Kopnina, H. (2015) Revisiting the Lorax complex: Deep ecology and biophilia in cross-cultural perspective. *Environmental Sociology*. **43**(4), pp. 315–24.

Kopnina, H. (2016a) Half the earth for people (or more)? Addressing ethical questions in conservation. *Biological Conservation*. **203**, pp. 176–85.

Kopnina, H. (2016b) Wild animals and justice: The case of the dead elephant in the room. *Journal of International Wildlife Law & Policy*. **19**(3), pp. 219–35.

Kopnina, H. (2016c) Of big hegemonies and little tigers: Ecocentrism and environmental justice. *The Journal of Environmental Education*. **47**(2), pp. 132–50.

Kopnina, H., Washington, H., Gray, J. and Piccolo, J. (2020) Celebrate the Anthropocene? Why techno-eco-optimism is a strategy of ultimate denial. In: Grušovnik, T., Spannring, R. and Syse, K.L. (eds) *Environmental and Animal Abuse Denial: Averting our Gaze*. London: Lexington Books, pp. 169–85.

Kopnina, H., Washington, H., Gray, J. and Taylor, B. (2018) The 'future of conservation' debate: Defending ecocentrism and the Nature Needs Half movement. *Biological Conservation*. **217**, pp. 140–48.

Laville, S. (2018) Artist Gavin Turk arrested in London climate change protest. *The Guardian*. Available from: https://www.theguardian.com/world/2018/nov/18/artist-gavin-turk-arrested-in-london-climate-change-protest.

Leopold, A. (1949) *A Sand County Almanac and Sketches Here and There*. New York, NY: Oxford University Press.

Liddick, D. (2006) *Eco-terrorism: Radical Environmental and Animal Liberation Movements*. Westport, CT: Praeger.

Lindsay, J.A., Boghossian, P. and Pluckrose, H. (2018) Academic grievance studies and the corruption of scholarship. *Areo Magazine*. Available from: https://areomagazine.com/2018/10/02/academic-grievance-studies-and-the-corruption-of-scholarship/.

Lomborg, B. (2001) *The Skeptical Environmentalist: Measuring the Real State of the World*. Cambridge: Cambridge University Press.

Lomborg, B. (ed.) (2010) *Smart Solutions to Climate Change: Comparing Costs and Benefits*. Copenhagen: Copenhagen Business School.

Margit, M. (2019) War on science: Iran arrests environmental activists. *The Jerusalem Post*. Available from: https://www.jpost.com/Magazine/Irans-war-on-science-580567.

Milfont, T. and Schultz, P.W. (2016) Culture and the natural environment. *Current Opinion in Psychology*. **8**, pp. 194–9.

Miller, B., Soule, M. and Terborgh, J. (2014) The 'New Conservation's' surrender to development. *Rewilding Institute*. Available from: http://rewilding.org/rewildit/the-new-conservations-surrender-to-development/.

Milman, O. (2019) Endangered species face 'disaster' under Trump administration. *The Guardian*. Available from: https://www.theguardian.com/environment/2019/mar/06/endangered-species-face-disaster-under-trump-administration.

Minter, T., van der Ploeg, J., Pedrablanca, M.R., Sunderland, T. and Persoon, G.A. (2014) Limits to indigenous participation. The Agta and the Northern Sierra Madre Natural Park, the Philippines. *Human Ecology*. **42**, pp. 769–78.

Naess, A. (1973) The shallow and the deep: Long-range ecology movement. A summary. *Inquiry*. **16**(1–4), pp. 95–9.

Nguen, T.D. and Datzberger, S. (2018) Environmentalism and authoritarian politics in Vietnam. *The Transnational Institute*. Available from: https://www.tni.org/en/publication/environmentalism-and-authoritarian-politics-in-vietnam.

Nixon, R. (1996) Pipe dreams: Ken Saro-Wiwa, environmental justice, and micro-minority rights. *Black Renaissance*. **1**(1), p. 39.

Nonini, D. (2013) Hallsworth plenary debate: Justice for people should come before justice for environment. Paper presented for the World Anthropology Congress. ASA-IUAES conference, 5–10 August, Manchester. Available from: http://www.youtube.com/watch?v=oldnYTYMx-k.

Norgaard, K.M. (2006) 'People want to protect themselves a little bit': Emotions, denial, and social movement nonparticipation. *Sociological Inquiry*. **76**(3), pp. 372–96.

Noske, B. (1989) *Humans and Other Animals*. London: Pluto Press.

Piccolo, J., Washington, H., Kopnina, H. and Taylor, B. (2018) Back to the future: Why conservation biologists should re-embrace their ecocentric roots. *Conservation Biology*. **32**(4), pp. 959–61.

Ripple, W.J., Abernethy, K., Betts, M.G., Chapron, G., Dirzo, R., Galetti, M., Levi, T. et al. (2016) Bushmeat hunting and extinction risk to the world's mammals. *Royal Society Open Science*. **3**(10), p. 160498.

Rolston III, H. (2012) *A New Environmental Ethics: The Next Millennium for Life on Earth*. New York, NY: Routledge.

Schantz, J. (2003) Scarcity and the emergence of fundamentalist ecology. *Critique of Anthropology*. **23**(2), pp. 144–54.

Shellenberger, M. and Nordhaus, T. (2004) The death of environmentalism: Global warming politics in a post-environmental world. *The Breakthrough Institute*. Available from: https://s3.us-east-2.amazonaws.com/uploads.thebreakthrough.org/legacy/images/Death_of_Environmentalism.pdf.

Shoreman-Ouimet, E. and Kopnina, H. (2015a) Reconciling ecological and social justice to promote biodiversity conservation. *Biological Conservation*. **184**, pp. 320–26.

Shoreman-Ouimet, E. and Kopnina, H. (2015b) *Culture and Conservation: Beyond Anthropocentrism*. New York, NY: Routledge Earthscan.

Sinclair, A.R.E. (2015) Protected areas are necessary for conservation. In: Wuerthner, G., Crist, E. and Butler, T. (eds) *Protecting the Wild: Parks and Wilderness, The Foundation for Conservation*. London: Island Press, pp. 72–81.

Spanne, A. (2016) Why is Honduras the world's deadliest country for environmentalists? *The Guardian*. Available from: https://www.theguardian.com/environment/2016/apr/07/honduras-environment-killing-human-rights-berta-caceres-flores-murder.

Standaert, M. (2017) As it looks to go green, China keeps a tight lid on dissent. *Yale Environment 360*. Available from: https://e360.yale.edu/features/as-it-looks-to-go-green-china-keeps-a-tight-lid-on-dissent.

Stern, P.C. (2000) Towards a coherent theory of environmentally significant behavior. *Journal of Social Issues*. **56**(3), pp. 407–24.

Strang, V. (2017) Justice for all: Inconvenient truths – and reconciliation – in human-non-human relations. In: Kopnina, H. and Shoreman-Ouimet, E. (eds) *Handbook of Environmental Anthropology*. New York, NY: Routledge, pp. 263–78.

Tatlow, D. K. (2016) Chinese man's death in custody prompts suspicion of police brutality. *The New York Times*. Available from: https://www.nytimes.com/2016/05/13/world/asia/china-lei-yang-police-death.html.

The Economist (2014) The dam bursts: French eco-politics. *The Economist*. Available from: https://www.economist.com/europe/2014/11/08/the-dam-bursts.

The Economist (2015) If a tree falls: The Internet in Vietnam. *The Economist*. Available from: https://www.economist.com/asia/2015/04/18/if-a-tree-falls.

The Economist (2016) Cambodian politics: The velvet glove frays. *The Economist*. Available from: https://www.economist.com/asia/2016/09/29/the-velvet-glove-frays.

The Guardian (2018) 83 environmental defenders had been confirmed killed by October 2018. *The Guardian*. Available from: https://www.theguardian.com/environment/ng-interactive/2018/feb/27/the-defenders-recording-the-deaths-of-environmental-defenders-around-the-world.

The Moscow Times (2018) Russian environmentalist's beating tied to Medvedev's alleged mansion. *The Moscow Times*. Available from: https://www.themoscowtimes.com/2018/01/15/russian-environmentalists-beating-tied-to-medvedevs-alleged-mansion-a60183.

Van der Zee, B. (2018) Top ivory investigator murdered in Kenya. *The Guardian*. Available from: https://www.theguardian.com/environment/2018/feb/05/leading-ivory-trade-investigator-killed-in-kenya.

Vidal, J. (2016) On the frontline of Africa's wildlife wars. *The Guardian*. Available from: https://www.theguardian.com/environment/2016/may/07/africa-frontline-of-wildlife-wars.

Vidal, J. (2018) 2018 is on pace to be another bloody year for environmental defenders around the world. *Huffington Post*. Available from: https://www.huffingtonpost.com.au/entry/2018-grim-year-environmental-defenders-around-world_n_5bbd0b80e4b0876edaa3016b.

Vilkka, L. (1997) *The Intrinsic Value of Nature*. Amsterdam: Rodolpi.

Von Hellermann, P. (2007) Things fall apart? Management, environment, and Taungya farming in Edo State, Southern Nigeria. *Africa*. **77**(3), pp. 371–92.

Vrieze, P. and Naren, K. (2012) SOLD: In the race to exploit Cambodia's forests new maps reveal the rapid spread of plantations and mining across the country. *The Cambodia Daily*. 10–11 March, pp. 4–11.

Wakild, E. (2015) Parks, people, and perspectives: Historicizing conservation in Latin America. In: Wuerthner, G., Crist, E. and Butler, T. (eds) *Protecting the Wild: Parks and Wilderness, The Foundation for Conservation*. Washington, DC, USA and London, UK: Island Press, pp. 41–53.

Washington, H. (2019). *A Sense of Wonder Towards Nature: Healing the World Through Belonging*. London: Routledge.

Washington, H., Taylor, B., Kopnina, H., Cryer, P. and Piccolo, J. (2017) Why ecocentrism is the key pathway to sustainability. *The Ecological Citizen*. **1**, pp. 35–41. Available from: https://www.ecologicalcitizen.net/pdfs/v01n1-08.pdf.

Washington, H., Chapron, G., Kopnina, H., Curry, P., Gray, J. and Piccolo, J. (2018) Foregrounding ecojustice in conservation. *Biological Conservation*. **228**, pp. 367–74.

Watts, J. (2018) Almost four environmental defenders a week killed in 2017. *The Guardian*. Available from: https://www.theguardian.com/environment/2018/feb/02/almost-four-environmental-defenders-a-week-killed-in-2017.

Watts, J. and Vidal, J. (2017) Environmental defenders being killed in record numbers globally, new research reveals. *The Guardian*. Available from: https://www.theguardian.com/environment/2017/jul/13/environmental-defenders-being-killed-in-record-numbers-globally-new-research-reveals.

West, P. and Brockington, D. (2012) Introduction: Capitalism and the environment. *Environment and Society: Advances in Research*. **3**(1), pp. 1–3.

Wuerthner, G., Crist, E. and Butler, T. (eds) (2014) *Keeping the Wild: Against the Domestication of Earth*. Washington, DC: Island Press.

PART X

CONCLUSION

23. Moving forward in the study of anti-environmentalism: combining tools from different tool kits

David Tindall, Mark C.J. Stoddart and Riley E. Dunlap

INTRODUCTION

In the Introduction, we provided an overview of the history of environmentalism, and introduced and discussed the distinction between classic anti-environmentalism and reflexive anti-environmentalism.[1] In this final chapter, we have a different set of objectives. Here we identify and describe a series of perspectives and orienting topics that could be used to develop a more integrated explanatory framework for future research on anti-environmentalism, as well as relating them to prior chapters.

Under some conditions, anti-environmentalism can be considered a countermovement, as Staggenborg and Meyer note in this volume. But anti-environmentalism also describes a wider variety of phenomena (as we discuss in the Introduction). Scholars have studied anti-environmentalism from a variety of disciplinary and theoretical lenses. By integrating concepts from environmental sociology, political sociology, social movements and network analysis, this chapter sets out to sketch an innovative theoretical framework that we hope may facilitate future studies of anti-environmentalism.

We focus on the following: (1) Location on the Human Exemptionalist-Ecological Paradigm (HEP/NEP) Dimension; (2) Political Ideology and the Left/Right Spectrum; (3) Networks of Relations: The Structural Location of Actors, and of Ecosystems; (4) Political Economy and the Role of Capitalism; (5) Resources and Political Opportunity Structures; (6) Framing, Culture, Narratives and Emotion. These conceptual tool kits help us connect the social-cultural, political and economic dimensions of anti-environmentalism. We then turn to, (7) Field theory as a unifying overarching framework for connecting these dimensions. Finally, we discuss how this theoretical framework can be applied to analyze the (8) Outcomes and impacts of anti-environmentalism.

These various perspectives we draw on are associated with the scholarly areas of social movements, environmental sociology, political science, political sociology and social networks (amongst others). We are motivated in part by the observation that scholars of anti-environmentalism often work in one of these areas but could benefit from conceptual tools available outside their main area of focus. A second motivation is the hope that we can encourage people to develop synthesized approaches by combining several of these perspectives in their scholarship. In some cases, this has been done before in varying degrees; for example, social movement scholars have combined resource mobilization, political process theory and framing perspectives (as discussed in Staggenborg and Meyer's chapter). However, many potentially fruitful combinations of the perspectives described below have not been utilized. In this chapter we do not attempt to formally synthesize all these perspectives, but we will make suggestions where concepts, approaches or methodologies could be productively combined into a broader framework for analyzing anti-environmentalism.

There are several potential benefits to the suggested syntheses. First, as Fligstein and McAdam (2012) have suggested, the field concept provides a useful vehicle for bringing together several of these conceptual frameworks (such as resources, political opportunities and framing). Second, and perhaps more importantly, we encourage researchers to consider where both phenomena (e.g. environmental and/or anti-environmental movement mobilization) and research (studies of environmental/anti-environmental movement mobilization) fit within the HEP–NEP dimension,[2] and thereby bring a more distinctive social-ecological sensibility to the field perspective. We build upon this by also encouraging network-relational perspectives, including ideas from social-ecological networks perspectives that relationally link social and ecological phenomena together. Third, this integrative strategy enhances the possibility for the development of theoretical hypotheses about the interrelations amongst phenomena that would otherwise be analyzed in isolation from one another. Fourth, we also encourage researchers to consider the outcomes and impacts of anti-environmentalism, something that is often assumed or inferred, but often not rigorously examined.

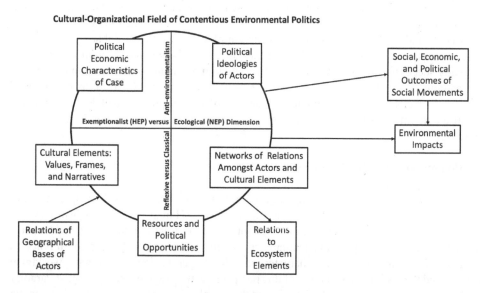

Figure 23.1   A cultural-organizational field framework for understanding anti-environmentalism

Figure 23.1 illustrates our effort to integrate the perspectives described below, in the context of a cultural-organizational field of contentious environmental politics. The field is visually represented by the circle. The characteristics of its elements are depicted by the various components listed in Figure 23.1 inside or on the edge of the circle. In particular, we can think about different types of phenomena in terms of their location on the HEP–NEP dimension, and whether they are characteristic of classic or reflexive anti-environmentalism (as discussed in the Introduction). A given case may be described in terms of the political ideologies of its actors, the political economic characteristics of the case, and various cultural elements that are part of the field, such as values, frames and narratives. Other elements of the field include the resources mobilized by various actors, and the political opportunities they face. Networks can be used to model several aspects of relations amongst elements of the field. Actors can be linked together through social networks. The linkages amongst elements of discourse and actors can be represented through multi-mode networks (Knoke et al., 2021). Also, the linkages amongst actors and ecosystem elements can also be depicted in multi-mode network relations. The boxes fully outside the circle in Figure 23.1, at the bottom of the diagram, represent the observation that the geographical bases of actors, and the ecosystem elements that they are in contention over, may be different. Finally, the boxes to the right of the diagram represent the notion that various outcomes and impacts can occur as results of the dynamics that take place within the cultural-organizational field. For example, anti-environmental movements and mobilizations can result in various outcomes such as changes in policy or public opinion. Such dynamics can also have various environmental impacts, such as increases in carbon emissions, greater deforestation, increases in pollution, and so on.

We acknowledge that many of the examples we give in this chapter are from the US or Canada. This is a consequence of the authors of this chapter all being residents of North America and also reflects that much of the research on anti-environmentalism focuses on Anglo-American societies. As a qualification, both countries are home to liberal market economies (Hall and Soskice, 2001), and majoritarian/pluralist polities (Lijphart, 2012). Classic anti-environmentalism (as described in the Introduction) has generally been more visible and politically successful in these types of societies, though elements of anti-environmentalism—such as climate skepticism—have diffused throughout much of the world, as examined by McKie in her chapter in this volume. At the end of the chapter we call for future studies of anti-environmentalism to explore cases in a broader range of economic and political conditions.

Location on the HEP–NEP Dimension

In the late 1970s, Catton and Dunlap (Catton and Dunlap, 1978, 1980; Dunlap and Catton, 1979) developed the HEP–NEP distinction in sociology (Human Exemptionalism Paradigm versus New Ecological Paradigm) in an attempt to demonstrate the need for a field of environmental sociology. Catton and Dunlap argued that sociology had come to embrace the fundamental 'anthropocentrism' characterizing the larger society's dominant worldview. They labeled the sociological version of this perspective, the Human Exemptionalist Paradigm (HEP), as at the time most sociologists viewed the bio-physical environment as little more than a stage upon which human affairs took place and as largely irrelevant. Sociologists likewise shared the larger society's optimistic expectation of endless growth and progress, based on the assumption that, with their advanced technologies and social organization, modern societies were largely 'exempt' from the ecological constraints.

While this distinction was originally applied to sociology, Dunlap (1980) argued that human exemptionalism underlies nearly all of the social sciences, and one can argue many of the humanities as well. In their chapter in this volume, for example, Kopnina et al. identify several particular 'progressive' subdisciplines that have taken an anthropocentric perspective in critiquing conservation. Catton and Dunlap stated that sociological acceptance of this optimistic worldview was shaped by the doctrine of progress inherent in Western culture. At the time they wrote their initial work on this topic (1978–1980), they argued that the majority of the public maintained a strong belief that the present was better than the past and the future would be even better. Their work focused mostly on the US, and thus this characterization applies most strongly there, but also in varying degrees to other Western industrialized liberal democracies. By contrast, Catton and Dunlap argued that it was possible to identify an emerging set of assumptions about the nature of social reality that stands in stark contrast to the HEP. Catton and Dunlap called this the 'New Ecological Paradigm', or NEP. In his chapter in this volume, Dunlap describes the context of the mid-1970s US, and concludes that environmental protection was not a dominant or even important American value, and that was one reason why anti-environmentalism was able to emerge quickly in response to the initial efforts of the environmental movement.

We believe it is useful to consider the dynamics of environmentalism/anti-environmentalism in the context of the HEP–NEP continuum. In our view, the HEP–NEP distinction is a useful analytical tool for situating movement/countermovement phenomena as well as studies of them. Aspects of the HEP–NEP continuum might be used to classify both the substance of movements, and the scholarship of movements. With regard to the latter point, to the extent that studies of environmentalism/anti-environmentalism constitute a traditional social movement analysis using categories of social movement scholarship without consideration of sustainability issues, then one might classify such analyses as examples of HEP scholarship. For such studies, environmentalism is merely a nominal characteristic (e.g. the explanatory framework and key variables might easily apply to some other type of social movement).

As suggested in the Introduction and in Nicholas Scott's chapter in this volume, there is significant variation amongst anti-environmental movements. Classic anti-environmentalism tends to be based on the assumptions of the dominant Western worldview and its human exemptionalist outlook (Catton and Dunlap, 1978, 1980). However, some reflexive anti-environmentalism movements are more often based on assumptions of the alternative worldview (or NEP).

In a certain sense the HEP–NEP distinction can be thought of as providing a couple of ideal types (Weber, 2009). For a variety of reasons, many empirical cases fall somewhere in between the two poles. Further, there may be other ways of judging environmentalism. Huddart Kennedy (2020), for example, has suggested that some commonly used measures of environmentalism (such as the NEP Scale developed by Dunlap and Van Liere, 1978; also see Dunlap et al., 2000) may be biased, and may overlook the environmental sensibilities that rural conservatives have. Semi-relatedly, in interviews with the first author (as part of the study discussed in Tindall, Stoddart and Berseth's chapter), members of anti-environmentalist countermovement organizations in Canada talked about the notion that they were the 'real environmentalists' because they were out and about in nature on a regular basis, unlike city-based environmentalists. Further, they had practical, rather than abstract, knowledge of nature (see also Dunk, 1994). While the researchers see some of their interpretations of issues as being couched in anthropocentric terms, the informants believed they demonstrated environmental sensitivities.

Despite the need for some qualification under certain circumstances, the HEP–NEP analytic framework can be combined with a number of the other perspectives we describe here (such as political economy, for example). However, as we will describe below, we think there is potential for extending this framework by linking it to the social-ecological network approach, and also by emphasizing connections to social movement outcomes and environmental impacts. Further, we suggest the fields approach as a potential integrating perspective (e.g., see Fligstein and McAdam, 2012, for one version of this analytical strategy) for studies of anti-environmentalism, and integrating a HEP–NEP dimension into fields analyses would be a useful development.

Political Ideology and the Left/Right Spectrum

Political ideology (Marger, 1987) is a factor that tends to correlate with the views of individuals on environmental issues. Political scholars often distinguish between social liberalism/conservativism and economic liberalism/conservatism (Brint, 1984). Economic liberalism/conservativism is of most direct relevance to considering anti-environmentalism, though social liberalism/conservatism tends to also be correlated with economic liberalism/conservativism (Dunlap et al., 2001; Hochschild, 2018). As illustrated in a number of chapters in this volume, the political ideology of key actors is an important aspect of anti-environmental mobilization and framing (see those by Afanasyeva et al., Ali, Ard et al., Dunlap, Doreian and Mrvar, and Lucas).

In this chapter, we use the term 'liberal' as roughly equivalent with 'left wing' and 'conservative' as roughly equivalent to 'right wing' on the ideological continuum, which is consistent with usage in North America.[3] Elsewhere, in some contexts, 'neoliberal' is used as a synonym of conservative, and socialist or social democratic is used to describe those on the left. Ideological terms vary depending, in part, on different political traditions, and on the width of the political spectrum that describes different political jurisdictions.

Analytically, conservative political ideologies have been linked to system justification tendencies, or the tendency to support the maintenance of the status quo and resist social change (Jost et al., 2008). Empirically, scholarship has also shown that those holding more conservative economic views (e.g. preference for the free market over government intervention) are less likely to support environmental protection (Dunlap and Van Liere, 1984). Empirically, people who identify as more liberal/left wing are also more likely to support environmental protection and more likely to be affiliated with environmental movements (Dunlap et al., 2001; McCright et al., 2014; Tindall et al., 2022). However, as Krueger shows in his study of food sovereignty movements, these distinctions can become complicated when applied to specific cases. In some countries, such as the United States, political polarization has grown, and the correlation between political affiliation and views about environmental issues has increased (McCright and Dunlap, 2011a, 2011b). As Dunlap notes in the Preface to his chapter, by the 1990s the Conservative Movement in the US had become a primary force behind anti-environmentalism (see also McCright and Dunlap, 2000, 2011a). Similar dynamics of institutionalizing anti-environmentalism through conservative or right-leaning populist political parties can be seen in other places, such as Brazil under President Jair Bolsonaro, or in Australia or the Czech Republic, as examined in this volume by Lucas and Ocelík in their respective chapters.

Substantively, those with liberal/left orientations are more supportive of government intervention in general (such as regulations), are more supportive of taxation measures (for environmental protection) and tend to be more trusting of science (Gauchat, 2012; Kozlowski, 2021; McCright et al., 2013, 2014). To some extent, those with more conservative/right-wing views tend in the opposite direction on these issues. The strong impact of political orientation, however, seems to be much more pronounced in the United States, and the other Anglophone nations of Australia, Canada and the UK than in other Western countries (Smith and Mayer, 2019), with the US leading the pack in terms of political polarization (Capstick et al., 2015).

Aside from topics such as taxation and tolerance for regulation and other forms of government intervention, it is not necessarily obvious that there is any inherent affinity between liberalism and environmentalism. Indeed, various authors have pointed out that 'conservative' and 'conservation' are etymologically related. Macy et al. (2019) have argued that on many political issues where there is substantial polarization, initial positions may have been somewhat arbitrary, but cascading processes develop from initial conditions, and tipping points eventually occur, making an issue become partisan when there may not have been an inherent reason for it to become partisan (e.g. see Macy et al., 2019).[4]

Dunlap and McCright (e.g. Dunlap and McCright, 2015) have argued that a neoliberal political ideological shift occurred in the late 1970s and early 1980s with the election of the Margaret Thatcher government in the UK and the Ronald Reagan administration in the US. These politicians ushered in a new form of conservatism that sought to reduce taxes and regulations and decrease the power of labor unions. Relatedly, a number of right-wing think-tanks were founded by conservative philanthropists and corporate leaders in the US and elsewhere to combat the progressive gains in the 1960s and 1970s (Stefancic and Delgado, 1996), and many of them played a key role in combating environmental protection (Jacques et al., 2008). Wendy Brown (2015) and Nancy MacLean (2017) have also documented how the libertarian right and neoliberal ideology have reshaped American democracy more generally (especially via extensive privatization), and journalist Jane Mayer (2017) has examined the role of big money in funding the multi-faceted conservative movement (also see Ard et al., 2017).

In this volume, Doreian and Mrvar examine the social network ties of the US billionaires, David and Charles Koch, and their efforts to stifle environmentalism and other forms of progressivism. Ard et al. analyze pro-environmental voting behavior by US Congressional representatives and assess the relative influence of public opinion and lobbying from industry interest groups. Lucas examines the movement of corporate and political actors back and forth between government and the corporate world, and how this network has hampered the development of effective climate change policy in Australia.

In their chapter, Afanasyeva et al. examine opposition to wind power in Alberta. At the time of their study, a left-wing progressive government was in power at the provincial level (which is extremely unusual for the region). As Afanasyeva et al. discuss, affiliation with conservative parties and conservative ideology was an important factor in opposition to wind turbines. Afanasyeva et al. also stress that the views of their informants were nuanced, a mixture of local environmental sensitivities combined with a rejection of policies that they saw designed to remedy problems at a global level—for which the policies would likely prove ineffective.

While liberals are more likely to be supportive of environmental movements (Dunlap et al., 2001; Tindall et al., 2022), and conservatives have been more likely to be involved in anti-environmentalism (Jacques et al., 2008), there are, nevertheless, conservatives who are supportive of measures to deal with climate change and other environmental issues. Often, conservative environmentalists embrace a different vision of environmentalism, such as stressing technological developments, green consumerism, and the power of the market in solving environmental problems. This is reflected in the 'Ecological Modernization' theoretical perspective (Mol and Spaargaren, 2000) and also characteristic of much 'green growth' discourse used to justify continued economic growth.

We argue that scholars of anti-environmentalism need to consider the liberal–conservative dimension in a nuanced and contextual way. For example, there is an important difference between Red Tories (as they are known in Canada and the UK) and Libertarians. Similarly, while in the US many conservative Christian religious organizations are connected to the climate change denial movement (Veldman, 2019), Christians are not monolithic, and there is a significant group of progressive evangelical Christians who believe climate change is real, and are concerned with Creation Care (Wilkinson, 2012). In his chapter, for example, Victor Lam highlights variation amongst Christian groups in their views about climate change and related support for Indigenous peoples and their lands. While political ideology needs to be considered by analysts, it needs to be employed in a reflexive way.

Networks of Relations: The Structural Location of Actors, and of Ecosystems

While network analysts from a variety of disciplinary backgrounds have done work on environmentalism and anti-environmentalism, network analysis as a perspective has not been central in environmental sociology scholarship. It has gained more traction in the social movements literature (e.g., see Diani and McAdam, 2003), and social network techniques are often embraced by those working in political economy (e.g. Carroll, 2017, 2018; Carroll et al., 2018). Several examples of social network approaches are provided in this volume in chapters by Carroll et al., Doreian and Mvrar, Lucas, McKie, and Ocelík.

At the heart of network analysis is a focus on relationships (Wellman, 1988; Crossley, 2011). Often these are amongst individuals or groups, but other relational perspectives are possible, such as in discourse network analysis (see Stoddart and Tindall, 2015; Crossley, 2011; Leifeld, 2020). A variety of structural perspectives (as exemplified by network analysis) have been undertaken in social science studies of environmental issues including by scholars of anti-environmentalism (Brulle, 2018, 2019; Carroll et al., 2018; Dunlap and Jacques, 2013; Farrell, 2016a, 2016b, 2019; Jacques et al., 2008; Tindall et al., 2021), yet there are opportunities to integrate this perspective more fully in this field of study.

One area where there has been considerable attention to social networks is in the study of social movements, including environmental movements. Networks are important in social movements for coordinating collective activities, linking organizations (Heaney and Rojas, 2008; Andrews and Edwards, 2005), recruiting individuals (Klandermans and Oegema, 1987) and groups from past events to participate in new campaigns (McAdam et al., 1988) and diffusing information (McAdam and Rucht, 1993; Granovetter, 1973). Movement identities are also formed through social networks (Tindall et al., 2014), and new networks are a key outcome of mobilization (Diani, 1997; Tindall et al., 2012).

While the social network perspective has been used quite widely within the more general social movements literature (Diani and McAdam, 2003), it has only been employed to a limited extent in research on countermovements in general, and anti-environmentalism in particular. Some works that might be considered part of this literature include Brulle (2018, 2019); Carroll (2017, 2018); Carroll et al. (2018); Dunlap and Jacques (2013); Farrell (2016a, 2016b, 2019); Fisher et al. (2013a, 2013b); Jacques et al. (2008); Jasny et al. (2015); and Tindall et al. (2021).

An ego-network or personal network approach examines a social network from the vantage point of an individual and the patterns of actors she is tied to (her alters). (Sometimes the ties amongst the alters are also examined.) Relatively few personal network studies have been conducted on anti-environmentalism countermovements. Paralleling previous research on the participants of environmental movements (Tindall, 2002; Diani, 1995; Tindall and Robinson, 2017), a study conducted by Tindall et al. (2021) examined countermovement activism and personal social networks amongst members of an anti-environmentalism countermovement (also discussed by Tindall, Stoddart and Berseth in this volume). They found that while many of the same factors that explain participation in social movements (such as intra-movement social network ties, and support of movement-related values) explained participation in this countermovement, a novel finding was that the strongest predictor of countermovement activism was out-movement social network ties (ties to people in the environmental movement). Further investigation suggested that this is likely to be due to a mixture of 'selection' and 'influence' effects. There is some evidence that repeated interactions in conflictual contexts with environmentalists motivated countermovement members to become involved in anti-environmentalism movement activities. On the other hand, the more active that people were in the countermovement, the more ties they had to others within the environmental movement.

Social units other than individuals can also serve as nodes in social networks. Some researchers who have examined countermovements have focused on organizations. Indeed, much more research on social networks and anti-environmentalism has been done in the context of interorganizational networks. In particular, several environmental sociologists studying climate change denial and policy obstruction have examined social networks of ties amongst organizations.

Robert Brulle and his colleagues have undertaken several studies that examine the role of social networks in promoting denial and obstructing climate policy-making. Brulle (2019) argues that the climate change countermovement (CCCM) in the US has played a significant role in delaying actions to address climate change. He analyzed twelve prominent CCCM coalitions from 1989 to 2015. He found that over 2000 organizations were members of these coalitions and that a core of 179 organizations belonged to multiple coalitions. Brulle's analysis showed that organizations from the coal and electrical utility sectors were the most numerous and influential organizations in these coalitions. One of the key activities taken by anti-environmental social networks is lobbying government to make policy decisions that favor their interests.

Brulle (2018) has also examined lobbying with regard to climate change legislation. He notes that the major sectors involved in lobbying were fossil fuel and transportation corporations, utilities, and affiliated trade associations. The amount of money spent by these sectors was enormous compared to that spent by environmental organizations and renewable energy corporations. Brulle (2018) argues that the amount of money invested in lobbying is correlated with the introduction and potential passage of significant climate legislation.

Riley Dunlap and his colleagues Aaron McCright and Peter Jacques have examined various aspects of the Conservative Movement in the US and its role in promoting climate change denial. McCright and Dunlap (2003) examined the role of Conservative Movement actors in opposing the United States adoption of the Kyoto Protocol concerning global warming. They showed how conservative think-tanks mobilized to contest the global warming claims of mainstream climate science, enlisting the services of several high-profile contrarian scientists who were well known for their criticism of mainstream climate research (and often for their affiliations with the fossil fuels industry). The think-tanks promoted the contrarians in the media and in congressional hearings where they were often invited to testify by Republicans.

Dunlap and Jacques (2013) adopt a social network perspective in analyzing the production of books that promote climate change denial, as they did in an earlier study of books promoting anti-environmentalism more generally (Jacques et al., 2008). They argue that in order to block or delay action to ameliorate climate change, CCCM actors deny the reality and seriousness of climate change, and a primary strategy is manufacturing uncertainty over climate science. Conservative think-tanks (CTT) play a central role by supporting publication of books espousing climate change denial. Dunlap and Jacques found links between CTTs and a majority of 108 climate change denial books published through 2010, and noted that the diffusion of such books from the US to other nations was largely due to links between American CTTs and CTTs in those countries.

Recently, as part of their Corporate Mapping Project (some aspects of which they report in their chapter in this volume) William Carroll and colleagues have provided social network analyses of 'carbon capital' in Canada (Carroll, 2017, 2018; Carroll et al., 2018, and their chapter in this volume). In this research the focus is on 'ownership relations', which unearth 'views of the powerful interests that dominate fossil-fuel activities in Canada [and] reveal how the financial benefits from fossil-fuel production go predominantly to a small number of corporations, investment funds, wealthy families and governments' (Carroll, 2018, p. 9). Longitudinal social network analysis graphs highlight ownership relations for fossil-fuel corporations among the top 50 corporations in Canada between 2010 and 2015 (Carroll, 2018). The network is primarily composed of weak ties (ownership of 1 to 2 percent) originating from banks and insurers, along with 'a few dozen large holdings that give clear-cut strategic control to corporate or personal owners' (Carroll, 2018, p. 7). Important policy coalition actors include industry associations (e.g. the Canadian Association of Petroleum Producers); business advocacy groups representing broad class interests (e.g. chambers of commerce and business councils); 'astroturf' business advocacy groups (e.g. the Canadian Taxpayers Federation); think-tanks that take direction from large corporations (e.g. the CD Howe Institute); universities and other public research institutes (e.g. the University of Calgary's School of Public Policy) (Carroll et al., 2018). Carroll's work illustrates one fruitful synthesis of conceptual tools: combining social network analysis with a political economy perspective.

Other researchers have also examined the social structure of climate change denial and other forms of anti-environmentalism using a social network approach. Dana Fisher, Lorien Jasny, Philip Leifeld and their colleagues have examined political polarization, policy networks, and the role of echo-chambers in climate change policy-making, and climate change communication more generally (e.g. see Fisher et al., 2013a, 2013b; Fisher et al., 2015; Jasny et al., 2015, 2018; Jasny and Fisher, 2019). Fisher et al. note that US climate change policy networks are marked by a great deal of homophily—actors tend to be tied to others who are similar to themselves in terms of party and ideological affiliation. This results in polarized social networks, and the formation of echo-chambers where climate change deniers tend to receive and send information with others who also doubt the existence of anthropogenic climate change, and the need for policy measures to deal with climate change.

Justin Farrell (2016a, 2016b, 2019) has employed computational methods to explore the linkages between US actors involved in promoting climate change denial, ties to their supporters and the discourse the actors produce. For example, Farrell (2016a, 2016b) examines how polarization over climate change in the US is shaped by a patterned network of political and financial actors. He built and analyzed a data set that included all the individual and organizational actors in the climate change countermovement (164 organizations and 4556 individuals), all written and verbal texts produced by this network between 1993 and 2013 (40,785 texts, more than 39 million words) and the influence of corporate (ExxonMobil) and conservative foundation (Koch Family Foundations) funding on the centrality of organizations and their output of denial discourse. He found that organizations that received ExxonMobil or Koch funding were more central to the network, more likely to have produced and disseminated denial material and more likely to see their discourse reflected in the mass media and policy circles.

In a subsequent analysis, Farrell (2019) used natural language processing techniques to build a data set that enabled him to analyze the relationship between the key actors responsible for producing scientific misinformation about climate change and US philanthropy (primarily conservative in orientation). His analysis showed that from 1997 to 2006 (when Al Gore's movie, *An Inconvenient Truth*, was issued and received enormous visibility and accolades) social networks of individuals and organizations promoting scientific misinformation regarding climate change were increasingly embraced and supported by institutional philanthropy in the US, before tapering off a bit over the next decade but remaining at significant levels.

In general, there is potential for much more work applying social network perspectives to anti-environmentalism, and there is a significant amount of literature beyond that located in the realms of social movements, political economy and political sociology. One promising approach is the socio-ecological network approach. This approach has been developed by Örjan Bodin, Beatrice Crona and their colleagues who are part of the 'Naseberry' group. Much of this research uses SNA tools to examine social-ecological relations around natural resource management and governance.

These scholars have undertaken a program of research that often uses multi-mode-networks to understand socio-ecological systems (see Bodin and Crona, 2009; Bodin et al., 2006; Bodin and Prell, 2011; Sayles et al., 2019; Barnes et al., 2019; Ernston, 2013). One mode consists of ties amongst social actors, and another mode consists of ties from social actors to ecosystem elements. A number of works use SNA tools to examine social-ecological relations around natural resource management/governance. Thus far, much of this emerging research has focused on how to build/improve collaboration across diverse actors that rely on shared resource pools (e.g. fisheries), but recently there have been calls to devote more attention to applying social-ecological network analysis to study and better understand conflict in environmental governance – an obvious point of connection to studies of anti-environmental actors and their impact on environmental governance (Bodin et al., 2020).

While these researchers do not explicitly draw upon the HEP–NEP conceptualization developed by Catton and Dunlap (1978; 1980), they have essentially developed an approach that situates social network analysis within a NEP framework. We would encourage scholars of anti-environmentalism movements to draw upon this synthesis. For example, researchers taking a social-ecological networks approach might examine the networks amongst environmentalists, and amongst anti-environmentalists, and the extent to which members of each group have ties to different or similar ecosystem units. They might also examine ties between the two opposing movements (see Tindall et al., 2021). These suggestions are illustrated in Figure 23.1.

Political Economy and the Role of Capitalism

A fundamental divide within both environmental social science, and within the environmental movement, is between those who view capitalism as the root cause of environmental problems (Foster and Clark, 2020; Schnaiberg, 1980; Gould et al., 2004; Klein, 2015) and those who see the potential for capitalism to create market-oriented solutions to environmental problems (Mol and Spaargaren, 2002). In sociology and other social sciences, neo-Marxist perspectives, such as Schnaiberg's Treadmill of Production perspective (TOP) (1980), argue that the ideological commitment of dominant social actors to economic growth, and the political power of actors committed to economic growth and neoliberal policies, tends to push capitalist societies on unsustainable paths. By contrast, Ecological Modernization (EMT) (Mol and Spaargaren, 2002) is a 'capitalism friendly' perspective, which argues that sustainable growth can occur/ is occurring within capitalist economic systems. Keys to green growth, according to the ecological modernization perspective, are the implementation of green technology, use of market mechanisms (such as carbon pricing), and having the state step back from a 'command role' and play more of a coordinating role (Mol, 1997). The empirical support for these respective perspectives is mixed, with EMT being more heavily criticized regarding its claims about the potential of green growth. However, as Carrillo notes in this volume, both perspectives suffer from race-blind approaches to the intersection of environmental harm, racism, and projects of racial state formation. Yet, we would assert that TOP is more compatible with environmental justice scholarship that focuses on how environmental harms are disproportionately borne by racialized communities (see, for example, Pellow, 2004).

While we do not have space to explore this issue in depth, it is worth noting that capitalism can take a variety of forms (Hall and Soskice, 2001). There are the liberal market economies (US, UK, Australia, New Zealand), where classic anti-environmentalism has arguably been most prevalent and had greater political efficacy (Jacques et al., 2008). In contrast, there are countries that are better characterized as coordinated market economies (Germany and much of the rest of the EU, Japan, etc.), which includes several countries where policies associated with Ecological Modernization have been more successfully implemented. We tend to see weaker signs of classic anti-environmentalism in coordinated market economies (where there is typically closer coordination and collaboration across state, industry actors, unions, and civil society). The details of the processes described by the TOP and EMT perspectives will vary to some extent, depending on the form of capitalism that is present in a given country.

Within the broad 'environmental movement', there are a number of diverse movements and a variety of actors who have differing views about how to address environmental degradation. Views differ on a number of issues, but most notably in the context of this discussion, there are different perspectives about political-economic issues. Within the environmental movement, actors such as former US Vice-President Al Gore assert that the climate crisis can be largely solved through existing technologies and the application of key policy measures (2006, 2009), which is consistent with the ecological modernization view.[5] On the other hand, there are critics, such as Marxist sociologists (Foster and Clark, 2020) and social commentators like Naomi Klein (2015, 2020), who see capitalism (notably neoliberal market capitalism) as at the root of ecological problems, and argue for rearranging the socio-political-economic structure in order to solve the climate crisis and simultaneously address a number of social justice issues, which resonates more with the TOP view.[6]

With respect to anti-environmentalism, some commentators engage in pro-capitalistic rhetoric (Lomborg, 2003, 2010; Moore, 2000), while others simultaneously critique environmentalism and capitalism or at least some forms of environmentalism. This echoes the distinctions made in the Introduction to this volume between classic and reflexive anti-environmentalism. Those who embrace the former perspective argue that the climate crisis and other purported environmental problems are exaggerated (or even untrue), that there are more important problems to deal with (e.g. Lomborg, 2003, 2010), and that proposed government intervention to deal with environmental problems is unwarranted. Those who embrace the latter perspective argue that there are simultaneous environmental and social justice crises, and that both are linked to capitalism—particularly neoliberal capitalism (Gould et al., 2015).

Some social movement scholars have criticized the social movements literature for insufficiently considering the role that capitalism plays in shaping social movement mobilization and political contestation (Hetland and Goodwin, 2013; della Porta, 2015), and for overlooking many useful conceptual tools from Marxist analyses. The chapter in this volume by Carroll et al. provides a useful counter to this criticism, while also incorporating an ecological sensitivity (thus working within a NEP framework). We believe scholars of anti-environmentalism could pay more attention to capitalism as a system, and the role of capital in particular, as well as the particular 'flavor' of capitalism that typifies a particular case, in trying to understand the dynamics of anti-environmentalism. Attention to capitalist economic systems should also be incorporated into analyses of the impacts of anti-environmentalism on the environment.

A problem with single-case studies is that key contextual conditions in which cases are embedded do not vary. Put the same actors in another context, and their actions and the dynamics between them may well differ substantially. One solution is to undertake comparative analyses, a suggestion Dunlap makes in the Preface to his chapter. Comparative studies should consider cases where political-economic conditions vary, and consider whether such variation has an effect on the form that anti-environmentalism takes (McAdam et al., 2001).

Resources and Political Opportunity Structures

In the next several sections, we consider perspectives that are front and center in the social movement literature, and are often employed together by social movement scholars. Two of these are the related notions of resource mobilization (McCarthy and Zald, 1977) and political opportunity structures (McAdam, 1982). The former perspective is associated with resource mobilization theory, and the latter with political process theory.[7] In their chapter, Staggenborg and Meyer provide considerable attention to resources and political opportunities in their discussion of the dynamics of movements and countermovements. They focus on the conditions under which countermovements emerge and succeed. An important observation they make is that social media have changed the balance of communication resources for movements and countermovements. Here we will provide some additional commentary on resources and opportunity structures.

Another important point Staggenborg and Meyer make in the context of considering environmental movements and anti-environmental countermovements, is that the resources available to these two movements are not symmetrical. While the availability of different types of resources might vary, the financial resources available to anti-environmental actors are greater by many magnitudes.[8] We would add further that this imbalance is due to the fact that actors with greater access to capital are seemingly more likely to be allied with anti-environmental actors than with environmental movement actors. In many cases, this is part of a strategy to protect financial investments and future growth opportunities.

A number of studies have examined environmental organizations by focusing on resources (e.g., Walsh, 1981; McLaughlin and Khawaja, 2000). Scholars studying climate change denial countermovements have noted how countermovement leaders have leveraged and redirected the resources of pre-existing groups involved in conservative politics (Dunlap and Jacques, 2013) to actions that cast doubt on anthropogenic climate change, and that resist policy measures to reduce emissions. To take the climate denial movement as an example of anti-environmentalism, supporters of this movement have been very effective at leveraging financial resources into media coverage. In particular, resources have been mobilized directly and indirectly from beneficiaries of fossil fuel production to other actors in the climate denial network (Dunlap and McCright, 2015; see also Farrell, 2016a, 2016b; 2019; Brulle, 2018, 2019).

In a sense, political process theory is an extension of resource mobilization theory, emphasizing the interactions that a social movement has with actors in its political environment. According to this perspective:

> 'exogenous factors' enhance or inhibit a social movement's prospects for (a) mobilising, (b) advancing particular claims rather than others, (c) cultivating some alliances rather than others, (d) employing particular political strategies and tactics rather than others, and (e) affecting mainstream institutional politics and policy. (Meyer, 2004, p. 126)

In this context, the distinction between majoritarian and consensus oriented political structures may be particularly important, as well as the distinction between corporatist and pluralist political cultures, as meta-characteristics of the political opportunity structure in different societies (Lijphart, 2012). As noted earlier, many of the strongholds of anti-environmentalism are also associated with more majoritarian and pluralist political cultures (which also often tend to be the more liberal market economies).

As discussed in both Riley Dunlap's chapter Preface and Harris Ali's chapter, shifts in federal administrations in both the US and Canada illustrate how political opportunities realigned for both the environmental movement and anti-environmentalism regarding climate change. In the US, under the George W. Bush administration (first elected in 2000), little was done to address climate change. Many members of the Bush administration were skeptical about anthropogenic climate change, and some had direct ties to the oil and gas industry. The Bush administration interfered with the activities of key government organizations charged to monitor climate change (such as NASA and NOAA), and muzzled federal scientists (McCright and Dunlap, 2010; Turner and Isenberg, 2018).

In Canada, as Ali discusses in this volume, the Stephen Harper-led Conservative government (first elected in 2006) did little to address climate change. During the tenure of the Harper administration, Canada pulled out of the Kyoto Protocol (the first country to do so), a number of federal cabinet ministers were skeptical of human-caused climate change, and environmentalists were labeled 'foreign-funded radicals'. Also, environmental groups were investigated by the Canadian Revenue Agency for violation of their charitable status for speaking out on climate change (yet charitable organizations who promoted right-wing policy agendas were not), and federal environmental scientists were 'muzzled' (Lakanen, 2018). In this volume, Harris Ali's chapter focuses in particular on the communication strategies employed by the

Harper government to define the environmental movement in Canada as a national security threat to Canada's economy and society.

Both the George W. Bush (as discussed by Dunlap in his Preface) and Harper (as discussed by Ali) administrations created hostile political opportunity structures for environmental movements, but were welcoming environments for climate change deniers and other anti-environmental actors. In their chapter, Staggenborg and Meyer note that one way in which environmental movement actors responded to this was by turning to other levels of government to try to make progress on climate action—such as state/provincial governments, and cities.

In the US, once the Barack Obama administration was elected (in 2008), possibilities for positive change increased. Amongst other things, during the Obama administration the Keystone XL pipeline was canceled, executive orders were implemented to shut down super polluters and deal with other environmental issues, and the US signed the Paris Agreement on Climate Change. The Obama administration thus provided a more positive context for environmental activists than the previous Bush administration, but its pro-environmental leanings were met with strong Republican opposition (Turner and Isenberg, 2018).

Under the subsequent Donald Trump administration (elected in 2016), by contrast, the US announced it was pulling out of the Paris Agreement, environmental regulations were rolled back, the EPA suffered large cuts, industry-friendly individuals were placed in charge of environmental regulatory agencies, the Keystone XL Pipeline was reapproved, drilling for oil was approved in environmentally sensitive areas, and so on (as discussed by both Ali and Dunlap; also see Turner and Isenberg, 2018). In addition, as Carrillo notes in this volume, the Trumpist project also worked to link anti-environmentalism to a racial politics that played to white supremacist tendencies among his supporters.

In Canada, a Liberal government came into power in 2015 led by Justin Trudeau. Under the Trudeau-led federal government, a new cabinet minister in charge of Climate Change and Environment was named (a first), Canada signed the Paris Agreement and pushed for a 1.5°C limit to global warming, and a new federal carbon pricing scheme was announced and eventually implemented. To a certain extent, political opportunities had opened up again for environmentalists. Yet, the Trudeau government has a mixed environmental legacy, especially its tendency to undertake actions to support the fossil fuel industry (e.g. see Tindall et al., 2020).

Other examples are also given in this volume about the dynamics amongst the environmental movement, anti-environmental countermovements, corporate actors, and governments. For example, Lukas' chapter in this volume examines mobilization by local communities against the Betung Kerihun National Park in West Kalimantan, Indonesia. Also, as Krueger notes, macro-level political processes of democratization following the end of Indonesian President Suharto's regime created openings for civil society and social movement activity. However, within this broader shift in the political opportunity structure, specific critical events brought to the surface tensions between the national park authority and local communities and sparked anti-environment mobilization and protest.

Framing, Culture, Narratives and Emotion

Another dimension of social movement scholarship, and social science research more generally, orients around framing, culture, narratives and emotion. While there are several origins for the framing concept within the social sciences (including Goffman, 1974), within social movement scholarship it was popularized by David Snow and Robert Benford (Snow et al., 1986; Snow and Benford, 1988, 1992; Benford and Snow, 2000). The study of frame alignment processes involves examining the linkages between the perceptions, values and interests of individuals and the recruitment strategies employed by social movement organizations. A frame was defined as a 'framework of interpretation' that allows individuals to locate, perceive, identify and label events in the world: 'By rendering events or occurrences meaningful, frames function to organize experience and guide action' (Snow et al., 1986, p. 464).

While some scholars have employed the framing perspective to emphasize particular substantive themes that might appear in environmental communications such as 'the need for environmental justice' (Capek, 1993) or 'jobs versus the environment' (Doyle et al., 1997), an important aspect of framing is that in addition to conveying content, frames play a particular communication function (Benford and Snow, 2000).[9]

Several of the chapters in this volume deal with aspects of framing, culture, narratives and emotion, including Tindall et al.'s examination of the Share Our Resources countermovement in British Columbia and Ocelík's study of climate skepticism in the Czech Republic. Ali examines how the Canadian federal government framed the interests of the fossil fuel industry as aligned with national interests. Similarly, Özen examines how the Turkish government reframed anti-mine activism as aligned with foreign interests that are inconsistent with national developmental aspirations. McMullin-Messier analyzes discourse about immigration in the context of environmentalism. Dunlap's discussion of the context of US environmentalism in the 1970s shows how early environmental movement proposals were portrayed as threats to dominant American values. Ali examines some of the framing strategies of the Canadian federal government under the Harper administration. During this period in Canada, framing strategies were used by the federal government to stigmatize environmentalists and to reframe environmental issues as security issues (Lakanen, 2018).

In their chapter, Staggenborg and Meyer note that framing efforts are also part of the interactive process that occurs between movements and countermovements, with countermovement frames designed to respond to movement actors and frames over time. Returning to substantive themes, one common theme in anti-environmentalism campaigns is 'jobs versus the environment', which has been used in environmental controversies from forestry (Doyle et al., 1997), to coal mining (Lewin, 2019), to oil production (Hackett and Adams, 2018). In this volume, Bible notes the resonance of the jobs-versus-environment frame in fueling suspicion of environmentalism among Australian extractive industry workers and farmers. Vachon examines the jobs versus the environment frame in the context of labor union anti-environmentalism in the US, while Dunlap also notes the salience of this frame in the US. In the substantially different context of mobilization against the Kalimantan National Park authority, Lukas similarly points to the use of anti-environmentalist frames that defined local villagers as sustainable resource users in opposition to the national park authority as an enemy force that severed communities from their livelihoods. Similar themes arise in the analysis presented in the chapter by Tindall, Stoddart and Berseth.

Another frequently used anti-environmentalist frame is 'hypocrites/hypocrisy'. Environmentalists are often portrayed as hypocrites for talking about the need to phase out use of fossil fuels, stop the use of forest products, and so on, while being seen as inconsistent in their actions.[10] Another tactic used by anti-environmentalists is to use the frames of environmentalists against them,[11] which is consistent with Staggenborg and Meyer's observation that the tactics and frames of countermovements are produced in continuing interactions with social movements.

A further commonly used anti-environmentalist framing technique is to allege that environmentalists pursue their goals out of 'self-interest' (Readfern, 2017). There are many examples. Anti-environmentalists often employ an implicit theory of resource mobilization in claiming that environmentalists artificially manufacture environmental problems because they need to raise money for their organizations. Climate scientists are depicted as constructing a hoax in order to enrich themselves with research grants (Mann, 2013, 2021), a claim noted by Staggenborg and Meyer in their chapter. Wilderness advocates are stereotyped as elites who are acting to protect their personal recreation areas. Advocates of alternative energy are seen as exaggerating anthropogenic climate change and advocating alternative energy in order to profit from their financial investments, often at the expenses of taxpayers through government subsidies (see Afanasyeva et al.'s chapter in this volume).

Another issue that frequently appears in anti-environmentalists' discourse is the notion that 'environmentalists are geographical and social outsiders'. For instance, the juxtaposition of local concerns of conservatives versus the global concerns of environmentalists is an issue discussed by Afanasyeva et al. in this volume. Disputes over natural resource extraction projects are often framed by anti-environmentalists as involving locals against outsiders (Dunk, 1994; Lewin, 2019; Tindall et al., 2021). This is despite the fact that most often multinational corporations headquartered hundreds or thousands of miles away control and/or own 'local' extraction projects, and that at least some of the environmentalists are often local residents. Past researchers have combined social constructionist and political economy approaches in investigating this theme (Dunk, 1994). But other tools suggested here could also be integrated, such as the social-ecological networks approach (Bodin et al., 2006). In Figure 23.1 we suggest that researchers might consider both the geographical location of actors, and the geographical location of contested ecosystems. This would add an additional dimension for analysis to the cultural-organizational field of environmental contestation.

Framing is one analytical perspective on cultural aspects of contentious politics, but there are other important approaches, especially those that unpack broader cultural contexts (as exemplified by Hochschild, 2018) and focus on narratives. Through ethnographic field work, Hochschild (2018) examines the puzzle of why southern white, conservative, mainly Christian Tea Party supporters, many of whom are working class and/or low income, seemingly act against their own interests by opposing government regulations protecting the environment, and government providing social welfare benefits. Further motivating her research is the observation that in many cases these were the same people who supported Donald Trump for president in 2016 (who did more than any US president in living memory to reverse environmental protections). The paradox is that many of the people who oppose government involvement in social programs and environmental protection are beneficiaries of such programs, and have been directly harmed by pollution resulting from deregulation of the environment.

Hochschild (2018) explains this by describing a 'deep story', a narrative that describes her informants as feeling that despite working hard, playing by the rules and paying taxes, they were facing a declining situation because others (such as minorities) were 'cutting in line' and receiving undeserved benefits, leapfrogging those who should be ahead of them in line. Hence, they oppose governments in general, and politicians in particular, that allow this perceived injustice to continue. Hochschild is not necessarily claiming that the empirical situation that the narrative depicts is accurate, just that this narrative captures the feelings of her informants.[12]

In the realm of climate change research, Norgaard (2011) has examined climate change denial amongst members of a small community in Norway. In her ethnographic study, she examines climate change denial as a cultural and psychological process. Norgaard's informants provided narratives that discounted evidence of climate change because, amongst other things, acknowledging such changes would necessitate questioning the fact that Norway's economy is heavily dependent on the fossil fuel industry.

There are also other perspectives that emphasize cultural and emotional aspects of contentious politics. A growing body of literature concludes that information deficit models of environmental communication that focus on providing scientific facts to people to stimulate social change are insufficient to change minds and elicit climate action (e.g. Boykoff, 2019; Marshall, 2015). Marshall (2015), complementing Hochschild's work, notes that the average person does not operate on the basis of recalled scientific facts and abstractions. Rather, people tend to learn, remember and communicate in the context of stories. Hence, according to Marshall, it is better to tell narratives about climate change (rather than regurgitate scientific facts), and to articulate these stories in the context of people's immediate and everyday lives and surroundings rather than to refer to phenomena and problems on other parts of the planet. In our view, Marshall's work is another call for scholars who are interested in anti-environmentalism to pay attention to culture and narrative in order to obtain a deeper understanding about aspects of this phenomenon. And if the goal is to engage in an intervention, then scholars should embrace narratives in the manner described by Marshall.[13]

Others, such as Jasper (2018), have argued that social movement scholars have overemphasized structural explanations and rationality, and have underemphasized emotion. It is argued that very often participants in social movements, or countermovements, are catalyzed by a deep sense of outrage about a particular situation. In the case of countermovements at the community level, this is often about a sense that local culture and identities have been disrespected (Dunk, 1994; Lewin, 2019; Tindall et al., 2021). In the present volume, Afanasyeva et al. touch upon this issue, as does Tindall et al.'s chapter.

Field Theory as a Unifying Approach

One potential unifying framework is the field theory approach. Figure 23.1 visually illustrates this objective. The idea of fields has received considerable attention recently in social science in general, and in the social movements area in particular. Martin (2003, 2009) has written some key works on this issue, tracing the use of this concept in both the natural sciences and social sciences. The concept of field has been employed in quite different ways by different scholars in the social sciences.

In the context of the social sciences, Martin (2003, p. 28) argues:

> there is a tendency for field theorists to use the word 'field' in three overlapping or interrelated senses: In the first, there is the purely topological sense ... the field is conceived as an analytic area of simplified dimensions in which we position persons or institutions. Second, there is the sense of a field as an organization of forces. Third, there is the sense of the field as a field of contestation, a battlefield.

Martin further notes that one distinctive aspect of field theories is that they offer explanations where 'effects' are not direct. For example, the concept of a field has been applied in organizational sociology to help understand the way organizations interact and influence each other (e.g. see DiMaggio and Powell, 1983). This definition draws heavily from the work of Pierre Bourdieu, who uses the concept of field to refer 'to both the totality of actors and organizations involved in an arena of social or cultural production and the dynamic relationships among them' (DiMaggio, 1979, p. 1463). An organizational field can be considered both a conceptual tool and a level of analysis (Scott, 2008a, 2008b). We can think about environmental movement organizations and anti-environmentalism groups as an organizational field (see, for example Ramos, 2015 and Carroll et al., 2021).

In the social movements literature a number of scholars have worked with versions of the field idea, including Diani (2015); Klandermans (1992); Evans and Kay (2008); Fligstein and McAdam (2011, 2012); and Jasper (2019) amongst others.[14] Within this context, Fligstein and McAdam (2011, p. 3) provide a definition of strategic action fields:

> We hold the view that strategic action fields (hereafter, SAFs) are the fundamental units of collective action in society. A strategic action field is a meso-level social order where actors (who can be individual or collective) interact with knowledge of one another under a set of common understandings about the purposes of the field, the relationships in the field (including who has power and why), and the field's rules.

Our argument here is that we can think of environmental and anti-environmental movement organizations and related cultural elements as constituting a field. Some of the cultural elements include collective identities, frames about environmental issues and other aspects of environmental discourse, values and repertoires of tactics (Ramos, 2015). Social network analyses can be used to model the relations amongst the elements. For example, in climate change denial movements in the US the field might include wealthy fossil-fuel corporations, conservative donors, conservative politicians, conservative think-tanks, right-wing media outlets, conservative religious organizations, networks of discourse, and so on (Brulle, 2014; Carroll, 2017; Carroll et al., 2018; Farrell, 2016a).

One aspect of Fligstein and McAdam's treatment of field theory is that it consolidates a number of different streams of social movement theory, such as resource mobilization, political opportunity structures, framing, and the dynamics of contention. We draw upon their suggestion, and encourage scholars of anti-environmentalism to synthesize these concepts, and others discussed in this chapter (such as the HEP–NEP continuum) in future studies of anti-environmentalism.

While we encourage researchers to embrace an integrated perspective on anti-environmentalism, and suggest field theory as a possible approach for this objective, we acknowledge that this is not easy. Collecting and integrating multiple types of data at potentially different scales is admittedly challenging. However, with enough time, resources and collaboration this is a goal to work toward.

Outcomes and Impacts

In this final section we would like to consider outcomes and impacts as analytical concepts that may be linked to the integrative research strategy we have discussed. While these terms overlap somewhat in meaning, we will use 'outcomes' to refer to social, economic and political outcomes of social movements, and 'impacts' to refer to environmental impacts. Also, as this book is focused on anti-environmentalism we will concentrate primarily on countermovement phenomena. However, the conceptual points we are making here apply more or less equally to both environmentalism and anti-environmentalism.

In the past few decades, social movement scholars have paid closer attention to social movement outcomes (Giugni, 1998; Giugni et al., 1999). Sometimes social movements have intended outcomes (e.g. getting a park or protected area legally recognized or having climate change legislation signed into law). Researchers have studied the extent to which the actions taken by movement actors (mobilization, protests, etc.) lead to changes that are consistent with their stated objectives. Much of the scholarship on outcomes focuses primarily on political outcomes (narrowly defined). While harder to measure, movements also have important cultural outcomes in terms of shaping broader cultural values over time (Stoddart, 2015; Jamison et al., 1990). Movements can also have economic outcomes in terms of helping to channel pro-environmental market trends, as Vasi (2011) argues in his analysis of the role of environmental movements in structuring the emergence and growth of renewable energy sectors. Other examples of social movement outcome studies include McAdam and Su (2002) and Soule and Olzak (2004).

Critics of studies that assume mobilization leads to the realization of movement objectives point out that there may be a variety of causal factors, and it is conceivable that, rather than being a causal factor, social movement mobilization might be an outcome of other changes. For example, it is possible that changes in the economy lead to changes in public opinion and the priorities of elected officials, and that these outcomes lead to changes in policy. Perhaps in these circumstances social movement mobilization is an epiphenomenon of other processes, or one of a constellation of contributing factors that are analytically difficult to parse out.

Similarly, the outcomes from countermovements like anti-environmentalism should be examined carefully by scholars, who will face the same sorts of challenges. Here, another factor of potential interest to scholars of anti-environmentalism is the notion of 'impacts', especially environmental impacts. Conducting social research built on the new ecological paradigm as advocated by Catton and Dunlap means taking the environment seriously in empirical analyses. In environmental sociology, many scholars have begun to take environmental impacts more seriously by incorporating environmental measures into their research as dependent variables (e.g., Marquart-Pyatt et al., 2015; York et al., 2003). In Figure 23.1, we depict outcomes and impacts as arising from the interactions in the cultural-organizational field. In addition, environmental impacts are also affected by social movement outcomes.

Some issues for anti-environmentalism scholars to consider include the following: how contestation between environmental and anti-environmental players has outcomes across political (e.g. policy outcomes; McCright and Dunlap, 2003), economic (e.g. shaping the fortunes of fossil fuel versus green-tech companies; Vasi, 2011), and cultural spheres (e.g. broader social values; Stoddart, 2015) as well as impacts on environmental quality.

A related set of tools is 'impact analysis' (White, 2009, 2010; Gertler et al., 2016; Khandker et al., 2009), and the concept of 'counterfactuals' (Morgan and Winship, 2015). Impact analysis is already a significant part of environmental sociology and related disciplines. Impact analysis can be undertaken to examine social outcomes and environmental impacts of projects and programs, and events like natural and human-caused disasters (Freudenburg, 1986; Freudenburg et al., 2009; Freudenburg and Gramling, 2011). Here we would like to highlight that scholars of anti-environmentalism could bring such studies further into the NEP paradigm by trying to consider the outcomes and impacts of anti-environmental movements, both socially and environmentally, and perhaps try to estimate the environmental impacts that would have resulted from pro-environmental campaigns if such countermovements had not materialized (an example of counterfactual analysis) (this is illustrated in Figure 23.1). Again, this is an ideal to work towards. Measuring social movement outcomes and environmental impacts is hard work, and cannot be undertaken in every study.

CONCLUSION

In this chapter we set out to describe a variety of conceptual tools that exist within the social movements literature, the environmental sociology literature, as well as cognate literature. We argue that research on environmental movements and countermovements have both tended to be embedded within particular theoretical literatures with insufficient connection across these perspectives. A research program for anti-environmentalism studies would benefit from drawing on a greater synthesis across these bodies of literature. Figure 23.1 provides a visual illustration of this suggestion. For example, combining some of the insights of the HEP–NEP continuum with other perspectives, and perhaps also trying to link these to social/political/economic outcomes and environmental impacts, might facilitate more powerful analyses.

The array of conceptual tools we have presented is not exhaustive, and we do not intend it to be. We have selected from the literature with which we are familiar. However, a case can certainly be made that other sets of conceptual tools could be added to this collection, such as those associated with gender analyses (Bell et al., 2019; Huddart Kennedy and Dzialo, 2015), studies of ethnicity and race (Mohai et al., 2009; Park and Pellow, 2011; Taylor, 2014; Waldron, 2018), and perspectives on colonization (Bacon, 2019; Callison, 2020; McKay et al., 2020; Norgaard, 2020; Whyte, 2018).[15] In particular, these analytical issues often arise in the context of environmental/climate justice movements (Agyeman et al., 2010; Roberts and Parks, 2006), and anti-environmental countermovement responses to them. While we have not included a detailed discussion of these issues in this chapter, we refer readers back to Carrillo's chapter, which examines race and racism in our understanding of the social and political dynamics of anti-environmentalism, and to McMullin-Messier's chapter, which investigates anti-immigration discourses in the context of environmentalism. Bible's chapter also highlights the ways in which colonial legacies continue to inform the social dynamics of anti-environmentalism in Australia.

While we have provided research from a variety of cases in this volume, there is still a vital need for further work that expands an anti-environmentalism research program to cover the diversity of anti-environmentalisms (as per our Introduction) playing out across a broader range of cases, particularly in regions that are characterized by diverse economic systems (e.g. coordinated market economies) and political systems (e.g. more consensus-oriented or corporatist political systems), as well as across the global north and global south, including in post-socialist or more authoritarian political systems. Such a program of work is consistent with calls made by several authors in this volume for more comparative research. This type of approach will help us better understand the societal conditions and dynamics that facilitate or mitigate the emergence and efficacy (in terms of outcomes) of different forms of anti-environmentalism.

Our main objectives here are to encourage scholars of anti-environmentalism to consider other analytical tools besides the ones they are most familiar with, to synthesize amongst multiple approaches, and to examine the multiple social and environmental dimensions that are associated with anti-environmentalism phenomena.

In this volume we have endeavored to shine light on different cases and processes in order to provide an understanding of various forms of anti-environmentalism. The cases presented here come from a variety of countries, from several continents. We have not set out to develop a 'how to' guide for combating anti-environmentalism, though some helpful suggestions are made by James Hoggan in his Foreword to this volume (see also Boykoff, 2019). Instead, we argue that providing a deeper and more nuanced understanding of the variety of anti-environmentalisms is a vital first step. But also, in some cases it might be that instead of simply responding to anti-environmentalism from a pre-formulated environmentalist perspective, there are also important lessons to be learned, particularly from cases of more constructive reflexive anti-environmentalist critiques. As we are faced with intersecting social-ecological crises, including climate change, biodiversity loss, ocean acidification and ecological decline, time is of the essence in developing constructive responses to such lessons.

NOTES

1. We would like to thank Victor Lam and Valerie Berseth for their very helpful feedback on an earlier version of this chapter. We would also like to thank Erick Lachapelle and Marjolaine Martel-Morin for their contributions to our thinking about political ideology and the left/right spectrum.
2. The HEP–NEP dimension (the Human Exemptionalist Paradigm versus the New Ecological Paradigm) describes the extent to which (1) actors and analyses embrace an anthropocentric worldview that sees modern human societies as separate from and no longer dependent on the biophysical environment because their complex social organization, science and technology frees them from the ecological constraints facing other species, thus allowing for unlimited growth and progress, versus (2) actors and analyses that adopt an alternative biocentric worldview that sees human societies as embedded in and dependent upon ecological systems which place constraints on their development, often in the form of unintended negative consequences of scientific-technological advances and economic growth, thus hampering endless growth and progress (Catton and Dunlap, 1978, 1980; Dunlap and Catton, 1979).
3. The term 'liberal' or 'liberalism' is particularly complicated as this word can be used to describe ideologies embraced by individual actors, it can be used to describe a broad political philosophy, and it can be used to describe an economic philosophy. These labels have somewhat different meanings in these different contexts, and consequently we use the word somewhat differently in different parts of the chapter. In some contexts (e.g. the US), it may refer broadly to the left-leaning part of the political spectrum, while in other contexts (Canada, UK), it has stronger connotations/linkages with specific political parties. There are also some ambiguities in distinguishing between the term 'liberalism' and 'neoliberalism'. We use the term 'liberalism' as synonymous with modern liberalism (which has its roots in social liberalism), which is distinct from neoliberalism. The latter is closely associated with classical liberalism. In some parts of the chapter we use the term 'neoliberalism' when this label has been used by authors we cite, or in cases where this refers to neoliberal (or free market) policies or policy directions.
4. While environmentalism on the surface seems to be a liberal/left-wing issue, some seeming paradoxes exist (in North America at least): arguably the first 'environmental' US President was a Republican (Theodore Roosevelt), Republican President Richard Nixon established the Environmental Protection Agency (EPA), the first carbon tax in North America was instituted by a right-wing party in British Columbia, Canada, one of the early leaders in fighting climate change at the state level in the US was a Republican Governor (Arnold Schwarzenegger of California), and until recently, arguably the most 'green' Canadian Prime Minister was a conservative (Brian Mulroney).

5. Most recently, Bill Gates (2021)—someone who is not exactly known for his opposition to capitalism—makes similar arguments.
6. An alternative to the TOP and EMT perspectives is a focus on disproportionality (Freudenburg, 2005; Davidson and Grant, 2012). This work highlights the strategic value of targeting the 'worst actors' within highly polluting sectors (which are fields of heterogeneous actors with significantly varied environmental practices and footprints), rather than focusing on 'capitalism' more generally.
7. Sometimes these two perspectives are categorized as different strains of resource mobilization theory, with the former referred to as the entrepreneurial model, and the latter labeled the political process model.
8. On this note, spokespersons for anti-environmental actors frequently make the opposite claim in the media, and contend that the environmental movement has unlimited resources, and actors such as those who support the fossil fuel industry are Davids in a David and Goliath struggle (Jacques et al., 2008; Dunlap and Jacques, 2013).
9. Snow et al. use the term 'frame amplification' to refer to the process of highlighting aspects of a message (while sometimes downplaying other parts) to achieve clarity with audiences. For example, in Cormier and Tindall's (2005) study, environmental activists emphasized protecting 'giant trees'. They were ultimately interested in protecting animal habitat and biodiversity, but emphasizing charismatic mega-fauna was an effective communication tactic for getting attention.
10. Climate change deniers like to talk about Al Gore's jet-setting lifestyle and its contrast with his speeches about reducing carbon emissions. At protests against fossil fuel pipeline expansion in remote locations, activists are often grilled as to how they arrived on location, the implication being that they benefited from the use of fossil fuel to travel. Activists working to protect old-growth forests are often quizzed at protests about whether or not they use toilet paper.
11. For example, in the early days of the wilderness preservation movement in British Columbia (Tindall, 2002; Cormier and Tindall, 2005) environmental activists argued for protecting the few remaining tracts of old growth forests. Activists used the term 'preservation' to protect these areas. But they were not 'preservationist' per se, in that generally most of the environmentalists were 'conservationists' who were not necessarily against logging in other areas, as long as trees were regrown. However, anti-environmentalists soon started using the term 'preservationists' against the environmentalists (Doyle et al., 1997) in order to claim that their goal was to stop all logging and destroy the forest (timber) industry. Similar frame reversals have been used in other cases.
12. Hochschild's account has been criticized on various grounds, including its lack of accounting for the role of right-wing media outlets (such as Fox News) in formulating this narrative in the first place (e.g. see Shapira, 2017).
13. On this topic see also Callison (2015) on vernaculars to communicate climate change with different audiences, the use of messengers, and weighing considerations of context, shared cultural narratives, audience and trust.
14. Some authors such as Jasper (2019), and Staggenborg and Meyer in their chapter, use the term 'arena' instead of 'field'.
15. Though some scholars might argue that these issues can be covered under perspectives such as political economy, framing, political opportunities, and so on, gender, race and colonialism are gaining increasing use as theoretical perspectives on their own, as the references indicate.

REFERENCES

Agyeman, J., Cole, P., Haluza-DeLay, R. and O'Riley, P. (eds) (2010) *Speaking for Ourselves: Environmental Justice in Canada*. Vancouver: University of British Columbia Press.

Andrews, K. and Edwards, B. (2005) The organizational structure of local environmentalism. *Mobilization: An International Quarterly*. **10**(2), pp. 213–34.

Ard, K., Garcia, N. and Kelly, P. (2017) Another avenue of action: An examination of climate change countermovement industries' use of PAC donations and their relationship to Congressional voting over time. *Environmental Politics*. **26**(6), pp. 1107–31.

Bacon, J.M. (2019) Settler colonialism as eco-social structure and the production of colonial ecological violence. *Environmental Sociology.* **5**(1), pp. 59–69.

Barnes, M.L., Bodin, Ö., McClanahan, T.R., Kittinger, J.N., Hoey, A.S., Gaoue, O.G. and Graham, N.A.J. (2019) Social-ecological alignment and ecological conditions in coral reefs. *Nature Communications.* **10**, 2039. Available from DOI: 10.1038/s41467-019-09994-1.

Bell, S.E., Fitzgerald, J. and York, R. (2019) Protecting the power to pollute: Identity co-optation, gender, and the public relations strategies of fossil fuel industries in the United States. *Environmental Sociology.* **5**(3), pp. 323–88.

Benford, R.D. and Snow, D.A. (2000) Framing processes and social movements: An overview and assessment. *Annual Review of Sociology.* **26**(1), pp. 611–39.

Bodin, Ö. and Crona, B.I. (2009) The role of social networks in natural resource governance: What relational patterns make a difference? *Global Environmental Change.* **19**(3), pp. 366–74.

Bodin, Ö. and Prell, C. (eds) (2011) *Social Networks and Natural Resource Management: Uncovering the Social Fabric of Environmental Governance.* New York, NY: Cambridge University Press.

Bodin, Ö., Crona, B. and Ernstson, H. (2006) Social networks in natural resource management: What is there to learn from a structural perspective? *Ecology and Society.* **11**(2). Available from: http://www.ecologyandsociety.org/vol11/iss2/resp2/.

Bodin, Ö., García, M.M. and Robins, G. (2020) Reconciling conflict and cooperation in environmental governance: A social network perspective. *Annual Review of Environment and Resources.* **45**, 2.1–2.25. Available from DOI: 10.1146/annurev-environ-011020-064352.

Boykoff, M. (2019) *Creative (Climate) Communications.* Cambridge: Cambridge University Press.

Brint, S. (1984) 'New-class' and cumulative trend explanations of the liberal political attitudes of professionals. *American Journal of Sociology.* **90**(1), 30–71.

Brown, W. (2015) *Undoing the Demos: Neoliberalism's Stealth Revolution.* Brooklyn, NY: Zone Books.

Brulle, R.J. (2014) Institutionalizing delay: Foundation funding and the creation of US climate change counter-movement organizations. *Climatic Change.* **122**(4), pp. 681–94.

Brulle, R.J. (2018) The climate lobby: A sectoral analysis of lobbying spending on climate change in the USA, 2000 to 2016. *Climatic Change.* **149**(3–4), pp. 289–303. Available from DOI: 10.1007/s10584-018-2241-z.

Brulle, R.J. (2019) Networks of opposition: A structural analysis of US climate change countermovement coalitions 1989–2015. *Sociological Inquiry.* Available from DOI: 10.1111/soin.12333.

Callison, C. (2015) *How Climate Change Comes to Matter: The Communal Life of Facts.* Durham, NC: Duke University Press.

Callison, C. (2020) The Twelve-Year Warning. *Isis.* **111**(1), pp. 129–37.

Capek, S.M. (1993) The 'environmental justice' frame: A conceptual discussion and an application. *Social Problems.* **40**(1), pp. 5–24.

Capstick, S., Whitmarsh, L., Poortinga, W., Pidgeon, N. and Upham, P. (2015) International trends in public perceptions of climate change over the past quarter century. *Wiley Interdisciplinary Reviews: Climate Change.* **6**(1), pp. 35–61. Available from DOI: 10.1002/wcc.321.

Carroll, W.K. (2017) Canada's carbon-capital elite: A tangled web of corporate power. *Canadian Journal of Sociology/Cahiers Canadiens de Sociologie.* **42**(3), pp. 225–60.

Carroll, W.K. (2018) *Who Owns Canada's Fossil-Fuel Sector?: Mapping the Network of Ownership.* Vancouver: Canadian Centre for Policy Alternatives.

Carroll, W.K., Graham, N. and Shakespear M. (2021) Mapping the environmental field: Networks of foundations, ENGOs and think tanks. *Canadian Review of Sociology.* **58**(3), pp. 284–305.

Carroll, W., Graham, N., Lang, M.K., Yunker, Z. and McCartney, K.D. (2018) The corporate elite and the architecture of climate change denial: A network analysis of carbon capital's reach into civil society. *Canadian Review of Sociology/Revue Canadienne de Sociologie.* **55**(3), pp. 425–50.

Catton, W.R. and Dunlap, R.E. (1978) Environmental sociology: A new paradigm. *The American Sociologist.* **13**(1), pp. 41–9.

Catton, W.R. and Dunlap, R.E. (1980) A new ecological paradigm for post-exuberant sociology. *American Behavioral Scientist.* **24**(1), pp. 15–47.

Cormier, J.J. and Tindall, D.B. (2005) Wood frames: Framing the forests in British Columbia. *Sociological Focus.* **38**(1), pp. 1–24.

Crossley, N. (2011) *Towards Relational Sociology.* London: Routledge.

Davidson, D.J. and Grant, D. (2012) The double diversion: Mapping its roots and projecting its future in environmental studies. *Journal of Environmental Studies and Sciences.* **2**, pp. 69–77.

Della Porta, D. (2015) *Social Movements in Times of Austerity: Bringing Capitalism Back into Protest Analysis.* Cambridge: Polity.

Diani, M. (1995) *Green Networks: A Structural Analysis of the Italian Environmental Movement.* Edinburgh: Edinburgh University Press.

Diani, M. (1997) Social movements and social capital: A network perspective on movement outcomes. *Mobilization: An International Journal.* **2**, pp. 129–47.

Diani, M. (2015) *The Cement of Civil Society.* New York, NY: Cambridge University Press.

Diani, M. and McAdam, D. (eds) (2003) *Social Movements and Networks: Relational Approaches to Collective Action.* Oxford: Oxford University Press.

DiMaggio, P. (1979) On Pierre Bourdieu. Review essay on *Outline of a Theory of Practice* by Pierre Bourdieu and *Reproduction: In Education, Society and Culture* by Pierre Bourdieu and Jean-Claude Passeron. *American Journal of Sociology.* **84**(6), pp. 1460–74.

DiMaggio, P.J. and Powell, W.W. (1983) The iron cage revisited: Institutional isomorphism and collective rationality in organizational fields. *American Sociological Review.* **48**(2), pp. 147–60.

Doyle, A., Elliott, B. and Tindall, D. (1997) Framing the forests: Corporations, the B.C. forest alliance and the media. In: Carroll, W.K. (ed.) *Organizing Dissent. Contemporary Social Movements in Theory and Practice* (2nd edn). Toronto: Garamond Press, pp. 240–68.

Dunk, T. (1994) Talking about trees: Environment and society in forest workers' culture. *Canadian Review of Sociology/Revue Canadienne de Sociologie.* **31**(1), pp. 14–34.

Dunlap, R.E. (1980) Paradigmatic change in social science: From human exemptionalism to an ecological paradigm. *American Behavioral Scientist.* **24**(1), pp. 5–14.

Dunlap, R.E. and Catton, Jr, W.R. (1979) Environmental Sociology. *Annual Review of Sociology.* **5**, pp. 243–73.

Dunlap, R.E. and Jacques, P.J. (2013) Climate change denial books and conservative think tanks: Exploring the connection. *American Behavioral Scientist.* **57**(6), pp. 699–731.

Dunlap, R.E. and McCright, A. (2015) Challenging climate change. In: Dunlap, R.E. and Brulle, R.G. (eds) *Climate Change and Society: Sociological Perspectives.* New York, NY: Oxford University Press, pp. 300–332.

Dunlap, R.E. and Van Liere, K.D. (1978) The 'New Environmental Paradigm': A proposed measuring instrument and preliminary results. *Journal of Environmental Education.* **9**(4), pp.10–11.

Dunlap, R.E. and Van Liere, K.D. (1984) Commitment to the dominant social paradigm and concern for environmental quality. *Social Science Quarterly.* **65**, pp. 1013–28.

Dunlap, R.E., Xiao, C. and McCright, A.M. (2001) Politics and environment in America: Partisan and ideological cleavages in public support for environmentalism. *Environmental Politics.* **10**(4), pp. 23–48.

Dunlap, R.E., Van Liere, K.D., Mertig, A.G. and Jones, R.E. (2000) Measuring endorsement of the new ecological paradigm: A revised NEP scale. *Journal of Social Issues.* **56**, pp. 425–42.

Ernstson, H. (2013) The social production of ecosystem services: A framework for studying environmental justice and ecological complexity in urbanized landscapes. *Landscape and Urban Planning.* **109**, pp. 7–17. Available from DOI: 10.1016/j.landurbplan.2012.10.005.

Evans, R. and Kay, T. (2008) How environmentalists 'greened' trade policy: Strategic action and the architecture of field overlap. *American Sociological Review.* **73**(6), pp. 970–91.

Farrell, J. (2016a) Corporate funding and ideological polarization about climate change. *Proceedings of the National Academy of Sciences.* **113**(1), pp. 92–7.

Farrell, J. (2016b) Network structure and influence of the climate change counter-movement. *Nature Climate Change.* **6**(4), pp. 370–74.

Farrell, J. (2019) The growth of climate change misinformation in us philanthropy: Evidence from natural language processing. *Environmental Research Letters.* **14**(3), 034013.

Fisher, D.R., Leifeld, P. and Iwaki, Y. (2013a) Mapping the ideological networks of American climate politics. *Climatic Change.* **116**(3), pp. 523–45.

Fisher, D.R., Waggle, J. and Jasny, L. (2015) Not a snowball's chance for science. *Contexts.* **14**(4), pp. 44–9.

Fisher, D.R., Waggle, J. and Leifeld, P. (2013b) Where does political polarization come from? Locating polarization within the US climate change debate. *American Behavioral Scientist.* **57**(1), pp. 70–92.

Fligstein, N. and McAdam, D. (2011) Toward a general theory of strategic action fields. *Sociological Theory.* **29**(1), pp. 1–26.

Fligstein, N. and McAdam, D. (2012) *A Theory of Fields.* New York, NY: Oxford University Press.

Foster, J.B. and Clark, B. (2020) *The Robbery of Nature: Capitalism and the Ecological Rift.* New York, NY: Monthly Review Press.

Freudenburg, W.R. (1986) Social impact assessment. *Annual Review of Sociology.* **12**, pp. 451–78.

Freudenburg, W.R. (2005) Privileged access, privileged accounts: Toward a socially structured theory of resources and discourses. *Social Forces.* **84**(1), pp. 89–114.

Freudenburg, W.R. and Gramling, R. (2011) *Blowout in the Gulf: The BP Oil Spill Disaster and the Future of Energy in America.* Cambridge, MA: MIT Press.

Freudenburg, W.R., Gramling, RB., Laska, S. and Erikson, K. (2009) *Catastrophe in the Making: The Engineering of Katrina and the Disasters of Tomorrow.* Washington, DC: Island Press.

Gates, B. (2021) *How to Avoid a Climate Disaster: The Solutions We Have and the Breakthroughs We Need.* New York, NY: Knopf.

Gauchat, G. (2012) Politicization of science in the public sphere: A study of public trust in the United States, 1974–2010. *American Sociological Review.* **77**(2), pp. 167–87.

Gertler, P.J., Martinez, S., Premand, P., Rawlings, L.B. and Vermeersch, C.M. (2016) *Impact Evaluation in Practice.* Washington, DC: The World Bank.

Giugni, M.G. (1998) Was it worth the effort? The outcomes and consequences of social movements. *Annual Review of Sociology.* **24**(1), pp. 371–93.

Giugni, M., McAdam, D. and Tilly, C. (eds) (1999) *How Social Movements Matter (Vol. 10).* Minneapolis, MN: University of Minnesota Press.

Goffman, E. (1974) *Frame Analysis: An Essay on the Organization of Experience.* Cambridge, MA: Harvard University Press.

Gore, A. (2006) *An Inconvenient Truth: The Planetary Emergency of Global Warming and What We Can Do about It.* Emmaus, PA: Rodale.

Gore, A. (2009) *Our Choice: A Plan to Solve the Climate Crisis.* Emmaus, PA: Rodale.

Gould, K.A., Pellow, D.N. and Schnaiberg, A. (2004) Interrogating the treadmill of production: Everything you wanted to know about the treadmill but were afraid to ask. *Organization & Environment.* **17**(3), pp. 296–316.

Gould, K.A., Pellow, D.N. and Schnaiberg, A. (2015) *Treadmill of Production: Injustice and Unsustainability in the Global Economy.* Abingdon: Routledge.

Granovetter, M. (1973) The strength of weak ties. *American Journal of Sociology.* **78**(6), pp. 1360–80.

Hackett, R.A. and Adams, P.R. (2018) *Jobs vs the Environment?* Vancouver: Canadian Centre for Policy Alternatives.

Hall, P.A. and Soskice, D. (2001) An introduction to varieties of capitalism. In: Hall, P.A. and Soskice, D. (eds) *Varieties of Capitalism: The Institutional Foundations of Comparative Advantage.* Oxford: Oxford University Press, pp. 1–70.

Heaney, M.T. and Rojas, F. (2008) Coalition dissolution, mobilization, and network dynamics in the US antiwar movement. In: Coy, P.G. (ed.) *Research in Social Movements, Conflicts and Change.* Bingley: Emerald Publishing, pp. 39–82.

Hetland, G. and Goodwin, J. (2013) The strange disappearance of capitalism from social movement studies. In: Barker, C., Cox, L., Krinsky, J. and Nilsen, A.G. (eds) *Marxism and Social Movements.* Leiden: Brill Academic Publishers, pp. 82–102.

Hochschild, A.R. (2018) *Strangers in their Own Land: Anger and Mourning on the American Right.* New York, NY: The New Press.

Huddart Kennedy, E. (2020) Measuring human–environment relationships: Introducing the 'Eco-Social Relationship' (ESR) framework. Unpublished manuscript.

Huddart Kennedy, E. and Dzialo, L. (2015) Locating gender in environmental sociology. *Sociology Compass.* **9**(10), pp. 920–29.

Jacques, P.J., Dunlap, R.E. and Freeman, M. (2008) The organisation of denial: Conservative think tanks and environmental scepticism. *Environmental Politics.* **17**(3), pp. 349–85. Available from DOI: 10.1080/09644010802055576.

Jamison, A., Eyerman, R., Cramer, J. and Laessoe, J. (1990) *The Making of a New Environmental Consciousness: A Comparative Study of the Environmental Movements in Sweden, Denmark and the Netherlands*. Edinburgh: Edinburgh University Press.

Jasny, L. and Fisher, D.R. (2019) Echo chambers in climate science. *Environmental Research Communications*. **1**(10), p. 101003.

Jasny, L., Waggle, J. and Fisher, D.R. (2015) An empirical examination of echo chambers in US climate policy networks. *Nature Climate Change*. **5**(8), pp. 782–6.

Jasny, L., Dewey, A.M., Robertson, A.G., Yagatich, W., Dubin, A.H., Waggle, J.M. and Fisher, D.R. (2018) Shifting echo chambers in US climate policy networks. *PlosOne*. **13**(9), p. e0203463.

Jasper, J.M. (2018) *The Emotions of Protest*. Chicago, IL: University of Chicago Press.

Jasper, J.M. (2019) Linking arenas: Structuring concepts in the study of politics and protest. *Social Movement Studies*. **20**(2), pp. 1–15.

Jost, J.T., Nosek, B.A. and Gosling, S.D. (2008) Ideology: Its resurgence in social, personality, and political psychology. *Perspectives on Psychological Science*. **3**(2), pp. 126–36.

Khandker, S.R., Koolwal, G.B. and Samad, H.A. (2009) *Handbook on Impact Evaluation: Quantitative Methods and Practices*. Washington, DC: The World Bank.

Klandermans, B. (1992) The social construction of protest and multiorganizational fields. In: Morris, A.D. and Mueller, C.M. (eds) *Frontiers in Social Movement Theory*. New Haven, CT: Yale University Press, pp. 77–103.

Klandermans, B. and Oegema, D. (1987) Potentials, networks, motivations, and barriers: Steps towards participation in social movements. *American Sociological Review*. **52**(4), pp. 519–31.

Klein, N. (2015) *This Changes Everything: Capitalism vs. the Climate*. New York, NY: Simon & Schuster.

Klein, N. (2020) *On Fire: The (Burning) Case for a Green New Deal*. New York, NY: Simon & Schuster.

Knoke, D., Diani, M., Hollway, J. and Christopoulos, D. (2021) *Multimodal Political Networks*. Cambridge, UK: Cambridge University Press.

Kozlowski, A.C. (2021) How conservatives lost confidence in science: The role of ideological alignment in political polarization. *Social Forces*. Available from DOI: 10.1093/sf/soab020.

Lakanen, R. (2018) Dissent and descent: Tracing Canada's environmental governance from regulatory beginnings to dismissal and reversals by the Harper government. *Local Environment*. **23**(5), pp. 549–64.

Leifeld, P. (2020) Policy debates and discourse network analysis: A research agenda. *Politics and Governance*. **8**(2), pp. 180–83.

Lewin, P.G. (2019) 'Coal is not just a job, it's a way of life': The cultural politics of coal production in Central Appalachia. *Social Problems*. **66**(1), pp. 51–68.

Lijphart, A. (2012) *Patterns of Democracy: Government Forms and Performance in Thirty-Six Countries* (2nd edn). New Haven, CT: Yale University Press.

Lomborg, B. (2003) *The Skeptical Environmentalist: Measuring the Real State of the World (Vol. 1)*. Cambridge: Cambridge University Press.

Lomborg, B. (2010) *Cool it: The Skeptical Environmentalist's Guide to Global Warming*. Vintage.

MacLean, N. (2017) *Democracy in Chains: The Deep History of the Radical Right's Stealth Plan for America*. New York, NY: Penguin.

Macy, M., Deri, S., Ruch, A. and Tong, N. (2019) Opinion cascades and the unpredictability of partisan polarization. *Science Advances*. **5**(8), p. eaax0754.

Mann, M.E. (2013) *The Hockey Stick and the Climate Wars: Dispatches from the Front Lines*. New York, NY: Columbia University Press.

Mann, M.E. (2021) *The New Climate War: The Fight to Take Back Our Planet*. New York, NY: Public Affairs.

Marger, M. (1987) *Elites and Masses: An Introduction to Political Sociology*. Belmont, CA: Wadsworth Publishing Company.

Marquart-Pyatt, S.T., Jorgenson, A.K. and Hamilton, L.C. (2015) Methodological approaches for sociological research on climate change. In: Dunlap, R.E. and Brulle, R.J. (eds) *Climate Change and Society: Sociological Approaches*. New York, NY: Oxford University Press, pp. 369–411.

Marshall, G. (2015) *Don't Even Think About It: Why Our Brains Are Wired to Ignore Climate Change*. New York, NY: Bloomsbury Publishing USA.

Martin, J.L. (2003) What is field theory? *American Journal of Sociology*. **109**(1), pp. 1–49.
Martin, J.L. (2009) *Social Structures*. Princeton, NJ: Princeton University Press.
Mayer, J. (2017) *Dark Money: The Hidden History of the Billionaires Behind the Rise of the Radical Right*. Anchor Books.
McAdam, D. (1982) *Political Process and the Development of Black Insurgency*. Chicago, IL: University of Chicago Press.
McAdam, D. and Rucht, D. (1993) The cross-national diffusion of movement ideas. *The Annals of the American Academy of Political and Social Science*. **528**(1), pp. 56–74.
McAdam, D. and Su, Y. (2002) The war at home: Antiwar protests and congressional voting, 1965 to 1973. *American Sociological Review*. **67**(5), pp. 696–721.
McAdam, D., McCarthy, J. and Zald, M. (1988) Social movements. In: Smelser, N.J. (ed.) *Handbook of Sociology*. Newbury Park, CA: Sage, pp. 695–737.
McAdam, D., Tarrow, S. and Tilly, C. (2001) *Dynamics of Contention*. Cambridge: Cambridge University Press.
McCarthy, J.D. and Zald, M.N. (1977) Resource mobilization and social movements: A partial theory. *American Journal of Sociology*. **86**(6), pp. 1214–41.
McCright, A.M. and Dunlap, R.E. (2000) Challenging global warming as a social problem: An analysis of the conservative movement's counter-claims. *Social Problems*. **47**(4), pp. 499–522.
McCright, A.M. and Dunlap, R.E. (2003) Defeating Kyoto: The conservative movement's impact on US climate change policy. *Social Problems*. **50**(3), pp. 348–73.
McCright, A.M. and Dunlap, R.E. (2010) Anti-reflexivity: The American conservative movement's success in undermining climate science and policy. *Theory, Culture and Society*. **27**(2–3), pp. 100–133.
McCright, A.M. and Dunlap, R.E. (2011a) Cool dudes: The denial of climate change among conservative white males in the United States. *Global Environmental Change*. **21**(4), pp. 1163–72.
McCright, A.M. and Dunlap, R.E. (2011b) The politicization of climate change and polarization in the American public's views of global warming, 2001–2010. *The Sociological Quarterly*. **52**(2), pp. 155–94.
McCright, A.M., Dunlap, R.E. and Xiao, C. (2013) Perceived scientific agreement and support for government action on climate change in the USA. *Climatic Change*. **119**(2), pp. 511–18.
McCright, A.M., Dunlap, R.E. and Xiao, C. (2014) Political polarization on support for government spending on environmental protection in the USA, 1974–2012. *Social Science Research*. **48**, pp. 251–60.
McKay, D.L., Vinyeta, K. and Norgaard, K.M. (2020) Theorizing race and settler colonialism within US sociology. *Sociology Compass*. **14**(9), p. e12821.
McLaughlin, P. and Khawaja, M. (2000) The organizational dynamics of the US environmental movement: Legitimation, resource mobilization, and political opportunity. *Rural Sociology*. **65**(3), pp. 422–39.
Meyer, D.S. (2004) Protest and political opportunities. *Annual Review of Sociology*. **30**, 125–45.
Mohai, P., Pellow, D. and Roberts, T. (2009) Environmental justice. *Annual Review of Environment and Resources*. **34**, pp. 405–30.
Mol, A.P.J. (1997) Ecological modernization: Industrial transformations and environmental reform. In: Redclift, M. and Woodgate, G. (eds) *The International Handbook of Environmental Sociology*. Cheltenham, UK and Northampton, MA, USA: Edward Elgar Publishing, pp. 138–99.
Mol, A.P.J. and Spaargaren, G. (2000) Ecological modernisation theory in debate: A review. *Environmental Politics*. **9**(1), pp. 17–49.
Mol, A.P.J. and Spaargaren, G. (2002) Ecological modernization and the environmental state. In Mol, A.P.J. and Buttel, F.H. (eds) *The Environmental State Under Pressure (Research in Social Problems and Public Policy, Volume 10*. Bingley: Emerald Publishing, pp. 33–52.
Moore, P.A. (2000) *Green Spirit: Trees are the Answer*. Vancouver: Greenspirit Enterprises.
Morgan, S.L. and Winship, C. (2015) *Counterfactuals and Causal Inference*. Cambridge: Cambridge University Press.
Norgaard, K.M. (2011) *Living in Denial: Climate Change, Emotions, and Everyday Life*. Cambridge, MA: MIT Press.
Norgaard, K.M. (2020) Whose energy future? Whose imagination? Revitalizing sociological theory in the service of human survival. *Society & Natural Resources*. **33**(11), pp. 1438–45.

Park, L.S.-H. and Pellow, D.N. (2011) *The Slums of Aspen: Immigrants vs. the Environment in America's Eden.* New York, NY: New York University Press.

Pellow, D.N. (2004) *Garbage Wars: The Struggle for Environmental Justice in Chicago.* Cambridge, MA: MIT Press.

Ramos, H. (2015) Mapping the field of environmental justice: Redistribution, recognition and representation in ENGO Press Advocacy. *Canadian Journal of Sociology.* **43**(3), pp. 355–75.

Readfern, G. (2017) The idea that climate scientists are in it for the cash has deep ideological roots. *The Guardian.* Available from: https://www.theguardian.com/environment/planet-oz/2017/sep/15/the-idea-that-climate-scientists-are-in-it-for-the-cash-has-deep-ideological-roots.

Roberts, T.J. and Parks, B.C. (2006) *A Climate of Injustice: Global Inequality, North-South Politics, and Climate Policy.* Cambridge, MA: MIT Press.

Sayles, J.S., Garcia, M.G., Hamilton, M., Alexander, S.M., Baggio, J.A., Fischer, A.P., Ingold, K. et al. (2019) Social-ecological network analysis for sustainability sciences: A systematic review and innovative research agenda for the future. *Environmental Research Letters.* **14**(9), pp. 1–18. Available from DOI: 10.1088/1748-9326/ab2619.

Schnaiberg, A. (1980) *The Environment: From Surplus to Scarcity.* New York, NY: Oxford University Press.

Scott, W.R. (2008a) *Institutions and Organizations: Ideas and Interests* (3rd edn). Thousand Oaks, CA: Sage.

Scott, W.R. (2008b) Approaching adulthood: The maturing of institutional theory. *Theory and Society.* **37**(5), pp. 427–42.

Shapira, H. (2017) Who cares what they think? Going about the right the wrong way. *Contemporary Sociology.* **46**(5), pp. 512–17.

Smith, E.K. and Mayer, A. (2019) Anomalous Anglophones? Contours of free market ideology, political polarization, and climate change attitudes in English-speaking countries, Western European and post-Communist states. *Climatic Change.* **152**(1), pp. 17–34.

Snow, D.A. and Benford, R.D. (1988) Ideology, frame resonance, and participant mobilization. *International Social Movement Research.* **1**(1), pp. 197–217.

Snow, D.A. and Benford, R.D. (1992) Master frames and cycles of protest. In: Snow, D.A., Soule, S.A. and Kresi, H. (eds) *Frontiers in Social Movement Theory.* Oxford: Blackwell, pp. 133–55.

Snow, D.A., Rochford Jr, E.B., Worden, S.K. and Benford, R.D. (1986) Frame alignment processes, micromobilization, and movement participation. *American Sociological Review.* **51**(4), pp. 464–81.

Soule, S.A. and Olzak, S. (2004) When do movements matter? The politics of contingency and the equal rights amendment. *American Sociological Review.* **69**(4), pp. 473–97.

Stefancic, J. and Delgado, R. (1996) *No Mercy: How Conservative Think Tanks and Foundations Changed America's Social Agenda.* Philadelphia, PN: Temple University Press.

Stoddart, M.C.J. (2015) Wilderness revisited: Canadian environmental movements and the eco-politics of special places. In: Ramos, H. and Rodgers, K. (eds) *Protest and Politics: The Promise of Social Movement Societies.* Vancouver, BC: UBC Press, pp. 255–73.

Stoddart, M.C. and Tindall, D.B. (2015) Canadian news media and the cultural dynamics of multilevel climate governance. *Environmental Politics.* **24**(3), pp. 401–22.

Taylor, D.E. (2014) *Toxic Communities: Environmental Racism, Industrial Pollution, and Residential Mobility.* New York, NY: NYU Press.

Tindall, D.B. (2002) Social networks, identification, and participation in an environmental movement: Low-medium cost activism within the British Columbia wilderness preservation movement. *Canadian Review of Sociology and Anthropology.* **39**(4), pp. 413–52.

Tindall, D.B. and Robinson, J.L. (2017) Collective action to save the ancient temperate rainforest: Social networks and environmental activism in Clayoquot Sound. *Ecology and Society.* **22**(1), p. 40.

Tindall, D.B., Cormier, J. and Diani, M. (2012) Network social capital as an outcome of social movement mobilization. *Social Networks.* **34**, pp. 387–95.

Tindall, D.B., Howe, A.C. and Mauboulès, C. (2021) Tangled roots: Personal networks and the participation of individuals in an anti-environmentalism countermovement. *Sociological Perspectives.* **64**(1), pp. 5–36.

Tindall, D.B., Robinson, J.L. and Stoddart, M.C.J. (2014) Social network centrality, movement identification, and the participation of individuals in a social movement: The case of the Canadian environmental movement. In: Dehmer, M. and Emmert-Streib, F. (eds) *Quantitative Graph Theory: Mathematical Foundations and Applications*. Oxford: Chapman and Hall/CRC, pp. 407–23.

Tindall, D.B., Stoddart, M.C. and Howe, A.C. (2020) Social networks and climate change policy preferences: Structural location and policy actor support for fossil fuel production. *Society & Natural Resources*. **33**(11), pp. 1359–79.

Tindall, D.B., Berseth, V., Martel-Morin, M. and Lachapelle. E. (2022) Political values and socialization. In: Grasso, M. and Giugni, M. (eds) *Routledge Handbook of Environmental Movements*. London: Routledge, pp. 374–89.

Turner, J.M. and Isenberg, A.C. (2018) *The Republican Reversal: Conservatives and the Environment from Nixon to Trump*. Cambridge, MA: MIT Press.

Vasi, I.B. (2011) *Winds of Change: The Environmental Movement and the Global Development of the Wind Energy Industry*. New York, NY: Oxford University Press.

Veldman, R.G. (2019) *The Gospel of Climate Skepticism: Why Evangelical Christians Oppose Action on Climate Change*. Oakland, CA: University of California Press.

Waldron, I. (2018) Re-thinking waste: Mapping racial geographies of violence on the colonial landscape. *Environmental Sociology*. **4**(1), pp. 36–53.

Walsh, E.J. (1981) Resource mobilization and citizen protest in communities around Three Mile Island. *Social Problems*. **29**(1), pp. 1–21.

Weber, M. (2009) *The Theory of Social and Economic Organization*. New York, NY: Simon & Schuster.

Wellman, B. (1988) Structural analysis: From metaphor and method to theory and substance. In: Wellman, B. and Berkowitz, S.D. (eds) *Social Structures: A Network Approach*. Cambridge: Cambridge University Press, pp. 19–61.

White, H. (2009) Theory-based impact evaluation: Principles and practice. *Journal of Development Effectiveness*. **1**(3), pp. 271–84.

White, H. (2010) A contribution to current debates in impact evaluation. *Evaluation*. **16**(2), pp. 153–64.

Whyte, K.P. (2018) Indigenous science (fiction) for the Anthropocene: Ancestral dystopias and fantasies of climate change crises. *Environment and Planning E: Nature and Space*. **1**(1–2), pp. 224–42.

Wilkinson, K.K. (2012) *Between God and Green: How Evangelicals are Cultivating a Middle Ground on Climate Change*. New York, NY: Oxford University Press.

York, R., Rosa, E.A. and Dietz, T. (2003) Footprints on the earth: The environmental consequences of modernity. *American Sociological Review*. **68**, pp. 279–300.

Index

Abbey, E. 426
Aberle, D.F. 124
Abernethy, V. 349
Aboriginal Australians 157, 158, 159, 296
abortion conflict 23, 24, 25, 28, 31, 34–5, 36
Abortion and the Politics of Motherhood 28
'acceptance-rejection' strategy 250
Ackland, R. 235
activism/activists 5, 23, 24, 38, 49
    climate change 31–2, 35, 36, 37, 166
    food sovereignty 285, 287, 288, 291, 300
    murder and violence against 424–5
    portrayals *see* terrorist label
    social media 32
    see also dis/ability activists; micro-activism; youth activism
actor congruence network, climate sceptics and ACC exponents 93, 94, 96
Adani coalmine 167, 203
adaptability/adaptation 13, 85, 86, 91, 92, 94, 97, 99
adat law 317, 320–21
adversarial framing 251–2, 255, 259–61, 262
Africa 10, 174, 182, 183, 399–400, 424, 427
African Americans 147
age, and environmentalism 138
agenda setters, media as 84
AGRA (land reform movement) 305–6, 307, 319–24, 325
agribusiness 167, 431
agriculture
    Big Scrub, Northern NSW 155
    influence on pro-environmental voting 147
    legislation and knowledge monoculture 288–9
    state regulation 285
    see also farmers and farming; industrial agriculture; shifting cultivation
agrobiodiversity 290, 296
agroecology 285, 290, 294–5
Ainsworth, J. 157
Alaimo, S. 161
Alberta
    climate change denial 217, 329
    extractive populism 224–5
    fossil capital elite 218
    oil sands 11, 50, 54, 216, 217, 221, 225
    wind energy study 332–41

ally support, and countermovement emergence 30–32
Alstonville 159
alternative knowledges 288–91
alternativists 111, 113, 124, 125, 130
American Conservative Union 139
American Federation of Labor-Council of Industrial Organizations (AFL-CIO) 382, 383, 384, 385, 390, 394
American values 6, 108, 109, 117–20, 125, 128, 237
Americans for Prosperity 6
Amnesty International of Canada 258
Anderson, S.E. 137
Anglo-American model (AMM), climate scepticism 98–9
animal rights (AR) movements 50–51, 53, 56
animal victimhood 427
anthropocentrism 71, 442
anti-coal mining 166
anti-environmentalism
    in academia 425–32, 432–3
    business unionism 391–2
    countermovements *see* countermovements
    defining 331, 366, 423
    direct 424–5
    in farming 167
    future research 440–60
    grassroots-level 153
    immigration 346
    labor unions 396
    literature 7, 448
    moral versatility 57
    pluralist governance 395
    population environmentalism 349
    in the post-Harper era 258–9
    racial identity politics 371–2
    religious environmental movements as a response to 400–402
    spectrum 2, 6–13
    Turkey 271–9
    wind energy 332–6
    see also climate change denial/scepticism
anti-gas mining rally 164–5
anti-government discourses 332–4, 337
anti-nationalism 252
anti-nuclear movement 30, 308, 384
anti-population environmentalism 362
anti-reflexivity 249–50, 257, 259–60

anti-regulation 86, 284–300, 332–4
anti-sealing campaigns 12
anti-smoking movement 30–31
Appalachian coal workers 9
Appeal to Higher Loyalties (AHL) 177, 178, 179, 180, 181, 182, 183
Ard, K. 134, 445
Ashwood, L. 373
Asia 114, 182, 183, 424–5
Associated Country Sawmillers of NSW 163
astroturf organizations/astroturfing 2, 7, 8, 48, 79, 227, 238
Attack on the American Free Enterprise System 240
attacks on collective character 85, 91, 95, 98
attitudes 65, 71–4, 160
Atwater, L. 369
auditing, environmental groups 255–6, 259
Audubon Society 3, 4, 350
Aulby, H. 195, 197
Austin, A. 271
Australia 98
    anti-environmentalism 2, 9, 153
    CCCM organisations 174
    conservative political ideology 444
    politics of decarbonisation 192–208
    white supremacy and environmental policy 375
    see also Northern New South Wales
Australian Petroleum Producers and Exploration Association (APPEA) 199
Australian school of natural science 156
authoritarianism 50, 51

Babiš, A. 99
balance bias 85–6
Banaszak, L.A. 31
Banks, J. 154
Bardon, A. 239–40
bargaining power 387
Barkemeyer, R. 84
Bartell, T. 129
Battershill, C. 227
Bauman, Z. 261
Beck, U. 64
Beder, S. 192
behavioural change 123
behaviour(s) 75, 77–8, 176, 423
beliefs 8, 65, 68–71, 187, 392, 393
Bell, S.E. 9
belonging 10, 153–4, 162, 164, 166, 167, 235, 275, 375
Benford, R.D. 85
Bentley Blockade 164
Bergama movement 268, 270–71

anti-environmental campaign against 271–9
Betung Kerihun National Park 304–26
    hunter–gatherer communities 304, 309–16
    implementation programmes and regulation 316–17
    mobilization against 305–6, 307, 319–24
    villager–park relations 318–19
Bichler, S. 204
Big Scrub 154–5, 156, 157, 158, 159, 160, 162
billionaires 31, 196, 234
bio-divinity 400
biological conservation 423–4, 427
Biologie, Oder Philosophie der lebenden Natur 156
biospheric egalitarianism 427, 432
birds' nests 313
Bishop, B.H. 136, 149
Black community activism 5
Blacks, environmental concerns 138
Blanket Exercise (KAIROS) 413
Block Island Offshore Wind Farm 389
blue collar workers, resistance to climate protection 387
Blue Planet in Green Shackles 87
Bodin, O. 449
Böhm, S. 78
Bolsonaro, J. 50, 186
Boltanski, L. 44–5
Bolton, G. 155, 159
Bonyhady, T. 156, 157
Border Ranges (Northern NSW) 158, 160–62, 166
Borneo 304, 309, 310, 312, 315, 316, 322–3, 326
Bourdieu, P. 457
Boussalis, C. 181
Bower, R. 349
Bowling Alone 51
Boykoff, J.M. 85, 252, 262
Boykoff, M.T. 85
Brabec, R. 96–7
Bradley Foundation 237
Braun, Y.A. 9
Bray, J. 157
Breakthrough Institute 425, 427, 431
British Columbia 63–80
British Columbia Civil Liberties Association (BCLA) 258
Brockington, D. 426, 427, 429
Brodbeck, J. 136
Brower, D. 349
Brown, K. 86
Brown, W. 445
Brownlee, J. 240
Brulle, R.J. 7, 99, 134, 137, 187, 219, 240, 446, 447

Buchanan, J. 234
Buckley v. Valeo (1976) 136
Bundjalung people 154, 155, 157, 158, 164
Bundock, M. and W. 157–8
Bungan Jaya 304, 309, 316
Bush, G.H.W. 111, 369
Bush, G.W 111, 243, 263, 452, 453
business
    political influence 135–6
    state relationship with large 367
    see also Climate Change Counter Movement (CCCM)
Business Council of Canada 219, 223
business interests 29, 31, 32, 38
business unionism 391–2
Bustamante, J. 355
Bwindi Impenetrable National Park 10

Calhoun, J. 234
Callison, C. 11
Calls to Action (TRCC) 408
Campbell, M.M. 346
Canada 25, 208
    agricultural law and policy 288
    anti-environmentalism 2, 9, 443
        climate change denial 98, 217, 220–24
        moral assemblages 46–50, 52, 53–4
        portrayal and surveillance of environmentalists 252–4
        reflexive religious 404–415
    CCCM organisations 174
    fossil fuel industry *see* fossil fuel industry
    neoliberal governance of environmentalism 248–64
    political opportunity structure and climate change 453
    white supremacy and environmental policy 375
    see also Alberta; British Columbia
Canada Action 47, 227
Canada Revenue Agency (CRA) 255, 256, 259
Canada's Energy Citizens (CEC) 227
Canadian Association of Petroleum Producers 47, 218, 219, 223, 227, 228
Canadian Environmental Assessment Agency (CEAA) 254
Canadian Security Intelligence Service (CSIS) 253, 254, 258, 259
Canadian Taxpayer Federation (CTF) 48, 49
Cann, H.W. 98
capital power 218–20
capital as power theory 204–5
capitalism 401
    environmental sociology 13
    political economy and role of 450–51

    see also consumer capitalism; corporate capitalism; fossil capitalism; industrial capitalism
Capstick, S.B. 85
carbon (CO_2) emissions 92, 173, 178, 181, 216
carbon lock-in 206
Carbon Pledge 243
carbon pricing plan 46, 50
carbon-centred scientific industrial complex 219
Caren, N. 33
Carroll, W. 7, 186, 218, 240, 446, 448
Carson, R. 4
Carter, J. 29, 111
Cato Institute 237, 242
Catton, W.R. 108, 442, 443, 458
cedar-getters 155, 157, 158, 159
celebrity environmentalism 32, 226, 426, 429
celebrity species 55
Center for Economics and Politics 87
Center for Public Integrity 197, 241
Center for Responsive Politics 134, 140
Chalupa, T. 87
China 181, 185, 425, 430
Chinatown (Vancouver) 52
Christianity 399, 401, 406, 407, 408, 413, 414, 417
Christoff, P. 156
Čílek, V. 93, 96
Citizen United v. FEC (2010) 136, 139, 140, 244
Citizens for Government Waste 181
Citizens for Public Justice 408
Civil Democratic Party (Czech) 87, 98, 99–100
civil disobedience 4, 31, 54, 65, 292, 409, 412
civil rights movements (US) 4, 31, 43
Claeys, P. 291
Clark, M. 155
class 12, 27, 51, 80, 129, 351, 355, 361, 362, 367, 370, 374, 391, 403, 412, 414
classic anti-environmentalism 2, 6–9, 63, 443, 450
Clawson, D. 136
Clayoquot Sound protests (1990s) 64, 65
Clexit 178
climate change
    'acceptance-rejection' strategy 250
    activists 31–2, 35, 36, 37, 166
    Czech Republic
        media coverage 88
        public acceptance 87–8
    exponents 93–4, 98, 99
    labor resistance to climate protection 385–93
    lobbying 134
    media consensus 98, 100
    polarizing nature of 330
    policy networks 448

political polarization 137, 448–9
questioning premise of 334–6
racial prejudice and views on 371
and reconciliation, Canada 410–12
Climate Change Counter Movement (CCCM) 133, 173–88
as an international deviant network 186–7
influence of PAC donations 134, 142–4, 149
international scope 174–6
neutralization techniques 178–85, 186
social networks 447
climate change denial/scepticism 7, 23, 30
Canada 216, 217, 220–24
conservatives 137
criminology 176–8
Czech Republic (case study) 86–100
Copenhagen conference and aftermath 90–94
data and methods 88–90
media coverage 97–100
towards expertization 94–7
donor foundations 134
emotions 425
Koch Brothers 239–43
literature 448
mass media and strategies 84–6
misinformation 33
narrative 456
neoliberalism 186
political opportunity structures 452, 453
racial prejudice and 372
resources 38, 451
social networks 447, 448
social organisation and structure 222
support from allies 31–2
Climate Change Performance Index 87
climate science/scientists
attacks on 85, 87, 98, 240
demonisation and criticism of 182
depiction of 455
questioning of work 33
racial prejudice and views on 371–2
Climategate controversy 87, 88
Clinton, B. 35, 112
Clyde River community 12
coal industry
Australia 202, 203
Czech Republic 86, 93
United States 9, 177, 244, 384, 392
Coan, T.G. 181
Coast Salish peoples 409
Coates, T. 374
Coats, E. 11
coded racism 369–70
coercive action 285

collective action 34, 35, 129, 149, 262, 270, 284, 308, 356, 360, 390, 395, 396, 457
collective avoiding 425
Collective Behavior 108
collective continuance 375
collective property 293, 299
collective responsibility 299
collective rights 292, 299
colonialism 10, 154–6, 289, 401, 402, 427
see also settler colonialism
The Colonial Earth 156
Committee for a Constructive Tomorrow 181
Committee for Women, Population and the Environment 356
common good, anti-environmentalism for 43–58
commons, nonstate regulation of 296
communication 456
see also distorted communication; social media
Communications Security Establishment of Canada (CSEC) 253
community courts 299
Competitive Enterprise Institute 242
concession costs 31
Condemnation of the Condemner (COC) 177, 178, 179, 180, 181, 182, 183
Condra, A. 293
conflicts
over Indigenous land 412
see also abortion conflict; environmental conflicts; movement–countermovement conflict; value conflicts
conformist journalists 92
congressional voting (study) 133, 138–50
Connors, L. 160
consensus movements 26
conservation 3, 10
Alberta oil sands 11
conflicts over 306–7
local resistance to 427
Northern NSW 156–7, 159–160, 161, 162–3
conservationists 426, 427, 429, 430, 431
conservative denial movement, extractive populism 224–7
Conservative Movement 109, 110, 128, 447
conservative think tanks (CTT) 7, 9, 87, 109, 174, 221, 239, 445, 447, 448
see also Breakthrough Institute; Heritage Foundation
conservative values 98
conservatives 46, 48, 137, 373, 374, 444
Conservators of Forests 159
conspiracy theories 272, 273, 280
construction industry 388–9, 389–90, 391

consumer capitalism 12
consumer rights 292
Conway, E.M. 240
Cook, J. 154
cooperation 290, 383
cooptation 288
coordinated market economies 450
Coors, J. 237
Copenhagen Conference of Parties 87, 88, 90–94
core-periphery structure, climate sceptics and ACC exponents 96
Cornwall Alliance 399
corporate anti-environmentalism 2, 6, 7, 8, 9, 192, 216
corporate capitalism 430–31
corporate elites 218, 219, 223, 228, 240
corporate freedom 238
corporate influence 193, 195–9, 204–6, 226
corporate interests 6, 8, 9, 13, 187, 194, 195, 200, 205, 240, 262, 263
Corporate Mapping Project (CMP) 216, 219, 220, 448
corporate power 204, 205, 216–17, 219, 396
corporate responsibility 74, 221
corporate state capture 199
corporatist governments 395–6
corruption and misconduct 197, 201–4, 307
Coulthard, G.S. 408
counter attributions 85, 92, 95
counter prognoses 85, 92, 95
counter-framing 85, 91–2, 95, 98, 100
counterfactuals 458
countermovements 23–39
    anti-environmental 2, 6–7, 26, 30, 109–10, 280, 458
        climate denial, US 221–2
        for the common good 43–58
        see also AGRA (land reform movement); Canada Action; Climate Change Counter Movement (CCCM); Share Our Resources; Wise Use Movement
    literature 109
    reasons for emergence 24–33
    size and scope 26
    see also movement–countermovement dynamics
Coutinho, A. 222, 249, 250
covert corporate funding 244
covert networks 193, 195–9, 206, 207
Covid-19 global pandemic 38, 99
Covid-19 Market Crisis Joint Working Group 228
criminology 176–8
Crist, E. 428

critical anti-environmentalism *see* reflexive anti-environmentalism
critical conversations/reflection 2, 12, 414
critical events, triggering mobilization 307–9, 319–24, 325
critical infrastructure protection (CIP) 260–61
critical political economy 204
critical social science 426, 427–32
Crona, B. 449
Cronon, W. 12
Crowley, S.L. 307, 324
Cubbie Station 167
cultural conflict 29
cultural interests 27
cultural revolution (1960s) 125
culture(s) 8, 9, 38, 80, 280, 408, 454, 455
Curry, P. 432
Curtis, K. 165
customary land tenure 296
customary law 291
cynicism 33
Czech Academy of Sciences 87–8
Czech Republic 86–100, 444

Dagan, H. 297
Dakota Access Pipeline (DAPL) 114, 384, 385, 390
dark money 31, 38, 208
Dark Money 234, 235
data suppression 251
Davis, H. 411
Davis, K. 349
Dayak 309
decarbonization, politics of 192–308
decisions/decision-making 66–7, 287, 293, 294, 308
Declaration of Nyéléni 293
decolonization 400, 404, 405–7, 408, 412, 414, 415–16
deep ecology 11, 427, 431
'deep story' narrative 8, 455
deep value change 112–13
demobilization 262, 288
Democracy in Chains 234, 235
Democratic Party 134, 137, 147, 369, 373
demographics *see* age; class; education; gender; race
demonization 9, 178, 182, 204, 226, 274, 280
Denial of Injury (DOI1 and DOI2) 177, 178, 179, 180, 181, 182, 183, 184
denial machine 84, 85, 239
denial regime 216
Denial of Responsibility (DOR) 177, 178, 179, 180, 181, 182, 183, 184

Denial of Victim (DOV) 177, 179, 180, 181, 182, 183, 184
Derber, C. 216, 217
DESMOG 242
Desmond, J. 427
destabilization 410, 414
deviancy 176, 177, 186–7
Dewey, S. 382
Diani, M. 457
diffusion 184, 185, 187
direct action tactics 166, 250, 410
direct anti-environmentalism 424–5
direct environmental impacts 423
direct mail campaigns 5, 51
Dirty Dozen Campaign 130
dis/ability activists 51
discourse network analysis 84, 89, 446
discursive approaches 6
discursive obstruction 249, 251–2, 255, 257–8, 262
discursive opportunity structure 260
disinvestment 369
disruption costs 31
distorted communication 219
Doctrine of Discovery 407, 408
dog-whistle politics 369, 372
domestication, media coverage, climate change 88, 95, 99
Donaldson, S. 56
donations
    from right-wing movements 31
    to environmental NGOs 255
    see also political donations
Donora death fog 382
Doulton, H. 86
drunk driving movement 27
Dryzek, J.S. 86
Duddy, T. 166
Dudley, M.R. 136, 149
Duffy, R. 426–7, 428
Dunford, D.T. 260
Dunk, T. 8, 80
Dunlap, R.E. 30, 99, 137, 174, 182, 184, 186, 239, 240, 243, 244, 249, 442, 443, 444, 445, 446, 447, 448, 454, 458
Dunphy, M. 159

Earth Day 4, 25, 49, 111, 123, 252, 345, 349, 362, 383
Earth First! 5, 431
Earthkeepers 409, 411, 412, 413
Ebell, M. 238
echo-chambers 448
eco-centrism 11, 12–13, 432
eco-fiscal compromise 46, 50, 54

eco-Marxist perspective 13
eco-modernism 431
eco-terrorism 263
    see also terrorist label
ecodemocracy 432–3
ecojustice 432
Ecological Modernization Theory (EMT) 13, 222, 365, 367, 370–71, 374, 375, 450
ecology 4, 45
    see also agroecology; deep ecology; invasion ecology; organizational ecology
economic development
    and gold mining, Turkey 268, 269, 272, 273
    interests v. conservation 11
    and sustainability 5, 10
economic elites 135, 249
economic growth 86, 384
    and anti-environmentalism 163, 276, 425
    climate protection as threat to 91
    environmental degradation/destruction 117, 173, 367, 431
    extractivism 225
    labor–environmental conflict 384
    race, racism and 366
    TOP theory 13
    see also green growth; Treadmill of Production (TOP)
economic outcomes 458
economic values 71
economics
    and anti-environmentalism 8, 133
    countermovement emergence 27
    Czech climate sceptic countermovement 98
    declining support for environmentalism 117–18
    trade-off between environmentalism and 173
ecotage 4, 122
Edelman, M. 287
education 138, 147–8, 289
Education Action Group Foundation 181
Eghenter, C. 312
Ehrlich, P. 349, 357
Eisinger, P.K. 307
elections, racial identity politics 371–4
electricity sector, Australia 200, 201
elite closure 219
elite cohesion 219
elite cues 99
elite legitimation 227
elite support 26, 30, 31, 36
elite-driven green gentrification 52
elite-generated countermovements 26, 27
elites *see* corporate elites; economic elites; political elites; urban elites
elitist power 51

Ellis, C. 166–7
Elsasser, S.W. 239
Emanuel, R. 112
emotion(s) 425, 454, 456
empathy walls 8
employer support, countermovement emergency 30
Enbridge Inc. 248, 254
energy conservation 75, 78
'energy lifeworld' discourse 224
energy policy 193, 199, 200, 205, 390
energy transition 11, 200, 329, 331, 332, 338, 339, 340, 341, 394
Environmental Action 4, 130
environmental conflicts
  forestry-related 63, 64–5
    see also Northern New South Wales
  over conservation 306–7, 325
  resource disparities 31, 32, 36, 38
  Turkey 269
  United States 4
  see also Indigenous–environmental conflict; jobs v. the environment
environmental degradation
  differing view on addressing 450
  economic growth 117, 173, 367
  focus on 4
  population growth and 345, 352, 356, 359
  Turkey 269
environmental deregulation 87, 112, 372
environmental harms 176
  racialized distribution see environmental racism
environmental identification 75–6, 78
environmental impacts
  as an analytical concept 457–9
  direct and indirect 423
environmental injustice 58, 374, 375, 376, 403, 410–12
environmental issues
  political polarization 137
  public concern/opinion, United States 133, 137
  Turkey 268, 269–70, 276–7, 280
environmental justice 50, 51, 64, 366, 403
  activism 5, 49
  collective continuance 375
  demographics 9, 138
  growth of 112
  inequitable distribution of environmental harms 12, 370
  population environmentalism 348, 351, 356, 358
  religious settlers 407
environmental knowledge 160, 161, 165

environmental legislation
  Australia 156, 159
  lobbying and 447
  Turkey 269
  United States 25, 28–9, 112, 136, 176
environmental movement(s)
  business backlash against 133
  defined 330
  goals 111, 118–19, 121–2
  radical, Czech Republic 99
  solidarity and fracture in 415–16
  understanding opposition to 108–30
    changing nature of the movement 120–27
    dominant American values 117–20
    preface 108–14
  see also Bergama movement; environmental justice; food sovereignty; religious environmental movement
environmental policy 133–50
  drivers of 136–8
  eroding power of public opinion 133
  inclusion of traditional and Indigenous knowledge 57
  rolling back of 2
  white identity politics 371, 375
environmental politics
  evangelicalism 372
  loss of place and influence on 167
  managed scarcity 13
  religion 399
environmental problems
  anti-racism as imperative for resolving 376
  discovery of neglected 121
  explanations for origin of 119
  as racialized minority problems 371
environmental protection 423, 443
  costs 117
  forestry job loss 68–71
  political ideology 444, 445
  race and 369
  Turkey 269
  United States 111, 138–50, 382, 385–93
Environmental Protection Agency (EPA) 25, 28, 32, 35, 244, 370
environmental quality
  achieving 117, 119
  dominant American values 118–20
  value-conflict 127
environmental racism 5, 10, 12, 50, 356, 366, 368–71, 374, 403
environmental regulation
  coded racism 369–70
  costs of 117
  countermovement opposition 26, 29

use of money to influence 177
see also environmental deregulation
environmental restorative justice 299
environmental skepticism 221, 276
environmental state
   competing views on 365
   racial state in tension with 366–8
The Environmental State Under Pressure 367
environmental taxation 185, 393–4
environmental values 65, 77
environmentalism
   Australia 156, 159–60, 164–5, 166, 167, 330
   brief history of 3–5
   British Columbia 63–4
   critics 12–13
   as a cross-cultural phenomenon 429
   Czech Republic 87
   defining 329–30, 366
   demographic characteristics 138
   different aspects of 423–4
   discourses, wind energy 336–9
   labor advocacy 381
   measures 443
   neo-Marxist ideology 431
   suppression of 262–3
   see also environmental movements;
      labor-environmentalism;
      mainstream environmentalism;
      population-environmentalism;
      religious environmentalism
environmentalists/environmental groups
   Aboriginal Australians 159
   adversarial framing 251–2, 255
   alliances between NSW farmers and 166
   anthropocentrically motivated attacks on 426
   auditing 255–6, 259
   classification 130
   demonisation and criticism of 182, 280
   false claims against 427–32
   and forestry job loss 68–71
   ideal types 111
   negative encounters with 392
   portrayals 226, 260, 261, 263, 426, 454–5
      see also framing; terrorist label
   surveillance 252–3
   violent repression 114
   see also activism/activists; conservationists;
      environmental movement(s)
environmentally friendly behaviours (EFBs) 75, 77–8
epistemic scepticism 85–6, 91, 95, 98
epistemic subsidiarity 290–91
Esch, E. 375
ethical extensionalism 432
ethical responsibilities 54

ethics 164, 359, 361–2, 427, 428, 431–2
eugenics 352, 357, 373
Euro-scepticism 98
Europe/European Union (EU) 91–2, 98, 99, 182, 183, 185, 269
European colonists 154–5
Eurostat survey (2017) 88
Evangelical Environmental Network 399
evangelicalism 372, 373, 413
Evans, R. 457
eventful protests 308
eventful temporality 308–9
evictions, of local communities 427–9
exemptionalist paradigm 222
expert knowledge power 290, 291
expertization, media coverage 99
Extinction Rebellion (XR) 5, 54, 424
extractive populism 224–7
'extremism' frame/label 252, 253
ExxonMobil 7, 134, 449
Eyerman, R. 7

Fagan, A. 87
faith-based actions 409–10, 412–13
family planning 347, 348, 350, 351, 352, 353, 357
family size 359
family values 238
farmers and farming
   anti-environmentalism 167
   environmentalism 159–160, 164–5, 166, 167, 330, 338–9, 340
   see also agriculture; human–livestock
      relations; small-scale farmers
farmer–science experimentation 290
Farrell, J. 137, 187, 238, 446, 448–9
Feagin, J. 373
fear and anxiety 280, 295, 359, 372
Federal Bureau of Investigation (FBI) 252
Federal Housing Administration (FHA) 369
federal structures, movement–countermovement conflict 25, 36
Federation for American Immigration Reform (FAIR) 347, 352, 358–9
Ferguson, M. 198, 199
field theory 441, 456–7
financial resources 255, 262, 451–2
   see also donations
Finney, C.M. 156
First Nation peoples 12, 54, 250, 405, 408–9
first wave environmentalism 3, 10, 349
Fischer, K. 184
Fisher, D.R. 2, 446, 448
Fligstein, N. 441, 457
Floyd, A. 160–61
folk devils 261, 263

food sovereignty 284–300
  internal regulations 298
  non-state regulation 295–8
  political ideology 444
  social control and non-state laws 299
  state regulation 287–95
Forcese, C. 260
forestry
  anti-environmentalism 6–7, 8–9
  beliefs about job loss, BC 68–71
  environmental conflicts 63, 64–5
  lifestyle 71
  Northern NSW *see* Northern New South Wales
  resource control, use and depletion, Kalimantan 310–16
Forestry Commission (NSW) 159, 160, 161, 162
fossil capitalism 183, 193, 217, 218–20
fossil fuel industry 37, 86
  Australia
    corrosive influence on politics 206–7
    cross-party solidarity 200–201
    overt and covert influences on policy-making 195–9
    profit and negative externalities 194
    structural bias and soft corruption 201–4
  Canada
    capital power structure 218–20
    climate denial 7, 221
    corporate influence and corruption 204
    corporate power 216–17
    environmentally friendly policies 54
    extractive populism and conservative denial movement 224–7
    inefficient environmentalism 46
    landscape 217–18
    oil price collapse 228
    policies and notoriety 216
    regime of obstruction 217–18, 220
  climate denial 32, 177, 186, 244, 452
  environmental destruction/harm 173, 176
  labor-environmental conflict 384, 386
  ownership relations 448
  see also coal industry; oil and gas industry
Foster, J.B. 8
Foucault, M. 277
fourth wave environmentalism 4
Fowler, A. 136
frames/framing 30, 43, 85, 109, 113, 186, 203, 259–61, 453–5
  see also adversarial framing; counter-framing; neutralization techniques
France 25
free enterprise 237, 238

free market 237, 238, 385, 393
Freedman, L. 28
freedom 238
Friends of the Earth 4, 383
fringe groups 33
frontier masculinity 27
Fry, O. 155
functional territorialisation 317
fusion centres 253
fusion knowledge 295
Future of Conservation 426

gaharu 312–13, 317
Gallup trend data (1989–91) 110
Garbutt, R. 166
Gasteen, J. 161–2
gatekeepers 32, 33
gender 9, 28, 51, 138, 147, 351, 356, 403, 412, 414
General Social Survey (1973–2014) 138, 141
genetically modified organisms (GMOs) 291, 292
gentailers 200, 201
geographic-economic factors, resistance to climate protection 388
George Mason University (GMU) 234
George, W. 409
Germany 25, 98, 274, 275, 278
gerrymandering 373
Gilens, M. 135
Glencore 203
global warming 91, 92, 137, 238, 447
Goddard Institute for Space Studies (GISS) 31–2
gold mining 268
  conservation conflict, Kalimantan, 311–12, 317, 319
  Turkey
    anti-environmental campaign and discourse 271–9
    mobilization against 270–71
golden escalator 196–9
Goodall, J. 429
Gore, A. 112, 450
government
  anti-environmentalism 2, 395–6
  climate change scepticism 87
  environmentalism 3
  limiting 238
  responsiveness to public opinion 149
  support, countermovement emergence 30, 31
  TOP theory 13
grassroots movements
  anti-environmental 2, 8, 47, 153
  environmental 5, 112, 159, 429
Gray, J. 432
Greasing the Wheels 195–6

Great Paradox 8
green building management 394
green consumerism 111, 113, 365, 367, 445
green gentrification 52
'green on green' debate 330, 340
green growth 112, 445, 450
Green, J. 159
Green New Deal 38, 112, 113, 393–4, 394–5
Green Revolution 289, 290
greenhouse gas (GHG) emissions 92, 171, 173, 178, 216, 221, 223, 250, 334, 381, 388
greening of hate 345, 346, 348, 349, 351, 354, 356, 357, 359, 362
greening of religion 400, 401, 402, 403, 404, 414, 417
Greenpeace 4, 5, 6, 12, 50, 51, 242, 409
Griffiths, T. 154
Grossman, R.L. 386
group membership, and nonstate regulation 296
Guber, D. 138
gun control movement 27

Hablemitoğlu, N. 278
Hanley, S. 87
Hansen, J. 31
Hardin, G. 129, 355
Harper, S. 2, 219, 220, 221, 225, 226, 248, 250, 257, 263, 452–3
Harred, J.L. 178
Havel, V. 87
Hayek Institute 178
Hayes, D. 383
Hayes, H. 161
Head, B.W. 100
health, and human rights 356–7
health industries 147
Heartland Institute 30, 36, 181, 185, 237, 242
Heller, M.A. 297
helmeted hornbill 314
Helvarg, D. 425
heritage 238
Heritage Foundation 31, 109, 237
Hertel-Fernandez, A. 234, 238, 239, 244
higher-income neutralisation techniques 183, 184
Hirschman, A.O. 33
Hoberg, G. 63
Hochschild, A.R. 8, 372, 455–6
Hodinott, T. 164
Hoff, J. 157
Hogan, R.E. 136
Holmes, O. 427
Hong Kong 196, 308
Huber, M. 224
Human Exemptionalist-Ecological Paradigm (HEP/NEP) 440, 441, 442–4

human rights
  as opposed to state regulation 291–3
  and population-environmentalism 354–60, 361
  punishment of poachers as violation of 429
  and resource exploitation 428
human-caused climate change 30, 44, 173, 176, 177, 187, 452
human–livestock relations 166–7
Hunt, S. 85
hunter–gatherer communities 304, 309–16, 322–3
Hutchins, B. 277
Hutton, D. 160
hypocrites/hypocrisy frame 454

identity see place identities; regional identity; religious identities
ideology
  CCCM organisations 184
  and pro-environmental voting 144–8
  see also political ideology; population-environmentalism
Idle No More 254, 403
illegal logging/deforestation 314, 427
'immediate return' turn of mind 315
immigration 11, 346, 347–9, 351, 355, 357, 373
impact analysis 458
An Inconvenient Truth 43, 87, 88, 449
Independent Commission Against Corruption (ICAC) 197
India 55, 181, 185, 196, 400
Indian Residential School system 408
Indigenous knowledge 57, 402
Indigenous nonhuman species 428, 430
Indigenous peoples
  AGRA activists' projection of imagined 325
  assimilation into settler society 408
  experiences of climate injustice 410–12
  food sovereignty and non-state regulation 296
  and the natural environment 54, 55
  right to collective property 293
  see also Aboriginal Australians; Bundjalung people; First Nations peoples
Indigenous religions 400
Indigenous rights 11, 54, 412
Indigenous–environmental conflict 11–12, 411–12
  see also forestry; pipeline expansion; renewable energy
Indigenous–settler relations 403, 406
indirect anti-environmentalism 425–7
indirect environmental impacts 423
individual-level environmentalism 13
Indonesia 196, 304–26, 400, 453

industrial agriculture 55, 285, 300
industrial capitalism 48, 173, 177, 204–5, 221, 222, 426
industrial donations 136–7, 244
industrial pollution 74
industry
    opposition to environmental protection 133, 134
    v. conservation, Northern NSW 161, 162–3
    see also Climate Change Counter Movement (CCCM)
inefficient environmentalism 45, 46–8, 53, 57
inequalities, personalizing climate change through lens of 411
inequitable environmentalism 45, 50–52, 53, 57
information dissemination 84
information gathering 253, 258
Inglehart, R. 72–3
insider support 31
Institute for Humane Studies (GMU) 234
institutionalization 5, 7, 111, 112, 113, 194, 220, 288
'instrumental logic of containment' 277
Integrated Service Unit (ISU) 253
Integrated Threat Assessment Centre (ITAC) 253
intellectuals 3, 4, 7–8
intelligence and security agencies 253
intended outcomes 458
inter-media agenda setters 84
interest coalitions 192, 223, 331
interest groups
    policy formation 135–6
    population environmentalism 349
    use of neutralization techniques 177
interests
    threats to, and countermovement emergence 26–30
    see also business interests; corporate interests; self-interest; worker-citizen interests
Intergovernmental Panel on Climate Change (IPCC) 43, 88, 239
internal regulations, food sovereignty 298
International Climate Science Coalition 178
international environmentalism 5
International Tropical Timber Organization (ITTO) 316
interorganizational networks 447
intimidation 256, 262–3
Inuit 12, 54, 408
invasion ecology 53
Ireland 98, 99, 208
Izaak Walton League 3, 350

Jacques, P.J. 99, 221, 222, 446, 447, 448

Jamison, A. 7
Jansen, K. 290
Japan 185
Jarrett, Charles 158
Jasanoff, S. 290
Jasny, L. 446, 448
Jasper, J.M. 308, 456
Jenkins, W. 402
Jirásek, V. 94
job blackmail 386
job bribery 389–90
job consciousness 391, 392, 394
job loss 68–71, 386–7
jobs v. the environment 6, 8, 29, 167, 381, 383–4, 395
Johnston, H. 260
joint security response, climate change messaging 184
Joosse, P. 263
Jorgenson, A.K. 2
just sustainabilities 12
just transition 393, 394
justice *see* environmental justice; social justice
justice-based messaging 407–10
Justification by Comparison (JBC) 178, 179, 180, 181, 182, 183

KAIROS 408, 413
Kaiser, D. 91, 93
Kalland, A. 426
Katznelson, I. 368
Kay, T. 457
Kazis, R. 386
Kelly, R. 163
Kennedy, H. 443
Kenney, J. 49–50
Kent, P. 255–6
Keskitalo, A. 11
Keystone XL pipeline 248, 381, 384, 385, 390, 453
Kijas, J. 158
Killian, L.M. 108, 118, 120, 122, 123, 129
Kinder Morgan 54, 221, 405, 409
Klandermans, B. 457
Klaus, V. 87, 88, 91, 92, 93, 94, 95, 98, 99
Klein, N. 51, 450
Klein, R. 225
knowledge interests 7
knowledge monoculture 288–90
knowledge production 174
Koch Brothers 6, 8, 134
    Charles 234, 237
    climate change denial 7, 31, 239–43, 449
    David 234, 243
    network 235–9

Kopnina, H. 442
Krajhanzl, J. 88
Kramer, R.C. 176
Krause, V. 8, 256
Kretschmer, K. 28
Kristof, N. 374
Krueger, J.S. 444
Krugman, P. 243, 244
Kymlicka, W. 56
Kyoto Protocol 223, 384, 447, 452

La Vía Campesina 286, 288, 291, 294, 298
Labor Network for Sustainability and Trade Unions 395
labor unions
 countermovement emergence 30
 environmentalism 381, 382–5
 fight for climate protection 393–4
 influence on pro-environmental voting 147
 portrayed as anti-environmental organizations 381
 resistance to climate protection 385–93
 use of PACs 135–6
Lake Erie Bill of Rights 55
Lambek, N. 291
land acts (NSW, 1861) 155
Land, C. 412
land dispossession 375–6
land ethic 164, 427
landowner perspectives/opposition 330, 331, 332–4, 335, 336, 337, 338–9, 340, 341
Langton, M. 296
Largest Oil and Gas Rally in Canadian History 47, 49
Latin America *see* South America
Laudati, A. 10
Layzer, J. 135
leadership, labor unions 393
Leadnow and Dogwood Initiative 254–5
League of Conservation Voters (LCV) 113, 137, 138–9
left-liberal countermovements 45, 49
left/right political ideology 444–6
legal pluralism 295, 296, 297
legislation
 anti-environmental, Turkey 278–9
 anti-terrorist 253, 278
 food sovereignty 288
 knowledge monoculture in agriculture 288–9
 racist 373
 see also adat law; environmental legislation; land acts; Tjukurpa law
legitimacy
 of environmental regulators 286
 of nonstate regulation 299

Lehotský, L. 86, 88, 99
Leifeld, P. 448
Leonard, C. 234, 238, 241
Leopold, A. 427
Lester, L. 277
Lever, J. 160, 161
Lewin, P.G. 9, 80, 280
Lewondowsky, S. 187
LGBTQ rights 38
liberal market economies 450, 452
liberal/left political ideology 444–5
libertarianism 36, 46, 184, 237, 239, 240, 284, 285, 287, 300, 445, 446
liberty 238
Limbaugh, R. 110
Lindblom, C. 204
linkages of issues 28
lived experiences 392, 415, 431
livelihoods 153, 154, 156, 161, 162–3, 165, 166, 167
lobbying
 on climate change 134
 and climate change legislation 447
 covert networks 196, 197
 fossil capitalism 219
 see also political action committees (PACs)
local communities, evictions of 427–9
local knowledges 52, 160, 161, 288, 290
localization, food sovereignty and 293–4
Lock the Gate Alliance (LTG) 166
Lockwood, M. 98
logging *see* cedar-getters; forestry
Lomborg, B. 8, 46, 86, 91, 92, 93, 425
low-income countries, neutralisation techniques 183, 184
Luders, J.E. 31
Luke, T.W. 12
Luker, K. 28
Lumley Park 159–60
Lynch, M.J. 176
Lynn White thesis 400–401
Lysack, M. 403–4

McAdam, D. 309, 441, 457, 458
McCarthy, J. 27, 109, 331
McCright, A.M. 30, 137, 174, 182, 184, 186, 239, 240, 445, 447
McFarlane, I. 198, 199
McGregor, D. 54
Machiavellian politics 193, 204, 205, 208
McKie, R.E. 174
MacLean, N. 238, 240, 445
McMichael, P. 287
MacTavish, K. 373
Macy, M. 445

mainstream environmentalism 49
    blurred line between religious
        environmentalism and 403
    and population-environmentalism 348, 349,
        350–52, 354, 361
    refuting 336
mainstreaming of climate protection 222
majoritarianism 373–4
managed scarcity 13
managerialism 289–90
Mann, M. 243–4
Mannkal Economic Foundation (Canada) 178
market conditions, forestry job loss 70, 71
Marshall, G. 456
Martin, J.L. 456–7
masculinity 9, 10, 27
Maslen, R. 162
mass media, climate change sceptics' strategies
    84–6
Matalunai 304, 305, 309, 311, 315
material interests 27, 30, 392
materialist values 77
Matza, D. 177, 178, 186
Mayer, J. 238–9, 240, 244, 445
Mazzocchi, T. 393
mechanization 68, 70, 71, 160, 311–12
media
    consensus, climate change 98, 100
    demonisation and criticism of 182
    shaping of public opinion 167
    see also mass media; social media
media coverage
    climate change/climate change denial 88, 95,
        97–100, 186
    countering Bergama movement 274, 276
    immigration discussions and racial overtones
        353
Melayu 309, 311
meliorists 111, 113, 125, 130
Mellon Scaife, R. 237
Mercatus Center 234, 237
Merchants of Doubt 240
meta-rules 298
Methmann, C.P. 222
Métis communities 54, 408
Metro Vancouver 47, 48, 54
Meyer, D.S. 2, 109, 451, 454
Meyer, J.W. 184
micro-activism 78
Millar, M. 254
Mining Association of Canada 219
mining industry *see* fossil fuel industry; gold
    mining
misinformation 33, 37, 185, 239, 449
mobilization

countermovement 23
critical events tiggering 307–9, 319–24, 325
impact of opposing movements on 34–5
insider support and 31
and outcomes 458
social media and 5, 227
see also resource mobilization
modern environmentalism 405
Mohai, P. 371
Mol, A. 367
Monaghan, J. 252, 255, 262
The Monkey Wrench Gang 426
Montreal Economic Institute 178
Moore, P. 8
Moore, S. 33
moral assemblages 44, 45–56, 57
moral conflicts 28, 38
moral panic 261, 263
moral terrains 375
Morrison, D.E. 129
Morrison, S. 186
movement influence, and countermovement
    emergence 24–6
movement threats, and countermovement
    emergency 24–6
movement–countermovement dynamics 8, 25,
    33–6, 37, 63, 65
Moyal, A. 156
Muir, J. 3
Müller, G. 309
Mulroney, B. 222
Multi-Issue Extremism 253
multi-level regulation 293
Murphy, R. 8
Myrdal, G. 355

Nanga Bungan 304, 305, 310, 311, 317, 319, 323,
    324
narratives 8, 9, 225, 226, 454, 455–6
National Energy Board (NEB) 54, 220, 251, 254,
    262, 405, 409
National Energy Program (NEP) 224–5
National Network for Immigrant and Refugee
    Rights 356
national parks 3, 4, 10, 156, 159, 161, 162
    see also Betung Kerihun National Park
National Research Council 239
National Rifle Association 27
National Security and Intelligence Review
    Agency (NSIRA) 258
National Wildlife Association 350
nationalism 224–5, 260, 268, 275, 280
native genocide 375–6
nativism 355, 372–3

natural environment, relationships with 54, 55, 160, 161, 164
natural resource(s)
    conditional access to 296
    conflicts 306–7, 412
    donations 147
    early environmentalism 3
    exploitation 54, 156, 193–4, 269, 311, 315, 401, 428
    extraction 156, 185, 194
    god-given right to 399
    over-consumption of 72
    preservation 72
Natural Resources Defense Council (NRDC) 4
natural science 156
nature protection, movement against, Kalimantan 304–26
necessity, for labour-intensive practices 295
negative externalities, racialization of 368–71
Neilsen, M. 164
neo-Marxism 431, 450
neoliberal capitalism 48, 431, 450, 451
neoliberal conservationists 426, 430
neoliberalism 297, 300, 384
    and anti-environmentalism 6, 110, 112, 113, 184, 186
    Czech Republic 87
    environmental issues and policies, Turkey 269–70
    governance of environmentalism, Canada 248–64
    influence on policy, Australia 205
    labor resistance to climate protection 385
    shift towards, 1970s 445
Netherlands 178, 196
neutralization techniques 177, 178–85, 186
new conservationists 426, 427, 430, 431
New Deal 368, 370
new denialism 219, 221, 222, 223, 224
New Ecological Paradigm (NEP) 443, 449, 458
    see also Human Exemptionalist-Ecological Paradigm (HEP/NEP)
new exemptionalism 222
New Right 26, 29, 31, 87
New South Wales (NSW)
    ICAC hearings 197
    see also Northern New South Wales (NSW)
New Zealand 55, 98, 181, 375
Newman, C. 198
Nicholson, N. 163
Nicholson, P. 298
Nigeria 174, 183
Nita, M. 403
Nitzan, J. 204
Nixon, R. 10, 28, 117, 370

NNU 392, 393
Noakes, J.A. 260
non-economic values 71
non-interference, defensive right to 292–3
non-state regulation, food sovereignty and 295–8, 299
nonhuman rights 55, 57
nonhuman species, Indigenous 428, 430
Nordhaus, T. 362, 431
Nordic countries 11, 98, 196, 208, 456
Norgaard, K.M. 222, 425, 456
norm-oriented movements 120, 121
normative change 111, 113, 121–2, 125
Northern Gateway pipeline 248–9, 254, 256, 258
Northern New South Wales 153–68
    colonialism 154–6
    conservationism 156–7, 159–60, 161
    farmers v. gas drilling 164–5
    forestry
        Border Ranges campaign 160–62
        Terania Creek campaign 162–5
        v. farming 158–60
    Indigenous landscape 157–8
The Northern Star 163
Noske, B. 427
Not in My Backyard (NIMBYism) 330, 356, 370, 371
Notley, R. 224
Numbers Impact 354, 355, 358–60, 361

Obach, B.K. 392
Obama, B. 23, 93, 112, 372, 385, 453
Ogge, M. 195, 197
Ogilvie, E. 157
Oil, Chemical and Atomic Workers (OCAW) Union 383, 393
oil and gas industry
    Australia 164–5, 202, 203
    Canada
        oil sands development 250–51, 254–5
        pipeline expansion 49, 220–21, 225, 263–4
        pipeline opponents 226, 254–5, 258, 408
        pro-petroleum movements 47, 48, 49
        social media campaigns 227
        see also Alberta; Dakota Access Pipeline (DAPL); Keystone XL pipeline; Trans Mountain pipeline
    climate change denial 7, 240, 241
    Indigenous–environmental conflict 12
    influence on environmental regulation 177
Olausson, U. 88
oligarchy 51–2, 205
Oliver, J. 251

Olson, M. 129
Omi, M. 366
On Justification 44
O'Neill, T. 254
opposing movements 23, 33–6, 37, 123–4
oral history 153
Oreskes, N. 240
organizational ecology 219
organizational fields 457
organizations/astroturfing 7, 26
organized opposition 109
OSHA Environmental Network 383
Ostrom, E. 296
Otis Group 201
Our Common Future (Brundtland Report) 5
out-movement social network ties 447
outsiders, environmentalists portrayed as 455
over-exploitation 428
overcutting 71
overpopulation 350, 352, 357, 358, 425
ownership relations 448

Page, B.I. 135
paid protesters 226
partisanship 28
Patel, R. 287
patriotism 260, 264, 275, 280
peasant union, Kalimantan 305, 319–20
penalties, regulation violations 241, 296–7, 317
Pence, M. 243
People for the Ethical Treatment of Animals (PETA) 51, 253–4
Perlman, S. 394
personal contact, in individual recruitment 130
personal social networks 447
'personal transformation' strategy 111, 122–3, 125, 129
persuasion 129, 130
Petráček, Z. 96
Pew Research Center 133
Philosophical Society of Australasia 156
Pidgeon, N.F. 85
Pilarski, C. 227
Pinchot, G. 3
Pithart, D. 96
place identities 330
Planck Foundation (Netherlands) 178
Planned Parenthood of Southeastern Pennsylvania v. Casey (1992) 35
Plehwe, D. 184
pluralist governments 395
policy coalition actors 448
policy failure 206
policy-making
    environmental *see* environmental policy
    exposing corporate influences 204–6
    history of interest groups 135–6
    limiting of environmentalists' participation in 251
    overt and covert influences, Australia 195–9
policymakers, demonisation and criticism of 182
political action committees (PACs) 31, 134, 135–6, 136–7, 140, 142–50
political donations
    and environmental voting 142–50
    from the coal industry to Republicans 244
    funding of media campaigns 207
    influence on policy 134, 136–7
    lack of transparency, Australia 198
Political Ecology Group 348
political economy
    of environmental change 365, 368
    and the role of capitalism 450–51
    social network analysis and 448
    see also critical political economy
political elites 46, 47, 48, 87, 194, 249
political ideology 29, 36, 444–6
    see also libertarianism; neo-Marxism; neoliberalism
political lock-in 206
political mobilization 226
political opportunity structure 24, 37, 49, 87, 109, 111, 112, 149, 308, 452–3
political outcomes 458
political polarization 28, 110, 137, 445, 448–9
political process theory 451, 452
political responsibility, in reconciliation 405–7
political service personnel 196, 198–9
political units (small-scale) 294
'politically correct' people 49
Politics and Markets 204
Pollack, H.N. 85
Polluter Watch 242
polluting activities, deregulation of 372
polluting companies, racism and siting decisions 370
pollution 121, 241
pollution control, labor support for 382, 383
'pollution is a people problem' 122–3
Pompeo, M. 243
Pondělíček, M. 96
Population Action International (PAI) 352
population advocacy 345, 349, 352–4, 361
Population Connection 352
population control 345, 348, 357
Population Ecology Group (PEG) 356
population growth
    environmental impacts 345, 352, 353, 356, 359
    immigration and 355, 359

neo-Marxist discounting of 431
slowing of non-white 373
see also Zero Population Growth (ZPG)
population-environmentalism 345–62
connection/partnership 349–54
controversy surrounding immigration 347–9
human rights v. societal goals 354–60
interest in 345
negotiating 360–62
populism 48–9, 98, 186, 224–7
Port Alberni 63, 65–7, 68
Porta, D.D. 308
Portugal 98
post-9/11 securitization 259–61
post-environmental approach 431
post-truth techniques 268, 272
postmaterialist values 72–4, 77
Powell, L. 240
power
and construction of deviancy 176
Indigenous–settler relations 406
of public opinion 133
silence as instrument and effect of 277
see also bargaining power; corporate power; elitist power, capital power
power tactics 123, 124
power v. participation strategies 129
Powys-Whyte, K. 414
pragmatic sociology 44–5
preservation(ism) 3, 72, 157, 160
Pretel, J. 94
print media 84
private ordering 297–8
privatization 200, 238, 269
problem denial 85, 92, 95
Professional Institute of the Public Service of Canada (PIPSC) 257–8
progress 442–3
progressive anti-environmentalism 46
project labor agreements (PLAs) 389–90
Promethean discourse 86, 193–5, 202, 203
property rights movement 292–3, 300
proportional representation 207
Protect the Inlet 409
protected areas 10
protest cycle, 1960s 4, 8
protest movements, and countermovement emergence 24
protest tactics (out-of-system) 5
Protestantism 401
Pruitt, S. 372
pseudo-science 173–4, 178, 184
public concern, environmental issues 133
public good(s) 129, 224, 225, 368–71
public office 196–9

public opinion
elite cues 99
on environmental issues 137
environmental voting 133, 137, 142–50
eroding power of 133
government responsiveness 149
impact of climate change denial on 187
media shaping of 167
and policy 84–5, 133, 135
Pulido, L. 374
Punan Hovongan tribe 309, 310, 315, 320
Putnam, R. 48, 51
Putussibau 304, 310, 311, 314, 316, 318

Quadagno, J. 371
quality of life 347, 351–2, 356–7
quality press 84, 85, 86
Quarry Australia 193–5
'quotidian disruptions' 308

race 51, 138, 147, 351, 356, 361, 367, 368, 370, 403, 412, 414
race-blindness 450
racial conservatives 373, 374
racial diversity 354–5
racial formation 366
racial identity politics 371–4
racial inequalities 5, 365–6, 367, 372
racial projects 366, 373
racial state
and environmental state in tension 366–8
framework 365–6
racialization 368–71
racism
immigration and 353, 355
see also environmental racism; greening of hate
radical critiques 46, 52, 54, 57
radical environmentalism 5, 99
radical movements 120, 121, 123–4
Rainforest Action Network 218
rainforest regeneration 159–60
Ramos, H. 308
rationalist discourse 86
Raymond, L. 98
re-regulation 200
Reagan, R. 29, 30, 34, 35, 110, 111, 112, 369, 370
Reason Foundation 237
recreation-led environmentalism 3, 10
recycling 75, 78
Red Tories 446
redefining critical events 308
redemptive movements 124

reflexive anti-environmentalism 2, 10–13, 400, 443
reflexive environmental skepticism 340
reflexive religious anti-environmentalism 402–4
    Canada 404–15
    contending a decolonial reality in 415–16
reformist critiques 46, 52, 54, 57
reformists 111, 113, 120, 121, 124, 125, 126, 130
region, and pro-environmental voting 148
regional identity 9
regional values 9
regulation(s)
    Betung Kerihun National Park 316–17
    legitimacy of 286
    see also internal regulations; non-state regulation; re-regulation; state regulation
Reich, C.A. 122
religious environmental organizations (REOs) 400, 404, 408–10
religious environmentalism 399–400, 400–402, 403
religious identities 275, 403, 405–7, 410–15
Remington, C. 349
renewable energy 178, 200
    Australia 201–2
    and job loss 386
    labor support 381
    see also energy transition; wind energy
repression 114, 262, 277–8, 424–5
Republican Party 27, 29, 35, 36, 109, 111–12, 137, 147, 148, 244, 249, 372, 373
research
    anti-environmental 7, 167, 280
        topics for future 440–60
    environmental 6, 31–2
    need for comparative 37
Reskin, B. 369
resource(s)
    depletion, demobilization and 262
    disparities, environmental conflicts 31
    future anti-environmentalist research 451–2
    movements/countermovements 32, 36, 38
    see also financial resources; natural resource(s)
resource mobilization 109, 451, 452
respectable movements 120, 121
response skepticism 86, 91, 95, 98
restorative justice 296–7, 299
retail industry 147
revolutionary critique 46
revolutionary movements 120, 121, 124
'revolving door' strategy 193, 196
rhetoric of reaction 33
Richardson, S.B. 288

Richmond River 154, 155, 158
Rieder, M. 94, 96
right-wing movements 25–6, 29, 31, 36, 48–9, 256
'rights master frame' 291
'rights of nature' movement 55
Riley, G.D. 382
Roach, K. 260
Roberts, A. 165
Roberts, C. 394
Robertson, G. 47
Roe v. Wade (1973) 34
Roediger, D. 375
Rokeach, M. 119
romanticism 3, 10
Roosevelt, F.D. 3
Rossi, L. 153
Rous, J.H. 154
Rovenský, J. 93
Royal Canadian Mounted Police (RCMP) 253, 254
Royal Commission of Inquiry into Forestry (1908) 158
Ruggiero, V. 176
Rummery Park forestry camp 159
rural environmentalists 72, 75, 76
Russia 182, 183, 185

Sagebrush Rebellion 6, 109
Sagy, T. 297–8
St George, A. 129
St John, F.A.V. 426–7
Salatin, J. 287
Sámi territories 11
Sanders, B. 374
Sanger, M. 352
Sapinski, J.P. 186
scapegoating 225, 261, 348, 357, 428
Scheer, A. 49
Schnaiberg, A. 130, 367, 450
Schrepfer, S.R. 10
science trap 222
science/scientists 240, 289, 290
scientific consensus 7, 30, 31, 91, 92
scientific information 239, 257–8, 264
scientific uncertainty 85, 98
second wave conservative mobilization 237
second wave environmentalism 3
securitization 259–61, 264
security threats, environmentalists portrayed as 252–4, 260
segregation 370, 371
self-interest 455
self-protection 222
self-reflexivity 413

Sellato, B. 310, 315, 322
Sercombe, P.G. 315
settler colonialism 11, 156, 157, 163, 375, 400, 405–7, 408, 411, 412–15
settler environmentalism 45, 52–4, 56, 57
Sewell, W.H. 308
Shantz, J. 431
Shapiro, R.Y. 135
Share Our Resources 6–7, 66–7, 70, 71–2, 73–4, 75, 76, 77–8, 79, 454
Shearman, L. 164, 165
Shellenberger, M. 362, 431
Shields, J.A. 28
shifting cultivation 289, 304, 305, 311, 317, 321, 322
Shriver, T. 249
Sierra Club 3, 4, 35, 112, 129, 254, 345, 346, 347–8, 349, 350, 356, 358, 383
Sierrans for US Population Stabilization (SUSPS) 347, 348, 349, 358
silence, on environmental issues 9, 268, 276–7, 280
Silent Spring 4
siting decisions, racialized 370, 371, 374
Skocpol, R. 234, 238, 239, 244
Skoglund, A. 78
small government 238
small-scale farmers 288, 289, 290, 291, 294–5
small-scale markets 293–4
Smelser, N.J. 120, 121
Snow, D.A. 308
social control 262, 278, 284, 286, 299
social hierarchy, nonstate regulation 297–8
social inequalities 10, 50, 52, 57
social infrastructures, contested 45, 47, 49, 51, 53, 55, 57
social justice 2, 11, 12, 33, 49, 50, 51, 52, 64, 356
social media 5, 6, 12, 32–3, 37, 53, 226, 227
social movements
    classifying 124–7
    congruence between goals and societal values 118
    costs 31
    critical events in 307–9
    fragmentation of 358
    individual recruitment 130
    Koch Brothers and climate denial 234–44
    outcomes 441, 457–9
    study of 108–9
    unionism 391, 393
    see also countermovements; environmental movements; movement influence; movement threats; right-wing movements
social networks
    fossil capitalism, Canada 218, 219, 228
    Koch Brothers 235–9, 241–2
    study of anti-environmentalism 441, 446–9
    see also covert networks; social media
social safety net, US weak 387–8
societal goals, human rights versus 354–60
'societal manipulation' strategy 111, 122, 123, 124, 127, 129
societal values 118, 120, 121, 122, 123, 127, 129
society–nature relationships 400, 414
socio-cultural dynamics 9, 110, 416, 425
socio-ecological network approach 449, 455
sociology 442
solidarity 200–201, 294, 391–2, 409, 412, 414
Soon, W. 185
South America 74, 114, 174, 182, 183, 184, 185, 444
South, N. 176
Spaargaren, G. 367
spectacular racism 374
splinter groups, population-environmentalism 347–9, 352, 354, 358
Šrámek, J. 96
Staggenborg, S. 2, 109, 308, 451, 454
state regulation
    agricultural 285
    environmentalists' positioning against 284
    of externalities 368
    food sovereignty and 287–95
    nonstate law overridden by 297
state structures 25
status quo
    defenders of 37, 86, 127
    threats to 127, 184–5
'Steady-State Society' concept 125–6
Stern, P.C. 65, 423
stewardship 159, 330, 338, 339, 340, 353, 399
Steyer, T. 36
stigmatization 251, 262, 357, 362, 386
Stoddart, M.C.J. 99
Straight Arrow Coalition 128–9
Strangers in their Own Land 8
strategic action fields 457
strategic invisibility 277
strategies and tactics
    climate change sceptics 84–6
    environmental movements 122–3, 129, 130, 250
    interaction between values, opposition and 123–4
    of opposing movements 35–6
    see also direct action tactics; discursive obstruction
Stratford, E. 167
Streams of Justice 410, 411, 413–14

Su, Y. 458
subsidized publics 227
'suddenly realised/imposed' grievances 308
'sundown town' practices 370
support from allies, countermovement emergence 30–33
suppression 251, 262–3, 373, 408
Supran, G. 240
surveillance 252–5
sustainability
    anti-racism as imperative for 376
    and economic development 5
    environmental sociology 13
    in farming *see* agroecology
    food sovereignty and 285
    forestry, British Columbia 68, 71
    population and 353
    reflexive anti-environmentalism 2
    shared decision-making 66–7
    voluntary market transactions 370–71
Sykes, G. 177, 178, 186
symbolic interests, threats to 27–8, 30
symbolic nationalization 224, 225
systems of responsibility 375
Szarka, J. 330

Tanjung Lokang 304, 305, 309, 310, 311, 316, 317, 319, 323, 324
Tea Party 6, 8, 36, 238, 372, 455
technical knowledge 219
techno-institutional complexes 206
techno-scientific efficiency 46, 48, 53–4
technology *see* mechanization; social media
Terania Creek campaign 162–4
terminal values 119
terrorist label 113–14, 252, 260, 278, 425
Thévenot, L. 44–5
think tanks 2, 203, 219, 237
    see also conservative think tanks (CTT)
third wave environmentalism 4
Thompson, W.E. 178
Thoreau, H.D. 3
threats 26–30, 91, 123, 167
tightly coupled conflict 35–6
Tillman Act (1907) 136
Tilly, C. 307
Tindall, D. 7, 26, 446, 447, 453, 454
Tjukurpa law 375
tobacco industry 30, 240
Todd, Z. 411
Tomalin, E. 400
tor fish 314, 317
tourism 10, 158, 317, 375, 426
Toxic Wastes and Race in the United States 403
traditional denialism 221, 222, 223–4

traditional knowledge 52, 54, 55, 57
Trans Canada Corporation 248, 254
Trans Mountain pipeline 54, 221, 224, 248–9, 258, 259, 400, 404, 405, 408, 409, 412
transcendentalism 125
transcorporeal experience of nature 161
transformationists 111, 112–13, 124, 125–6, 127, 130
transparency, lack of 51, 197
transportation industry 147
Trauger, A. 294
Treadmill of Production (TOP) 13, 365, 367, 370, 374, 375, 450
Treviranus, G.R. 156
Trudeau, J. 46, 47, 49, 50, 54, 219, 220, 224, 228, 248, 257, 258, 453
True the Vote 238
Trumka, R. 388
Trump, D. 2, 23, 35, 36, 48, 49, 50, 95, 96, 110, 111, 112, 186, 228, 239, 244, 248, 371, 372–3, 374, 425, 453, 455
Truth and Reconciliation Commission (Canada) 403, 406, 408
Tsleil-Waututh Nation 409
Turkey 268–80, 424
Turkish Institute of Scientific and Technical Research 271
Turner, R.H. 108, 118, 120, 123, 129

Uehlein, J. 391
Uluru rock 375
unecological environmentalism 45, 55–6, 57
union democracy 392–3
Unitarian Church of Vancouver 409
unitary state structures 25
United Church of Christ's Commission for Racial Justice 403
United Conservative Party (UCP) 49
United Kingdom 9, 25, 39, 86, 98, 110, 174, 204, 403
United Mine workers of America 384, 394
United Nations 5, 52, 239, 291, 350, 356
United Nations Declaration for the Rights of Indigenous Peoples (UNDRIP) 405, 408
United Nations Declaration on the Rights of Peasants and Other People Working in Rural Areas 291
United Nations Environment Programme (UNEP) 5
United Nations Framework Convention of Climate Change (UNFCCC) 173, 223
United States
    anti-environmentalism 2, 6, 8, 9, 11, 25–6, 29, 111–12, 243
    climate denial 23, 98, 221

understanding opposition to 108–30
anti-reflexivity movement 249–50, 257
climate protection and labor movement 381–96
environmental conflicts 37
environmental state and racial state in tension 365–76
environmentalism 3–5, 8, 25, 31–2, 112–13
movement–countermovement conflict 23, 25, 27–32
neoliberalism 110
neutralisation techniques 182, 183
population-environmentalism 345–62
public opinion and environmental policy 133–50
quality press 85
United Steelworkers (USW) union 382, 384
United We Roll 49
unlearning 407, 413, 414
unprofitable environmentalism 45, 46, 47, 48–50, 57
Unruh, G. 206
urban elites 47, 48
urban environmentalists 72, 75, 76
Urquhart, I. 220

value change 111, 112–13, 121–2, 125, 127
value conflicts 108, 120, 127
value-belief-norm (VBN) theory 65
value-oriented movements 120, 121, 124
values 71–4
    anti-environmental 160, 225
    construction of deviance and criminal behaviour 176
    democratic unionism 392, 393
    food sovereignty 298
    interaction between strategies, opposition and 123–4
    see also American values; conservative values; family values; regional values; societal values
Van Rensburg, W. 100
Vancouver Quakers 409, 413
Vancouverism 52
Vandeweerdt, C. 133
Vasi, I.B. 458
Vávra, J. 99
Veblen, T. 204
veganism 50–51
Vesa, J. 99
Vidomus, P. 98
Vietnam 424–5, 430
Vikka, L. 432
villager–park relations (Kalimantan) 318–29
violent repression 114, 424–5

Vogel, D. 135
Von Hellerman, P. 427
Voss, K. 30
Voter Integrity Party 238

Walby, K. 252, 255, 262
Walker, E. 227
Walker, R. 159
Walsh, E.J. 308
The War Against the Greens 425
Washington, H. 432
Watson, I. 160
Watt, J. 29
Webster v. Reproductive Health Services (1989) 34
Weinberg, A. 367
Weiss, M. 91, 92, 93
Weitz, T. 28
West, M. 196
Western neo-colonial elitism, false accusation of 429–30
When Affirmative Action Was White 368
Whian Whian 159
white identity politics 371–3, 374
white majoritarian status 374
white supremacy 50, 357, 372, 374, 375, 376
whites
    climate change denial 137
    environmental concerns 138
Whyte, K. 375
Wiangaree 157–8
Wickard v. Filburn (1942) 292
wilderness
    BC environmentalism 64
    cultural construction of 12
    labor concern for 382–3
Wilderness Movement 4
Wilderness Society 4, 35, 350
wilful pollution 241
Wilkie, R. 166
Willer, R. 372
Wilson, W. 157
Winant, H. 366
wind energy
    Alberta (study)
        characterization of opposition 339–40
        discourses of anti-environmentalism 332–6
        discourses of environmentalism 336–9
        reconsidering anti-environmentalism 340–41
        research setting and methods 331–2
    anti-environmentalist stance 330, 332–6
    arguments for 330
    union support for, US 389

Wise Use Movement 6, 29, 36, 63, 109, 173, 331
Wolfson, M. 27
worker-citizen interests 13
World Commission on Environment and
    Development (UN) 5
World Trade Organization (WTO) 383
World Wide Fund for Nature (WWF) 5–6, 304,
    316, 319, 321

Yasmi, Y. 306
Ylä-Anttila, T. 99

Young, N. 222, 249, 250
youth activism 5, 36, 52, 112, 305

Zald, M.N. 109
Zeman, M. 99
Zero Population Growth (ZPG) 126, 345, 346,
    347, 349, 350, 352
Zona Khusus 317, 322
zoopolis 56, 57
Zvěřinová, I. 88